S. Ackman
455-9700

DIGITAL COMPUTER FUNDAMENTALS

DIGITAL COMPUTER FUNDAMENTALS

Fifth Edition

Thomas C. Bartee
Harvard University

McGraw-Hill Book Company
New York   St. Louis   San Francisco
Auckland   Bogotá   Hamburg
Johannesburg   London   Madrid
Mexico   Montreal   New Delhi
Panama   Paris   São Paulo
Singapore   Sydney   Tokyo   Toronto

DIGITAL COMPUTER FUNDAMENTALS

34567890   FGFG   8987654321

Library of Congress Cataloging in Publication Data

Bartee, Thomas C
   Digital computer fundamentals.
   Bibliography: p.
   Includes index.
     1. Electronic digital computers.   I. Title.
QA76.5.B297   1981   001.64   80–12855
ISBN 0–07–003894–5

This book was set in Helvetica Light by Cobb/Dunlop Publisher Services Incorporated. The editor was Charles E. Stewart; the production supervisor was Diane Renda. The cover was designed by Raphael Hernandez. Fairfield Graphics was printer and binder.

CONTENTS

v

PREFACE

The purpose of this book is to present, as clearly as possible, the principles of modern digital computers. Many questions are included in a separate section of each chapter, and answers to selected odd-numbered questions are given at the end of the book.

This edition of the book includes major recent computer developments such as microprocessors, IC memories, interfacing a microcomputer or a minicomputer, and several new computers. A considerable amount of the book has been rewritten, and there are also many new questions. I have received a number of suggestions and comments from users of the book, and these have been used to improve the presentation and coverage.

Chapter 1 describes the uses of the computer in business, industry, and science. It also presents a brief introduction to programming. Some historical material is included, as are some basic concepts relating to computer usage.

Chapters 2 through 5 introduce some of the basic ideas and principles which are used in all digital computers and also in digital instruments, digital communications systems, digital control systems, and in fact in all digital devices. These chapters describe number systems, Boolean algebra, logic design, and the major digital circuit lines. The sections on counters and logic design using NAND and NOR gates have been expanded in this edition. Also, the material on digital circuits has been updated, and the major new circuit advances including IIL have been included.

Chapters 6, 7, and 8 treat arithmetic operations, memories, and input-output devices. The material on arithmetic operations first explains how arithmetic is performed in computers and then how arithmetic-logic units in computers are organized. The chapter on memories presents integrated circuit memories followed by core, drum, disk, tape, bubble, CCD, and other storage devices. The latest developments in this area, such as floppy disks, Winchester drives, and dynamic IC memories, are included here. The chapter on input and output describes the major input-output devices and also includes some material on analog-to-digital converters, digital-to-analog converters, terminals, modems, and acoustic couplers. Several new sections showing how to interface a keyboard and a printer to a microcomputer bus have been added.

The two final chapters, Chapters 9 and 10, first discuss the control unit in modern computers, including a description of both conventional logic design of control circuitry and microprogramming for computer control. The overall organization of computers is then discussed, as are the major topics in computer architecture—addressing techniques, interrupt servicing, etc. Existing computers are used as examples of the ideas presented. There is emphasis on microcomputers and minicomputers, but the basic ideas in large systems are also discussed.

The book is arranged so that the material on electronic circuits can be skipped. There are several reasons for this. In some schools, circuits are covered in a separate course. Other schools wish to treat circuit material lightly, since an understanding of circuit details is not essential to comprehending the functions performed by the circuits. Also, the widespread use of integrated circuits makes it possible to study the operation of a computer from a module, or block, viewpoint, as in Chapters 3 and 4, so that computer operation can be understood by considering flip-flops and gates from a functional, or operational, viewpoint.

The block diagram symbols in this book are those that have been adopted by the American National Standards Institute and also in Military Standards.

I have had considerable help and advice during the preparation of the various editions of this book. The first edition was written at M.I.T. Lincoln Laboratory, and I will always be indebted to M.I.T. and the laboratory members for the considerable support provided me.

Many friends and users of the book have contributed to later editions. I regret that I cannot name them all. Certainly Professors Glen Goff, W. W. Peterson, M. A. Miller, Robert Carroll, Irving Reed, and Irwin Lebow should be singled out. I must also thank the teaching assistants in my courses for their many suggestions.

I am indebted to Thomas Quentin Bartee for his work on the manuscript and the new figures. His help was essential to the preparation of this book.

Thomas C. Bartee

DIGITAL
COMPUTER
FUNDAMENTALS

1
COMPUTER OPERATION

The computer industry continues to be the fastest growing major industry. This year's government statistics indicate that the salaries of beginning computer personnel increased by 30 percent, more than the cost-of-living increase.

The great success of microcomputers along with the fast-growing minicomputer business have been a major factor in the widespread acceleration of computer sales. The prices of microcomputers have reached a point where these computers are widely used in some consumer products. Minicomputer prices continue to fall, with the result that smaller businesses and laboratories can make use of them as well as schools, factories, and small government offices. At the same time the sales of larger computers continue to grow.

Minicomputers and microcomputers lead to exciting new application areas for computers because of their low cost, reliability, small size, and low weight. These small computers are able to calculate at a rate of hundreds of thousands to millions of operations per second and offer computing power which was available in only the larger computers as recently as 10 years ago. The places where small computers can be used appear endless: such areas as process control, medical monitoring, production testing, scientific instrument recording, store checkout systems, and automobile test and evaluation systems were among the first to appear.

Well over a million people now work in the computer industry, and this does not include the millions who work with computers indirectly, such as bank clerks who put all their transactions into computers, airline and motel employees who work with computers to make reservations, and machinists who use computer-controlled power tools.

In fact, computers now route our long-distance telephone calls, process and issue the checks in our banks, schedule our planes and trains, make our weather forecasts, predict and process our elections, and figure in so many things that

1

entire books will be (and have been) written just documenting the types of applications.

Computers now use the major share of the electronics components being manufactured, and this share will continue to rise. The need for computer personnel in all areas continues to grow: over a quarter of a million new programmers are needed each year; the federal government's Department of Labor continues to maintain business machine service personnel and electronic computer operating personnel in first and second place in a list of five "fastest-growing employment areas."

1 • 1 CALCULATORS AND COMPUTERS

From the time individuals first started using arithmetic, they have been inventing devices to aid in handling numbers. One of the earliest and most ingenious examples of an aid to computation is the abacus. This primitive (4000 to 3000 B.C.) predecessor of modern computers consists of a rectangular frame carrying several parallel wires. Each wire supports a number of beads which are free to slide along the length of the wire. The Romans called these beads *calculi,* the plural of *calculus,* meaning pebble. This Latin root gave rise to our word *calculate.* By manipulating the beads, a skillful operator can add, subtract, multiply, and divide with amazing speed. In a contest between a Japanese proponent of this ancient invention and the trained operator of a modern manually operated calculating machine, the abacus won easily. Science will have the last word, however, for the computers described in this book perform operations several million times faster than the best of the abacus experts.

Calculating machines, including such familiar devices as adding machines, desk calculators, and cash registers, were invented more recently. The first successful mechanical calculator was constructed by Blaise Pascal in the seventeenth century. It was completed in 1642, and authentic models are still in existence. The primary conception which this machine introduced was the mechanization of the carry. The machine consists of a series of numbered wheels, or dials, each numbered from 0 to 9 and arranged to be read from left to right. When one of the dials passes from 9 to 0, a ratchet causes the wheel on its left to be moved one unit forward. The machine adds and subtracts directly, but multiplication and division are accomplished by repeated additions and subtractions.

In 1671 Leibniz constructed a calculating machine that could not only add and subtract, but also multiply. Addition and subtraction were accomplished in the same manner as in Pascal's machine, but additional gears were included which enabled the machine to multiply directly.

Leibniz commented that although the device was not completely automatic, the slight effort involved in using it was certainly preferable to the tedious and often erroneous procedures required in manual arithmetic. The calculator designed by Leibniz was the model for most later machines and embodied almost all the principles now used in the design of calculators.

As business techniques and science progressed, the need for the mechanization of simple arithmetic operations increased. The amount of arithmetic done by business concerns increased vastly and became far more complex, and bookkeepers increased in number, as did all types of white-collar workers. The paper work required to manage government functions efficiently also reached staggering proportions. For instance, it took so long to process the data gathered during the United States government census that the information was not available in a convenient summary form until after it had lost its timeliness. The problems of the Bureau of the Census were so acute that it became the developer of the punched card, using punched cards for its tabulating as early as in the 1890s.†

In the fields of science and engineering, many problems were being reduced to mathematical expressions which were so complex that it took a prohibitive amount of time to perform the arithmetic necessary to evaluate them for the various sets of parameters. For example, when the mathematical formulas describing the flight of an artillery shell along a ballistics trajectory were first known with considerable accuracy, the solution of these formulas (involving many different gun-elevation angles, distances, etc.) required the services of a large staff of human computers for long periods of time. Further, the tables had to be recalculated for new types of shells and weapons. This often introduced a lag from the time the weapons became available until they could be accurately used.

Fortunately the calculator was progressing also. Improvements in design and construction increased the speed and the number and variety of operations which could be performed by these devices, and at the same time improved manufacturing techniques made them more readily available. In early models, hand cranks were replaced by electric motors, and the speed of calculation was increased. Numerous aids to the operator were also introduced, thus increasing the speed of computation and decreasing the chances of error. Various types of desk calculating machines were common, and most business arithmetic was performed by these devices.

The final step in calculator development came with the introduction of electronic calculators. The speed of these devices is electronic—not mechanical—and in the larger models there are even small electronic memories or sometimes tape strips or metal cards which can store short "programs" containing instructions to the calculator. The calculator can then perform these short programs at electronic speeds at the will of the operator.

The fact remains that the data (generally numbers) operated on must be inserted by the human operating the calculator. The remarkable functions provided by electronic calculators greatly help but do not remove the need for computers.

For instance, many computers operate on large files of data which are stored in computer memory devices, such as magnetic tape or disks. These data would occupy many filing cabinets, and it would take human operators long periods of time to find items in these files. The computer, however, can search these files, often in fractions of a second, but occasionally in seconds, and find and update

---

†Herman Hollerith, who developed the punched card for the Census Bureau, later formed his own company, which still later was incorporated into IBM.

records automatically. For instance, the larger banking computers contain millions of records relating to customers' accounts. All transactions made in the branches of a large bank must be recorded and the appropriate records updated at the end of each day. The computer can accomplish this automatically, and banks and insurance companies are large users of computers as are businesses which use computers to maintain their inventories, such as large grocery chains which use computers to order automatically, to bookkeep their operations, etc.

Computers are used to control production devices in industry, monitor the operation of industrial processes, and help set type for newspapers and books. They perform many functions automatically and often at speeds and with accuracy and precision not possible for humans.

For scientific applications, some calculations are extremely complicated and long, requiring hundreds of millions of calculations. The speed and lack of errors in computer calculations make computers ideal for performing these calculations. Often scientific calculation involves large amounts of test data (from satellites or nuclear experiments or from medical laboratories, for instance). These data must be analyzed using mathematical techniques which require many calculations. While such calculations could be performed on electronic calculators, the amount of human effort and time required would make the cost of such calculations prohibitive.

The sequence of instructions which tells the computer how to solve a particular problem is called a *program*. The program tells the computer what to do, step by step, including all decisions that are to be made. It is apparent from this that the computer does not plan for itself, but that all planning must be done in advance. The growth of the computer industry created the need for trained personnel who do nothing but prepare the programs, or sequences of instructions, which direct the computer. The preparation of the list of instructions to the computer is called *programming,* and the personnel who perform this function are called *programmers.*

1 • 2 ELECTRONIC DIGITAL COMPUTERS

The history of attempts to make machines which would perform long sequences of calculations automatically is fairly long. The best known early attempt was made in the nineteenth century by Charles Babbage, an English scientist and mathematician. Babbage attempted to mechanize sequences of calculations, eliminating the operator and designing a machine so that it would perform all the necessary operations in a predetermined sequence. The machine designed by Babbage used cardboard cards with holes punched in them to introduce both instructions and the necessary data (numbers) into the machine. The machine was to perform the instructions dictated by the cards automatically, not stopping until an entire sequence of instructions had been completed. The punched cards used to control the machine had already been used to control the operation of weaving machines. Surprisingly enough, Babbage obtained some money for his project from the

English government and started construction. Although he was severely limited by the technology of his time and the machine was never completed, Babbage succeeded in establishing the basic principles upon which modern computers are constructed. There is even some speculation that if he had not run short of money, he might have constructed a successful machine. Although Babbage died without realizing his dream, he had established the fundamental concepts which were used to construct machines elaborated beyond even his expectations.

By the 1930s punched cards were in wide use in large businesses, and various types of punched-card-handling machines were available. In 1937 Howard Aiken, at Harvard, proposed to IBM that a machine could be constructed (using some of the parts and techniques from the punched-card machines) which would automatically sequence the operations and calculations performed. This machine used a combination of electromechanical devices, including many relays. The machine was in operation for some time, generating many tables of mathematical functions (particularly Bessel functions), and was used for trajectory calculations in World War II.

Aiken's machine was remarkable for its time, but limited in speed by its use of relays rather than electronic devices, and by its use of punched cards for sequencing the operations. In 1943 S. P. Eckert and J. W. Mauchly, of the Moore School of Engineering of the University of Pennsylvania, started the Eniac, which used electronic components (primarily vacuum tubes) and was therefore faster, but which also used switches and a wired plug board to implement the programming of operations. Later Eckert and Mauchly built the Edvac, which had its program stored in the computer's memory, not depending on external sequencing. This was an important innovation, and a computer which stores its list of operations, or program, internally is called a *stored-program computer*. Actually the Edsac, at the University of Manchester, started later but completed before Edvac, was the first operational stored-program computer.

A year or so later, John Von Neumann, at the Institute for Advanced Study in Princeton, started the IAS in conjunction with the Moore School of Engineering, and this machine incorporated most of the general concepts of parallel binary stored-program computers.

The Univac I was the first commercially available electronic digital computer and was designed by Eckert and Mauchly at their own company, which was later bought by Sperry Rand. The U.S. Bureau of the Census bought the first Univac. (Later Univac and half of Aiken's machine were placed in the Smithsonian Institution, where they may now be seen.) IBM entered the competition with the IBM 701, a large machine, in 1953, and in 1954 with the IBM 650, a much smaller machine which was very successful. The IBM 701 was the forerunner of the 704–709–7094 series of IBM machines, the first "big winners" in the large-machine category.

There were quite a few vacuum-tube electronic computers available and in use by the late 1950s, but at this time an important innovation in electronics appeared—the transistor. The replacement of large, expensive (hot) vacuum tubes with small, inexpensive, reliable, comparatively low heat-dissipating transistors led to what are called "second-generation computers," and the size and importance of the computer industry grew at amazing rates, while the costs of individual computers dropped substantially.

By 1965 a third generation of computers was introduced. (The IBM Corporation, in introducing their 360 series, used the term "third-generation" as a key phrase in their advertising, and it remains as a catch word in describing all machines of this era.) The machines of this period began making heavy use of *integrated circuits* in which many transistors and other components are fabricated and packaged together in a single small container. The low prices and high packing densities of these circuits plus lessons learned from prior machines led to some differences in computer-system design, and these machines proliferated and expanded the computer industry to its present multibillion-dollar size.

Fourth-generation machines are less easily distinguished from earlier generations. There are some striking and important differences, however. The manufacture of integrated circuits has become so advanced as to incorporate thousands of active components in volumes of a fraction of an inch, leading to what is called medium-scale integration (MSI) and large-scale integration (LSI). This has led to small-size, lower-cost, large-memory, ultrafast computers. Large computers have become increasingly complex; medium-sized computers now perform as large computers of the near past did; and there is a new breed of computers called microcomputers and minicomputers which are small and inexpensive, are manufactured by many different companies, and are proliferating at a surprising rate.

1 • 3 APPLICATION OF COMPUTERS TO PROBLEMS

Large office forces have for many years been employed in the accounting departments of business firms. The clerks employed by these businesses spend most of their time performing arithmetic computations and then entering their results into company books and on paychecks, invoices, order forms, etc. Most of the arithmetic consists of repetitious sequences of simple calculations which the clerks perform over and over on different sets of figures. Few decisions are required, rules having usually been defined covering almost all problems that might arise.

A typical task in a payroll office is the processing of paychecks for company employees who work at an hourly rate.† This job involves calculating total earnings by multiplying each employee's hourly wage rate by the number of hours worked, taking into consideration any overtime; figuring and then deducting taxes, insurance, contributions to charity, etc.; then making out the necessary check and entering a record of all figures. Figure 1·1 is a flowchart of a possible procedure. Flowcharts such as this are standard tools of business and are often used by the computing industry. Such flowcharts are very useful when reducing problems to the necessary steps required and are an invaluable aid in the field of programming. The example given deliberately omits overtime rates, irregular taxes such as FICA,

---

† It is interesting to note that 95 percent of the checks issued by the federal government are made out by computers.

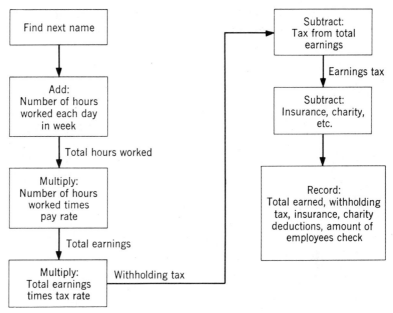

FIG. 1 • 1 Flowchart of paycheck calculation.

and other such complicating features. The procedure followed by a clerk in performing this sequence of computations might be as follows:

1. The clerk looks up the employee's daily work record and adds the number of hours worked each day, obtaining the total number of hours worked during the week.
2. The total number of hours worked is multiplied by the pay rate, and the total earnings for the week are obtained.
3. The total earnings are multiplied by the tax rate for the employee, and the amount of withholding tax is found.
4. The withholding tax is subtracted from the total earnings.
5. Any regular deductions such as insurance are subtracted.
6. A record of each of the above operations is entered in the company books, and a check is made out for the correct amount.

It can be seen that almost all of the above procedure can be mechanized by a machine which can be caused to add, multiply, and subtract in the correct sequence. The machine must also have the following less obvious features:

1. The ability to remember the intermediate results which have been obtained. For instance, the total amount earned must be remembered while the tax is being figured. It is also convenient to keep the employee's pay rate, rate of withholding tax, insurance rates, and the amount regularly given to charity in the machine.

2. The ability to accept information. The records of time worked, changes in pay rates, deduction amounts, etc., must be entered into the machine.

3. The ability to print out the results obtained.

The widespread acceptance of digital computing machines in payroll offices is largely due to the repetitious type of work which is normally done in such offices. Mechanization of such tasks is straightforward, although often complicated; but the additional accuracy and speed, as well as the lower operating costs, which electronic business machines make possible, have made their use especially popular in this field. Most large companies now use special time clocks which enter the time each employee arrives and leaves by punching holes in time cards. The time cards are "read into" a computer which interprets the holes in the cards, then automatically performs all the necessary arithmetic operations, and prints a record of all totals, subtotals, etc., for the company books. The computer also keeps a record of the total amount paid each week and each year to the employee, as well as a record of the various deductions, such as withholding tax. The computer can determine the total number of hours worked by all employees during any given week, the average pay for all workers during any selected period, the number of people contributing to various charities, and practically any other type of payroll information.

1 • 4 BUSINESS APPLICATIONS

It can be readily seen that the use of computers is not restricted to the area of scientific calculation. In fact, far more machines are produced for business than for laboratory or scientific use. The main difference between the use of digital machines in business and in scientific work lies in the ratio of operations performed to total data processed. While the business machine performs only a few calculations using each datum, a great volume of data must be processed. The scientific problem generally starts with fewer data, but a great many calculations are performed using each datum. Both types of machines still fall under the heading of automatic digital computers, and either type of work may be done on all computers, although some machines may be better adapted to one or the other type of problem.

One of the first uses for the digital computer has been in the mechanizing of the more routine and clerical aspects of management. The description of the use of a computer in figuring payrolls (Sec. 1·3) is an example of a business application and illustrates the similarity in programming the operation of a computer and figuring out employee office procedures. First, the problem to be solved is reduced to a series of simple operations: finding the name of the next employee whose wages are to be computed, figuring how many hours he or she has worked, and multiplying this figure by the hourly rate of pay. After the procedure to be used has been worked out and explained to the clerk, the clerk is provided with the necessary numerical information, such as pay rates, insurance rates, etc. If the operations are further simplified, each step in Fig. 1·1 may be performed by a different clerk. For instance, the first clerk may find the employee's record and send it to the second clerk, who computes the total number of hours worked and presents this to the next clerk, who multiplies by the wage rate, and so on until all the operations have been performed. It may be seen from this that the breaking down of business procedures into basic steps is a very old practice indeed.

The procedure for preparing a list of instructions for a digital computer is basically the same. All the operations the computer is to perform are written in flowchart form (Fig. 1·1). The problem is then broken down into a list of instructions to the machine which specify exactly how the solution is to be obtained. After the problem has been programmed, the list of instructions is transferred onto some medium which the machine can "read" (punched cards, for instance) and is then read into the machine. The machine automatically performs the required steps. Notice that once the procedure has been established and the programmed steps have been read in, the programming is finished until a change in procedure is desired. Changes in rates, for instance, can be inserted by simply reading the new pay rates into the machine. This does not affect the procedure.

1 • 5 SCIENTIFIC APPLICATIONS

Modern science and engineering use mathematics as a language for expressing physical laws in precise terms. The electronic digital computer is a valuable tool for studying the consequences of these laws. Often the exact procedure for solving a problem has been found, but the time required to perform the necessary calculations manually is prohibitive. Sometimes it is necessary to solve the same problem many times using different sets of parameters, and the computer is especially useful for solving problems of this type. The computer is not only able to evaluate types of mathematical expressions at high speeds, but if a set of calculations is performed repeatedly on different sets of numerical values, the computer is able to compare the results and determine the optimum values that were used.

An algebraic formula is an expression of a mathematical relationship. Many of the laws of physics, electronics, chemistry, etc., are expressed in this form, in which case digital computers may be easily used, because algebraic formulas may be directly changed to the basic steps they represent. Figure 1·2 is a flowchart illustrating the steps necessary to evaluate the expression $ax^3 + bx^2 + cx + d$, given numerical values for a, b, c, d, and x. The required steps are as follows:

1. Multiply a times x, yielding ax.
2. Add b, yielding $ax + b$.
3. Multiply this by x, forming $ax^2 + bx$.
4. Add c, yielding $ax^2 + bx + c$.
5. Multiply this by x: $x(ax^2 + bx + c)$ or $ax^3 + bx^2 + cx$.
6. Add d, obtaining $ax^3 + bx^2 + cx + d$.

It would take several minutes to perform the calculations necessary to evaluate this algebraic expression for a single set of values using manually operated cal-

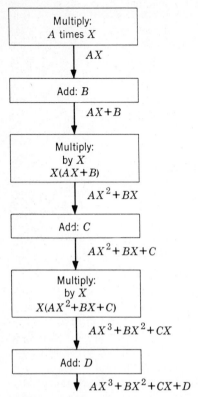

FIG. 1 • 2 Flowchart of evaluation of expression.

culators, but practically any computer could perform this series of operations several thousand times per second. While the algebraic expression shown is certainly much simpler than many formulas encountered by members of the engineering and scientific professions, the value of using a computer for certain types of problems may be readily seen.

1 • 6 SOME DIFFERENT TYPES OF COMPUTER SYSTEMS

The most familiar use of computers is in operating programs punched into cards (or perhaps recorded on paper or magnetic tape) and run by a computer which then prepares printouts, checks, or some form of data presentation recording the results. This is an example of what is called *batch processing*. When a computer is used in this way, the input data (and often the program) are introduced into the computer and processed automatically, generally without operator intervention. Often many different jobs (or sets of data) are processed, one right after the other, or even at the same time, but without any interaction from the system's user during program operation. For instance, the keypunch operators may punch many decks of punched cards containing data on customers and claims. These cards are then stacked together and transported to a large computer which processes the cards, issuing checks, sending out bills, printing records for the company, etc. This is batch processing.

Similarly, the user of a computer in a scientific laboratory may submit program cards and data cards as a *job,* with the familiar elastic band around these, along with any notes to the operators of the machine. A number of these decks of cards are collected and then stacked together, and finally run by the machine. Later the results are printed out and, perhaps even the next day, delivered to the individual users. This is also batch processing.

In other types of systems, users interact with the computer directly, inserting and receiving the data as desired. For instance, an airline ticket agent wishes to make a reservation. The agent types the desired aircraft flight number and passenger identification on a special typewriter which communicates, via the telephone lines, with a computer. The computer looks in its memory, sees if the flight is full, and if not, enters the passenger's name on its list for the flight, and then communicates this fact back to the airline ticket agent. If no seats are available, the computer sends this information to the ticket agent, who attempts to interest the passenger in another flight. In this way an airline connects all its ticket agents together, keeping a constant record of flights, passengers, and payments and doing all the bookkeeping. The terminals where the ticket agents are located are scattered throughout the world, but communicate with the computer via telephone lines. Motels, hotels, stockbrokers, and many other businesses have similar systems for reservations, information transferral, and bookkeeping.

All these are called *online interactive* systems, for the users of the system communicate directly with the computer, and the computer responds directly. The development of these systems has progressed in parallel with the development of keyboard input devices, as well as output devices for users of various types, including television displays, printers, and other data display devices.

Online systems are also widely used in scientific applications where users operate their programs at a terminal connected to the computer, perhaps by telephone lines, trying changes and variations at will. Experimenters can try a set of inputs and study the results, then try other inputs and study these results. The technique of online interactive computing is used by circuit designers, architects, and chemists, and in almost any area, including medical systems for hospital use.

A widely used input–output device is the *terminal,* shown in Fig. 1·3. This is an example of a keyboard which is "typewriterlike," generating a printed record when used, but also generating electrical signals which can be used as computer input. Similarly, electronic signals from a computer can be used to control the terminal, and the terminal's printer will type, under the computer's control, the results of calculations.

Terminals are often used in systems where the console terminal is some distance from the computer. A special attachment called a *modem* is used, which makes it possible to transmit the electrical signals generated by the terminal to the computer and receive the computer's response back over telephone lines. At the computer another modem is located which can also transmit or receive, and this pair of modems allows communication in both directions over telephone lines. The user of the terminal simply dials the number at which the computer is located, establishes a connection and the user's identity and right to use the computer (the computer generally checks a password), and then proceeds to use the computer.

Terminal characteristics are fairly well standardized, and the same terminals often can use several different computers, when available. There are now many companies that provide computer service to users who have terminals at their disposal. The users simply dial the computer they prefer.

Figure 1·4 shows a keyboard similar to a typewriter for data entry, but the computer responses are sent to an oscilloscope display which is similar to a television, thus providing a temporary display (instead of "hard copy," which is the printed page). (Sometimes some means for making a copy of what is displayed, at the user's convenience, is provided.) This type of output device is called a *display device* and enables the computer to draw pictures or make graphs as well as use printed characters.

The computer terminal in Fig. 1·4 is portable. An attachment which holds a telephone handset is provided so that when the telephone handset is placed in the attachment, a computer can be dialed, and once the connection is made, the terminal then generates audio tones into the handset when keys are depressed on the keyboard. The terminal receiver also decodes coded tones representing char-

FIG. 1 • 3 A computer terminal. (Courtesy of DEC, Inc.)

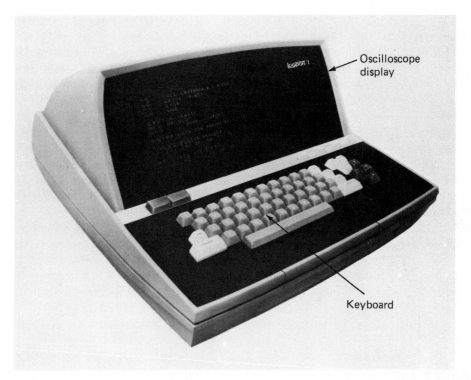

FIG. 1 • 4 Portable computer terminal with cathode-ray-tube display. (Courtesy of Logitron, Inc.)

acters generated by the computer, displaying the information received on the oscilloscope display device. In this way the user of a terminal can "converse," or communicate, with any compatible computer connected to the telephone system.

When a number of users share a computer, using the computer, often via telephone lines, at the same time, the computer is said to be *time shared.* By time sharing is meant that the computer is able to alternate and interweave the running of its programs so that several jobs or users can be on at the same time. This makes for more efficient use, and the airline, motel, and hotel reservation systems and most online systems use time sharing. We shall return to these systems in Sec. 1·9.

1 • 7 COMPUTERS IN CONTROL SYSTEMS

The ability of digital computers to make precise calculations and decisions at high speeds has made it possible to use them as parts of control systems. The first example of the use of a computer in a large control system was the SAGE Air Defense System. In this system, data from a network of radar stations, which are used to detect the positions of all aircraft in the area, are fed via communication links into a high-speed computer. The computer stores all the incoming positional information from the radar stations, and from this calculates the future positions of the aircraft, their speed and altitude, and all other pertinent information. A number of other types of information are also relayed into the computer, including information from picket ships, AEW aircraft, Ground Observer Corps aircraft spotters, flight plans for both military and civilian aircraft, and weather information.

A single computer receives all this information and from it calculates a composite picture of the complete air situation. The computer then generates displays on special oscilloscopes which are used by members of the military services to make tactical decisions. The computer further aids these operators by calculating the most effective use of the interceptor aircraft, antiaircraft guns, and also antiaircraft missiles. By means of radio links, the computer automatically guides both interceptor aircraft and missiles to their targets.

It may be seen that the computer in this system is truly a high-speed data processing machine. The computer receives data from many sources, processes these data, and then "controls" the defending air power.

A system of this sort is called a *real-time control system* because information must be processed and decisions must be made in real time. When a computer is used to process business data or to perform most scientific calculations, time is not as critical a factor. In real-time systems the computer must "keep up," processing all data at high speeds in order to be effective.†

Other examples of real-time control applications include oil refineries and other manufacturing areas which use the computer to control the manufacturing processes automatically. Digital computers are also used to guide machine tools which perform precision-machining operations automatically, as shown in Fig. 1·5. Further, both manned and unmanned space vehicles carry digital computers which perform the necessary guidance functions, while a network of computers on the ground monitors and directs the progress of the flight.

Most real-time control systems require an important device known as an *analog-to-digital converter*. The inputs to these systems in many cases are in the form of *analog quantities* such as mechanical displacements (for instance, shaft positions) or temperatures, voltages, pressures, etc. Since the digital computer operates on digital rather than analog data, a fundamental "language" problem arises which requires the conversion of the analog quantities into digital representations. The analog-to-digital converter does this.

The same problem occurs at the computer output, where it is often necessary to convert numerical output data from the computer into mechanical displacements or analog-type electrical signals. For instance, a "number" output from the computer might be used to rotate a shaft through the number of revolutions indicated by the output number. A device which converts digital-type information into analog quantities is called a *digital-to-analog converter*. A description of both analog-to-digital and digital-to-analog converters will be found in Chap. 8.

---

†Most reservation systems would be considered real-time systems by their operators, since delays of any consequence would be detrimental to business.

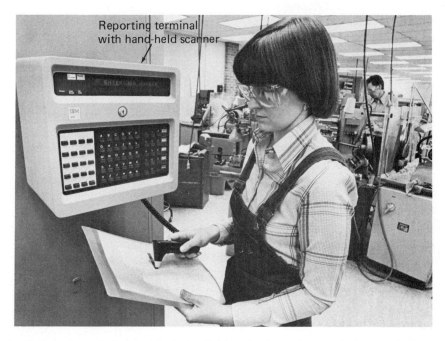

FIG. 1 • 5 Computer-controlled machine tools with interactive terminal-based plant communication system. (Courtesy IBM)

The basic elements of a control system using a digital computer consist of (1) the data-gathering devices which perform measurements on the external environment and, if necessary, also perform analog-to-digital conversion on the data from the system which is to be controlled; (2) the digital computer itself, which performs calculations on the data supplied and makes the necessary decisions; and (3) the means of communication with, or control over, certain of the elements in the external environment. If no person aids the computer in its calculations or decisions, the system is considered to be fully automatic; if a human being also enters the control loop, the system is defined as semiautomatic.

Figure 1·5 shows a computer being used in a manufacturing application. Because of their high speed, computers can measure, test, analyze, and control manufacturing functions as they occur, often operating unattended. Computers can handle shop floor control, quality-control testing, materials handling, and production monitoring. The typewriterlike station to the left of the computer in Fig. 1·5 is used to communicate with the system.

1 • 8 SPECIAL-PURPOSE AND GENERAL-PURPOSE COMPUTERS

In general there are two types of digital computers. The first is the *special-purpose digital computer,* which performs a fixed and preset sequence of calculations. This type of computer may be constructed more efficiently in that it can be lighter and smaller and may consume less power, etc., than the general-purpose computer. Because of the advantages in construction, small special-purpose computers are used where such factors as weight, power consumption, etc., are critical, as in aircraft control systems, missile guidance systems, special checkout equipment for military devices used in the field, etc.

The second type of computer is defined as a *general-purpose digital computer.* The sequence of instructions which the machine follows is generally read into this type of machine and stored in the memory of the machine. The machine can be made to follow another sequence of instructions by simply reading in the desired set of instructions. Since the sequence of operations performed by the general-purpose digital computer may be easily changed, the machine possesses great flexibility, and this is the type of machine generally used in business and for scientific computations. The general-purpose computer can process a stack of payroll cards, and then, after another program has been read into it, can perform an inventory of a company's stock. In scientific applications a general-purpose computer can calculate the orbit of a satellite, and then, after a new program has been read in, design a set of lenses for a movie projector. The general-purpose computer may be used to solve a wide variety of problems, the details of which may have been unknown when the machine was designed. The special-purpose computer is generally only capable of solving a special type of problem.

1 • 9 TIME-SHARED COMPUTER SYSTEMS

Among the more important real-time computer systems are those designed to aid research operations, businesses, and military decision making. These systems provide users with a large file of information and a computational facility by means of which they can communicate in a direct manner. As has been mentioned, the user of the system is able to introduce instructions to the computer by utilizing some device such as a teletype keyboard or a set of push buttons at a console. The computer responds by either printing the results or displaying them on an oscilloscope. The interaction between the user and the computer is direct; the computer is made to respond immediately. In general the time that elapses from when a command is given to a computer to when results are obtained is called *turnaround* time. The designer of a time-shared online system tries to minimize turnaround time.

These systems are used in many ways. Computer-aided design systems have consoles and displays such that a designer can work out the details of a design by using the computer to perform all calculations and to display the effects of changes in the design. The designer then attempts to optimize the design by changing the parameters and noting the effects of those changes in the design.

The business manager or military leader uses large digital systems in a manner which relies heavily on the enormous number of records that can be stored in the memory of a digital machine. The business systems are called *management control systems,* and the military systems are called *command and control systems.* The business systems contain the files and records for the business, as well as any other pertinent data, and the military systems store the military information required by officers to make critical decisions. In either case the information is continually updated, using communications facilities. When a category of data is requested, the computer locates it in its memory and provides selected features upon request. For instance, the computer might store the types of aircraft available at each airport in the world, along with the range and ability of each aircraft to carry bombs. If aircraft were flown from one place to another, or if they were in the air or had been lost, this information would be entered into the computer. If air force personnel then wanted to design a bombing raid, they would ask the computer for the data and then try to use aircraft that were favorably placed and suited for their tasks. The computer could also supply data concerning the fuel and ammunition available at each place to further facilitate decision making.

Similarly, an executive in a business would have access to all the company's sales records, salaries, current stock levels, overhead figures, and any other data he or she might wish to calculate using the company records.

In the above systems the computer is liable to be *time shared,* since it has many input and output information channels, each with different users, and these users share the main computer.

1 • 10 BASIC COMPONENTS OF A DIGITAL COMPUTER

The block diagram in Fig. 1·6 illustrates the five major operational divisions of an electronic digital computer. Although presently available machines vary greatly in the construction details of various components, the overall system concepts

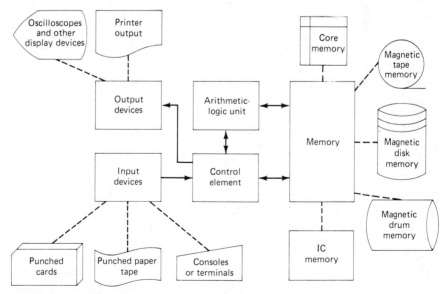

FIG. 1 • 6 Block diagram of typical digital computer.

remain roughly the same. It is interesting to note that present-day machines are basically designed according to the precepts which Charles Babbage proposed for his "analytic engine." Although Babbage's machine was of mechanical construction whereas present-day computers are electronic, the functions which the various sections of the machines perform are much the same.

Perhaps the outstanding conceptual difference lies in the ability of the modern computer's memory to store either instructions or the data to be used in the same location. This permits more efficient use of the memory and also enables the computer to alter the instructions which constitute the program while the computer is operating.

A digital computer may be divided into the following fundamental units:

1. *Input*　The input devices read the necessary data into the machine. In most general-purpose computers the instructions which constitute the program must be read into the machine along with all the data to be used in the computations. Some of the more common input devices are keyboards, punched-card and punched-paper-tape readers, magnetic-tape readers, and various manual input devices such as toggle switches and push buttons.

2. *Control*　The control section of a computer sequences the operation of the computer, controlling the actions of all other units. The control circuitry interprets the instructions which constitute the program and then directs the rest of the machine in its operation.

3. *Memory*　The memory, or storage, section of the computer consists of the devices used to store the information that will be used during the computations. The memory section of the computer is also used to hold both intermediate and final results as the computer proceeds through the program. The principal or high-speed memory devices for a computer are divided into pieces of equal size, each of which is then identified with what is called an *address,* or *location in memory.* If the control unit is looking for a specific piece of information or an instruction located in the memory section, it calls for it by means of its address. Memory devices are constructed so that it is possible for control to obtain the information contained at any address. The length of time required to obtain information may vary somewhat, however, and is determined by the type of device used to store the information. Common storage devices are integrated circuit memories, magnetic cores, magnetic drums, magnetic tape, and magnetic disks.

4. *Arithmetic-logic unit*　The arithmetic-logic units of most computers are capable of performing the operations of addition, subtraction, division, and multiplication, as well as some "logical operations" which will be described. The control unit tells the arithmetic-logic unit which of these operations to perform and then sees that the necessary numbers are supplied. The arithmetic element can be compared to the calculating machines described previously in that the numbers to be used are inserted, and it is then directed to perform the necessary operations.

5. *Output*　The output devices are used to record the results obtained by the computer and present them to the "outside world." Most output devices are

directed by the control element, which also causes the necessary information to be supplied to them. Common output devices are card-punching machines, magnetic-tape machines, special electromechanical typewriters, cathode-ray tubes, and high-speed printing devices. There are also many unusual types of output devices, such as lights, buzzers, and loudspeakers.

1 • 11 CONSTRUCTION OF MEMORY

It has been mentioned that the inner or high-speed memory is broken into a number of addresses, or locations. At each of these addresses a group of digits is stored and is handled by the computer as a unit. The group of digits stored at each address in memory is generally referred to as a "word."† Each address in memory is assigned a number, and the address is then referred to by that number. We say that address 100 contains the value 300, or that address 50 contains an instruction word. In most computers instruction words may be stored in the same locations as number or data words, which makes the memory more flexible. Notice also that instruction words consist of a group of digits when stored in the computer.

The time it takes to obtain a word from a storage device is called the *access time.* The access time of the storage devices used in a machine has a profound effect on the speed of the computer. One of the factors which for a long time impeded the construction of high-speed computers was the lack of reliable storage devices with short access times. The development of storage devices (such as magnetic cores) with very short access times plus the ability to store information for an indefinite time was a great forward step.

1 • 12 INSTRUCTIONS

It has been mentioned that computers can make simple logical decisions. Many of these decisions are based on numbers and are therefore quantitative rather than qualitative decisions. The sort of numerical decision the computer might make is whether one number is larger than another, or whether the result of some series of calculations is positive or negative. However, most of the decisions made by clerical workers and scientists are also based on figures. For instance, once physical phenomena have been expressed in formulas, the solutions to specific problems are expressed by means of numbers.

The digital computer does not figure out its own solution to problems, but must

---

†There are actually two ways of organizing a memory now in general use. One way is to store a character at each address (a character is a 1 or 2, an A or B, etc.). These systems are called *character addressable* systems. The second way is to store a complete *operand* or instruction word at each address. These systems are called *word addressable* systems. As might be guessed, character addressable systems have smaller amounts of information at each address than word addressable systems. There are, quite naturally, pros and cons for each type of system. We shall simplify the description by assuming that each successive address contains a word, as in word addressable systems, but we will describe other systems later.

be told exactly how to solve any given problem, as well as how to make all decisions. As mentioned, preparing a list of instructions which tells the computer how
to perform its calculations is called programming. The procedure for programming
a problem generally consists of two separate steps. The first step, planning the
program, involves determining the sequence of operations required to solve the
problem. It consists, generally, in breaking the problem down into flow diagrams
such as those illustrated in the preceding section. Once the problem has been
reduced to this form, it is ready to be *coded;* this is the second step. *Coding* consists in writing the steps outlined in the flowchart in a special language which can
be interpreted by the machine. The final coded program consists of a list of instructions to the computer, written in a special format which details the operations the
computer is to perform.

The instruction words which direct the computer are stored in the machine in
numerical form. The programmer rarely writes instructions in numerical form, however; instead, each instruction to the computer is written using a letter code to
designate the operation to be performed, plus the address in memory of the number to be used in this step of the calculation.† Later the alphabetic section of the
instruction word is converted to numerical form by a computer program called an
assembler. This will be described in a later section.

An instruction word as written by the programmer consists of two parts: (1) the
operation-code part which designates the operation (addition, subtraction, multiplication, etc.) to be performed, and (2) the *address* of the number to be used. A
typical instruction word written by the programmer is

ADD 535

This instruction word is divided into two main parts: first, the operation-code part,
consisting of the letters ADD, which directs the computer to perform the arithmetic
operation of addition; and second, the address part, which tells the computer the
address in storage of the number to be used.

It is important to notice that the second section of the instruction word gives
only the location (address) in storage of the number to be added. The number 535
in the instruction shown is not the actual number to be added, but only tells the
computer where to find the desired number. To what is the number at address 535
added? It is to be added to the number which is already in the arithmetic-logic unit
in a storage device or register called an *accumulator.* If the accumulator contains
zero before the instruction is executed, the accumulator will contain the number
which is stored at address 535 after the instruction has been performed. If the
accumulator contains the number 500 before the instruction is performed, and the

---

†The instructions described are typical instructions for a *single-address* computer. Computers are also constructed which use two, three, and four addresses in each computer instruction word. These computers are called
multiple-address computers, and will be described in Chap. 9. The single-address type of instruction is very straightforward, and will be used in the illustrations in this chapter. The two-address computer is equally popular and equally
easy to learn, and will be discussed later in the book. Learning two-address coding after single-address coding has
been mastered is very simple indeed.

TABLE 1 • 1

INSTRUCTION WORD		FUNCTION PERFORMED BY INSTRUCTION
OPERATION CODE	ADDRESS PART	
CLA	430	The accumulator is emptied of all previous numbers and the number at address 430 is added into it. After the instruction is performed, the accumulator contains the number in storage at address 430. CLA is a mnemonic code for "clear and add."
ADD	530	The number located at address 530 is added to the number in the accumulator. After the instruction, the accumulator contains the sum of the number it previously contained and the number in address 530.
SUB	235	Subtracts the number located at address 235 in the memory from the number in the accumulator and places the difference in the accumulator.
STO	433	The number in the accumulator is stored at address 433. Any information previously in this address is destroyed. The number which was in the accumulator before the instruction was performed remains in the accumulator. This is generally referred to as a STORE instruction.
HLT	000	The machine is ordered to stop. The number in the accumulator remains.

number stored at address 535 is 200, the number stored in the accumulator after the ADD operation will be 700. To illustrate this principle more fully, several more instructions are explained in Table 1·1.

A short program which adds three numbers together using these instructions is shown in Table 1·2.

The program operates as follows: The control section starts with the instruction word at address 1, which clears the accumulator and then adds the number at address 6 into it. The instruction at address 2 adds the number at address 7 to the number already in the accumulator. This produces the sum of 200 + 300, or 500. The third instruction adds the contents of address 8 to this sum, giving 900 in the accumulator. This number is then stored in memory at location 9 in the memory.

TABLE 1 • 2

| ADDRESS IN MEMORY | INSTRUCTION WORD | | CONTENTS OF ARITHMETIC ELEMENT AFTER INSTRUCTION IS PERFORMED |
	OPERATION CODE	ADDRESS PART	
1	CLA	6	200
2	ADD	7	500
3	ADD	8	900
4	STO	9	900
5	HLT	0	900

6 contains the number 200
7 contains the number 300
8 contains the number 400

The machine is then ordered to halt. Notice that the machine is stopped before it reaches the data. This is to prevent the control element from picking up the data, for instance, the number 200, which is at address 6, and trying to use it as an instruction.

There is no difference between a number and an instruction as far as storage is concerned. Both are stored in the same basic form. From this it can be seen that the instructions are generally placed in a different section of the memory than the data to be used. The computer progresses through the instructions and is stopped before it reaches the data. The fact that either instructions or data may be stored at all addresses makes the machine more flexible. It may be seen that either a large amount of data and a few instructions, or many instructions and few data, can be used as long as the total amount of storage available is not exceeded.

1 • 13 MULTIPLICATION INSTRUCTION

By adding another instruction, that of multiplication, it will be possible to write more sophisticated programs (see Table 1·3).

The program in Table 1·4 evaluates the expression $ax^3 + bx^2 + cx + d$. The actual quantities for $a, b, c, d,$ and x are stored in memory at locations 22, 23, 24, 25, and 26, respectively. It is important to notice that the program shown evaluates the expression for any values which might be read into these locations. The expression could be evaluated for any number of values for x by running the pro-

TABLE 1 • 3

| INSTRUCTION WORD | | |
OPERATION CODE	ADDRESS PART	FUNCTION
MUL	400	The number at address 400 is multiplied by the number already in the accumulator and the product placed in the accumulator.

TABLE 1 · 4

| ADDRESS IN MEMORY | INSTRUCTION WORD | | CONTENTS OF ACCUMULATOR AFTER INSTRUCTION IS PERFORMED |
	OPERATION CODE	ADDRESS PART	
1	CLA	22	a
2	MUL	26	ax
3	ADD	23	$ax + b$
4	MUL	26	$x(ax + b)$ or $ax^2 + bx$
5	ADD	24	$ax^2 + bx + c$
6	MUL	26	$x(ax^2 + bx + c)$ or $ax^3 + bx^2 + cx$
7	ADD	25	$ax^3 + bx^2 + cx + d$
8	STO	27	$ax^3 + bx^2 + cx + d$
9	HLT	000	$ax^3 + bx^2 + cx + d$

22 contains a
23 contains b
24 contains c
25 contains d
26 contains x
27 contains 0

gram for one value of x, then substituting the succeeding values of x into register 26 and rerunning the program for each value. In practice it is possible to have the program automatically repeat itself by means of special instructions. All the various desired values for x can then be stored and the equation solved for each x without stopping the computer.

It can be seen from Table 1·4 that very complicated algebraic functions can be evaluated using only a very few instructions. The program shown can be performed by a high-speed computer in less than 1/100,000 s. The value of such speed in the solution of the more complex problems encountered in engineering and science may readily be seen. Computers are making possible engineering techniques which were previously unusable because of the high costs in time and money of lengthy computations.

1 · 14 BRANCH, SKIP, OR JUMP INSTRUCTIONS

All the instructions explained so far have been used to perform problems in simple arithmetic. It has been pointed out, however, that the computer is able to repeat the same sequence of instructions without being stopped and restarted. This facility is provided by a group of instructions referred to as *branch, skip,* or *jump* instructions. These instructions tell the computer not to perform the instruction at the address following that of the instruction being performed, but to skip to some other instruction. Some branch instructions are *unconditional* in nature and cause the computer to skip regardless of what the conditions may be. Other branch

TABLE 1 • 5

OPERATION CODE	ADDRESS PART	FUNCTION
BRA	420	This instruction tells the computer to perform the instruction at address 420 next. The computer will skip or branch from the instruction it would have performed and perform instruction 420 instead. The computer will then perform instruction 421, followed by 422, etc.
BRM	420	The computer will branch to instruction 420 only if the number in the accumulator is negative. If the number is positive or zero, the computer will not branch, but will perform the instruction stored at the next address in memory. BRM is a mnemonic code for "branch or minus."

instructions are *conditional* and tell the computer to skip only if certain things are true. Branch instructions enable the computer to make logical choices which alter its future actions.

Two typical instructions are shown in Table 1·5.

The short program shown in Table 1·6 illustrates several very important principles. The purpose of the program is to add all the even integers from 2 to 100. The program is of the repetitious sort where a few short orders are used to generate a program which runs for some time by repeating the same sequence of

TABLE 1 • 6

ADDRESS	INSTRUCTION WORD		CONTENTS OF ACCUMULATOR		
	OPERATION CODE	ADDRESS PART	1ST TIME	2D TIME	LAST TIME
1	CLA	39	0	2	98
2	ADD	41	2	4	100
3	STO	39	2	4	100
4	ADD	43	2	6	$2 + 4 + 6 + \ldots + 100$
5	STO	43	2	6	$2 + 4 + 6 + \ldots + 100$
6	CLA	40	-50	-49	-1
7	ADD	42	-49	-48	$+0$
8	STO	40	-49	-48	$+0$
9	BRM	1	-49	-48	$+0$
10	HLT	000			

39 contains 000
40 contains -50
41 contains 2
42 contains 1
43 contains 0

instructions. The program illustrates how the ability to branch on a negative number can be used to form a counter that will determine how many times a part of a program is repeated.

The number stored in location 39 increases by 2 each time the program runs through. The total of these numbers is stored in address 43 which, after the program has halted, contains the total of all the numbers that have been in location 39. The number stored at address 40 decreases in magnitude by 1 each time the program runs through, until the number stored at 40 is no longer negative. When the program "falls through" the BRANCH WHEN MINUS (BRM) instruction, it then performs the next instruction in sequence, which is a HALT instruction. Zero is considered to be a positive number, although this varies with different machines. Notice that the first section of the program will cycle a number of times equal to the negative number stored in register 40. A simulated counter is formed by the −50 stored at address 40, the 1 stored in location 42, and the instructions at addresses 6 through 9. Any sequence of instructions which precedes a counter of this sort will be run through the number of times determined by the counter. This is an especially useful device for iterative schemes when the number of iterations required is known.

1 • 15 READING THE PROGRAM INTO THE COMPUTER

After the programmer has written the list of instructions that the computer is to perform, another step must be taken before the written program can be read into the machine. This generally consists in recording the program in some medium, such as punched cards or punched paper tape, which the computer's input devices can read. If the input medium is perforated paper tape, the written program will be given to an operator of a paper-tape-punching machine. The tape-punching machine has a keyboard resembling a typewriter which contains both alphabetic and numeric characters. A long strip of paper tape is fed through the punching section of the machine as the operator of the machine operates the keyboard. Each time the operator depresses a key of the keyboard, several holes are punched into the paper tape. The keyboard mechanism is arranged so that a different combination of holes is punched into the tape for each key that is depressed. The operator of the tape-punching machine types the program just as a secretary types a letter. The result is a strip of paper tape which has been perforated with coded groups of holes.

A paper-tape reader connected to the digital computer is used to read this tape into the computer. The paper-tape reader "senses" the holes perforated into the tape and delivers the locations of these holes in the tape to the computer in the form of electrical signals. The computer then stores this information. A description of paper-tape readers, punches, and the way the paper tape is coded will be presented in Chap. 8.

Figure 1·7 shows a teletype that can punch or read paper tape with a keyboard which can also be attached to telephone lines (notice the dial on the lower right corner). A small section of tape can be seen extending from the tape-punching

Paper for
"hard copy"

Telephone dial for dialing
computer when teletype is used
at a remote location

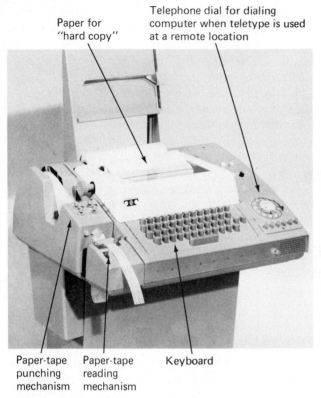

Paper-tape   Paper-tape   Keyboard
punching   reading
mechanism   mechanism

FIG. 1 • 7 Teletype console with tape punch. (Courtesy of AT&T.)

device. After a tape is punched, the tape can be read by a high-speed computer tape reader. Often, however, a teletype is connected directly to a computer, and its tape reader is used to read the tape into the computer.

The preparation of punched cards is similar. The operator of a card punch (refer to Fig. 1·8) depresses keys of a keyboard which punches holes into succeeding columns of a rectangular "punched card." The set of cards thus punched is then assembled in order into a "deck" of cards which can be read by a punched-card reader.

The general procedure for punched cards is for the programmer to write the program on a special coding form such as that shown in Fig. 1·9. A keyboard is then used to type, or *keyboard,* the program written on the form. Figure 1·9 also shows a punched card containing the first line of page 2 of the program. In general, one line of writing on a coding form is entered into a single card.†

---

†The program on the coding form in Fig. 1·9 is a section of a business data processing program written in a "higher-level" programming language called PL/1 (see Sec. 1·19). Notice that the language is similar to that used by accountants. (In this, PL/1 resembles an earlier business language called Cobol.)

Card   Column   Printing   Card
stacker   indicator   mechanism   hopper

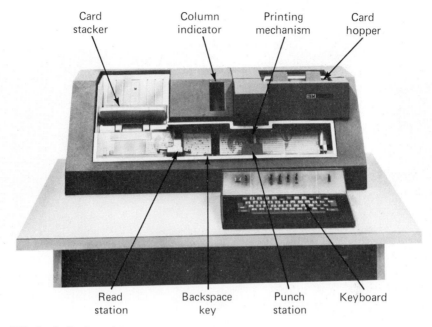

Read   Backspace   Punch   Keyboard
station   key   station

FIG. 1 • 8 Card punch.

There are a number of other techniques for data and program entry into computers. Figure 1·10 shows a special card on which data can be entered by simply marking boxes on the card with a soft lead pencil. A special "mark sense" reading device can sense the position of the boxes which have been marked and transmit their location on the card to a computer.†

An important mode of program entry is in *online* systems, where the operator of a keyboard types the program directly into the computer. In this case the keyboard contains electrical circuitry which generates signals to the computer each time a key is depressed. Generally a printing mechanism also types or prints the characters the operator keyboards on paper. The computer generally has the ability to write responses using the same printing mechanism that was used to record the program and data entered, or sometimes the computer gives the responses by means of an oscilloscope display or some other graphic device. Such systems enable the computer and its user to communicate directly instead of using some intermediate medium such as cards or tape.

Figure 1·11 shows a keyboard and an oscilloscope display in a system where the information keyboarded at the console is recorded on paper (notice the roll of paper in the printer above the keyboard) as well as displayed on the oscilloscope. Both the printer and the oscilloscope are also used to print or display computer output information.

---

†The particular card shown has a single statement from a programming language called Basic written on it.

FORTRAN Coding Form

IBM

GX28-7327-6 U/M 050**
Printed in U.S.A.

PAGE 1 OF 2

PROGRAM RECORD-ORIENTED DATA TRANSMISSION

PROGRAMMER R.L. TONN

```
UPDATE: PROCEDURE OPTIONS (MAIN);
       DECLARE INFILE FILE RECORD INPUT;
       DECLARE WAGES FILE RECORD OUTPUT;
       DECLARE 1 PAYROLL,
               2 NAME,
                 3 LAST CHARACTER (12),
                 3 FIRST CHARACTER (8),
                 3 MIDDLE CHARACTER (1),
               2 PAY-NO CHARACTER (5),
               2 RATE
                 (3 REGULAR,
                  3 OVERTIME)
                  FIXED DECIMAL (3,2);
AGAIN: READ FILE (INFILE) INTO (PAYROLL);
       DECLARE 1 PAY-RECORD,
               2 NAME,
                 3 LAST CHARACTER (12),
                 3 FIRST CHARACTER (8),
                 3 MIDDLE CHARACTER (1),
               2 HOURS,
                 (3 REGULAR, 3 OVERTIME) FIXED DECIMAL (2),
               2 PAY,
                 (3 REGULAR, 3 OVERTIME) FIXED DECIMAL (5,2);
       GET LIST (PAY-RECORD.NAME, PAY-RECORD.HOURS);
```

FIG. 1 • 9 Coding forms and a punch card.

28

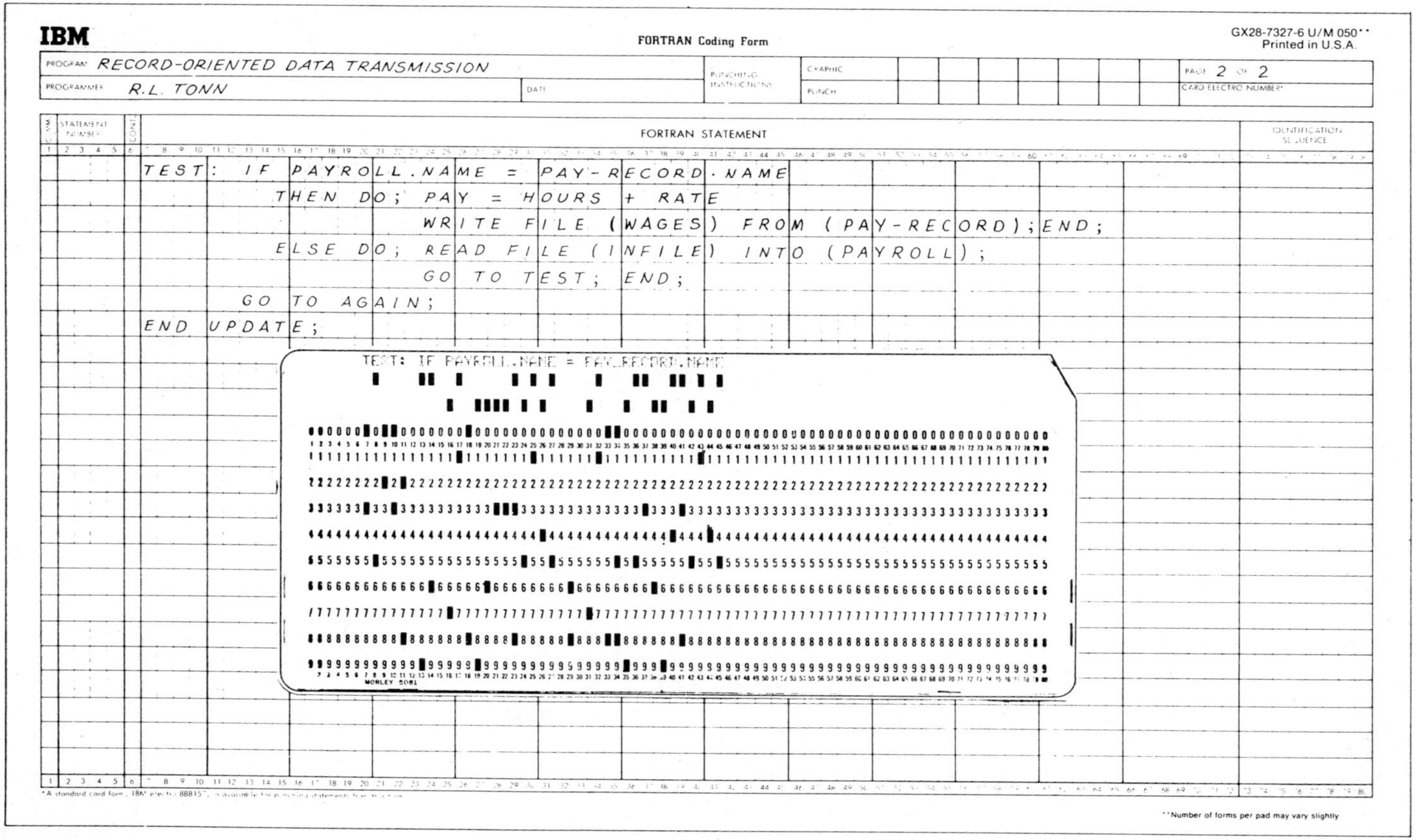
IBM
FORTRAN Coding Form
GX28-7327-6 U/M 050**
Printed in U.S.A.
PROGRAM RECORD-ORIENTED DATA TRANSMISSION
PROGRAMMER R.L. TONN
DATE
PUNCHING INSTRUCTIONS
GRAPHIC
PUNCH
PAGE 2 OF 2
CARD ELECTRO NUMBER*
STATEMENT NUMBER
CONT.
FORTRAN STATEMENT
IDENTIFICATION SEQUENCE
TEST: IF PAYROLL.NAME = PAY-RECORD.NAME
THEN DO; PAY = HOURS + RATE
WRITE FILE (WAGES) FROM (PAY-RECORD);END;
ELSE DO; READ FILE (INFILE) INTO (PAYROLL);
GO TO TEST; END;
GO TO AGAIN;
END UPDATE;
TEST: IF PAYROLL.NAME = PAY_RECORD.NAME
MORLEY 5081
*A standard card form, IBM electro 888157, is available for punching statements from this form.
**Number of forms per pad may vary slightly

FIG. 1 • 9 (*Continued.*)

Notes: BASIC language statements have three elements: <u>statement number</u>,
statement type, and operands. The card below is marked for the
statement: 15Ø LET A = B + C − 5

The statement number (15Ø) is indicated in the STATEMENT NUMBER
field by a single pencil mark in the boxes labeled 1, 5, and Ø.

The statement type (LET) is indicated in the STATEMENT
field by a single mark in the box labeled LET.

The operand (A = B + C − 5) is indicated in the FORMULA field.

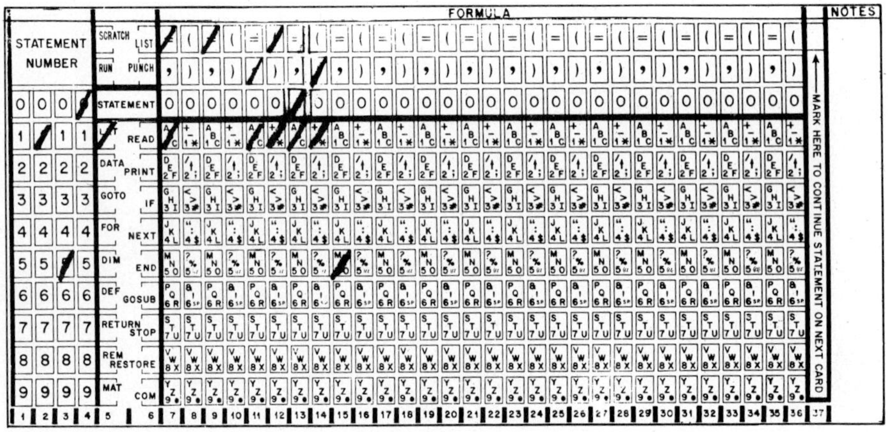

FIG. 1 • 10 Card with pencil marks which can be read by a mark sense reader.

Most of the data entered into computers are still in the form of punched cards.
(There are over 500,000 card punches now in active use.) The use of online systems and other input media is growing, however, and represents a substantial portion of the overall usage of computers.

The preceding description of the steps in preparing a program should make it
apparent that it is not always economical to use a large digital computer to perform
very simple sequences of calculations which need be performed only once or
twice. The computer is valuable when very repetitious sets of calculations must be
performed.

Consider the payroll accounting procedure described earlier. Once a program
has been written which will calculate the weekly gross earnings, taxes, deductions,
etc., for the employees of a large manufacturer, the same program can be used
to compute each of thousands of employees' checks. If a combined clock and
card-punching device is used to punch the time an employee enters a factory and
the time the employee leaves into a time card which also records, in punched form,
an identifying number for the employee, the entire operation can be made automatic. The time cards can then be "read" by the computer, which will compute
the amount of time worked, total weekly earnings, etc., and will actually print the

paycheck and then record in printed form all the data required by the bookkeeping system.

Figure 1· 12 shows a system where ledger cards are used to record printed data from the computer (and keyboarded data, if desired). Ledger cards are widely used in accounting systems for billing, bookkeeping, and general record handling. The ledger cards are dropped into the feed slot in the center just above the keyboard. Different sizes of ledger cards can be used for different applications. This type of printer is typical of those used in many business applications.

1 • 16 PROGRAMMING SYSTEMS

The preceding discussion showed a basic procedure for writing a program and introducing it into the computer. There are, however, various types of *programming languages* which greatly facilitate the actual writing of programs. One of the first things the programming profession discovered was that the greatest aid to

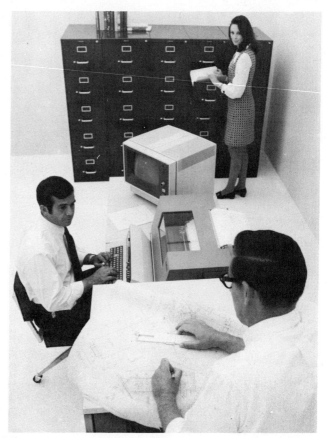

FIG. 1 • 11 Keyboard with attached printer and oscilloscope display.

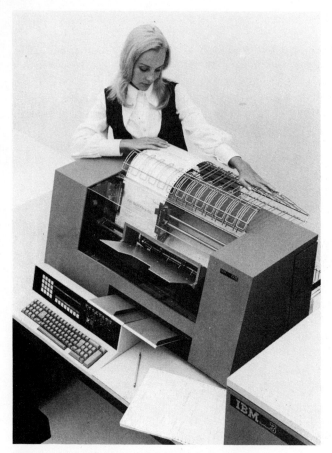

FIG. 1 • 12 Keyboard and ledger-card printer.

programming was the computer itself. It was found to be capable of translating written programs from a language which was straightforward and natural for the programmer into computer, or machine, language.

As a result, programs were written whose purpose was to read other programs written in a language natural for the programmer and to translate them into the machine's language. The program systems now in use are primarily of two types: *assemblers* and *compilers*.† The assembler and the compiler are intended for the same basic purpose; each is a program designed to read a program written in a programming language and to translate it. The assembler or compiler is read into the machine first, and is then followed by the program to be tranlated. After translation the assembler or compiler stores the machine-language program on punched

---

†There is also a translator type of program that translates one line or statement at a time, called an *interpreter*, and is used with such programming languages as Basic.

cards, on magnetic or paper tape, or in some large memory so that it can be performed when desired.

The purpose of this procedure is to enable programmers to write the operations they want the computer to perform in a manner that is simpler than machine language. The language which the programmer writes is called a *programming language,* and a program written in such a language is called a *source program.* The translated program in machine (or some intermediate) language is called an *object program.*

To return to the subject of the translator programs, an assembly language differs from a compiler language in that most assembly languages closely resemble machine languages, primarily because each instruction to the computer in assembly language is translated into a single computer word. In compiler systems a single instruction to the computer may be converted into many computer words.

1 • 17 ASSEMBLY LANGUAGES

Each instruction to the computer in an artificial programming language is called a *statement.* The basic characteristic which most distinguishes an assembly language is that each statement is translated by the assembly program into a single machine instruction word.† As a result, an assembly language somewhat resembles machine language. The facilities offered the programmer are substantial, however, and generally include:

1. *Mnemonic operation codes* The programmer can write instructions to the computer using letters instead of binary numbers, and the letters which designate a given operation are arranged into a mnemonic code which conveys the ''sense'' of the instruction. In our preceding example of coding, the mnemonic codes ADD, MUL, CLA, etc., were used. The assembler would translate these mnemonic codes into the correct machine binary or binary-coded-decimal numbers and ''package'' these into the instruction words constituting the object program.

2. *Symbolic referencing of storage addresses* One of the greatest facilities offered the programmer is the ability to name the different pieces of data used in the program and to have the assembler automatically assign addresses to each name.

   If we wish to evaluate the algebraic expression $y = ax^3 + bx^2 + cx + d$ as in Sec. 1·13, the program can appear as shown in Table 1·7.

   Notice that the address of the first instruction was simply given the name FST, consisting of three letters, and that no further addresses in memory were specified. If we tell the assembler that FST = 1, the assembler then will see that the instructions are placed in memory as in the program in Sec. 1·13. Notice also that the operands were simply given the variable names X, A, B,

---

†This is not, of course, strictly the case (sometimes a single statement may be translated into several words), but generally translation is into a single instruction word that can require one or more memory locations or words.

TABLE 1 • 7

ADDRESS IN MEMORY	INSTRUCTION WORD	
	OPERATION	OPERAND
FST	CLA	A
	MUL	X
	ADD	B
	MUL	X
	ADD	C
	MUL	X
	ADD	D
	STO	Y
	HLT	

C, and D, as in the equation, instead of assigning addresses in memory to them. The assembly program will assign addresses to these names of variables, and if it assigns A to 22, B to 23, C to 24, etc., the final program will look as in Sec. 1·13.

The assembler will also see that actual arithmetic values for X, A, B, C, and D are placed in the correct locations in memory when the data are read into the computer.

3. *Convenient data representation* This simply means that the programmer can write input data as, for instance, decimal numbers or letters, or perhaps in some form specific to the problem, and that the assembly program will convert the data from this form into the form required for machine computation.

4. *Program listings* An important feature of most assemblers is their ability to print for the programmer a listing of the source program and also a listing of the object program which is in machine language. A study of these listings will greatly help the programmer in finding any errors made in writing the program and also in modifying the program when this is required.

5. *Error detection* An assembler program will also notify the programmer if an error has been made in the usage of the assembly language. For example, the programmer may use the same variable name, for instance, X, twice, and then give X two different values, or the programmer may write illegal operation codes, etc. This sort of diagnosis of a program's errors is very useful during the checking out of a new program.

Assemblers provide many other facilities which help the programmer, such as the ability to use programs which have already been written as part of a new program and the ability to use routines from these programs as part of a new program. Often programmers have a set of different programs which they will run together in different combinations. This is made possible simply by specifying to the assembler the variable names in the different programs which are to be the same variable, the entry and exit points for the programs, etc. This means that programs written in an assembly language can be linked together in various ways.

TABLE 1 • 8

| ADDRESS | INSTRUCTION WORDS | | COMMENTS |
	OPERATION	OPERAND	
A	DEC	0	
B	DEC	− 50	
C	DEC	2	
D	DEC	1	
E	DEC	0	
N	CLA	A	Last value of integer
	ADD	C	
	STO	A	Stores sum for next time
	ADD	E	
	STO	E	
	CLA	B	
	ADD	D	
	STO	B	
	BRM	N	
	HLT		

Let us consider the short program in Table 1·6 which sums the even integers from 0 to 100. This will illustrate the use of symbolic names for addresses when a branch instruction is used. The assembly-language program is shown in Table 1·8.

Notice that the values of the variables were specified before the program was begun; the DECs indicate that the values given for A, B, C, D, and E are in decimal. This enables the assembler to locate the variables in the memory and assign values to them.† Also, note that the transfer instruction BRM was to the symbolic address N.

If the assembler were told to start the program at address 1 in the memory, conversion into object or machine language would make it look similar to the one in Sec. 1·14, provided the assembler decided to store A, B, C, D, and E in locations 39 through 43. Also, the operation codes of CLA, MUL, etc., would be converted to numerical or machine form, if this were necessary.

1 • 18 COMPILER LANGUAGES

More advanced types of programming languages are called *compiler languages, high-level languages,* or *problem-oriented languages.* These are the simplest languages to use for most problems and are also the simplest to learn. These languages often reveal very little about the digital machines on which they are run,

---

†In a sense, the operation code DEC says "assign the decimal value in the operational column to the variable name in the address column."

however. The designer of the language generally concentrates on specifying a programming language that is simple enough for the casual user of a digital computer and yet has enough facilities to make the language and its associated compiler valuable to professional programmers. In fact, many languages are almost completely computer-independent, and programs written in one of these languages may be run on any computer that has a compiler or translator for the language in its program library.

Certain languages have been very successful and have found extremely wide usage in the computer industry. The most famous language is Fortran, which is the earliest of the languages and has been regularly updated. A program written in Fortran can be run on most commercial computers that have a memory size large enough to accommodate a Fortran compiler, because most manufacturers will prepare a Fortran compiler for their computer.

There are a number of other languages in active use. Algol, a language that was designed for international use, is widely used in describing algorithms in technical journals and has had moderate success in actual practice; Cobol is a language especially for business systems; Mad and several other languages have been developed by universities for educational purposes; Formac does symbolic manipulation; Jovial is a language for real-time systems; Basic is a very simple, easy-to-use language which is often used in online systems and which has become quite popular. About all that can be said is that there is no truly universal programming language but that there are several good languages. Fortunately there is no staggering difference in these languages from a conceptual viewpoint, and when one of the languages has been learned, learning another presents no great problem.

A popular programming language is called *Programming Language One* (abbreviated PL/1). Some of the features of this language will suffice for illustrating the general appearance of compiler languages. PL/1 has been chosen because of its simplicity for algebraic equations and because of the very elementary format for reading in data and printing results. Also, PL/1 at this level looks almost like Fortran except that we need not worry about mixing real variables with integer variables, nor about format statements for printing or reading, provided we are willing to use the standard PL/1 format (in this we adopt the attitude of Basic, and our programs will be quite similar). Finally, several simple versions of PL/1 have been developed by microprocessor and microprogrammed computer manufacturers. For example, a version of PL/1 called PL/M is widely used in microcomputer systems.

Since the following section gives an introduction to a specific compiler language, those who are familiar with compiler languages such as Fortran or Cobol may omit it. Others may wish to skip over this material until later. The text is arranged so that subsequent material in the book does not depend on the following section, and this section can be omitted or studied at a later time. The material is introduced at this point because many believe that it is a good idea to look at a compiler language fairly early in studying computers (or else there may be a misconception that computer programmers must actually write their programs in computer or machine language, which would greatly limit the use of computers). Merely a reading of this material will be sufficient in many cases. For those who wish to study it in more depth, quite a few questions have been provided at the end of the chapter which call for a study of some additional features of PL/1, and these can be used as a supplement.

*1 • 19 A SHORT INTRODUCTION TO PL/1

As has been mentioned, the distinguishing feature of compilers and their programming languages is that a single statement which the programmer writes may be converted by the compiler into a number of machine-language instructions. In PL/1, for instance, a single statement to the computer can generate quite a number of instructions in object or machine language. As a result, the language is not particularly dependent on the structure of the computer on which the program is run, and the following programs may be run on any computer with a PL/1 compiler.

The PL/1 compiler is written in machine language, and a PL/1 program is ultimately run in machine language. For this reason, knowledge of the machine and its organization can be of great use to those writing and checking out programs. Further, for the systems programmers (those who maintain, modify, and prepare the compilers, assemblers, load programs, etc.) a knowledge of the machine on which the program is operated is indispensable. The fact that compilers and computers are backed up by an army of technical personnel, from systems programmers through design and maintenance engineers, technicians, and computer operators, is often overlooked by the user of the machine whose program is miraculously debugged and operated. Like most electronic devices, digital computers are not as independent and self-supporting as they may appear to casual users.

Thus forewarned, let us examine the structure of PL/1 in a little detail, leaving a more complete exposition to one of the references.

The first thing to be learned in writing statements is the use of the = symbol. This is treated somewhat as a command to the computer, for when we write Y = A + B, what is meant is "replace the current value of Y with that of A + B." So therefore, if we write

$$A = 50;$$
$$B = 20;$$
$$Y = A + B;$$
$$END;$$

we find that after this is run, A will be equal to 50, B to 20, and Y to 70. Notice that each statement is followed by a semicolon. As a further example, we can increase,

---

*This section can be omitted on a first reading without loss of continuity or overall understanding.

decrease, or otherwise change the current value of Y by adding or subtracting from it. Consider

$$Y = 30;$$
$$A = 40;$$
$$Y = Y + A;$$
$$END;$$

After these four statements are operated, Y will have the value of 70; that is, the location in memory that has been used to store Y will have the value 70 in it. Notice that the statements above took the form of algebraic equations. Here is one further example:

$$Y = 20;$$
$$Z = 50;$$
$$W = Y + Z;$$
$$M = W - 30;$$
$$END;$$

After this is run, W will have the value 70 and M the value 40.

In PL/1, the addition symbol is the familiar + and the subtraction symbol is the usual −, but multiplication is indicated by an asterisk (*), and exponentiation (raising to a power) by two asterisks. Thus A*B means "multiply A by B" and A**B means A^B or "raise A to the Bth power." Therefore the program statements

$$A = 20;$$
$$B = 30;$$
$$C = A*B;$$
$$END;$$

give a value of 600 for C, and the program

$$A = 20;$$
$$B = 2;$$
$$C = A**B;$$
$$END;$$

gives a value of 400 to C.

Division is indicated by a / symbol. Thus

$$A = 20;$$
$$B = 2;$$
$$Y = A/B;$$
$$END;$$

will place the value 10 in the location in memory delegated to Y.

Let us examine one simple way to form a loop in the program, that is, to repeat a sequence of instructions until we desire to stop. Here are two PL/1 statements:

LOOP. DO WHILE X LE Y;

and

END LOOP;

The first of these says "do the following set of statements up to the END LOOP, while X is less than or equal to Y." In other words, "repeat the following instructions until Y is greater than X." If we write the following statements:

```
T = 0;
M = 4;
N = 2;
P = 6;
LOOP. DO WHILE N LE M;
S = P*N;
T = T + S;
N = N + 1;
END LOOP;
Y = T*2;
END;
```

then the statements between the LOOP and END LOOP will be repeated until N is greater than M. Since N starts with the value 2 (and as 1 is added each time) while M starts with the value 4, N will take the values 2, 3, 4, 5. But when N equals 5, it will be greater than M, and the program will proceed with the instruction Y = T*2; and then END. The LOOP statements will therefore be repeated three times. The first time S will equal P times N, or 12, T will be equal to 0 + S, or 12, and N will then be increased from 2 to 3. The second time, S will equal P times N, or 6 times 3, which is 18; T will be equal to 12 + 18, or 30; and N will be increased to 4. The third and last time through the loop, S will equal 6 times 4, or 24, T will take the value 30 + 24, or 54, and N will be increased to 5. N will then be greater than M, and the END LOOP statement will be operated. T, which has the value 54, will then be multiplied by 2, giving 108, and the program will stop with Y equal to 108.

Let us examine two other features. To read data we simply write

READ (X, Y, Z);

and this will tell the compiler to arrange for reading the value of X, Y, and Z from cards and continue with the values read as the current values of X, Y, and Z. We must therefore supply values of X, Y, and Z on punched cards. The advantage of this is that we can change the values of X, Y, and Z by simply replacing our data cards with cards containing new values. If we write

```
READ (X, Y, Z);
M = X + (Y*Z);
END;
```

and attach cards with the values X = 20, Y = 30, and Z = 2, we shall have M = 80. If we change our data cards to read X = 5, Y = 3, and Z = 4, we shall then have M = 17 after we run the program.

To print out data, we write the statement

$$WRITE\ (X, Y, Z, A)$$

and the computer will print out the current values of X, Y, Z, and A.

It should be noted that the READ and WRITE statements assume that the programmer will be satisfied with the standard format for the input data and print statements. Assuming that this is the case, we can write the following program, which will first evaluate the equation $y = ax^3 + bx^2 + cx + d$ for values of A, B, D, and X which are read in on data cards or tape and for C = 1. If the value of Y for these particular values is greater than 2,000, the program will print the value of Y as calculated and also the value C = 1. If, however, Y is less than or equal to 2,000, the program will calculate the smallest positive integer which, when substituted into C, will make $ax^3 + bx^2 + cx + d$ greater than 2,000. The program will then print this value of C and the value of $ax^3 + bx^2 + cx + d$ associated with the value of C.

```
READ (A, B, D, X);
       C = 0;
       Y = 0;
LOOP. DO WHILE Y LE 2000;
       C = C + 1;
       Y = A*X**3 + B*X**2 + C*X + D;
END LOOP;
PRINT (C, Y);
END;
```

We have only touched on the power of this language. It is not possible in a short exposition to do more than show several statements and give a general idea of how such a language operates. Nevertheless, a clever programmer could do quite a lot with the limited vocabulary we have introduced.

PL/M, the microprocessor version of PL/1, is widely used. The translators (compilers) for PL/M produce machine language that can be run on a microprocessor. This simplifies writing programs for a microprocessor, since a program can be written in PL/M and not machine language.

PL/M provides many of the facilities of PL/1, except that arithmetic operations and file operations are not emphasized (for instance, arithmetic is integer arithmetic, not including fractions). On the other hand, PL/M provides substantial facilities for interfacing input–output devices to a microcomputer. For example, PL/M includes an INPUT statement that reads from a selected input device and an OUT-PUT statement that causes a selected output device to be written into. PL/M even has provision for servicing interrupts, a subject to be discussed in Chap. 8. It is, however, necessary to be familiar with the general characteristics of the micro-computer on which the translated PL/M program is to be run in order for programs to be truly effective.

One thing which should become apparent from this brief introduction is that once the statement types and details of a high-level language are learned, the job of programming a given problem is greatly facilitated.

QUESTIONS

1. Discuss possible applications of microprocessors in real-time control systems.
2. The computer's ability to translate languages such as PL/1 and Fortran greatly simplifies programming. Comment on the difficulty a computer might have in translating English. What about ambiguities? Must programming languages avoid them?
3. Sometimes the same computer is used by several different companies during the day, and the computer is time shared between these companies. Discuss problems which might arise in billing the companies for the computer's services.
4. Discuss online computer systems and give examples of businesses and industries that might use online systems.
5. Discuss batch processing and give several examples of businesses and industries that might use batch processing.
6. Give examples of industries that might use real-time control systems for manufacturing.
7. Values for X, Y, and Z are stored at memory addresses 40, 41, and 42, respectively. Using the instructions for the generalized single-address computer described in Secs. 1·12 to 1·14, write a program that will form the sum $X + Y + Z$ and store it at memory address 43.
8. Explain the difference between the *address* of a word in memory and the *word* itself.
9. Given that values for X, Y, and Z are stored in locations 20, 21, and 22, respectively, use the instructions for the computer given in Secs. 1·12 to 1·14 to write a program that will form $X^2 + Y^2 + Z^2$ and store this at memory address 40.
10. The program in Table 1·4 is run with the following values when it is started: 5 in address 22, 4 in address 23, 6 in address 24, 4 in address 25, and 2 in address 26. What value will be in address 27 after the program has been run?
11. Convert the flowchart in Fig. 1·2 into a computer assembly-language program using the instructions described in the chapter.
12. If the program in Table 1·4 is started with location 22 containing 4, location 23 containing 4, location 24 containing 4, location 25 containing 1, and loca-

tion 26 containing 2, what number will be stored in location 27 after the program is run?

13. Write a program that will store $X^5 + X$ in register 40, using the assembly language in Secs. $1 \cdot 12$ to $1 \cdot 14$, given that X is in register 20. Use fewer than 20 instructions. Now rewrite this program using the assembly language in Sec. $1 \cdot 17$.

14. If the program in Table $1 \cdot 6$ were operated but the number at address 40 were -30 instead of -50 when the program was started, the number at address 43 would be the sum of all even integers from 2 to ___ instead of 2 to 100.

15. Draw a flowchart for the program in Sec. $1 \cdot 14$.

16. Given that a value for X is stored at address 39, write a program that will form X^4 and store it at address 42, using the assembly language in Secs. $1 \cdot 12$ to $1 \cdot 14$.

17. Draw a flowchart showing how to find the largest number in a set of five numbers stored at locations 30, 31, 32, 33, and 34 in memory.

18. Values for X and Y are stored at addresses 30 and 31. Write a program that will store the larger of the two values at address 40, using the assembly language in Secs. $1 \cdot 12$ to $1 \cdot 14$.

19. Given three different numbers, determine whether they are in ascending or descending order. Draw a flowchart for the problem, and write a program using the assembly language in Secs. $1 \cdot 13$ to $1 \cdot 14$. Assume that the numbers are stored in memory locations 30, 31, and 32.

20. A value for Y is stored at location 55 and a value for A at location 59. Write an assembly-language program to store AY^3 at location 40.

21. Write a program to find $ax^2 + by + cz^2$, with A in location 20, B in location 21, C in location 22, X in location 23, Y in location 24, and Z in location 25. Store your result in location 40.

22. A value for X is stored at address 40. Write a program that will store X^9 at address 45, using fewer than 10 instruction words.

23. Using the assembly language described in Secs. $1 \cdot 12$ to $1 \cdot 14$, write a program that will branch to location 300 if the number stored in memory register 25 is larger than the number stored in register 26, and which will transfer or branch to location 400 if the number at address 26 is equal to or larger than the number at address 25.

24. Write a program that will produce the value $Y - X$ or X, whichever is larger, in both the assembly language in Secs. $1 \cdot 12$ to $1 \cdot 14$ and the compiler language in Sec. $1 \cdot 19$. Store this value in location 300 for the assembly program and assign the variable B to this value for the program written in the compiler language. For the assembly program, assume that X is in location 100 and Y in 101.

25. Calculate the largest of the three numbers A, B, and C and assign the largest of the numbers to the variable X, using the assembly language in Sec. $1 \cdot 17$ to write the program.

26. Write a PL/1 program that will assign the value 40 to variable C and the value 60 to variable D.

27. Write a program in PL/1 that will assign the value of 10 to A, 20 to B, and 5 to C, and which will then calculate the value $(A \times B)^C$ and assign this value to a variable D.

28. In PL/1 what will be the value of D if we execute the statement D = X + $(Y^{**}Z)$ when X has value 5, Y has value 2, and Z has value 2?

29. If the PL/1 program which was used to illustrate the LOOP command is run with P having value 4, but with T, M, and N as in the program in the text, what will be the value of Y after the program is run?

30. Suppose that the final PL/1 program in the text is run with values of 4 for A, 3 for B, 2 for C, and 2 for X. What values of C and Y will the program cause to be printed?

31. Using the compiler language in Sec. 1·19, write a program that will determine which of X − Y or Y − X is positive (or equal to 0) and which will print the value of this positive number or 0, assigning the variable Z to this number.

32. Modify the program in Sec. 1·14 so that it will sum all the odd numbers from 1 through 79.

33. We have 30 numbers stored in successive registers in our memory, starting at location 300. Write a program that will convert any negative numbers in the 30 to positive form. That is, write a program that will take the 30 numbers, convert each number to its positive value without changing its magnitude, and restore it in the same location. Use assembly language.

34. Write a program, using the assembly language in Secs. 1·12 to 1·14, which will rearrange five numbers stored in addresses 200 through 204 so that they are in descending order (for example, 10, 3, 0, −5, −7).

Additional questions on PL/1

35. In a nonparenthesized section of a given statement, the PL/1 language, like Fortran and Algol, first performs exponentiation, or raising to a power, then multiplication and division, and then addition and subtraction. Within this hierarchy, statements are evaluated from left to right. Thus the statement A = $((B/C) − (D^*E))/(C^{**}D)$ can be written as A = $(B/C − D^*E)/(C^{**}D)$. The following are four more examples of the way in which the compiler evaluates arithmetic statements:

(1) $a^b + c \cdot d + e/f$ can be written $A^{**}B + C^*D + E/F$.

(2) $(a \cdot b \cdot c)\, e^b + (g/h)$ can be written $A^*B^*C^*E^{**}F + G/H$.

(3) $\dfrac{a \cdot b \cdot c}{d \cdot e}$ must be written $(A^*B^*C)/(D^*E)$.

(4) $a \cdot b + (c/d) + ef$ is written $A^*B + C/D + E^*F$.

Find the value of X in the following statements if A = 5, B = 2, C = 20, and D = 15:

(a) X = $A^{**}B + C$ (c) X = $A^*C^{**}B$

(b) X = $C + D^*B + A$ (d) X = $C + D^{**}B/A + A$

36. Using the compiler language in Sec. 1·19, assume that we have read in values for the variables X, Y, and Z. Assign the largest of these values to the variable A, the second largest to the variable B, and the third largest to the variable C. For instance, if X is read in as 29, Y as 31, and Z as 23, after the program operates we would like the value A $=$ 33, B $=$ 29, and C $=$ 21.

37. Write PL/1 statements that correspond to the following algebraic formulas written in conventional mathematical notation:

(a) $\dfrac{a^c}{b^d}$ (b) $a^2 + b^2 + cd$ (c) $\left(\dfrac{a}{b}\right) + \left(\dfrac{c}{d}\right)^e$ (d) $(a \cdot b)^c + \dfrac{bd}{e}$

38. In PL/1 it is possible to write mathematical statements with subscripted variables, which are called *array variables*; that is, if we have a set of variables X_1, X_2, X_3, and X_4, we can write these in PL/1 as X(1), X(2), X(3), and X(4). Notice that the parentheses do not indicate multiplication, but rather the fact that the variable is an array variable or a subscripted variable. Now, if we write in a program X(K), whether this indicates X(1) or X(2) or X(3) or X(4), for instance, depends upon the value of the variable K at that particular time. What are the values of X in each of the following statements if A(1) $=$ 3, A(2) $=$ 4, A(3) $=$ 5, and K $=$ 1:

(a) X $=$ A(1) $+$ A(2)   (b) Y $=$ A(2)**A(1) $+$ A(3)
(c) X $=$ A(K) $+$ A(2)*A(3)   (d) Y $=$ A(K $+$ 2) $+$ A(K)

39. There is a class of statements in PL/1 called *control statements*. These statements make it possible to iterate many times through a given set of instructions, providing indexing facilities during these iterations. The general form of the most important one of these statements, which is the DO statement, is DO N K $=$ P, Q. Here N is the statement number or location of some executable statement, K is a simple variable, and P and Q are either constants or nonarray variables. A typical DO statement might therefore appear as DO 30 K $=$ 1, 25. This statement in a program will cause the instructions or statements following the DO statement up to statement 30 to be repeated, with the variable K equal to 1 through 25; that is, the loop from the DO statement to statement 30 in the program is repeated 25 times, the first time with the variable K equal to 1, the second time with the variable K equal to 2, the third time with the variable K equal to 3, etc., until K $=$ 25. This time the program will pass through statement 30 to the next statement. If we therefore write

$$X = 2$$
$$B(1) = 5$$
$$B(2) = 6$$
$$B(3) = 7$$
$$B(4) = 8$$
$$DO\ 19\ K = 1, 4$$
$$A(K) = B(K) + 6$$
$$19 \qquad X = X^{**} 2$$

After this program has been run, A(1) will equal 11, A(2) will equal 12, A(3) will equal 13, and A(4) will equal 14, while X $=$ 65,536.

Using the DO statement in PL/1, write a program that will rearrange a set of 20 numbers that are stored in successive registers. These variables are A(1) through A(20), where each value is assumed to be positive. Assign these values to a set of variables B(1) through B(20) so that B(1) is equal to the smallest of the values of A, B(2) is equal to the second smallest of the values of A, and, finally, B(20) is equal to the largest value of the A variables.

40. Using the DO statement explained in Question 39, write a program that will examine and form an average of the values of a set of variables A(1) through A(10), where A(1) through A(10) are assumed to be already stored in the memory of the computer when the program begins. Call this average of the 10 values the *mean* of these values, and give a variable named M this value when the program has operated.

2 NUMBER SYSTEMS

It is India that gave us the ingenious method of expressing all numbers by means of ten symbols, each symbol receiving a value of position as well as an absolute value; a profound and important idea which appears so simple to us now that we ignore its true merit.

Marquis de Laplace

As a mathematician, Laplace could well appreciate the decimal number system. He was fully aware of the centuries of mental effort and sheer good luck which had gone into the development of the number system we use, and he was in a position to appreciate its advantages. Our present number system provides modern mathematicians and scientists with a great advantage over those of previous civilizations and is an important factor in our rapid advancement.

Since hands are the most convenient tools nature has provided, human beings have always tended to use them in counting. It is both natural and fortunate that our number system is based on the number of digits we possess. It was quite some time after we learned to count, however, that we attempted to represent numbers graphically. The earliest numerals which have been found consist of either vertical or horizontal marks. Our 1 is an example of this sort of symbol, and it is interesting to note that the symbol for 2 consists of two horizontal marks with a connecting line, and 3 consists of three horizontal lines with connections. Roman numerals are good examples of lines used as the basis for numerals.

The decimal system for counting has been so widely adopted throughout our present civilization that we rarely consider the possibilities of other number systems. Nevertheless, it is not reasonable to expect a system based on the number of fingers we possess to be the most efficient number system for machine construction. The fact is that a little used but very simple system, the binary number system, has proved the most natural and efficient system for machine use.

2 • 1 THE DECIMAL SYSTEM

Our present system of numbers has 10 separate symbols, 0, 1, 2, 3, . . . , 9, which are called arabic numerals. We would be forced to stop at 9 or to invent more symbols if it were not for the use of *positional notation.* An example of earlier types of notation can be found in roman numerals, which are essentially additive: III = I + I + I, XXV = X + X + V. New symbols (X, C, M, etc.) were used as the numbers increased in value: thus V rather than IIIII = 5. The only importance of position in Roman numerals lies in whether a symbol precedes or follows another symbol (IV = 4, while VI = 6). The clumsiness of this system can easily be seen if we try to multiply XII by XIV. Calculating with roman numerals was so difficult that early mathematicians were forced to perform arithmetic operations almost entirely on abaci, or counting boards, translating their results back into roman-number form. Pencil-and-paper computations are unbelievably intricate and difficult in such systems. In fact, the ability to perform such operations as addition and multiplication was considered a great accomplishment in earlier civilizations.

The great beauty and simplicity of our number system can now be seen. It is necessary to learn only the 10 basic numerals and the *positional notation system* in order to count to any desired figure. After memorizing the addition and multiplication tables and learning a few simple rules, it is possible to perform all arithmetic operations. Notice the simplicity of multiplying 12 × 14 using the present system:

$$
\begin{array}{r}
14 \\
\underline{12} \\
28 \\
\underline{14} \\
168
\end{array}
$$

The actual meaning of the number 168 can be seen more clearly if we notice that it is spoken as "one hundred and sixty-eight." Basically, the number is a contraction of $(1 \times 100) + (6 \times 10) + 8$. The important point is that the value of each digit is determined by its position. For example, the 2 in 2,000 has a different value than the 2 in 20. We show this verbally by saying "two thousand" and "twenty." Different verbal representations have been invented for numbers from 10 to 20 (eleven, twelve . . .), but from 20 upward we break only at powers of 10 (hundreds, thousands, millions, billions). Written numbers are always contracted, however, and only the basic 10 numerals are used, regardless of the size of the integer written. The general rule for representing numbers in the decimal system using positional notation is as follows: $a_1 10^{n-1} + a_2 10^{n-2} + \cdots + a_n$ is expressed as $a_1 a_2 \ldots a_n$, where n is the number of digits to the left of the decimal point.

The base, or *radix,* of a number system is defined as the number of different digits which can occur in each position in the number system. The decimal number system has a base, or radix, of 10. This means that the system has 10 different digits (0, 1, 2, . . . , 9), any one of which may be used in each position in a number. History records the use of several other number systems. The quinary system, which has 5 for its base, was prevalent among Eskimos and North American Indians. Examples of the duodecimal system (base 12) may be seen in clocks, inches and feet, and dozens or grosses.

2 • 2 THE BINARY SYSTEM

A seventeenth-century German mathematician, Gottfried Wilhelm von Leibniz, was an advocate of the binary number system which has 2 for a base, using only the symbols 0 and 1. If it seems strange for an eminent mathematician to advocate such a simple number system, it should be noted that he was also a philosopher. Leibniz's reasons for advocating the binary system seem to have been mystical. He felt there was great beauty in the analogy between zero, representing the void, and one, representing the Deity.

Regardless of how good Leibniz's reasons for advocating it were, the binary system has become very popular in the last decade. Present-day digital computers are constructed to operate in binary or binary-coded number systems, and present indications are that future machines will also be constructed to operate in these systems.

The basic elements in early computers were relays and switches. The operation of a switch, or relay, can be seen to be essentially binary in nature; that is, the switch is either on (1) or off (0). The principal circuit elements in more modern computers are transistors similar to those used in radios and television sets. The desire for reliability led designers to use these devices so that they were essentially in one of two states, fully conducting or nonconducting. A simple analogy may be made between this type of circuit and an electric light. At any given time the light (or transistor) is either on (conducting) or off (not conducting). Even after a bulb is old and weak, it is generally easy to tell if it is on or off. The same sort of thing may be seen in radios. As a radio ages, the volume generally decreases, and we compensate by turning the volume control up. Even when the radio becomes very weak, however, it is still possible to tell easily whether it is on or off.

Because of the large number of electronic parts used in computers, it is highly desirable to utilize them in such a manner that slight changes in their characteristics will not affect their performance. The best way of accomplishing this is using circuits which are basically *bistable* (having two possible states).

2 • 3 COUNTING IN THE BINARY SYSTEM

The same type of positional notation is used in the binary number system as in the decimal system. Table 2·1 lists the first 20 binary numbers.

While the same positional notation system is used, the decimal system uses powers of 10, and the binary system powers of 2. As was previously explained, the number 125 actually means $(1 \times 10^2) + (2 \times 10^1) + (5 \times 10^0)$. In the binary system, the same number (125) is represented as 1111101, meaning $(1 \times 2^6) + (1 \times 2^5) + (1 \times 2^4) + (1 \times 2^3) + (1 \times 2^2) + (0 \times 2^1) + (1 \times 2^0)$.

To express the value of a binary number, therefore, $a_1 2^{n-1} + a_2 2^{n-2} + \cdots + a_n$ is represented as $a_1 a_2 \ldots a_n$, where a is either 1 or 0, and n is the number of digits to the left of the binary (radix) point.

TABLE 2 • 1

DECIMAL		BINARY	DECIMAL		BINARY
1	=	1	11	=	1011
2	=	10	12	=	1100
3	=	11	13	=	1101
4	=	100	14	=	1110
5	=	101	15	=	1111
6	=	110	16	=	10000
7	=	111	17	=	10001
8	=	1000	18	=	10010
9	=	1001	19	=	10011
10	=	1010	20	=	10100

The following examples illustrate the conversion of binary numbers to the decimal system:

$$
\begin{aligned}
101 &= (1 \times 2^{3-1}) + (0 \times 2^{3-2}) + (1 \times 2^{3-3}) \\
&= (1 \times 2^2) + (0 \times 2^1) + (1 \times 2^0) \\
&= 4 + 1 = 5 \\
1001 &= (1 \times 2^{4-1}) + (0 \times 2^{4-2}) + (0 \times 2^{4-3}) + (1 \times 2^{4-4}) \\
&= (1 \times 2^3) + (0 \times 2^2) + (0 \times 2^1) + (1 \times 2^0) \\
&= 8 + 1 = 9 \\
11.011 &= (1 \times 2^{2-1}) + (1 \times 2^{2-2}) + (0 \times 2^{2-3}) + (1 \times 2^{2-4}) + (1 \times 2^{2-5}) \\
&= (1 \times 2^1) + (1 \times 2^0) + (0 \times 2^{-1}) + (1 \times 2^{-2}) + (1 \times 2^{-3}) \\
&= 2 + 1 + \tfrac{1}{4} + \tfrac{1}{8} \\
&= 3\tfrac{3}{8}
\end{aligned}
$$

Notice that fractional numbers are formed in the same general way as in the decimal system. Just as

$$
0.123 = (1 \times 10^{-1}) + (2 \times 10^{-2}) + (3 \times 10^{-3})
$$

in the decimal system,

$$
0.101 = (1 \times 2^{-1}) + (0 \times 2^{-2}) + (1 \times 2^{-3})
$$

in the binary system.

2 • 4 BINARY ADDITION AND SUBTRACTION

Binary addition is performed in the same manner as decimal addition. Actually, binary arithmetic is much simpler to learn. The complete table for binary addition is as follows:

$$0 + 0 = 0$$
$$0 + 1 = 1$$
$$1 + 0 = 1$$
$$1 + 1 = 0 \qquad \text{plus a carry-over of 1}$$

"Carry-overs" are performed in the same manner as in decimal arithmetic. Since 1 is the largest digit in the binary system, any sum greater than 1 requires that a digit be carried over. For instance, 100 plus 100 binary requires the addition of the two 1s in the third position to the left, with a carry-over. Since $1 + 1 = 0$ plus a carry-over of 1, the sum of 100 and 100 is 1000. Here are three more examples of binary addition:

DECIMAL	BINARY	DECIMAL	BINARY	DECIMAL	BINARY
5	101	15	1111	$3\frac{1}{4}$	11.01
6	110	20	10100	$5\frac{3}{4}$	101.11
11	1011	35	100011	9	1001.00

Subtraction is the inverse operation of addition. To subtract, it is necessary to establish a procedure for subtracting a larger from a smaller digit. The only case in which this occurs using binary numbers is when 1 is subtracted from 0. The remainder is 1, but it is necessary to borrow 1 from the next column to the left. This is the binary subtraction table:

$$0 - 0 = 0$$
$$1 - 0 = 1$$
$$1 - 1 = 0$$
$$0 - 1 = 1 \qquad \text{with a borrow of 1}$$

A few examples will make the procedure for binary subtraction clear.

DECIMAL	BINARY	DECIMAL	BINARY	DECIMAL	BINARY
9	1001	16	10000	$6\frac{1}{4}$	110.01
−5	−101	−3	−11	$-4\frac{1}{2}$	−100.1
4	100	13	1101	$1\frac{3}{4}$	1.11

2 • 5 BINARY MULTIPLICATION AND DIVISION

The table for binary multiplication is very short, with only four entries instead of the 100 necessary for decimal multiplication. The binary multiplication table is

$$0 \times 0 = 0$$
$$1 \times 0 = 0$$
$$0 \times 1 = 0$$
$$1 \times 1 = 1$$

The following three examples of binary multiplication illustrate the simplicity of each operation. It is only necessary to copy the multiplicand if the digit in the multiplier is 1, and to copy all 0s if the digit in the multiplier is a 0. The ease with which each step of the operation is performed is apparent.

DECIMAL	BINARY	DECIMAL	BINARY	DECIMAL	BINARY
12	1100	102	1100110	1.25	1.01
× 10	× 1010	×8	× 1000	×2.5	× 10.1
120	0000	816	1100110000	625	101
	1100			250	1010
	0000			3.125	11.001
	1100				
	1111000				

Binary division is, again, very simple. As in the decimal system (or in any other), division by zero is meaningless. The complete table is

$$0 \div 1 = 0$$
$$1 \div 1 = 1$$

Here are two examples of division:

DECIMAL	BINARY
5	101
5) 25	101) 11001
	101
	101
	101

DECIMAL	BINARY
2.416···	10.011010101···
12) 29.0000	1100) 11101.00
24	1100
50	10100
48	1100
20	10000
12	1100
80	10000
72	1100
8	······

Converting the quotient obtained in the second example from binary to decimal would proceed as follows:

$$
\begin{aligned}
10.0110101 = 1 \times 2^{1} &= 2.0 \\
0 \times 2^{0} &= 0.0 \\
0 \times 2^{-1} &= 0.0 \\
1 \times 2^{-2} &= 0.25 \\
1 \times 2^{-3} &= 0.125 \\
0 \times 2^{-4} &= 0.0 \\
1 \times 2^{-5} &= 0.03125 \\
0 \times 2^{-6} &= 0.0 \\
1 \times 2^{-7} &= 0.0078125 \\
0 \times 2^{-8} &= 0.0 \\
1 \times 2^{-9} &= \underline{0.001953125} \\
&\ 2.416015625
\end{aligned}
$$

Therefore 10.0110101 binary equals approximately 2.416 decimal.

2 • 6 CONVERTING DECIMAL NUMBERS TO BINARY

There are several methods for converting a decimal number to a binary number. The first and most obvious method is simply to subtract all powers of 2 which can be subtracted from the decimal number until nothing remains. The highest power of 2 is subtracted first, then the second highest, etc. To convert the decimal integer 25 into the binary number system, first the highest power of 2 which can be subtracted from 25 is found. This is $2^{4} = 16$. Then $25 - 16 = 9$. The highest power of 2 which can be subtracted from 9 is 2^{3}, or 8. The remainder after subtraction is 1, or 2^{0}. The binary representation for 25 is therefore 11001.

This is a laborious method for converting numbers. It is convenient for small numbers when it can be performed mentally, but is less used for larger numbers. Instead, the decimal number is repeatedly divided by 2, and the remainder after each division is used to indicate the coefficients of the binary number to be formed. Notice that the binary number derived is written from the bottom up.

$$
\begin{aligned}
125 \div 2 &= 62 + \text{remainder of } 1 \\
62 \div 2 &= 31 + \text{remainder of } 0 \\
31 \div 2 &= 15 + \text{remainder of } 1 \\
15 \div 2 &= 7\ \ + \text{remainder of } 1 \\
7 \div 2 &= 3\ \ + \text{remainder of } 1 \\
3 \div 2 &= 1\ \ + \text{remainder of } 1 \\
1 \div 2 &= 0\ \ + \text{remainder of } 1
\end{aligned}
$$

The binary representation of 125 is therefore 1111101. Checking this result gives

$$1 \times 2^6 = 64$$
$$1 \times 2^5 = 32$$
$$1 \times 2^4 = 16$$
$$1 \times 2^3 = 8$$
$$1 \times 2^2 = 4$$
$$0 \times 2^1 = 0$$
$$1 \times 2^0 = \underline{1}$$
$$125$$

This method will not work for mixed numbers. If similar methods are to be used, it is necessary first to divide the number into its whole and fractional parts; that is, 102.247 would be divided into 102 and 0.247 and the binary representation for each part found, and then the two parts added together.

The conversion of decimal fractions to binary fractions may be accomplished using several techniques. Again, the most obvious method is to subtract the highest negative power of 2 which may be subtracted from the decimal fraction. The next highest negative power of 2 is then subtracted from the remainder of the first subtraction, and this process is continued until there is no remainder, or to the desired precision.

$$0.875 - (1 \times 2^{-1}) = 0.875 - 0.5 = 0.375$$
$$0.375 - (1 \times 2^{-2}) = 0.375 - 0.25 = 0.125$$
$$0.125 - (1 \times 2^{-3}) = 0.125 - 0.125 = 0$$

Therefore 0.875 decimal is represented by 0.111 binary. A much simpler method for longer fractions consists of repeatedly "doubling" the decimal fraction. If a 1 appears to the left of the decimal point after a multiplication by 2 is performed, a 1 is added to the right of the binary fraction being formed. If after a multiplication by 2, a 0 remains to the left of the decimal point of the decimal number, a 0 is added to the right of the binary number. The following example illustrates the use of this technique in converting 0.4375 decimal to the binary system:

	BINARY REPRESENTATION
$2 \times 0.4375 = 0.8750$	0.0
$2 \times 0.875 = 1.750$	0.01
$2 \times 0.75 = 1.50$	0.011
$2 \times 0.5 = 1.0$	0.0111

The binary representation of 0.4375 is therefore 0.0111.

2 • 7 NEGATIVE NUMBERS

A standard convention adopted for writing negative numbers consists of placing a "sign symbol" before a number that is negative. For instance, negative 39 is written as −39. If −39 is to be added to +70, we write

$$+70 + (-39) = 31$$

When a negative number is subtracted from a positive number, we write $+70 - (-39) = +70 + 39 = 109$. The rules for handling negative numbers are well known and will not be repeated here, but since negative numbers constitute an important part of our number system, the techniques used to represent negative numbers in digital machines will be described.

In binary machines, numbers are represented by a set of bistable storage devices, each of which represents one binary digit. As an example, given a set of five switches, any number from 00000 to 11111 may be represented by the switches, if we define a switch with its contacts closed as representing a 1 and a switch with open contacts as representing a 0. If we desire to increase the total range of numbers that we can represent so that it will include the negative numbers from 00000 to −11111, another bit (or switch) will be required. We then treat this bit as a *sign bit* and place it before the magnitude of the number to be represented.

Generally, the convention is adopted that when the sign bit is a 0, the number represented is positive, and when the sign bit is a 1, the number is negative. If the previous situation, where five switches are used to store the magnitude of a number, is extended so that both positive and negative numbers may be stored, a sixth switch will be required. When the contacts of this switch are open, the number will be a positive number equal to the magnitude of the number stored in the other five switches, and if the switch for the sign bit is closed, the number represented by the six switches will be a negative number with a magnitude determined by the other five switches. An example is shown in Fig. 2·1.

Sets of storage devices which represent a number or are handled as an entity are referred to as *registers,* and they are given names such as register A, register B, register C, etc. We can then write that register A contains − 12 and register B contains +22. In writing a signed number in binary form, the sign bit is generally set apart from the magnitude of the number by means of a period, so that 0.0111

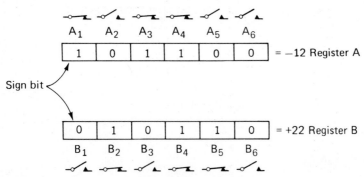

FIG. 2 • 1 Example of negative number representation.

represents positive 0111, or positive 7 decimal, and 1.0111 represents −0111, or negative 7 decimal.

The confusion which arises from separating the sign bit from the magnitude of the number with a period which can also be a radix (binary or decimal) point is compensated for when negative numbers are handled in what is known as the "complemented form," as we shall see in the following section. It should be emphasized that a symbol other than the period could be used to separate the sign and magnitude bits, such as a hyphen or a star. Then − 1011 (negative 11 decimal) could be written 1-1011 or 1*1011, and + 1100 as 0-1100 or 0*1100. There is no particular objection to these conventions, but the use of a period to separate the sign bit from the magnitude is fairly well established and will be adhered to in this text.

2 • 8 THE USE OF COMPLEMENTS TO REPRESENT NEGATIVE NUMBERS

The convention of using a sign bit to indicate whether a stored number is negative or positive has been described. The magnitude of the number stored is not always represented in normal form, however, but quite often negative numbers are stored in "complemented form." By using this technique, a machine can be made to both add and subtract, using only circuitry for adding. The actual technique involved will be described in Chap. 6.

There are two basic types of complements which are useful in the binary and also in the decimal number systems. In the decimal system the two types are referred to as the 10s *complement* and the 9s *complement*.

The 10s complement of any number may be formed by subtracting each digit of the number from 9 and then adding 1 to the least significant digit of the number thus formed. For instance, the 10s complement of 87 is 13, and the 10s complement of 23 is 77. Subtraction may be performed by simply adding the 10s complement of the subtrahend to the minuend and discarding the final carry, if any. For instance:

NORMAL SUBTRACTION	10s COMPLEMENT SUBTRACTION
89	89 89
− 23	− 23 = + 77
66	┌ 166
	└→ the carry is dropped
98	98 98
− 87	− 87 = + 13
11	┌ 111
	└→ the carry is dropped

The 9s complement of a decimal number is formed by subtracting each digit of the number from 9. For instance, the 9s complement of 23 is 76, and the 9s complement of 87 is 12. When subtraction is performed using the 9s complement, the complement of the subtrahend is added as before, but any carry generated must be added to the rightmost digit of the result.

NORMAL SUBTRACTION	9s COMPLEMENT SUBTRACTION

$$
\begin{array}{r}
89 \\
-23 \\
\hline
66
\end{array}
\qquad
\begin{array}{r}
89 \quad 89 \\
-23 = 76 \\
\hline
\underset{\llcorner\rightarrow}{\overline{165}} \\
\underline{1} \\
66
\end{array}
$$

$$
\begin{array}{r}
98 \\
-87 \\
\hline
11
\end{array}
\qquad
\begin{array}{r}
98 \quad 98 \\
-87 = 12 \\
\hline
\underset{\llcorner\rightarrow}{\overline{110}} \\
\underline{1} \\
11
\end{array}
$$

The rules for handling signs during the subtraction process and for handling all combinations of positive and negative numbers will be explained in Chap. 6. If this seems, at first, to be an unwieldy technique, it should be noted that the majority of machines now being constructed subtract using a complemented number.

2 • 9 COMPLEMENTS IN OTHER NUMBER SYSTEMS

There are two types of complements for each number system. Since only binary and binary-coded-decimal machines are now being constructed in quantity, only these number systems will be explained in any detail. The two types of complements and the rules for obtaining them are:

1. *True complement* This is formed by subtracting each digit of the number from the radix-minus-one of the number system and then adding 1 to the least significant digit of the number formed. The true complement of a number in the decimal system is referred to as the 10s complement, and in the binary system as the 2s complement.
2. *Radix-minus-one complement* The radix-minus-one is 9 for the decimal system and 1 for the binary system. The complement in each system is formed by subtracting each digit of the number from the radix-minus-one. For instance, the radix-minus-one complement of decimal 72 is 27.

2 • 10 BINARY NUMBER COMPLEMENTS

According to the rule in the preceding section, the 2s complement of a binary number is formed by simply subtracting each digit (bit) of the number from the radix-minus-one and adding a 1 to the least significant bit. Since the radix in the binary number system is 2, each bit of the binary number is subtracted from 1. The application of this rule is actually very simple; every 1 in the number is changed to a 0 and every 0 to a 1. A 1 is then added to the least significant bit of the number formed. For instance, the 2s complement of 10110 is 01010, and the 2s complement of 11010 is 00110. Subtraction using the 2s complement system involves forming the 2s complement of the subtrahend and then adding this "true complement" to the minuend. For instance:

$$\begin{array}{r} 11011 \\ -10100 \\ \hline 00111 \end{array} = \begin{array}{r} 11011 \\ +01100 \\ \hline 1\ 00111 \end{array} \quad \text{and} \quad \begin{array}{r} 11100 \\ 00100 \\ \hline 11000 \end{array} = \begin{array}{r} 11100 \\ 11100 \\ \hline 1\ 11000 \end{array}$$

the carry is dropped   dropped

Subtraction using the 1s complement system is also straightforward. The 1s complement of a binary number is formed by changing each 1 in the number to a 0 and each 0 in the number to a 1. For instance, the 1s complement of 10111 is 01000, and the 1s complement of 11000 is 00111.

When subtraction is performed in the 1s complement system, any end-around carry is added to the least significant bit. For instance:

$$\begin{array}{r} 11001 \\ -10110 \\ \hline 00011 \end{array} = \begin{array}{r} 11001 \\ +01001 \\ \hline 1\ 00010 \\ \rightarrow 1 \\ \hline 00011 \end{array} \quad \text{and} \quad \begin{array}{r} 11110 \\ -01101 \\ \hline 10001 \end{array} = \begin{array}{r} 11110 \\ 10010 \\ \hline 10000 \\ \rightarrow 1 \\ \hline 10001 \end{array}$$

2 • 11 BINARY-CODED-DECIMAL NUMBER REPRESENTATION

Since most of the electronic circuit elements used to construct digital computers are inherently binary in operation, the binary number system is the most natural number system for a computer. Also, computers constructed using the binary number system require a smaller amount of circuitry and are therefore more efficient than machines operating in other number systems. On the other hand, the decimal system has been used for a long time, and there is a natural reaction to performing calculations in a binary number system. Also, since checks, bills, tax rates, prices, etc., are all figured in the decimal system, the values of most things must be converted from decimal to binary before computations can begin. For these and other reasons most of the early machines operated in binary-coded-decimal number systems. In such systems a coded group of binary bits is used to represent each of the 10 decimal digits. For instance, an obvious and natural code is a simple "weighted binary code," as shown in Table 2·2.

This is known as a *binary-coded-decimal 8, 4, 2, 1 code*, or simply BCD. Notice that 4 binary bits are required for each decimal digit, and each bit is assigned a weight; for instance, the rightmost bit has a weight of 1 and the leftmost bit in each code group has a weight of 8. By adding the weights of the positions in which 1s

TABLE 2 • 2

BINARY CODE	DECIMAL DIGIT
0000	0
0001	1
0010	2
0011	3
0100	4
0101	5
0110	6
0111	7
1000	8
1001	9

appear, the decimal digit represented by a code group may be derived. This is somewhat uneconomical since $2^4 = 16$, and therefore the 4 bits could actually represent 15 different values; but the next lesser choice, 3 bits, gives only 2^3, or 8, values, which are insufficient. If the decimal number 214 is to be represented in this type of code, 12 binary bits are required as follows: 0010 0001 0100. For the decimal number 1246 to be represented, 16 bits are required: 0001 0010 0100 0110.

This is a very useful code and has been much used. One difficulty with the code, however, lies in forming the complements of numbers in this system. It is common practice to perform subtraction in a computer by adding the complement of the subtrahend; however, when the BCD 8, 4, 2, 1 system is used, the most natural complement of the number stored is not useful because the most direct way for a computer to complement a number is simply to change each 0 to a 1 and each 1 to a 0. However, the natural complement of 0010 (2 decimal) is 1101, which is 13, and not an acceptable BCD character in this system. To get around this difficulty, several other codes have been used. One of the first, a code that was used in the early Mark machines built at Harvard and has been used a good deal since, is known as the _excess 3_ code and is formed by adding 3 to the decimal number and then forming the binary-coded number in the normal weighted binary code. For instance, to form the excess 3 representation for 4, first 3 is added, yielding 7, and then the "normal" BCD is used, which is 0111. Therefore 0111 is the excess 3 code for the decimal digit 4. Table 2·3 shows all 10 decimal digits and the code for each.

By complementing each digit of the binary code representing a decimal digit, the 9s complement of that digit may be formed. For instance, the complement of 0100 (1 decimal) is 1011, which is 8 decimal.

The decimal number 243 coded in the excess 3 system would be 0101 0111 0110, and the decimal number 347 would be 0110 0111 1010. The 9s complement of 243 is 756 decimal, or 1010 1000 1001 binary. Table 2·4 lists the excess 3 code representation for each of the 10 decimal digits along with the 9s comple-

TABLE 2 • 3

EXCESS 3 CODE	
DECIMAL	BINARY CODE
0	0011
1	0100
2	0101
3	0110
4	0111
5	1000
6	1001
7	1010
8	1011
9	1100

ments listed below. It may be seen that the 9s complement of each code group may be formed by changing each 0 to a 1 and each 1 to a 0 in the code group.

The excess 3 code is not a weighted code, however, because weights cannot be assigned to the bits so that their sum equals the decimal digits represented.

A weighted code in which the 9s complement may be formed by complementing each binary digit is the 2, 4, 2, 1 code (see Table 2·5). If each bit of a code group is complemented, the 9s complement of the decimal digit represented is formed. For instance, 0010 (2 decimal) complemented is 1101 (7 decimal), and 1011 (5 decimal) complemented is 0100 (4 decimal). This code is widely used in instruments and electronic calculators.

The following convention is generally adopted to distinguish binary from decimal. A binary number is identified by a subscript of 2 placed at the end of the number (00110_2), and a decimal number by the subscript 10 (for instance, decimal

TABLE 2 • 4

DECIMAL DIGIT	EXCESS 3 CODE	9s COMPLEMENT
0	0011	1100
1	0100	1011
2	0101	1010
3	0110	1001
4	0111	1000
5	1000	0111
6	1001	0110
7	1010	0101
8	1011	0100
9	1100	0011

TABLE 2 • 5 2, 4, 2, 1 CODE

| | CODED BINARY | | | |
| | WEIGHT OF BIT | | | |
DECIMAL	2	4	2	1
0	0	0	0	0
1	0	0	0	1
2	0	0	1	0
3	0	0	1	1
4	0	1	0	0
5	1	0	1	1
6	1	1	0	0
7	1	1	0	1
8	1	1	1	0
9	1	1	1	1

948 may be written 948_{10}). We may then write 0111_2 as 7_{10}. This convention will be used when necessary.

2 • 12 OCTAL AND HEXADECIMAL NUMBER SYSTEMS

There are two other number systems which are very useful in the computer industry: the octal number system and the hexadecimal number system.

The octal number system has a base, or radix, of 8; eight different symbols are used to represent numbers. These are commonly 0, 1, 2, 3, 4, 5, 6, and 7. Using positional notation, the first few octal numbers and their decimal equivalents are as shown in Table 2·6.

To convert an octal number to a decimal number, we use the same sort of polynomial as was used in the binary case, except that we now have a radix of 8

TABLE 2 • 6

OCTAL	DECIMAL	OCTAL	DECIMAL
0	0	11	9
1	1	12	10
2	2	13	11
3	3	14	12
4	4	15	13
5	5	16	14
6	6	17	15
7	7	20	16
10	8	21	17

instead of 2. Therefore 1213 in octal is $(1 \times 8^3) + (2 \times 8^2) + (1 \times 8^1) + (3 \times 8^0) = 512 + 128 + 8 + 3 = 651$ in decimal. Also, 1.123 in octal is $(1 \times 8^0) + (1 \times 8^{-1}) + (2 \times 8^{-2}) + (3 \times 8^{-3})$, or $1 + \frac{1}{8} + \frac{2}{64} + \frac{3}{512} = 1\frac{83}{512}$ in decimal.

There is a simple trick for converting a binary number to an octal number. Simply group the binary digits into groups of 3s, starting at the octal point, and read each set of three binary digits according to Table 2·7.

Let us convert the binary number 011101. First we break it into 3s (thus 011 101), and then, converting each group of three binary digits, we get 35 in octal. Therefore 011101 binary = 35 octal. Here are several more examples:

$$
\begin{aligned}
111110111_2 &= 767_8 \\
110110101_2 &= 665_8 \\
11011_2 &= 33_8 \\
1001_2 &= 11_8 \\
10101.11_2 &= 25.6_8 \\
1100.111_2 &= 14.7_8 \\
1011.1111_2 &= 13.74_8
\end{aligned}
$$

Conversion from decimal to octal can be performed by repeatedly dividing the decimal number by 8 and using each remainder as a digit in the octal number being formed. For instance, to convert 200_{10} to an octal representation, we divide as follows:

$$
\begin{aligned}
200 \div 8 &= 25 \qquad \text{remainder is 0} \\
25 \div 8 &= 3 \qquad \text{remainder is 1} \\
3 \div 8 &= 0 \qquad \text{remainder is 3}
\end{aligned}
$$

Therefore $200_{10} = 310_8$.

Notice that when the number to be divided is less than 8, we use 0 as the quotient and the number as the remainder. Let us check this:

$$
310_8 = (3_{10} \times 8^2_{10}) + (1_{10} \times 8^1_{10}) + (0_{10} \times 8^0_{10}) = 192_{10} + 8_{10} = 200_{10}
$$

TABLE 2 • 7

THREE BINARY DIGITS	OCTAL DIGIT
000	0
001	1
010	2
011	3
100	4
101	5
110	6
111	7

Here is another example. We wish to convert 3964_{10} to octal:

$$
\begin{aligned}
3964 \div 8 &= 495 && \text{with a remainder of 4} \\
495 \div 8 &= 61 && \text{with a remainder of 7} \\
61 \div 8 &= 7 && \text{with a remainder of 5} \\
7 \div 8 &= 0 && \text{with a remainder of 7}
\end{aligned}
$$

Therefore $7574_8 = 3964_{10}$. Checking,

$$
\begin{aligned}
7574_8 &= (7_{10} \times 8_{10}^3) + (5_{10} \times 8_{10}^2) + (7_{10} \times 8_{10}) + 4_{10} \\
&= (7_{10} \times 512_{10}) + (5_{10} \times 64_{10}) + (7_{10} \times 8_{10}) + (4_{10} \times 1_{10}) \\
&= 3584_{10} + 320_{10} + 56_{10} + 4_{10} \\
&= 3964_{10}
\end{aligned}
$$

There are several other techniques for converting octal to decimal and decimal to octal, but they are not used very frequently manually, and tables prove to be of about as much value as anything in this process. Octal-to-decimal and decimal-to-octal tables are readily available in a number of places, including the manuals distributed by manufacturers of binary machines.

An important use for octal is in listings of programs and for memory "dumps" for binary machines, thus making the printouts more compact. The manuals for several of the largest manufacturers use octal numbers to represent binary numbers because of ease of conversion and compactness.

The hexadecimal number system is useful for a similar reason. All the IBM 370 series of computers, and a great many other computers, in particular most minicomputers and microcomputers, have their memories organized into sets of *bytes,* each consisting of eight binary digits. Each byte either is used as a single entity to represent a single alphanumeric character or is broken into two 4-bit pieces. (We shall examine the coding of alphanumeric characters using bytes in Chap. 8.) When the bytes are handled in two 4-bit pieces, the programmer is given the option of declaring each 4-bit character as a piece of a binary number or as two binary-coded-decimal numbers. For instance, the byte 00011000 can be declared a binary number, in which case it is equal to 24 decimal, or as two binary-coded-decimal characters, in which case it represents the decimal number 18.

When the machine is handling numbers in binary, but in groups of four digits, it is convenient to have a code for representing each of these sets of four digits. Since there are 16 possible different numbers that can be represented, the digits 0 through 9 will not suffice; so the letters A, B, C, D, E, and F are also used (see Table 2·8).

To convert binary to hexadecimal we simply break a binary number into groups of four digits and convert each group of four digits according to the preceding code. Thus $10111011_2 = BB_{16}$, $10010101_2 = 95_{16}$, $11000111_2 = C7_{16}$, and $10001011_2 = 8B_{16}$. The mixture of letters and decimal digits may seem strange at first, but these are simply convenient symbols, just as decimal digits are.

The conversion of hexadecimal to decimal is straightforward but time-consum-

TABLE 2 • 8

BINARY	HEXADECIMAL	DECIMAL
0000	0	0
0001	1	1
0010	2	2
0011	3	3
0100	4	4
0101	5	5
0110	6	6
0111	7	7
1000	8	8
1001	9	9
1010	A	10
1011	B	11
1100	C	12
1101	D	13
1110	E	14
1111	F	15

ing. For instance, BB represents $(B \times 16^1) + (B \times 16^0) = (11 \times 16) + (11 \times 1) = 176 + 11 = 187$. Similarly,

$$
\begin{aligned}
AB6_{16} &= (10_{10} \times 16^2_{10}) + (11_{10} \times 16_{10}) + 6_{10} \\
&= (10_{10} \times 256_{10}) + 176_{10} + 6_{10} \\
&= 2560_{10} + 176_{10} + 6_{10} \\
&= 2742_{10}
\end{aligned}
$$

To convert, for instance, $3A6_{16}$ to decimal:

$$
\begin{aligned}
3A6_{16} &= (3_{10} \times 16^2_{10}) + (10_{10} \times 16_{10}) + 6_{10} \\
&= (3_{10} \times 256_{10}) + (10_{10} \times 16_{10}) + 6_{10} \\
&= 768_{10} + 160_{10} + 6_{10} \\
&= 934_{10}
\end{aligned}
$$

Again, tables are convenient for converting hexadecimal to decimal and decimal to hexadecimal. Table 2·9 is useful for converting in either direction.

The chief use of the hexadecimal system is in connection with byte-organized machines. Users of these computers become amazingly adept, with experience, at handling the hexadecimal system.

Quite a large number of questions have been included below for this chapter. For those desiring to study octal and hexadecimal number systems further, Questions 58 through 67 contain information and exercises on octal addition and multiplication, and Questions 68 through 72 can be used to supplement the study of the hexadecimal system.

TABLE 2 • 9 HEXADECIMAL-TO-DECIMAL CONVERSION TABLE

A. INTEGER CONVERSION

EXAMPLE: 2322_{16} is
$8192_{10} + 768_{10} + 32_{10} + 2_{10}$
$= 8994.0.$

HEX	DEC	HEX	DEC	HEX	DEC	HEX	DEC
0	0	0	0	0	0	0	0
1	4,096	1	256	1	16	1	1
2	8,192	2	512	2	32	2	2
3	12,288	3	768	3	48	3	3
4	16,384	4	1,024	4	64	4	4
5	20,480	5	1,280	5	80	5	5
6	24,576	6	1,536	6	96	6	6
7	28,672	7	1,792	7	112	7	7
8	32,768	8	2,048	8	128	8	8
9	36,864	9	2,304	9	144	9	9
A	40,960	A	2,560	A	160	A	10
B	45,056	B	2,816	B	176	B	11
C	49,152	C	3,072	C	192	C	12
D	53,248	D	3,328	D	208	D	13
E	57,344	E	3,584	E	224	E	14
F	61,440	F	3,840	F	240	F	15

Hexadecimal Positions: 4, 3, 2, 1

B. FRACTIONAL CONVERSION

HEX 0123	DEC	HEX 4567	DECIMAL	HEX 0123	DECIMAL	HEX 4567	DECIMAL EQUIVALENT
.0	.0000	.00	.0000 0000	.000	.0000 0000 0000	.0000	.0000 0000 0000 0000
.1	.0625	.01	.0039 0625	.001	.0002 4414 0625	.0001	.0000 1525 8789 0625
.2	.1250	.02	.0078 1250	.002	.0004 8828 1250	.0002	.0000 3051 7578 1250
.3	.1875	.03	.0117 1875	.003	.0007 3242 1875	.0003	.0000 4577 6367 1875
.4	.2500	.04	.0156 2500	.004	.0009 7656 2500	.0004	.0000 6103 5156 2500
.5	.3125	.05	.0195 3125	.005	.0012 2070 3125	.0005	.0000 7629 3945 3125
.6	.3750	.06	.0234 3750	.006	.0014 6484 3750	.0006	.0000 9155 2734 3750
.7	.4375	.07	.0273 4375	.007	.0017 0898 4375	.0007	.0001 0681 1523 4375
.8	.5000	.08	.0312 5000	.008	.0019 5312 5000	.0008	.0001 2207 0312 5000
.9	.5625	.09	.0351 5625	.009	.0021 9726 5625	.0009	.0001 3732 9101 5625
.A	.6250	.0A	.0390 6250	.00A	.0024 4140 6250	.000A	.0001 5258 7890 6250
.B	.6875	.0B	.0429 6875	.00B	.0026 8554 6875	.000B	.0001 6784 6679 6875
.C	.7500	.0C	.0468 7500	.00C	.0029 2968 7500	.000C	.0001 8310 5468 7500
.D	.8125	.0D	.0507 8125	.00D	.0031 7382 8125	.000D	.0001 9836 4257 8125
.E	.8750	.0E	.0546 8750	.00E	.0034 1796 8750	.000E	.0002 1362 3046 8750
.F	.9375	.0F	.0585 9375	.00F	.0036 6210 9375	.000F	.0002 2888 1835 9375

Hexadecimal Positions: 1, 2, 3, 4

QUESTIONS

1. Convert the following decimal numbers to equivalent binary numbers:
   (a) 43   (b) 64   (c) 4096
   (d) 0.375   (e) $\frac{27}{32}$ (f) 0.4375
   (g) 512.5   (h) 131.5625   (i) 2048.0625
2. Convert the following numbers to the equivalent binary numbers:
   (a) 12   (b) 0.25   (c) $3\frac{5}{16}$
   (d) 5.4   (e) $2\frac{3}{8}$ (f) 0.775

3. Convert the following binary numbers to equivalent decimal numbers:

(a) 1101	*(b)* 11011	*(c)* 1011
(d) 0.1011	*(e)* 0.001101	*(f)* 0.001101101
(g) 111011.1011	*(h)* 1011011.001101	*(i)* 10110.0101011101

4. Convert the following binary numbers to equivalent decimal numbers:

(a) 101	*(b)* 1100	*(c)* 100011
(d) 1101	*(e)* 11100	*(f)* 101101

5. Convert the following binary numbers to equivalent decimal numbers:

(a) 1011	*(b)* 100100	*(c)* 10011
(d) 0.1101	*(e)* 0.1001	*(f)* 0.0101
(g) 1011.0011	*(h)* 1001.1001	*(i)* 101.011

6. Convert the following binary numbers to equivalent decimal numbers:

(a) 0.11	*(b)* 0.1101	*(c)* 1.011
(d) 111.1011	*(e)* 0110.0101	*(f)* 101.10101

7. Perform the following additions and check by converting the binary numbers to decimal:

(a) 1001.1 + 1011.01	*(b)* 100101 + 100101
(c) 0.1011 + 0.1101	*(d)* 1011.01 + 1001.11

8. Perform the following additions and check by converting the binary numbers to decimal and adding:

(a) 1011 + 1110	*(b)* 1010 + 1111	*(c)* 10.11 + 10.011
(d) 1101.11 + 1.11	*(e)* 11111.1 + 10010.1	*(f)* 101.1 + 111.11

9. Perform the following additions and check by converting the binary numbers to decimal:

(a) 1101.1 + 1011.1	*(b)* 101101 + 1101101
(c) 0.0011 + 0.1110	*(d)* 1100.011 + 1011.011

10. Perform the following subtractions in binary and check by converting the numbers to decimal and subtracting:

(a) 1101 − 1000	*(b)* 1101 − 1001	*(c)* 1011.1 − 101.1
(d) 1101.01 − 1011.1	*(e)* 111.11 − 101.1	*(f)* 1101.1 − 1010.01

11. Perform the following subtractions in the binary number system:

(a) 64 − 32	*(b)* 127 − 63
(c) 93.5 − 42.75	*(d)* $84\frac{9}{32} - 48\frac{5}{16}$

12. Perform the following subtractions in the binary number system:

(a) 128 − 32	*(b)* $\frac{1}{8} - \frac{1}{16}$	*(c)* $2\frac{1}{8} - 4\frac{3}{32}$
(d) $31 - \frac{5}{8}$	*(e)* $62 - 31\frac{1}{16}$	*(f)* 129 − 35

13. Perform the following subtractions in the binary number system:

(a) 37 − 35	*(c)* 94.5 − 43.75
(b) 128 − 64	*(d)* 255 − 127

14. Perform the following multiplications and divisions in the binary number system:

(a) 16 × 8	*(b)* 31 × 14	*(c)* 23 × 3.525
(d) 15 × 8.625	*(e)* 6 ÷ 2	*(f)* 16 ÷ 8

15. Perform the following multiplications and divisions in the binary number system:

(a) 24 × 12	*(b)* 18 × 14	*(c)* 32 ÷ 8
(d) 27 ÷ 18	*(e)* 49.5 × 51.75	*(f)* 58.75 ÷ 23.5

16. Perform the following multiplications and divisions in the binary number system:

(a) 16×2.75 (b) $19 \div 6$ (c) $256\frac{1}{2} \div 128\frac{1}{4}$

(d) $31.5 \div 15.75$ (e) $3 \div \frac{5}{8}$ (f) $2\frac{2}{8} \times 1\frac{5}{8}$

17. Perform the following multiplications and divisions in the binary number system:

(a) 15×13 (b) 10×15 (c) $44 \div 11$

(d) $42 \div 12$ (e) 7.75×2.5 (f) 22.5×4.75

18. Convert the following decimal numbers into both their 9s and 10s complements:

(a) 9   (b) 19   (c) 8

(d) 24   (e) 25   (f) 99

19. Convert the following decimal numbers into both their 9s and 10s complements:

(a) 5436   (b) 1932   (c) 45.15   (d) 18.293

20. Convert the following decimal numbers into both their 9s and 10s complements:

(a) 95   (b) 79   (c) 0.83

(d) 0.16   (e) 298.64   (f) 332.52

21. Convert the following decimal numbers into both their 9s and 10s complements:

(a) 3654   (b) 2122   (c) 54.19   (d) 37.263

22. Convert the following binary numbers into both their 1s and 2s complements:

(a) 1101   (b) 1010   (c) 1111

(d) 1110   (e) 1011   (f) 1001

23. Convert the following binary numbers into both their 1s and 2s complements:

(a) 1011   (b) 11011   (c) 1011.01   (d) 11011.01

24. Convert the following binary numbers into both their 1s and 2s complements:

(a) 1011   (b) 1101   (c) 0.0111

(d) 0.101   (e) 11.101   (f) 101.011

25. Convert the following binary numbers into both their 1s and 2s complements:

(a) 101111   (b) 100100   (c) 10111.10   (d) 10011.11

26. Perform the following subtractions using both 9s and 10s complements:

(a) $8 - 4$ (b) $16 - 8$ (c) $198 - 124$

(d) $28.5 - 23.4$ (e) $27.6 - 23.4$ (f) $0.55 - 0.42$

27. Perform the following subtractions using both 9s and 10s complements:

(a) $948 - 234$ (b) $347 - 263$

(c) $349.5 - 245.3$ (d) $412.7 - 409.2$

28. Perform the following subtractions using both 9s and 10s complements:

(a) $14 - 9$ (b) $15 - 9$ (c) $0.5 - 40.24$

(d) $0.41 - 0.4$ (e) $0.434 - 0.33$ (f) $1.2 - 0.34$

29. Perform the following subtractions using both 9s and 10s complements:

(a) $1024 - 913$ (b) $249 - 137$ (c) $24.1 - 13.4$ (d) $239.3 - 119.4$

30. Perform the following subtractions of binary numbers using both 1s and 2s complements:

(a) $1010 - 1011$ (b) $110 - 10$ (c) $110 - 0.111$

(d) $0.111 - 0.1001$ (e) $0.1111 - 0.101$ (f) $11.11 - 10.111$

31. Perform the following subtractions using both 1s and 2s complements:
(a) $1011 - 101$ (b) $11011 - 11001$
(c) $10111.1 - 10011.1$ (d) $11011 - 10011.11$

32. How many different numbers can be stored in a set of four switches, each having three different positions (four three-position switches)?

33. How many different binary numbers can be stored in a register consisting of six switches?

34. How many different BCD numbers can be stored in 12 switches? (Assume two-position or ON–OFF switches.)

35. How many different BCD numbers can be stored in a register containing 12 switches using an 8, 4, 2, 1 code? Using an excess 3 code?

36. Write the first 12 numbers in the base 4 (or quaternary) number system.

37. Write the first 10 numbers in the quaternary number system, which has a base, or radix, of 4. Use the digits 0, 1, 2, and 3 to express these numbers.

38. Write the first 20 numbers in the base 12 (or *duodecimal*) number system. Use A for 10 and B for 11.

39. Write the first 25 numbers in a base 11 number system, using the digits 0, 1, 2, 3, 4, 5, 6, 7, 8, 9, and A to express the 25 numbers that you write. (Decimal 10 = A, for instance.)

40. Perform the following subtractions in the binary number system using 1s complements:
(a) $1111 - 1001$ (b) $1110 - 1011$
(c) $101.11 - 101.01$ (d) $111.1 - 100.1$

41. Using the 1s complement number system, perform the following subtractions:
(a) $0.1001 - 0.0110$ (b) $0.1110 - 0.0110$ (c) $0.01111 - 0.01001$
(d) $11011 - 11001$ (e) $1110101 - 1010010$

42. Perform the following subtractions in the binary number system using 2s complements:
(a) $1111 - 110$ (b) $1110 - 1100$
(c) $1011.11 - 101.001$ (d) $111.1 - 110.1$

43. Using the 2s complement number system, perform the following subtractions and also represent the answers as decimal fractions:
(a) $0.101010 - 0.010101$ (b) $0.11001 - 0.00100$
(c) $0.111000 - 0.000111$ (d) $0.101100 - 0.010011$

44. Convert the following hexadecimal numbers to decimal numbers:
(a) 15 (b) B8 (c) AB4
(d) 9.B (e) 9.1A

45. Convert the following hexadecimal numbers to decimal:
(a) B6C7 (b) 64AC (c) A492 (d) D2763

46. Convert the following octal numbers to decimal:
(a) 15 (b) 125 (c) 115
(d) 124 (e) 156 (f) 15.6

47. Convert the following octal numbers to decimal:
(a) 2376 (b) 2473 (c) 276431 (d) 22632

48. Convert the following binary numbers to octal:
(a) 110 (b) 111001 (c) 111.111
(d) 0.11111 (e) 10.11 (f) 1111.1101

49. Convert the following binary numbers to octal:
    (a) 101101   *(b)* 101101110   *(c)* 10110111
    (d) 110110.011   *(e)* 011.1011011
50. Convert the following octal numbers to binary:
    (a) 54   *(b)* 44   *(c)* 232.2
    (d) 232.4   *(e)* 453.45   *(f)* 31.234
51. Convert the following octal numbers to binary:
    (a) 7423   *(b)* 3364   *(c)* 33762   *(d)* 3232.14   *(e)* 3146.52
52. Convert the following decimal numbers to octal:
    (a) 17   *(b)* 8   *(c)* 19
    (d) 0.55   *(e)* 0.625   *(f)* 2.125
53. Convert the following decimal numbers to octal:
    (a) 932   *(b)* 332   *(c)* 545.375   *(d)* 632.97   *(e)* 4429.625
54. Convert the following hexadecimal numbers to binary:
    (a) 9   *(b)* 1B   *(c)* 0.A1
    (d) 0.AB   *(e)* A.B   *(f)* 12.B
55. Convert the following hexadecimal numbers to binary:
    (a) CD   *(b)* 6A9   *(c)* A14   *(d)* AA.1A   *(e)* AB2.234
56. Convert the following binary numbers to hexadecimal:
    (a) 1101.0110   *(b)* 11011110   *(c)* 1111
    (d) 11101   *(e)* 11110.01011   *(f)* 1011.11010
57. Convert the following binary numbers to hexadecimal:
    (a) 10110111   *(b)* 10011100   *(c)* 1001111
    (d) 0.01111110   *(e)* 101101111010
58. A simple rule for multiplying two digits in any radix is simply to multiply the two digits in decimal. If the product is less than the radix, take it; if greater, divide (in decimal) by the radix and use the remainder as the first, or least significant, position and the quotient as the carry, or most significant, digit. Thus, in base 6, $2 \times 2 = 4$, $3 \times 1 = 3$, etc.; however, $2 \times 4 = 8$, and

$$\begin{array}{r} 1 \\ 6\overline{)8} \end{array}$$

So $2_6 \times 4_6 = 12_6$. Similarly, in base 7, $3 \times 4 = 12$ and

$$\begin{array}{r} 1 \\ 7\overline{)12} \\ \underline{7} \\ 5 \end{array}$$

So $3_7 \times 4_7 = 15_7$. Using this rule perform, in base 7:
    (a) $2_7 \times 3_7$ *(b)* $2_7 \times 2_7$
    (c) $4_7 \times 4_7$ *(d)* $4_7 \times 3_7$
59. Using the rule in Question 58 perform:
    (a) $3_6 \times 4_6$ *(b)* $3_6 \times 3_6$ *(c)* $3_9 \times 4_9$
    (d) $4_9 \times 5_9$ *(e)* $5_9 \times 15_9$

60. An addition table for octal is as follows:

+	0	1	2	3	5	5	6	7
0	0	1	2	3	4	5	6	7
1	1	2	3	4	5	6	7	10
2	2	3	4	5	6	7	10	11
3	3	4	5	6	7	10	11	12
4	4	5	6	7	10	11	12	13
5	5	6	7	10	11	12	13	14
6	6	7	10	11	12	13	14	15
7	7	10	11	12	13	14	15	16

$$1\ 1 \longleftarrow \text{carries}$$

Using this table, we add in octal 1 2 6
                                    3 5 7
                                   ‾‾‾‾‾
                                    5 0 5

Perform the following additions:

(a) $7_8 + 7_8$ (b) $6_8 + 5_8$ (c) $7_8 + 16_8$

(d) $5_8 + 4_8$ (e) $5_8 + 14_8$

61. Using the table in Question 60, perform:

(a) $15_8 + 14_8$ (b) $24_8 + 36_8$ (c) $126_8 + 347_8$

(d) $67_8 + 45_8$ (e) $136_8 + 636_8$

62. Make up a hexadecimal addition table.

63. Using the table in Question 60, perform:

(a) $6_{16} + A1_{16}$ (b) $7_{16} + 17_{16}$ (c) $8_{16} + 28_{16}$

(d) $A16A_{16} + B16A_{16}$ (e) $A84_{16} + A83_{16}$

64. Perform the additions in Question 63 in binary and convert back to hexadecimal.

65. Perform the additions in Question 61 in binary and convert back to octal.

66. To multiply two numbers in octal we use the rule given in Question 58 and then proceed as follows:

$$6 \times 27 = 6 \times 20 = (6 \times 20) + (6 \times 7)$$
$$= 140 + 52 = 212$$

Multiply the following in octal:

(a) 6×7 (b) 6×10 (c) 5×14

67. To multiply numbers of more than one digit, proceed as in Question 66, then add in octal:

$$
\begin{array}{r}
23 \\
\underline{23} \\
70 \\
\underline{46} \\
550
\end{array}
$$

Multiply the following octal numbers:
(a) 3 × 14   (b) 23 × 12   (c) 11 × 22
(d) 22 × 44   (e) 13 × 13   (f) 14 × 15

68. Perform the following multiplications of hexadecimal numbers:
(a) A × 8   (b) 9 × 14   (c) A1 × 8
(d) A11 × 9   (e) A12 × 6   (f) A13 × 2B

69. Using the rule in Question 58, perform the following multiplications of hexa-decimal numbers:
(a) 15 × B   (b) 14 × B   (c) 11 × A
(d) 142 × A   (e) 13 × 14

70. Perform the multiplications in Question 68 in binary, then convert back to hexadecimal.

71. Perform the multiplications in Question 69 in binary, then convert back to hexadecimal.

72. In converting decimal numbers to hexadecimal, it is convenient to go first to octal, then to binary, then to hexadecimal. For instance, to convert 412_{10} to hexadecimal, we go first to octal:

$$
\begin{array}{r}
51 \\
8\overline{)412} \\
\underline{40} \\
12 \\
\underline{8} \\
4
\end{array}
\qquad
\begin{array}{r}
6 \\
8\overline{)51} \\
\underline{48} \\
3
\end{array}
$$

                   2d digit   6 ← 1st digit

3d digit

Now $412_{10} = 634_8$; converting this to binary, $634_8 = \underbrace{110}_{6}\ \underbrace{011}_{3}\ \underbrace{100}_{4}$; then regrouping, $\underbrace{1}_{1}\ \underbrace{1001}_{9}\ \underbrace{1100}_{C}$; so $412_{10} = 19C$.

Convert the following decimal numbers to hexadecimal:
(a) 24   (b) 397   (c) 1343   (d) 513   (e) 262

3

BOOLEAN ALGEBRA AND GATE NETWORKS

Modern digital computers are designed, maintained, and their operation is analyzed using techniques and symbology from a field of mathematics called *modern algebra*. Algebraists have studied for a period of over a hundred years mathematical systems called *Boolean algebras*. Nothing could be more simple and normal to human reasoning than the rules of a Boolean algebra, for these originated in studies of how we reason, what lines of reasoning are valid, what constitutes proof, and other allied subjects.

The name Boolean algebra honors a fascinating† English mathematician, George Boole, who in 1854 published a classic book, *An Investigation of the Laws of Thought, on Which Are Founded the Mathematical Theories of Logic and Probabilities*. Boole's stated intention was to perform a mathematical analysis of logic.

Starting with his investigation of the laws of thought, Boole constructed a "logical algebra." This investigation into the nature of logic and ultimately of mathematics led subsequent mathematicians and logicians into several new fields of mathematics. Two of these, known as "the calculus of propositions" and "the algebra of sets," were based principally on Boole's work. This book will designate the algebra now used in the design and maintenance of logical circuitry as *Boolean algebra*.‡

Boolean algebra was first brought to bear on problems which had arisen in the design of relay switching circuits in 1938 by Claude E. Shannon, a research assist-

---

†George Boole was the son of a shoemaker. His formal education ended in the third grade. Despite this, he was a brilliant scholar, teaching Greek and Latin in his own school, and an accepted mathematician who made lasting contributions in the areas of differential and difference equations as well as in algebra.

‡This algebra is sometimes called *switching algebra*. It is, in fact, only one of several realizations of what modern algebraists call Boolean algebra.

ant in the department of electrical engineering at the Massachusetts Institute of Technology. A version of Shannon's thesis, written at MIT for the degree of Master of Science, was published under the title, "A Symbolic Analysis of Relay and Switching Circuits." This paper presented a method for representing any circuit consisting of combinations of switches and relays by a set of mathematical expressions, and a calculus was developed for manipulating these expressions. The calculus used was shown to be based on the rules of Boolean algebra. The basic techniques described by Shannon were adopted almost universally for the design and analysis of switching circuits. Because of the analogous relationship between the actions of relays and of modern electronic circuits, the same techniques which were developed for the design of relay circuits are still being used in the design of modern high-speed computers.

There are several advantages in having a mathematical technique for the description of the internal workings of a computer. For one thing, it is often far more convenient to calculate with expressions used to represent switching circuits than it is to use schematic or even logical diagrams. Further, just as an ordinary algebraic expression may be simplified by means of the basic theorems, the expression describing a given switching circuit network may also be reduced or simplified. This enables the logical designer to simplify the circuitry used, achieving economy of construction and reliability of operation. Boolean algebra also provides an economical and straightforward way of describing the circuitry used in computers. In all, a knowledge of Boolean algebra is indispensable in the computing field.

3 • 1 FUNDAMENTAL CONCEPTS OF BOOLEAN ALGEBRA

When a variable is used in an algebraic formula, it is generally assumed that the variable may take any numerical value. For instance, in the formula $2X + 5Y = Z$, we assume that X, Y, and Z may range through the entire field of real numbers.

The variables used in Boolean equations have a unique characteristic, however; they may assume only one of two possible values. These two values may be represented by the symbols 0 and 1.† If an equation describing logical circuitry has several variables, it is still understood that each of the variables can assume only the value 0 or 1. For instance, in the equation $X + Y = Z$ each of the variables X, Y, and Z may have only the values 0 or 1.

This concept will become clearer if another symbol is defined, the $+$, or *logical addition,* symbol. When the $+$ symbol is placed between two variables, say X and Y, since both X and Y can take only the role 0 or 1, we can define the $+$ symbol by listing all possible combinations for X and Y and the resulting values of $X + Y$.

The possible input and output combinations may be arranged as follows:

$$0 + 0 = 0$$
$$0 + 1 = 1$$

---

† Or T and F, or $+$ and $-$, etc. 0 and 1 are almost universally used in computer work, however.

$$1 + 0 = 1$$
$$1 + 1 = 1$$

This is a logical addition table and could represent a standard binary addition table except for the last entry. When both X and Y represent 1s, the value of $X + Y$ is 1. The + symbol therefore does not have the "normal" meaning, but is a logical addition symbol. The equation $X + Y = Z$ can be read "X or Y equals Z" or "X plus Y equals Z." This concept may be extended to any number of variables; for instance, in the equation $A + B + C + D = E$, even if $A, B, C,$ and D all had the value of 1, the sum of the values, or E, would represent only a 1.

To avoid ambiguity, a number of other symbols have been recommended as replacements for the + sign. Some of these are $\cup$,† **v**, and **V**. The majority of computer people still use the + sign, however, which was the symbol originally proposed by Boole.

3 • 2 LOGICAL MULTIPLICATION

A second important operation in Boolean algebra is the operation which we will call *logical multiplication*. The rules for logical multiplication can again be given by simply listing all values that might occur. These are

$$0 \cdot 0 = 0$$
$$0 \cdot 1 = 0$$
$$1 \cdot 0 = 0$$
$$1 \cdot 1 = 1$$

Thus, for instance, if we write $Z = X \cdot Y$, and find $X = 0$ and $Y = 1$, then $Z = 0$. Only when X and Y are both 1s would Z be a 1.

Both + and · obey a mathematical rule called the *associative law*. This law says, for +, that $(X + Y) + Z = X + (Y + Z)$, and for ·, that $X \cdot (Y \cdot Z) = (X \cdot Y) \cdot Z$. What this means is that, for instance, we can write $X + Y + Z$ without ambiguity, for no matter in what order the logical addition is performed, the result is the same; that is, adding X to Y and then adding Z gives the same result as adding Y to Z and then adding this to X. We can test this for both + and · by again trying all combinations.

Note that while either +'s and ·'s can be used freely, the two cannot be "mixed" without ambiguity in the absence of further rules. For instance, does $A \cdot B + C$ mean $(A \cdot B) + C$ or $A \cdot (B + C)$? The two form different values for $A = 0$, $B = 0$, and $C = 1$, for then we have $(0 \cdot 0) + 1 = 1$ and $0 \cdot (0 + 1) = 0$, which differ. (Always operating from left to right will alleviate this, and is used in some programming languages, but not usually by algebraists or computer designers or

---

†The preceding equation might then be written $A \cup B \cup C \cup D = E$.

maintenance personnel.) The rule which is used is that $\cdot$ is always performed before $+$. Thus $X \cdot Y + Z$ is $(X \cdot Y) + Z$, and $X \cdot Y + X \cdot Z$ means $(X \cdot Y) + (X \cdot Z)$.

3 • 3 OR GATES & AND GATES

The $+$ and $\cdot$ operations are physically realized by two types of electronic circuits, called *OR gates* and *AND gates*. We shall treat these as "black boxes," deferring until later any discussion of how the actual circuitry operates.

A *gate* is simply an electronic circuit which operates on one or more input signals to produce an output signal. One of the simplest and most frequently used gates is called the OR gate, and the block diagram symbol for the OR gate is shown in Fig. 3·1, as is the table of combinations for the inputs and outputs for the OR gate. Since the inputs X and Y are signals with values either 0 or 1 at any given time, the output signal Z can be described by simply listing all values for X and Y and the resulting value for Z. A study of the table in Fig. 3·1 indicates that the OR gate performs logical addition on its inputs.

Similarly, the AND gate in Fig. 3·2 performs logical multiplication on input values, yielding an output Z with value $X \cdot Y$, so that Z is a 1 only when both X and Y are 1s.

Just as the $+$ and $\cdot$ operations could be extended to several variables using the associative law, OR gates and AND gates can have more than two inputs. Figure 3·3 shows three input OR and AND gates and the table of all input combinations for each. As might be hoped, the OR gate with input X, Y, and Z has a 1 output if X or Y or Z is a 1, so that we can write $X + Y + Z$ for its output. Also, the output of the AND gate with inputs X, Y, and Z is a 1 only when all three of the inputs are 1s, so that we can write the output as $X \cdot Y \cdot Z$.

The above argument can be extended. A four-input OR gate has a 1 output when any of its inputs is a 1, and a four-input AND gate has a 1 output only when all four inputs are 1s.

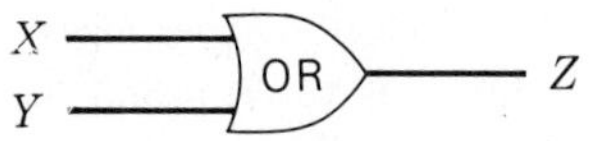

INPUT		OUTPUT
X	Y	Z
0	0	0
0	1	1
1	0	1
1	1	1

FIG. 3 • 1 The OR gate.

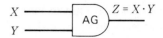

$$Z = X \cdot Y$$

INPUT		OUTPUT	
X	Y	Z	
0	0	0	$0 \cdot 0 = 0$
0	1	0	$0 \cdot 1 = 0$
1	0	0	$1 \cdot 0 = 0$
1	1	1	$1 \cdot 1 = 1$

FIG. 3 • 2 The AND gate.

It is often convenient to shorten $X \cdot Y \cdot Z$ to XYZ, and we will sometimes use this convention.

3 • 4 COMPLEMENTATION AND INVERTERS

The two operations defined so far have been what algebraists would call *binary operations* in that they define an operation on two variables. There are also *singularly*, or *unary*, *operations*, which define an operation on a single variable. A familiar example of unary operation is $-$, for we can write -5 or -10 or $-X$,

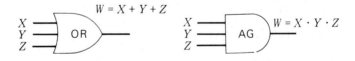

INPUT			OUTPUT
X	Y	Z	W
0	0	0	0
0	0	1	1
0	1	0	1
0	1	1	1
1	0	0	1
1	0	1	1
1	1	0	1
1	1	1	1

INPUT			OUTPUT
X	Y	Z	W
0	0	0	0
0	0	1	0
0	1	0	0
0	1	1	0
1	0	0	0
1	0	1	0
1	1	0	0
1	1	1	1

FIG. 3 • 3 Three-input OR and AND gates.

meaning that we are to take the negative of these values. ($-$ is also used as a binary operation symbol for subtraction, which makes it a familiar but ambiguous example.)

In Boolean algebra we have an operation called *complementation,* and the symbol we shall use is $^{-}$. Thus we write $\overline{X}$, meaning "take the complement of X," or $\overline{(X + Y)}$, meaning "take the complement of $X + Y$." The complement operation can be defined quite simply:

$$\overline{0} = 1$$
$$\overline{1} = 0$$

The complement of a value can be taken repeatedly. For instance, we can find $\overline{\overline{X}}$; for $X = 0$ it is $\overline{\overline{0}} = \overline{1} = \overline{0} = 1$. For $X = 1$ it is $\overline{\overline{1}} = \overline{\overline{0}} = \overline{1} = 0$.

A useful rule is based on the fact that $\overline{\overline{X}} = X$; checking, we find that $\overline{\overline{0}} = \overline{1} = 0$ and $\overline{\overline{1}} = \overline{0} = 1$. [This rule, that double complementation gives the original value, is an important characteristic of a Boolean algebra which does not generally hold for most unary operations. For instance, notice that for the operation of squaring a real number, the rule does not hold: $(3^2)^2 = 81$, not 3.]

The complementation operation is physically realized by a gate or circuit called the *inverter.* Figure 3·4(*a*) shows an inverter and the table of combinations for its input and output. Figure 3·4(*b*) shows also that connecting two inverters in series gives an output equal to the input, and this is the gating counterpart to the law of double complementation, $\overline{\overline{X}} = X$.

Several other symbols have been used for the complementation symbol. For instance, $\sim$ is often used by logicians who write $\sim X$ and read this "the negation of X." The symbol $'$ has been used by mathematicians and computer people; thus X' is the complement of X in these systems. The overbar symbol is now used by the American National Standards Institute and Military Standards, as well as by most journals and manufacturers, and we will use it.

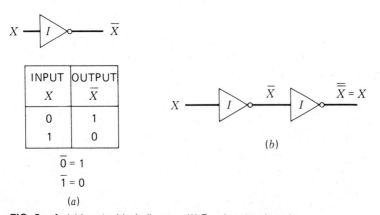

INPUT	OUTPUT
X	$\overline{X}$
0	1
1	0

$\overline{0} = 1$
$\overline{1} = 0$

(*a*)

(*b*)

FIG. 3 • 4 (*a*) Inverter block diagram. (*b*) Two inverters in series.

TABLE 3 • 1

X	Y	Z
0	0	0
0	0	1
0	1	0
0	1	1
1	0	0
1	0	1
1	1	0
1	1	1

TABLE 3 • 2

X	Y	Z	$\overline{Z}$
0	0	0	1
0	0	1	0
0	1	0	1
0	1	1	0
1	0	0	1
1	0	1	0
1	1	0	1
1	1	1	0

3 • 5 EVALUATION OF LOGICAL EXPRESSIONS

The tables of values for the three operations that have been explained are some-times called *truth tables,* or *tables of combinations.* To study a logical expression it is very useful to construct a table of values for the variables and then to evaluate the expression for each of the possible combinations of variables in turn. Consider the expression $X + Y\overline{Z}$. There are three variables in this expression, X, Y, and Z, each of which can assume the value 0 or 1. The possible combinations of values may be arranged in ascending order,† as in Table 3·1.

One of the variables, Z, is complemented in the expression $X + Y\overline{Z}$. So a column is now added to the table listing values of $\overline{Z}$ (see Table 3·2).

A column is now added listing the values that $Y\overline{Z}$ assumes for each value of X, Y, and Z. This column will contain the value 1 only when both Y is a 1 and $\overline{Z}$ is a 1 (see Table 3·3).

TABLE 3 • 3

X	Y	Z	$\overline{Z}$	$Y\overline{Z}$
0	0	0	1	0
0	0	1	0	0
0	1	0	1	1
0	1	1	0	0
1	0	0	1	0
1	0	1	0	0
1	1	0	1	1
1	1	1	0	0

---

† Notice that the variables in each row of this table may be combined into a binary number. The binary numbers will then count from 000 to 111 in binary, or from 0 to 7 decimal. Sometimes each row is numbered in decimal according to the number represented. Reference may then be made to the row by using the decimal number. For instance, row 0 has values of 0, 0, 0 for X, Y, and Z, row 6 has values of 1, 1, 0, and row 7 has values of 1, 1, 1.

TABLE 3 • 4

X	Y	Z	$\bar{Z}$	$Y\bar{Z}$	$X + Y\bar{Z}$
0	0	0	1	0	0
0	0	1	0	0	0
0	1	0	1	1	1
0	1	1	0	0	0
1	0	0	1	0	1
1	0	1	0	0	1
1	1	0	1	1	1
1	1	1	0	0	1

Now the logical addition of the values of X to the values which have been calculated for $Y\bar{Z}$ is performed in a final column (see Table 3·4).

The final column contains the value of $X + Y\bar{Z}$ for each set of input values which X, Y, and Z may take. For instance, when $X = 1$, $Y = 0$, and $Z = 1$, the expression has the value of 1.

3 • 6 EVALUATION OF AN EXPRESSION CONTAINING PARENTHESES

The following example illustrates the procedure for constructing a truth table for the expression $X + Y(\bar{X} + \bar{Y})$. There are only two variables in the expression, X and Y. First a table of the values which X and Y may assume is constructed (see Table 3·5).

Now, since the expression contains both $\bar{X}$ and $\bar{Y}$, two columns are added listing complements of the original values of the variables (see Table 3·6).

The various values which the term inside parentheses, $(\bar{X} + \bar{Y})$, assumes are now calculated (see Table 3·7).

The values for $\bar{X} + \bar{Y}$ are now multiplied by the values of Y in the table, forming another column representing $Y(\bar{X} + \bar{Y})$ (see Table 3·8).

Finally the values for $Y(\bar{X} + \bar{Y})$ are added to the values for X which are listed, forming the final column and completing the table (see Table 3·9).

Inspection of the final column of the table indicates that the values taken by the function $X + Y(\bar{X} + \bar{Y})$ are identical with the values found in the logical addition

TABLE 3 • 5

X	Y
0	0
0	1
1	0
1	1

TABLE 3 • 6

X	Y	$\bar{X}$	$\bar{Y}$
0	0	1	1
0	1	1	0
1	0	0	1
1	1	0	0

TABLE 3 • 7

X	Y	$\overline{X}$	$\overline{Y}$	$(\overline{X}+\overline{Y})$
0	0	1	1	1
0	1	1	0	1
1	0	0	1	1
1	1	0	0	0

TABLE 3 • 8

X	Y	$\overline{X}$	$\overline{Y}$	$\overline{X}+\overline{Y}$	$Y(\overline{X}+\overline{Y})$
0	0	1	1	1	0
0	1	1	0	1	1
1	0	0	1	1	0
1	1	0	0	0	0

TABLE 3 • 9

X	Y	$\overline{X}$	$\overline{Y}$	$\overline{X}+\overline{Y}$	$Y(\overline{X}+\overline{Y})$	$X+Y(\overline{X}+\overline{Y})$
0	0	1	1	1	0	0
0	1	1	0	1	1	1
1	0	0	1	1	0	1
1	1	0	0	0	0	1

table. This indicates that the function $X + Y(\overline{X} + \overline{Y})$ is equivalent to the function $X + Y$. This equivalence has been established by the *proof by perfect induction*. If a logical circuit were constructed for each of the two expressions, one circuit would require two inverters, two OR circuits, and an AND circuit, while the other circuit would require only an OR circuit. Both circuits would perform the same function, yielding identical outputs for each combination of inputs.

3 • 7 BASIC LAWS OF BOOLEAN ALGEBRA

Some fundamental relations of Boolean algebra have been presented. A complete set of the basic operations is listed below.† Although simple in appearance, these

---

†There are, actually, a number of possible sets of postulates which may be used to define the algebra. The particular treatment of Boolean algebra given here is derived from that of E. V. Huntington and M. H. Stone. The author would also like to acknowledge the influence of I. S. Reed and S. H. Caldwell on this development of the concepts of the algebra.

rules may be used to construct a Boolean algebra,† determining all the relations that follow:

$$\text{If } X \neq 0, \text{ then } X = 1$$

and

$$\text{If } X \neq 1, \text{ then } X = 0$$

LOGICAL ADDITION	LOGICAL MULTIPLICATION	COMPLEMENT RULES
$0 + 0 = 0$	$0 \cdot 0 = 0$	$\bar{0} = 1$
$0 + 1 = 1$	$0 \cdot 0 = 0$	$\bar{1} = 0$
$1 + 0 = 1$	$1 \cdot 0 = 0$	
$1 + 1 = 1$	$1 \cdot 1 = 1$	

A list of useful relations is presented in Table 3·10. Most of the basic rules by which Boolean algebra expressions may be manipulated are contained in this table. Each of these rules may be proved using the proof by perfect induction. An example of this proof for rule 3 in Table 3·10 is as follows: The variable X can have only the value 0 or 1; if X has the value 0, then $0 + 0 = 0$; if X has the value 1, then $1 + 1 = 1$. Therefore $X + X = X$.

The same basic technique may be used to prove the remainder of the rules. Rule 9 states that double complementation of a variable results in the original variable. If X equals 0, then the first complement is 1 and the second will be 0, the original value. If the original value for X is 1, then the first complement will be 0 and the second 1, the original value. Therefore $X = \bar{\bar{X}}$.

Rules 10 and 11, which are known as the *commutative laws,* express the fact that the order in which a combination of terms is performed does not affect the result of the combination. Rule 10 is the commutative law of addition, which states that the order of addition does not affect the sum $(X + Y = Y + X)$. Rule 11 is the commutative law of multiplication $(XY = YX)$, which states that the order of multiplication does not affect the product.

Rules 12 and 13 are the *associative laws.* Rule 12 states that in the addition of several terms, the sum which will be obtained if the first term is added to the second and then the third term is added will be the same as the sum obtained if the second term is added to the third and then the first term is added $[X + (Y + Z) = (X + Y) + Z]$. Rule 13 is the associative law of multiplication, stating that in a product with three factors, *any* two may be multiplied together, followed by the third, $X(YZ) = (XY)Z$.

---

†Notice that these rules are used to construct an *example,* or *realization,* of a Boolean algebra. We note that, strictly speaking, this Boolean algebra consists of a set B of two elements which we call 0 and 1, an addition operation $+$, a multiplication operation $\cdot$, and a complement operation $\overline{}$. There are other Boolean algebras (an infinite number), but this was Boole's original algebra. This algebra is sometimes called *switching algebra* to identify it more closely, but it is the same as "propositional calculus," for instance.

TABLE 3 • 10 BOOLEAN ALGEBRA RULES

1. $0 + X = X$
2. $1 + X = 1$
3. $X + X = X$
4. $X + \overline{X} = 1$
5. $0 \cdot X = 0$
6. $1 \cdot X = X$
7. $X \cdot X = X$
8. $X \cdot \overline{X} = 0$
9. $\overline{\overline{X}} = X$
10. $X + Y = Y + X$ _comm law of add_
11. $X \cdot Y = Y \cdot X$ _" " of mult_
12. $X + (Y + Z) = (X + Y) + Z$ _assoc law over mult_
13. $X(YZ) = (XY)Z$ _assoc law over add law_
14. $X(Y + Z) = XY + XZ$ _distrub._
15. $X + XZ = X$
16. $X(X + Y) = X$
17. $(X + Y)(X + Z) = X + YZ$ _XX + XZ + XY + YZ_
18. $X + \overline{X}Y = X + Y$
19. $XY + YZ + \overline{Y}Z = XY + Z$

$Z(Y + \overline{Y})$

Rule 14, the *distributive law,* states that the product of a monomial (X) multiplied by a polynomial $(Y + Z)$ is equal to the sum of the products of the monomial multiplied by each term of the polynomial, $X(Y + Z) = XY + XZ$.

The three laws, commutative, associative, and distributive, may be extended to include any number of terms. For instance, the commutative law for addition states that $X + Y = Y + X$. This may be extended to

$$X + Y + Z + A = A + Y + Z + X$$

The commutative law for multiplication may also be extended: $XYZ = YZX$. These two laws are useful in rearranging the terms of an equation.

The terms may also be combined:

$$(X + Y) + (Z + A) = (A + Y) + (X + Z)$$

and $(XY)(ZA) = (XA)(ZY)$. These two laws are useful in regrouping the terms of an equation.

The distributive law may be extended in several ways:

$$X(Y + Z + A) = XY + XZ + XA$$

If two polynomials, such as $(W + X)$ and $(Y + Z)$, are to be multiplied together, one of the polynomials is treated as a monomial and multiplied by the individual terms of the other polynomial. The results are then multiplied out according to the distributive law. For instance,

$$(W + X)(Y + Z) = W(Y + Z) + X(Y + Z) = WY + WZ + XY + XZ$$

3 • 8 PROOF BY PERFECT INDUCTION

Notice that, among others, rule 17 does not apply to "normal" algebra. The rule may be obtained from the preceding rules as follows:

$$
\begin{aligned}
(X + Y)(X + Z) &= XX + XZ + XY + YZ &\quad \text{where } XX = X, \text{ rule 7, so} \\
&= X + XZ + XY + YZ \\
&= X + XY + XZ + YZ \\
&= X(1 + Y) + Z(X + Y) &\quad \text{where } (1 + Y) = 1, \text{ rule 2, so} \\
&= X + Z(X + Y) \\
&= X + XZ + YZ \\
&= X(1 + Z) + YZ &\quad \text{where } (1 + Z) = 1, \text{ rule 2, so} \\
&= X + YZ
\end{aligned}
$$

Therefore

$$(X + Y)(X + Z) = X + YZ$$

Since rule 17 does not apply to normal algebra, it is interesting to test the rule using the proof by perfect induction. It will therefore be necessary to construct truth tables for the right-hand $(X + YZ)$ and the left-hand $(X + Y)(X + Z)$ members of the equation and compare the results (see Tables 3·11 and 3·12).

The last column of the table for the function $X + YZ$ is identical with the last column of the table for $(X + Y)(X + Z)$. This proves (by means of the proof by perfect induction) that the expressions are equivalent.

TABLE 3 • 11

X	Y	Z	YZ	X + YZ
0	0	0	0	0
0	0	1	0	0
0	1	0	0	0
0	1	1	1	1
1	0	0	0	1
1	0	1	0	1
1	1	0	0	1
1	1	1	1	1

TABLE 3 • 12

X	Y	Z	$X + Y$	$X + Z$	$(X + Y)(X + Z)$
0	0	0	0	0	0
0	0	1	0	1	0
0	1	0	1	0	0
0	1	1	1	1	1
1	0	0	1	1	1
1	0	1	1	1	1
1	1	0	1	1	1
1	1	1	1	1	1

Rules 15 and 16 are also not rules in "normal" algebra. The following is a proof of rule 15 using preceding rules:

$X + XZ = X(1 + Z)$ distributive law, and since $(1 + Z) = 1$ by rule 2
$X + XZ = X(1)$ and $X(1) = X$ by rule 6

Therefore

$$X + XZ = X$$

It is worthwhile to try and prove rule 15 using the proof by perfect induction at this point. Here is a proof of rule 16 using rules that precede it.

$$\begin{aligned} X(X + Y) &= XX + XY \quad &\text{distributive law, and since } XX = X \\ &= X + XY \\ &= X(1 + Y) \quad &\text{where } 1 + Y = 1, \text{ rule 2, so} \\ &= X \end{aligned}$$

It is instructive to prove this rule also by perfect induction at this point.

3 • 9 SIMPLIFICATION OF EXPRESSIONS

The rules given may be used to simplify Boolean expressions, just as the rules of normal algebra may be used to simplify expressions. Consider the expression

$$(X + Y)(X + \overline{Y})(\overline{X} + Z)$$

The first two terms consist of $(X + Y)(X + \overline{Y})$; these terms may be multiplied together and, since $X + X\overline{Y} + XY = X$ and $Y\overline{Y} = 0$, reduced to X.

The expression has now been reduced to $X(\overline{X} + Z)$, which may be expressed as $X\overline{X} + XZ$ (rule 14), and since $X\overline{X}$ is equal to 0, the entire expression $(X + Y)(X + \overline{Y})(\overline{X} + Z)$ may be reduced to XZ.

Another expression that may be simplified is $XYZ + X\overline{Y}Z + XY\overline{Z}$. First the three terms $XYZ + X\overline{Y}Z + XY\overline{Z}$ may be written $X(YZ + \overline{Y}Z + Y\overline{Z})$, using rule 14. Then, using rule 14 again, $X[\,Y(Z + \overline{Z}) + \overline{Y}Z\,]$; and since $Z + \overline{Z}$ equals 1, we have $X(Y + \overline{Y}Z)$.

The expression $X(Y + \overline{Y}Z)$ may be further reduced to $X(Y + Z)$ by using rule 18. The final expression can be written in two ways: $X(Y + Z)$ or $XY + XZ$. The first expression is generally preferable if the equation is to be constructed as an electronic circuit, because it requires only one AND circuit and one OR circuit.

3 • 10 DE MORGAN'S THEOREMS

The following two rules are known as De Morgan's theorems:

$$\overline{(X + Y)} = \overline{X} \cdot \overline{Y}$$
$$\overline{(X \cdot Y)} = \overline{X} + \overline{Y}$$

The complement of any Boolean expression, or a part of any expression, may be found by means of these theorems. In these rules, two steps are used to form a complement:

1. Addition symbols are replaced with multiplication symbols or multiplication symbols with addition symbols.
2. Each of the terms in the expression is complemented.

The use of De Morgan's theorem may be demonstrated by finding the complement of the expression $(X + YZ)$. First it is important to notice that a multiplication sign has been omitted and the expression could be written $X + (Y \cdot Z)$. To complement this, the addition symbol is replaced with a multiplication symbol and the two terms are complemented, giving $\overline{X} \cdot \overline{(Y \cdot Z)}$; then the remaining term is complemented, $\overline{X}(\overline{Y} + \overline{Z})$. The following equivalence has been found: $\overline{(X + YZ)} = \overline{X}(\overline{Y} + \overline{Z})$.

The complement of $\overline{(WX + Y\overline{Z})}$ may be formed by two steps:

1. The addition symbol is changed.
2. The complement of each term is formed:

$$(\overline{\overline{W} \cdot X})(\overline{Y \cdot \overline{Z}})$$

this becomes $(W + \overline{X})(\overline{Y} + Z)$.

Notice that since W and Z were already complemented, they become uncomplemented by the theorem $\overline{\overline{X}} = X$.

It is sometimes necessary to complement both sides of an equation. This may be done in the same way as before:

$$WX + YZ = 0$$

Complementing both sides, $\qquad \overline{(WX + YZ)} = \overline{0}$
$$(\overline{W} + \overline{X})(\overline{Y} + \overline{Z}) = 1$$

3 · 11 BASIC DUALITY OF BOOLEAN ALGEBRA

De Morgan's theorem expresses a basic duality which underlies all Boolean algebra. The postulates and theorems which have been presented can all be divided into pairs. For example, $(X + Y) + Z = X + (Y + Z)$ is the "dual" of $(XY)Z = X(YZ)$, and $X + 0 = X$ is the dual of $X \cdot 1 = X$.

Often the rules of theorems are listed in an order which illustrates the duality of the algebra. In proving the theorems or rules of the algebra, it is then necessary only to prove one theorem, and the "dual" of the theorem follows necessarily. For instance, if you prove that $X + XY = X$, you can immediately add the theorem $X(X + Y) = X$ to the list of theorems as the "dual" of the first expression.† In effect, all Boolean algebra is predicated on this "two-for-one" basis.

3 · 12 DERIVATION OF A BOOLEAN EXPRESSION

When designing a logical circuit, the logical designer works from two sets of known values: (1) the various states which the inputs to the logical network can take, and (2) the desired outputs for each input condition. The logical expression is derived from these sets of values.

Consider a specific problem. A logical network has two inputs X and Y and an output Z. The relationship between inputs and outputs is to be as follows:

1. When both X and Y are 0s, the output Z is to be 1.
2. When X is 0 and Y is 1, the output Z is to be 0.
3. When X is 1 and Y is 0, the output Z is to be 1.
4. When X is 1 and Y is 1, the output Z is to be 1.

These relations may be expressed in tabular form as shown in Table 3·13.

It is now necessary to add another column to the table. This column will consist of a list of *product terms* obtained from the values of the input variables. The new column will contain each of the input variables listed in each row of the table, with the letter representing the respective input complemented when the input value for this variable is 0, and not complemented when the input value is 1. The terms obtained in this manner are designated as product terms. With two input variables X and Y, each row of the table will contain a product term consisting of X and Y,

---

†When the first expression, $X + XY = X$, has been complemented, $\overline{X}(\overline{X} + \overline{Y}) = \overline{X}$ is obtained. Uncomplemented variables may then be substituted on both sides of the equation without changing the basic equivalence of the expression.

TABLE 3 • 13

INPUTS		OUTPUT
X	Y	Z
0	0	1
0	1	0
1	0	1
1	1	1

TABLE 3 • 14

INPUTS		OUTPUT	PRODUCT TERMS
X	Y	Z	
0	0	1	$\overline{X}\,\overline{Y}$
0	1	0	$\overline{X}Y$
1	0	1	$X\overline{Y}$
1	1	1	XY

with X or Y complemented or not, depending on the input values for that row (see Table 3·14).

Whenever Z is equal to 1, the X and Y product term from the same row is removed and formed into a *sum-of-products* expression. Therefore the product terms from the first, third, and fourth rows are selected. These are $\overline{X}\,\overline{Y}$, $X\overline{Y}$, and XY.

There are now three terms, each the product of two variables. The sum of these products is equal to the expression desired. This type of expression is often referred to as a *canonical expansion* for the function. The complete expression in normal form is

$$\overline{X}\,\overline{Y} + X\overline{Y} + XY = Z$$

The left-hand side of this expression may be simplified as follows:

$$\overline{X}\,\overline{Y} + X\overline{Y} + XY = Z$$
$$\overline{X}\,\overline{Y} + X(\overline{Y} + Y) = Z$$
$$\overline{X}\,\overline{Y} + X = Z$$

and finally, by rule 18 in Table 3·10, $X + \overline{Y} = Z$

The truth table may then be constructed to check the function that has been derived (see Table 3·15). The last column of this table agrees with the last column of the truth table of the desired function, showing that the expressions are equivalent.

TABLE 3 • 15

X	Y	$\overline{Y}$	$X + \overline{Y}$
0	0	1	1
0	1	0	0
1	0	1	1
1	1	0	1

TABLE 3 • 16

INPUTS			OUTPUT
When: $X = 0$,	$Y = 0$,	$Z = 0$	1
0	0	1	0
0	1	0	1
0	1	1	0
1	0	0	1
1	0	1	0
1	1	0	1
1	1	1	0

The expression $X + \overline{Y}$ may be constructed in one of two ways. If only the inputs X and Y are available, as might be the case if the inputs to the circuit were from another logical network or from certain types of storage devices, an inverter would be required to form $\overline{Y}$. The circuit would then require an inverter plus an OR gate. Generally the complement of the Y input would be available, however, and only one OR gate would be required for the second way the expression would be constructed.

Another expression, with three inputs (designated as X, Y, and Z), will be derived. Assume that the desired relationships between the inputs and the output have been determined, as shown in Table 3·16.

1. A truth table is formed (see Table 3·17).
2. A column is added listing the inputs X, Y, and Z according to their values in the input columns (see Table 3·18).
3. The product terms from each row in which the output is a 1 are collected $(\overline{X}\overline{Y}\overline{Z}, \overline{X}Y\overline{Z}, X\overline{Y}\overline{Z},$ and $XY\overline{Z})$, and the desired expression is the sum of these products $(\overline{X}\overline{Y}\overline{Z} + \overline{X}Y\overline{Z} + X\overline{Y}\overline{Z} + XY\overline{Z})$. Therefore the complete expression in standard form for the desired network is

$$\overline{X}\overline{Y}\overline{Z} + \overline{X}Y\overline{Z} + X\overline{Y}\overline{Z} + XY\overline{Z} = A$$

This expression may be simplified as shown below:

$$\overline{X}\overline{Y}\overline{Z} + \overline{X}Y\overline{Z} + X\overline{Y}\overline{Z} + XY\overline{Z} = A$$
$$\overline{X}(\overline{Y}\overline{Z} + Y\overline{Z}) + X(\overline{Y}\overline{Z} + Y\overline{Z}) = A$$
$$\overline{X}[\overline{Z}(\overline{Y} + Y)] + X[\overline{Z}(\overline{Y} + Y)] = A$$
$$\overline{X}\overline{Z} + X\overline{Z} = A$$
$$\overline{Z} = A$$

The function can therefore be performed by a single inverter connected to the Z input. Inspection of the truth table will indicate that the output A is always equal to the complement of the input variable Z.

TABLE 3 • 17

INPUTS			OUTPUT
X	Y	Z	A
0	0	0	1
0	0	1	0
0	1	0	1
0	1	1	0
1	0	0	1
1	0	1	0
1	1	0	1
1	1	1	0

TABLE 3 • 18

INPUTS			OUTPUT	PRODUCT TERMS
X	Y	Z	A	
0	0	0	1	$\overline{X}\overline{Y}\overline{Z}$
0	0	1	0	$\overline{X}\overline{Y}Z$
0	1	0	1	$\overline{X}Y\overline{Z}$
0	1	1	0	$\overline{X}YZ$
1	0	0	1	$X\overline{Y}\overline{Z}$
1	0	1	0	$X\overline{Y}Z$
1	1	0	1	$XY\overline{Z}$
1	1	1	0	XYZ

3 • 13 COMBINATION OF GATES

The OR gates, AND gates, and inverters described in Secs. $3 \cdot 3$ and $3 \cdot 4$ can be interconnected to form *gating,* or *logic, networks.* (Those who study switching theory would also call these *combinational networks.*) The Boolean algebra expression corresponding to a given gating network can be derived by systematically progressing from input to output on the gates. Figure $3 \cdot 5(a)$ shows a gating network with three inputs X, Y, and Z and an output expression $(X \cdot Y) + \overline{Z}$. A network that forms $(X \cdot Y) + (\overline{X} \cdot \overline{Y})$ and another network that forms $(X + Y) \cdot (\overline{X} + \overline{Y})$ are shown in Fig. $3 \cdot 5(b)$ and (c).

We can analyze the operation of these gating networks using the Boolean algebra expressions, and can, for instance, in troubleshooting a computer, determine

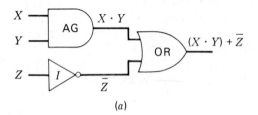

(a)

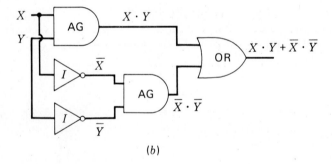

(b)

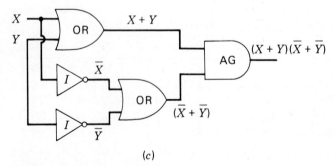

(c)

FIG. 3 • 5 Three gating networks.

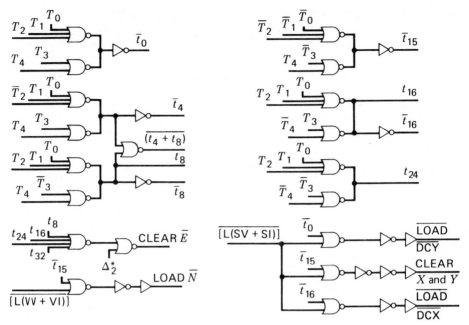

FIG. 3 • 6 Block diagram from a computer.

which gates have failed by examining the inputs to the gating network and the outputs and seeing if the Boolean operations are properly performed. The bookkeeping for computer circuitry is done by means of block diagrams, as in Fig. 3·6, which shows a typical print. The use of Boolean algebra is spread completely throughout the computer industry.

3 • 14 SUM-OF-PRODUCTS AND PRODUCT-OF-SUMS

An important consideration in dealing with gating circuits and their algebraic counterparts is the *form* of the Boolean algebra expression and the resulting form of the gating network. Certain types of Boolean algebra expressions lead to gating networks which are more desirable from most implementation viewpoints. We will now define the two most used and usable forms for Boolean expressions.

First let us define terms:

1. *Product term* A product term is a single variable or the logical product of several variables. The variables may or may not be complemented.

2. *Sum term* A sum term is a single variable or the sum of several variables. The variables may or may not be complemented.

For example, the term $X \cdot Y \cdot Z$ is a product term; $X + Y$ is a sum term; X is both a product term and a sum term; $X + Y \cdot Z$ is neither a product term nor a sum term; $X + \overline{Y}$ is a sum term; $X \cdot \overline{Y} \cdot \overline{Z}$ is a product term; $\overline{Y}$ is both a sum term and a product term. (*Comment:* Calling single variables sum terms and product terms is disagreeable but necessary. Since we must suffer with it, remember that some apples are red, round, and shiny, that is, more than one thing.)

We now define two most important forms:

1. *Sum-of-products expression* A sum-of-products expression is a product term or several product terms logically added together.
2. *Product-of-sums expression* A product-of-sums expression is a sum term or several sum terms logically multiplied together.

For example, the expression $\overline{X} \cdot Y + X \cdot \overline{Y}$ is a sum-of-products expression; $(X + Y)(\overline{X} + \overline{Y})$ is a product-of-sums expression. The following are all sum-of-products expressions:

$$X$$
$$X \cdot Y + Z$$
$$\overline{X} \cdot \overline{Y} + \overline{X} \cdot \overline{Y} \cdot \overline{Z}$$
$$X + Y$$

The following are product-of-sums expressions:

$$(X + Y) \cdot (X + \overline{Y}) \cdot (\overline{X} + \overline{Y})$$
$$(X + Y + Z) \cdot (X + \overline{Y}) \cdot (\overline{X} + \overline{Y})$$
$$(\overline{X} + Z)$$
$$\overline{X}$$
$$(X + Y)X$$

One prime reason for liking sum-of-products or product-of-sums expressions is their straightforward conversion to very nice gating networks.

In their purest, nicest form they go into *two-level networks,* which are networks for which the longest path through which a signal must pass from input to output is two gates.

Note: In the following discussion it will be assumed that when a signal is available, its complement $\overline{X}$ is also available; that is, no inverters are required to complement inputs. This is quite important and quite realistic, since most signals come from flip-flops, which we shall study later, and which provide both an output and its complement.

Figure 3·7 shows several gating networks. Section (*a*) of the figure shows sum-of-products networks, and section (*b*) shows product-of-sums networks. The gating networks for sum-of-products expressions in "conventional" form, that is, expressions with at least two product terms and with at least two variables in each product term, go directly into an AND-to-OR gate network, while "conventional" product-of-sums expressions go directly into OR-to-AND gate networks as shown in the figure.

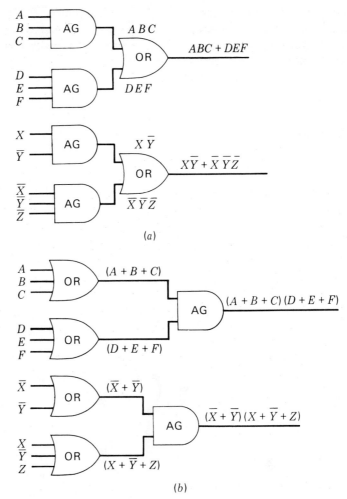

FIG. 3 • 7 (a) AND-to-OR gate networks. (b) OR-to-AND gate networks.

3 • 15 DERIVATION OF PRODUCT-OF-SUMS EXPRESSIONS

The sequence of steps described in Sec. 3·12 derived a sum-of-products expression for a given circuit. Another technique, really a dual of the first, forms the required expression as a product-of-sums. The expression derived in this manner is made up, before simplification, of terms each consisting of sums of variables such as $(X + Y + Z) \cdots$. The final expression is the product of these sum terms and has the form $(X + Y + Z)(X + Y + \overline{Z}) \cdots (\overline{X} + \overline{Y} + \overline{Z})$.

The method for arriving at the desired expression is as follows:

1. Construct a table of the input and output values.
2. Construct an additional column of sum terms containing complemented and

TABLE 3 • 19

INPUTS		OUTPUT
X	Y	Z
0	0	1
0	1	0
1	0	0
1	1	1

TABLE 3 • 20

INPUTS		OUTPUT	SUM TERMS
X	Y	Z	
0	0	1	$(X + Y)$
0	1	0	$(X + \overline{Y})$
1	0	0	$(\overline{X} + Y)$
1	1	1	$(\overline{X} + \overline{Y})$

uncomplemented variables (depending on the values in the input columns) for each row of the table. In each row of the table, a sum term is formed; however, in this case, if the input value for a given variable is 1, the variable will be complemented, and if 0, not complemented.

3. The desired expression is the product of the sum terms from the rows in which the output is 0.

The use of these rules will be illustrated by working examples in this and the following sections.

Table 3·19 contains the input and output values which describe a function to be realized by a logical network.

A column containing the input variables in sum-term form is now added in each row. A given variable is complemented if the input value for the variable is 1 in the same row, and not complemented if the value is 0 (see Table 3·20). Each sum term is therefore simply the complement of the product term which occurs in the same row in the previous table for sum-of-products expressions. Notice that the sum term $(\overline{X} + Y)$ in the third row of Table 3·20 is the complement of the product term $X\overline{Y}$ used in the sum-of-products derivation.

A product-of-sums expression is now formed by selecting those sum terms for which the output is 0 and multiplying them together. In this case 0s appear in the second and third rows, showing that the desired expression is $(X + \overline{Y})(\overline{X} + Y)$. A sum-of-products expression may be found by multiplying the two terms of this expression together, yielding $XY + \overline{X}\overline{Y}$. In this case the same number of gates would be required to construct circuits corresponding to both the sum-of-products and the product-of-sums expressions.

3 • 16 DERIVATION OF A THREE-INPUT-VARIABLE EXPRESSION

Consider Table 3·21, expressing an input-to-output relationship for which an expression is to be derived.

Two columns will be added this time, one containing the sum-of-products terms and the other the product-of-sums terms (see Table 3·22).

The two expressions may now be written in the following way:

TABLE 3 • 21

INPUTS			OUTPUT
X	Y	Z	A
0	0	0	0
0	0	1	0
0	1	0	1
0	1	1	1
1	0	0	0
1	0	1	0
1	1	0	1
1	1	1	0

TABLE 3 • 22

INPUTS			OUTPUT	PRODUCT TERMS	SUM TERMS
X	Y	Z	A		
0	0	0	0	$\overline{X}\overline{Y}\overline{Z}$	$X + Y + Z$
0	0	1	0	$\overline{X}\overline{Y}Z$	$X + Y + \overline{Z}$
0	1	0	1	$\overline{X}Y\overline{Z}$	$X + \overline{Y} + Z$
0	1	1	1	$\overline{X}YZ$	$X + \overline{Y} + \overline{Z}$
1	0	0	0	$X\overline{Y}\overline{Z}$	$\overline{X} + Y + Z$
1	0	1	0	$X\overline{Y}Z$	$\overline{X} + Y + \overline{Z}$
1	1	0	1	$XY\overline{Z}$	$\overline{X} + \overline{Y} + Z$
1	1	1	0	XYZ	$\overline{X} + \overline{Y} + \overline{Z}$

Sum-of-products:

$$(\overline{X}\,Y\overline{Z}) + (\overline{X}\,YZ) + (XY\overline{Z}) = A$$

Product-of-sums:

$$(X + Y + Z)(X + Y + \overline{Z})(\overline{X} + Y + Z)(\overline{X} + Y + \overline{Z})(\overline{X} + \overline{Y} + \overline{Z}) = A$$

The two expressions may be simplified as shown below:

SUM-OF-PRODUCTS

$$(\overline{X}\,Y\overline{Z}) + (\overline{X}\,YZ) + (XY\overline{Z}) = A$$
$$\overline{X}(Y\overline{Z} + YZ) + (XY\overline{Z}) = A$$
$$\overline{X}Y + XY\overline{Z} = A$$
$$Y(\overline{X} + X\overline{Z}) = A$$
$$\overline{X}Y + Y\overline{Z} = A$$

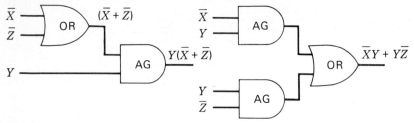

FIG. 3 • 8 Networks for $Y(\overline{X} + \overline{Z})$ and $\overline{X}Y + Y\overline{Z}$.

PRODUCT-OF-SUMS

$$(X + Y + Z)(X + Y + \overline{Z})(\overline{X} + Y + Z)(\overline{X} + Y + \overline{Z})(\overline{X} + \overline{Y} + \overline{Z}) = A$$
$$(X + Y)(\overline{X} + Y)(\overline{X} + \overline{Z}) = A$$
$$Y(\overline{X} + \overline{Z}) = A$$

The two final expressions can clearly be seen to be equivalent. Notice, however, that the shortest sum-of-products expression, which is $\overline{X}Y + Y\overline{Z}$, requires two AND gates and an OR gate, as is shown in Fig. 3·8, while the shortest product-of-sums expression, $Y(\overline{X} + \overline{Z})$, requires only a single AND gate and a single OR gate. In some cases the minimal sum-of-products expression will require fewer logical elements to construct, and in other instances the construction of the minimal product-of-sums will require fewer elements. If the sole criterion is the number of logical elements, it is necessary to obtain both a minimal sum-of-products expression and also a minimal product-of-sums expression to compare the two. It is possible to derive the canonical expansion expression for the network to be designed in one of the forms—for instance, product-of-sums—to simplify the expression, and then to convert the simplified expression to the other form, using the distributive laws. Any additional simplification which is required can then be performed. In this way, minimal expressions in each form may be obtained without deriving both canonical expansions, although this may be desirable.

The simplification techniques which have been described are algebraic and depend on judicious use of the theorems that have been presented. The problem of simplifying Boolean expressions so that the shortest expression is always found is quite complex; however, it is possible, by means of the repeated use of certain algorithms, to derive minimal sum-of-products and product-of-sums expressions. We shall examine this problem in following sections.

3 • 17 NAND GATES AND NOR GATES

Two other types of gates, NAND gates and NOR gates, are often used in computers. It is fortunate that the Boolean algebra which has been described can be easily made to analyze the operation of these gates.

A NAND gate is shown in Fig. 3·9. The inputs are A, B, and C, and the output

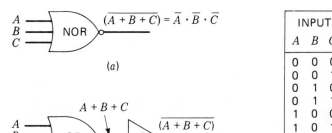

FIG. 3 • 9 The NAND gate.

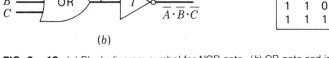

(a)

$$A + B + C$$

$$\overline{(A + B + C)}$$
$$\overline{A \cdot B \cdot C}$$

(b)

INPUT			OUTPUT
A	B	C	
0	0	0	1
0	0	1	0
0	1	0	0
0	1	1	0
1	0	0	0
1	0	1	0
1	1	0	0
1	1	1	0

FIG. 3 • 10 (a) Block diagram symbol for NOR gate. (b) OR gate and inverter equivalent circuit to NOR gate.

from the gate is written $\overline{A} + \overline{B} + \overline{C}$. The output will therefore be a 1 if A is a 0 or B is a 0 or C is a 0, and the output will be a 0 only if A and B and C are all 1s.

The operation of the gate can be analyzed using the equivalent block diagram circuit shown in Fig. 3·9, which has an AND gate followed by an inverter. If the inputs are A, B, and C the output of the AND gate will be $A \cdot B \cdot C$, and the complement of this is $(\overline{A \cdot B \cdot C}) = \overline{A} + \overline{B} + \overline{C}$, as shown in the figure.

The NOR gate can be analyzed in a similar manner. Figure 3·10 shows the NOR gate block diagram symbol with inputs A, B, C and output $\overline{A}\overline{B}\overline{C}$. This says the NOR gate's output will be a 1 only when all three inputs are 0s. If any input represents a 1, the output of a NOR gate will therefore be a 0.

Below the NOR gate block diagram symbol in Fig. 3·10 is an equivalent circuit showing an OR gate and an inverter.† The inputs A, B, and C are ORed by the OR gate, giving $A + B + C$, which is complemented by the inverter, giving $(\overline{A + B + C}) = \overline{A}\overline{B}\overline{C}$.

Multiple-input NAND gates can be analyzed similarly. A four-input NAND gate with inputs A, B, C, and D has an output $\overline{A} + \overline{B} + \overline{C} + \overline{D}$, which says that the

---

†The "bubble," or small circle, on the output of the NAND and NOR gates represents complementation. The NAND can then be seen to be an AND symbol followed by a complementer, and the NOR can be analyzed similarly.

output will be a 1 if any one of the inputs is a 0 and will be a 0 only when all four inputs are 1s.

Similar reasoning will show that the output of a four-input NOR gate with inputs A, B, C, and D can be represented by the Boolean algebra expression $\overline{A}\,\overline{B}\,\overline{C}\,\overline{D}$, which will be equal to 1 only when A, B, C, and D are all 0s.

If one of the two input lines to a two-input NAND gate contained the inputs $A + B$ and the other contained $C + D$, as shown in Fig. 3·11(a), the output from the NAND gate would be

$$\overline{[(A + B)(C + D)]} = \overline{A}\,\overline{B} + \overline{C}\,\overline{D}$$

We can show this by noting that the NAND gate first ANDs the inputs (in this case $A + B$ and $C + D$) and then complements this.

If one of the input lines to a two-input NOR gate contained the signal $A \cdot B$ and the other input line contained the signal $C \cdot D$, the output from the NOR gate would be $(\overline{A \cdot B + C \cdot D}) = (\overline{A} + \overline{B})(\overline{C} + \overline{D})$, as shown in Fig. 3·11($b$).

Notice that we can make an AND gate from two NAND gates, using the trick shown in Fig. 3·12, and a two-input OR gate from three NAND gates, as is also shown in the figure. A set of NAND gates can therefore be used to make any combinational network by substituting the block diagrams shown in Fig. 3·12 for the AND and OR blocks. (Complementation of a variable, when needed, can be obtained from a single NAND gate by connecting the variable to all inputs.)

The NOR gate can also be used to form any Boolean function which is desired, and the fundamental tricks are shown in Fig. 3·13.

Actually, it is not necessary to use the boxes shown in Figs. 3·12 and 3·13 to replace AND and OR gates singly, for a two-level NAND gate network yields the same function as a two-level AND-to-OR gate network, and a two-level NOR gate

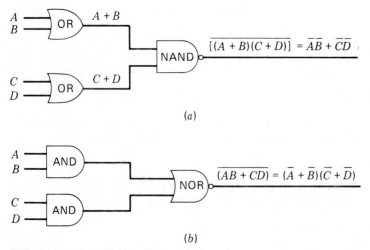

(a)

(b)

FIG. 3 • 11 Two types of gating networks. (a) OR-to-NAND gate network. (b) AND-to-NOR gate networks.

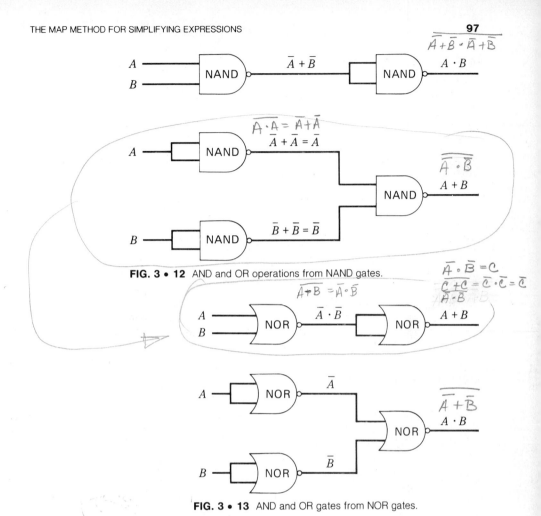

FIG. 3 • 12   AND and OR operations from NAND gates.

FIG. 3 • 13   AND and OR gates from NOR gates.

network yields the same function as a two-level OR-to-AND gate network. This is shown in Fig. 3·14. Compare the output of the NAND gate network with that in Fig. 3·7, for example. In Secs. 3·21 and 3·22 design procedures for NAND and NOR gate networks will be given.

*3 • 18   THE MAP METHOD FOR SIMPLIFYING EXPRESSIONS

We have examined the derivation of a Boolean algebra expression for a given function using a table of combinations to list the desired function values. To derive a sum-of-products expression for the function, a set of product terms was listed, and those terms for which the function was to have value 1 were selected and logically added together to form the desired expression.

---

*This and the following sections are optional. Subsequent chapters can be read without this material.

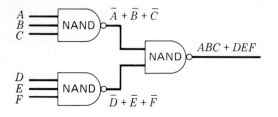

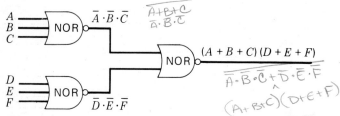

FIG. 3 • 14 NAND and NOR gates in two-level networks.

The table of combinations provides a nice natural way to list all values of a Boolean function. There are several other ways to represent or list function values, and the use of certain kinds of maps, which we will examine, will also permit minimization of the expression formed in a nice graphic way.

The particular type of map we will use is called the *Karnaugh map* after its originator.† Figure 3·15 shows the layouts for Karnaugh maps of from two to four variables. The diagram in each case lists the 2^n different product terms which can be formed in exactly n variables, each in a different square. For a function of n variables, a product term in exactly these n variables is called a *minterm*. Thus for three variables X, Y, and Z there are 2^3, or 8, different *minterms*, which are $\overline{X}\overline{Y}\overline{Z}$, $\overline{X}\overline{Y}Z$, $\overline{X}Y\overline{Z}$, $\overline{X}YZ$, $X\overline{Y}\overline{Z}$, $X\overline{Y}Z$, $XY\overline{Z}$, and XYZ. For four variables there are 2^4, or 16, terms, for five variables there are 32 terms, etc. As a result, a map of n variables will have 2^n squares, each representing a single minterm. The minterm in each box, or cell, of the map is the product of the variables listed at the abscissa and ordinate of the cell. Thus $\overline{X}YZ$ is at the intersection of $\overline{X}Y$ and Z.

Given a Karnaugh map form, the map is filled in by placing 1s in the squares, or cells, for each term which leads to a 1 output.

As an example, consider a function of three variables which for the following input values are to be 1:

$$X = 0, Y = 1, Z = 0$$
$$X = 0, Y = 1, Z = 1$$
$$X = 1, Y = 1, Z = 0$$
$$X = 1, Y = 1, Z = 1$$

---

†Similar maps are sometimes called *Veitch diagrams*.

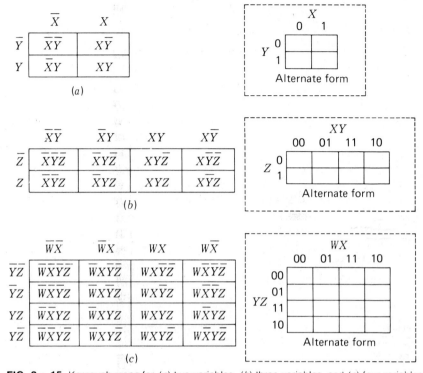

FIG. 3 • 15 Karnaugh maps for (a) two variables, (b) three variables, and (c) four variables.

This function is shown in Fig. 3·16(a) in both table-of-combinations and Karnaugh map form. Another function of four variables is shown in Fig. 3·16(b).

As a means for displaying the values of a function, the Karnaugh map is convenient and provides some "feeling" for the function because of its graphic presentation. Its chief use, however, is due to the arrangement of cells. Each cell differs from its adjacent cell by having exactly one variable complemented in the minterm in one cell which is not complemented in the minterm in the adjacent cell.

As an example of this, consider the four-variable map in Fig. 3·16 and the minterm $\overline{W}X\overline{Y}Z$. There are four cells adjacent to the cell containing $\overline{W}X\overline{Y}Z$. These contain (1) $WX\overline{Y}Z$, which differs in the variable W; (2) $\overline{W}\,\overline{X}\,\overline{Y}\,Z$, which differs from $\overline{W}X\overline{Y}Z$ in X; (3) $\overline{W}XYZ$, which differs from $\overline{W}X\overline{Y}Z$ in Y; and (4) $\overline{W}X\overline{Y}\,\overline{Z}$, which differs from $\overline{W}X\overline{Y}Z$ in Z.

One trick should be noted at this point. The maps are considered to be "rolled," or continuous, so that top and bottom edges or left and right side edges are touching. For the three-variable map, consider the left side edge and the right side edge to be touching, so that the map is considered to be rolled like a hoop horizontally on the page. This places the cell containing $\overline{X}\,\overline{Y}\,\overline{Z}$ next to $X\overline{Y}\,\overline{Z}$, as well as to $\overline{X}\,\overline{Y}\,Z$ and $\overline{X}\,Y\overline{Z}$. Also, for this map it places $\overline{X}\,\overline{Y}\,Z$ next to $X\overline{Y}\,Z$, which touches because of the rolling, as well as to $\overline{X}\,YZ$ and $\overline{X}\,\overline{Y}\,\overline{Z}$.

X Y Z	FUNCTION VALUES
0 0 0	0
0 0 1	0
0 1 0	1
0 1 1	1
1 0 0	0
1 0 1	0
1 1 0	1
1 1 1	1

	$\bar{X}\bar{Y}$	$\bar{X}Y$	XY	$X\bar{Y}$
$\bar{Z}$	0	1	1	0
Z	0	1	1	0

(a)

W X Y Z	FUNCTION VALUES
0 0 0 0	1
0 0 0 1	1
0 0 1 0	0
0 0 1 1	0
0 1 0 0	0
0 1 0 1	1
0 1 1 0	1
0 1 1 1	0
1 0 0 0	0
1 0 0 1	1
1 0 1 0	1
1 0 1 1	0
1 1 0 0	0
1 1 0 1	0
1 1 1 0	0
1 1 1 1	1

	$\bar{W}\bar{X}$	$\bar{W}X$	WX	$W\bar{X}$
$\bar{Y}\bar{Z}$	1	0	0	0
$\bar{Y}Z$	1	1	0	1
YZ	0	0	1	0
$Y\bar{Z}$	0	1	0	1

(b)

FIG. 3 • 16 Two Karnaugh maps. (a) Map of Boolean expression $\bar{X}Y\bar{Z} + \bar{X}YZ + XY\bar{Z} + XYZ$. (b) Map of four-variable function.

For the four-variable map the map is rolled so that the top edge touches the bottom edge, and the left side touches the right side. The touching of top and bottom places $\bar{W}X\bar{Y}\bar{Z}$ next to $\bar{W}XY\bar{Z}$, and the left side to the right side edges touching places $W\bar{X}YZ$ next to $\bar{W}\bar{X}YZ$.

A good rule to remember is that there are two minterms adjacent to a given minterm in a two-variable map; there are three minterms next to a given minterm in a three-variable map; there are four minterms next to a given minterm in a four-variable map; etc.

3 • 19 SUBCUBES AND COVERING

A *subcube* is defined as a set of exactly 2^m adjacent cells containing 1s. For $m = 0$ the subcube consists of a single cell (and thus of a single minterm). For $m = 1$ a subcube consists of two adjacent cells; for instance, the cells containing $\overline{X}\overline{Y}Z$ and $\overline{X}YZ$ form a subcube as shown in Fig. 3·17(a), as do $X\overline{Y}\overline{Z}$ and $\overline{X}\overline{Y}\overline{Z}$ (since the map is rolled).

For $m = 2$ the subcube has four adjacent cells, and several such subcubes are shown in Fig. 3·17(c). Notice that we have here omitted 0s for clarity, and filled in only the 1s for the function. This policy will be continued.

Finally, a subcube containing eight cells (for $m = 3$) is shown in Fig. 3·17(d).

(It is sometimes convenient to call a subcube containing two cells a 2-cube, a subcube of four cells a 4-cube, a subcube of eight cells an 8-cube, etc., and this will be often used.)

To demonstrate the use of maps and subcubes in minimizing Boolean algebra expressions we need to examine a rule of Boolean algebra:

$$AX + A\overline{X} = A$$

In the above equation the variable A can stand for more than one variable. For instance, let $A = WY$; we then have

$$(WY)X + (WY)\overline{X} = (WY)$$

Or let $A = W\overline{Y}\overline{Z}$; we then have

$$W\overline{Y}\overline{Z}\overline{X} + W\overline{Y}\overline{Z}X = W\overline{Y}\overline{Z}$$

The basic rule can be proved by factoring

$$AX + A\overline{X} = A(X + \overline{X})$$

Then since $X + \overline{X} = 1$, we have

$$AX + A\overline{X} = A(X + \overline{X}) = A\cdot 1 = A$$

Each of the examples given can be checked similarly; for instance,

$$W\overline{Y}\overline{Z}\overline{X} + W\overline{Y}\overline{Z}X = W\overline{Y}\overline{Z}(\overline{X} + X) = W\overline{Y}\overline{Z}\cdot 1 = W\overline{Y}\overline{Z}$$

This rule can be extended. Consider

$$WX\overline{Y}\overline{Z} + WX\overline{Y}Z + WXY\overline{Z} + WXYZ$$

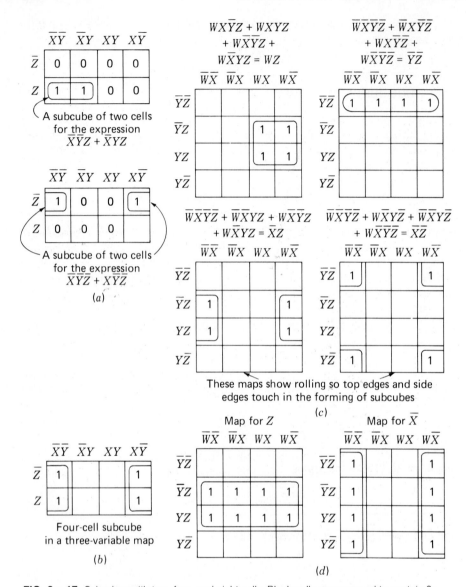

FIG. 3 • 17 Subcubes with two, four, and eight cells. Blank cells are assumed to contain 0s.

There are four terms here, each with two variables WX constant while the other two variables Y and Z take all possible values. The term WX is then equal to the sum of the other terms, for

$$WX\overline{Y}\overline{Z} + WX\overline{Y}Z + WXY\overline{Z} + WXYZ = WX\overline{Y}(\overline{Z} + Z) + WXY(Z + \overline{Z})$$
$$= WX\overline{Y} + WXY$$
$$= WX(\overline{Y} + Y)$$
$$= WX$$

Thus *WX* could be substituted for the other four terms in an expression without changing the values the expression takes for any input values to the variables, that is, $WX = WX\overline{Y}\overline{Z} + WX\overline{Y}Z + WXY\overline{Z} + WXYZ$.

On a map the above algebraic moves may be performed easily. Since a sub-cube of two cells has both cells with a single variable differing, a product term in just those variables which do not differ will cover (can be substituted for) the two minterms in the two cells.

Consider the subcube of two cells for $\overline{X}\overline{Y}Z$ and $\overline{X}YZ$ on the three-variable map in Fig. 3·17(*a*). The single product term $\overline{X}Z$ is equal to the sum of these two min-terms; that is,

$$\overline{X}\overline{Y}Z + \overline{X}YZ = \overline{X}Z$$

Similarly, the two cells containing minterms $\overline{X}\overline{Y}\overline{Z}$ and $X\overline{Y}\overline{Z}$ form a subcube of two cells, as shown in Fig. 3·17(*a*), from which we form $\overline{Y}\overline{Z}$, which can be sub-stituted for $\overline{X}\overline{Y}\overline{Z} + X\overline{Y}\overline{Z}$ in an expression.

Similarly, the subcube of four cells in a three-variable map [Fig. 3·17(*b*)] with terms $\overline{X}\overline{Y}\overline{Z}$, $\overline{X}\overline{Y}Z$, $X\overline{Y}\overline{Z}$, $X\overline{Y}Z$ has a single-variable constant $\overline{Y}$; and we find $\overline{Y} = \overline{X}\overline{Y}\overline{Z} + \overline{X}\overline{Y}Z + X\overline{Y}\overline{Z} + X\overline{Y}Z$.

In general a subcube with 2^m cells in an *n*-variable map will have $n - m$ vari-ables, which are the same in all the minterms, and *m* variables which take all pos-sible combinations of being complemented or not complemented. Thus for a four-variable map for $m = 3$, any eight adjacent cells which form a subcube will have $4 - 3 = 1$ variable constant and three variables which change complementation from cell to cell. Then a subcube of eight cells in a four-variable map can be used to determine a single variable which can be substituted for the sum of the minterm in all eight cells.

As an example in Fig. 3·17(*d*) we find a subcube of eight cells with the minterms $\overline{W}\overline{X}\overline{Y}Z$, $\overline{W}\overline{X}YZ$, $\overline{W}X\overline{Y}Z$, $\overline{W}XYZ$, $W\overline{X}\overline{Y}Z$, $W\overline{X}YZ$, $WX\overline{Y}Z$, and $WXYZ$, and the sum of these will be found to be equivalent to Z.

The set of minterms in an expression does not necessarily form a single sub-cube, however, and there are two cases to be dealt with. Call a *maximal subcube* the largest subcube that can be found around a given minterm. Then the two cases are:

1. All maximal subcubes are nonintersecting; that is, no cell in a maximal subcube is a part of another maximal subcube. Several examples are shown in Fig. 3·18.

2. The maximal subcubes intersect; that is, cells in one maximal subcube are also in other maximal subcubes. Figure 3·19 shows examples of this.

Case 1 is the more easily dealt with. In this case the product terms correspond-ing to the maximal subcubes are selected, and the sum of these forms a minimal sum-of-products expression. (In switching theory, the product term corresponding to a maximal subcube is called a *prime implicant*.)

Figure 3·18 shows an example of this in four variables. There is a subcube of two cells containing *WXYZ* and $WX\overline{Y}Z$ which can be covered by the product term

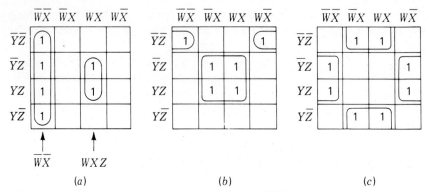

FIG. 3 • 18 Maps with disjoint subcubes. (a) Map for $\overline{WX}$ + WXZ. (b) Map for XZ + $\overline{X}\,\overline{Y}\overline{Z}$. (c) Map for $X\overline{Z}$ + $\overline{X}\,Z$.

WXZ. There is also a subcube of four cells containing $\overline{WX}\,\overline{Y}\overline{Z}$, $\overline{WX}\,\overline{Y}Z$, $\overline{WX}Y\overline{Z}$, and $\overline{WX}\,YZ$ which can be covered by $\overline{WX}$. The minimal expression is therefore $\overline{WX} + WXZ$.

Two other examples are shown in Fig. 3·18(b) and (c). In each case the subcubes do not intersect or share cells, and so the product term (prime implicant) which corresponds to a given maximal subcube can be readily derived, and the sum of these for a given map forms the minimal expression.

When the subcubes intersect, the situation can be more complicated. The first principle to note is: *Each cell containing a 1 (that is, each 1-cell) must be contained in some subcube which is selected.*

Figure 3·19(a) shows a map with an intersecting pair of subcubes plus another subcube. The minimal expression is, in this case, formed by simply adding together the three product terms associated with the three maximal subcubes. Notice that a single term, $\overline{W}\,XYZ$, is shared between two subcubes and, because of this, is effectively in the minimal expression twice. This is permissible because of the idempotent rule of Boolean algebra, $A + A = A$, which states that repetition of terms does not change functional equivalence.

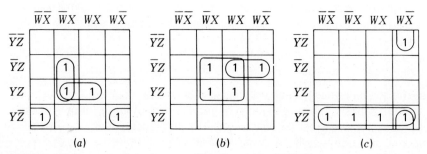

FIG. 3 • 19 Intersecting subcubes. (a) $\overline{W}XZ$ + XYZ + $\overline{X}Y\overline{Z}$. (b) XZ + $W\overline{Y}Z$. (c) $\overline{Y}\overline{Z}$ + $W\overline{X}\overline{Z}$.

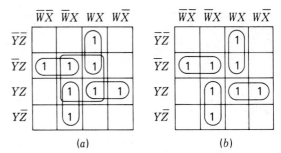

FIG. 3 • 20 Intersecting subcubes and solution. (a) $XZ + WYZ + \overline{W}\,\overline{Y}Z + \overline{W}XY + WX\overline{Y}$. (b) $WX\overline{Y} + WYZ + \overline{W}XY + \overline{W}\,\overline{Y}Z$.

Two other examples of intersecting maximal subcubes are shown in Fig. 3·19(b) and (c).

As long as the maximal subcubes can be readily found and there are no options in subcube selection, the minimization problem is straightforward. In some cases the problem is more complicated. Figure 3·20 shows an expression with a sub-cube of four cells in the center of the map, which is maximal. The selection of this maximal subcube does not lead to a minimal expression, however, because the four cells with 1s around this subcube must also be covered. In each case these 1-cells can be found to have a single adjacent cell and therefore to be part of maximal subcubes consisting of 2-cells. In Fig. 3·20(a) $\overline{W}X\overline{Y}Z$ is in a cell adjacent to only $\overline{W}X\overline{Y}Z$, and so forms part of a 2-cell. Figure 3·20(b) shows another way to form subcubes for the map, and this leads to the minimal expression $WX\overline{Y} + WYZ + \overline{W}XY + \overline{W}\,\overline{Y}Z$.

The finding of minimal expressions for such maps is not direct. The rules to be followed are:

1. Begin with cells that are adjacent to no other cells. The minterms in these cells cannot be shortened and must be used as they are.
2. Find all cells that are adjacent to only one other cell. These form subcubes of two cells each.
3. Find those cells that lead to maximal subcubes of four cells. Then find sub-cubes of eight cells, etc.
4. The minimal expression is formed from a collection of as few cubes as possi-ble, each of which is as large as possible, that is, each of which is a maximal subcube.

Figure 3·21 shows an example of a difficult map. The maximal subcubes can be selected in several ways so that all cells are covered. The figure shows three maps, of which only one leads to a minimal expression. Practice with various maps will lead to skill in finding minimal expressions. For difficult cases there are alge-braic techniques which guarantee a minimal expression, and these may be found in Bartee, Lebow, and Reed, Birkhoff and Bartee, McCluskey, and others listed in the Bibliography.

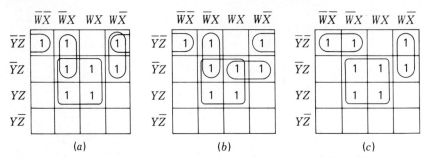

FIG. 3 • 21 Three coverings of the same map. (a) $XZ + \overline{X}\,\overline{Y}\overline{Z} + W\overline{X}\overline{Y} + \overline{W}X\overline{Y}$. (b) $XZ +$ $\overline{X}\,\overline{Y}\overline{Z} + \overline{W}X\overline{Y} + W\overline{Y}Z$. (c) $XZ + \overline{W}\,\overline{Y}\overline{Z} + W\overline{X}\overline{Y}$.

3 • 20 PRODUCT-OF-SUMS EXPRESSIONS—DON'T-CARES

The technique for product-of-sums expressions is almost identical with the design procedure using sum-of-products expressions. The basic rule can be stated quite simply: *Solve for 0s, then complement the resulting expression.*

Let us examine an example. Figure 3·22(a) shows a table of combinations and a Karnaugh map for a four-variable problem. In Fig. 3·22(a) the sum-of-products expression is derived, and in minimal form is found to be $\overline{X}\,\overline{Y} + YZ + WY$.

In Fig. 3·22(b) the same problem is solved for the 0s, which gives $X\overline{Y} +$ $\overline{W}\,Y\overline{Z}$. Since we have solved for 0s, we have solved for the complement of the desired problem. If the output is called *F,* then we have solved for $\overline{F}$. We then write $\overline{F} = X\overline{Y} + \overline{W}\,Y\overline{Z}$.

Now, what is wanted is *F*; so both sides of this expression are complemented, and we have

$$F = (\overline{X} + Y)(W + \overline{Y} + Z)$$

This expression is in product-of-sums form and is somewhat simpler than the sum-of-products expression.

If sum-of-products and product-of-sums expressions are equally easy to implement, then a given problem must be solved in both forms and the simpler solution chosen. There is no way to determine which will be simpler other than by a complete working of the problem.

There is another frequently encountered situation where certain outputs are not specified in a problem. Such outputs are called *don't-care* outputs, for the designer does not care what the outputs are for these particular inputs.

Figure 3·23(a) shows such a problem with six of the possible 16 output values listed as d's (don't-cares). This is a part of a BCD translator, and so these particular six input combinations are never used.

Since d output values are of no importance, they may be filled in with 1s and 0s in any way that is advantageous. Figure 3·23(a) shows a Karnaugh map of the table of combinations in the figure, with d's in the appropriate places. In solving this table, a d may be used as either a 1 or a 0; so the d's are used to enlarge or

INPUTS	FUNCTION
$W\ X\ Y\ Z$	VALUES
0 0 0 0	1
0 0 0 1	1
0 0 1 0	0
0 0 1 1	1
0 1 0 0	0
0 1 0 1	0
0 1 1 0	0
0 1 1 1	1
1 0 0 0	1
1 0 0 1	1
1 0 1 0	1
1 0 1 1	1
1 1 0 0	0
1 1 0 1	0
1 1 1 0	1
1 1 1 1	1

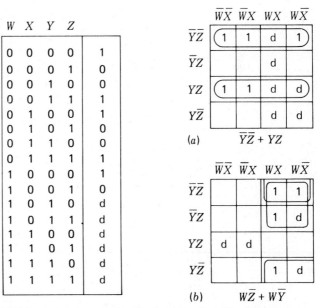

FIG. 3 • 22 Solving for product-of-sums. (a) $\overline{X}\overline{Y} + YZ + WY$ (b) $(\overline{X} + Y)(W + \overline{Y} + Z)$.

$W\ X\ Y\ Z$	
0 0 0 0	1
0 0 0 1	0
0 0 1 0	0
0 0 1 1	1
0 1 0 0	1
0 1 0 1	0
0 1 1 0	0
0 1 1 1	1
1 0 0 0	1
1 0 0 1	0
1 0 1 0	d
1 0 1 1	d
1 1 0 0	d
1 1 0 1	d
1 1 1 0	d
1 1 1 1	d

FIG. 3 • 23 Don't-care conditions. (a) Map for table with don't-cares. (b) Solving another map with don't-cares.

complete a subcube whenever possible, but are otherwise ignored (that is, made 0). *The d's need not be covered by the subcubes selected, but are used only to enlarge subcubes containing 1s, which must be covered.*

In Fig. 3·23(a), the vertical string of four d's in the WX column are of use twice, once in filling out, or completing, the top row of 1s and once in completing the third row. These subcubes give the terms $\overline{Y}\overline{Z}$ and YZ; so the minimal sum-of-products expression is $\overline{Y}\overline{Z} + YZ$. Notice that if all the d's were made 0s, the solution would require more terms.

Another problem is worked in Fig. 3·23(b). For this problem the solution is $W\overline{Z} + W\overline{Y}$. Notice that two of the d's are made 0s. In effect, the d's are chosen so that they lead to the best solution.

3 • 21 DESIGN USING NAND GATES

Section 3.17 introduced NAND gates and showed the block-diagram symbol for the NAND gate. NAND gates are widely used in modern computers, and an understanding of their use is invaluable.

Any NAND gate network can be analyzed using Boolean algebra, as previously indicated. Sometimes it is convenient, however, to substitute a functionally equivalent block diagram symbol for the conventional NAND gate symbol in order to analyze a block diagram. Figure 3·24 shows a gate symbol that consists of an OR gate symbol with "bubbles" (inverters) at each input. The two block-diagram symbols in Fig. 3·24 perform the same function on inputs, as shown, for the NAND gate yields $\overline{A} + \overline{B} + \overline{C}$ on these inputs A, B, and C, as does the functionally equivalent gate.

As an example of the use of an equivalent symbol to simplify the analysis of a NAND gate network, we examine Fig. 3·25(a). This shows a two-level NAND-to-NAND gate network with inputs A, B, C, D, E, and F. Figure 3·25(b) shows the same network, but with the rightmost NAND gate replaced by the functionally equivalent block-diagram symbol for a NAND gate previously shown in Fig. 3·24. Notice that the output function is the same for Fig. 3·25(b) as for Fig. 3·25(a), as it should be. Finally, an examination of the fact that the bubbles in Fig. 3·25(b) always occur in pairs, and can therefore be eliminated from the drawing from a functional viewpoint (since $\overline{\overline{X}} = X$), leads to Fig. 3·25(c) which is an AND-to-OR gate network. This shows that the NAND-to-NAND gate network in Fig. 3·25(a) yields the same function as the AND-to-OR gate network in Fig. 3·25(c).

The substitution of the equivalent symbols followed by the removal or the "dou-

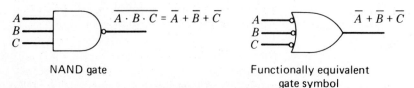

NAND gate   Functionally equivalent
                                          gate symbol

FIG. 3 • 24 NAND gate and functionally equivalent gate.

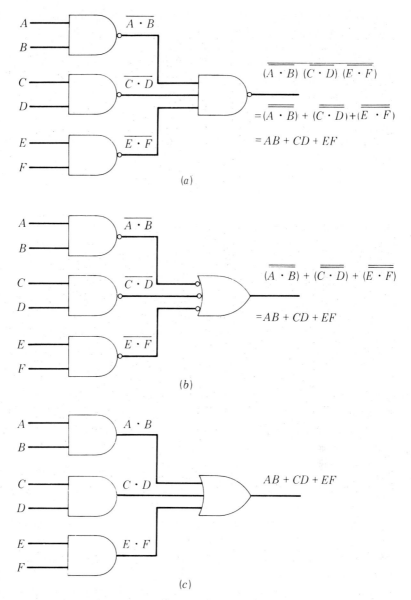

FIG. 3 • 25 NAND-to-NAND gate analysis. (*a*) NAND gate network. (*b*) Network in (*a*) with equivalent gate. (*c*) AND-to-OR gate network.

ble bubbles'' in Fig. 3·25 is a visual presentation of the following use of De Morgan's rule, which should be compared with the transformation in the figure:

$$\overline{(\overline{A\cdot B})\cdot(\overline{C\cdot D})\cdot(\overline{E\cdot F})} = (\overline{\overline{A\cdot B}}) + (\overline{\overline{C\cdot D}}) + (\overline{\overline{E\cdot F}}) = A\cdot B + C\cdot D + E\cdot F$$

Study of the above will show that the same principle applies to NAND-to-NAND gates in general. As a further example, Fig. 3·26 shows another NAND-to-NAND gate network and the transformation to an AND-to-OR gate network. The algebraic moves equivalent to the symbology substitutions are also shown.

A question may arise as to why drawings of NAND gate networks in computer diagrams do not use either the equivalent symbol (as in Fig. 3·24) or even the AND-to-OR gate symbols in Figs. 3·25 and 3·26. There are several reasons. First the industrial and military specifications call for gate symbols to reflect the actual circuit operation. Therefore if a circuit ANDs the inputs and then complements the result, the circuit is a NAND gate and, strictly speaking, the original NAND gate symbol should be used. Also, if the circuits used are contained in integrated-circuit packages and the computer drawing calls out the part number for the integrated-circuit packages, an examination of the manufacturer's integrated-circuit package drawings will show NAND gate symbols (if NAND gates are in the integrated-circuit package). The next chapter will show such packages and clarify this. In any case, substitution of symbols might easily lead to confusion, and it seems best to use the NAND gate symbol when NAND gates are used.

The above analysis of two-level NAND gate networks leads to a direct procedure for designing a NAND-to-NAND gate network.

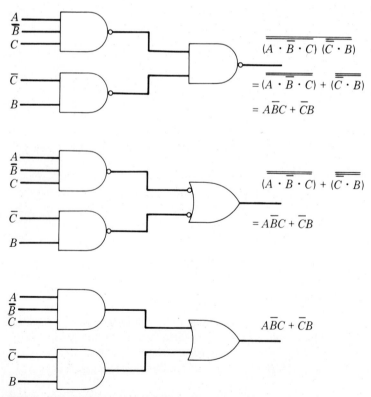

$$(\overline{\overline{A \cdot \overline{B} \cdot C})\,(\overline{\overline{C} \cdot B})}$$

$$= \overline{(\overline{A \cdot \overline{B} \cdot C})} + \overline{(\overline{\overline{C} \cdot B})}$$

$$= A\overline{B}C + \overline{C}B$$

$$\overline{(\overline{A \cdot \overline{B} \cdot C})} + \overline{(\overline{\overline{C} \cdot B})}$$

$$= A\overline{B}C + \overline{C}B$$

$$A\overline{B}C + \overline{C}B$$

FIG. 3 • 26 NAND-to-NAND to AND-to-OR gate transformation.

TABLE 3 • 23

	INPUTS		OUTPUT
For: $A = 0$	$B = 0$	$C = 0$	1
0	0	1	1
0	1	0	0
0	1	1	1
1	0	0	0
1	0	1	0
1	1	0	1
1	1	1	1

NAND — NAND
AND — OR

Design rule

> To design a two-level NAND-to-NAND gate network, use the table-of-combinations procedure for a sum-of-products expression. Simplify this sum-of-products expression using maps, as has been shown. Finally draw a NAND-to-NAND gate network in the two-level form and write the same inputs as would have been used in an AND-to-OR gate network, except that NAND gates are used in place of the AND and OR gates.

For example, let us design a NAND-to-NAND gate network for a problem with three inputs A, B, and C and the problem definition in Table 3·23.

The table of combinations for this function, map, simplified expression, and NAND-to-NAND gate network is shown in Fig. 3·27. (It would be possible to go directly to the map from the above specification. The table of combinations is shown for completeness.)

An adjustment is necessary if the simplified expression contains a single variable as a product term. For instance, if the simplified expression is $A + BC + \overline{B}\overline{C}$, then the "natural" network is as shown in Fig. 3·28(a). Notice, however, that the NAND gate at the A input is unnecessary if $\overline{A}$ is available, and this leads to the form shown in Fig. 3·28(b), which eliminates this gate. [The same simplification could be repeated if several single variables occur (as product terms) in the simplified expression.]

3 • 22 DESIGN USING NOR GATES

NOR gates are often used in computers because the integrated circuit technology now in use yields NOR gates in efficient, fast circuit designs. Fortunately the design of a NOR-to-NOR gate network, which is the fastest form in which all functions can be realized using only NOR gates, follows naturally from previous design techniques, as will be shown.

First note that a symbol functionally equivalent to the NOR gate exists and is

Inputs A	B	C	Output	Product terms		
0	0	0	1	$\overline{A}$	$\overline{B}$	$\overline{C}$
0	0	1	1	$\overline{A}$	$\overline{B}$	C
0	0	0	0	$\overline{A}$	B	$\overline{C}$
0	1	1	1	$\overline{A}$	B	C
1	0	0	0	A	$\overline{B}$	$\overline{C}$
1	0	1	0	A	$\overline{B}$	C
1	1	0	1	A	B	$\overline{C}$
1	1	1	1	A	B	C

$$\overline{A}\,\overline{B}\,\overline{C} + \overline{A}\,\overline{B}C + \overline{A}BC + AB\overline{C} + ABC$$

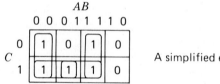

A simplified expression is $\overline{A}\,\overline{B} + \overline{A}C + AB$

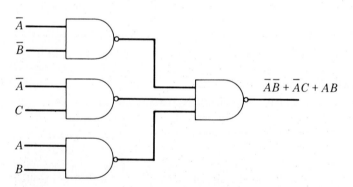

$$\overline{A}\,\overline{B} + \overline{A}C + AB$$

FIG. 3 • 27 Design of a two-level NAND-to-NAND gate.

shown in Fig. 3·29. The change of the block-design symbols mirrors De Morgan's rule:

$$\overline{A + B + C} = \overline{A}\cdot\overline{B}\cdot\overline{C}$$

Figure 3·30(a) shows a NOR-to-NOR gate network having the output function $(A + B)(C + D)(E + F)$. In order to analyze this network, we substitute the functionally equivalent symbol for the rightmost NOR gate, as shown in Fig. 3·30(b). This yields the same function, but an examination of Fig. 3·30(b) shows

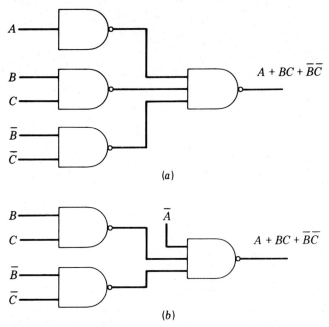

(a)

(b)

FIG. 3 • 28 Equivalent NAND-to-NAND gate designs. (a) Natural NAND-to-NAND gate design. (b) Equivalent NAND-to-NAND gate network.

the bubbles occurring in pairs. Since $\overline{\overline{X}} = X$, these can be eliminated as shown in Fig. 3·30(c), which is for OR-to-AND gate networks.

The transformation in the block diagrams of Fig. 3·30 from (a) to (b) to (c) mirrors the following Boolean algebra moves:

$$\overline{\overline{(A + B)} + \overline{(C + D)} \ \overline{(E + F)}} = \overline{\overline{(A + B)}} \ \overline{\overline{(C + D)}} \ \overline{\overline{(E + F)}}$$
$$= (A + B) \ (C + D) \ (E + F)$$

This shows that a NOR-to-NOR gate network is functionally equivalent to an OR-to-AND gate network. Figure 3·31 shows another example of this. A NOR-to-NOR gate network is transformed into an OR-to-AND gate network, and the corresponding algebraic transformations are shown.

Examination of the above leads to a rule for the design of a NOR-to-NOR gate network, given the input–output specifications.

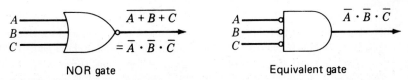

NOR gate   Equivalent gate

FIG. 3 • 29 NOR gate symbol and equivalent gate.

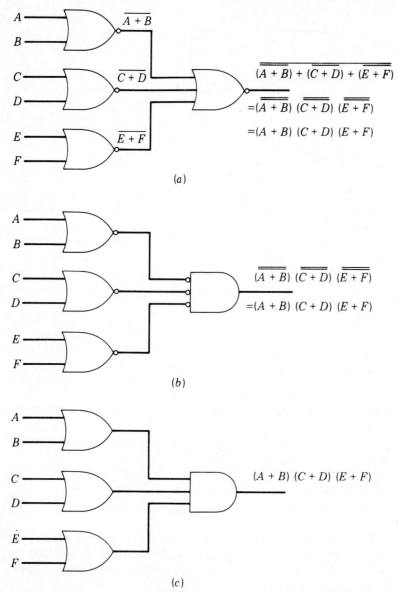

FIG. 3 • 30 NOR-to-NOR gate network analysis.

Design rule

> To design a NOR-to-NOR gate network, use the procedures for designing an
> OR-to-AND gate network. Simplify using maps as for the OR-to-AND gate
> networks. Finally draw the block diagram in the same form as for the OR-to-
> AND gate networks, but substitute NOR gates for the OR and AND gates.

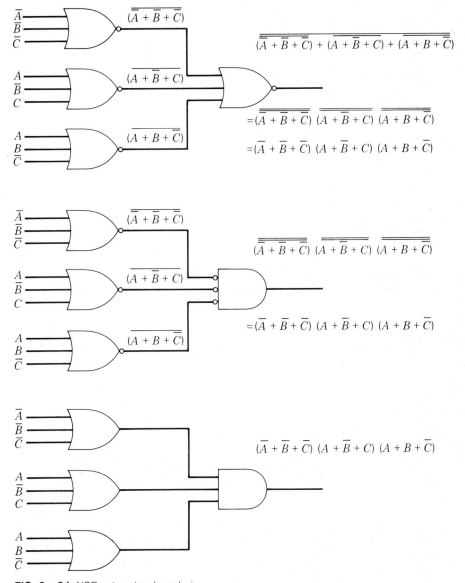

FIG. 3 • 31 NOR gate network analysis.

Figure 3·32 shows two examples of NOR-to-NOR gate designs, including the simplification of networks where a single variable occurs as a sum term.

3 • 23 NAND-TO-AND AND NOR-TO-OR GATE NETWORKS

The two preceding sections showed how to analyze and design networks using NAND and NOR gates in NAND-to-NAND and NOR-to-NOR forms. There are two other forms in common usage: the NAND-to-AND and the NOR-to-OR forms.

A	B	C	OUTPUT	SUM TERMS
0	0	0	1	$A + B + C$
0	0	1	0	$A + B + \bar{C}$
0	1	0	1	$A + \bar{B} + C$
0	1	1	0	$A + \bar{B} + \bar{C}$
1	0	0	0	$\bar{A} + B + C$
1	0	1	1	$\bar{A} + B + \bar{C}$
1	1	0	0	$\bar{A} + \bar{B} + C$
1	1	1	1	$\bar{A} + \bar{B} + \bar{C}$

$(A + B + C)\ (A + \bar{B} + C)\ (\bar{A} + B + \bar{C})\ (\bar{A} + \bar{B} + \bar{C})$

$\bar{A}\bar{B}$ $\bar{A}B$ AB $A\bar{B}$

	0 0	0 1	1 1	1 0
$\bar{C}$ 0	1	1	0	0
C 1	0	0	1	1

$(\bar{A} + C)\ (A + \bar{C})$

$\overline{(\bar{A} + C)}$

$\overline{(A + \bar{C})}$

$\overline{\overline{(\bar{A} + C)} + \overline{(A + \bar{C})}}$

$= \overline{\overline{(\bar{A} + C)}} \cdot \overline{\overline{(A + \bar{C})}}$

$= (\bar{A} + C)\ (A + \bar{C})$

A	B	C	OUTPUT	SUM TERMS
0	0	0	0	$A + B + C$
0	0	1	0	$A + B + \bar{C}$
0	1	0	0	$A + \bar{B} + C$
0	1	1	0	$A + \bar{B} + \bar{C}$
1	0	0	1	$\bar{A} + B + C$
1	0	1	1	$\bar{A} + B + \bar{C}$
1	1	0	0	$\bar{A} + \bar{B} + C$
1	1	1	1	$\bar{A} + \bar{B} + \bar{C}$

AB

	0 0	0 1	1 1	1 0
C 0	0	0	0	1
1	0	0	1	1

$A(\bar{B} + C)$

$\overline{(\bar{A} + \overline{(\bar{B} + C)}})$

$= A\overline{(\bar{B} + C)}$

$= A(\bar{B} + C)$

FIG. 3 • 32 Two NOR gate designs.

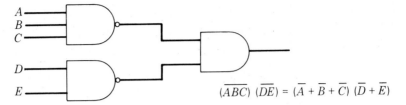

$$(\overline{ABC})\,(\overline{DE}) = (\overline{A} + \overline{B} + \overline{C})\,(\overline{D} + \overline{E})$$

a. Conventional NAND to AND gate network

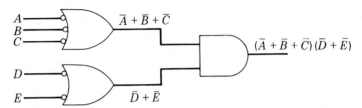

b. NAND-to-AND in (a) but with equivalent gates substituted for NANDs.

FIG. 3 • 33 NAND-to-AND gate networks. (*a*) Conventional NAND-to-AND gate network. (*b*) NAND-to-AND with equivalent gates substituted.

Since NAND gates are quite popular, and since the outputs from NAND gates can sometimes be ANDed by a simple connection, as will be shown, it is desirable to have analysis and design procedures for NAND-to-AND gate networks. To facilitate this, we again use our equivalent NAND gate symbol from Fig. 3·24, redrawing Fig. 3·33a as shown in Fig. 3·33b. This figure mirrors the Boolean algebra rule

$$(\overline{A \cdot B \cdot C}) \cdot (\overline{D \cdot E}) = (\overline{A} + \overline{B} + \overline{C}) \cdot (\overline{D} + \overline{E})$$

Examination of Fig. 3·33b shows that a NAND-to-AND gate network performs the same function as an OR-to-AND gate network, but with each input complemented. This gives us a design rule.

Design rule

> To design a NAND-to-AND gate network use the procedure for an OR-to-AND gate network, then draw the block diagram using a NAND-to-AND form, but compliment each input.

Example: Design a NAND-to-AND gate network for the conditions given in Table 3·24.
We add the sum term column (Table 3·25).

---

†NAND gates with this property are designated as such by the integrated-circuit manufacturer. Not all TTL NAND gates can be wire ANDed.

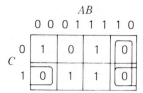

$(A + \overline{B} + C) \, (\overline{A} + B) \, (B + \overline{C})$ is simplified expression

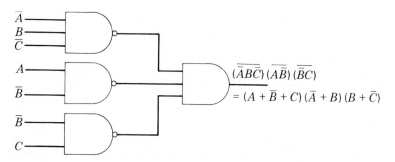

FIG. 3 • 34 Design of a NAND-to-AND network.

Our product-of-sums expression is therefore $(A + B + \overline{C}) \, (A + \overline{B} + C) \, (\overline{A} + B + C) \, (\overline{A} + B + \overline{C})$. This must be simplified. The simplified expression is $(A + \overline{B} + C) \, (\overline{A} + B) \, (B + \overline{C})$. The rule states that we must now form a NAND-to-AND gate network, but that each input should be complemented. The resulting block diagram is shown in Fig. 3·34.

For certain integrated circuit technologies (TTL, for instance) it is sometimes possible to form an AND gate by simply connecting together the outputs from several NAND gates.† In essence this gate is "free" as no circuits are needed; the gate is formed by a simple connection. Also, the network is faster since there is no delay through a second gate level.

The manufacturer of a given set of NAND gates will specify when and if this is possible. In a given computer block diagram, when the AND gate is made by a simple connection, as shown as in Fig. 3·35a, the dashed AND symbol will be used.

Figure 3.35b shows a net which performs the same as the NAND-to-AND gate network in 3.34 but uses a wired AND gate. Notice that the AND gate is drawn with

TABLE 3 • 24

A	B	C	OUTPUT
0	0	0	1
0	0	1	0
0	1	0	0
0	1	1	1
1	0	0	0
1	0	1	0
1	1	0	1
1	1	1	0

TABLE 3 • 25

A	B	C	OUTPUT	SUM TERM
0	0	0	1	$A + B + C$
0	0	1	0	$A + B + \overline{C}$
0	1	0	0	$A + \overline{B} + C$
0	1	1	1	$A + \overline{B} + \overline{C}$
1	0	0	0	$\overline{A} + B + C$
1	0	1	0	$\overline{A} + B + \overline{C}$
1	1	0	1	$\overline{A} + \overline{B} + C$
1	1	1	1	$\overline{A} + \overline{B} + \overline{C}$

a dashed line. It must be emphasized that not all NAND gates can be wire ANDed using a simple connection. When this is possible, however, the saving in circuitry and speed improvement makes the configuration desirable.

An important observation should be made here: if inputs are wire ANDed using a simple connection, *a single variable cannot be tied to the AND connection. A single input NAND gate* (inverter) *must be used.* If an input were connected directly to this connection, there could be a "tug-of-war" between the input value and the wire junction. Refer to Fig. 3·36, which shows a design where a single variable B occurs in the minimal expression.

For instance, if in Fig. 3·36 A and C are each 1 and B is 0, then the NAND gate's output should be 0, while the value of $\overline{B}$ is 1. What would the value at the wired AND junction be? Will the NAND gate's output pull $\overline{B}$ down, or will $\overline{B}$ win?

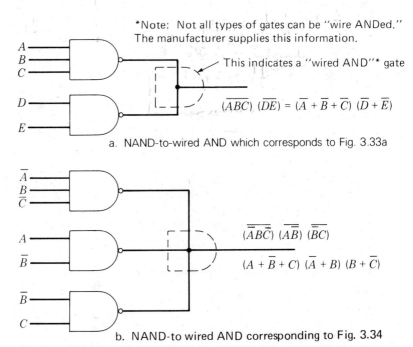

*Note: Not all types of gates can be "wire ANDed." The manufacturer supplies this information.

This indicates a "wired AND"* gate

$(\overline{ABC})\ (\overline{DE}) = (\overline{A} + \overline{B} + \overline{C})\ (\overline{D} + \overline{E})$

a. NAND-to-wired AND which corresponds to Fig. 3.33a

$(\overline{\overline{A}\overline{B}\overline{C}})\ (\overline{\overline{A}\overline{B}})\ (\overline{\overline{B}\overline{C}})$

$(A + \overline{B} + C)\ (\overline{A} + B)\ (B + \overline{C})$

b. NAND-to wired AND corresponding to Fig. 3.34

FIG. 3 • 35 NAND-to-AND with wired AND gate. (a) NAND-to-AND with wired AND for Figure 3·33(a). (b) NAND to wired AND for Figure 3·34.

A	B	C	OUTPUT
0	0	0	1
0	0	1	1
0	1	0	0
0	1	1	0
1	0	0	1
1	0	1	0
1	1	0	0
1	1	1	0

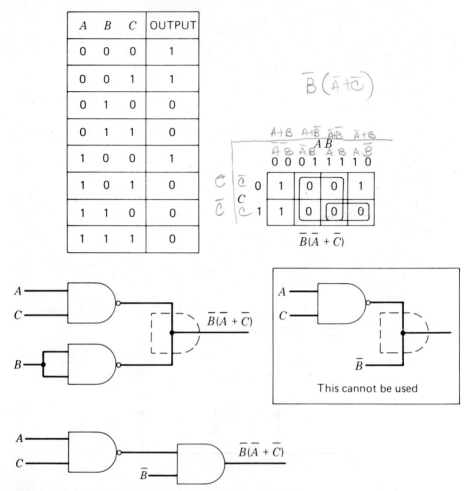

FIG. 3 • 36 NAND-to-AND gate design with single variable.

Smart designers do not find out in actual designs, but use an actual AND circuit (not a wired AND) or, more likely, use a NAND at the input, as shown in Fig. 3·36.

NOR-to-OR gate networks are similar to NAND-to-AND gate networks. Questions 59, 72, and 82 show NOR-to-OR gate networks. Some NOR gates will form an OR gate at their output when connected together and Fig 3.37 shows a NOR-to wired-OR net with output function $(\overline{A + B}) + (\overline{C + D}) = \overline{A}\cdot\overline{B} + \overline{C}\cdot\overline{D}$. This expression, $\overline{A}\cdot\overline{B} + \overline{C}\cdot\overline{D}$, shows us that the NOR-to-OR gate network functions like an AND-to-OR gate network, but with each variable complemented. Figure 3·37b shows this using the equivalent gate from Fig. 3·29.

We now design a NOR-to-OR gate network for the problem given in Table 3·26. The sum-of-products expression for this, after simplification, is $AB + BC + \overline{A}\overline{C}$. To form the block diagram we draw three NOR gates for the inputs, as shown

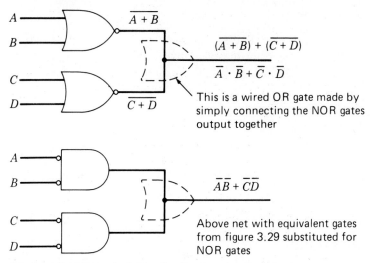

FIG. 3 • 37 NOR-to wired OR gate network and equivalent net.

TABLE 3 • 26

A	B	C	OUTPUT
0	0	0	1
0	0	1	0
0	1	0	1
0	1	1	1
1	0	0	0
1	0	1	0
1	1	0	1
1	1	1	1

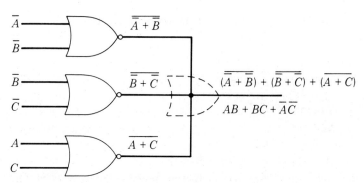

FIG. 3 • 38 Design for NOR-to-wired OR gate network.

in Fig. 3·38, then an OR gate to OR their outputs. The inputs from the expression to be realized, $AB + BC + \overline{A}\overline{C}$, must each be complemented, however, as shown in Fig. 3·38. The design rule is therefore as follows.

Design rule

> To design a NOR-to-OR gate network, develop and simplify the sum-of-products expression for the described function. Then draw the NOR-to-OR gate network, but complement each input in the sum-of-products expression.

Only certain NOR gates can be wire ORed. The design technique has been developed using wired OR gates because simply replacing the wired OR gate with an equivalent conventional gate gives an equivalent design.

The same rules for not ANDing single variables for wired AND gates apply to wired OR gates when inverters or NOR gates are required to "buffer" single inputs.

QUESTIONS

1. Prepare a truth table for the following Boolean expressions:
   (a) $XYZ + \overline{X}\,\overline{Y}\,\overline{Z}$ (b) $ABC + A\overline{B}C + \overline{A}\,\overline{B}\,\overline{C}$
   (c) $A(B\overline{C} + \overline{B}C)$ (d) $(A + B)(A + C)(\overline{A} + \overline{B})$

2. Prepare a table of combinations for the following Boolean algebra expressions:
   (a) $\overline{X}\,\overline{Y} + \overline{X}Y$ (b) $XY\overline{Z} + \overline{X}\,\overline{Y}Z$ (c) $\overline{X}\,YZ + \overline{X}\,\overline{Y}$
   (d) $\overline{X}\,\overline{Y}\,\overline{Z} + X\overline{Y}\,\overline{Z} + \overline{X}\,Y\overline{Z}$ (e) $\overline{X}\,\overline{Z} + \overline{Y}\,\overline{Z}$ (f) $\overline{A}\,B(\overline{A}\,\overline{B}\,\overline{C} + \overline{B}\,C)$

3. Prepare a truth table for the following Boolean expressions:
   (a) $A\overline{B} + \overline{A}\,B$ (b) $A\overline{B} + B\overline{C}$
   (c) $A\overline{C} + AC$ (d) $\overline{A}\,\overline{B}\,C + AB\overline{C} + \overline{A}\,BC$
   (e) $AB(\overline{A}\,\overline{B}\,C + A\overline{B}\,\overline{C} + A\overline{B}\,\overline{C})$

4. Prepare a table of combinations for the following Boolean algebra expressions:
   (a) $X(\overline{Y} + \overline{Z}) + X\overline{Y}$ (b) $X\overline{Y}(Z + YZ) + \overline{Z}$
   (c) $[X(Y + \overline{Y}) + \overline{X}(\overline{Y} + Y)]\cdot\overline{Z}$ (d) $\overline{A}\,B(\overline{A}\,B + \overline{A}\,B)$
   (e) $A[(\overline{B} + C) + \overline{C}]$ (f) $\overline{A}\,\overline{B}\,C(\overline{A}\,BC + \overline{A}\,B\,C)$

5. Prepare a table of combinations for the following Boolean algebra expressions:
   (a) $XY + \overline{X}\,\overline{Y}\,Z$ (b) $ABC + \overline{A}\,\overline{B} + \overline{A}\,B$
   (c) $ABC + \overline{A}\,\overline{C}$

6. Prepare a truth table for the following Boolean algebra expressions:
   (a) $A\overline{B}\,\overline{C} + \overline{A}\,B$ (b) $\overline{A}\,\overline{B}\,\overline{C} + AC + AB$
   (c) $XZ + XY + \overline{X}\,\overline{Z}$

7. Simplify the following expressions and draw a block diagram of the circuit for each simplified expression, using AND and OR gates. Assume the inputs are from flip-flops.
   (a) $A\overline{B}\,\overline{C} + \overline{A}\,\overline{B}\,\overline{C} + \overline{A}\,B\overline{C} + \overline{A}\,\overline{B}\,C$
   (b) $ABC + \overline{A}\,BC + A\overline{B}\,C + AB\overline{C} + A\overline{B}\,\overline{C} + \overline{A}\,B\overline{C} + \overline{A}\,\overline{B}\,\overline{C}$
   (c) $A(A + B + C)(\overline{A} + B + C)(A + \overline{B} + C)(A + B + \overline{C})$
   (d) $(A + B + C)(A + \overline{B} + \overline{C})(A + B + \overline{C})(A + \overline{B} + C)$

8. Simplify the expressions in Question 4 and draw block diagrams of gating

networks for your simplified expressions, using AND gates, OR gates, and inverters.

9. Simplify the following expressions:

(a) $ABC \, (AB\overline{C} + A\overline{B}C + \overline{A} \, BC)$ (b) $AB + A\overline{B} + \overline{A}\,C + \overline{A}\overline{C}$

(c) $XY + XYZ + X\overline{Y}\overline{Z} + XZY$ (d) $XY(\overline{X}\overline{Y}\overline{Z} + X\overline{Y}\overline{Z} + \overline{X}\,Y\overline{Z})$

10. Simplify the expressions in Question 6 and draw block diagrams of gating networks for your simplified expressions, using AND gates, OR gates, and inverters.

11. Form the complements of the following expressions. For instance, the complement of $(XY + XZ)$ is equal to $\overline{(XY + XZ)} = (\overline{X} + \overline{Y})\,(\overline{X} + \overline{Z}) = \overline{X} + \overline{Y}\overline{Z}$.

(a) $(A + BC + AB)$ (b) $(A + B)\,(B + C)\,(A + C)$

(c) $AB + \overline{B}C + CD$ (d) $AB(\overline{C}D + \overline{B}\,C)$

(e) $A(B + C)\,(\overline{C} + \overline{D})$

12. Complement the following expressions (as in Question 11):

(a) $\overline{X}\,\overline{Y} + X\overline{Y}$ (b) $X\overline{Y}Z + \overline{X}\,Y$

(c) $\overline{X}\,(Y + \overline{Z})$ (d) $X(Y\overline{Z} + \overline{Y}Z)$

(e) $XY(\overline{Y}Z + X\overline{Z})$ (f) $XY + \overline{X}\,\overline{Y}\,(YZ + \overline{X}\,\overline{Y})$

13. Prove the two basic De Morgan theorems using the proof by perfect induction.

14. Prove the following rules using the proof by perfect induction:

(a) $X\overline{Y} + XY = X$

(b) $X + \overline{X}\,Y = X + Y$

15. Convert the following expressions to sum-of-products form:

(a) $(A + B)\,(\overline{B} + C)\,(\overline{A} + C)$

(b) $(\overline{A} + C)\,(\overline{A} + \overline{B} + \overline{C})\,(A + \overline{B})$

(c) $(A + C)\,(A\overline{B} + AC)\,(\overline{A}\,C + B)$

16. Convert the following expressions to sum-of-products form: *and simplify using P.89*

(a) $(\overline{A} + \overline{B})\,(\overline{C} + \overline{B})$ (b) $\overline{A}\,B\,(\overline{B}\,C + \overline{B}\,C)$

(c) $(A + B\overline{C})\,(\overline{A}\,B + \overline{A}B)$ (d) $AB\,(A\overline{B}\,\overline{C} + \overline{A}\,C)$

(e) $(\overline{A} + B)\,(A\overline{C} + (B + \overline{C}))$ (f) $(\overline{A} + C)\,(AB + AB + AC)$

17. Which rule is the dual of rule 12 in Table 3·10?

18. Give a dual of the rule $X + \overline{X}\,Y = X + Y$.

19. Multiply the following sum terms together, forming a sum-of-products expression in each case. Simplify while multiplying when possible.

(a) $(A + C)\,(B + D)$

(b) $(A + C + D)\,(B + D + C)$

(c) $AB + C + DC)\,(AB + BC + D)$

(d) $(A\overline{B} + \overline{A}B + A\overline{C})\,(\overline{A}\overline{B} + AB + A\overline{C})$

20. Convert the following expressions to product-of-sums form:

(a) $A + \overline{A}\,B + \overline{A}\,C$ (b) $BC + \overline{A}\overline{B}$

(c) $AB\,(\overline{B} + \overline{C})$ (d) $\overline{A}\overline{B}\,(\overline{B}\,C + \overline{B}\overline{C})$

(e) $(A + \overline{B} + C)\,(AB + AC)$ (f) $(\overline{A} + \overline{B})\,A\overline{B}C$

21. Write the Boolean expression (in sum-of-products form) for a logical circuit that will have a 1 output when $X = 0$, $Y = 0$, $Z = 1$, and $X = 1$, $Y = 1$, $Z = 0$; and a 0 output for all other input states. Draw the block diagram for this circuit, assuming that the inputs are from flip-flops.

TABLE 3 • 27

INPUTS			OUTPUT	OUTPUT	OUTPUT
X	Y	Z	F_1	F_2	F_3
0	0	0	0	0	1
0	0	1	0	1	1
0	1	0	1	1	1
0	1	1	1	1	0
1	0	0	1	0	0
1	0	1	0	1	0
1	1	0	1	1	1
1	1	1	1	0	1

24. Prove the following theorem using the rules in Table 3·10:

$$(X + Y)(X + \overline{Y}) = X$$

25. Write the Boolean expression (in sum-of-products form) for a logical network that will have a 1 output when $X = 1$, $Y = 0$, $Z = 0$; $X = 1$, $Y = 1$, $Z = 0$; $X = 1$, $Y = 1$, $Z = 0$; and $X = 1$, $Y = 1$, $Z = 1$. The circuit will have a 0 output for all other sets of input values. Simplify the expression derived and draw a block diagram for the simplified expression.

26. Derive the Boolean algebra expression for a gating network that will have outputs 0 only when $X = 1$, $Y = 1$, $Z = 1$; $X = 0$, $Y = 0$, $Z = 0$; $X = 1$, $Y = 0$, $Z = 0$. The outputs are to be 1 for all other cases.

27. Prove rule 18 in Table 3·10 using the proof by perfect induction.

28. Develop sum-of-products and product-of-sums expressions for F_1, F_2, and F_3 in Table 3·27.

29. Develop both the sum-of-products and the product-of-sums expressions that describe Table 3·28, and then simplify both expressions. Draw a block dia-

TABLE 3 • 28

INPUTS			OUTPUT
X	Y	Z	A
0	0	0	0
0	0	1	1
0	1	0	1
0	1	1	0
1	0	0	0
1	0	1	1
1	1	0	1
1	1	1	0

TABLE 3 • 29

INPUTS			OUTPUT
A	B	C	Z
0	0	0	0
0	0	1	1
0	1	0	1
0	1	1	0
1	0	0	1
1	0	1	1
1	1	0	0
1	1	1	0

TABLE 3 • 30

INPUTS			OUTPUT
A	B	C	Z
0	0	0	1
0	0	1	0
0	1	0	0
0	1	1	1
1	0	0	1
1	0	1	0
1	1	0	0
1	1	1	1

TABLE 3 • 31

INPUTS			OUTPUT
X	Y	Z	P
0	0	0	1
0	0	1	1
0	1	0	1
0	1	1	1
1	0	0	1
1	0	1	0
1	1	0	0
1	1	1	0

gram for logical circuitry that corresponds to the simplified expressions, using only NAND gates for sum-of-products and NOR gates for product-of-sums.

30. Draw block diagrams for the F_1, F_2, and F_3 in Question 28 using only NAND gates.

31. Write the Boolean algebra expressions for Tables 3·29 to 3·31, showing expressions in sum-of-products form; then simplify the expressions and draw a block diagram of the circuit corresponding to each expression.

32. Draw block diagrams for the F_1, F_2, and F_3 in Question 28, using only NOR gates.

33. Draw a block diagram for F_1, F_2, and F_3 in Question 28, using OR-to-NAND networks.

34. Draw block diagrams for F_1, F_2, and F_3 in Question 28, using AND-to-NOR gate networks.

35. Draw Karnaugh maps for the expressions in Question 2.

36. Draw Karnaugh maps for the expressions in Question 3.

37. For a four-variable map in W, X, Y, and Z draw the subcubes for:
  (a) $WX\overline{Y}$ (b) WX (c) $XY\overline{Z}$ (d) Y

38. For a four-variable map in W, X, Y, and Z draw the subcubes for:
(a) $\overline{W}X\overline{Y}\overline{Z}$ (b) $W\overline{Z}$ (c) $\overline{W}Z$ (d) $\overline{Y}$

39. Draw maps of the expressions in Question 40, then draw the subcubes for the shortened terms you found.

40. Apply the rule $AY + A\overline{Y} = A$ where possible to the following expressions:
(a) $X\overline{Y} + \overline{X}Y$ (b) $\overline{A}\,\overline{B}\,C + A\overline{B}\,C$
(c) $A\overline{B}\,C + ABC$ (d) $ABC + A\overline{B}\,\overline{C} + A\overline{B}\,C + AB\overline{C}$
(e) $ABC + \overline{A}\,\overline{B}\,\overline{C} + A\overline{B}\,C$ (f) $ABC + \overline{A}BC + \overline{A}\,\overline{B}\,C$

Note: There is a technique for writing minterms that is widely used. It consists in writing the letter *m* (to represent *minterm*) along with the value of the binary number given by the row of the table and combinations in which the minterm lies. For instance, in the variables X, Y, Z we have the unfinished table of combinations given in Table 3·32.

For this table $m_0 = \overline{X}\,\overline{Y}\,\overline{Z}$, $m_1 = \overline{X}\,\overline{Y}\,Z$, $m_2 = \overline{X}\,Y\overline{Z}$, $m_3 = \overline{X}\,YZ$, and so to $m_7 = XYZ$. Now we can substitute m_is for actual terms and shorten the writing of expressions. For instance, $m_1 + m_2 + m_4$ means $\overline{X}\,\overline{Y}\,Z + \overline{X}\,Y\overline{Z} + X\overline{Y}\,\overline{Z}$. Similarly, $m_0 + m_3 + m_5 + m_7$ means $\overline{X}\,\overline{Y}\,\overline{Z} + \overline{X}\,YZ + X\overline{Y}\,Z + XYZ$.

This can be extended to four or more variables. An expression in W, X, Y, Z can be written as $m_0 + m_{13} + m_{15} = \overline{W}\,\overline{X}\,\overline{Y}\,\overline{Z} + WX\overline{Y}\,Z + WXYZ$. Or $m_2 + m_5 + m_9 = \overline{W}\,\overline{X}\,Y\overline{Z} + \overline{W}X\overline{Y}\,Z + W\overline{X}\,\overline{Y}\,Z$. As can be seen, to change a minterm to its m_i, simply make uncomplemented variables 1s and complemented variables 0s. Thus $\overline{W}XY\overline{Z}$ would be 0110, or 6 decimal, $\overline{W}X\,\overline{Y}\,Z$ would be 0010, or 2 decimal. These two terms would then be written m_6 and m_2. (Notice that we must know how many variables a minterm is in.)

41. Draw the Karnaugh maps in X, Y, Z for:
(a) $m_0 + m_1 + m_5 + m_7$ (b) $m_1 + m_3 + m_5 + m_4$
(c) $m_1 + m_2 + m_3 + m_5$ (d) $m_0 + m_5 + m_7$

42. Draw the subcubes for a three-variable map in X, Y, Z for:
(a) $m_1 + m_3 + m_5 + m_0$ (b) $m_4 + m_7$ (c) $m_0 + m_3$

43. Find the maximal subcubes for the maps drawn for Question 42.

	$\overline{X}\,\overline{Y}$	$\overline{X}Y$	XY	$X\overline{Y}$
$\overline{Z}$	m_0	m_2	m_6	m_4
Z	m_1	m_3	m_7	m_5

TABLE 3 • 32

INPUT			OUTPUT	PRODUCT TERMS	DESIGNATION AS m_i
X	Y	Z			
0	0	0		$\overline{X}\,\overline{Y}\,\overline{Z}$	m_0
0	0	1		$\overline{X}\,\overline{Y}\,Z$	m_1
0	1	0		$\overline{X}\,Y\overline{Z}$	m_2
0	1	1		$\overline{X}\,YZ$	m_3
1	0	0		$X\overline{Y}\,\overline{Z}$	m_4
1	0	1		$X\overline{Y}\,Z$	m_5
1	1	0		$XY\overline{Z}$	m_6
1	1	1		XYZ	m_7

P.104

44. Find minimal expressions for the maps drawn in Question 42.
45. Using maps, simplify the following expressions in four variables W, X, Y, and Z.
    (a) $m_2 + m_3 + m_5 + m_6 + m_7 + m_9 + m_{11} + m_{13}$
    (b) $m_0 + m_2 + m_4 + m_8 + m_9 + m_{10} + m_{11} + m_{12} + m_{13}$
46. Using maps, simplify the following expressions in four variables W, X, Y, and Z:
    (a) $m_1 + m_3 + m_5 + m_7 + m_{12} + m_{13} + m_8 + m_9$
    (b) $m_0 + m_5 + m_7 + m_8 + m_{11} + m_{13} + m_{15}$
47. Using maps, derive minimal product-of-sums expressions for the functions given in Question 46.
48. Using maps, derive minimal product-of-sums expressions for the functions given in Question 42.
49. Using maps, simplify the following expressions, using sum-of-products form:

$$\text{(a)}\quad \overbrace{}^{\text{don't-cares}}$$

(a) $\overline{A}\,\overline{B}\,\overline{C} + A\overline{B}\,\overline{C} + \overbrace{ABC + \overline{A}B\overline{C} + \overline{A}\,\overline{B}\,C}^{\text{don't-cares}}$

(b) $ABC + \overline{A}\,\overline{B}\,\overline{C} + \overbrace{AB\overline{C} + A\overline{B}C}^{\text{don't-cares}}$

(c) $ABCD + \overline{A}\,\overline{B}\,\overline{C}D + \overline{A}\,BCD + \overbrace{A\overline{B}CD + \overline{A}\,\overline{B}CD + ABC\overline{D}}^{\text{don't-cares}}$

50. Using maps, derive minimal product-of-sums expressions for the functions given in Question 49.
51. Using maps, simplify the following expressions, using sum-of-products form:

(a) $ABC + \overline{A}\,\overline{B}\,C + \overbrace{\overline{A}\,BC + A\overline{B}C + AB\overline{C}}^{\text{don't-cares}}$

(b) $ABCD + \overline{A}\,\overline{B}CD + \overbrace{\overline{A}BCD + A\overline{B}CD + \overline{A}\,\overline{B}\,\overline{C}D}^{\text{don't-cares}}$

(c) $A\overline{B}C\overline{D} + A\overline{B}CD + \overbrace{\overline{A}\,BC\overline{D} + \overline{A}\,BC\overline{D}}^{\text{don't-cares}}$

52. (a) Design an AND-to-OR gate combinational network for the Boolean algebra expression

$$ABCD + AB\overline{C}\,\overline{D} + \overline{A}\,\overline{B}CD + \overline{A}B\overline{C}D + ABC\overline{D} + \overline{A}BCD$$

   Use as few gates as you can.
   (b) Design a NOR-to-NOR gate combinational network for the Boolean algebra function in part (a), again using as few gates as you can.
53. The following is a NAND-to-NAND gate network. Draw a block diagram for a NOR-to-NOR gate network that realizes the same function, using as few gates as possible.

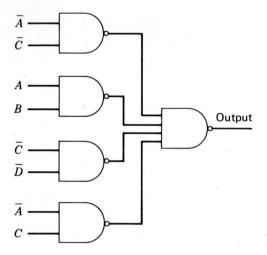

54. *(a)* Derive a Boolean algebra expression for the output Y of the network shown below.

(b) Convert the expression for Y derived in *(a)* to product-of-sums form.

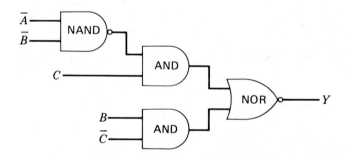

55. *(a)* Design an OR-to-AND gate combinational network for the Boolean algebra expression

$$ABCD + \overline{A}B\overline{C}D + \overline{A}B\overline{C}D + \overline{A}BC\overline{D} + (\overline{A}\,\overline{B}\,\overline{C}\overline{D} + \overline{A}B\,CD)$$

The two terms in parentheses are don't-care terms.

(b) Using only NAND gates, design a combinational network for the Boolean algebra function given in part *(a)*.

56. *(a)* Design an OR-to-AND gate combinatorial network for the Boolean algebra expression

$$\overline{A}\,BCD + \overline{A}BC\overline{D} + \overline{A}B\overline{C}D + \overline{A}B\overline{C}\overline{D} + (\overline{A}\,\overline{B}\,\overline{C}\overline{D} + \overline{A}B\,CD)$$

The two terms in parentheses are don't-care terms.

(b) Using only NOR gates design a combinatorial network for the Boolean algebra function given in part *(a)*.

57. The following NAND-to-AND gate network is to be redesigned using a NOR-to-OR gate configuration. Make the change using as few gates as possible.

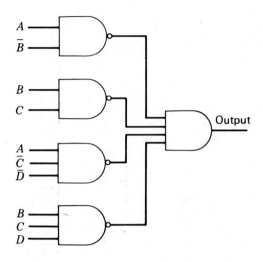

58. *(a)* Design an AND-to-OR gate combinational network for the Boolean algebra expression

$$ABCD + AB\overline{C}D + \overline{A}\,\overline{B}\,C\overline{D} + AB\overline{C}\,\overline{D} + ABC\overline{D} + \overline{A}\,B\overline{C}\,\overline{D}$$

Use as few gates as you can.

(b) Design a NOR-gate combinational network for the Boolean algebra function in part *(a)*, again using as few gates as you can.

59. Convert the following NOR-to-OR gate network into a NAND-to-AND gate network. Use as few gates as possible.

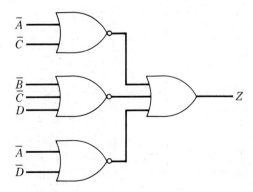

60. *(a)* Design an AND-to-OR gate combinational network for the Boolean algebra expression

$$A\overline{B}CD + AB\overline{C}D + \overline{A}\,\overline{B}CD + AB\overline{C}\,\overline{D} + A\overline{B}\,\overline{C}\,\overline{D} + \overline{A}BCD$$

Use as few gates as you can.

(b) Design a NOR-to-NOR gate combinational network for the Boolean algebra function in part *(a)*, again using as few gates as you can.

61. A combinational network has three control inputs C_1, C_2, and C_3; three data inputs A_1, A_2, and A_3; and a single output Z. ($\overline{A}_1$, $\overline{A}_2$, $\overline{A}_3$, $\overline{C}_1$, $\overline{C}_2$, and $\overline{C}_3$ are also available as inputs.) Each input is a binary valued signal. Only one of the control inputs can be a 1 at any given time, and all three can be 0s simultaneously. When C_1 is a 1, the value of Z is to be the value of A_1; when C_2 is a 1, the value of Z is to be the value of A_2; and when C_3 is a 1, the value of the output is to be the value of A_3. If C_1, C_2, and C_3 are 0s, the output Z is to have value 0. Design this network using only NOR gates. Make the network have two levels and use as few gates as possible.

62. The following NAND-to-AND gate network is to be redesigned using a NOR-to-OR gate configuration. Make the change using as few gates as possible.

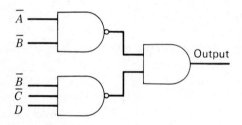

63. Convert the following NOR-to-NOR gate network into a NAND-to-AND gate network. Use as few gates as possible in your network.

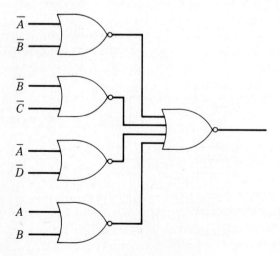

TABLE 3 • 33

X_1	X_2	X_3	X_4	OUTPUT
0	0	0	0	0
0	0	0	1	1
0	0	1	0	1
0	0	1	1	0
0	1	0	0	0
0	1	0	1	d
0	1	1	0	1
0	1	1	1	d
1	0	0	0	d
1	0	0	1	1
1	0	1	0	0
1	0	1	1	0
1	1	0	0	d
1	1	0	1	0
1	1	1	0	d
1	1	1	1	0

64. Will the minimal expression of the function in Table 3·33 require fewer NAND gates or NOR gates? (d means don't-care.) Assume complements are available. How many gates for each? Give your minimal expressions.

65. The following NAND-to-AND gate network must be converted to a NOR-to-OR gate network. Make the conversion using as few gates as possible in your final design.

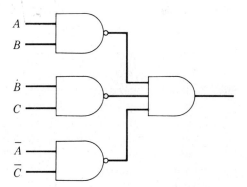

66. Will the minimal expression for the function in Table 3·34 require fewer NAND gates or NOR gates? (d means don't-care.) Assume complements are available. How many gates for each? Give your minimal expressions.

TABLE 3 • 34

X_1	X_2	X_3	X_4	OUTPUT
0	0	0	0	0
0	0	0	1	1
0	0	1	0	1
0	0	1	1	0
0	1	0	0	0
0	1	0	1	0
0	1	1	0	1
0	1	1	1	d
1	0	0	0	d
1	0	0	1	1
1	0	1	0	1
1	0	1	1	0
1	1	0	0	d
1	1	0	1	0
1	1	1	0	1
1	1	1	1	0

67. Simplify

(a)

$$(\overline{W} + \overline{X} + Y + Z)(\overline{W} + X + \overline{Y} + Z)(\overline{W} + X + Y + Z)$$

$$\overbrace{(W + X + \overline{Y} + Z)(W + \overline{X} + Y + Z)(\overline{W} + \overline{X} + Y + \overline{Z})}^{\text{don't-cares}}$$
$$(W + X + Y + Z)$$

(b) $\overline{A}\,\overline{B}\,\overline{C}\,\overline{D} + \overline{A}\,\overline{B}\,\overline{C}\,D + ABC\overline{D} +$

$$\overbrace{\overline{A}\,\overline{B}\,\overline{C}\,D + \overline{A}\,BCD + ABCD + \overline{A}\,BC\overline{D} + A\overline{B}\,C\overline{D}}^{\text{don't-cares}}$$

(c) For parts (a) and (b) design block diagrams for the logical circuitry of the simplified expressions using either NAND gates only or NOR gates only. Assume that complements of the inputs are available. The same type gates do not have to be used for both (a) and (b).

68. Write a Boolean algebra expression in sum-of-products form for a gating network with three inputs A, B, and C (and their complements $\overline{A}$, $\overline{B}$, and $\overline{C}$) that is to have a 1 output only when two (or) three of the inputs have a 1 value. Implement using a NAND-to-wired AND gate network.

69. Draw a block diagram for a gate network having a NOR-to-OR gate network with three inputs A, B, and C (and their complements) that have a 1 output only when two or three of the inputs have a 1 value as in Question 68.

70. Will the minimal expression for the function in Table 3·35 require fewer NAND gates or NOR gates? (d means don't-care.) Assume that complements are available. How many gates for each? Give your minimal expressions.

71. The following is a NAND-to-NAND gate network. Draw a block diagram for a NOR-to-NOR gate network that realizes the same function, using as few gates as possible.

TABLE 3 • 35

X_1	X_2	X_3	X_4	OUTPUT
0	0	0	0	0
0	0	0	1	1
0	0	1	0	1
0	0	1	1	0
0	1	0	0	d
0	1	0	1	0
0	1	1	0	1
0	1	1	1	d
1	0	0	0	d
1	0	0	1	1
1	0	1	0	1
1	0	1	1	d
1	1	0	0	d
1	1	0	1	0
1	1	1	0	1
1	1	1	1	0

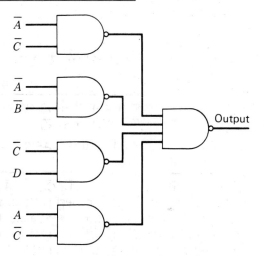

72. Convert the following NOR-to-OR gate network into a NAND-to-NAND gate network. Use as few gates as possible in your network.

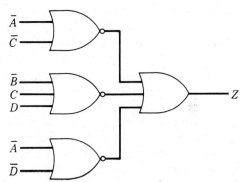

73. (a) Design an AND-to-OR gate combinational network for the Boolean algebra function

$$F = \overline{W}\overline{X}\overline{Y}\overline{Z} + W\overline{X}\,\overline{Y}Z + W\overline{X}\overline{Y}\overline{Z} + W\overline{X}\,YZ + \overline{W}X\overline{Y}\overline{Z}$$

Use as few gates as you can.

(b) Design a NOR gate combinational network for the Boolean algebra function in part (a), again using as few gates as you can.

74. This chapter has explained a number of two-level networks that can be used to implement all possible functions of a given number of variables. There are also two-level networks that can only implement a few of the many functions possible. For instance, an AND-to-AND gate network is only the AND function as shown below:

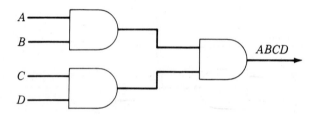

Similarly, a NAND-to-OR implements only an OR function with complemented inputs as shown below:

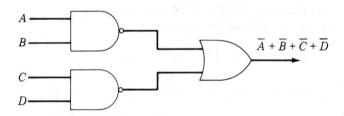

In all, eight of the possible 16 two-level network arrangements that can be made using NAND, OR, and AND gates will realize all functions, while eight are degenerate and only yield a few of the functions. Identify the degenerate forms and the forms that will yield all functions.

75. This chapter did not treat the two-level form AND-to-NOR. Derive a rule for designing AND-to-NOR gate networks and show how it works for a problem of your choice.

76. This chapter did not treat OR-to-NAND gate networks, although all Boolean functions can be realized using that configuration. Derive a design rule for using OR-to-NAND gate forms and design a sample network using your rule.

77. Show how the NOR-to-NAND gate network shown below can be replaced by a single gate.

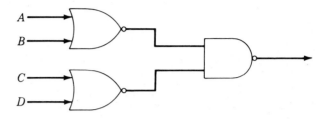

78. Convert the following NAND-to-NAND gate network into a (two-level) NOR-to-OR gate network:

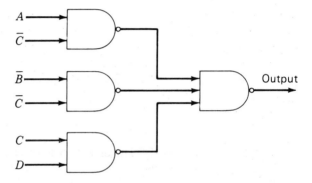

79. Using as few gates as possible, design a NAND-to-AND gate network that realizes the following Boolean algebra expression:

$$\overline{A}B\overline{C}D + AB\overline{C}\,\overline{D} + A\overline{B}\,C\overline{D} + ABC\overline{D} + A\overline{B}\,\overline{C}\,\overline{D}$$

80. Convert the following NAND-to-NAND gate network into a (two-level) NOR-to-AND gate network:

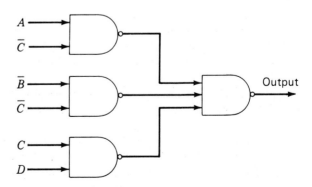

81. Convert the following NAND-to-NAND gate network to a NOR-to-NOR gate network:

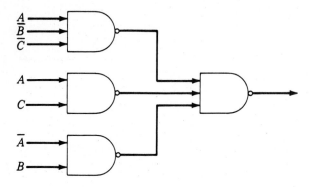

82. Convert the following NOR-to-OR gate network to a NAND-to-AND gate network. Use as few gates as possible.

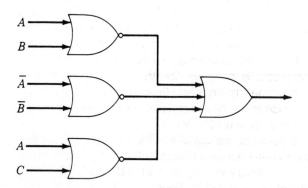

83. Convert the following NOR-to-OR gate network into a NAND-to-AND gate network. Use as few gates as possible in your network.

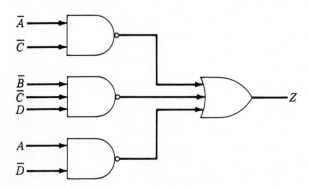

4
LOGIC DESIGN

The preceding chapter described gates and the analysis of gating networks using Boolean algebra. The basic devices used in the operational or calculating sections of digital computers consist of gates and devices called *flip-flops.* It is remarkable that even the largest of computers is primarily constructed of these devices. Accordingly, this chapter first describes flip-flops and their characteristics. From an intuitive viewpoint flip-flops provide memory and gates provide operations on, or functions of, the values stored in these memory devices.

Following the introduction to flip-flops, the use of flip-flops and gates to perform several of the most useful functions in computers is presented. The particular functions described include counting in binary and binary-coded-decimal, transferring values, and shifting or scaling values stored in flip-flops.

There are, incidentally, several other names which have been used instead of flip-flop. These include *binary* and *toggle,* but flip-flop has been the most frequently used. Also, there are several other types of memory devices in computers, and these will be studied in Chap. 7. For actual operations flip-flops remain dominant, however, because of their high speed, the ease with which they can be set or read, and the natural way gates and flip-flops can be interconnected.

This chapter also contains a section on clocks in digital computers. Computers do not run by taking steps at random times, but proceed from step to step at intervals precisely controlled by a clock which provides a carefully regulated time base for all operations. Some knowledge of the uses of clocks in computers is indispensable, and the subject is introduced here.

All the above material is presented without recourse to the study of electronic digital circuitry. In many cases students have gained familiarity with digital circuits prior to studying this material; in other cases, where courses and users of the book are pressed for time, it is decided to progress without studying the actual circuit details of the gates and flip-flop circuits which are used. Accordingly, this book has been constructed so that it is possible to proceed while omitting the material on circuits, which is given in Chap. 5. (Material can also be selected from Chap. 5 at the instructor's discretion.)

It is the fact that computers have come to be constructed of circuits which operate in a modular, or block, fashion that makes it possible to treat circuit material in this way. As integrated circuits have become increasingly complex, it has become necessary to examine them from a functional viewpoint rather than a component viewpoint in both computer design and maintenance. We ask first, "What does the circuit do?" then, only later, "How does it work?"

4 • 1 THE FLIP-FLOP

The basic circuit for storing information in a digital machine is called a *flip-flop*. There are several fundamental types of flip-flops and many circuit designs; however, there are two characteristics shared by all flip-flops.

1. The flip-flop is a bistable device, that is, a circuit with only two stable states, which we will designate the 0 state and the 1 state.

The flip-flop circuit can remember, or store, a binary bit of information because of its bistable characteristic. The flip-flop responds to inputs. If an input causes it to go to its 1 state, it will remain there and "remember" a 1 until some signal causes it to go to the 0 state. Similarly, once placed in the 0 state, it will remain there until told to go to the 1 state. This simple characteristic, the ability of the flip-flop to retain its state, is the basis for information storage in the operating or calculating sections of a digital computer.

2. The flip-flop has two output signals, one of which is the complement of the other.

Figure 4·1 shows the block diagram for a particular type of flip-flop, the *RS flip-flop*. There are two inputs, designated as S and R, and two outputs, marked with X and $\overline{X}$. To describe and analyze flip-flop operation, there are several conventions that are standard in the computer industry.

1. Each flip-flop is given a "name." Convenient names are generally letters such as X or Y or A or B, or letter-number combinations such as A_1 or B_2, or sometimes, because of difficulty in subscripting on typewriters or printers, simply $A1$ or $B2$. The flip-flop in Fig. 4·1 is called X. It has two outputs, the X output and the $\overline{X}$ output.

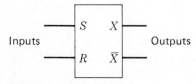

FIG. 4 • 1 *RS* flip-flop.

The X and $\overline{X}$ output lines are always complements; that is, if the X output line has a 1 signal, the $\overline{X}$ output line has a 0 signal; and if the X output line has a 0 signal, output line $\overline{X}$ has a 1 signal.

2. The state of the flip-flop is taken to be the state of the X output. Thus if the output line X has a 1 signal on it, we say that "flip-flop X is in the 1 state." Similarly, if the X line contains a 0 signal, we say that "flip-flop X is in the 0 state."

These two sets of conventions are very important and convenient. Notice that when flip-flop X is in the 1 state, the output line $\overline{X}$ has a 0 on it, and when flip-flop X is in the 0 state, the output line $\overline{X}$ has a 1 on it.

There are two input lines to the RS flip-flop. These are used to control the state of the flip-flop. The rules are as follows:

1. As long as both input lines S and R carry 0 signals, the flip-flop remains in the same state, that is, it does not change state.
2. A 1 signal on the S line (the SET line) and a 0 signal on the R line cause the flip-flop to "set" to the 1 state.
3. A 1 signal on the R line (the RESET line) and a 0 signal on the S line cause the flip-flop to "reset" to the 0 state.
4. Placing a 1 on the S and a 1 on the R lines at the same time is forbidden. If this occurs, the flip-flop can go to either state. (This is in effect an ambiguous input in that it is telling the flip-flop to both SET and RESET at the same time.)

An example of a possible sequence of input signals and the resulting state of the flip-flop is as follows:

S	R	X	
			X is the state of the flip-flop after inputs S and R are applied.
1	0	1	
0	0	1	Flip-flop remains in same state.
0	0	1	
0	1	0	Flip-flop is reset.
0	0	0	
0	0	0	
0	1	0	Flip-flop is told to reset but is already reset.
0	0	0	
1	0	1	Flip-flop is set.
0	0	1	

While the above conventions may seem formidable at first, they can be simply summarized by seeing that a 1 on the S line causes the flip-flop to SET (that is, assume the 1 state) and a 1 on the R line causes the flip-flop to RESET (that is, assume the 0 state). The flip-flop does nothing in the absence of 1 inputs and would be hopelessly confused by 1s on both S and R inputs.

It is very convenient to be able to draw graphs of the inputs and outputs from computer circuits to show how they act as inputs vary. We shall assume the con-

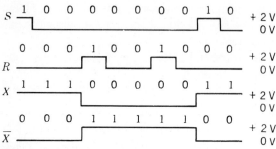

FIG. 4 • 2 *RS* flip-flop waveforms.

vention that a 1 signal is a positive signal and a 0 signal a ground, or 0 V, signal. This is conventional in most present-day circuits and is called *positive logic.* Figure 4·2 shows several signals as they progress in time, with the current binary values of each signal written above it. The signals in Fig. 4·2 are the sequence of signals given in the list above along with both the X and $\overline{X}$ output line signals from the flip-flop. We have arbitrarily chosen +2 V for the 1 state of the signals and 0 V for the 0 state because these are very frequently used levels. Notice that the flip-flop changes only when the input levels command it to, and that it changes at once. (Actually, there would be a slight delay from when the flip-flop is told to change states and when it changes, since no physical device can respond instantly; so we assume that the flip-flop's delay in responding is quite small, perhaps a small fraction of a microsecond.)

4 • 2 THE TRANSFER

The *RS* flip-flop, although simple in operation, is adequate for all purposes and is the basic flip-flop circuit. Let us examine the operation of this flip-flop in a configuration called a *transfer circuit*. Figure 4·3 shows two sets of flip-flops named X_1, X_2, and X_3 and Y_1, Y_2, and Y_3. The function of this configuration is to transfer the states or *contents* of Y_1 into X_1, Y_2 into X_2, and Y_3 into X_3 upon the TRANSFER command which consists of a 1 on the TRANSFER line.

Assume that Y_1, Y_2, and Y_3 have been set to some states that we want to remember or store in X_1, X_2, and X_3, while the Y flip-flops are used for further calculations. Placing a 1 on the TRANSFER line will cause this desired transfer of information. Understanding the transfer of the state of Y_1 into X_1 depends on seeing that if Y_1 is in the 0 state, the Y_1 output line has a 0 on it, and so the input line connected to the AND gate will be a 0 and the AND gate will place a 0 on the S input line of X_1, while the $\overline{Y}_1$ output from Y_1 will be a 1, causing, in the presence of a 1 on the TRANSFER line, a 1 on the R input of X_1. Similar reasoning will show that a 1 in Y_1 will cause a 1 to be placed in X_1 in the presence of a 1 on the TRANSFER line. As long as the TRANSFER line is a 0, both inputs to the X flip-flops will be 0s, and the flip-flop will remain in the last state it assumed.

The above simple operation, the *transfer operation,* is quite important. Related

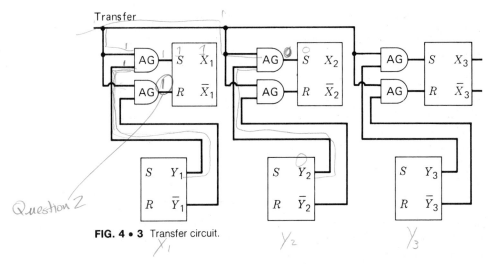

FIG. 4 • 3 Transfer circuit.

sets of flip-flops in a computer are called *registers,* and we might call the three flip-flops Y_1, Y_2, and Y_3 simply *register Y,* and the three flip-flops X_1, X_2, and X_3 would be called *register X.* Then a 1 on the TRANSFER line would transfer the contents of register Y into register X. We shall return to this important concept.

4 • 3 THE CLOCK

A very important fact about digital computers (and flip-flops) as we now conceive of them is that they are almost invariably clocked. This means that there is some "master clock" somewhere sending out signals which are carefully regulated in time.

There are excellent reasons why machines are designed this way. The alternative way, with operations triggering other operations as they occur, is called *asynchronous operation* (the clocked way is called *synchronous operation*) and leads to considerable difficulty in design and maintenance. As a result, genuinely asynchronous operation is rarely used.

The clock is therefore the mover of the computer in that it carefully measures time and sends out regularly spaced clock signals which cause things to happen. We can then examine the operation of the flip-flops and gates before and after the clock "initiates an action." Initiating signals are often called, for historical reasons, *clock pulses.*†

Figure 4·4 shows a clock. The clock waveform in Fig. 4·4(*a*) and (*b*) is called a *square wave.* The figure shows two important portions of a square wave, the *leading edge,* or *rising edge,* or sometimes *positive-going edge,* and the *falling edge,* or *negative-going edge.* These are particularly important since most flip-

---

†The term *clock pulse* has a historical origin. The early computers used short electrical pulses to initiate operations, and these were naturally called *clock pulses.* Few circuits still use these narrow pulses, and the majority of circuits now respond to edges of square waves as in Fig. 4·4.

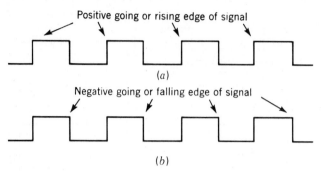

Positive going or rising edge of signal

(a)

Negative going or falling edge of signal

(b)

FIG. 4 • 4 Clock waveforms.

flops now in use respond to either (but not both) a falling edge or a rising edge. In effect, a system which responds to rising edges of the clock "rests" between such edges and changes state only when such positive-going edges occur. (The reason for the rest periods is to give the circuits time to assume their new states and to give all transients time to die down. The frequency at which such edges occur is generally determined by the speed with which the circuits can go to their new states, the delay times for the gates since they must process the new signals, etc.)

Since clock signals are used to initiate flip-flop actions, a clock input is included on most flip-flops. This input is marked with a CL, as shown in Fig. 4·5. A clocked flip-flop can respond to either the positive-going edge of the clock signal or the negative-going edge.† If a given flip-flop responds to the positive-going edge of the signal, there is no "bubble" at the CL input on the block diagram, as in Fig. 4·5(a). If the flip-flop responds to a negative-going edge, or signal, a bubble is placed at the CL input, as in Fig. 4·5(b).

It is important to understand the above convention because clocked flip-flops actually respond to a *change* in clock input level, not to the level itself.

This is shown in Fig. 4·5(c) and (d). The flip-flop in Fig. 4·5(a) responds to positive-going clock edges (positive shifts), and a typical set of signals for the *clocked RS flip-flop* in Fig. 4·5(a) is shown in Fig. 4·5(c).

The flip-flop is operated according to these rules:

1. If the S and R inputs are 0s when the clock edge (pulse) occurs, the flip-flop does not change states but remains in its present state.
2. If the S input is a 1 and the R input is a 0 when the clock pulse (positive-going edge) occurs, the flip-flop goes to the 1 state.
3. If the S input is a 0 and the R input a 1 when the clock pulse occurs, the flip-flop is cleared to the 0 state.
4. Both the S and R inputs should not be 1s when a clock signal's positive-going edge occurs.

---

†A flip-flop which responds to a rising or falling clock signal (as opposed to responding to a dc level) is called an *edge-triggering,* or *master-slave,* flip-flop for reasons that will be explained. Sometimes the clock input on the block diagram symbol for an edge-triggering flip-flop contains a small triangle, but this symbol is not widely used.

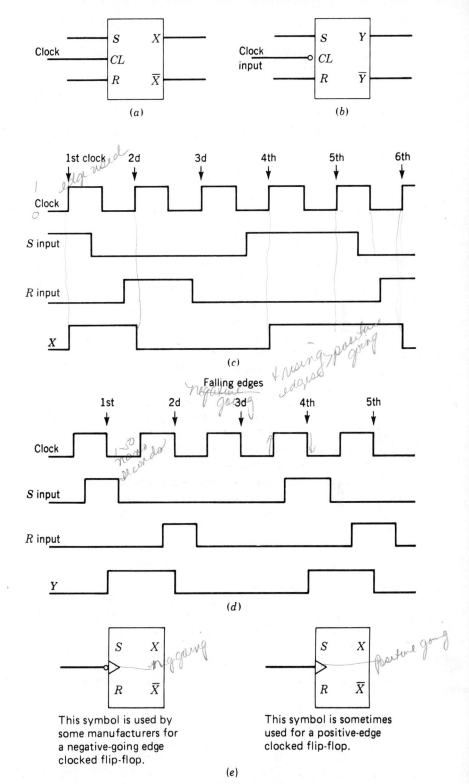

FIG. 4 • 5 Clocked flip-flops and waveforms. (*a*) Positive-edge-triggering flip-flop. (*b*) Negative-edge-triggering flip-flop. (*c*) Waveforms for positive-edge-triggering flip-flop in (*a*). (*d*) Waveforms for flip-flop in (*b*). (*e*) Alternate symbol for edge-triggering flip-flop.

Of course, nothing happens to the flip-flop's state between occurrences of the initiating positive-going clock signal.†

Figure 4·5(c) shows this with a square-wave clock signal. The flip-flop is set to a 1 by the first clock positive-going edge; a 0 at the occurrence of the second clock signal; no change occurs at the third positive-going clock edge; the flip-flop is set to 1 again on the fourth edge; and remains a 1 until the sixth clock edge occurs. Notice that the S and R inputs can be anything between the clock edges without affecting the operation of the flip-flop. (They can even both be 1s without effect, except when the positive-going edge occurs.)

Figure 4·5(d) shows typical waveforms for the flip-flop in Fig. 4·5(b). This flip-flop is *negative-edge triggering* because it responds to shifts in the clock level which are negative-going. The rules of operation are as before: 0s on S and R lead to no change; a 1 on S sets the flip-flop; and a 1 on R clears the flip-flop. The flip-flop responds to the S and R inputs only at the precise time the clock, or CL, input, goes negative.

In order to bring out the edge-triggering feature of a flip-flop, a special symbol is sometimes used. This is shown in Fig. 4·5(e). The more conventional symbol in Fig. 4·5(a) will be used in this book. The symbol in Fig. 4·5(e) is included for completeness.

4 • 4 THE SHIFT REGISTER

Figure 4·6 shows a *shift register*. This circuit accepts information from some input source and then shifts this information along the chain of flip-flops, moving it one flip-flop each time a positive-going clock signal occurs.

Figure 4·6 also shows a typical sequence of input signals and flip-flop signals in the shift register. The input value is taken by X_1 when the first positive-going clock signal arrives. Anything in this and the remaining flip-flops is shifted right at this time. We have assumed that all the flip-flops are initially in their 0 states. In the figure, the input waveform is at 1 when the first clock occurs; so X_1 goes to the 1 state.

When the second positive-going clock signal arrives, the input is at 0; so X_1 goes to the 0 state, but the 1 in X_1 is shifted into X_2. When the third clock edge appears, the input is a 1; so X_1 takes a 1, the 0 previously in X_1 is shifted into X_2, and the 1 in X_2 goes into X_3. This process continues. The values in X_3 are simply dropped off the end of the register.

Notice that each flip-flop takes the value in the flip-flop on its left when the shift register is stepped. The reasoning is as follows: If, for instance, X_1 is in the 1 state,

---

†There is some delay from the time the positive-going edge of the clock signal tells a flip-flop to "go" until the flip-flop's outputs are able to change values. The clock signal itself will also require some small amount of time to rise, for physical reasons. For present systems the rise time on the clock signals, that is, the time to rise 90 percent of total rise, ranges from about 1×10^{-9} to about 50×10^{-9} s. The delay from the clock-signal change until a flip-flop's output changes 90 percent, which is called the *delay time*, ranges from 10.5×10^{-9} to 50×10^{-9} s for most circuits.

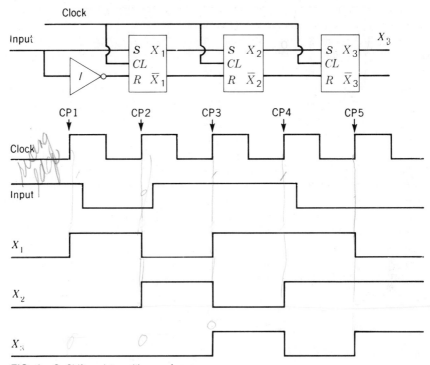

FIG. 4 • 6 Shift register with waveforms.

its X output line is a 1 and thus the S input to X_2 will be a 1; and the $\overline{X}$ output of X_1 will be a 0, and so the R input of X_2 will be a 0. This causes X_2 to take its 1 state when the clock pulse occurs. A 0 in X_1 will cause X_2 to go to 0 when the clock pulse occurs, and the reason for this should be analyzed.

There is one problem that could occur if certain design precautions were not taken with the flip-flops. If the flip-flop outputs changed too fast, a state could ripple, or race, down the chain. This is called the *race problem;* it is handled by designing the flip-flops so that they take the value at their inputs just as the clock positive-going edge occurs and not slightly after or during the clock's rise time. This leads to a certain complexity in flip-flop design, which we will not at this time consider. The designer and manufacturer of circuits provide us with this protection, and we shall accept it for the present, but an explanation in detail is given in the final sections of this chapter and can be read now, if desired.

4 • 5 THE BINARY COUNTER

Inasmuch as the binary counter is one of the most useful of logical circuits, there are many kinds of binary counters. The fundamental purpose of the binary counter is to record the number of occurrences of some input. This is a basic function, that of counting, and it is used over and over.

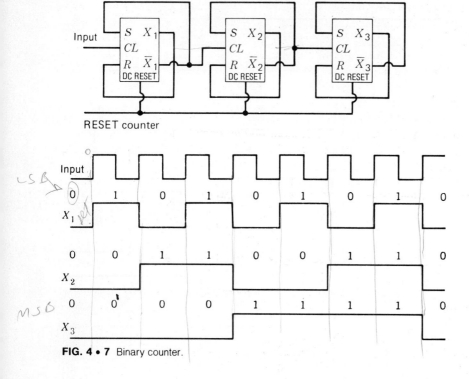

FIG. 4 • 7 Binary counter.

The first type of binary counter to be explained is shown in Fig. 4·7. This counter records the number of occurrences of a positive-going edge (or pulse) at the input.

It is desirable to start this counter with 0s in all three flip-flops; so one further line is added to each flip-flop, a DC RESET line. This line is normally at the 0 level; when it goes positive, or 1, it places a 0 in the flip-flop. This action does not depend on the clock; when a DC RESET line is at the 1 level, the flip-flop goes to 0 regardless of any other input and in the absence or presence of a clock pulse.

It is quite common for flip-flops to have a DC RESET line. Notice that this input "overrides" all other inputs when it is a 1, forcing the flip-flop to the 0 state. A 0 on this line, however, does not affect flip-flop operation in any way.

Before counting begins, then, a 1 is placed temporarily on the RESET COUNTER line, and the three flip-flops are cleared to 0. The RESET COUNTER line is then returned to 0.

When the first clock positive edge occurs, the flip-flop X_1 goes to its 1 state. This is because when the flip-flop X_1 is in the 0 state, the $\overline{X}_1$ output is high, or 1, placing a 1 on the S input (refer to Fig. 4·7), and the X_1 output is low, or 0, placing a 0 on the R input; so a 1 goes into flip-flop X_1.

Flip-flops X_2 and X_3 are not affected by this change, for although the $\overline{X}_1$ output is connected to the CL input of X_2, the signal has gone from 1 to 0. This is a negative shift, which does nothing to X_2.

The counter now has $X_3 = 0$, $X_2 = 0$, $X_1 = 1$, or binary 001; so the first input clock edge has stepped the counter from 000 to 001.†

The occurrence of the second positive-going clock edge causes flip-flop X_1 to go from the 1 state to the 0 state. The reasoning is as follows: When X_1 is a 1, the X_1 output is a 1 and is connected to the R input, and the $\overline{X}_1$ output is a 0 and is connected to the S input. This tells the flip-flop to "go to 0," and when the second clock pulse occurs, it goes.

This is important. When a flip-flop is cross-coupled, that is, when its uncomplemented output is connected to its R input and its complemented output to its S input, the occurrence of a clock edge will always cause it to "complement," or change values.

The change of value from 1 to 0 of flip-flop X_1 causes X_2 to change from a 0 to a 1. This is because $\overline{X}_1$'s output is connected to the CL input of X_2 and has gone from 0 to 1, a positive shift, and since X_2 is cross-coupled, it will complement (change values) and go from 0 to 1. This does not affect X_3, because the CL input of X_3 has gone from 1 to 0, a negative shift.

The counter has now progressed to $X_1 = 0$, $X_2 = 1$, and $X_3 = 0$; so the sequence of states has been 000, 001, 010.

Reasoning of this type will show that the progression of states by the counter will be as follows:

X_3	X_2	X_1
0	0	0
0	0	1
0	1	0
0	1	1
1	0	0
1	0	1
1	1	0
1	1	1
0	0	0
0	0	1
0	1	0

This is a list of binary numbers from 0 to 7, which repeats over and over. Thus after five input pulses the counter contains 101, or binary 5; after seven pulses the counter contains 111, or binary 7. The maximum number of pulses this counter can handle, without ambiguity, is 7. After eight pulses the counter contains 0; after nine pulses, 1; etc. In the trade this is called a *modulo 8*, or *three-stage,* counter.

The counter can be extended by another flip-flop, X_4, which is cross-coupled and which has its CL input connected to the output of flip-flop $\overline{X}_3$. This forms a

---

†Notice that the binary numbers are written in the opposite direction from the block diagram layout, which has the least significant bit on the left. This makes for a neater block diagram and is frequently used. The standards, in fact, ask for left-to-right signal flow.

ENABLE

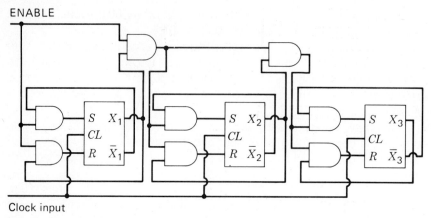

Clock input

Fig. 4 • 8 Gated-clocked binary counter.

four-stage, or *modulo 16,* counter, which can handle up to 15 counts. A fifth flip-flop would form a counter which would count to 31, a sixth to 63, etc.

We now consider a *gated-clocked binary counter.* This is an exceedingly pop-ular counter in modern integrated circuit computers, and it demonstrates the fact that most operations are *enabled* by logic levels and activated by clock signals. The preceding counter is called a *ripple counter* because changes ripple down the flip-flop chain.

In Fig. 4·8 the ENABLE input to the first flip-flop in the chain X_1 goes to two AND gates, which also have the output of the flip-flop as inputs. Notice, if the ENABLE signal is a 0, the two AND gates will have 0 outputs and X_1 will remain in the same state regardless of how many clock pulses occur.

When the ENABLE signal is a 1, however, the outputs from flip-flop X_1 cause that flip-flop to always change values when a clock pulse occurs. Thus the counter records the number of clock pulses that occur while the ENABLE is on. Then the flip-flop X_2 will change only when X_1 is a 1, the ENABLE signal is a 1, and a positive-going clock signal occurs. Similarly, X_3 will change states only when X_1 and X_2 are 1s, the ENABLE is a 1, and a clock positive edge occurs.

The two AND gates combined with an *RS* flip-flop in Fig. 4·8 are so useful that most popular lines of flip-flops contain in a single integrated circuit container the flip-flop and its two AND gates, as shown in Fig. 4·9(a).

Figure 4·9(b) shows another very popular and useful flip-flop, which consists of the *RS* flip-flop and its two AND gates, but with the AND gates having the cross-coupling already permanently made inside the container. In this form the two lines taken outside are called *J* and *K,* and the flip-flop is called a *JK flip-flop.* This is most useful because analysis indicates that the *J* and *K* inputs act just as *RS* inputs for two 0 inputs—in this case the flip-flop never changes states. However, with a 0 on *J* and a 1 on *K* the flip-flop goes to the 0 state when a clock positive edge appears, and with a 1 on *J* and a 0 on *K* the flip-flop goes to 1 when a clock positive edge appears. The significant fact is that when both *J* and *K* are 1s, the flip-flop always changes states when a clock positive edge appears.

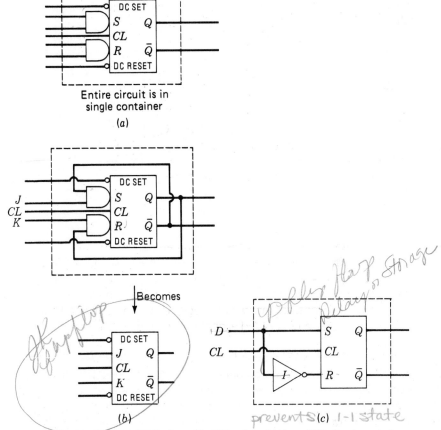

FIG. 4 • 9 *JK* and *D* flip-flops. (*a*) *RS* flip-flop with AND gates. (*b*) How *JK* flip-flop is made from *RS* flip-flops. (*c*) *D* flip-flop.

The flip-flops in Fig. 4·9(*a*) and (*b*) both have DC RESET and DC SET inputs. The bubbles at the input on the block diagram indicate that these are activated by 0 inputs and are normally held at a 1 level. When, for instance, a 0 is placed on the DC SET input, the flip-flop goes to a 1 level regardless of the clock or other inputs. DC SET and DC RESET should not be 0s at the same time, because this is forbidden and leads to an undetermined next state.

It is a general rule that bubbles, or small circles, at the DC SET and DC RESET inputs mean that these inputs are activated by 0 levels. The absence of these bubbles would mean that the inputs are activated by 1 levels and are normally at 0.

There is one other type of circuit now in general use, the *D flip-flop*. This flip-flop simply takes the value at its input when a clock pulse appears and remains in its same state until the next clock pulse appears. As shown in Fig. 4·9(*c*), the *D* flip-flop can be made from an *RS* flip-flop and an inverter.

The D flip-flop is very useful because when clocked it takes the state on its input and holds it until clocked again. Only a single input line is needed for a transfer, whereas the RS or JK flip-flops require two input lines.

An example of the use of JK flip-flops is shown in Fig. 4·10(a) and (b). Figure 4·10(a) shows the simplicity of a gated binary counter with JK flip-flops. Figure 4·10(b) shows a block diagram for a *binary up-down counter*. When the UP ENABLE line is high or a 1, the counter will count up, that is, 0, 1, 2, 3, 4, ... When the DOWN ENABLE line is a 1, the counter will count down, that is, 6, 5, 4, ... In general, the counter will increase its value by 1 if the UP ENABLE line is a 1 and a clock pulse arrives, or will decrease its value by 1 if the DOWN ENABLE input is a 1 and a clock pulse occurs.

A RESET line is provided which is used to DC RESET the counter to 0. This is activated by a 1 on the RESET line.

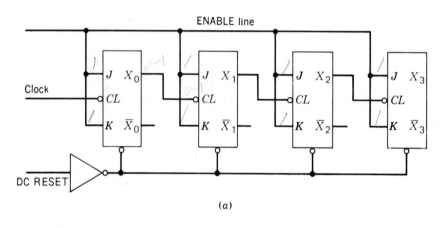

(a)

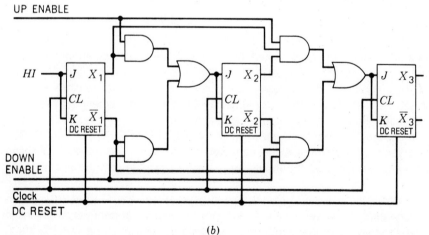

(b)

FIG. 4 • 10 Binary counters with JK flip-flops. (a) Gated-ripple counter. (b) Up-down counter.

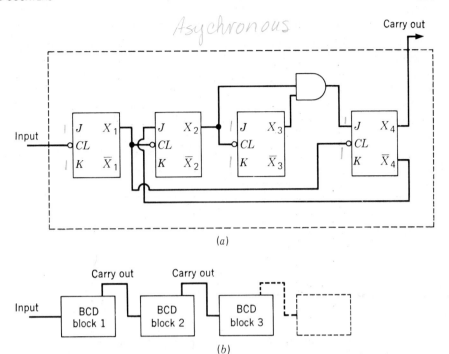

(a)

(b)

FIG. 4 • 11 BCD counters. *(a)* Decade, or BCD, counter. (*Note:* Unconnected inputs are 1s.)
(b) Cascading BCD counter blocks.

4 • 6 BCD COUNTERS

The binary counters considered so far all count to their limit before resetting to all
0s. Often it is desired to have counters count in binary-coded-decimal (BCD). Figure 4·11(a) shows a typical BCD counter. Examination of this counter shows that
it counts normally until it reaches 1001; that is, the sequence until that time is as
follows:

X_4	X_3	X_2	X_1
0	0	0	0
0	0	0	1
0	0	1	0
0	0	1	1
0	1	0	0
0	1	0	1
0	1	1	0
0	1	1	1
1	0	0	0
1	0	0	1
0	0	0	0

When the next negative-going edge at the input occurs, however, the BCD
counter returns to all 0s. At the same time (that is, during the interval when the

counter goes from 9 to 0) a negative-going signal edge occurs at the CARRY output. This CARRY output can be connected to the INPUT of another BCD counter, which will then be stepped by 1 when the first BCD stage goes from 9 to 0. This is shown in Fig. 4·11(b), where several four-flip-flop BCD stages are combined to make a large counter.

If we consider just two of the "BCD boxes," we find the sequence to be as follows:

8	4	2	1	8	4	2	1 value of bits
Y_4	Y_3	Y_2	Y_1	X_4	X_3	X_2	X_1
0	0	0	0	0	0	0	0
0	0	0	0	0	0	0	1
0	0	0	0	0	0	1	0
0	0	0	0	0	0	1	1
0	0	0	0	0	1	0	0
0	0	0	0	0	1	0	1
0	0	0	0	0	1	1	0
0	0	0	0	0	1	1	1
0	0	0	0	1	0	0	0
0	0	0	0	1	0	0	1
0	0	0	1	0	0	0	0
0	0	0	1	0	0	0	1
.	.	.	.	.	.	.	.
0	0	0	1	1	0	0	1
0	0	1	0	0	0	0	0
0	0	1	0	0	0	0	1
.	.	.	.	.	.	.	.

We have here counted to 21; this would continue until the counter reached 99, when the Y part would put out a signal which could be used to gate another stage to form a counter that could count to 999.

This sort of repetition of various "boxes," or "modules," such as a BCD counter, is facilitated by manufacturers placing an entire four-stage BCD counter in a single integrated circuit container, as is often the case.

One thing should be noted about the block diagram in Fig. 4·11(b). The flip-flops trigger (that is, are activated by) negative-going shifts in input levels at the input. This is indicated by the small circles of "bubbles" at the inputs. As a result, a flip-flop such as X_3 is activated when X_2 goes from a 1 to a 0, that is, when the 1 output makes a negative transition.

Also, note that unconnected inputs, such as the K inputs of all the flip-flops and the J inputs of X_1 and X_3, are assumed to be at 1 levels. This is due to the circuit construction.

4 • 7 INTEGRATED CIRCUITS

The flip-flops and gates used in modern computing machines—which range from calculators and microcomputers through the large high-speed computers—are constructed and packaged using what is called *integrated circuit technology*. When integrated circuits are used, one or more complete gates or flip-flops are packaged in a single integrated circuit (IC) container. The IC containers provide input and output pins or connections which are then interconnected using plated strips on circuit boards, wires, or other means to form complete computing devices.

In earlier computers, flip-flop and gate circuits were constructed using discrete electrical components such as resistors, capacitors, transistors, and before that, vacuum tubes and relays. Individual components were interconnected to form flip-flops and gates which were then interconnected to form computers. With the present-day IC technology, flip-flops and gates are fabricated in containers, and only the IC containers (or "cans") need be interconnected.

Two typical IC containers are shown in Fig. 4·12(a). One is called a *dual inline package* (in the trade it is called a "coffin" or a DIP), and this particular package has 14 pins which provide for external connections. For years this 14-pin package was a standard in the industry, and plastic and ceramic DIPs of this sort have been the largest selling IC package for some years.

There has been a tendency as IC technology improved, however, to increase the number of pins per package. Packages with 16 and 20 pins are becoming popular, and up to 70 pins per package can now be found in some IC manufacturers' products.

Figure 4·12(b) through (e) shows how several gates and flip-flops are packaged in a single container. The inputs and outputs are numbered, and each number refers to an external pin on the IC container. A ground connection and a positive power voltage are both required for each container so that only 12 pins remain to be used for the actual inputs and outputs to gates and flip-flops. (For these circuits, each V_{CC} pin is connected to a 5.5-V power supply and GND to 0 V or system ground.)

The particular circuits in Fig. 4·12 are called *transistor-transistor-logic* (TTL) circuits and are widely used high-speed circuits (see Chap. 5). These particular configurations with identical pin connections are manufactured by just about every major IC manufacturer, and packages from one manufacturer can be fairly easily substituted for another manufacturer's packages (provided the speed requirements or loading capabilities are not violated). There are many other packages with, for instance, 3 three-input NAND gates, 2 *RS* flip-flops, exclusive OR gates, etc.

In order to illustrate the use of IC packages in logic design we now examine an implementation of Fig. 4·13, using the packages shown in Fig. 4·12. The logic circuit in Fig. 4·13 is called a *shift register with feedback*,† for it consists of four

---

†This particular type of shift register with feedback is so widely used that complete books have been written about it. It is sometimes called a *linear shift register*, a *random sequence generation*, or a *linear recurring sequence generator*. With similar feedback connections, a register with as many flip-flops as desired can be made, thus forming counters with sequences of $2^N - 1$ for any reasonable N (where N is the number of flip-flops).

Consider the set of consecutive states taken by X_4 in the shift register in Fig. 4·13 to be its output sequence. Each nonzero 4-tuple occurs once in any 15-bit segment of this sequence, each nonzero 3-tuple occurs twice, etc. Adding a 15-bit segment of this sequence to another 15-bit segment bit-by-bit mod 2 (exclusive OR) will give still another 15-bit segment. These sequences are used in instruments to form random number generators and to generate bandpass noise; in radar for interplanetary observations; in communications systems to generate noise and encode or encrypt; and for many other purposes. See Birkhoff and Bartee for more information and references.

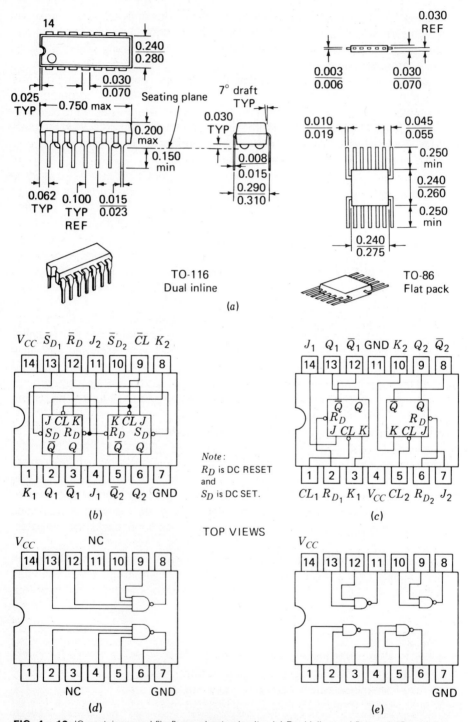

FIG. 4 • 12 IC containers and flip-flop and gate circuits. (*a*) Dual inline and flat pack IC containers. (*b*) Dual *JK* flip-flops with common clock and resets and separate sets. (*c*) Dual *JK* flip-flop with separate resets and clocks. (*d*) Dual four-input NAND gates. (*e*) Quad two-input NAND gates.

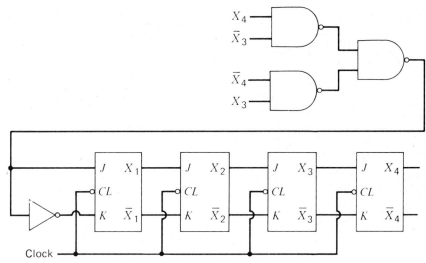

FIG. 4 • 13 Shift register with feedback.

flip-flops connected in a shift register configuration and "feedback" from these four flip-flops to the first flip-flop's inputs. This particular counter is started by setting a 1 in X_1 and 0s in X_2, X_3, and X_4. The sequence of states taken is then

$$
\left.
\begin{array}{cccc}
1 & 0 & 0 & 0 \\
0 & 1 & 0 & 0 \\
0 & 0 & 1 & 0 \\
1 & 0 & 0 & 1 \\
1 & 1 & 0 & 0 \\
0 & 1 & 1 & 0 \\
1 & 0 & 1 & 1 \\
0 & 1 & 0 & 1 \\
1 & 0 & 1 & 0 \\
1 & 1 & 0 & 1 \\
1 & 1 & 1 & 0 \\
1 & 1 & 1 & 1 \\
0 & 1 & 1 & 1 \\
0 & 0 & 1 & 1 \\
0 & 0 & 0 & 1 \\
\end{array}
\right\} \text{ basic sequence which repeats}
$$

$$
\begin{array}{cccc}
1 & 0 & 0 & 0 \\
0 & 1 & 0 & 0 \\
\end{array}
$$

Notice that this sequence contains 15 of the 16 possible 4-bit numbers that might be taken by this circuit. (Only the all 0 combination is excluded.) This is a widely used sequence which occurs in many instruments and has many uses in radar systems, sonar systems, coding encryption boxes, etc.

Quite often the sequence of states taken by a logic circuit is written in a *counter table*. The counter table for the above sequence is

X_1	X_2	X_3	X_4
1	0	0	0
0	1	0	0
0	0	1	0
1	0	0	1
1	1	0	0
0	1	1	0
1	0	1	1
0	1	0	1
1	0	1	0
1	1	0	1
1	1	1	0
1	1	1	1
0	1	1	1
0	0	1	1
0	0	0	1

In the counter table the flip-flops' names are first listed, followed by the starting states. Then the successive states taken are listed in order, and the final line contains the state preceding the starting state.

There is a straightforward technique for designing a logic circuit to realize a counter table; this technique is developed in Sec. 4·12. For now we return to the implementation of the counter in Fig. 4·13.

In order to implement this counter, we require four flip-flops and a gate circuit which will yield the function $\overline{X}_3 X_4 + X_3 \overline{X}_4$. As shown, this can be made with a NAND-to-NAND gate network with 3 two-input NAND gates. An inverter is also required. (A NAND gate can be used for this by connecting both inputs together.)

One problem remains: We need to start the counter with X_1 in state 1 and the other three flip-flops in state 0. Since DC RESET inputs are connected together on the flip-flops [see Fig. 4·12 (b)], it is necessary to use a trick for flip-flop X_1. This simply involves renaming the J and K inputs and the two outputs so that J becomes K, K becomes J, and the two output names are reversed. The DC RESET input then becomes a DC SET input for the new (renamed) flip-flop.

Figure 4·14 shows the circuit as finally designed. Notice how X_1 differs in connections from X_2 and X_3.

The logic circuit in Fig. 4·14 could be implemented using a printed circuit board to make the connections between IC containers, or the connections could be made by individual wires using any one of a number of interconnection boards manufactured by various companies. Placing a 0 (ground) on the DC RESET input sets the flip-flops to the desired starting conditions, and the circuit will then step through the desired states.

There are ten major lines of integrated circuits now being produced in substantial quantities. Table 4·1 lists these lines and gives some of the characteristics of each line. The first six IC lines in the table are called *bipolar logic* because they utilize conventional transistors in the IC packages, and the final three of the lines use what are called field effect transistors (FETs) and are fabricated using metallic

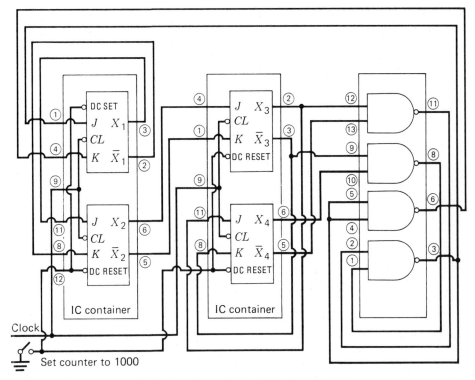

FIG. 4 • 14 Design of shift register in Fig. 4·13 using TTL. Circled numbers are pin numbers on IC containers.

oxide semiconductor (MOS) technology. The bipolar logic lines are widely used for constructing configurations on circuit boards which realize high-speed logic. Generally there are not so many gates and flip-flops in a package using bipolar logic, but these lines are fast and can be interconnected more readily than the MOS lines. The reason for this is that the bipolar logic lines use more power (primarily more current) for each gate or flip-flop and can, as a result, produce more current drive and therefore drive long cables, long wires, and, in general, more other circuits.

Associated with each gate and flip-flop in a line of integrated circuits are data concerning the gate's or flip-flop's ability to drive other circuits and be driven by other circuits. Typically the manufacturer gives data concerning the delays through the circuit, rise and fall times for output waveforms, the circuit's ability to drive other electrical loads, circuits, and long wires or cables. The manufacturer also generally provides information on how many other inputs to gates of a similar type a given gate can drive. In its simplest form, every input to every gate and flip-flop is the same, and the manufacturer simply stipulates how many inputs can be connected to a given output. Each input is then called a *standard load* and an output is said to be able to drive, for instance, eight standard loads. For some circuit lines, different gates and flip-flop inputs present different loads, and so an input to a particular kind of gate might have a number such as 2 or 3 associated with it and an

TABLE 4 • 1 INTEGRATED CIRCUIT LINES

NAME OF CIRCUIT LINE	ACRONYM	SPEED (DELAY PER GATE), ns	POWER PER GATE	GOOD FEATURES	PROBLEMS
Resistor-transistor logic	RTL	40	20 mW	Simple to manufacture and inexpensive. Easy to inter-connect.	Sensitive to noise. Low fan-out ratios. Low packing density.
Diode-transistor logic	DTL	20	8 mW	Inexpensive, good noise rejection, easy to use and interconnect.	Relatively low speed. _Low_ _medium_ packing density.
High-level diode-transistor logic	HLDTL	30	15 mW	A line of DTL specially made for industrial applications because of high noise rejection. Easy to use and interconnect.	Low speed, relatively high power dissipation, low packing density.
Transistor-transistor logic	TTL	4 (1.5 ns for Schottky clamped)	10 mW (20 mW for Schottky clamped)	Most popular line at present. Easy to interconnect; fast, wide selection of circuits available. MSI packages available, inexpensive.	Generates noise spikes, relatively high power dissipation, modest packing density.
Low-power transistor-transistor logic	LPTTL	20	1 mW	A low-power per gate TTL developed for space and other portable applications, easy to use and interconnect.	Low speed.

12-15 operations to manufacture.

158

Emitter-coupled logic	ECL	0.3	60 mW	Highest speed, generates little noise internally.	Difficult to interconnect. Low packing density. Difficult to cool.
p-channel metal oxide silicon	PMOS	50	0.1 mW	Low power, good packing density, easy to manufacture, inexpensive.	Slow and delicate, has limited ability to drive lines and to interface with other circuit lines.
n-channel metal oxide silicon	NMOS	10	0.1 mW	Faster than PMOS, relatively low power, good packing density, inexpensive and relatively easy to manufacture.	Has limited ability to drive lines and to interface with other circuits.
Complementary metal oxide silicon	CMOS	5	10 nW	Very low standby power required. Modest speed and packing density, reasonably priced.	Difficult to manufacture. Power consumption increases when switched at high speeds.
Integrated injection logic	IIL	1	0.1 mW	Fast, low power	Difficult to manufacture. Nonstandard logic gate formations.

Note: In this table W stands for watts, n for nano (= 10^{-9}), m for milli (= 10^{-3}), and s for seconds.

Very High Speed Integrated Circuit Technology   VHSIC

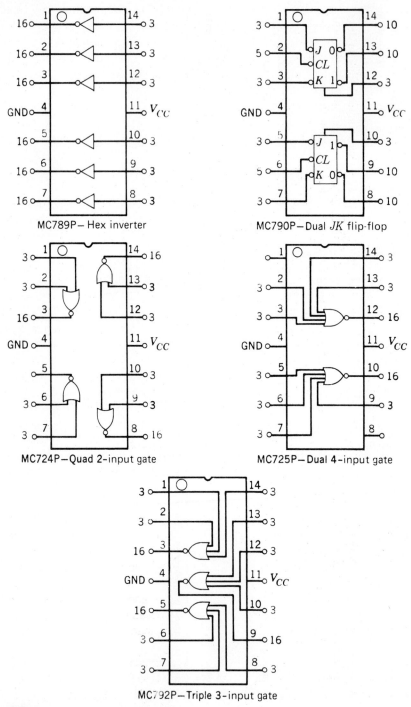

MC789P— Hex inverter

MC790P—Dual *JK* flip-flop

MC724P—Quad 2-input gate

MC725P—Dual 4-input gate

MC792P—Triple 3-input gate

FIG. 4 • 15 IC packages (top views).

output drive number such as 12. Then the designer must see that the sum of the input loads does not exceed the output drive number for a given output. As an example, Fig. 4·15 shows several RTL IC packages. Notice the numbers on the input and output pins. These give the input load for inputs and the output drive capability for outputs. The total of the input loads connected to an output must not exceed the output drive capability for that output.

The following chapter and the questions in this chapter develop this subject in more detail.

4 • 8 MEDIUM- AND LARGE-SCALE INTEGRATION

As has been explained, most circuits are now fabricated using the general technology of integrated circuitry. In this case the transistors, diodes, resistors, and any other components are fabricated together, using solid-state physics techniques, in a single container. In the most common technology, called *monolithic integrated circuitry,* a single semiconductor wafer is processed by photomasking, etching, diffusions, and other steps, thus producing a complete array of diodes, transistors, and resistors already interconnected to form one or more logic gates or flip-flops.

Two terms find wide use in discussing integrated circuitry. When more than one or two flip-flops or a few gates are packaged in a single container, the process is called *medium-scale integration* (MSI). Notice that medium-scale integration still refers to integrated circuits, except that even more circuits are housed in a single container. There are no fixed specific rules, but generally if more than 10 but less than 100 gates or flip-flops are in a single package, the manufacturer will refer to it as MSI.

When over 100 gates or flip-flops are manufactured in a single small container, the process is called *large-scale integration* (LSI). Some ideas of the complexity of arrays of this sort will be found in later chapters where memories and arithmetic-logic units consisting of thousands of flip-flops and gates in a single package will be studied.

Despite the various levels of integration, the circuits are surprisingly similar in principle, except that LSI tends to use a technology based on MOS, while MSI and "conventional" integrated circuits use "conventional" *npn* and sometimes *pnp* transistors fabricated on silicon chips. There are good reasons for this. MOS circuits require very small areas on a chip and use very little power, which is quite important considering the volume/complexity factor. On the other hand, as has been mentioned, conventional bipolar circuits are faster and more readily interconnected. As a result the MOS technology is more often used for larger arrays which can be treated only as complete single units rather than on a circuit-by-circuit basis.

Figure 4·16(a) shows a typical MSI package containing a complete BCD counter. This counter steps from 0 to 9 and then resets to 0 when X_1 (which is pin 5) is connected to clock 2 (which is pin 6). The counter is stepped each time an input clock waveform connected to clock 1 (pin 8) goes negative (on negative edges). The counter can be reset to the all 0s by connecting a 0 to the reset line

FIG. 4 • 16 (*a*) BCD counter in IC package. (*b*) Logic diagram for seven-segment decoder. (*c*) Designation for the seven segments. (*d*) Numbers formed by seven segments. (*e*) General arrangement for connecting seven-segment decoder. (Courtesy Fairchild Semiconductor.)

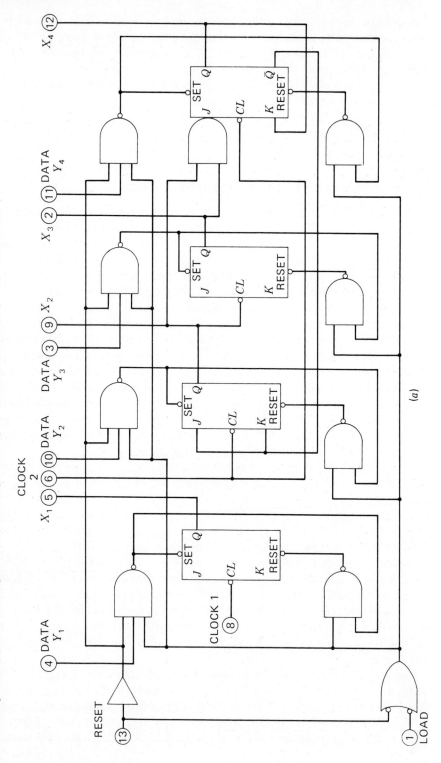

(*a*)

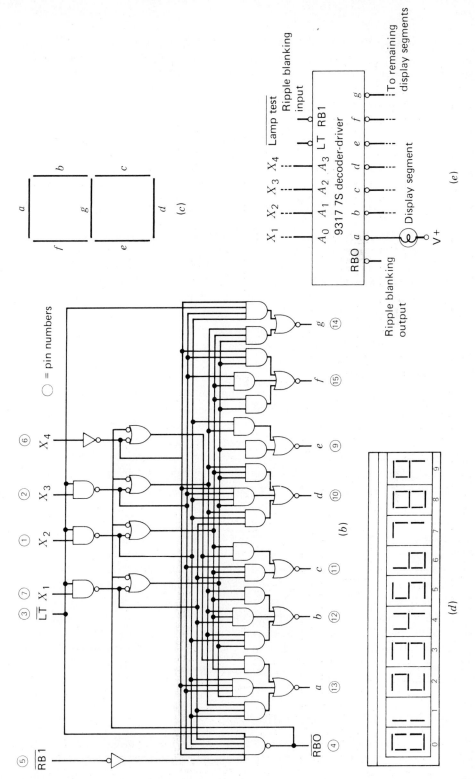

(c)

(e)

(b)

(d)

163

(pin 13). Data from four input wires connected to Y_1, Y_2, Y_3, and Y_4 will be loaded into flip-flops X_1, X_2, X_3, and X_4, respectively, if the LOAD input is pulled down to a 0. (It is normally a 1.)

An example of gate networks in MSI packages is shown in Fig. 4·16(b), which shows a *seven-segment decoder.* When decimal numbers are to be read from a digital calculator, instrument, microcomputer, etc., display devices using light-emitting diodes (LEDS) or liquid crystals are often used. Each digit of the display is formed from seven segments, each consisting of one light-emitting diode or crystal which can be turned on or off. A typical arrangement is shown in Fig. 4·16(c) which assigns the letters *a* through *g* to the segments. To make the digit 5, for example, segments *a, f, g, c,* and *d* are turned on. The set of digits as formed by these segments is shown in Fig. 4·16(d).

The seven-segment decoder in Fig. 4·16(b) can be connected to the outputs of the four flip-flops in the BCD counter in Fig. 4·16(a) by connecting the X_1, X_2, X_3, and X_4 outputs from Fig. 4·16(a) to the X_1, X_2, X_3, and X_4 inputs of Fig. 4·16(b). If the seven outputs *a* through *f* of Fig. 4·16(b) are then connected to a decimal digital display device, a counter with a decimal digit display, such as those in the familiar calculator, will be formed.

The BCD counter in Fig. 4·16(a) can be extended to several digits by connecting the X_4 output from one digit to the clock 1 input of the next-highest-order digit in the counter.

The seven-segment decoder in Fig. 4·16(b) has the ability to blank leading zeroes in a multidigit display, which is commonly done on calculators. Consider that a multistage BCD counter has been connected to several seven-segment decoders with one decoder per BCD counter stage. If the ripple blanking output (RBO) of each seven-segment decoder is connected to the ripple blanking input (RBI) of the seven-segment decoder of the next-higher-order digit in the counter and the ripple blanking input of the most significant digit's seven-segment decoder is connected to a 0 input, a blanking circuit will be formed. Then, for instance, in a four-stage counter the number 0014 will have the leading two 0s turned off or "blanked"; the number 0005 will be displayed as simply 5, with the 0 displays not turned on, etc. In effect, the circuit tests for a 0 value at its input and if the value is 0 and all the digits to its left are 0, then it turns off all seven segments and generates a blanking signal for the next rightmost digits light driver. The light test (LT) input can be used to test all seven segments simultaneously. Notice that making the light test input a 0 will cause all seven segments to go on.

In the MSI products of some manufacturers both a four-stage BCD counter and a seven-segment decoder are placed in the same package complete with a blanking input and output for each digit. This gives some feeling for the more complex MSI packages.

4·9 GATED FLIP-FLOP DESIGNS

It is important to note that flip-flops can be made from gates and, in fact, that this is a common practice. Figure 4·17 shows two NOR gates cross-coupled to form

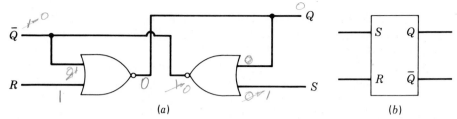

(a)   (b)

FIG. 4 • 17 *RS* flip-flop formed by cross-coupling NOR gates. (*a*) Cross-coupled NOR gates. (*b*) *RS* flip-flop corresponding to (*a*).

an *RS* flip-flop. The cross-coupled NOR gates in Fig. 4·17(*a*) have two inputs, *S* and *R,* and two outputs, *Q,* and $\overline{Q}$. This configuration realizes the *RS* flip-flop in Fig. 4·17(*b*).

The operation of the NOR gates is as follows: Consider both *S* and *R* to be 0s. If *Q* is a 1, then the rightmost NOR gate has a 1 and a 0 input and its output will be a 0. This places a 0 on the $\overline{Q}$ output and two 0s at the point to the leftmost NOR gate which will have a 1 output and the configuration will be stable. Similar reasoning will show that the configuration will be stable with a 1 on $\overline{Q}$ and a 0 on *Q.*

The *S* and *R* inputs work as follows: If a 1 is placed on the *R* input and a 0 on the *S* input, this will force the leftmost NOR gate to a 0 output, and this will cause the rightmost NOR gate to have two 0s as inputs and a 1 output. The flip-flop has now been cleared with a 0 on the *Q* output and a 1 on the $\overline{Q}$ output. Similar reasoning will show that a 1 on the *S* input and a 0 on the *R* input will force the NOR gate to flip-flop to the 1 state with *Q* a 1 and $\overline{Q}$ a 0.

4 • 10 THE GATED FLIP-FLOP

Just as Fig. 4·17 showed that two NOR gates can be used to form an *RS* flip-flop, Fig. 4·18 shows that two NAND gates can be used to form an *RS* flip-flop. In this case the inputs operate as follows: When both *S* and *R* are 1s, the flip-flop will remain in its present state, that is, it will not change states. If, however, the *R* input

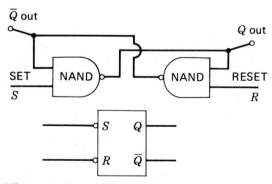

FIG. 4 • 18 Two NAND gates used to form an *RS* flip-flop.

goes to a 0, the NAND gate connected to R will have a 1 output regardless of the other feedback input to the NAND gate, and this will force the flip-flop to the 0 state (provided the S input is kept high or a 1).

Similar reasoning shows that making the S input a 0 will cause the NAND gate at the S input to have a 0 output, forcing the flip-flop to the 1 state (again provided the R input is kept high or 1).

If both inputs R and S are made 0s, the next state will depend on which input is returned to 1 first, and if both are returned to 1 simultaneously, the resulting state of the flip-flop will be indeterminate. As a result, this is a "forbidden," or "restricted," input combination.

The block diagram in Fig. 4·18 shows the flip-flop to be a conventional RS flip-flop, except that the two inputs are inverted. This is shown by the two "bubbles" at the R and S inputs. The circuit is therefore activated by 0s, and inputs are normally at 1.

A limited form of clocked flip-flop can be formed by using four NAND gates, as shown in Fig. 4·19(a). The circuit has an R and an S input and also a clock input CL. This flip-flop is activated by a postive level on the clock input, and not on a positive transition. Thus the flip-flop "takes" its input levels during the positive portion of clock signals, not changes in clock levels. To see how the circuit works, if the clock signal is at the 0 level, both NAND gates A and B will have 1 outputs, and so the NAND gate inputs to C and D will be 1 and, as before, the flip-flop will remain in its present state with either C or D on. (Both cannot be on because of the cross-coupling.)

If the clock signal goes to the 1 level and both inputs R and S are at the 0 level, the NAND gate outputs of A and B will still be 1s, and the flip-flop will remain in the same state.

If the R input is a 1 and the S input a 0, when the clock input goes positive (a 1), the NAND gate connected to R will have a 0 output and the NAND gate connected to S a 1 output, forcing the flip-flop consisting of C and D to the 0 state.

Similarly, a 1 at the S input and a 0 at the R input will cause the S input gate A to have a 0 output and the R input gate B a 1 output, forcing the flip-flop to the 1 state.

If both S and R are 1s and a clock pulse (1 level) occurs, the next state of the circuit is indeterminate.

A major problem with this circuit is that the R and S inputs should remain unchanged during the time the clock is a 1. This considerably limits the use of the circuit, leading to more complicated circuits to give the designer more flexibility. The primary value of the circuit is its simplicity.

The clocked RS flip-flop in Fig. 4·19(a) is often called a *latch*. The block diagram for a latch is the same as for an edge-triggered flip-flop, unfortunately, and it is necessary to "name" latches on block diagrams so that users will realize that the state taken by the flip-flop is determined by the R and S inputs during the positive clock level and not at the edge of the clock signal.

Manufacturers often put a number of latches in a single IC package. In this case the D-type latch shown in Fig. 4·19(c) is generally used. It takes the value at its input whenever the clock pulse input is high. It will effectively "track" input levels

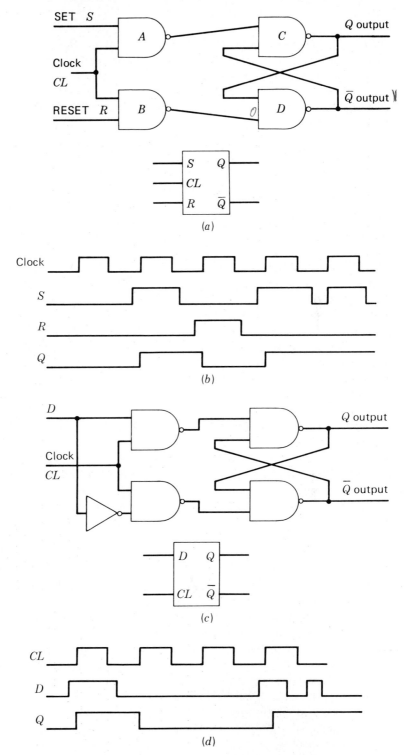

FIG. 4 • 19 Latches. (*a*) *RS* latch. (*b*) *RS* flip-flop waveforms. (*c*) *D* latch. (*d*) Waveforms for *D* latch.

as long as the clock input is high, as shown in Fig. $4 \cdot 19(d)$. If the clock input is lowered, the state will be the state the flip-flop had when the clock input was high. If the input returns to 0 just before or during a transistion in the input to the D latch, the final state the flip-flop takes will depend on the delay time for the flip-flop. Allowing input transitions during the time period when the clock is high is dangerous, unless there is assurance that the D input will not change for a safe period before the clock input is lowered.

4 • 11 THE MASTER-SLAVE FLIP-FLOP

In a computer the flip-flops are connected, either directly or through gates, to other flip-flops, and when clock edges occur, the resulting changes in a given flip-flop's output may lead to a change in the input to another flip-flop. This race problem is generally alleviated by using flip-flops that take the input information applied at the time of the clock's change in value or at the time just before the clock's change in value. Naturally these flip-flops are more complicated logically, but the elimination of worry about the effects of interaction between circuits has led to widespread use of such flip-flops.

To effect this "safety factor" in flip-flop operation, discrete component circuits use capacitors to store input signals and thus to "smooth out" and delay changes in input values.

Integrated circuits use pure logic to effect the same thing. The most used flip-flop design for IC flip-flops is that shown in Fig. $4 \cdot 20$. It is a *JK* flip-flop which actually consists of two flip-flops plus some gating. The two flip-flops are called *master* and *slave.* In Fig. $4 \cdot 20(a)$ the master flip-flop is comprised of the leftmost NAND gates, and the slave flip-flop of the rightmost NAND gates.

The flip-flop's output changes on the negative-going edge of the clock pulse. The basic timing is shown in Fig. $4 \cdot 20(a)$. First, on the positive-going edge and during the positive section of the clock pulse, the master flip-flop is loaded by the two leftmost NAND gates. Then, during the negative-going edge of the clock signal, the two rightmost NAND gates load the contents of the master flip-flop into the slave flip-flop just after the two input NAND gates are disabled. This means that the master flip-flop will not change in value while the clock is low (0); so the slave remains attached to a stable flip-flop, with a value taken during the positive section of the clock pulse.

A more detailed account of the action of the flip-flop is as follows: If the clock signal is low, the two input NAND gates both have 1 outputs; so the master flip-flop does not change states since it is a NAND gate flip-flop and can be set or cleared only by 0 inputs.

At the same time, as long as the clock signal is low (a 0), the inverter causes the inputs to the E and F NAND gates to force the value of the master flip-flop into the slave flip-flop. The situation is stable. The master cannot change, and the output flip-flop is "slaved" to the master.

When the clock starts positive, however, the circuit thresholds are arranged so that first the E and F NAND gates are disabled, and the NAND gates A and B to

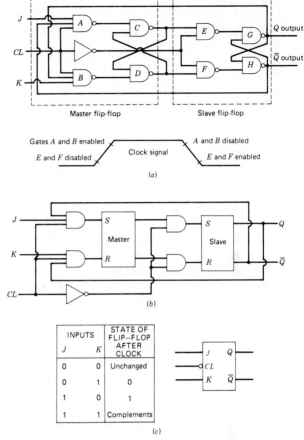

FIG. 4 • 20 (*a*) Gate arrangement for master-slave flip-flop. (*b*) *RS* flip-flop equivalent of (*a*). (*c*) Master-slave flip-flop state table and symbol.

the master flip-flop are then enabled. That is, the natural slope of the input signal plus delays and circuit values ensure that the two NAND gates *E* and *F* both have 1s at their output before any change in the master flip-flop can affect the slave flip-flop.

When the input clock signal is a 1, then the master flip-flop will accept information from the *J* and *K* inputs, and the slave flip-flop is now isolated from the master and will not change states regardless of changes in the master.

The operation of the master flip-flop is according to the following rules when the clock level is a 1:

1. If both *J* and *K* are at 0 levels, the two input NAND gates will have 1 outputs and the master flip-flop will not change values.
2. If the *J* input is a 1 and the *K* input a 0, the master flip-flop will go to its 1 state, with the upper master NAND gate having a 1 output.

3. If the J input is a 0 and the K input a 1, the master flip-flop will go to its 0 state, with the upper NAND gate having a 0 output.
4. If both J and K are 1s, the master flip-flop will take the value of the complement of the slave flip-flop (that is, a 0 if the slave is a 1 or a 1 if the slave is a 0).

When the clock signal goes negative to its 0 level, first the input NAND gates to the master flip-flop are disabled, that is, each output goes to a 1, then the E and F NAND gates are enabled (by the inverted clock signal). This causes the state of the master flip-flop to be transferred into the slave flip-flop.

The effects of all this are shown in the next-state table in Fig. 4·20(c), which indicates that the flip-flop is a JK flip-flop activated by a negative-going clock signal.

*4 • 12 COUNTER DESIGN

The design of a counter to sequence through a given set of states is straightforward, using the technique to be shown.

First, a counter table is made up listing the states to be taken. Let us assume that we wish a counter using three flip-flops to sequence as follows:

	A	B	C	
Starting state →	0	0	0	⎫
	1	1	1	
	1	0	1	
	1	1	0	⎬ this repeats
	0	0	1	
	0	1	0	⎭
	0	0	0	
	1	1	1	
	1	0	1	
	•	•	•	
	•	•	•	

This table shows that if the counter is in the state $A = 0$, $B = 0$, $C = 0$ and a clock pulse (edge) is applied, the counter is to step to $A = 1$, $B = 1$, $C = 1$. As another example, if $A = 0$, $B = 1$, and $C = 0$ and a clock pulse occurs, the counter is to step to $A = 0$, $B = 0$, $C = 0$. As can be seen, the counter "cycles" because after taking the state 010 it returns to 000 and then goes to 111, as before. If clock pulses continue, the counter will cycle through the six different states shown indefinitely.

We first use RS flip-flops for our first design, and JK flip-flops for the second.

---

*This section can be omitted at a first reading.

Now each flip-flop has two inputs, an R input and an S input. We therefore give the R input to A the name A^R, the S input to A the name A^S, the R input to B the name B^R, and so on through C^S.

The problem is now to derive Boolean algebra expressions for each of the six inputs to the flip-flops. To do this, we place the state table in a *counter design table* listing the three flip-flops and their states and also listing the six inputs to the flip-flops. This is shown in Fig. 4·21(a).

The values for A^R, A^S, B^R, B^S, C^R, C^S are then filled in using the following rule.

Design rule

Consider a row in the table and a specific flip-flop:

1. If the flip-flop's state is a 0 in the row and a 0 in the next row, place a 0 in the S input column and a d in the R input column for the flip-flop inputs.
2. If the flip-flop is a 1 in the row and a 1 in the next row, place a 0 in the R input column and a d in the S input column.
3. If the flip-flop is a 0 in the row and changes to a 1 in the next row, place a 1 in the S column and a 0 in the R column.
4. If the flip-flop is a 1 in the row and changes to a 0 in the next row, place a 1 in the R column and a 0 in the S column.

As an example, consider flip-flop A in Fig. 4·21(a). The flip-flop has value 0 in the first row and changes to a 1 in the second row. We therefore place a 1 in A^S in row 1 and a 0 in A^R in row 1. In row 2, A has value 1 and remains a 1 in row 3. We therefore fill a d in A^S and a 0 in A^R.

The reasoning behind these rules is as follows: Suppose that flip-flop A is in the 0 state and should stay in the 0 state when the next clock pulse is applied. The S input must then be 0 and the R input can be a 1 *or* a 0. Thus we must have 0 at A^R, but can place a d (for don't-care) at the A^S input.

If A is a 0 and should change to a 1, however, the S input to A must be a 1 and the R input a 0 when the next clock pulse is applied, so a 1 is placed in A^S and 0 in A^R.

It is instructive to examine several of the entries in the counter table in Fig. 4·21(a) to see how this rule applies.

Our goal is to generate the flip-flop inputs (A^R, A^S, etc.) in a *given* row so that when the counter is in the state in that row, each input will take the value listed. The next clock pulse will then cause the counter to step to the state in the next row below in the counter table.

The design of the counter now progresses as a Boolean algebra expression is formed from this table for A^R, A^S, B^R, B^S, C^R, and C^S, the inputs to the flip-flops, and then each expression is minimized. This is shown in Fig. 4·21(b), which gives the maps for the flip-flops' inputs. Notice that any unused counter states can be included as d's in the map as they are don't-cares because the counter never uses them. The minimal expressions are shown beside each map.

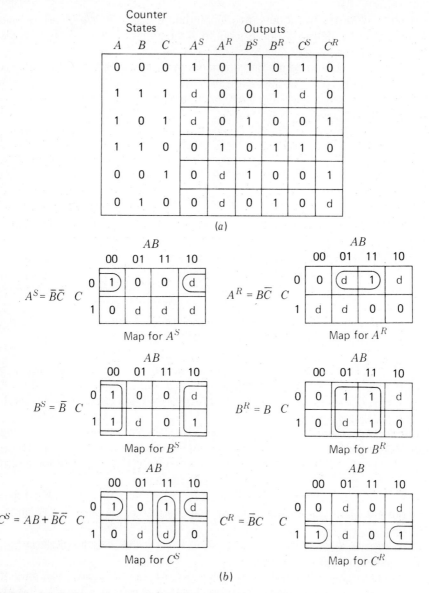

FIG. 4 • 21 Designing a counter using *RS* flip-flops.

The final step is to draw the block diagram for the counter using the minimal expressions. The final design for this counter is shown in Fig. 4·22.

Now suppose that we desire to design the above counter using *JK* flip-flops. The procedure will be basically the same, except that the rules for filling in the counter design using *JK* flip-flops will be different.

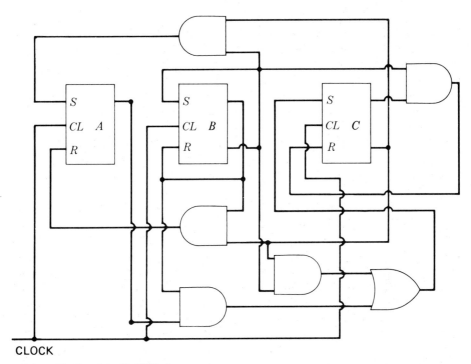

FIG. 4 • 22 Counter with *RS* flip-flops.

The inputs will now be A^J, A^K, B^J, B^K, C^J, and C^K. The rules for *JK* flip-flops are given in the following.

Design rule

For a given flip-flop in a selected row, the *J* and *K* inputs to the flip-flop are filled in as follows:

1. If the flip-flop is a 0 in the row and remains a 0 in the next row, place a 0 in the *J* input column and a d in the *K* input column.
2. If the flip-flop is a 1 in the row and remains a 1 in the next row, place a 0 in the *K* input column and a d in the *J* input column.
3. If the flip-flop is a 0 in the row and changes to a 1 in the next row, place a 1 in the *J* input column and a d in the *K* input column.
4. If the flip-flop is a 1 in the row and changes to a 0 in the next row, place a d in the *J* input column and a 1 in the *K* input column.

The reasoning behind the above rules is as follows: Suppose that a given flip-flop, say *A*, is in the 0 state and should stay in the same state when the next clock pulse occurs. The input A^K must be a 0 at that time, but A^J can be either a 0 at that time or a 1, so the A^J input is essentially a d (or don't-care) input. If *A* must go from a 0 to a 1, however, the A^K input *must* be a 1 but the A^J input can be either a 0 or a 1 (since the flip-flop will change states if both inputs are 1s). Notice that

A	B	C	A^J	A^K	B^J	B^K	C^J	C^K
0	0	0	1	d	1	d	1	d
1	1	1	d	0	d	1	d	0
1	0	1	d	0	1	d	d	1
1	1	0	d	1	d	1	1	d
0	0	1	0	d	1	d	d	1
0	1	0	0	d	d	1	0	d

$A^J = \bar{B}\bar{C}$

$$\begin{array}{c} AB \\ \begin{array}{cccc} 00 & 01 & 11 & 10 \end{array} \\ \begin{array}{c|c|c|c|c|} 0 & 1 & 0 & d & d \\ \hline 1 & 0 & d & d & d \end{array} \end{array}$$

C

$A^K = \bar{C}$

$$\begin{array}{c} AB \\ \begin{array}{cccc} 00 & 01 & 11 & 10 \end{array} \\ \begin{array}{c|c|c|c|c|} 0 & d & d & 1 & d \\ \hline 1 & d & d & 0 & 0 \end{array} \end{array}$$

C

$B^J = 1$

$$\begin{array}{c} AB \\ \begin{array}{cccc} 00 & 01 & 11 & 10 \end{array} \\ \begin{array}{c|c|c|c|c|} 0 & 1 & d & d & d \\ \hline 1 & 1 & d & d & 1 \end{array} \end{array}$$

C

$B^K = 1$

$$\begin{array}{c} AB \\ \begin{array}{cccc} 00 & 01 & 11 & 10 \end{array} \\ \begin{array}{c|c|c|c|c|} 0 & d & 1 & 1 & d \\ \hline 1 & d & d & 1 & d \end{array} \end{array}$$

C

$C^J = A + \bar{B}$

$$\begin{array}{c} AB \\ \begin{array}{cccc} 00 & 01 & 11 & 10 \end{array} \\ \begin{array}{c|c|c|c|c|} 0 & 1 & 0 & 1 & d \\ \hline 1 & d & d & d & d \end{array} \end{array}$$

C

$C^K = \bar{B}$

$$\begin{array}{c} AB \\ \begin{array}{cccc} 00 & 01 & 11 & 10 \end{array} \\ \begin{array}{c|c|c|c|c|} 0 & d & d & d & d \\ \hline 1 & 1 & d & 0 & 1 \end{array} \end{array}$$

C

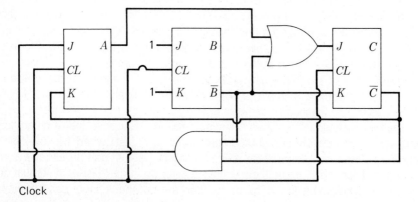

Clock

FIG. 4 • 23 Design for a *JK* flip-flop counter.

there are more d's in the rules for *JK* flip-flops than for *RS* flip-flops because of the ability of the flip-flops to change states when both inputs are 1s.

The maps for each input to the flip-flops A^J, A^K, B^J, B^K, C^J, and C^K are drawn as before, the expression for each flip-flop's input is minimized, and the block diagram for the counter is then drawn as in Fig. 4·23. Notice that fewer gates are used for the counter in Fig. 4·23 than for that in Fig. 4·22. This is because of the additional d's in the maps, and it will generally, although not always, be the case. (Sometimes the *RS* and *JK* designs will be the same; *JK* flip-flops cannot require more gates for a given counter sequence.)

QUESTIONS

1. Draw a set of waveforms for *S* and *R* and *X* and $\overline{X}$ (as in Fig. 4·2) so that the flip-flop in Fig. 4·1 will have the output signals 0011010 on the output line.

2. If the AND gate connected to the *R* input of X_1 in Fig. 4·3 fails so that its p.141 output is always 1, we would expect, after a few transfers, that X_1 would always be in the _____ state. Why?

3. Draw a set of waveforms for *S* and *R* (as in Fig. 4·2) so that the flip-flop in Fig. 4·1 will have the output signals 101110001 on the *X* output line.

4. If the $\overline{X}$ output of flip-flop *X* is connected to an inverter, the inverter's output will always be the same as the *X* output of the flip-flop. True or false? Why?

5. Draw a set of waveforms as in Fig. 4·5(*d*) for the flip-flop in Fig. 4·5(*b*) so that the flip-flop will have the output signals 0010110 on its *Y* output line.

6. In Fig. 4·6, if flip-flop X_2 "sticks" (that is, fails) in its 0 state, X_3 will have a 1 output after (*a*) clock pulse 1, (*b*) clock pulse 2, (*c*) clock pulse 3, and for each clock pulse thereafter.

7. Draw an input waveform as in Fig. 4·6 so that X_3 will have the output signal p. 145 00010011010 if X_1, X_2, and X_3 are started in the 0 state.

8. Draw a set of waveforms as in Fig. 4·5(*c*) for the flip-flop in Fig. 4·5(*a*) so that the flip-flop will have the output signals 10111001 on its *X* output line.

9. The binary counter in Fig. 4·7 uses flip-flops which act on positive transitions. Draw a block diagram of a binary counter with "bubbles" on the CL inputs (that is, with flip-flops which act on *negative*-going clock, or CL, inputs).

10. If the X_3 line (the output of X_3) is connected to the input line in Fig. 4·6, a *ring counter* is formed. If this circuit is started with $X_1 = 0$, $X_2 = 1$, and $X_3 = 1$, draw the waveform at X_1, X_2, and X_3 for six clock pulses.

11. Redraw Fig. 4·7 as it is but place bubbles on each CL input to X_1, X_2, and X_3 [that is, make the same drawing but use the flip-flop in Fig. 4·5(*b*) instead of that in Fig. 4·5(*a*)]. Redraw the waveforms in Fig. 4·7 for this circuit.

12. Does the counter in Question 11 count up or down?

13. Make a single change in Fig. 4·7 by connecting the output of flip-flop X_2 to the CL input of X_3 instead of the $\overline{X}_2$ output of X_2. Now redraw the waveforms in Fig. 4·7 for this changed configuration. p. 146

14. After answering Question 13, using the flip-flop in Fig. 4·5(*a*), design a counter that counts as follows:

X_3	X_2	X_1
0	0	0
0	1	1
0	1	0
1	0	1
1	0	0
1	1	1
1	1	0
0	0	1
0	0	0
0	1	1
0	1	0
1	0	1
.	.	.

15. After answering Question 13, using only the flip-flop in Fig. 4·5(a), design a counter that counts as follows:

X_3	X_2	X_1
0	0	0
1	1	1
1	1	0
1	0	1
1	0	0
0	1	1
0	1	0
0	0	1
0	0	0
1	1	1

This counter counts *down*. Figure 4·7 counts *up*.

16. For Fig. 4·10(b) draw up enable, down enable, and clock waveforms so that the counter starts at 000 and counts as follows:

X_3	X_2	X_1
0	0	0
0	0	1
0	1	0
0	1	1
1	0	0
0	1	1
0	1	0
0	1	1

p. 150

17. In Fig. 4·10(a), when the ENABLE line is a 1, the counter counts at the occurrence of a negative-going clock edge. Draw the output waveforms for FF0, FF1, and FF2 for these waveforms. Start the flip-flops at 0.

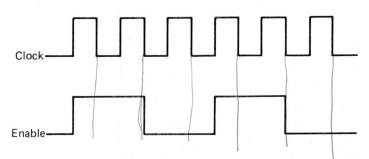

18. Draw a clock waveform and waveforms for the output of the AND gate connected to the S input of X_1, the R input of X_2, and the 1 output of X_1, X_2, and X_3 for Fig. 4·8.

19. Suppose that the AND gate in Fig. 4·11(a) fails so that its output is always a 0. Write the sequence or show the waveform through which this counter will go in response to clock signals.

20. Suppose that the AND gate's output in Fig. 4·11(a) is connected to the K input of X_4 instead of the J input. How will the computer count?

21. For Fig. 4·11(b), the carry-out from block 1 to block 2 goes from 1 to 0 every _____ clock pulses. The carry-out from block 3 to block 4 goes from 1 to 0 every _____ clock pulses.

22. (a) If we replace block 2 in Fig. 4·11(b) with the four-stage ripple counter in Fig. 4·10(a), using the 1 output of FF3 in that counter as the carry-out line, the carry-out line from block 2 will go from 1 to 0 after how many clock pulses?

(b) For the configuration in (a), after how many clock pulses will the carry-out from block 2 go from 0 to 1?

23. Using the circuits in Fig. 4·12, design a gated-clocked binary counter. *p. 154*

24. Design a BCD counter using the flip-flops in Fig. 4·12.   *b) synchronous J-K*

25. Using the circuits in Fig. 4·12, design a gating network with inputs A, B, and C which will have output 1 when $\overline{A}\,\overline{B}\,C$ or $A\overline{B}\,\overline{C}$ are 1s.

26. Using the circuits in Fig. 4·12, design a BCD counter.

27. The inputs to the NOR gates in Fig. 4·15 have 0s on them when not connected. Does connecting only two inputs of a four-input NOR gate give a gate which acts as a two-input gate? Explain your answer. *Note:* Inputs to TTL gates, such as in Fig. 4·12, which are left unconnected, automatically act as if they have 1s on them.

28. Does a three-input NAND gate, as in Fig. 4·12, act as a two-input gate would if only two inputs were used? Explain your answer.

29. Design the counter in Fig. 4·13 using the blocks in Fig. 4·15.

30. Give the states of the flip-flops in the following circuit after each of the first five clock signals (pulses) are applied. The circuit is started in the state A_1 = 0, A_2 = 0, A_3 = 1.

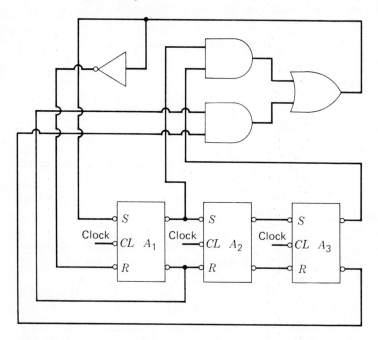

31. Redesign the following circuit using only RS flip-flops and NOR gates:

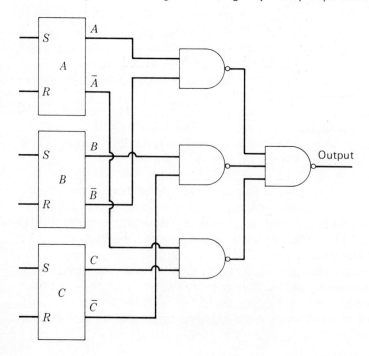

32. The gate block in the following circuit is an "equal to" combinational network realizing the Boolean function $\overline{X}_3\overline{X}_2 + X_3X_2$. If this set of three flip-flops is started in $X_1 = 1$, $X_2 = 0$, and $X_3 = 0$, what will the sequence of internal states be? As a start, the first three states can be listed as follows:

X_1	X_2	X_3	
1	0	0	
1	1	0	after first clock pulse
0	1	1	after second clock pulse
.	.	.	(you are to continue this list)

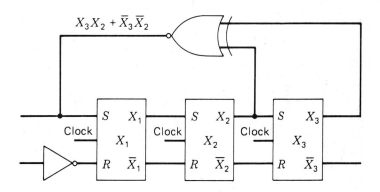

33. The following circuit is started in $C_1 = 1$ and $C_2 = 0$. The circuit divides the number of positive-going input edges (positive pulses) by what number? (That is, every _____ input pulses the output will return to 0.) Justify your answer.

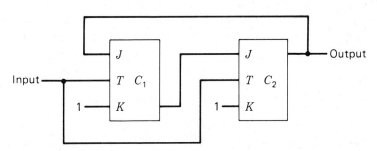

34. In Fig. 4·20, write 0s and 1s for all gate inputs and outputs when the CL input is 1, J is a 1, K is a 1, and the flip-flop is in the 1 state.

35. In Fig. 4·20, why are E and F enabled at a lower level than A and B?

36. In Fig. 4·20, if the feedback connection from the C NAND gate output to the input of the D NAND gate is broken (open), in what state will we probably find the flip-flop?

37. Using your result from Question 34, explain how the flip-flop in Fig. 4·20 complements when J and K are 1s and a negative edge appears.

38. The following sequence is to be realized by a counter consisting of three *RS* flip-flops. Use AND and OR gates in your design.

	A_1	A_2	A_3	
	0	0	0	starting state
	0	1	0	
Sequence repeats after this segment	0	1	1	
	0	0	1	
	1	0	0	
	1	1	0	
	0	0	0	
	.	.	.	

39. Design a counter using only *JK* flip-flops, AND gates, and OR gates which counts in the following sequence:

0	0	0	
0	1	0	
0	1	1	this repeats
1	0	0	
0	0	0	
0	1	0	
0	1	1	
1	0	0	
0	0	0	

40. Design a counter using three *JK* flip-flops X_1, X_2, and X_3, and whatever gates you would like, which counts as follows:

X_1	X_2	X_3	
0	0	0	starting state
0	1	1	after first clock pulse
0	1	0	after second clock pulse
1	1	1	after third clock pulse
1	0	1	after fourth clock pulse
0	0	0	after fifth clock pulse
0	1	1	
0	1	0	

41. The following sequence is to be realized by a counter consisting of three *JK* flip-flops. Use AND and OR gates in your design.

	A_1	A_2	A_3	
	0	0	0	starting state
	0	1	1	
Sequence repeats after this segment	0	1	0	
	0	0	1	
	1	0	1	
	1	1	0	
	0	0	0	
	.	.	.	

42. If the S and R inputs to Fig. 4·18 are both made 0s and the S is made a 1 followed by R, what will be the resulting state of the flip-flop?

43. The NAND gate flip-flop in Fig. 4·18 will have what outputs on the 0 and 1 lines if both SET and RESET are made 0s?

44. Design a counter using three JK flip-flops X_1, X_2, and X_3, and whatever gates you would like, which counts as follows:

X_1	X_2	X_3	
0	0	1	starting state
0	1	1	after first clock pulse
0	1	0	after second clock pulse
1	1	1	after third clock pulse
1	0	1	after fourth clock pulse
0	0	1	after fifth clock pulse
0	1	1	
0	1	0	

45. The rules for designing counters using JK and RS flip-flops have been given. Derive the rules for designing a counter using D flip-flops.

46. Design a counter using D flip-flops which count in the same manner as the example given for JK and RS flip-flops.

5
DIGITAL
CIRCUITS

Electronics circuitry and electronic devices have undergone vast improvements since the digital computer was first introduced. The large arrays of vacuum tubes with their glass shells and heated filaments have been squeezed into small plastic integrated circuit (IC) containers by industrious solid-state physicists and electronic circuit designers. Even the past 10 years have brought a significant change, and smaller, faster, less expensive devices and circuits are continually being introduced. Basic changes are not quite so rapid, however, and most of the improvements are now due to refinements of existing technology rather than radical new ideas. It should be noted, though, that the digital integrated electronics circuit industry is the largest segment of the electronics industry, and descriptions of new designs and improvements on old designs continue to fill the pages of the computer journals.

The study of the actual circuits used in electronic computers—from microcomputers to the largest systems—centers around IC technology. Further, the integrated circuits now in general use are generally variations of several basic circuit designs. In fact, it is safe to say that over 98 percent of all computers now contain circuits using the basic circuits described in Table 4·1.

The intent of this chapter is first to explain some of the circuit principles which relate to all digital circuits and then to examine, one at a time, the major circuit technologies. Basic facts about the general properties of each circuit technology are given, and some of the advantages and disadvantages of each type of circuit are pointed out. No attempt is made to be comprehensive; only representative circuits have been selected and explained.

It is possible to omit this chapter on a first reading without loss of continuity, and it is also possible to sample selected sections and examine some, but not all, of the circuit lines. However, the author feels that an overview of this subject matter is well worth the effort involved, and having spent many hours designing circuits, he has strong personal feelings concerning the value of this material. He also realizes, however, that this subject is often taught in other courses and that time limitations may not permit inclusion of the material.

5 • 1 COMPUTER CIRCUITS

Although a modern electronic computer is composed of a large number of electronic components, an entire machine will usually contain only a few types of basic circuits. The current theory of computer construction dictates the use of a few basic "blocks" which are used over and over. Construction of this sort greatly simplifies the design of the machines, increases reliability—since only a few well-tested circuits are used—and makes maintenance of machines easier and faster. The circuits used in these blocks are simple in principle. They are simpler, for instance, than most of the circuits used in modern radio and television sets. There are several types of circuits: circuits which perform logical operations on input signals; storage elements, such as flip-flops, which store bits of information; and accessory circuits, such as coaxial line drivers, neon-light indicator circuits, etc.

The circuits which will be described have been classified according to the functions they perform. For instance, following the description of diode and transistor characteristics, the first type of circuit to be described is the diode AND gate. This is followed by a diode-and-transistor AND gate. Then, finally, an all-transistor AND gate is described. The intent here is, therefore, to describe the function each circuit performs and how one circuit differs from another and, at the same time, to explain the manner in which the circuits function.

No attempt has been made to describe every circuit configuration now in use; only representative circuits of each type are included in the discussion.

5 • 2 CHARACTERISTICS OF DIODES AND TRANSISTORS USED IN SWITCHING CIRCUITS

Before analyzing logic circuits, we shall briefly describe the general characteristics of junction transistors and diodes when used as switching devices. This does not imply that the characteristics of these devices in switching circuits are radically different from those used in audio or other circuitry; however, most general introductions to transistors treat them as linear amplifying devices. When transistors are used in switching circuits, they are generally operated at or near the extremes of their operating points. That is, they are quite often operated either in a "cutoff" or in a "saturated" condition. Therefore some of the characteristics which are most important to the computer circuit are of less importance in other fields.

Also, no attempt will be made to explain the physics of junction semiconductor devices. Semiconductor physics and a detailed analysis of the operating characteristics of junction devices are so interwoven with the manufacturing techniques, the geometry of the junctions, and many other considerations that the subject has grown into a highly specialized (and very fascinating) field, which is treated in detail in other books. For our purposes, and for the purposes of most users of circuit devices, the operational characteristics of these devices are what are important, and we shall limit our discussion to these operational characteristics.

The characteristics of semiconductor diodes will first be briefly noted. A semiconductor diode is made of two pieces of semiconductor material† of different types joined together. One type of semiconductor material is called *p-type* material, and the other *n-type* material [refer to Fig. 5·1(a)].‡ When two differing types of semiconductor material are joined together, a *semiconductor junction* is formed, and a single junction is also called a *diode*. In Fig. 5·1(a) the *p*-type material is referred to as the *anode* of the diode and the *n*-type material is called the *cathode* of the diode. Figure 5·1(a) also shows the schematic symbol for the diode.

A study of semiconductor, or solid-state, devices would explain the physical internal workings of the diode. However, our sole interest here is to view the diode as a component in electronic switching circuits; so we will examine the diode from the viewpoint of its electrical characteristics only. When we apply an electric voltage, possibly through a resistor as in Fig. 5·1(b), so that the anode of the diode is positive with respect to the cathode, the diode is said to be *forward biased*. A diode which is forward biased will conduct current rather freely. (*Conventional current* will be used in our discussion; conventional current flows from positive to negative.)

Figure 5·1(c) shows a typical characteristic curve for a semiconductor germanium diode and silicon diode. Most of the diodes in computer use are silicon diodes. Notice that, when forward biased, the silicon diode drops on the order of 0.7 V.§ Notice that the forward-biased region on the graph lies to the right of the ordinate of the graph.

When the cathode of a diode is positive with respect to the anode, the diode is said to be *reversed biased,* and it will present a very high resistance to current flow [refer to Fig. 5·1(b) and (c)]. This ranges from tens to hundreds of megohms.¶

A diode may therefore be thought of as a kind of electronic switch which is closed (freely passes current) when forward biased and open (passes almost no current) when reverse biased.

The most commonly used transistors in computer circuits are *junction transistors,* constructed of either a piece of *n* material between two pieces of *p* material or a piece of *p* material between two pieces of *n* material. The first of these is

---

†A semiconductor has a conductivity roughly halfway between those of metals, which are "good" conductors, and insulators, which conduct poorly.

‡*n*-type material has an excess of negative current carriers (electrons), while *p*-type material has an excess of positive current carriers (holes). Thus current flows readily when the *p*-type material is positive and the *n*-type material negative. Alternatively, very little current flows when the *p*-type material is negative and the *n*-type material is positive.

§Provided 1 mA or more of current flows (1mA = 1 milliampere, or 1×10^{-3} A).

¶The part of the curve for silicon diodes which is below the 0 current level is somewhat distorted since a diode actually passes less than a few hundred nanoamperes when reverse biased (1nA = 10^{-9} A).

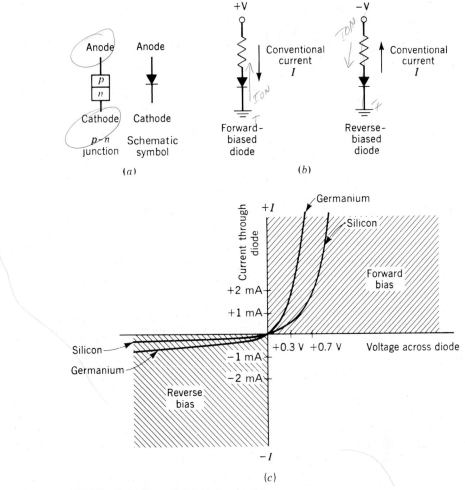

FIG. 5 • 1 Diode symbol and characteristics.

called a *pnp* transistor, and the second an *npn* transistor. Figure 5·2(*a*) and (*b*) shows this. The pieces of *n* and *p* material are named; for the *pnp* transistor the "middle" piece is *n*-type and is called the *base,* while the two *p*-type pieces are called the *collector* and *emitter* and are further identified with the schematic symbols shown in Fig. 5·2(*a*). For the *npn* transistor the *p*-type material is the base, and the two pieces of *n*-type material are the emitter and collector.

A transistor's operating characteristics are generally studied by connecting the transistor in a circuit, varying the input currents and voltages, and plotting the resulting output currents and voltages.

Figure 5·3 shows an *npn* transistor in a circuit with the emitter grounded. The currents and voltages in the circuit are identified as follows: The current *into* the

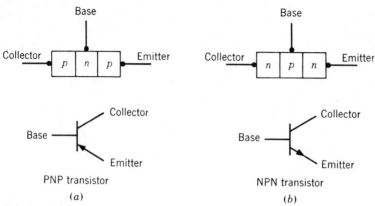

FIG. 5 • 2 Transistor symbols and designations.

base of the transistor is called I_b; the current *into* the collector is called I_c; the current *into* the emitter is called I_e; the voltage of the collector is called V_{ce} (this is the voltage between the collector and the emitter); the voltage at the base is called V_{be} (the voltage between base and emitter).

In this configuration the transistor can be operated in three modes: (1) *active region,* (2) *saturated,* and (3) *cutoff.*

First let us define these terms and then examine the transistor's characteristics in each region of operation.

1. *Active*   The *npn* transistor in Fig. 5·3(a) is in the *active region* when current flows into the base, that is, when I_b is positive and when V_{ce} is more positive than V_{be} (the collector is more positive than the base).
2. *Saturated*   The *npn* transistor in Fig. 5·3(a) is in the *saturated region* when positive current flows into the base (I_b is positive) and when V_{ce} is equal to or less than V_{be} (the collector is less positive than the base).
3. *Cutoff*   The *npn* transistor is said to be *cut off* when either no current flows into the base or current flows out of the base (when I_b is either 0 or negative).

Active   When transistors are used in television or radio circuits, they are most often operated in the active region, because a small change in base current then causes a large change in collector current, thus making it possible to amplify the input. To examine this, a set of curves is presented in Fig. 5·3(b) for a widely used transistor, the 2N706.

To see an example of the current gain, notice that if in Fig. 5·3(b) the voltage V_{ce} is held at 8 V and I_b, the base current, is at 0.45 mA, then I_c, the collector current, will be about 15 mA. If I_b is changed to 0.85 mA, a change of 0.4 mA, I_c changes to 30 mA, a change of 10 mA. Thus the collector current has changed more than the base current by a factor of 30.

In the active region the base-emitter junction is forward biased and the base-collector junction is reverse biased. This means that current flows easily from base to emitter but that base-to-collector current is small. As current is increased

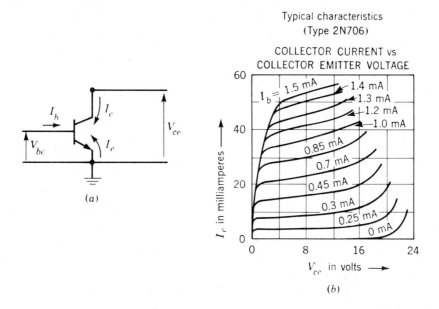

Typical characteristics
(Type 2N706)

COLLECTOR CURRENT vs
COLLECTOR EMITTER VOLTAGE

(a)

(b)

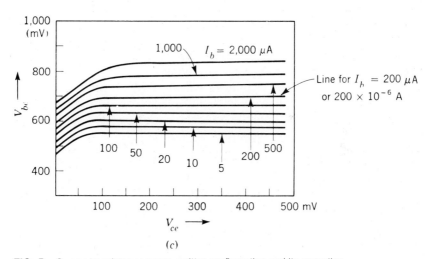

(c)

FIG. 5 • 3 *npn*-transistor common-emitter configuration and its operation.

through the base-emitter junction, however, this stimulates current flow through the base from the collector to the emitter. The fact that a small change in base current causes a large change in current from the collector to the emitter is the "secret" of the transistor's usefulness as an amplifier. The base of a transistor is made very thin, which encourages the flow of current through the base (from collector to emitter), once the base area begins to "break down" (that is, to permit current flow) due to the current from base to emitter. Notice that this base-emitter current also controls the collector-emitter current.

Saturated　When the input current I_b is positive but V_{ce} is less than V_{be}, then the base-collector and the base-emitter junctions will both be forward biased and the transistor will "look like" two forward-biased diodes. Current will flow freely in both the base and the base-collector junctions.†

Cutoff　When no current or negative current flows into the base (that is, V_{be} is negative), the transistor is cut off and virtually no current flows in the collector (I_c = 0). This can be seen in Fig. 5·3(b), for with 0.25 mA into the base, less than 3 mA will flow in the collector, and for I_b equal to 0, virtually no current flows in the collector (I_c = 0).‡ If V_{be} is negative (the base is negative with respect to the emitter), both junctions of the transistor will be reverse biased and virtually no current will flow in the circuit (I_c and I_b will be 0).

Let us now examine the operation of the circuit in Fig. 5·4(a). A load resistor of 500 Ω has been added to the collector circuit, and an input resistor of 2,000 Ω to the base circuit. The plot of an input–output signal for this circuit is shown in Fig. 5·4(b).

In Fig. 5·4(b) the input starts at 0 V, so that no base current flows in the transistor, and it is cut off. As a result the output is at +5 V, since no current flows in the collector and no voltage is dropped across R2.

As the input starts positive, current begins to flow into the base and the transistor passes into the active region. This causes current to flow in the collector circuit, and this current flows through resistor R2, and so the output begins to fall. At some point the output will fall below the voltage at the base, which will be held at about 0.8 V—the base-emitter junction is well forward biased by the current through the resistor R1—and the transistor will be saturated.

When the voltage at the input goes back to 0 V, the process is reversed; the transistor passes from saturation through the active region and is again cut off.

Notice that the output from the transistor is an "inverted" near-replica of the input; so the circuit is generally called an *inverter*.

Note: One general comment should be made. An *npn* transistor is, strictly speaking, "cut off" when the base current is 0 or negative, which means, for our circuits, when the base voltage V_{be} is 0 or negative. In general practice, a transistor is said to be cut off when "negligible" current flows. This is, of course, not precise, nor can it be made so. What is meant is that so little current flows into the base that virtually no current flows in the collector circuit.

The operation of a *pnp* transistor is essentially the same as that of the *npn* transistor, except that all the polarities discussed are reversed. For instance, the

---

†Some curves for a saturated transistor are shown in Fig. 5·3(c). Notice that the collector voltages are less than the base voltages. Also notice that the base voltages are very "flat" for wide ranges of collector voltage. For instance, with a base current I_b of 1,000 μA (microampere) (1 μA = 10^{-6} A), the base voltage will be about 0.75 V when the collector is from 0.1 to 0.5 V.

‡The slight "turnup" in the ends of the curves in Fig. 5·3(b) is due to junction breakdown at higher voltages. The transistor is to be operated with collector voltage of less than + 10V.

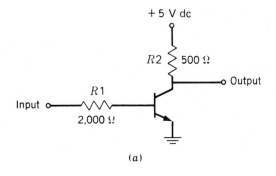

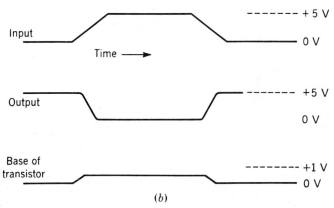

FIG. 5 • 4 The transistor inverter. (*a*) Inverter circuit. (*b*) Waveforms for inverter circuit.

pnp transistor is cut off when I_b is positive or into the base. The voltage V_{ce} is made negative for *pnp* transistors in the common-base circuit.

For completeness, a *pnp* transistor and its characteristics are shown in Table 5·1. The currents I_e and I_c are as before, but since the base and not the emitter is grounded, the voltages are measured from emitter to base (and not from base to emitter) and from collector to base (and not from emitter to collector), and so are called V_{eb} and V_{cb}. Table 5·1 also shows several curves for values of emitter currents. Some characteristics of the active, cutoff, and saturated regions are also noted.

5 • 3 THE EMITTER FOLLOWER

There are three transistor configurations which produce a power gain from input to output. The common-base and common-emitter configurations are shown in Fig. 5·3 and Table 5·1; the third configuration is the *common collector* shown in Fig.

TABLE 5 • 1   *pnp* TRANSISTOR CHARACTERISTICS FOR A COMMON-BASE CIRCUIT

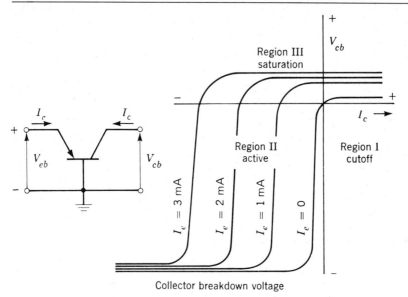

Collector breakdown voltage

DEFINITIONS

1. *Cutoff*   The *pnp* transistor is defined as being "cut off" when the input current flowing from the emitter (I_e) of the transistor is 0, or when current flows from the emitter, and when the collector potential is negative with respect to the base. The cutoff region in the figure above lies to the right of the curve plotted for an emitter current equal to 0. This is designated as Region I on the figure, and extends vertically up to the x axis of the graph. The important thing to note is that the emitter-base junction is reverse biased. For the *pnp* transistor this means that the base is positive with respect to the emitter. (For the *npn* transistor, the base was negative.)

2. *Active*   In this region the *pnp* transistor has a normal, or forward, emitter-to-base bias (the emitter is positive with respect to the base), and the collector is negative with respect to the base. The active region is designated as Region II in the figure. This is the normal operating region for the transistor, and most transistor amplifiers operate in this region.

3. *Saturation*   When the collector is positive with respect to the base, the transistor is said to be saturated. This is Region III in the above figure.

CHARACTERISTICS OF THE THREE MODES OF OPERATION

The transistor exhibits different input and output characteristics in each of the three regions. Referring again to the figure, the three regions of operation have the following characteristics:

1. When the *pnp* transistor is cut off, the emitter and collector are both negative with respect to the base. As a result, both the emitter and the collector appear as large resistances, and little current flows from either the collector or the emitter. Some reverse current will flow, however, because of leakage current across the surface and reverse current through the junction.* The magnitude of this current varies with the

voltage across the junction and the temperature of the transistor, but generally lies somewhere between 1 to 100 nA for silicon transistors.

2. In the active region the transistor exhibits all the characteristics common to signal amplifier circuits. The transistor possesses a power gain from input to output in this region, and the current which flows in the collector circuit is a function of the current into the emitter. The current gain from the emitter to the collector is designated as α, the ratio of small change in the emitter current to the resulting change in the collector current $\Delta I_c/\Delta I_e$, with the collector voltage held constant. This value generally lies between 0.9 and 0.99 for junction transistors. For a particular transistor, the value of α varies somewhat throughout the active region.†

   If the positive collector voltage is increased beyond a certain point, known as the *breakdown voltage*, the collector current will increase rapidly with virtually no change in collector voltage. This may be caused either by avalanche of the minority carriers or by another phenomenon, known as *punchthrough*, which occurs when the collector space charge region extends to the emitter. Care is generally taken to see that transistors are not operated with voltages that will cause breakdown.

3. When the *pnp* transistor is saturated, both the emitter and the collector are positive (forward biased) with respect to the base, and both the emitter-base and the collector-base junctions present small resistance to current flow.

*The leakage current is often designated as "cutoff current" and identified as I_{co}.
†Notice that $1/(1 - \alpha)$ gives the current gain from base to collector.

5·5. In actual practice the common collector is connected and used as in Fig. 5·5(a) and (b), which shows a single resistor at the emitter, an input to the base, and an output from the emitter. In this form the circuit is called an *emitter follower,* for as long as the input level does not exceed $+ V$ or $- V$, the output at the emitter will be an exact replica of the input; that is, the emitter *follows* the base, except for a slight shift in level. (For the *npn* circuit the shift is *down* about 0.5 V, and for the *pnp* it is *up* about 0.5 V.) Because of its ability to simply follow the input signal level, the emitter follower is generally used to provide current gain. The emitter follower is operated in the active region. The characteristics of the emitter follower are:

1. The voltage gain of the circuit is approximately unity. A change of 3 V in the input voltage will cause a change of approximately 3 V at the output.

2. The dc output level from the emitter follower is approximately equal to the dc input level. If the input to the base of an emitter follower is a dc level of $+3$ V and the transistor is operating in the active region, the output level at the emitter will also be at approximately $+3$ V dc. For the circuit in Fig. 5·5(a) the output level at the emitter will be slightly negative with respect to the base because of the base-emitter junction drop, and the output dc level will effectively "follow" the input level.

3. The current gain of the emitter follower is greater than unity. For most transistors the current gain through the emitter follower will be greater than 25. Since the voltage gain of the circuit is approximately unity and the current gain is greater than unity, the emitter follower has power gain.

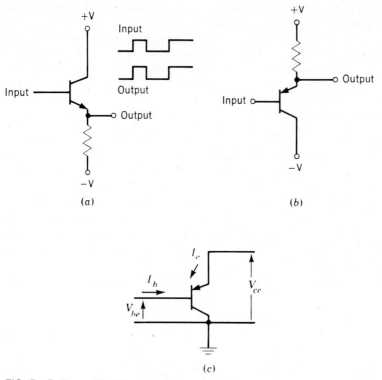

FIG. 5 • 5 The emitter follower. (*a*) *npn* emitter follower. (*b*) *pnp* emitter follower. (*c*) Common-collector configuration.

4. The output of the emitter follower is *in phase,* or follows the input. This applies to both input and output currents and input and output voltages.
5. The emitter follower has a high input resistance and a low output resistance. (The input resistance is usually at least an order of magnitude greater than the load resistance at the emitter.)

5 • 4 THE AND GATE

Since the information processed by a digital computer is represented by sets of electric signals which may be considered to represent binary values, a given signal may be thought of as representing either a 0 or a 1. Assume that a positive dc voltage represents a 1, and a negative voltage a 0. In this case the function of an AND gate with two inputs is to produce a positive output signal (a 1) only when both inputs are positive (1s). If the AND gate has three inputs, the output will be positive only when all three inputs are positive (in all other cases the output level will be negative, representing a 0).

In most systems 0s and 1s are represented by a positive dc signal (representing a 1) or a 0 V dc signal (representing a 0). The function of the AND gate circuit is then to produce a positive dc signal at its output only when a positive dc signal is applied to all the inputs to the circuit simultaneously. If the inputs to the circuit are labeled *X, Y,* and *Z,* the circuit will produce a positive dc signal only when a positive dc signal is simultaneously applied to *X* AND *Y* AND *Z.*

5 • 5 THE DIODE AND CIRCUIT

Figure 5·6 illustrates a two-input diode AND gate. In the circuit illustrated, a 0 V dc level represents a binary 0 and a +3 V signal a binary 1. If both inputs are at 0 V, both of the diodes will be forward biased and the output will be held at 0 V by the diodes. The total voltage drop across the resistor will be 5 V.†

If the *X* input line goes to 3 V and the *Y* input remains at 0 V, the diode connected to the *Y* input will still be forward biased, and the output will remain at 0 V dc. (Notice that in this case the *X* input diode will be reverse biased and 3 V will be dropped across the diode.) If the input at *Y* goes to +3 V and *X* remains at 0 V, the output will be at 0 V dc.

When the inputs at *X* and *Y* both go to the +3 V level, the output level will then rise to +3 V, and the output will represent a 1.

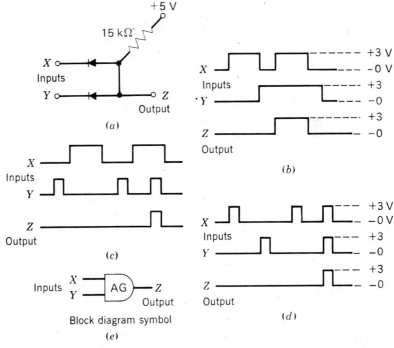

FIG. 5 • 6 Diode AND gate.

---

†We have assumed, for simplicity of explanation, that no voltage is dropped across a forward-biased diode. In fact, for silicon diodes, the output would be at approximately +0.7 V and the drop across the resistor about 4.3 V.

The responses of the diode AND gate to several types of inputs are illustrated in Fig. 5·6. The circuit in Fig. 5·6 could have more than two inputs. In this case a diode would be required for each input, and each additional diode would be connected just as the two diodes are connected in the figure. If four diodes are connected as shown in Fig. 5·6, the output will rise to the +3 V signal level only when the input signals to all four diodes are positive. There is a practical limit to the number of diodes which can be connected in this manner, however, due to the fact that the diodes do not actually have an infinite back resistance or zero forward resistance. With a large number of inputs, the finite forward and back resistances of the diodes will cause varying output levels, depending on the state of the inputs.

5 • 6 THE OR GATE

The OR gate has the property that a signal representing a 1 will appear at the output if any one of the inputs represents a 1. Figure 5·7 illustrates a diode OR gate circuit. There are two inputs to the circuit (X and Y) and one output. The input signals to the circuit consist of 0 V signals representing 0s and +3 V signals representing 1s. If both inputs to the circuit are at 0 V dc, both diodes will be forward biased and the output of the circuit will be at 0 V dc, representing a 0. If either of the inputs to the circuit rises to +3 V dc, the diode at this input will be forward biased and the output will rise to +3 V, representing a 1. The diode at the input

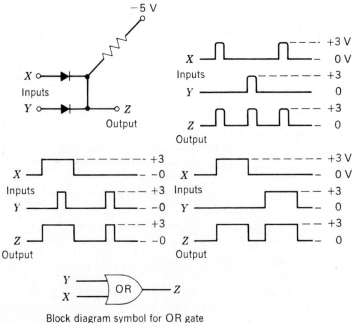

Block diagram symbol for OR gate

FIG. 5 • 7 Diode OR gate.

remaining at 0 V will then be reverse biased by the +3 V signal at the output. This circuit has the property that the output level will be at the level of the most positive input.

If both inputs to the circuit rise to +3 V, the output will again be at +3 V. (This circuit is sometimes referred to as an *inclusive* OR circuit, because the output is a 1 when both inputs are 1s.)

More inputs may be added to the circuit illustrated in Fig. 5·7. A diode is then required for each input. If any one or any combination of the inputs rises to the +3 V level, the output will be at +3 V.

As in the case of the diode AND gate, it is not practical to have too many inputs to the circuit because the forward and back resistances of the diodes are finite, and different combinations of input signals will then cause different signal levels at the outputs.

The logical block diagram symbol used for the OR gate is also illustrated in Fig. 5·7.

If the convention that a positive signal represents a 1 and a negative signal a 0 is reversed, the circuit of Fig. 5·7 will then perform the AND function. Also notice that if the AND gate which is illustrated in Fig. 5·6 has negative inputs representing 1s and positive input signals representing 0s, the circuit will then perform the OR function. To avoid confusion, the circuit in Fig. 5·7 is sometimes referred to as a *positive* OR gate or as a *negative* AND gate. The circuit in Fig. 5·6 would then be referred to as a *positive* AND gate or a *negative* OR gate. Unless otherwise noted, we will consider relatively positive signals to represent 1s and relatively negative signals to represent 0s. The term AND gate will then refer to a positive AND gate, such as the one in Fig. 5·6, and an OR gate will mean a positive OR gate, such as that in Fig. 5·7.

5 • 7 THE INVERTER CIRCUIT

The circuit shown in Fig. 5·8 is from an early and once very popular line of integrated circuits called RTL (resistor-transistor logic) circuits. These circuits have the advantage of being simple and quite inexpensive. Binary 0s are represented by 0 V signals and binary 1s by signals ranging from about +0.8 to +3.5 V. (The rea-

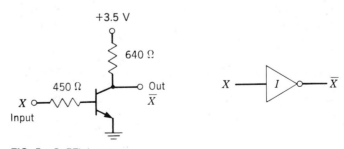

FIG. 5 • 8 RTL inverter.

son for the variation in 1 signals will be explained.) The logic for entire computers can be constructed from this simple circuit; so it is perhaps the most basic transistor circuit.

The input X in Fig. 5·8 can be a binary 0 which is 0 V, in which case, since the base will be at the same potential as the emitter, the transistor will be cut off, and no current will flow in the collector circuit; so the output will rise to a binary 1 or +3.5 V level.

If the input is at +3 V, a binary 1, the transistor will be turned on and in saturation and the collector will then be at 0 V, plus the emitter-collector drop, representing a binary 0.

This circuit can be used to illustrate an important point. If a single inverter output is connected to a single inverter as in Fig. 5·9(a), or to two inverters as in Fig. 5·9(b), or to three inverters as in Fig. 5·9(c), differing output voltages occur for the 1 level at the output of the first inverter.

If the input to the first inverter is a 0, the transistor will be off, and for the single-inverter load in Fig. 5·9(a) the resistor at the output of the first stage and the input to the second stage form a voltage divider in series with the base-emitter junction of the transistor of the second stage. Assuming that this drop is 0.5 V, the 640 Ω and 450 Ω resistors will drop 3 V and the point Z will be at +1.7 V.

With two inverters connected to the output of the first inverter, as in Fig. 5·9(b), point Z will be at +1.3 V, while with three inverters at the output, as in Fig. 5·9(c), point Z will be at +1.1 V.

Since all three of these voltages, 1.7, 1.3, and 1.1 V, represent 1s, and since even more circuits might be added, it is necessary to (1) limit the number of circuits connected to an output and (2) let 0s and 1s be represented by voltages lying in intervals.

As an example of (1) above, Fig. 4·15 shows several IC packages from the Motorola line. Included is a six-inverter package with six inverters in a single IC container of the sort shown in Figs. 5·8 and 5·9. The inner numbers on the MC 789P show the pin numbers; so the topmost inverter has pin 14 as an input and pin 1 as an output. The other numbers are for *loading,* or *fan-in, fan-out* purposes. For the topmost inverter we see that the input at pin 14 has a load factor of 3 and the output at pin 1 can drive 16 loads. Therefore we could connect five inverter inputs to a single inverter output (since 5 × 3 = 15, which is less than 16), but not six inverters, because that would overload a single output. Similarly, the pin 2 input of the dual *JK* flip-flop package is a CL input to a *JK* flip-flop with a load of 5; so only three of the CL inputs could be connected to an inverter output. Similarly, three inverters could be connected to pin 14 of the dual *JK* flip-flop package, since this would give a load factor of 9, which is less than the load of 10 the 0 output of the flip-flop can support.

Regarding voltage levels, the circuits are designed so that levels of less than +0.5 V represent binary 0s, while signals of greater than 0.8 V represent 1s. There is, therefore, a 0.3 V indeterminate interval† which gives some protection against

† This is sometimes called the "region of ambiguity."

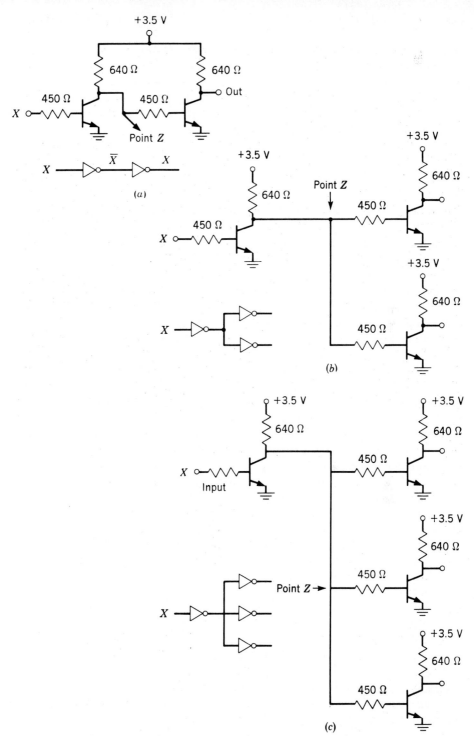

FIG. 5 • 9 Inverters connected together. (*a*) Two inverters in series. (*b*) Two inverters to a single output. (*c*) Three inverters to a single output.

noise and some immunity against variations in circuits. (Proper design can further provide protection against noise. RTL is generally conceded to be more sensitive to noise than some other systems, however.) V_{cc}, the power supply level, is to be 3.5 V dc $\pm$ 10 percent. Each of the circuits in Fig. 4·15 can be obtained in the IC packages described in Chap. 4, as can the RTL made by any of the major manufacturers.

5 • 8 NOR GATES

By combining two of the circuits in Fig. 5·8 it is possible to make a *two-input NOR gate*. Figure 5·10 shows this: the two collectors are tied together and share a single load resistor.

If either or both of the inputs X and Y to the circuit in Fig. 5·10 are high (or 1s), the transistor connected to that input will be turned on and saturated. This means that the collector will be at essentially ground, or 0, potential and the output will be a 0. For instance, if the input at X is at $+2$ V, $T1$ will be turned on and saturated, and the output will be at 0 V. If the input Y happens to be at 0 V, it will not affect the output, and the collector-base junction of $T2$ will be at about the same potential.

The same applies if both inputs are at a 1 or high input level: both $T1$ and $T2$ will be saturated and the output a 0.

If both inputs X and Y happen to be 0s, then both $T1$ and $T2$ will be off and the output will be at $+3.5$ V.

A truth table for the circuit is shown in Fig. 5·10. This indicates that the presence of a 1 at either or both inputs leads to a 0 output; so the circuit is a two-input NOR gate. This is one of the circuits in Fig. 4·15.

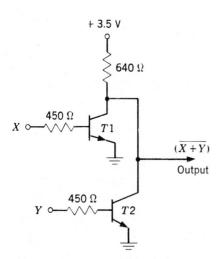

X	Y	Output
0	0	1
0	1	0
1	0	0
1	1	0

FIG. 5 • 10 Two-input NOR gates.

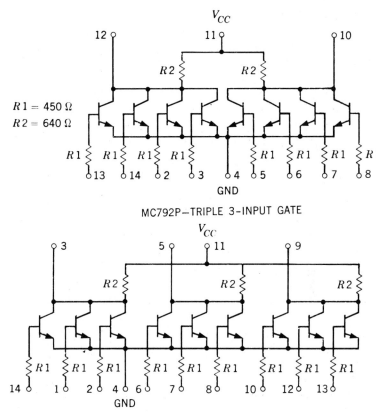

$R1 = 450 \, \Omega$

$R2 = 640 \, \Omega$

MC792P—TRIPLE 3-INPUT GATE

$R1 = 450 \, \Omega$

$R2 = 640 \, \Omega$

FIG. 5 • 11 Three- and four-input NOR gates. (Courtesy Motorola Corp.)

Figure 5·11 shows that the circuit can be extended. Connecting the collectors of three inverters together forms a three-input NOR gate; four transistors can form a four-input NOR gate; etc. Both of these circuits are RTL circuits and correspond to the block diagram in Fig. 4·15.

5 • 9 THE TRANSISTOR FLIP-FLOP

The basic characteristic of the flip-flop circuit is that it is bistable. This ability to be stable in only one of two possible states or conditions at a given time is almost always based on some variation of the basic two-transistor circuit shown in Fig. 5·12. The two-transistor circuits are arranged so that one of the transistors is always on and the other is always off.

Assume that transistor $T2$ is off. Then the 640 Ω resistor $R4$ at its collector "pulls

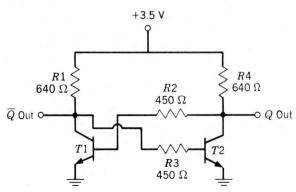

FIG. 5 • 12 Two-transistor flip-flop.

up'' on the base of transistor $T1$ through resistor $R2$. This turns transistor $T1$ on and saturates it. The output at the collector of $T1$ is then at essentially ground, which applies about 0 V to the base of $T2$ through $R3$, keeping it off. At this time the Q output is at about $+1.7$ V, depending on the base-to-emitter drop of $T1$, and the $\overline{Q}$ output is at perhaps $+0.3$ V. This is then the 1 state for the flip-flop.

If $T1$ is off, then $R1$ and $R2$ turn $T2$ on, and the collector of $T2$ then is near ground, keeping $T1$ off. The Q output is then at about ground (perhaps $+0.3$ V), and the $\overline{Q}$ output will be at about $+1.7$ V, and so the flip-flop is in the 0 state.

An examination will show that the circuit will not be stable in any condition but the 1 or 0 state outlined above.

This flip-flop has outputs but no inputs. Figure 5·13 shows an RS flip-flop with a SET and RESET input. The SET and RESET inputs are normally at 0. When a

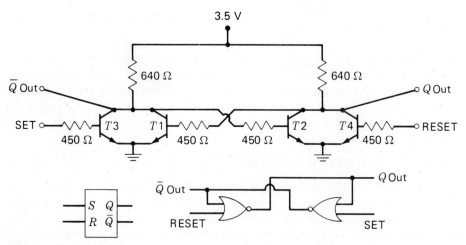

FIG. 5 • 13 SET-RESET flip-flop.

positive voltage is applied to the RESET input, transistor $T4$ goes on, and the collector of $T4$ goes to about ground; this turns $T1$ off, and the output of $T1$ rises, turning $T2$ on. If the positive voltage is now removed from the RESET input, the flip-flop will be in the 0 state, with $T1$ off and the $\overline{Q}$ output high and with $T2$ on and the Q output low.

A positive voltage applied to the SET input will turn $T3$ on, grounding the base of $T2$ and turning $T2$ off. This will turn $T1$ on and, removing the positive input voltage from the SET input, will leave the flip-flop with 1 state, with the Q output high and the $\overline{Q}$ output low.

Figure 5·13 also shows that this circuit consists of two NOR gates cross-coupled, which is how the basic RS flip-flop is made in RTL logic.

5 • 10 RESISTOR-TRANSISTOR LOGIC

We have already seen several examples of a class of logic circuits called RTL circuits. These circuits are distinguished by their use of only transistors and resistors as circuit elements and by the presence of a resistor at the input to each base. The circuits are also characterized by the use of the NOR gate as the standard gate. The circuits are generally medium speed and medium power, although low-power circuits are available.

These circuits are manufactured to standards throughout the industry, so that the circuit packages used are interchangeable in that one manufacturer's circuit can be replaced by another's. (An examination of the schematics of two circuits will generally show that both circuits are identical with regard to component values and configuration as well as external pin numbers.)

For the gates shown in Figs. 5·10 and 5·11, the delay through a single unloaded gate is on the order of 12 ns. The gates have an input load factor of 3 and an output capability of 16; so five inputs could be connected to a single output.

Figure 5·14 shows the schematic for a standard clocked JK flip-flop. This flip-flop has inverted inputs and outputs (notice the bubbles on the block diagram) because it is constructed of NOR gates which lead to inverted logic. Figure 5·14 shows a table of the clocked input operation values. This shows that if both inputs J and K are 1s when the negative-going edge of the clock pulse arrives, the flip-flop will remain in the same state. If, however, both inputs are 0s when the negative edge arrives, the flip-flop will change states. If the pin 3 input is a 1 and the pin 1 input is a 0 when the clock arrives, the flip-flop goes to the 0 state (since inputs are inverted), with pin 13 high (since the 1 output is inverted) and pin 14 low (since the 0 output is inverted). Similarly, if pin 3 is a 1 and pin 1 a 0 when the clock goes negative, afterward pin 13 will be low (a 0) and pin 14 high (a 1). This inverted input, inverted output requires some thinking in use, but it is common to all lines of RTL logic.

Pin 12 is used to clear the flip-flop to its 0 state, and a plus or 1 signal is used to activate the input. During normal clocked operation this input is at ground, or 0, potential.

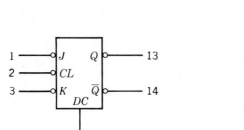

CLOCKED OPERATION

J	K	Q Output
0	0	Changes
0	1	Goes to 0
1	0	Gate 1
1	1	No change

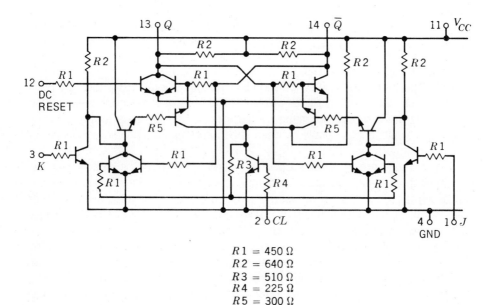

$$R1 = 450\ \Omega$$
$$R2 = 640\ \Omega$$
$$R3 = 510\ \Omega$$
$$R4 = 225\ \Omega$$
$$R5 = 300\ \Omega$$

FIG. 5 • 14 RTL flip-flop.

5 • 11 DIODE-TRANSISTOR LOGIC

Diode-transistor logic (DTL) was at one time the most frequently used circuit line. DTL is characterized by diode gates followed by transistor inverters, which leads to a NAND gate as the basic gate. DTL has more resistance to noise than RTL, and the logic is more "natural," but the circuits are more complicated. DTL was the largest selling line for some years and is still widely used, particularly in industrial applications where protection against noise is an important factor in evaluating logic circuit performance. DTL has reasonably good performance in this area, and there is a circuit line called HLDTL (or high-level DTL) where the power supply voltage is +25 V instead of the +5 V used in basic DTL. This line of circuits has excellent noise protection and is widely used in industrial applications where, for instance, machinery causes electrical noise and there are large power-line transients.

The basic DTL gate is shown in Fig. 5·15(a). This particular circuit is standard with virtually all manufacturers. It basically consists of a diode AND gate followed by a transistor inverter. There is also an additional transistor (an emitter follower) between the diode AND gate and the transistor inverter's input. This means that there is more gain through the input circuit, and therefore less input drive required. The extra transistor T1 also means that a higher input level is required to turn T2 on since there are now three junctions (a diode and the base-emitter junctions of T1 and T2) between the output of the AND gate and ground, and so a higher voltage is required to start significant current flowing. This increases the protection against noise.

To analyze the operation of the circuit in Fig. 5·15(a), if any one of the three inputs is at ground potential, the base of T1 will be only slightly positive (the amount of the drop across a diode), and the three junctions in series, the base emitter of T1, the diode D1, and the base-emitter junction of T2, will not conduct, particularly since R3 is also holding the base to ground. As a result, the output will tend to rise to the output voltage of +5 V.

If all inputs are at a high or 1 level (3 V or more), the output from the diode AND gate will be high and the emitter of T1 will be at about the input level (notice that the base-emitter junction of T1 drops a voltage about equal to the rise across the diodes), so that T2 is turned on hard and saturates. This gives a low or 0 output. The circuit therefore operates as a NAND gate.

A block diagram and schematic for the standard RS flip-flop in DTL are shown in Fig. 5·15(b). The standard flip-flop has 2 two-input AND gates which come connected to the S and R inputs. In DTL, unused inputs are 1s; so simply using one R and one S input will give a conventional RS flip-flop. A table of next-state values for this flip-flop is shown in the figure. The flip-flop is initiated by negative-going edges on the clock. DC RESET and DC SET lines are included, and these are normally at a high, or 1, level (unconnected, they will be 1s) and are activated by "grounding," or making the input a 0.

There is one frequently used trick with this flip-flop. Connecting the Q output to an R input and the $\overline{Q}$ output to an S input gives a JK flip-flop (which complements with two 1 inputs).

The circuit in Fig. 5·15(b) can be further analyzed using the logic diagram in Fig. 5·15(c), which shows the circuit reduced to its block form. This shows the flip-flop to be a master-slave flip-flop, as previously described.

5 • 12 TRANSISTOR-TRANSISTOR LOGIC

The line of circuits called transistor-transistor logic (TTL) is now the most widely used circuit line because of the high speed of TTL circuits. These circuits are characterized by a multiple emitter transistor at the inputs. Otherwise the circuits are very similar to DTL, with a standard NAND gate, except the output stage frequently contains two transistors.

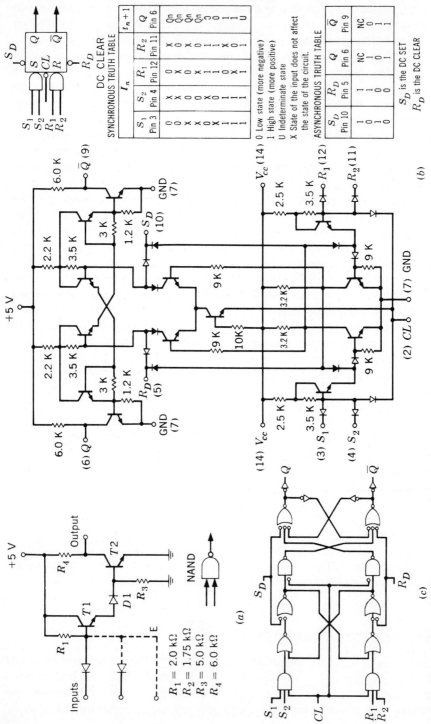

FIG. 5 · 15 (a) Basic DTL gate. (b) Block diagram and schematic for standard *RS* flip-flop in DTL. (c) Logic diagram.

The characteristic which distinguishes TTL circuits from other circuit lines is a multiple emitter transistor at the input circuit. The schematic diagram for this kind of transistor is shown as $T1$ in Fig. 5·16(a). The multiple emitter transistor simply has a larger than normal collector area and several base-emitter junctions. The two-emitter transistor in Fig. 5·16(a) functions like the two-transistor circuit because the two-emitter transistor is effectively two transistors with a common collector and base. Figure 5·16(b) and (c) shows the TTL input circuit in separate transistor and multiple emitter transistor form. The transistors $T1A$, $T1B$, and $T1C$ are combined to form a single multiple emitter transistor $T1$ in Fig. 5·16(c). This circuit operates as follows. If one of three inputs X, Y, and Z is at 0 V, current will flow through $R1$ and the base-emitter junction of $T1$ to the input. This will hold the base of $T1$ at about 0.5 V. The base collector of $T1$ and the base emitter of $T2$ form two junctions in series with resistor $R3$ to ground, and so the base of $T2$ will not be positive more than 0.2 V, which is insufficient to turn $T2$ on; and little (leakage only) current will flow in the collector circuit of $T1$, and $T2$ will be off. As a result, no current will flow through the resistors $R2$ and $R3$, and the emitter of $T2$ will be at ground and the collector at +5 V.

If all three inputs are at a level of +3.5 V (the 1 level), then current will flow through $R1$ and the base-collector junction of $T1$ (which is forward biased) into the

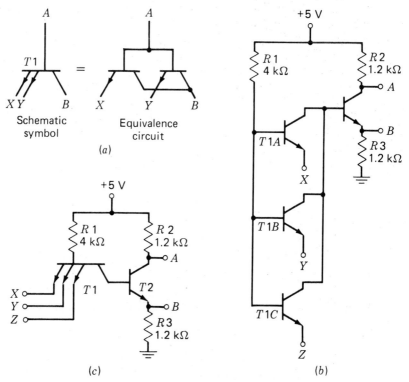

FIG. 5 • 16 TTL gate circuit. (a) Schematic symbol and equivalent circuit. (b) Discrete version of TTL gate. (c) Multiple emitter TTL gate.

base of $T2$, turning it on. Current will flow through $R1$ and $R2$ until the transistor $T2$ is saturated with its emitter and collector both at about 2.5 V. At this time, notice that the three emitter-base junctions of the multiple emitter transistor will be reverse biased.

The two outputs from the collector and emitter of $T2$ operate like scissors which close when $T2$ is on and open when $T2$ is off. That is, the emitter and collector of $T2$ will be at about the same voltage (closed) when $T2$ is on, and the emitter will be at ground and the collector at +5 V when $T2$ if off (open scissors).

Notice that $T2$ is on when the three inputs are high (1s) and $T2$ is off when any one of the three inputs is low (a 0), so the circuit operation is basically that of a NAND gate.

A complete TTL NAND gate is shown in Fig. 5·17. This is a "second genera-tion" TTL circuit and is typical of the circuits offered by the major TTL manufac-turers in their medium-speed lines.

Let us examine the operation of the circuit in Fig. 5·17 by assuming that input Y is at +3.5 V and X is at 0 V, and therefore $T1$ has its base-emitter junction connected to Y reversed biased, and the full current from $R1$ flows through the base-emitter junction connected to X. At this time, (1) $T2$ will be off; (2) $T4$ will be off because with no current through $R4$ its base will be at essentially ground; (3) $T3$ and $T5$ will be turned on by current flowing through $R2$. The transistors $T5$ and $T3$ are connected in what is called a *Darlington configuration* which gives large current gain. As a result, little current will be required through $R2$ to turn $T3$ on, and the output will be at +5 V minus the base-emitter drops for $T5$ and $T3$ and therefore at about +4 V.

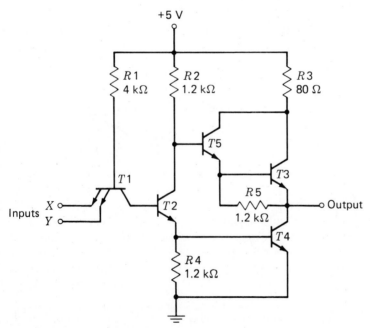

FIG. 5 • 17 Classic TTL NAND gate.

Let us consider that the input voltage at *X* is slowly raised positive. As a result, the collector of *T*1 goes positive, and *T*2 begins to conduct. As the emitter of *T*2 becomes more and more positive, *T*4 begins to conduct, and as the collector of *T*2 becomes more and more negative, the *T*5 to *T*3 combination begins to turn off. Finally (1) *T*2 will saturate; (2) *T*4 will be saturated, and therefore about $+0.5$ V or less.

The circuit in Fig. 5·17 will have about 4 ns turn-on delays and 7 ns turn-off delays and a power dissipation of about 10 mW.

The reason for the high speeds lies in the all-transistor construction of the TTL and in the fact that the final stage drives current in both directions. The standard transistor inverter (see Figs. 5·8 or 5·15 for examples in RTL and DTL) has an output which is "driven down" by the turning on of the output transistor. When the transistor is turned off, however, the rising edge is formed by the resistor at the circuit's output supplying current to all the stray capacity in this circuit and any circuits connected to the output. Therefore the rise time is exponential. With TTL's two-transistor output (the circuit is called a *totem pole*) the rising edge is "driven up" by the upper transistor turning on and the lower transistor turning off. This gives a sharp edge, and the falling edge is similarly sharp.

In many aerospace, military, and industrial applications it is desirable to have a much lower power dissipation. If the resistor values in the basic circuit design shown in Fig. 5·17 are raised, the circuit will consume far lower power, and circuit manufacturers offer low-power TTL circuits. Typical resistor values are: $R1 = 40$ kΩ, $R2 = 20$ kΩ, $R3 = 500$ Ω, $R4 = 12$ kΩ, and $R5 = 5$ kΩ. Naturally there will be a decrease in speed, but low-power gates are still capable of 33 ns delays at only 1 mW power dissipation.

There is a famous problem with TTL circuits which can be illustrated using Fig. 5·17. When TTL circuits are switched, they generate large "spikes" on their outputs, and interconnections must be carefully watched to prevent ringing or even circuit damage. Generally, capacitors are even placed across the $+5$ V to ground power supply on each circuit container to prevent spikes in the power supply voltage.

The problem develops because it is possible for both *T*3 and *T*4 to be on simultaneously when the circuit is switching. For instance, if the output is switching from a 0 to a 1 level, then *T*4 must go off and *T*3 must go on. But if *T*3 goes on before *T*4 is completely off, then both transistors will be on simultaneously, almost shorting the $+5$ V to ground.

The TTL current spike problem has plagued the TTL family and is clearly in evidence in the circuit of Fig. 5·17. While *T*3 and *T*4 can both be on during turn-on and turn-off, the turn-off case is usually worse since the storage time of *T*4 causes both transistors to be on for a greater time. Turn-on current spiking may be lowered by increasing the ratio of *R*2 to *R*4. In this way the collector of *T*2 reaches a lower voltage before *T*4 begins to conduct. There is a trade-off involved, however, since increasing *R*2 decreases the on drive for *T*4, decreasing its turn-on time. The increased value of *R*2 also results in decreased noise immunity. So far, no "perfect" answer to current spiking has been found.

Although the standard TTL circuits are fast, there is always a desire to speed up circuit lines. In order to increase still further the speeds of TTL logic, a basic

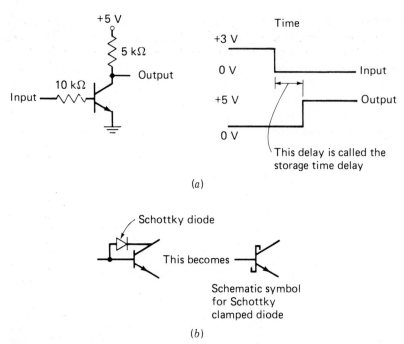

(a)

(b)

FIG. 5 • 18 Schottky clamped transistor. (a) Storage delay. (b) Schottky diode and transistor.

problem must be dealt with. When a transistor is saturated and must be turned off, before the transistor begins to go off there is a delay (caused by the minority carriers) called the *storage time delay*. This is shown in Fig. 5·18(a) where a transistor inverter is turned off from saturation. While this delay is on the order of nanoseconds, it is still significant since several of the TTL circuit transistors become saturated at various times.†

In order to alleviate this problem, the newest TTL circuits use a diode clamp between base and collector. This is shown in Fig. 5·18(b). The diode used is not a conventional diode, however, but a special diode (called a Schottky diode) formed by the junction of a metal and a semiconductor.

The Schottky diode is faster than conventional diodes because electrons which have crossed the junction and entered the metal when current is flowing are not distinguishable from the conduction electrons of the metal. Since these electrons are majority carriers, there is no delay associated with minority carrier recombination as in semiconductor diodes. As a result, reverse recovery times for Schottky diodes are generally in the low picosecond range. Further, because of the choice of materials (aluminum or platinum silicides), the forward drop of the Schottky diode is less than for a conventional diode.

The transistor with a Schottky diode connected from base to collector will switch faster because the transistor is not allowed to saturate. The minority carrier

---

†Gold doping is often used to reduce minority carrier storage times in switching transistors.

storage time normally associated with the transistor's operation when coming out of saturation is avoided and the circuit can operate faster.

When a transistor is fabricated with a Schottky diode connected from base to collector, the combination is given a special schematic diagram symbol as shown in Fig. 5·18(b).

The use of Schottky clamped transistors has resulted in a series of high-speed TTL circuits with delays on the order of 2 ns (rise and fall times are on the order of 3 ns). Figure 5·19(b) shows a typical circuit. Notice that the transistors which

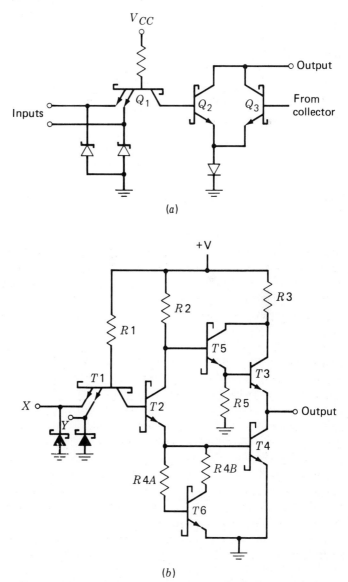

FIG. 5 • 19 (a) Schottky MSI circuit. (b) Schottky clamped TTL logic gate.

TABLE 5 • 2 TTL CHARACTERISTICS

	VERY HIGH SPEED 74 S (SCHOTTKY CLAMPED)	HIGH SPEED	MEDIUM SPEED 74	LOW SPEED 74 L
High-level input (minimum)	2 V	1.8 V	2 V	2 V
Low-level input (maximum)	0.8 V	0.9 V	0.8 V	0.7 V
High-level output (minimum)	2.7 V	2.5 V	2.4 V	2.4 V
Low-level output (maximum)	0.5 V	0.4 V	0.4 V	0.3 V
High-level noise margin (minimum)	700 mV	700 mV	400 mV	400 mV
Low-level noise margin (minimum)	300 mV	500 mV	400 mV	400 mV
Maximum input load current	−2 mA	−2 mA	−1.6 mA	−1.8 mA
Average power per gate	20 mW	22 mW	10 mW	1 mW
Typical delay, high to low	1.5 ns	4 ns	8 ns	31 ns
Typical delay, low to high	1.5 ns	4 ns	12 ns	35 ns
Supply voltage	5 V	5 V	5 V	5 V

normally become saturated at some time are now Schottky clamped transistors, and so storage delays are reduced. The operation of this circuit is essentially the same as that of Fig. 5·17 except that the transistors do not saturate.

The diodes connected to ground at the inputs dampen negative spikes and negative-going signals which may occur during ringing. These circuits must be carefully interconnected, however, and wire or printed circuit connections of more than 8 in. in length should be treated with respect and terminated according to the rules given by the circuits' manufacturers.

Table 5·2 gives some of the characteristics for several TTL lines. Notice that speed is associated with power consumption.

TTL circuits are also available in MSI. The MSI seven-segment decoder and BCD counters in Chap. 4 were TTL. A simplified TTL gate is used internally for such MSI circuits, and this gate is shown in Fig. 5·19(a).

A TTL flip-flop is shown in Fig. 5·20, the Fairchild 9022. This operates like any JK flip-flop, except that it provides AND gates at the J and K inputs and a JK or "gate" input, which can be used to inhibit the flip-flop's operation. Notice that the clock input presents no bubble; so positive clock transitions activate the flip-flop (that is, 0 to 1 shifts). The block diagram in Fig. 5·20 shows the flip-flop to be a master-slave flip-flop. DC RESET and DC SET inputs are activated by grounding the respective input line. This gives some idea of the complexity of circuits in TTL logic packages. Two of these flip-flops are packaged in one 14-pin container as shown in Fig. 4·12.

5 • 13 EMITTER-COUPLED LOGIC

Emitter-coupled logic (ECL) has several other common names: *current-mode logic* (CML), *current-steering logic,* and *nonsaturating logic.* The latter term is the key to this type of circuit. When transistors are operated in a saturated condition, they turn off slowly due to the delay caused by a charge stored in the collector and

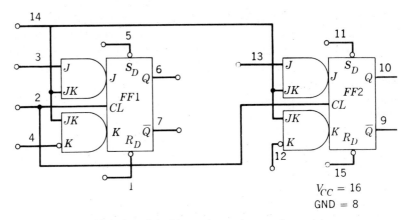

The numbers from 1 to 14 are pin numbers on the container.

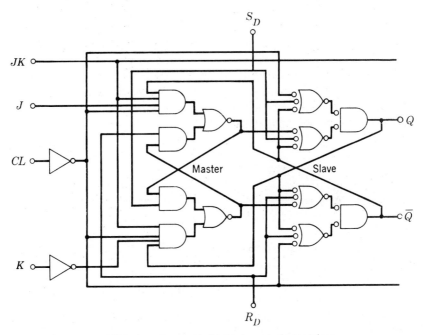

The above is repeated twice in a single container.

FIG. 5 • 20 TTL flip-flop. (Courtesy Fairchild Corp.)

base region.† This delay in "turn-off time" can be eliminated by operating transistors only in either the active or the off regions. As will be seen, in these circuits current is "steered" rather than having voltages or levels passed around.

The ECL logic line is the fastest currently available. Manufacturers of ECL have a number of basic circuits, each with different features and drawbacks. ECL has

_____

†This was called the storage delay in the preceding section.

not proved as popular as TTL, primarily because it is more expensive, harder to cool, and more difficult to interconnect, and is considered to have less noise immunity (this is debatable). Also, ECL may be faster than is necessary in many applications. On the other hand, the "superfast" computers use ECL as do a number of the highest speed special-purpose computers.

The basic ECL configuration can be best described by examining a particular inverter. Figure 5·21 shows an ECL inverter with an input X. The logic levels in this system are as follows: Binary 0 is represented by -1.55 V and binary 1 by -0.75 V. Notice that this is "positive logic," since, although both levels are negative, the more positive level, -0.75, is the binary 1. Also, notice the small signal difference between 0 and 1.

The circuit's operation is based on a *differential amplifier* consisting of $T4$ and $T3$. When the input to $T3$ is at -1.55 V, $T3$ will be off and current will flow through $R3$ and $R2$. Calculation will indicate a drop of about 0.8 V across $R2$; so figuring a base-emitter drop of 0.75 V for $T1$, the X output will be at -1.55 V.

Since $T2$ is cut off by the -1.55 V input, very little current will flow through $R1$, and the output $\overline{X}$ will be at the base-emitter drop voltage across $T2$; so the output will be at -0.75 V.

An examination will show that if the input is at -0.75 V, transistor $T3$ will be on, $T4$ will be off, the X output will be at -0.75 V, and the $\overline{X}$ output at -1.55 V. (The key to analyzing this circuit is to notice that in a "differential amplifier" circuit such as the $T3$ to $T4$ form, the current through the resistor $R3$ shared by the two emitters will be almost constant.) Notice that the transistors are never saturated. They are either in their active region or off.

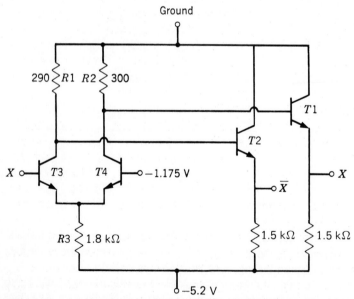

FIG. 5 • 21 ECL-gate basic circuit. (Courtesy Motorola Corp.; Motorola has the trade name MECL for Motorola ECL.)

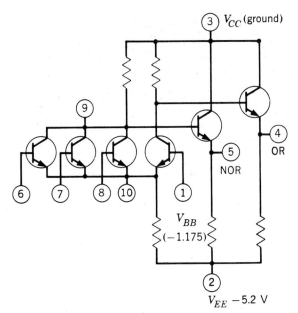

TRUTH TABLE

Inputs			Outputs	
8	7	6	5	4
0	0	0	1	0
0	0	1	0	1
0	1	0	0	1
0	1	1	0	1
1	0	0	0	1
1	0	1	0	1
1	1	0	0	1
1	1	1	0	1

FIG. 5 • 22 ECL three-input gate.

A three-input gate is shown in Fig. 5·22. This is a combined NOR and OR gate, as shown by the block diagram, depending on which output connection is used.

As time has passed, several generations of ECL circuits have evolved. In general the circuits have become faster and require more power with each generation. More facilities and more complicated logic per chip are also available in the new lines, including MSI chips. Notice that the circuits in Fig. 5·21 require three voltages: ground, −1.175 V, and −5.2 V. Later circuits provide a circuit on each chip to generate the intermediate (in this case −1.175 V) voltage, so that only a single power supply is required.

Figure 5·23 shows the four generations Motorola has gone through with their ECL logic which is called Motorola ECL or MECL, and also Fairchild's 10,000 series. Table 5·3 outlines some of the characteristics of these circuits, and the speed versus power and general noise characteristics can be deduced from the table. From Fig. 5·23 it is evident which variations were employed as technology advanced. For instance, notice that the circuit to produce the third −1.175 V bias voltage for the MECL I line is not included on the chip, whereas all subsequent lines have this as an internal feature.

Second, corresponding resistor values differ among MECL lines. This is necessary to achieve the varying speed and power improvements. Of course, speed is not determined by resistor values alone; transistor geometries, while not shown on a schematic, are a major factor. The transistor geometries in conjunction with the resistor values provide the speed and power characteristics of the different families.

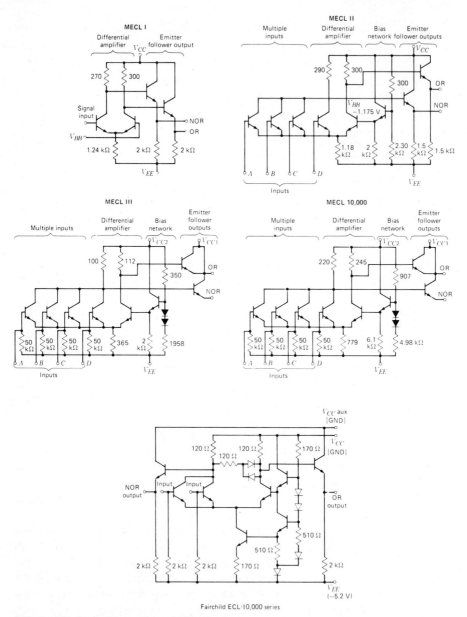

FIG. 5 • 23 Several generations of ECL circuits.

Notice also that Fairchild 10,000 and MECL III gates are supplied with base pull-down resistors (50 kΩ) to each of the input transistors, while the other two families are not. These resistors provide a path for base leakage current to unused input bases, causing them to be well turned off.

A final significant difference between the families is in the output circuits. MECL

TABLE 5 • 3 GENERAL CHARACTERISTICS OF ECL CIRCUITS

		FAIRCHILD			
FEATURE	MECL I	MECL II	10k SERIES	100k SERIES	MECL III
Gate propagation delay	8 ns	4 ns	2 ns	0.75 ns	1 ns
Gate edge speed	8.5 ns	4 ns	3.5 ns	1.5 ns	1 ns
Flip-flop toggle speed (minimum)	30 MHz	70 MHz	125 MHz	500 MHz	500 MHz
Gate power	31 mW	22 mW	25 mW	65 mW	60 mW
Input pull-down resistors	No	No	50 kΩ	50 kΩ	2 kΩ, 50 kΩ

I circuits normally are supplied with output pull-down resistors on the chip. MECL II circuits can be obtained with or without output resistors. MECL III and Fairchild 10,000 circuits normally have open outputs.

The use of on-chip output resistors has both advantages and limitations. An advantage is that fewer external components are required. However, with open outputs the designer can choose both the value and the location of the terminating resistance to meet system requirements. Finally the use of external resistors reduces on-chip heating and power dissipation, allowing more complex LSI and increasing chip life and reliability.

An *RS* flip-flop in this system is shown in Fig. 5·24. DC SET and RESET inputs are included. This flip-flop can be used in counters at rates up to 30 million counts per second. More complicated flip-flops operate at even higher rates.

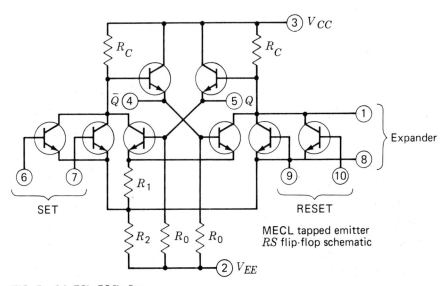

FIG. 5 • 24 ECL *RS* flip-flop.

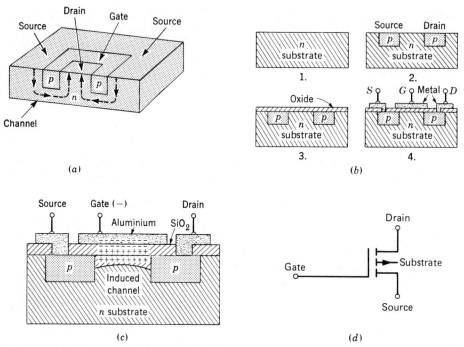

FIG. 5 • 25 MOSFET structure. (*a*) General configuration. (*b*) Fabrication steps. (*c*) Cross section with gate biased negative. (*d*) Schematic symbol. (Courtesy Motorola Corp.)

5 • 14 METAL-OXIDE SEMICONDUCTOR CIRCUITS

The circuits so far described are all termed *bipolar circuits* and use "conventional" transistors. For large-scale integration (LSI), quite often another type of transistor, called a *field effect transistor* (FET), is used. While the characteristics of these FETs have not proved desirable for some applications (because of their slowness, delicacy, and lack of drive characteristics), the ease of manufacture, small size, and small power dissipation have offset the negative factors and have led to FETs constructed of MOS (metal-oxide semiconductor) as the primary technology for use in large arrays. FETs constructed of MOS are called MOSFETs.

The manufacture of MOS circuits using FETs involves different techniques at different companies. Most MOSFET circuits now manufactured use a structure called *insulated gate p-channel enhancement mode field effect transistors* or *insulated gate n-channel enhancement mode field effect transistors,* We shall deal with these structures primarily.

Figure 5·25(*a*) shows a cross section of an FET of *p*-channel type. As shown in Fig. 5·25(*b*), a substrate of *n*-type (silicon) material is first formed, and two separate low-resistivity *p*-type regions are diffused into this substrate. Then the surface of this structure is covered with an insulating oxide layer. Holes are cut into the oxide, and two metal contacts are made to the two pieces of *p* material, and a thin piece of metal called the *gate* (G) is placed over what is called the *channel.*

With no voltages applied, the above structure (refer to Fig. 5·25) forms two diodes back to back, and if we attempt to force current from source to drain, the alternate *pn* junction followed by an *np* junction will not permit current flow (in either direction).

The gate is used to cause and control current flow in the following manner. Consider the source to be grounded and the drain connected to a negative voltage through a resistor. Figure 5·26 shows this. [The schematic symbol for the FET is shown in Fig. 5·25(*d*).] The metal area of the gate, along with the insulating oxide layer and semiconductor channel, form a capacitor, with the metal gate the top plate and the *n*-material substrate the lower plate. Making the gate potential negative causes a corresponding positive charge in the *n*-type semiconductor substrate along the channel, as shown in Fig. 5·25(*c*). Given sufficient negative potential on the gate, the positive charge induced in the channel finally causes this section of material to become *p*-type, and current begins to flow from source to drain—thus the term *current enhancement mode.*

The more negative the gate becomes, the more "*p*-type" the semiconductor channel becomes, and the more current flows. As a result, this type of MOS is also called PMOS.

As a switching circuit, an FET can be used to form an inverter. With a 0, or ground, input the output of the circuit shown in Fig. 5·26 will have a − 10 V output, and with a − 7 V or more negative input, the output will go to about 0 V.

Two things should be noted about this circuit. First, the voltages used are larger than for the circuits in preceding sections. Second, the FET circuit has a high input impedance (perhaps 10^{12} Ω) because the gate input is a capacitor, in effect.

One other fact should be noted. Instead of forming actual resistors for these circuits, another FET is used, thus simplifying manufacture. This is shown in Fig. 5·26. The FET resistor's gate areas are controlled so that the FET represents a high resistance (perhaps 10 to 100 kΩ) when the gate is at the drain potential. Some manufacturers show this FET using the regular symbol, and some show the resistor-plus-bar symbol, also seen in the figure.

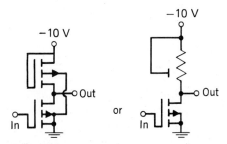

FIG. 5 • 26 Alternate schematic symbols for MOSFET resistive element.

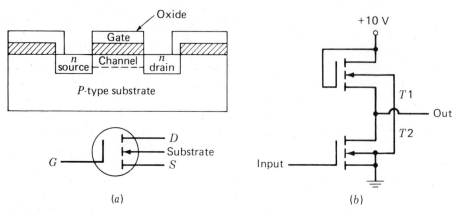

FIG. 5 • 27   (a) n-channel MOSFET transistor (NMOS). (b) n-channel inverter.

When a p-type substrate with n doping for the source and drain are used, as in Fig. 5·27, then the n-channel transistor is formed as shown in the figure. The schematic diagram symbols for the n-channel transistor and an inverter circuit are shown in Fig. 5·27(a) and (b). Notice that the circuit uses a positive voltage and behaves similarly to an npn transistor inverter circuit. This type of MOS is called NMOS.

A NOR gate can be formed in NMOS as shown in Fig. 5·28(a). The logic levels for this circuit are +1 to 0 V for a binary 0 and >+1.5 V for a binary 1. (This is positive logic.) If any of the inputs A, B, or C is a 1, the corresponding FET will conduct, causing the output to go to about +0.8 V or less. If all inputs are at +0.8 V or less, the FETs will all be off and the output will be at +0.4 V (or more).

Several different gates and flip-flops using NMOS are shown in Fig. 5·28. (PMOS is the same except for negative V_{CC} voltages and negative logic.) The high resistances used in these circuits mean low power dissipation. This, combined with the small areas needed to fabricate an FET, makes it possible to fabricate large numbers of circuits on a single small chip. Commonly one or two 1024-bit shift registers are included in a single container with 14 leads. Gating arrays with thousands of gates and flip-flops are also manufactured in standard containers, and these are often used in IC memories, which will be studied in Chap. 7, and in microprocessor chips, as described in Chap. 10.

5 • 15 CMOS LOGIC CIRCUITS

A series of circuits using MOSFET transistors called *complementary MOS* (CMOS) was originally developed for the aerospace and oceanographic industries. These circuits have very low power consumption and considerable resistance to noise. They are, however, slow relative to the high-speed logic lines, but large numbers of circuits can be placed on a single chip, the power supply voltage can vary over a large range, and the circuits are relatively economical to manufacture. The new-

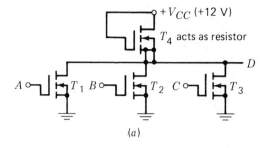

(a)

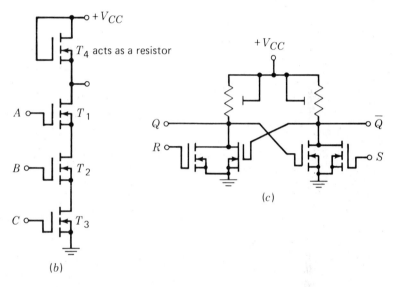

(b)

(c)

FIG. 5 • 28 FET logic circuit. (a) Three-input NOR gate. (b) Three-input NAND gate. (c) RS flip-flop.

est CMOS circuits have become relatively fast and are widely used for everything from electronic watches and calculators to microprocessors.

The CMOS circuits are fabricated as illustrated in Fig. 5·29(a), which shows that both n-channel and p-channel transistors can be fabricated on the same substrate.

The simplest form of CMOS integrated circuit consists of one n-channel and one p-channel MOS transistor, with both gate contacts tied together to form the input and both drain contacts tied together to form the output. This circuit is the basic CMOS inverter [Fig. 5·29(b)]. When the voltage at the input is near ground level, the gate-to-source voltage of the p-channel transistor approaches the value of the supply voltage + V, and the p channel is turned on. A low-resistance path is created between the supply voltage and the output, while a high-resistance path is between the output and ground, due to the n-channel transistor being off. The output voltage will approach that of the supply voltage $+V$. When the input voltage is near $+V$, the p channel turns off and the n channel turns on, causing the output voltage to approach ground.

Notice that in either state the circuit's power consumption is extremely low because one transistor is always off and because n- and p-channel transistors exhibit very high resistance when off, permitting very low leakage current to flow through the transistor which is in the off condition.

When conventional metal- and silicon-gate technologies are used, protective channel stops are provided to minimize leakage current between separate transistors as shown in Fig. 5·29(a). All p-channel devices must be surrounded by a continuous n-channel stop, which can also act as a conducting path for the external power supply to appropriate locations. Similarly, p-channel stops surround all n-channel devices and provide a conducting path between those n-channel devices which are electrically connected to the lowest potential and the external ground contact.

A two-input NOR gate can be constructed as shown in Fig. 5·30. Each additional input requires an additional p- and n-channel pair of MOS transistors.

A unique feature of CMOS circuits is the *transmission gate* shown in Fig. 5·30(b). This circuit presents a low resistance (impedance) from input to output when the gate is on and a very high resistance (impedance) when the gate is off. The gate is enabled when the gate input $G1$ is near ground and when $G2$ is near the $V+$ level. When $G1$ is near $V+$ and $G2$ is near ground, the gate is off and has a resistance from input to output which is generally greater than 10^9 Ω. Figure 5·28(b) also shows the logic diagram symbol for the transmission gate.

Transmission gates are widely used in CMOS designs. Often a three-state driver is used, and this will be described in later chapters. Figure 5·31 shows this circuit and its three states.

Figure 5·32 shows a D-type flip-flop in CMOS technology which uses transmission gates to simplify the design. Notice the simplicity of this configuration versus the TTL and DTL circuits shown earlier.

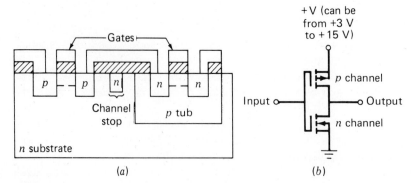

FIG. 5 • 29 CMOS inverter. (*a*) CMOS elements. (*b*) Circuit that is the basic CMOS inverter.

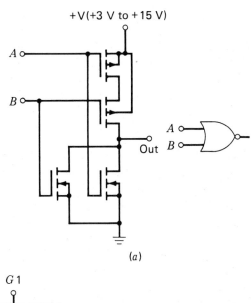

+V(+3 V to +15 V)

A

B

Out

A
B

(a)

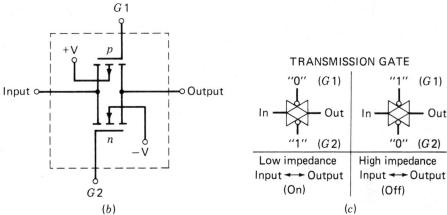

G1

+V   p

Input   Output

n
        −V

G2

(b)

TRANSMISSION GATE

"0" (G1)	"1" (G1)
In ⟶ Out	In ⟶ Out
"1" (G2)	"0" (G2)
Low impedance	High impedance
Input ⟷ Output	Input ⟷ Output
(On)	(Off)

(c)

FIG. 5 • 30 CMOS NOR gate and transmission gate. (a) NOR gate in which an additional transistor pair is required for each gate leg added. (b) Transmission gate schematic. (c) Schematic symbol.

Table 5·4 gives some details of CMOS operation versus other circuit lines. Notice the low power consumption (nanowatts when not being switched), competitive speeds, and noise protection.

5 • 16 IIL LOGIC CIRCUITS

Integrated injection logic (IIL or I²L) circuits represent an attempt to use bipolar junction transistor technology and still attain MOS transistor packing densities and low power consumption. Compared to MOS, the standard bipolar technology

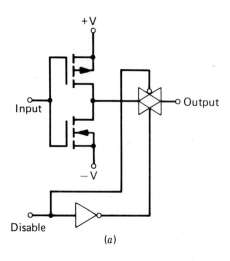

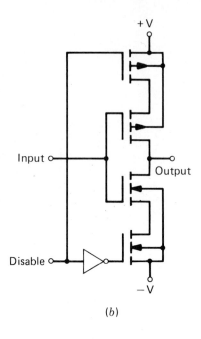

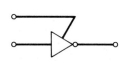

INPUT	DISABLE	OUTPUT
1	0	0
0	0	1
X	1	High impedance

X = Don't-care state

(c)

FIG. 5 • 31 Three-state CMOS circuit.

TABLE 5 • 4 CIRCUIT LINE CHARACTERISTICS

	STANDARD TTL 74	LOW-POWER TTL	DTL	SCHOTTKY CLAMPED TTL	CMOS 5 V SUPPLY	CMOS 10 V SUPPLY	ECL
Quiescent power	10 mW	1 mW	8.5 mW	20 mW	10 nW	10 nW	60 mW
Propagation delay	4 ns	20 ns	20 ns	1.5 ns	10 ns	7 ns	0.3 ns
Flip-flop toggle frequency	45 MHz	5 MHz	7 MHz	100 MHz	10 MHz	12 MHz	600 MHz
Noise immunity	1 V	1 V	1 V	0.8 V	2 V	4 V	0.5 V
Fan out	10	10	8	10	50	50	5

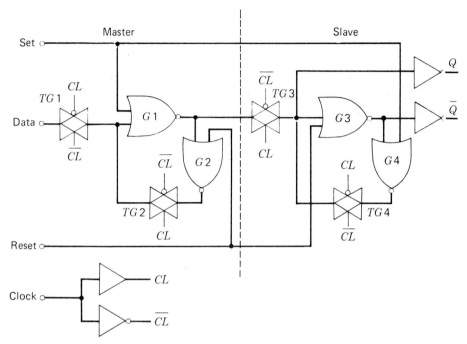

FIG. 5 • 32 *D*-type flip-flop in CMOS.

attains higher speeds but requires resistors, the transistors are larger, and an iso-lation diffusion is needed which wastes space on the chip. To alleviate these prob-lems, several designs have been made where the same transistor region is used as part of two or more devices. This technique is called *merging,* and IIL is the most used merged technology.

An example of merging is the move from the DTL NAND gate with a separate diode per input to the multiple emitter input transistor used in TTL. In IIL, multiple collectors are used instead of multiple emitters. Also, no resistors are used in these circuits, and these are their distinguishing features.

Figure 5·33 shows the basic IIL gate and a possible semiconductor layout. Each gate requires an injector transistor to feed current into the base. Notice the single input and multiple outputs (one collector junction per output). This is a nonstandard logic configuration, and no ANSI or MIL standard symbol exists for this circuit, although standards work is progressing. Figure 5·33(c) shows a symbol that is widely used at this time.

To show how gates can be formed from this configuration, which is basically an inverter with multiple outputs, Fig. 5·34(a) shows a NOR gate made from two of the circuits in Fig. 5·33. The IIL outputs are "open collector" outputs, and so con-necting them together forms a "wired AND." As a result in Fig. 5·34(a) the inputs A and B are first inverted and are then wire ANDed to form a $\overline{A}\cdot\overline{B}$, which is the same function as a NOR gate yields.

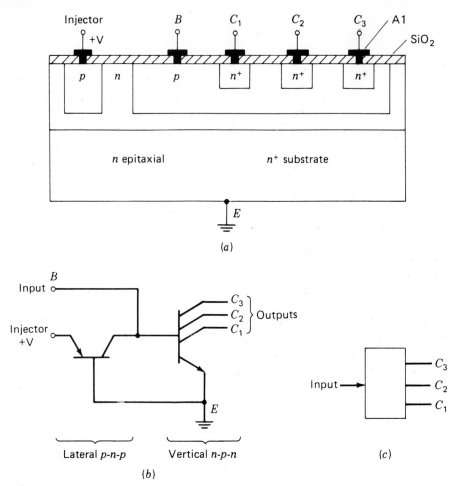

FIG. 5 • 33 IIL gate.

Figure 5·34(*b*) shows how IIL gates can be used to OR inputs. Notice that in this case several outputs are available, each with the value $A + B$.

Figure 5·34(*c*) shows how a NAND gate can be made using IIL gates. In this case the inputs must be outputs from the IIL gates since these are wire ANDed. Again, multiple outputs are available.

Because the basic IIL gate has a single input and multiple outputs, design does not proceed along regular lines. The advantages of this technology are sufficient to overcome this problem and IIL microprocessors are now available, as are some high-speed memories. IIL does not lend itself to chip interconnection in the way that TTL does, however, and seems primarily suited for large-scale integration (like MOS).

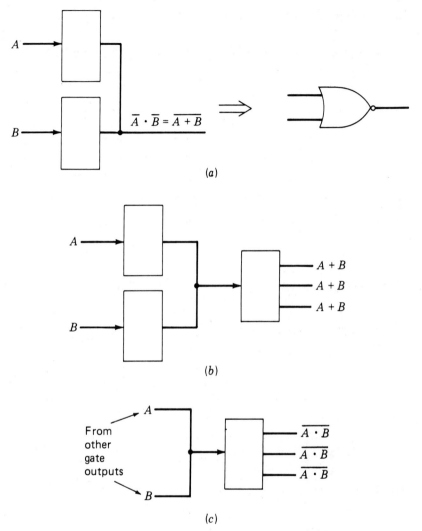

FIG. 5 • 34 IIL logic connections. (*a*) IIL NOR gate function. (*b*) IIL OR gate. (*c*) IIL NAND gate function.

QUESTIONS

1. For what current does the silicon diode graphed in Fig. $5 \cdot 1$ (*c*) have a voltage drop of $+0.6$ V?

2. For the saturated transistor graphed in Fig. $5 \cdot 3$ (*c*), what is the base voltage, which is also the base-emitter drop, when $I_b = 2000\ \mu\text{A}$ and V_{ce} is 200 mV?

3. For Question 2, what is the difference between the base voltage and the collector voltage at that time?

4. Consider this circuit (assume a silicon diode).

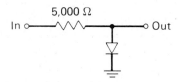

If we make IN a voltage of $+5$ V, the OUT point will be at about _____.

5. If, for Question 4, IN were -7 V, give the corresponding OUT voltage and resistor currents.

6. If V_{ce} is held at $+8$ V and I_b is changed from 0.85 to 1 mA, what is the resultant change in I_c for the 2N706 in Fig. 5·3?

7. What is the current gain through the transistor for Question 6 (the ratio of the change in I_b to I_c)?

8. The inputs to the following circuit are A, B, and C, each of which is a signal of 0 or $+2$ V, representing a binary 0 or 1, respectively. Draw a block diagram for this circuit using AND gates, NAND gates, flip-flops, or whatever you would like.

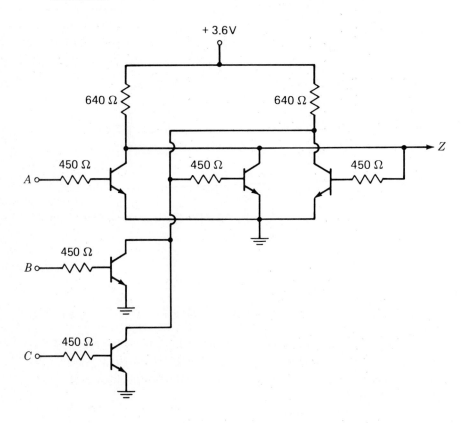

9. For the emitter follower in Fig. 5·5(a), if the $+V$ is 0 V and $-V$ is -5 V, the resistor is 1000 Ω, and the transistor base-emitter voltage drop is 0.75 V, a -2 V input will result in an output of _____ V. Is the transistor in the active region? Why?

10. For the emitter follower in Fig. 5·5(a), if $-V$ is ground, $+V$ is $+5$ V, the resistor is 3 kΩ, and the base-emitter drop of the transistor is 0.5 V, for a $+1$ V input give the output voltage and current through the resistor. Is the transistor in the active region? Why?

11. If the X input in Fig. 5·6 is at $+3.5$ V and the Y input at $+2$ V, what will the output voltage level at Z be? Assume a silicon diode with a forward drop of 0.6 V.

12. If the X input to the circuit in Fig. 5·6 is at $+0.5$ V and the Y input at 0.25 V, for a silicon diode with a forward drop of 0.5 V what will be the output voltage at Z?

13. Draw the schematic for a diode AND gate with four inputs.

14. If the X input to the OR gate in Fig. 5·7 is at $+3$ V and the Y input is at 0.5 V, what will the output voltage be? Assume a silicon diode with a forward drop of 0.6 V.

15. For the circuit described in the preceding question, what will be the output level if X is at 0.1 V and Y at 0.8 V?

16. Draw the schematic for a four-input diode OR gate.

17. Draw the schematic for a diode AND-to-OR gate network which realizes the Boolean algebra function $AB + CD$.

18. Analyze the output levels for the circuit you designed in the preceding question for input levels of $+3$ V for a logical 1 and $+0.5$ V for a logical 0.

19. Draw the block diagram and schematic for a single RTL inverter, as in Fig. 5·8, but with its output connected to four other inverters.

20. For the drawing you made in Question 19, calculate the output voltage for the first inverter when it has a 1 output.

21. Draw a block diagram for the following circuit. The inputs are A, B, and C and each carries a signal of 0 or $+2$ V, representing 0 or 1, respectively. What will the output levels be if the *output* is not connected to anything?

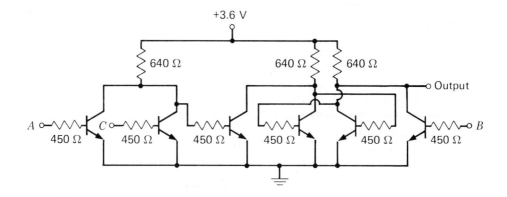

22. Assume the inputs A and B are both at ground potential (0 V) and that transistor $T2$ is off. If the input B is raised to $+2$ V and then lowered back to 0 V, describe the operation of the circuit.

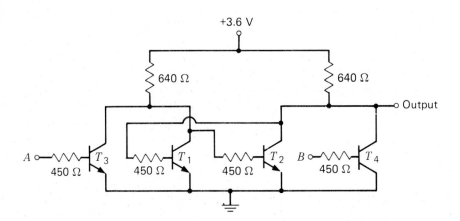

23. Discuss the noise protection of RTL circuits versus DTL circuits.
24. For the TTL circuit in Fig. 5·16(c), if all inputs are at $+3$ V, what will be the approximate voltages at the emitter and collector of $T2$?
25. Which transistors in the circuit in Fig. 5·17 are saturated when both inputs are low?
26. Which transistors in the circuit in Fig. 5·17 are saturated when both inputs are high?
27. Using the information gained in the preceding two questions, discuss how the use of Schottky clamped transistors might speed up the circuit in Fig. 5·17.
28. Does connecting the output of a DTL gate as in Fig. 5·15(a) to several DTL gate inputs tend to cause lower output levels when the output is a 1? Compare this with the RTL gate.
29. Comment on the simplicity and low power consumption of the circuit in Fig. 5·19(a).
30. Compare the virtues and problems of the TTL circuits in Table 5·2.
31. If we connect three inputs from DTL gates as in Fig. 5·15(a) to the output of a single gate, what will be the collector current of $T2$ when turned on? Assume that $T1$ has so much gain, its base draws 0 current.
32. The following is a schematic for a TTL NAND gate. If the X input is at $+3$ V and the Y input at 0 V, what will the approximate voltages be at points $A, B, C,$ and D?

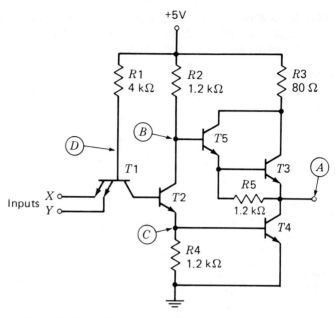

33. The following is a schematic for a logic circuit. Give the voltage values at points *A*, *B*, and *C* if the *X* input is +3 V and the *Y* input is at 0 V.

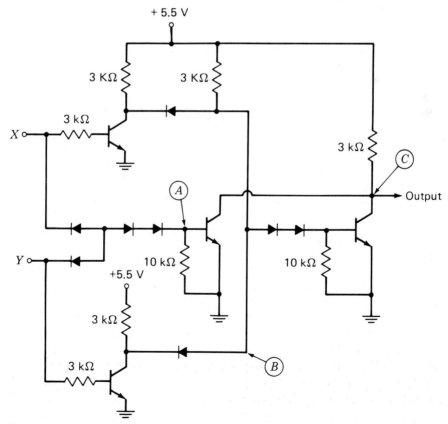

34. The following is an RTL circuit with three inputs A, B, and C and a single output Z. The input levels are either 0 V, representing a binary 0, or +2 V, representing a binary 1. Write the Boolean algebra expression for the function realized by this circuit.

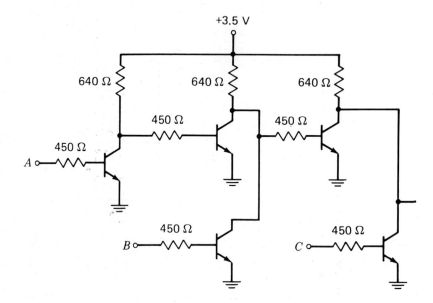

35. The inputs to the following circuit are *A, B, C,* and *D,* each of which is a signal of 0 or +3 V, representing 0 and 1, respectively, and the outputs are Output 0 and Output 1. Draw a block diagram for this circuit using AND, OR, NAND, NOR, or whatever gates you like.

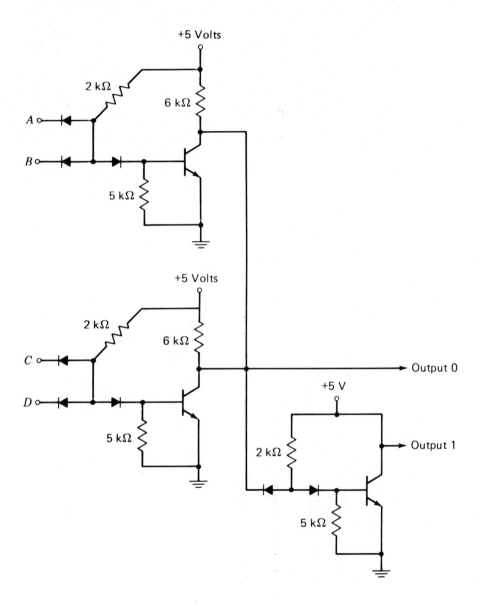

36. The following DTL circuit has inputs *A, B, C,* and *D* and a single output *Z*. Draw a block diagram of this circuit using AND, OR, NAND, NOR gates, inverters, or flip-flops.

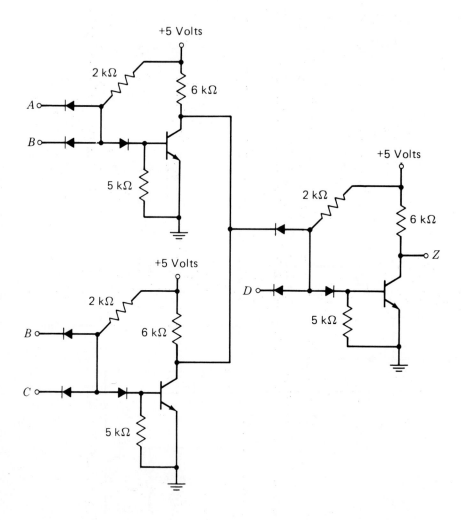

37. The following are three circuits from a survey of integrated circuits in *IEEE Transactions on Computers*. Identify each circuit type [that is, which is emitter-coupled logic (ECL), which is transistor-transistor logic (TTL), etc.]. Then briefly list or discuss the advantages of each circuit.

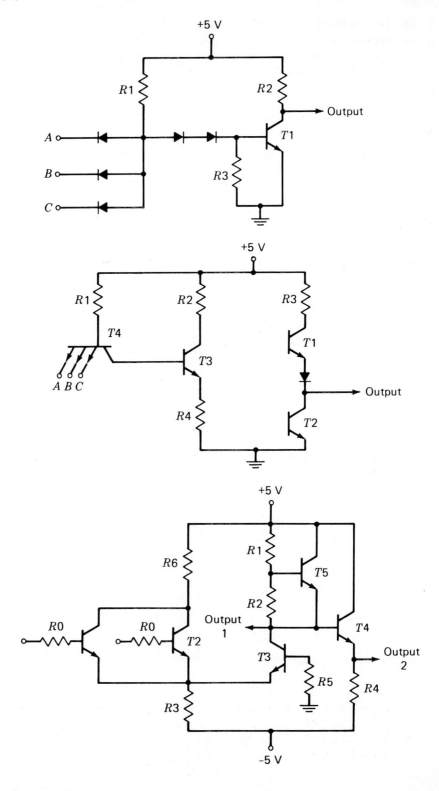

38. Explain the action of the two output transistors in the TTL gate in Fig. 5·17.

39. Write the values at the output of each gate in Fig. 5·15(c) for inputs of S_1 = 1, S_2 = 1, R_1 = 0, and R_2 = 1. Assume that CL = 1 and the flip-flop is in the 1 state.

40. Redo the above, but with S_1 = 0. To what state will the flip-flop go when CL goes to 0? Explain.

41. If T4 shorts in Fig. 5·21 so that the emitter and collector are both permanently connected to the base, what will be the output at $\overline{X}$? Explain.

42. Given a single *npn* transistor, how would you connect it to make the three-input MECL gate in Fig. 5·22 a four-input gate?

43. T4 in Fig. 5·28(a) and (b) acts as a resistor. Analyze the operation of both of these gates if A = 0, B = 1, and C = 1. Make V_{CC} equal to 30 V, 25 V a 1, and 0 V a 0.

44. Draw block diagrams for the flip-flop in Fig. 5·28(c).

45. In Fig. 5·28(c) does the Q output go positive or to 0 if R = 10 V and S = 0 V? Explain.

46. In Fig. 5·12, if the 640 Ω resistor from T1 to +3.5 V is open (or disconnected), the flip-flop will always be in the _____ state. Explain your answer.

47. If the RESET and SET inputs to the NOR gate flip-flop in Fig. 5·13 are both connected to +3.5 V, the 0 and 1 outputs will be at what levels?

48. Assume that the inputs X and Y to the following circuit are at ground potential and transistor T1 is off. Explain the operation of the circuit if the input X is made positive 5 V and then returned to ground.?

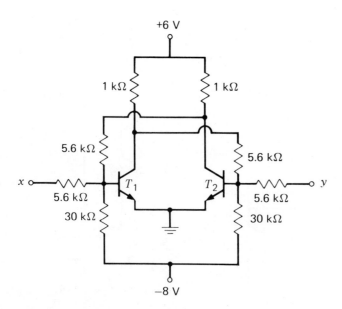

49. Write a Boolean algebra expression relating the inputs A, B, and C and their complements to the output Z for the following circuit:

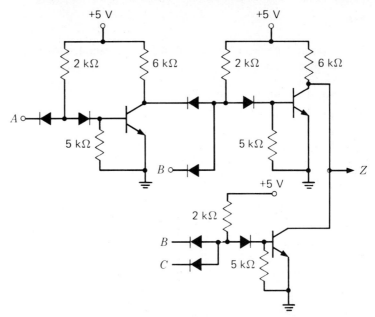

50. The inputs to the following circuit are *A*, *B*, *C*, and *D*, each of which is a

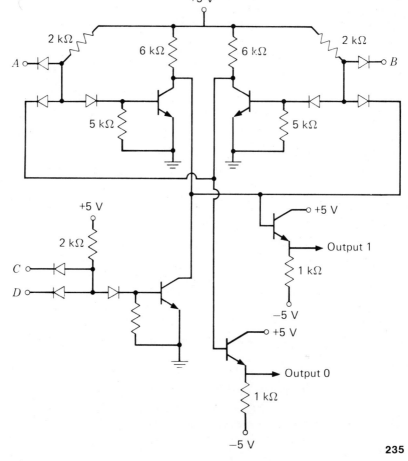

signal of 0 or +3 V, representing 0 and 1, respectively. Draw a block diagram for this circuit using AND, OR, NAND, NOR, or whatever gates you would like.

51. The following DTL circuit has inputs *A, B, C,* and *D* and a single output *Z*. Draw a block diagram of this circuit using AND, OR, NAND, NOR gates, inverters, or flip-flops.

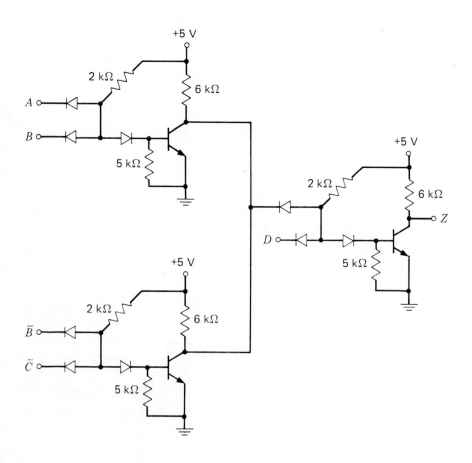

52. Draw a block diagram for the following circuit using any gates or flip-flops you choose. The inputs *A, B,* and *C* are signal levels of either 0 or + 3 V, representing 0 and 1, respectively.

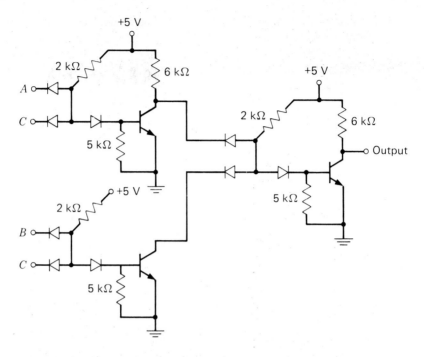

53. Draw a block diagram for the following circuit using any gates or flip-flops you choose. The inputs *A, B,* and *C* are signal levels of either 0 or +3 V, representing 0 and 1, respectively.

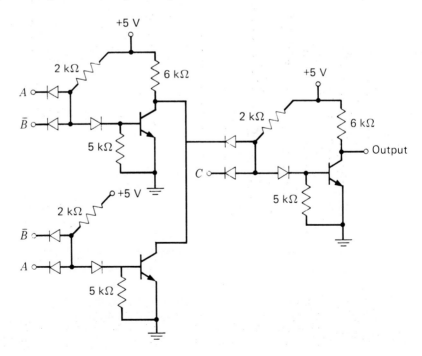

54. Write a Boolean algebra expression for the function realized by the following circuit. The inputs are *W, X, Y,* and *Z* and the output is to be expressed in these variables. Inputs are 0 or +3 V, representing binary 0 and 1, respectively.

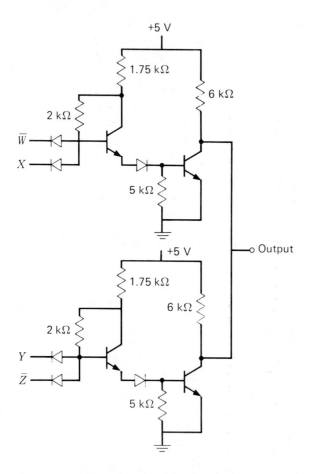

55. The ability of a given TTL circuit to drive other circuits is often given in terms of what is called a *unit load.* For Fairchild's 7400 series TTL a unit load is 40 μA (to ground) when the level is in the high state and is the ability to accept 1.6 mA in the low state. Then an input to a NAND gate in the 7400 series requires one unit load to be driven low or high. A NAND gate's output in the 7400 series can drive 20 unit loads when high and 10 unit loads when low. If a TTL NAND gate was connected to five inputs to other NAND gates and the output was high, how many amperes might the output supply to ground?

56. Using the data in the preceding question, how many gate inputs can be safely connected to a given gate output? (This is called the *fan-out* for the gate.)

57. Compare the *fan-out* ratios for the 7400 TTL gates with the RTL gates shown in Fig. 4·15.

58. Why is the unit load greater for the low level than the high level? Examine the basic TTL circuit to get your answer.

59. Explain why TTL outputs go from low to high faster than DTL when a long wire or other capacitative load must be driven.

60. What are some advantages of MOS over conventional bipolar circuits?

61. Why do CMOS gates require so little power when they are not changing states?

62. Compare speed and power consumption for Fairchild's 10,000 and Motorola's MECL III ECL circuits.

63. Explain the operation of the circuit in Fig. 5·28(a). Explain the operation of the circuit in Fig. 5·28(b).

64. Draw block diagram symbols for the circuit in Fig. 5·28(c).

65. Compare NMOS and PMOS circuits with regard to speed.

66. Explain the operation of the circuit in Fig. 5·30(a).

67. Explain the operation of the circuit in Fig. 5·30(b).

68. Why is the circuit in Fig. 5·31 called a three-state circuit? What is the third state?

69. For the data input a 1 explain the operation of the circuit in Fig. 5·32 during a clock pulse. Assume that the flip-flop starts in the 0 state.

70. For the data input a 0 and the flip-flop in the 1 state, show what happens to the flip-flop in Fig. 5·32 when a clock pulse is applied.

71. Compare CMOS with low-power TTL circuits. What might some disadvantages of CMOS be?

72. Discuss the problems and virtues of three of the circuit lines given in Table 5·4.

73. (a) Draw a block diagram which shows the logical operation of the following circuit. You can use AND gates, NAND gates, OR gates, NOR gates, etc., in your diagram.
    (b) Explain some advantages and disadvantages of the circuit.

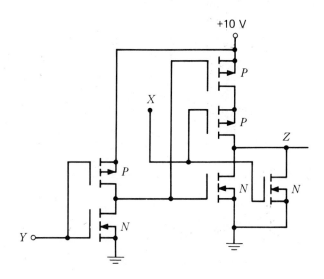

74. Calculate the power dissipated in resistor $R2$ when the ECL circuit in Fig. 5·21 is in both of its output states.

75. Compare the MECL III and Fairchild 10,000 ECL series of circuits with regard to the power dissipation. Are these circuits very similar?

6
THE ARITHMETIC-LOGIC UNIT

The arithmetic-logic unit (ALU) is the section of the computer that performs arithmetic and logical operations on the data processed by the computer. This section of the machine can be relatively small, consisting of perhaps one or more large-scale integration (LSI) chips, or, for large "number crunchers" (scientific-oriented computers), it can consist of a considerable array of high-speed logic components. Despite the variations in size and complexity, the small machines generally perform their arithmetic and logical operations using the same principles as the large machines. What changes is the speed of the logic gates and flip-flops used; also, special techniques are used for speeding up operations and performing several operations in parallel.

Although many functions can be performed by the ALUs of present-day machines, the basic arithmetic operations—addition, subtraction, multiplication, and division—continue to be "bread-and-butter" operations. Even the literature gives evidence of the fundamental nature of these operations, for when a new machine is described, the times required for addition and multiplication are always included as significant features. Accordingly, this chapter first describes the means by which a computer adds, subtracts, multiplies, and divides. Other basic operations, such as shifting, logical multiplication, and logical addition, are then described.

It should be remembered that the control unit directs the operation of the ALU. What the ALU does is to add, subtract, shift, etc., when it is provided with the correct sequence of input signals. It is up to the control element to provide these signals, as it is the function of the memory units to provide the arithmetic element with the information that is to be used. It will therefore be assumed that the control and memory sections of the machine are capable of delivering the correct control signals, and that the data on which the operations are to be performed are available. The function of the ALU is therefore to add, subtract, or perform whatever operation the control element directs.

6 • 1 CONSTRUCTION OF THE ALU

The information handled in a computer is generally divided into "words," each consisting of a fixed number of bits.† For instance, the words handled by a given binary machine may be 32 bits in length. In this case, the ALU would have to be capable of adding, subtracting, etc., words of 32 bits in length. The operands used are then supplied from computer storage, and the control element directs the operations that are performed. If addition is to be performed, the addend and augend will be supplied to the ALU which must add the numbers and then, at least temporarily, store the results (sum).

To introduce several concepts, let us consider the construction of a typical computer ALU. The storage devices will consist of a set of flip-flop *registers*, each of which consists of one or more flip-flops. The *length* of each register is defined as the maximum amount of information the register can store. In a binary register, the register length is equal to the maximum number of binary digits that can be stored; and in a binary-coded-decimal (BCD) register, the register length will be the number of decimal digits the register can store.

For convenience, the various registers of the ALU are generally given names such as X register, B register, MQ register, etc., and the flip-flops are then given the same names, so that the X register would contain flip-flops X_1, X_2, X_3, etc.

Most computers (especially microprocessors) have a register called an *accumulator* which is the principal register for arithmetic and logical operations. This register stores the result of each arithmetic or logical operation, and gating circuitry is attached to this register so that the necessary operations can be performed on its contents and any other registers involved.

An accumulator is therefore a basic storage register of the arithmetic element. If the machine is instructed to *load* the accumulator, the control element will first clear the accumulator of whatever may have been stored in it and then put the operand selected in storage into the accumulator register. If the computer is instructed to *add,* the number stored in the accumulator will represent the augend. The addend will then be located in memory, and the computer's circuitry will add this number (the addend) to the number previously stored in the accumulator (the augend) and store the sum in the accumulator. Notice that the original augend will no longer be stored in the accumulator after the addition. Furthermore, the sum may then either remain in the accumulator or be transferred to memory, depending on the type of computer. This chapter will deal only with the processes of adding, subtracting, etc., and not the process of locating the number to be added in mem-

---

† Some computers also provide the ability to handle variable length operands.

ory or the transferring of numbers to memory. These operations will be covered in following chapters.

Some computers, instead of having a single accumulator, will have two or more accumulators, and these are called, for instance, accumulator A and accumulator B (as in the 6800 Microprocessor) or ACC1, ACC2, etc. (as in the Data General Corporation computers). When the number of registers provided to hold operands becomes larger than four, however, the registers are often called *general registers,* and individual registers are given names, such as general register 4, general register 8, etc.

6 • 2 INTEGER REPRESENTATION

The numbers used in digital machines much be represented using such storage devices as flip-flops. The most direct number representation system for binary-valued storage devices is an *integer representation system.* Figure 6·1(a) shows a register of four flip-flops, X_1, X_2, X_3, and X_4, used to store numbers. Simply writing the values or states of the flip-flops gives the number in integer form, so that $X_1 = 1$, $X_2 = 1$, $X_3 = 0$, $X_4 = 0$ gives 1100, or decimal 12, while $X_1 = 0$, $X_2 = 1$, $X_3 = 0$, $X_4 = 1$ gives 0101, or decimal 5.

It is generally necessary to represent both positive and negative numbers; so an additional bit is required, called the *sign bit.* This is generally placed to the left of the magnitude bits. In Fig. 6·1(b) we choose X_0 as the sign bit, and X_1, X_2, X_3, and X_4 will give the magnitude. A 0 in X_0 means that the number is positive, and a 1 in X_0 means that the number is negative (this is the usual convention); so $X_0 = 0$, X_1

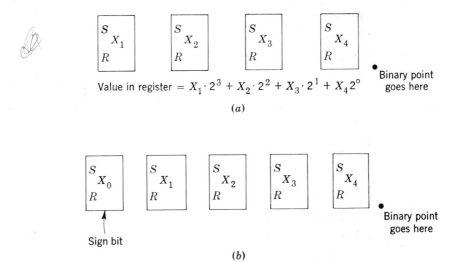

FIG. 6 • 1 Representation systems. (a) Integer representation. (b) Sign-plus-magnitude system.

= 1, X_2 = 1, X_3 = 0, and X_4 = 1 gives positive 1101, or +13 in decimal, and X_0 = 1, X_1 = 1, X_2 = 1, X_3 = 0, and X_4 = 1 gives negative 1101, or −13 in decimal.

This system is called the *signed-integer binary system,* or *signed magnitude binary integer system.*

If a register contains eight flip-flops, a signed binary number in the system would have 7 magnitude, or integer, bits and a single sign bit. So 00001111 would be +15 and 10001111 would be −15, since the leading 0 and 1 give the + and − only.

The magnitudes of numbers which can be stored in the two representative systems in Fig. 6·1 are as follows:

1. For binary integer representation, an *n*-flip-flop register can store from (decimal) 0 to 2^n − 1. Thus for a 6-bit register, we can store from 000000 to 111111, where 111111 is 63, which is 2^6 − 1, or 64 − 1.
2. The signed binary integer representation system has a range of from − (2^{n-1} − 1) to + (2^{n-1} − 1) for a binary register. For instance, a 7-flip-flop register can store from −111111 to +111111, which is −63 to +63 [− (2^6 − 1) to + (2^6 − 1)].

In the following sections we shall learn how to perform various arithmetic and logical operations on registers.

6 • 3 THE BINARY HALF ADDER

A basic module used in binary arithmetic elements is the *half adder.* The function of the half adder is to add two binary digits, producing a sum and a carry according to the binary addition rules shown in Table 6·1. Figure 6·2 shows a design for a half adder. There are two inputs to the half adder, designated as *X* and *Y* in Fig. 6·2, and two outputs, designated as *S* and *C.* The half adder performs the binary addition operation for two binary inputs shown in Table 6·1. This is *arithmetic addition,* not logical or Boolean algebra addition.

As shown in Fig. 6·2, there are two inputs to the half adder and two outputs. If either of the inputs is a 1, but not both, the output on the *S* line will be a 1. If both of the inputs are 1s, the output on the *C* (for carry) line will be a 1. For all other

TABLE 6 • 1

INPUTS	SUM BIT
0 + 0	0
0 + 1	1
1 + 0	1
1 + 1	0 with a carry of 1

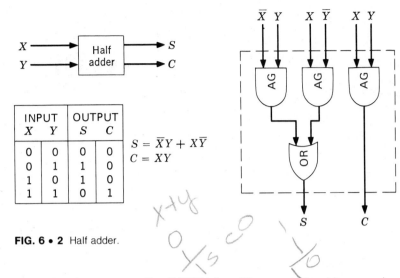

INPUT		OUTPUT	
X	Y	S	C
0	0	0	0
0	1	1	0
1	0	1	0
1	1	0	1

$$S = \overline{X}Y + X\overline{Y}$$
$$C = XY$$

FIG. 6 • 2 Half adder.

states there will be a 0 output on the CARRY line. These relationships may be written in Boolean form as follows:

$$S = X\overline{Y} + \overline{X}Y$$
$$C = XY$$

A *quarter adder* consists of the two inputs to the half adder and the S output only. The logical expression for this circuit is therefore $S = X\overline{Y} + \overline{X}Y$. This is also the *exclusive OR* relationship for Boolean algebra (refer to Chap. 3).

6 • 4 THE FULL ADDER

When more than two binary digits are to be added, several half adders will not be adequate, for the half adder has no input to handle carries from other digits.

Consider the addition of the following two binary numbers:

```
      1011              1011
  +  1110          +  1110
    11001 = sum        0101 = partial sum
                        1 1  = carry bits
                      11001 = complete sum
```

As shown, the carries generated in each column must be considered during the addition process. Therefore adder circuitry capable of adding the contents of two registers together must include provision for handling carries as well as addend and augend bits. There must therefore be three inputs to each stage of a multidigit adder—except the stage for the least significant bits—one for each input from the

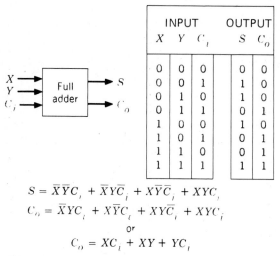

| INPUT | | | OUTPUT | |
X	Y	C_i	S	C_o
0	0	0	0	0
0	0	1	1	0
0	1	0	1	0
0	1	1	0	1
1	0	0	1	0
1	0	1	0	1
1	1	0	0	1
1	1	1	1	1

$$S = \overline{X}\,\overline{Y}C_i + \overline{X}YC_i + X\overline{Y}C_i + XYC_i$$
$$C_o = \overline{X}YC_i + X\overline{Y}C_i + XY\overline{C_i} + XYC_i$$

or

$$C_o = XC_i + XY + YC_i$$

FIG. 6 • 3 Full adder.

numbers being added and one for any carry that might have been generated or propagated by the previous stage.

The block diagram symbol for a *full binary adder,* which will handle these carries, is illustrated in Fig. 6·3, as is the complete table of input-output relationships for the full adder. There are three inputs to the full adder: the X and Y inputs from the respective digits of the registers to be added, and the C_i input, which is for any carry generated by the previous stage. The two outputs are S, which is the output value for that stage of the addition, and C_o, which produces the carry to be added into the next stage.† The Boolean expressions for the input-output relationships for each of the two outputs are also presented in Fig. 6·3, as is the expression for the C_o output in simplified form.

A full adder may be constructed of two half adders, as illustrated in Fig. 6·4. Constructing a full adder from two half adders may not necessarily be the most economical technique, however, and generally full adders are designed directly from the input–output relations illustrated in Fig. 6·3.

6 • 5 A PARALLEL BINARY ADDER

A 4-bit parallel binary adder is illustrated in Fig. 6·5. The purpose of this adder is to add together two 4-bit binary integers. The addend inputs are named X_1 through X_4, and the augend bits are represented by Y_1 through Y_4.‡ The adder shown does not possess the ability to handle sign bits for the binary words to be added, but

---

† C_i is for *carry-in* and C_o for *carry-out.*

‡ These inputs would normally be from flip-flop registers X and Y, and the adder would add the number in X to the number in Y, giving the sum, or S_1 through S_4.

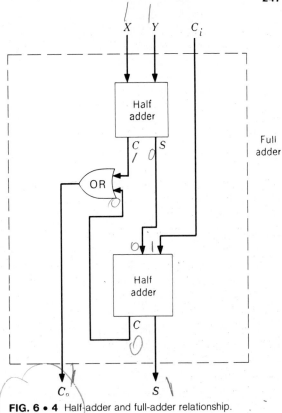

FIG. 6 • 4 Half-adder and full-adder relationship.

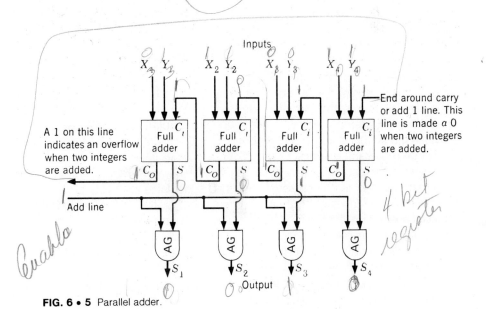

FIG. 6 • 5 Parallel adder.

only adds together the magnitudes of the numbers stored. The additional circuitry needed to handle sign bits is dependent on whether negative numbers are represented in true magnitude or in the 1s or 2s complement systems, and this problem will be described later.

Consider the addition of the following two 4-bit binary numbers:

$$0111 \text{ where } X_1 = 0, X_2 = 1, X_3 = 1, \text{ and } X_4 = 1$$
$$0011 \text{ where } Y_1 = 0, Y_2 = 0, Y_3 = 1, \text{ and } Y_4 = 1$$
$$\text{sum} = 1010$$

The sum should therefore be $S_1 = 1$, $S_2 = 0$, $S_3 = 1$, and $S_4 = 0$.

The operation of the adder may be checked as follows. Since X_4 and Y_4 are the least significant digits, they cannot receive a carry from a previous stage. In the problem above, X_4 and Y_4 are both 1s, their sum is therefore 0, and a carry is generated and added into the full adder for bits X_3 and Y_3. Bits X_3 and Y_3 are also both 1s, as is the carry input to this stage. Therefore the sum output line S_3 carries a 1 and the CARRY line to the next stage also carries a 1. Since X_2 is a 1, Y_2 a zero, and the carry input is 1, the sum output line S_2 will carry a 0, and the carry to the next stage will be a 1. Both inputs X_1 and Y_1 are equal to 0, and the CARRY input line to this adder stage is equal to 1. Therefore the sum output line S_1 will represent a 1 and the CARRY output line, designated as "overflow" in Fig. 6·5, will have a zero output.

The same basic configuration illustrated in Fig. 6·5 may be extended to any number of bits. A 7-bit adder may be constructed using 7 full adders, and a 20-bit adder using 20 full adders.

It should be noted that the OVERFLOW line could be used to enable the 4-bit adder in Fig. 6·5 to have a 5-bit output. This is not generally done, however, because the addend and augend both come from storage, and so their length is the length of the basic computer word, and a longer word cannot be readily stored by the machine. It was explained earlier that a machine with a word length of n bits [consisting of sign bit and $(n - 1)$ bits to designate the magnitude] could express binary numbers from $(-2^{n-1} + 1)$ to $(2^{n-1} - 1)$. A number within these limits is called *representable*. Since the simple 4-bit adder in Fig. 6·5 has no sign bit, it can only represent binary integers from 0 to 15. If 1100 and 1100 are added in the adder illustrated in Fig. 6·5, there will be a 1 output on the OVERFLOW line because the sum of these two numbers is 11000. This number is 24 decimal and cannot be represented in this system. Such a number is referred to as *nonrepresentable* for this particular very small register, and when two integers are added such that their sum is nonrepresentable (that is, contains too many bits), then we say the sum *overflows,* or an *overflow* occurs. A 1 on the CARRY line for the full adder connected to the most significant digits indicates this. The overflow generated in this case is often connected to circuitry which alerts the computer, generating an indication that an overflow operation has occurred. It is one of the functions of the arithmetic element to detect such overflows.

The AND gates connected to the S output lines from the four adders are used to gate the sum into the correct register.

6 • 6 POSITIVE AND NEGATIVE NUMBERS

When writing numbers in the decimal system, the common practice is to write the number as a magnitude preceded by a plus or minus sign, which indicates whether the number is positive or negative. Hence $+125$ is positive and -125 is negative 125. The same practice is generally used with binary numbers: $+111$ is positive 7, and -110 is negative 6. To handle both positive and negative numbers, the computer must have some means of distinguishing a positive from a negative number, and as was previously explained, the computer word usually contains a sign bit, generally adjacent to the most significant bit in the computer word. In the systems to be described, a 1 in the sign bit will indicate a negative number and a 0 in the sign bit a positive number.

We have examined the representation of numbers in Sec. 6·1 using a signed-integer magnitude representation system. There are two other representation systems, however, which are more often used—the 1s and 2s complement systems. (The 2s complement system is the most frequently used system at present.) The advantage of these systems is that both positive and negative numbers can be added or subtracted using only an adder of the type already explained.

Here are the three basic systems.

1. Negative numbers may be stored in their *true magnitude form.* The binary number -0011 will therefore be stored as 1.0011, where the 1 indicates that the number stored is negative and the 0011 indicates the magnitude of the number.†

2. The *1s complement* of the magnitude may be used to represent a negative number. The binary number -0111 will therefore be represented as 1.1000, where the 1 indicates that the number is negative and 1000 is the 1s complement of the magnitude. (The 1s complement is formed by simply complementing each bit of the positive magnitude.)

3. The *2s complement* may be used to represent a negative binary number. For instance, -0111 would be stored as 1.1001, where the 1 in the sign bit indicates that the number is negative and the 1001 is the 2s complement of the magnitude of the number. (The 2s complement is formed by 1s complementing the magnitude part 0111, giving 1000, and then adding 1 to the least significant digit, giving 1001.)

6 • 7 ADDITION IN THE 1S COMPLEMENT SYSTEM

The 1s complement system for representing negative numbers is often used in parallel binary machines. The main reason for this is the ease with which the 1s complement of a binary number may be formed, since only complementing each bit of a binary number stored in a flip-flop register is required. Before discussing

---

† Again we note that a binary point is used to separate the sign bit from the magnitude bits. Thus 0.011 is $+3$. Other symbols have been used, but this is conventional and we will use it.

the implementations of an adder for the 1s complement system, the four possible basic situations which may arise in adding combinations of positive and negative numbers in the 1s complement system will be noted:

1. When a positive number is added to another positive number, the addition of all bits, including the sign bit, is straightforward. Since both sign bits will be 0s, no sum or carry will be generated in the sign-bit adder and the output will remain 0. Here is an example of the addition of two 4-bit positive numbers.†

NORMAL NOTATION	COMPUTER WORD
+0011	0.0011
+0100	0.0100
+0111	0.0111

2. When a positive and a negative number are added together, the sum may be either positive or negative. If the positive number has a greater magnitude, the sum will be positive; and if the negative number is greater in magnitude, the sum will be negative. In the 1s complement system, the answer will be correct as is if the sum of the two numbers is negative in value. In this case no overflow will be generated when the numbers are added. For instance:

+0011	0.0011
−1100	1.0011
−1001	1.0110

In this case the output of the adder will be 10110, the last 4 bits of which are the 1s complement of 1001, the correct magnitude of the sum. The 1 in the sign bit is also correct, indicating a negative number.

3. If the positive number is larger than the negative number, the sum before the end-around carry is added will be incorrect. The addition of the end-around carrry will correct this sum. There will be a 0 in the sign bit, indicating that the sum is positive.

+1001 =	0.1001	+0011 =	0.0011
−0100 =	1.1011	−0010 =	1.1101
+0101	0.0100	+0001	0.0000
	→1		→1
	0.0101		0.0001

Notice what happens when two numbers of equal magnitude but opposite signs are added:

---

† In this, and in all discussions that follow, we assume that the result (sum) does not exceed the capacity of the number of digits being used. This will be discussed later.

$$+ 1011 = 0.1011 \qquad +0000 = 0.0000$$
$$\underline{- 1011 = 1.0100} \qquad \underline{-0000 = 1.1111}$$
$$ 0000 \quad 1.1111 \qquad 0000 \quad 1.1111$$

The result in these cases will be a negative zero (1.1111), which is correct.

4. When two negative numbers are added together, an end-around carry will always be generated, as will a carry from the adder for the first bits of the magnitudes of the numbers. This will place a 1 in the sign bit.

$$-0011 = \quad 1.1100 \qquad -0100 = \quad 1.1011$$
$$\underline{- 1011 = \quad 1.0100} \qquad \underline{-0111 = \quad 1.1000}$$
$$- 1110 \quad \boxed{-1.0000} \qquad - 1011 \quad \boxed{-1.0011}$$
$$ \longrightarrow 1 \qquad \longrightarrow 1$$
$$ \overline{1.0001} \qquad \overline{1.0100}$$

The output of the adder will be in 1s complement form in each case, with a 1 in the sign-bit position.

From the above we see that in order to implement an adder which will handle 4-bit magnitude signed 1s complement numbers, we can simply add another full adder to the configuration in Fig. 6·5. The sign inputs will be labeled X_0 and Y_0, and the C_o output from the adder connected to X_1 and Y_1 will be connected to the C_i input of the new full adder for X_0 and Y_0. The C_o output from the adder for X_0 and Y_0 will be connected to the C_i input for the adder for X_4 and Y_4. The S_0 output from the new adder will give the sign digit for the sum. (Overflow will not be detected in this adder, additional gates are required.)

6 · 8 ADDITION IN THE 2S COMPLEMENT SYSTEM

When negative numbers are represented in the 2s complement system, the operation of addition is very similar to that in the 1s complement system. In parallel machines, the 2s complement of a number stored in a register may be formed by first complementing the register and then adding 1 to the least significant bit of the register. This process requires two steps and is therefore more time-consuming† than the 1s complement system. However, the 2s complement system has the advantage of not requiring an end-around carry during addition.

The four situations which may occur in adding two numbers when the 2s complement system is used are as follows:

1. When both numbers are positive, the situation is completely identical with that in case 1 in the 1s complement system which has been discussed.
2. When one number is positive and the other negative, and the larger number is

---

† Generally this 1 is "sneaked in" during calculation, as will be shown.

the positive number, a carry will be generated through the sign bit. This carry may be discarded, since the outputs of the adder are correct, as shown below:

$$
\begin{array}{ll}
+0111 = & 0.0111 \\
-0011 = & +1.1101 \\
\hline
+0100 & \;\;\;0.0100 \\
& \rightarrow \text{carry is discarded}
\end{array}
\qquad
\begin{array}{ll}
+1000 = & 0.1000 \\
-0111 = & +1.1001 \\
\hline
+0001 & \;\;\;0.0001 \\
& \rightarrow \text{carry is discarded}
\end{array}
$$

3. When a positive and negative number are added and the negative number is the larger, no carry will result in the sign bit, and the answer will again be correct as it stands:

$$
\begin{array}{ll}
+0011 = & 0.0011 \\
-0100 = & 1.1100 \\
\hline
-0001 & 1.1111
\end{array}
\qquad
\begin{array}{ll}
+0100 = & 0.0100 \\
-1000 = & 1.1000 \\
\hline
-0100 & 1.1100
\end{array}
$$

Note: A 1 must be added to the least significant bit of a 2s complement negative number when converting it to a magnitude. For example:

$$
\begin{array}{ll}
1.0011 = & 1100 \text{ form the 1s complement} \\
& 0001 \text{ add 1} \\
\hline
-1101 &
\end{array}
$$

When both numbers are the same magnitude, the result is as follows:

$$
\begin{array}{ll}
+0011 = & 0.0011 \\
-0011 = & 1.1101 \\
\hline
0000 & 0.0000
\end{array}
$$

When a positive and a negative number of the same magnitude are added, the result will be a positive zero.

4. When the two negative numbers are added together, a carry will be generated in the sign bit and also in the bit to the right of the sign bit. This will cause a 1 to be placed in the sign bit, which is correct, and the carry from the sign bit may be discarded.

$$
\begin{array}{ll}
-0011 = & 1.1101 \\
-0100 = & 1.1100 \\
\hline
-0111 & \;\;\;1.1001 \\
& \rightarrow \text{carry is discarded}
\end{array}
\qquad
\begin{array}{ll}
-0011 = & 1.1101 \\
-1011 = & 1.0101 \\
\hline
1110 & 1.0010
\end{array}
$$

For parallel machines, addition of positive and negative numbers is quite simple, since any overflow from the sign bit is simply discarded. Thus for the parallel adder in Fig. 6·5 we simply add another full adder, with X_0 and Y_0 as inputs and with the CARRY line C_o from the full adder, which adds X_1 and Y_1, connected to the carry input C_i to the full adder for X_0 and Y_0. A 0 is placed on the C_i input to the adder connected to X_4 and Y_4.

This simplicity in adding and subtracting has made the 2s complement system the most popular for parallel machines. In fact, when signed-magnitude systems are used, the numbers generally are converted to 2s complement before addition of negative numbers or subtraction is performed. Then the numbers are changed back to signed magnitude.

6 • 9 ADDITION AND SUBTRACTION IN A PARALLEL ARITHMETIC ELEMENT

We now examine the design of a gating network which will either add or subtract two numbers. The network is to have an ADD input line and a SUBTRACT input line as well as the lines that carry the representation of the numbers to be added or subtracted. When the ADD line is a 1, the sum of the numbers is to be on the output lines, and when the SUBTRACT line is a 1, the difference is to be on the output lines. If both ADD and SUBTRACT are 0s, the output is to be 0.

First we note that if the machine is capable of adding both positive and negative numbers, subtraction may be performed by complementing the subtrahend and then adding. For instance, $8 - 4$ yields the same result as $8 + (-4)$, and $6 - (-2)$ yields the same result as $6 + 2$. Subtraction therefore may be performed by an arithmetic element capable of adding, by forming the complement of the subtrahend and then adding. For instance, in the 1s complement system, four cases may arise:

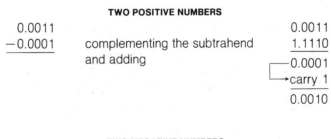

TWO POSITIVE NUMBERS

0.0011		0.0011
−0.0001	complementing the subtrahend	1.1110
	and adding	⌐0.0001
		└→carry 1
		0.0010

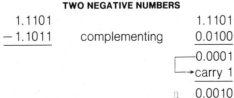

TWO NEGATIVE NUMBERS

1.1101		1.1101
−1.1011	complementing	0.0100
		⌐0.0001
		└→carry 1
		0.0010

POSITIVE MINUEND	NEGATIVE MINUEND
NEGATIVE SUBTRAHEND	POSITIVE SUBTRAHEND

$$\begin{aligned}\frac{\begin{array}{r}0.0010\\-1.1101\end{array}}{} &= \frac{\begin{array}{r}0.0010\\0.0010\end{array}}{}\\ &\quad\ \ 0.0100\end{aligned} \qquad \begin{aligned}\frac{\begin{array}{r}1.0101\\-0.0010\end{array}}{} &= \frac{\begin{array}{r}1.0101\\1.1101\end{array}}{}\\ &\quad\ \ 1.0010\\ &\rightarrow \text{carry } 1\\ &\quad\ \ 1.0011\end{aligned}$$

The same basic rules apply to subtraction in the 2s complement system, except that any carry generated in the sign-bit adders is simply dropped. In this case the 2s complement of the subtrahend is formed, and the complemented number is then added to the minuend with no end-around carry.

We now examine the implementation of a combined adder and subtracter network. The primary problem is to form the complement of the number to be subtracted. This complementation of the subtrahend may be performed in several ways. For the 1s complement system, if the storage register is composed of flip-flops, the 1s complement can be formed by simply connecting the complement of each input to the adder. The 1 which must be added to the least significant position to form a 2s complement may be added when the two numbers are added by connecting a 1 at the CARRY input of the adder for the least significant bits.

A complete logical circuit capable of adding or subtracting two signed 2s complement numbers is shown in Fig. 6·6. One number is represented by X_0, X_1, X_2, X_3, and X_4, and the other number by Y_0, Y_1, Y_2, Y_3, and Y_4. There are two control signals, ADD and SUBTRACT. If neither control signal is a 1 (that is, both are 0s), then the outputs from the five full adders, which are S_0, S_1, S_2, S_3, and S_4, will all be 0s. If the ADD control line is made a 1, the sum of the number X and the number Y will appear as S_0, S_1, S_2, S_3, and S_4. If the SUBTRACT line is made a 1, the difference between X and Y (that is, $X - Y$) will appear on S_0, S_1, S_2, S_3, and S_4.

Notice that the AND-to-OR gate network connected to each Y input selects either Y or $\bar{Y}$, so that, for instance, an ADD causes Y_1 to enter the appropriate full adder, while a SUBTRACT causes $\bar{Y}_1$ to enter the full adder.

To either add or subtract, each X input is connected to the appropriate full adder. When a subtraction is called for, the complement of each Y flip-flop is gated into the full adder, and a 1 is added by connecting the SUBTRACT signal to the C_i input of the full adder for the lowest order bits X_4 and Y_4. Since the SUBTRACT line will be a 0 when we add, a 0 carry will be on this line when addition is performed.

The simplicity of the operation of Fig. 6·6 makes 2s complement addition and subtraction very attractive for computer use, and it is the most frequently used system.†

The configuration in Fig. 6·6 is the most frequently used for addition and sub-

---

† A 1s complement parallel adder-subtracter can be made by connecting the CARRY-OUT line for the X_0, Y_0 adder to the CARRY-IN line for the X_4, Y_4 adder (disconnecting the SUBTRACT line to this full adder, of course).

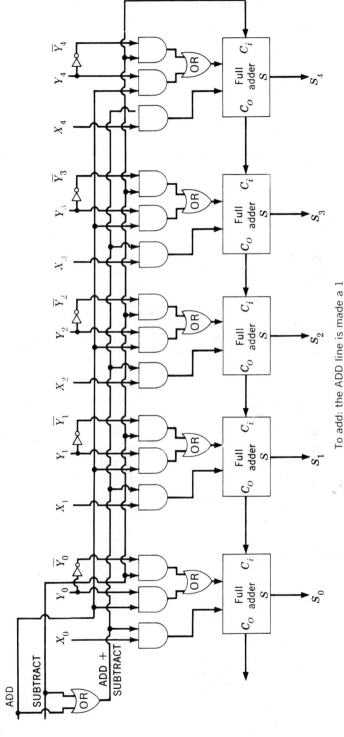

To add: the ADD line is made a 1
To subtract: the SUBTRACT line is made a 1
Numbers are to be in 2s complement form

FIG. 6 • 6 Parallel addition and subtraction.

255

traction because it provides a simple direct means for either adding or subtracting positive or negative numbers. Quite often the S_0, S_1, . . . , S_4 lines are gated back into the X flip-flops, so that the sum or difference or the numbers X and Y replaces the original value of X.

An important consideration is overflow. In digital computers an *overflow* is said to occur when the performance of an operation results in a quantity beyond the capacity of the register (or storage register) which is to receive the result. Since the registers in Fig. 6·6 have a sign bit plus 4 magnitude bits, they can store from $+15$ to -16 in 2s complement form. Therefore, if the result of an addition or subtraction were greater than $+15$ or less than -16, we would say that an overflow had occurred. Suppose we add $+8$ to $+12$; the result should be $+20$, and this cannot be represented (fairly) in 2s complement on the lines S_0, S_1, S_2, S_3, and S_4. The same thing happens if we add -13 and -7 or if we subtract -8 from $+12$. In each case logical circuitry is used to detect the overflow condition and signal the computer control element. Various options are then available, and what is done can depend on the type of instruction being executed. (Deliberate overflows are sometimes used in double-precision routines. Multiplication and division use the results as are.) We shall defer this to Chap. 9, except that one of the questions at the end of the chapter asks for a circuit to test for overflow.

The parallel adder-subtractor configuration in Fig. 6·6 is quite important, and it is instructive to try adding and subtracting several numbers in 2s complement form using pencil and paper and this logic circuit.

6 • 10 FULL ADDER DESIGNS

The full adder is a basic component of an arithmetic element. Figure 6·3 illustrated the block diagram symbol for the full adder, along with a table of combinations for the input-output values and the expressions describing the sum and carry lines. Succeeding figures and text described the operation of the full adder. Notice that a parallel addition system requires one full adder for each bit in the basic word.

There are of course many gate configurations for full binary adders. Examples of an IBM adder and an MSI package containing two full adders follow.

1. *Full binary adder*   Figure 6·7 illustrates the full binary adder configuration used in several IBM general-purpose digital computers. There are three inputs to the circuit: the X input is from one of the storage devices in the accumulator, the Y input is from the corresponding storage device in the register to be added to the accumulator register, and the third input is the CARRY input from the adder for the next least significant bit. The two outputs are the SUM output and the CARRY output. The SUM output will contain the sum value for this particular digit of the output. The CARRY output will be connected to the CARRY input of the next most significant bit's adder (refer to Fig. 6·5).

The outputs from the three AND gates connected directly to the X, Y, and C inputs are logically added together by the OR gate circuit directly beneath. If either the X and Y, X and C, or Y and C input lines contains a 1, there should

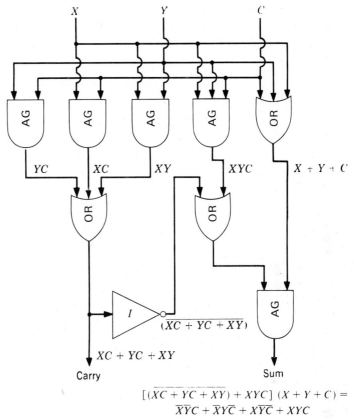

FIG. 6 • 7 Full adder used in IBM machines.

$$[(\overline{XC + YC + XY}) + XYC](X + Y + C) =$$
$$\overline{X}\overline{Y}C + \overline{X}Y\overline{C} + X\overline{Y}\overline{C} + XYC$$

be a CARRY output. The output of this circuit, written in logical equation form, is shown on the figure. This may be compared with the expression derived in Fig. 6·3.

The derivation of the SUM output is not so straightforward. The CARRY output expression $XY + XC + YC$ is first inverted (complemented), yielding $(\overline{XY + XC + YC})$. The logical product of X, Y, and C is formed by an AND gate and is logically added to this, forming $(\overline{XY + XC + YC}) + XYC$. The logical sum of X, Y, and C is then multiplied times this, forming the expression

$$[(\overline{XY + XC + YC}) + XYC](X + Y + C)$$

When multiplied out and simplified, this expression will be $\overline{X}\overline{Y}C + \overline{X}Y\overline{C} + X\overline{Y}\overline{C} + XYC$, the expression derived in Fig. 6·3. Tracing through the logical operation of the circuit for various values will indicate that the SUM output will be 1 when only one of the input values is equal to 1, or when all three input

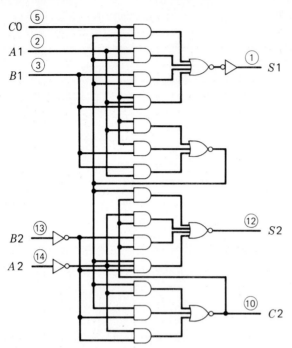

FIG. 6 • 8 Two full adders in an IC container. (Courtesy Texas Instruments.)

values are equal to 1. For all other combinations of inputs the output value will be a 0.

2. *Two full adders in an integrated circuit (IC) container* Figure 6·8 shows two full adders. This package was developed for integrated circuits using transistor-transistor logic (TTL). The entire circuitry is packaged in one IC container. The maximum delay from an input change to an output change for an *S* output is on the order of 8 nanoseconds (ns).† The maximum delay from input to the *C*2 output is about 6 ns.

The amount of delay associated with each carry is an important figure in evaluating a full adder for a parallel system, because the amount of time required to add two numbers is determined by the maximum time it takes for a carry to propagate through the adders. For instance, if we add 01111 to 10001 in the 2s complement system, the carry generated by the 1s in the least significant digit of each number must propagate through four carry stages and a sum stage before we can safely gate the sum into the accumulator. A study of the addition of these two numbers using the configuration in Fig. 6·5 will make this clear. The problem is called the *carry-ripple problem.*

There are a number of techniques which are used in high-speed machines

---

† 1 ns = 10^{-9} s.

to alleviate this problem. The most used is a bridging or carry-look-ahead circuit which calculates the carry-out of a number of stages simultaneously and then delivers this carry to the succeeding stages. (This is covered in the Questions.)

6 • 11 THE BINARY-CODED-DECIMAL (BCD) ADDER

Arithmetic units which perform operations on numbers stored in BCD form must have the ability to add 4-bit representations of decimal digits. To do this a BCD adder is used. A block diagram symbol for an adder is shown in Fig. 6·9. The adder has an augend digit input consisting of four lines, an addend digit input of four lines, a carry-in and a carry-out, and a sum digit with four output lines. The augend digit, addend digit, and sum digit are each represented in 8, 4, 2, 1 BCD code.

The purpose of the BCD adder in Fig. 6·9 is to add the augend and addend digits and the carry-in and produce a sum digit and carry-out. This adder could be designed using the techniques described in Chap. 3 and the rules for decimal addition. It is also possible to make a BCD adder using full adders and AND or OR gates. An adder made in this way is shown in Fig. 6·10.

There are eight inputs to the BCD adder, four X_i, or augend, inputs and four Y_i, or addend, digits. Each of these inputs will represent a 0 or a 1 during a given addition. If $3(0011)$ is to be added to $2(0010)$, then $X_8 = 0$, $X_4 = 0$, $X_2 = 1$, and $X_1 = 1$; $Y_8 = 0$, $Y_4 = 0$, $Y_2 = 1$, and $Y_1 = 0$.

The basic adder in Fig. 6·10 consists of the four binary adders at the top of the figure and performs base 16 addition when the intent is to perform base 10 addition. Some provision must therefore be made to (1) generate carries and (2) correct sums greater than 9. For instance, if $3_{10}(0011)$ is added to $8_{10}(1000)$, the result should be $1_{10}(0001)$ with a carry generated.

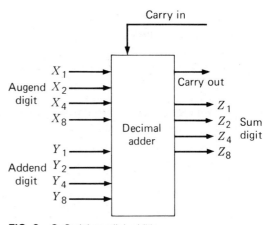

FIG. 6 • 9 Serial-parallel addition.

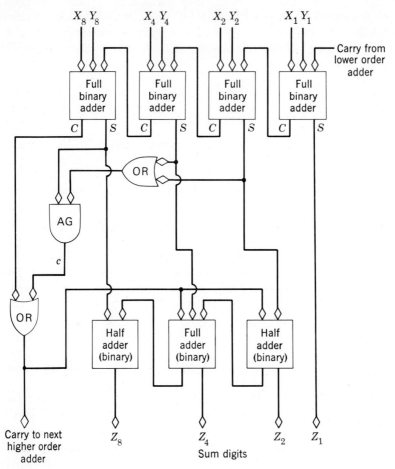

FIG. 6 • 10 BCD adder.

The actual circuitry which determines when a carry is to be transmitted to the next most significant digits to be added consists of the full binary adder to which sum (S) outputs from the adders for the 8, 4, 2 inputs are connected and of the OR gate to which the carry (C) from the eight-position bits is connected. An examination of the addition process indicates that a carry should be generated when the 8 AND 4, or 8 AND 2, or 8 AND 4 AND 2 sum outputs from the base 16 adder represent 1s, or when the CARRY output from the eight-position adder contains a 1. (This occurs when 8s or 9s are added together.)

Whenever the sum of two digits exceeds 9, the CARRY TO NEXT HIGHER ORDER ADDER line contains a 1 for the adder in Fig. 6·10.

A further difficulty arises when a carry is generated. If $7_{10}(0111)$ is added to $6_{10}(0110)$, a carry will be generated, but the output from the base 16 adder will be

1101. This 1101 does not represent any decimal digit in the 8, 4, 2, 1 system and must be corrected. The method used to correct this is to add 6_{10} (0110) to the sum from the base 16 adders whenever a carry is generated. This addition is performed by adding 1s to the weight 4 and weight 2 position output lines from the base 16 adder when a carry is generated. The two half adders and the full adder at the bottom of Fig. 6·10 perform this function. Essentially then, the adder performs base 16 addition and corrects the sum, if it is greater than 9, by adding 6. Several examples of this are shown below.

$$
\begin{array}{c}
\text{(8) (4) (2) (1)} \\
8 + 7 = 15 \quad 1000 + 0111 = \quad
\begin{array}{cccc}
1 & 1 & 1 & 1 \\
+\,0 & 1 & 1 & 0 \\
\hline
\end{array}
\end{array}
$$

$$
1 \quad\; 0 \quad 1 \quad 0 \quad 1 = 5
$$
$\llcorner$ with a carry generated

$$
\begin{array}{c}
\text{(8) (4) (2) (1)} \\
9 + 5 = 14 \quad
\begin{array}{cccc}
1 & 0 & 0 & 1 \\
0 & 1 & 0 & 1 \\
\hline
1 & 1 & 1 & 0 \\
+\,0 & 1 & 1 & 0 \\
\hline
\end{array}
\end{array}
$$

$$
1 \quad\; 0 \quad 1 \quad 0 \quad 0 \text{ or } 4
$$
$\llcorner$ with a carry generated

Figure 6·11 shows a complete BCD adder in an IC package.† The inputs are digits A and digits B, and the outputs are S. A carry-in and a carry-out are included. The circuit line used is CMOS.

6 • 12 POSITIVE AND NEGATIVE BCD NUMBERS

The techniques for handling BCD numbers greatly resemble those for handling binary numbers. A sign bit is used to indicate whether the number is positive or negative, and there are three methods of representing negative numbers which must be considered. The first and most obvious method is, of course, to represent a negative number in true magnitude form with a sign bit, so that -645 is represented as 1.645. The other two possibilities are to represent negative numbers in a 9s or a 10s complement form, which resembles the binary 1s and 2s complement forms.

---

† The IC packages in Figs. 6·11, 6·13, 6·14, and 6·15 are typical BCD MSI packages, The notation $A1$, $A2$, $A3$, $A4$ (instead of X_1, X_2, X_4, X_8) is often used for the 4 bits of a BCD digit, and the weights 1, 2, 4, 8 are understood. Thus a BCD digit in $B1$, $B2$, $B3$, $B4$ would have weight 1 or $B1$, weight 2 or $B2$, weight 4 or $B3$, and weight 8 or $B4$.

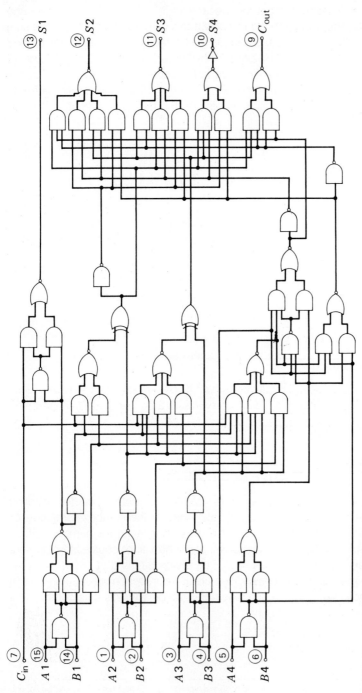

FIG. 6 • 11 Complete BCD adder in an IC package.

6 • 13 ADDITION AND SUBTRACTION
IN THE 9S COMPLEMENT SYSTEM

When decimal numbers are represented in a binary code in which the 9s complement is formed when the number is complemented, the situation is roughly the same as when the 1s complement is used to represent a binary number. Four cases may arise: two positive numbers may be added; a positive and negative number may be added, yielding a positive result; a positive and a negative number may be added, yielding a negative result; and two negative numbers may be added. Since there is no problem when two positive numbers are added, the three latter situations will be illustrated.

Negative and positive number—positive sum:

$$
\begin{array}{rl}
+692 = & 0.692 \\
-342 = & 1.657 \\
\hline
+350 & \llcorner 0.349 \\
& \quad \longrightarrow 1 \\
\hline
& 0.350
\end{array}
$$

Positive and negative number—negative sum:

$$
\begin{array}{rl}
-631 = & 1.368 \\
+342 = & 0.342 \\
\hline
-289 & 1.710 = -289
\end{array}
$$

Two negative numbers:

$$
\begin{array}{rl}
-248 = & 1.751 \\
-329 = & 1.670 \\
\hline
-577 & \llcorner 1.421 \\
& \quad \longrightarrow 1 \\
\hline
& 1.422 = -577
\end{array}
$$

The rules for handling negative numbers in the 10s complement system are the same as those for the binary 2s complement system in that no carry must be ended-around. A parallel BCD adder may therefore be constructed using only the full BCD adder as the basic component, and all combinations of positive and negative numbers may thus be handled.

There is an additional complexity in BCD addition, however, because the 9s complement of a BCD digit cannot be formed by simply complementing each bit in the representation. As a result, a gating block called a *complementer* must be used.

To illustrate the type of circuit which may be used to form complements of the code groups for BCD numbers, a block diagram of a logical circuit which will form the 9s complement of a code group representing a decimal number in 8, 4, 2, 1

Series parallel inputs

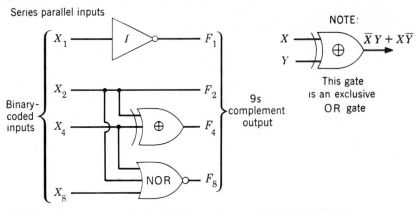

FIG. 6 • 12   Logical circuit for forming 9s complement of 8, 4, 2, 1 BCD digits.

BCD form is shown in Fig. 6·12. There are four inputs to the circuit, X_1, X_2, X_4, and X_8. Each of these inputs carries a different weight: X_1 has weight 1, X_2 has weight 2, X_4 has weight 4, and X_8 has weight 8. If the inputs represent a decimal digit of the number to be complemented, the outputs will represent the 9s complement of the input digit. For instance, if the input is 0010 (decimal 2), the output will be 0111 (decimal 7), the 9s complement of the input.

Figure 6·13 shows a complete 9s complementer in an IC package. The circuits used are CMOS, and so transmission gates† appear in the block diagram as well as conventional gates. (This does not bother the circuit's user because the user is primarily interested in the circuit's function.) When the COMP input is a 1, the outputs $F1$–$F4$ represent the complement of the digit on $A1$–$A4$; while if COMP is a 0, the $A1$–$A4$ inputs are simply placed on $F1$–$F4$ without change.

By connecting the IC packages in Figs. 6·11 and 6·13 together, a BCD adder-subtracter can be formed as shown in Fig. 6·14. This shows that a two-digit adder-subtracter IC package would be required for more digits. In order to add the digits in the inputs, the ADD-SUBTRACT input is made a 1; to subtract, this signal is made a 0. (Making the ZERO input a 1 will cause the value of B to pass through unchanged.) BCD numbers may also be represented in parallel form, as we have shown, but a mode of operation called *series-parallel* is often used. If a decimal number is written in binary-coded form, the resulting number consists of a set of code groups, each of which represents a single decimal digit. For instance, decimal 463 in a BCD 8, 4, 2, 1 code is 0100 0110 0011. Each group of 4 bits represents one decimal digit. It is convenient to handle each code group which represents a decimal digit as a unit, that is, in parallel. At the same time, as the word lengths for decimal computers are apt to be rather long, it is desirable to economize in the amount of equipment used.

---

† Transmission gates can be explained in terms of conventional gates. Figure 5·30 explains transmission gates.

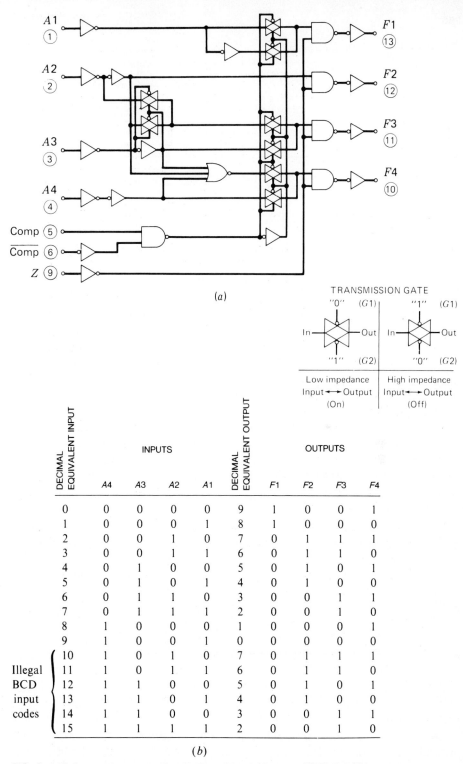

TRANSMISSION GATE

"0" (G1)	"1" (G1)
In —◇— Out	In —◇— Out
"1" (G2)	"0" (G2)
Low impedance	High impedance
Input ←→ Output	Input ←→ Output
(On)	(Off)

DECIMAL EQUIVALENT INPUT	INPUTS				DECIMAL EQUIVALENT OUTPUT	OUTPUTS			
	A4	A3	A2	A1		F1	F2	F3	F4
0	0	0	0	0	9	1	0	0	1
1	0	0	0	1	8	1	0	0	0
2	0	0	1	0	7	0	1	1	1
3	0	0	1	1	6	0	1	1	0
4	0	1	0	0	5	0	1	0	1
5	0	1	0	1	4	0	1	0	0
6	0	1	1	0	3	0	0	1	1
7	0	1	1	1	2	0	0	1	0
8	1	0	0	0	1	0	0	0	1
9	1	0	0	1	0	0	0	0	0
10	1	0	1	0	7	0	1	1	1
11	1	0	1	1	6	0	1	1	0
12	1	1	0	0	5	0	1	0	1
13	1	1	0	1	4	0	1	0	0
14	1	1	1	0	3	0	0	1	1
15	1	1	1	1	2	0	0	1	0

Illegal BCD input codes { 10 – 15 }

(a)

(b)

FIG. 6 • 13 9s complements in IC package. (a) Logic diagram. (b) Truth table.

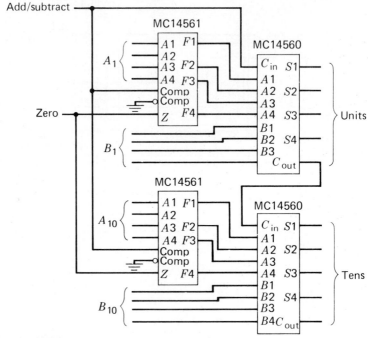

ZERO ADD/SUBTRACT RESULT

ZERO	ADD/SUBTRACT	RESULT
0	0	$B + A$
0	1	$B - A$
1	d	B

d = don't care

FIG. 6 • 14 Parallel add-subtract circuit (10s complement).

The *series-parallel* system provides a compromise in which each code group is handled in parallel, but the decimal digits are handled sequentially. This requires four lines for each 8, 4, 2, 1 BCD character, each input line of which carries a different weight. The block diagram for an adder operating in this system is shown in Fig. 6·15. There are two sets of inputs to the adder; one consists of the four input lines which carry the coded digit for the addend, and the other four input lines carry a coded augend digit. The sets of inputs arrive sequentially from the A and B registers, each of which consists of four shift registers; the least significant addend and augend BCD digits arrive first, followed by the more significant decimal digits.

If the 8, 4, 2, 1 code is used, let 324 represent the augend and 238 the addend. The ADD signal will be a 0. The adder will first receive 0100 on the augend lines, and at the same time it will receive 1000 on the addend lines. After the first clock pulse, these inputs will be replaced by 0010 on the augend lines and 0011 on the addend lines. Before the first clock signal, the sum lines should contain 0010, and

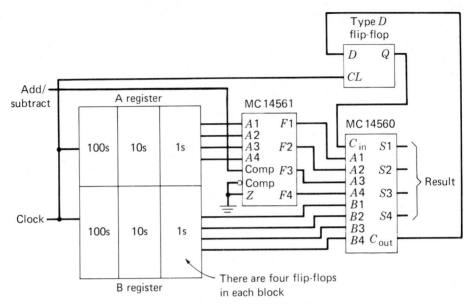

FIG. 6 • 15 Series-parallel BCD adder-subtracter using shift register.

before the second, 0110. A carry will be generated during the addition of the first two digits; this will be delayed and added in using the D flip-flop. The process will continue until each of the three digits has been added. To subtract B from A, we have only to make the ADD-SUBTRACT input a 1 and then apply the clocks.

6 • 14 THE SHIFT OPERATION

A *shift operation* is an operation which moves the digits *stored* in a register to new positions in the register. There are two distinct shift operations, a shift-left operation and a shift-right operation. A shift-left operation moves each bit of information stored in a register to the left by some specified number of digits. Consider the following six binary digits, 000110, which we will assume to be stored in a parallel binary register. If the contents of the register are shifted left 1, after the shift register will contain 001100. If a shift right of 1 is performed on the word 000110, after the shift the register will contain 000011. The shifting process in a decimal register is similar: if the register contains 0.01234, after a right shift of 1 the register will contain 0.00123, or after a left shift of 1 the register will contain 0.12340. The shift operation is used in the MULTIPLY and the DIVIDE instructions of most machines and also is provided as an instruction which may be used by programmers. For instance, a machine may have instructions SHR and SHL, where the letters represent in mnemonic form the order for SHIFT-RIGHT and SHIFT-LEFT instructions.

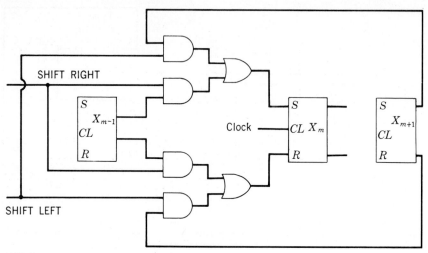

FIG. 6 • 16 Shift-left and shift-right stages of register.

A block diagram of logic circuitry for a single stage (flip-flop) in a register which can be shifted either left or right is shown in Fig. 6· 16. As can be seen, the bit to the left is shifted into X when SHIFT RIGHT is a 1 and the bit to the right is shifted into X when SHIFT LEFT is a 1.

Figure 6· 17 shows an MIS package which contains four flip-flops and gating circuitry so that the register can be shifted right or left, and also so that the four flip-flops can be parallel loaded from four input lines W, X, Y, and Z. The circuits are TTL circuits and are clocked in parallel. By combining modules such as this one, a register of a chosen length can be formed which can be shifted left or right or parallel loaded.

6 • 15 BASIC OPERATIONS

The arithmetic-logic unit of a digital computer consists of a number of registers in which information can be stored and a set of logic circuits which make it possible to perform certain operations on the information stored in the registers and to perform certain operations between registers.

As we have seen, the data stored in a given flip-flop register may be operated on in the following ways:

1. The register may be reset to all 0s.
2. The contents of a register may be complemented to either 1s or 2s complement form for binary, or for decimal to 9s or 10s complement form.
3. The contents of a register may be shifted right or left.
4. The contents of a register can be incremented or decremented.

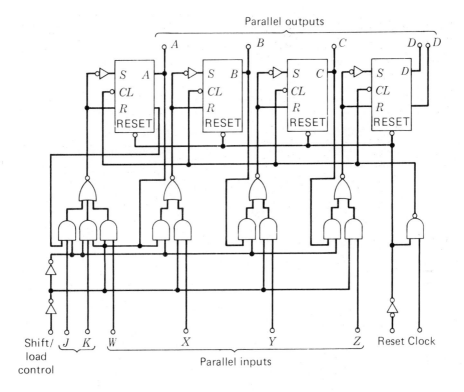

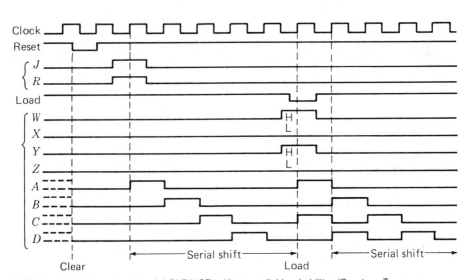

FIG. 6 • 17 Shift register (model SN74195) with a parallel load ability. (Courtesy Texas Instruments.)

Several operations between registers have also been described. These include:

1. Transferring the contents of one register to another register.
2. Adding to or subtracting from the contents of one register the contents of another register.

Most arithmetic operations which an ALU performs consist of these or sequenced sets of these two types of operations. Complicated instructions, such as multiplication and division, can require a large number of these operations, but these instructions may be performed using only sequences of the simple operations already described.

One other important point needs to be made. Certain operations which occur within instructions are *conditional;* that is, a given operation may or may not take place, depending on the value of certain bits of the numbers stored. For instance, it may be desirable to multiply using only positive numbers. In this case the sign bits of the two numbers to be multiplied together will be examined by control circuitry, and if either is a 1, the corresponding number will be complemented before the multiplication begins. This operation, complementing of the register, is a conditional one.

Many different sequences of operations can yield the same result. For instance, two numbers could be multiplied together by simply adding the multiplicand to itself the number of times indicated by the multiplier. If this were done with pencil and paper, 369 $\times$ 12 would be performed by adding 369 to itself 12 times. This would be a laborious process compared with the easier algorithm which we have developed for multiplying, but we would get the same result. The same principle applies to machine multiplication. Two numbers could be multiplied together by transferring one of the numbers into a counter which counted downward each time an addition was performed, and then adding the other number to itself until the counter reached zero. This technique has been used, but much faster techniques are also used and will be explained.

Many algorithms have been used to multiply and divide numbers in digital machines. Division, especially, is a complicated process, and in decimal machines in particular, many different techniques are used. The particular technique used by a machine is generally based on the cost of the machine and the premium on speed for the machine. As in almost all operations, speed is expensive, and a faster division process generally means a more expensive machine.

To explain the operations of binary multiplication and division, we will use a block diagram of a generalized binary machine. Figure 6·18 illustrates, in block diagram form, the registers of an ALU. The machine has three basic registers, an accumulator, a *Y* register, and a *B* register. The operations which can be performed have been described:

1. The accumulator can be cleared.
2. The contents of the accumulator can be shifted right or left. Further, the accumulator and the *B* register may be formed into one long shift register. If we then shift this register right two digits, the two least significant digits of the accumulator will be shifted into the first two places of the *B* register. Several

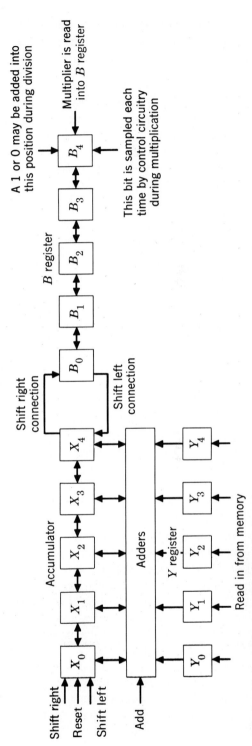

FIG. 6 • 18 Generalized parallel arithmetic element.

left shifts will shift the most significant digits of the *B* register into the accumulator. Since there are 5 bits in the basic machine word, there are five binary storage devices in each register. A right shift of five places will transfer the contents of the accumulator into the *B* register, and a left shift of five places will shift the contents of the *B* register into the accumulator.

3. The contents of the *Y* register can be either added to or subtracted from the accumulator. The sum or difference will then be stored in the accumulator register.

4. Words from memory may be read into the *Y* register. To read a word into the accumulator, it is necessary first to clear the accumulator, then to read the word from memory into the *Y* register, and then to add the *Y* register to the accumulator.

An arithmetic element which can perform these operations on its registers can be sequenced to perform all arithmetic operations. It is, in fact, possible to construct a machine using fewer operations than these, but most general-purpose computers will usually have an arithmetic element with at least these capabilities.

6 • 16 BINARY MULTIPLICATION

The process of multiplying binary numbers together may be best examined by writing out the multiplication of two binary numbers:

$$
\begin{array}{r}
1001 \quad = \text{multiplicand} \\
1101 \quad = \text{multiplier} \\
\hline
1001 \\
0000 \\
1001 \\
1001 \\
\hline
1110101 \quad = \text{product}
\end{array}
$$

partial products

The important thing to notice in this process is that there are really only two rules for multiplying a single binary *number* by a binary *digit:* (1) If the multiplier digit is a 1, the multiplicand is simply copied, and (2) if the multiplier digit is a 0, the product is 0. The above example illustrates these rules as follows: The first digit to the right of the multiplier is a 1; therefore the multiplicand is copied as the first partial product. The next digit of the multiplier to the left is a 0; therefore the partial product is a 0. Notice that each time a partial product is formed, it is shifted one place to the left of the previous partial product. Even if the partial product is a 0, the next partial product is shifted one place to the left of the previous partial product. This process is continued until all the multiplier digits have been used, and then the partial products are summed.

The three operations which the computer must be able to perform to multiply in this manner are therefore: (1) the ability to sense whether a multiplier bit is either a 1 or a 0, (2) the ability to shift partial products, and (3) the ability to add the partial products.

It is not necessary to wait until all the partial products have been formed before summing them. They may be summed two at a time. For instance, starting with the first two partial products in the above example,

$$
\begin{array}{r}
1001 \\
0000 \\
\hline
01001
\end{array}
$$

The next partial product may then be added to this sum, displacing it one position to the left:

$$
\begin{array}{r}
01001 \\
1001 \\
\hline
101101
\end{array}
$$

and finally,

$$
\begin{array}{r}
101101 \\
1001 \\
\hline
1110101
\end{array}
$$

A multiplier can be constructed in just this fashion. By sampling each bit of the multiplier in turn, adding the multiplicand into some register, and then shifting the multiplicand left each time a new multiplier bit was sampled, a product would be formed of the sum of the partial products. In fact, the process of multiplying in most binary machines is performed in a manner very similar to this.

To examine the typical technique for multiplying, the generalized arithmetic elements in Fig. 6·18 will be used. Referring to Fig. 6·18, let the multiplier be stored in the B register, and the multiplicand in the Y register; the accumulator contains all 0s as shown below:

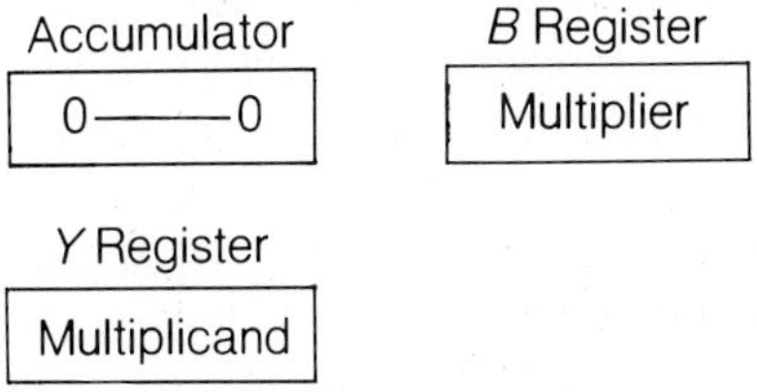

Accumulator	B Register
0———0	Multiplier

Y Register
Multiplicand

Let us also assume that both multiplier and multiplicand are positive. If either is negative, it must be converted to positive form before the multiplication begins. Assume n bits in each operand. For Fig. 6·18, $n = 4$.

The desired result format is shown below with the product being the combined accumulator and *B* register.

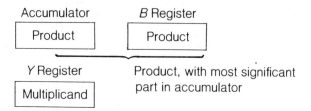

Accumulator   *B* Register

| Product | Product |

Y Register   Product, with most significant

| Multiplicand |

part in accumulator

A multiplication requires *n basic steps,* where *n* is the number of bits in the magnitude of the numbers to be multiplied, and a final right shift to position the product. Each basic step is initiated by the control circuitry examining the rightmost bit in the *B* register. The basic step is as follows.

> *Basic step* If the rightmost bit in the *B* register is a 0, the combined accumulator and *B* register is shifted right one place. If the rightmost bit in the *B* register is a 1, the number in the *Y* register is added to the contents of the accumulator, and the combined accumulator and *B* register is then shifted right one place.

After each basic step the new rightmost bit of the *B* register is again examined, and the next of the *n* steps is initiated.

Let us consider the same multiplication that was used in the previous example, that is, 1101 × 1001, where 1101 is the multiplier. In this case, in the beginning the accumulator contains 0.0000, the *B* register 0.1101, and the *Y* register 0.1001. Four steps will be required and a final shift.

Step 1. Since the rightmost bit of the *B* register contains a 1 (the least significant bit of the multiplier), during the first step the contents of the *Y* register are added to the accumulator, and the combined accumulator and *B* register are then shifted to the right. The second least significant bit of the multiplier will now occupy the rightmost bit of the *B* register and will control the next operation. The *Y* register will still contain the multiplicand 0.1001, the contents of the accumulator will be 0.0100, and the contents of the *B* register will be 1.0110.

Step 2. The rightmost bit of the *B* register is a 0, and since it controls the next operation, a SHIFT-RIGHT signal will be initiated, and the accumulator and *B* register will be shifted right, giving 0.0010 in the accumulator and 0.1011 in the *B* register.

Step 3. A 1 is now in the rightmost bit of the *B* register. The *Y* register will therefore again be added to the accumulator, and the combined accumulator and *B* register will again be shifted right, giving 0.0101 in the accumulator and 1.0101 in the B Register.

Step 4. The least significant bit of the *B* register will be another 1; so the *Y* register will again be added to the accumulator and the accumulator shifted right. After the above shift right, the combined accumulator and *B* register will contain 0.011101010. A final right shift gives 0.001110101, the correct product for our integer number system. The most significant digits will be stored in the accumulator, and the least significant digits in the B register.

Accumulator	B Register	
0.0000	0.1101	At beginning
0.0100	1.0110	After Step 1
0.0010	0.1011	After Step 2
0.0101	1.0101	After Step 3
0.0111	0.1010	After Step 4
0.0011	1.0101	After shift right

The reason for the combined accumulator and B register can now be seen. The product of two 5-bit signed numbers can contain up to nine significant digits (including the sign bit), and so two 5-bit registers, not one, are required to hold the product. The final product is treated like a 10-bit number extending through the two registers with the leftmost bits (most significant bits) in the left register, and the rightmost bits (least significant bits) in the right register, and the least significant binary digit in the product. Thus our result in the two combined registers was 0.001110101, which is $+117$ in decimal.

The control circuitry is designed to perform the examination of the multiplier bits, then either shift or add and shift the correct number of times, and then stop. In this case the length of the multiplier, or Y register, is 4 bits plus a sign bit; so four such steps are performed. The general practice is to examine each bit of the machine word except the sign bit, in turn. For instance, if the basic machine word is 25 bits, that is, 24 bits in which the magnitude of a number is stored plus a sign bit, each time a multiplication is performed, the machine will examine 24 bits, each in turn, performing the add-and-shift or just the shift operation 24 times. As may be seen, this makes the multiplication operation longer than such operations as add or subtract. Some parallel machines double their normal rate of operation during multiplication: if the machine performs such operations as addition, complement, transfers, etc., at a rate of 4 MHz/s for ordinary instructions, the rate will be increased to 8 MHz for the add-and-shift combinations performed while multiplying. Some machines are able to shift right while adding; that is, the sum of the accumulator and Y register appears shifted one place to the right each time, and the shift-right operation after each addition may be omitted.

The sign bits of the multiplier and multiplicand may be handled in a number of ways. For instance, the sign of the product can be determined by means of control circuitry before the multiplication procedure is initiated. This sign bit is stored during the multiplication process, after which it is placed into the sign bit of the accumulator, and the accumulator is then complemented, if necessary. Therefore the sign bits of the multiplier and multiplicand are first examined; if they are both 0s, the sign of the product should be 0; if both are 1s, the sign of the product should be 0; and if either but not both is a 1, the sign of the product should be 1. This information, retained in a flip-flop while the multiplication is taking place, may be transferred into the sign bit afterward. If the machine handles numbers in the 1s or 2s complement system, both multiplier and multiplicand may be handled as positive magnitudes during the multiplication, and if the sign of either number is negative, the number is complemented to a positive magnitude before the multiplication begins. Sometimes the multiplication is performed on complemented numbers using more complicated algorithms. These are described in the References.

6 • 17 DECIMAL MULTIPLICATION

Decimal multiplication is a more involved process than binary multiplication. Whereas the product of a binary digit and a binary number is either the number or 0, the product of a decimal digit and decimal number involves the use of a multiplication table plus carrying and adding. For instance,

$$7 \times 24 = (7 \times 4) + (7 \times 20) = 28 + 140 = 168$$

Even the multiplying of two decimal digits may involve two output digits; for instance, 7×8 equal 56. In the following discussion we call the two digits which may result when a decimal digit is multiplied times a decimal digit the *left-hand* and the *right-hand digits*. Thus for 3×6 we have 1 for the left-hand digit and 8 for the right-hand digit. For 2×3 we have 0 for the left-hand digit and 6 for the right-hand digit.

Except for simply adding the multiplicand to itself the number of times indicated by the multiplier, a simple but time-consuming process, the simplest method for decimal multiplication involves loading the rightmost digit of the multiplier into a counter that counts downward and then adding the multiplicand to itself and simultaneously indexing the counter until the counter reaches 0. The partial product thus formed may be shifted right one decimal digit, the next multiplier digit loaded into the counter, and the process repeated until all the multiplier digits have been used. This is a relatively slow but straightforward technique.

The process may be speeded up by forming products using the multiplicand and the rightmost digit of the multiplier as in the previous scheme, except by actually forming the left-hand and right-hand partial products obtained when multiplying a digit by a number and then summing them. For instance, 6×7164 would yield 2664 for the right-hand product digits and 4032 for the left-hand product digits. The sum would then be

$$
\begin{array}{r}
2664 \\
+ \ 4032 \\
\hline
42984
\end{array}
$$

Decimal-machine multiplication is in general a complicated process if speed is desired, and there are almost as many techniques for multiplying BCD numbers as there are types of machines.† IC packages are produced containing a gate net-

---

†Several machines use table-look-up techniques for forming products, where the product of each pair of digits is stored in the memory.

work that has two BCD characters as inputs which produce the two-digit output required. The Questions and References explore this in more detail.

*6 • 18 DIVISION

The operation of division is the most difficult and time-consuming that the ALU of most general-purpose machines performs. Although division may appear no more difficult than multiplication, there are several problems in connection with the division process which introduce time-consuming extra steps.

Division, using pencil and paper, is a trial-and-error process. For instance, if we are to divide 77 into 4610, we first notice that 77 will not "go" into 46; so we attempt to divide 77 into 461. We may guess that it will go six times; however,

$$
\begin{array}{r}
6 \\
77\overline{)4610} \\
462 \\
\hline
-1
\end{array}
$$

Therefore we have guessed too high and must reduce the first digit of the quotient, which we will develop, to 5.

The same problem confronts the computer when it attempts to divide in this manner. It must "try" a subtraction each step of the process and then see if the remainder is negative. Consider the division of 1111 by 11:

$$
\begin{array}{r}
101 \\
11\overline{)1111} \\
11 \\
\hline
0011 \\
11 \\
\hline
00
\end{array}
$$

It is easy to determine visually at any step of the process whether the quotient is to be a 1 or a 0, but the computer cannot determine this without making a trial subtraction each time. After a trial quotient has been tried and the divisor subtracted, if the result is negative, either the current dividend must be "restored" or some other technique for dividing used.

There are several points to be noted concerning binary fixed-point integer-value division. The division is generally performed with two signed binary integers of the same fixed length. The result, or quotient, is stored as a number, with as many digits as the divisor or dividend, and the remainder is also stored as a number of the same length.†

---

*This section can be omitted in a first reading.

†If we divide one integer into another, the quotient and remainder will both be integers. The rule is as follows: if a is the dividend, y the divisor, b the quotient, and r the remainder, then $a = y \times b + r$.

Using the registers shown in Fig. 6·18, we will show how to divide a number stored in the accumulator by a number in the Y register. The quotient is then stored in the B register and the remainder in the accumulator. This is the most common division format.

Assume the B and Y registers in Fig. 6·18 to be 5 bits in length (4 bits + sign bit) and the accumulator also 5 bits in length. Before starting the procedure, the dividend is read into the accumulator, and the divisor into the Y register. After the division, the quotient will be stored in the B register, and the remainder will be in the accumulator. Both divisor and dividend are to be positive.

The following shows an example. The accumulator (dividend) originally contains 11 (decimal) and the Y register (divisor) contains 4. The desired result then gives the quotient 2 in the B register and the remainder 3 in the accumulator.

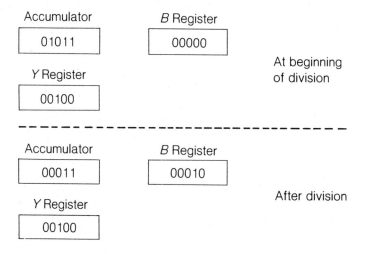

There are two general techniques for division for binary machines: the *restoring* and the *nonrestoring* techniques. Our first example will use the restoring technique.

Just as in multiplication, the restoring technique for division requires that a *basic step* be performed repeatedly (in this case as many times as there are significant bits in the subtrahend).

Basic step   In the restoring technique the basic step consists of a "trial division" which is made by first subtracting the Y register from the accumulator. After the subtraction, one of the following is executed.

1. If the result is negative, the divisor will not "go"; a 0 is therefore placed in the rightmost bit of the B register, and the dividend (accumulator) is restored by adding the divisor to the result of the subtraction. The combined B register and accumulator will then be shifted left.

2. If the result of a subtraction is positive or zero, there is no need to restore the partial dividend in the accumulator for the trial division has succeeded. The accumulator and B register are both shifted left and then a 1 is placed in the rightmost bit of the B register.

The computer determines whether or not the result of a trial division is positive or negative by examining the sign bit of the accumulator after each subtraction.

In order to demonstrate the entire procedure, it is first necessary to explain how to initiate the division and how to start and stop performing the basic steps. Unfortunately these are complicated procedures, just as determining the start, stop, and position of the decimal point is complicated for "ordinary" division.

1. As described above, if the divisor is larger than the dividend, then the quotient should be 0, and the remainder is the value of the dividend. (For instance, if we attempt to divide 7 by 17, the quotient is 0, and the remainder is 7.) To test this, the dividend in Y can be subtracted from the accumulator, and if the result is negative, all that remains is to restore the accumulator by adding the Y register to the accumulator. The B register now has value 0 which is right for the quotient, and the accumulator has the original value which is the remainder.

2. After the above test is made, it is necessary to align the leftmost 1 bit in the divisor with the leftmost 1 bit in the dividend by shifting the divisor left, and to record the number of shifts required to make this alignment. If the number of shifts is M, then the basic step must be performed $M + 1$ times.†

3. Now, the basic step is performed the necessary $M + 1$ times.

4. Finally, to adjust the remainder, the accumulator must be shifted right $M + 1$ times after the last basic step is performed. Examples are shown in Tables 6·2 and 6·3. Step 1 above, testing for a zero quotient, is not shown in the two examples.

Figure 6·19 shows a flowchart of the algorithm. Flowcharts are often used to represent algorithms. A more detailed flowchart would separate some of the steps, such as "shift the accumulator right $M + 1$ times," into single shifts performed in a loop which is controlled by a counter. Often, when algorithms are reasonably complicated, as this algorithm is, it is convenient to draw a flowchart of the algorithm before attempting to implement the control circuitry.

During division, the sign bits are handled in much the same way as during multiplication. The first step is to convert both the divisor and the dividend to positive magnitude form. The value of the sign bit for the quotient must be stored while the division is taking place. The rule is that if the signs of the dividend and divisor are both either 0s or 1s, the quotient will be positive. If either but not both of their signs is a 1, the quotient will be negative. The relationship of the sign bit of the quotient to the sign bit of the divisor and dividend is therefore the quarter adder, or exclusive OR, relationship, that is, $S = X\overline{Y} + \overline{X}Y$. The value for the correct sign of the quotient may be read into a flip-flop while the division is taking place, and this value may then be placed in the sign bit of the register containing the quotient after the division of magnitudes has been completed.

There are several techniques for nonrestoring division. One widely used algorithm employs a procedure in which the divisor is alternately subtracted and added.

---

†This can be accomplished by making Y a shift register and providing a counter to count the shifts until the first 1 bit of Y is aligned with the 1 bit of the accumulator. Both the accumulator and Y could be shifted left until there is a 1 bit in their first position, but the remainder will then have to be adjusted by moving it right in the accumulator.

TABLE 6 • 2

B REGISTER	ACCUMULATOR	Y REGISTER	REMARKS
0.0000	0.0110	0.0011	We divide 6 by 3.
0.0000	0.0110	0.0110	Y register is shifted left once, aligning 1s in accumulator and Y register. The basic step must be performed two times.
0.0000	0.0000	0.0110	Y register has been subtracted from accumulator. The result is 0, so B register and accumulator are shifted left, and a 1 is placed in the rightmost bit of B register.
0.0001	0.0000	0.0110	
0.0001	1.1010	0.0110	Y register is subtracted from accumulator.
0.0010	0.0000	0.0110	Y register is added to accumulator, and B register and accumulator are shifted left 1. A 0 is placed in B register's last bit.
0.0010	0.0000	0.0110	Accumulator must now be shifted right two times, but it is 0 so no change results. The quotient in B register is 2, and the remainder in accumulator is 0.

TABLE 6 • 3

B REGISTER	ACCUMULATOR	Y REGISTER	REMARKS
0.0000	0.1101	0.0011	We divide 13 by 3.
0.0000	0.1101	0.0110	Shift Y register left.
0.0000	0.1101	0.1100	Shift Y register left. Leftmost 1 bits in accumulator and Y register are aligned. Basic step will be performed three times.
0.0000	0.0001	0.1100	Y register has been subtracted from accumulator. Result is positive.
0.0001	0.0010	0.1100	B register and accumulator are shifted left, and 1 is placed in B register.
0.0001	1.0110	0.1100	Y register is subtracted from accumulator. Result is negative.
0.0010	0.0100	0.1100	Y register is added to accumulator. Both are then shifted left, and a 0 is placed in B register.
0.0010	1.1000	0.1100	Y register is subtracted from accumulator. Result is negative.
0.0100	0.1000	0.1100	Y register is added to accumulator. Accumulator and B register are shifted left. A 0 is placed in B register's bit.
0.0100	0.0001	0.1100	Accumulator has been shifted right three times. The quotient is 4, and the remainder is 1.

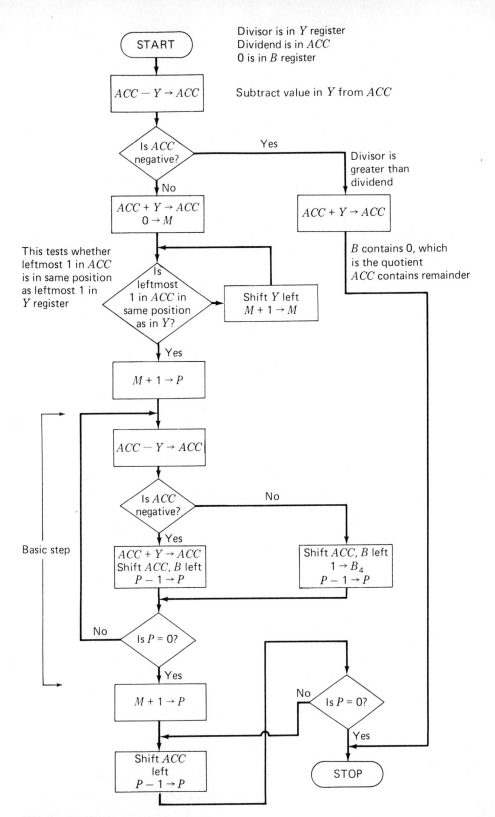

FIG. 6 • 19 Flowchart of division algorithm.

Another uses a technique where the divisor is compared to the dividend at each trial division. The references cover this material in detail.

6 • 19 LOGICAL OPERATIONS

In addition to the arithmetic operations, many logical operations are performed by ALUs. Three logical operations will be described here: logical multiplication, logical addition, and *sum modulo 2* addition (the exclusive OR operation). Each of these will be operations between registers, where the operation specified will be performed on each of the corresponding digits in the two registers. The result will be stored in one of the registers.

The first operation, logical multiplication, is often referred to as an *extract, masking,* or AND *operation.* The rules for logical multiplication have been defined in the chapter on logical algebra. The rules are $0 \cdot 0 = 0$; $0 \cdot 1 = 0$; $1 \cdot 0 = 0$; and $1 \cdot 1 = 1$. Suppose that the contents of the accumulator register are "logically multiplied" by another register. Let each register be five binary digits in length. If the accumulator contains 01101 and the other register 00111, the contents of the accumulator after the operation will be 00101.

The masking, or extracting, operation is useful in "packaging" computer words. To save space in memory and keep associated data together, several pieces of information may be stored in the same word. For instance, a word may contain an item number, wholesale price, and retail price, packaged as follows:

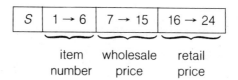

| item | wholesale | retail |
| number | price | price |

To extract the retail price, the programmer will simply logically multiply the word above by a word containing 0s in the sign digit through digit 15, and with 1s in positions 16 through 24. After the operation, only the retail price will remain in the word.

The logical addition operation, or the sum modulo 2 operation, is also provided in most computers. The rules for these operations are:

LOGICAL ADDITION	MODULO 2 ADDITION
$0 + 0 = 0$	$0 \oplus 0 = 0$
$0 + 1 = 1$	$0 \oplus 1 = 1$
$1 + 0 = 1$	$1 \oplus 0 = 1$
$1 + 1 = 1$	$1 \oplus 1 = 0$

Figure 6·20 shows how a single accumulator flip-flop and B flip-flop can be gated together so that all three of these logical operations can be performed. The circuit in Fig. 6·20 would be repeated for each stage of the accumulator register.

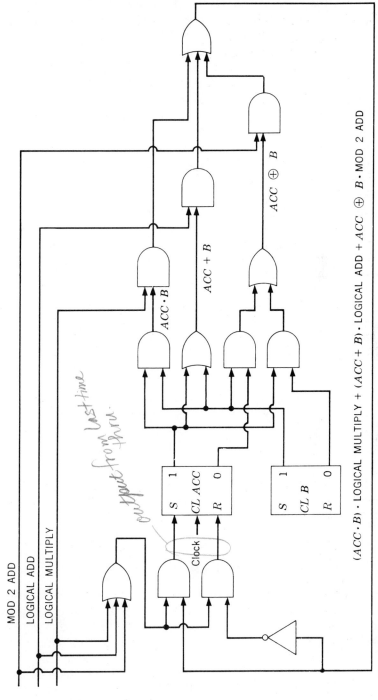

MOD 2 ADD

LOGICAL ADD

LOGICAL MULTIPLY

output from last time thru.

Clock

S 1

CL ACC

R 0

S 1

CL B

R 0

ACC · B

ACC + B

ACC ⊕ B

(ACC · B) · LOGICAL MULTIPLY + (ACC + B) · LOGICAL ADD + ACC ⊕ B · MOD 2 ADD

FIG. 6 · 20 Circuit for gating logical operations into accumulator flip-flop.

283

There are three control signals, LOGICAL MULTIPLY, LOGICAL ADD, and MOD 2 ADD. If one of these is up, or 1, when a clock pulse arrives, this operation is performed and the result placed in the ACC (accumulator) flip-flop. If none of the control signals is a 1, nothing happens, and the ACC remains as it is.

The actual values desired are found by three sets of gates; that is, $ACC \cdot B$, and $ACC + B$, and $ACC \oplus B$ are all formed first. Each of these is then AND-gated with the appropriate control signal. Finally the three control signals are ORed together, and this signal is used to gate the appropriate value into the ACC flip-flop when one of the control signals is a 1.

Figure $6 \cdot 20$ shows how a choice of several different function values can be gated into a single flip-flop using control signals. We could include an ADD signal and a SHIFT RIGHT and a SHIFT LEFT by simply adding more gates.

Figure $6 \cdot 21$ shows an example of the logic circuitry used in modern computers to form sections of an ALU. All the gates shown in this block diagram are contained in a single IC chip (package) with 24 pins. The chip is widely used (in the DEC PDP-11 series and Data General NOVAs, for example). With TTL (Schottky) circuits the maximum delay from input to output is 11 ns. (There is an ECL version with a 7 ns maximum delay.)

This chip is called a *4-bit arithmetic-logic unit* and can add, subtract, AND, OR, etc., two 4-bit register sections. Two chips could be used for the logic in an 8-bit accumulator, four chips would form a 16-bit accumulator, etc.

The function performed by this chip is controlled by the mode input M and four function select inputs S_0, S_1, S_2, and S_3. When the mode input M is low (a 0), the 74S181 performs such arithmetic operations as ADD or SUBTRACT. When the mode input M is high (a 1), the ALU does logic operations on the A and B inputs "a bit-at-a-time." (Notice in Fig. 6.21 that the carry generating gates are disabled by $M = 1$.) For instance, if M is a 0, S_1 and S_2 are also 0s, and S_0 and S_3 are 1s, the 74S181 performs arithmetic addition. If M is a 1, S_0 and S_3 are 1s, and S_1 and S_2 are 0s, the 74S181 chip exclusive ORs (mod 2 adds) A and B. (It forms $A_0 \oplus B_0$, $A_1 \oplus B_1$, $A_2 \oplus B_2$, and $A_3 \oplus B_3$.)

The table in Fig. $6 \cdot 21$ further describes the operation of this chip. Questions at the end of the chapter then further develop some operational characteristics of this 4-bit ALU section.

`6 • 20` FLOATING-POINT NUMBER SYSTEMS

The preceding sections describe number representation systems where positive and negative integers are stored in binary words. In the representation system used, the binary point is "fixed" in that it lies at the end of each word, and so each value represented is an integer. When computers calculate with binary numbers in this format, the operations are called *fixed-point arithmetic.*

In science it is often necessary to calculate with very large or very small num-

---

*This section can be omitted during a first reading.

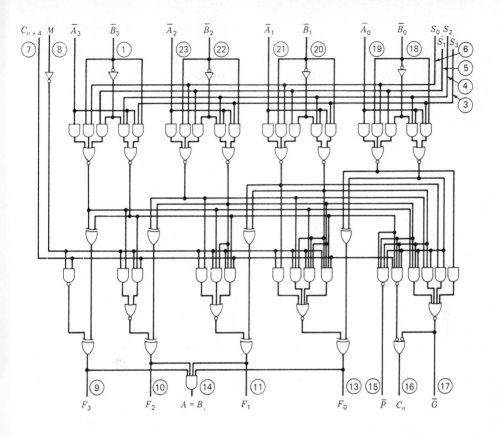

MODE SELECT INPUTS*				ACTIVE LOW INPUTS AND OUTPUTS	
				LOGIC	ARITHMETIC
S_3	S_2	S_1	S_0	$(M = H)$	$(M = L)$ $(C_n = L)$
L	L	L	L	$\overline{A}$	$A - 1$
L	L	L	H	$\overline{AB}$	$AB - 1$
L	L	H	L	$\overline{A} + B$	$A\overline{B} - 1$
L	L	H	H	Logical 1	-1
L	H	L	L	$\overline{A + B}$	$A \mp (A + \overline{B})$
L	H	L	H	$\overline{B}$	$AB \mp (A + \overline{B})$
L	H	H	L	$\overline{A \oplus B}$	$A - B - 1$
L	H	H	H	$A + \overline{B}$	$A + \overline{B}$
H	L	L	L	$\overline{A}B$	$A \mp (A + B)$
H	L	L	H	$A \oplus B$	$A \mp B$
H	L	H	L	B	$A\overline{B} \mp (A + B)$
H	L	H	H	$A + B$	$A + B$
H	H	L	L	Logical 0	$A \mp A*$
H	H	L	H	$A\overline{B}$	$AB \mp A$
H	H	H	L	AB	$A\overline{B} \mp A$
H	H	H	H	A	A

*$L = 0$; $H = 1$.

Note:

$x \overline{)\quad}\!\!\!\!\!\!\!\!\!\!\!\!\;z$ is the symbol for a mod 2 adder (exclusive OR gate)
$z = x \oplus y$

$\mp$ is the sign for arithmetic addition

FIG. 6 • 21 4-bit arithmetic-logic unit.

bers. Scientists have therefore adopted a convenient notation in which a *mantissa* plus an *exponent* are used to represent a number. For instance, 4,900,000 may be written as 0.49×10^7, where 0.49 is the mantissa and 7 is the value of the exponent, or 0.00023 may be written as 0.23×10^{-3}. The notation is based on the relation $y = a \times r^p$, where y is the number to be represented, a is the mantissa, r is the base of the number system ($r = 10$ for decimal, and $r = 2$ for binary), and p is the power to which the base is raised.

It is possible to calculate with this representation system. To multiply $a \times 10^n$ times $b \times 10^m$, we form $(a \times b) \times 10^{m+n}$. To divide $a \times 10^m$ by $b \times 10^n$, we form $a/b \times 10^{m-n}$. To add $a \times 10^m$ to $b \times 10^n$, we must first make m equal to n. If $m = n$, then $a \times 10^m + b \times 10^n = (a + b) \times 10^m$. The process of making m equal to n is called *scaling* the numbers.

Considerable "bookkeeping" can be involved in scaling the numbers, and there can be difficulty in maintaining precision during computations when the numbers vary over a very wide range of magnitudes. For computer usage these problems are alleviated by means of two techniques whereby the computer (not the programmer) keeps track of the radix (decimal) point, automatically scaling the numbers. In the first, programmed *floating-point routines* automatically scale the numbers used during the computations while maintaining the precision of the results and keeping track of the scale factors. These routines are used with small computers having only fixed-point operations. A second technique lies in building what are called *floating-point operations* into the computer's hardware. The logical circuitry of the computer is then used to perform the scaling automatically and to keep track of the exponents when calculations are performed. To effect this, a number representation system called the *floating-point system,* is used.

A floating-point number in a computer uses the exponential notation system described above, and during calculations the computer keeps track of the exponent as well as the mantissa. A computer number word in a floating-point system may be divided into three pieces: the first is the sign bit, indicating whether the number is negative or positive; the second part contains the exponent for the number to be represented; and the third part is the mantissa.

As an example, let us consider a 12-bit word length computer with a floating-point word. Figure 6·22 shows this. It is common practice to call the exponent part of the word the *characteristic* and the mantissa section the *integer part;* we shall adhere to this practice.

The integer part of the floating-point word shown represents its value in signed-magnitude form (rather than 2s complement, although this has been used). The

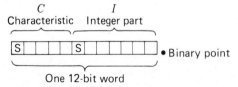

FIG. 6 • 22   12-bit floating-point word.

$$\overbrace{\hspace{2cm}}^{C}\quad\overbrace{\hspace{2cm}}^{I}$$

| 0 | 0 | 1 | 1 | 1 | 0 | 0 | 0 | 1 | 0 | 1 | 1 | Value is $2^7 \times 11 = 1408$

$C = +7$ $\quad\quad\quad I = +11$

| 0 | 0 | 0 | 1 | 1 | 1 | 0 | 0 | 0 | 1 | 1 | 1 | Value is $2^3 \times (-7) = -56$

$C = +3$ $\quad\quad\quad I = -7$

| 1 | 0 | 1 | 0 | 1 | 0 | 0 | 0 | 0 | 1 | 0 | 1 | Value is $2^{-5} \times 5 = \dfrac{5}{32}$

$C = -5$ $\quad\quad\quad I = +5$

| 1 | 0 | 1 | 1 | 0 | 1 | 0 | 0 | 1 | 0 | 0 | 1 | Value is $2^{-6} \times -9 = -\dfrac{9}{64}$

$C = -6$ $\quad\quad\quad I = -9$

FIG. 6 • 23 Values of floating-point numbers in 12-bit all-integer systems.

characteristic is also in signed-magnitude form. The value of the number expressed is $I \times 2^c$, where I is the value of the integer part, and C is the value of the characteristic.

Figure 6·23 shows several values of floating-point numbers both in binary form and after being converted to decimal. Since the characteristic has 5 bits and is in signed-magnitude form, the C in $I \times 2^c$ can have values from -15 to $+15$. The value of I is a sign-plus-magnitude binary integer of 7 bits, and so I can have values from -63 to $+63$. The largest number represented by this system would have a maximum I and would be 63×2^{15}. The least number would be -63×2^{15}.

This example shows the use of a floating-point number representation system to store "real" numbers of considerable range in a binary word.

One other widely followed practice is to express the mantissa of the word as a fraction instead of as an integer. This is in accord with common scientific usage since we commonly say that 0.93×10^4 is in "normal" form for exponential notation (and not 93×10^2). In this usage a mantissa in decimal normally has a value from 0.1 to 0.999 .... Similarly, a binary mantissa in normal form would have a value from 0.5 (decimal) to less than 1. Most computers maintain their mantissa sections in normal form, continually adjusting words so that a significant (1) bit is always in the leftmost mantissa position (next to the sign bit).

When the mantissa is in fraction form, this section is called the *fraction*. For our 12-bit example we can express floating-point numbers with characteristic and fraction by simply supposing the binary point to be to the left of the magnitude (and not to the right as in integer representation). In this system a number to be represented has value $F \times 2^c$, where F is the binary fraction and C is the characteristic.

For the 12-bit word considered before, fractions would have values from $1 - 2^{-6}$, which is 0.111111, to $-(1 - 2^{-6})$, which is 1.111111. Thus numbers from $(1 - 2^{-6}) \times 2^{15}$ to $-(1 - 2^{-6}) \times 2^{15}$ can be represented, or about $+32,000$ to $-32,000$. The smallest value the fraction part could have is now the fraction 0.1000000, which is 2^{-1}, and the smallest characteristic, which is 2^{-15}, so the smallest positive number representable is $2^{-1} \times 2^{-15}$ or 2^{-16}. Most computers use this fractional system for the mantissa, although computers of Burroughs Corporation and the National Cash Register Company use the integer system previously described.

The Univac 1108 represents single-precision floating-point numbers in this format:

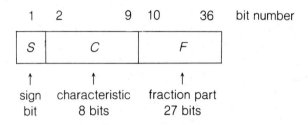

For positive numbers, the characteristic C is treated as a binary integer, the sign bit is a 0, and the fraction part is a binary fraction with value $0.5 \leqslant F < 1$. The value of the number represented is $2^{C-128} \times F$. This is called an *offset system* because the value of the characteristic is simply the integer value in that portion of the word minus an offset which in this case is 128. The exponent can therefore range from -128 to $+127$, since the integer in the characteristic section is 8 bits in length.

An an example, the binary word

$$0.1 0 0 0 0 0 0 1 \qquad 1 1 0 0 \ldots \ldots 0$$
$$\text{characteristic} \qquad\qquad \text{fraction}$$

has value $2^{129-128} \times \frac{3}{4} = 2 \times \frac{3}{4} = 1.5$. The representation for a negative number can be derived by forming the representation for the positive number with the same magnitude and then forming the 1s complement of this representation (considering all 36 bits as a single binary number).

In computers using 16-bit words (including some made by DEC, Hewlett-Packard, Data General, and IBM), floating-point words are represented by *two* adjacent words and thus have 32 bits per word. The actual format for floating-point words for several of these computers is shown in Fig. 6·24. In these computers the frac-

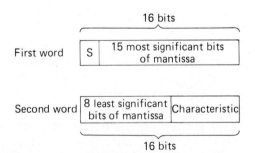

FIG. 6 • 24 Floating-point representation using two words.

tion part F consists of 24 bits representing a 23-bit fraction and a sign bit. The exponent or characteristic consists of 8 bits. (In Hewlett-Packard computers the fraction part and the characteristic part are represented in 2s complement form, as programmed for Fortran.) Each of these computers can represent magnitudes of up to 2^{127} (or about 10^{38}) and fractions of about as small as 2^{-138} (about 10^{-38}).

Another example of a computer with internal circuitry which performs floating-point operations and uses a single computer word representation of floating-point numbers is the IBM 360/370 series.

IBM calls the exponent part the *characteristic* and the mantissa part the *fraction*. In the 360/370 series floating-point data words can be either 32 or 64 bits in length. The basic formats are as follows:

short or single-word floating-point number:

S	characteristic	fraction
0	$1 \rightarrow 7$	$8 \rightarrow 31$

long or double-word floating-point number:

S	characteristic	fraction
0	$1 \rightarrow 7$	$8 \rightarrow 63$

In both cases the sign bit S is in the leftmost position and gives the sign of the number. The characteristic part of the word then comprises bits 1–7 and is simply a binary integer, which we shall call C, ranging from 0 to 127. The actual value of the scale factor is formed by subtracting 64 from this integer C and raising 16 to this power. Thus the value 64 in bits 1–7 gives a scale factor of $16^{C-64} = 16^{64-64} = 16^0$; a 93 (decimal) in bits 1–7 gives a scale factor of $16^{C-64} = 16^{93-64}$, which is 16^{29}; and a 24 in bits 1–7 gives a 16^{-40}.

The magnitude of the actual number represented in a given floating-point word is equal to this scale factor times the fraction contained in bits 8–31 for the short number, or 8–63 for a long number. The radix point is assumed to be to the left of bit 8 in either case. So if bits 8–31 contain 1000 . . . 00, the fraction has value $\frac{1}{2}$ (decimal); that is, the fraction is .1000 . . . 000 in binary. Similarly, if bits 8–31 contain 11000 . . . 000, the fraction value is $\frac{3}{4}$ decimal, or .11000 . . . 000 binary.

The actual number represented then has magnitude equal to the value of the fraction times the value determined by the characteristic. Consider a short number:

	sign	characteristic	fraction
floating-point number:	0	1 0 0 0 0 0 1	1 1 1 0 0 . . . 0
bit position:	0	1 2 3 4 5 6 7	8 9 10 11 12 . . . 31

The sign bit is a 0, and so the number represented is positive. The characteristic has binary value 1000001, which is 65 decimal, and so the scale factor is 16^1. The fraction part has value .111 binary, or $\frac{7}{8}$ decimal, and so the number represented is $\frac{7}{8} \times 16$, or 14 decimal.

Again, consider the following number:

	sign	characteristic	fraction
floating-point number:	1	1 0 0 0 0 0 1	1 1 1 0 0 . . . 0
bit position:	0	1 2 3 4 5 6 7	8 9 10 11 12 . . . 31

This has value -14 since every bit is the same as before, except for the sign bit. (The number representation system is signed magnitude.)

As further examples:

sign	characteristic	fraction	
0	1 0 0 0 0 1 1	1 1 0 . . . 0	$16^3 \times \frac{3}{4} = 3072$
0	0 1 1 1 1 1 1	1 1 0 . . . 0	$16^{-1} \times \frac{3}{4} = \frac{3}{64}$

6 • 21 PERFORMING ARITHMETIC OPERATIONS WITH FLOATING-POINT NUMBERS

A computer obviously requires additional circuitry to handle floating-point numbers automatically. Some machines come equipped with floating-point instructions. (For computers such as DEC PDP-11/45 and others, floating-point circuitry can be purchased and added to enable them to perform floating-point operations.)

To handle the floating-point numbers, the machine must be capable of extensive shifting and comparing operations. The rules for multiplying and dividing are

$$(a \times r^p) \times (b \times r^q) = ab \times r^{p+q}$$
$$(a \times r^p) \div (b \times r^q) = \frac{a}{b} \times r^{p-q}$$

The computer must be able to add or subtract the exponent sections of the floating-point numbers, and also to perform the multiplication or division operations on the mantissa sections of the numbers. In addition, precision is generally maintained by shifting the numbers stored until significant digits are in the leftmost sections of the word. With each shift the exponent must be changed. If the machine is shifting the mantissa section left, for each left shift the exponent must be decreased.

For instance, in a BCD computer, consider the word

0	10	0064
sign	exponent	mantissa

To attain precision, the computer shifts the mantissa section left until the 6 is in the most significant position. Since two shifts are required, the exponent must be decreased by 2, and the resulting word is 0.08 6400. If all numbers to be used are scaled in this manner, the maximum precision may be maintained throughout the calculations.

For addition and subtraction the exponent values must agree. For instance, to add 0.24×10^5 to 0.25×10^6, we must scale the numbers so that the exponents agree. Thus

$$(0.024 \times 10^6) + (0.25 \times 10^6) = 0.274 \times 10^6$$

The machine must also follow this procedure. The numbers are scaled as was described, so that the most significant digit of the computer mantissa section of each word contains the most significant digit of the number stored. Then the larger of the two exponents for the operands is selected, and the other number's mantissa is shifted and its exponent adjusted until the exponents for both numbers agree. The numbers may then be added or subtracted according to these rules:

$$(a \times r^p) + (b \times r^p) = (a + b) \times r^p$$
$$(a \times r^p) - (b \times r^p) = (a - b) \times r^p$$

QUESTIONS

1. Draw a block diagram of circuitry for two registers X and Y of three flip-flops each, so that Y can be transferred into X, or the 1s complement of Y can be transferred into X.

2. Two parallel binary registers, designated as register X and register Y, both consist of three flip-flops. Draw a block diagram of the registers and the necessary logic circuitry so that (a) register X can be cleared, or 1s complemented, and (b) the complement of the contents of register Y can be transferred into register X.

3. If a binary computer handles numbers in the sign-plus-magnitude integer system, and numbers are 5 bits (sign plus 4 bits) each, how would the following decimal numbers be represented? For example, $+5 = 0.0101$.
   (a) $+6$ (b) $+10$ (c) -12 (d) -16

4. If a binary computer represents numbers in a sign-plus magnitude with 5 bits per number, how would the following decimal numbers be represented:
   (a) $+8$ (b) $+11$ (c) -7
   (d) -4 (e) -15 (f) -12

5. If a binary machine handles negative numbers in the true magnitude form, how would -4 be stored in a register with a sign bit and 4 bits representing magnitude? If the same machine stored numbers in the 1s complement system, how would -4 be stored?

6. If a register contains five flip-flops as in Fig. 6·1(b) and the register contains $X_0 = 1$, $X_2 = 1$, $X_3 = 0$, $X_4 = 0$, $X_5 = 1$, give the decimal value of the number in the register if the 1s complement number system is used. What is the value if 2s complement is used?

7. The inputs to the full adder in Fig. 6·3 are as follows: $X = 1$, $Y = 1$, and $C = 1$. What will the output on the S and C lines represent?

8. If we use the $\oplus$ symbol to mean exclusive OR and define it as $X \oplus Y = \overline{X}Y + X\overline{Y}$, then the output S from a full adder can be written as $S = X \oplus Y \oplus C_i$. Show why this is the case.

9. If we load the binary number 1.0011 into the flip-flops in Fig. 6·1(b), that is, if $X_0 = 1$, $X_1 = 0$, $X_2 = 0$, $X_3 = 1$, and $X_4 = 1$, what will the value of the register be in the 1s complement number system? Give the answer in decimal. What will the value of this number be if the 2s complement number system is used?

10. If register X contains 0.0111 and register Y contains 1.1011, what do the two numbers represent in decimal if 1s complement is used? If 2s complement is used? Add the two numbers in 1s complement, then in 2s complement, and give the results in decimal.

11. Register X contains 0.1100, and register Y contains 0.1101 (where the 0s preceding the binary point designate that the number stored is positive). If the two registers are added together, what will the result be?

12. If 1s complement is used, for which of the following expressions will an overflow or end-around carry be generated? Why? Assume 5-bit registers, including a sign bit.
    (a) $+5 + (-7)$ (b) $+5 + (-4)$
    (c) $+12 + (-13)$ (d) $+12 + 3$

13. Add a stage to the load and shift register in Fig. 6·17. Copy only D in your drawing, omitting A, B, and C.

14. A binary register consists of five binary storage devices; one stores the sign bit, and the other four store the magnitude bits. If the number stored is 0.0110 and this number is then shifted right one binary place, what will be the result? Assume a 0 goes into the sign bit.

15. Design a half adder using only NOR gates.

16. Design a half adder using only NAND gates.

17. A binary half subtracter has two inputs x and y and two outputs which are the "difference" value $x - y$ and a "borrow" output which is 1 if the value of $x - y$ is negative ($x - y$ then is given the value 1). Draw a block diagram for a half subtracter using NAND gates and assuming x, $\overline{x}$, y, and $\overline{y}$ are all available as inputs.

18. Design a half subtracter using only NOR gates.

19. If a borrow input is added to the half subtracter in Questions 17 and 18, a full subtracter is formed. Design a full subtracter using only NAND gates.

20. Design a full subtracter using only NOR gates.

21. Design a full adder using only NAND gates.

22. Can an overflow occur during multiplication in a binary machine with numbers stored in fixed-point sign-plus magnitude? Assume a double-length product.

23. Explain how the 2s complement of the subtrahend is formed when we subtract using the configuration in Fig. 6·6. How is the 1 added in to form this complement?

24. Show how the configuration in Fig. 6·6 adds and subtracts by adding and subtracting +21 and +3 in binary, showing what each output will be.

25. Add and subtract +6 and −4 using the configuration in Fig. 6·6, showing what each output will be and checking correctness of the sum and difference.

26. The following is a *multiplexer* which is a logic circuit that selects from a number of input signals. The selection is done by the *select inputs* S_0, S_1, S_2, and the input selected is one of I_0–I_7. E is an enable input. Draw a multiplexer which selects from four inputs I_0–I_3 using two select inputs S_0 and S_1.

LOGIC DIAGRAM

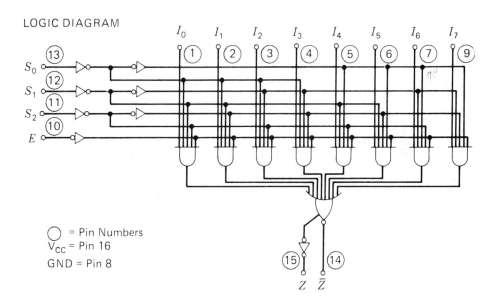

○ = Pin Numbers
V_{CC} = Pin 16
GND = Pin 8

27. Design a multiplexer for four inputs using a two-level NOR gate combinational network. The inputs are to be X_0, X_1, X_2, and X_3. The output is to be called W. The X_0, X_1, X_2, and X_3 are "selected" by S_0 and S_1. If S_0 and S_1 = 0, then W should equal X_0. If S_0 and S_1 = 01, then W should equal X_1. If S_0 and S_1 = 10, then W should equal X_2. If S_0 and S_1 = 11, then W should equal X.

28. Add a control line NAND and circuitry to Fig. 6·20 so that the NAND of ACC and B can be transferred into ACC.

29. If a register containing 0.110011 is logically added to a register containing 0.101010, what will the result be? What will be the result if the registers are logically multiplied? If the registers are exclusive ORed together?

30. Find a sequence of logical operations which will cause the ACC to have value 0 regardless of how ACC and B start in Fig. 6·20.

31. Referring to Fig. 6·20, show that a logical multiply followed by a logical addition will transfer the contents of B into ACC.

32. Add a control line NOR and circuitry to Fig. 6·20 so that the NOR of ACC and B can be transferred into ACC.

33. Demonstrate by means of a table of combinations that two half adders plus an OR gate do make a full adder as shown in Fig. 6·4.

34. Add gates and a flip-flop X_{m+2} so that we can shift left and right into X_{m+1} in Fig. 6·16.

35. Add gates to the following drawing so that if the control input signal C is made a 1, the value $\overline{X}\overline{Y}$ will appear on the output line. If A is a 1, then $X + Y$ appears on the output; if B is a 1, then $X \cdot Y$ appears on the output; if A, B, and C are 0s, then the output is to be a 0; and only one of A, B, or C can be a 1 at a given time.

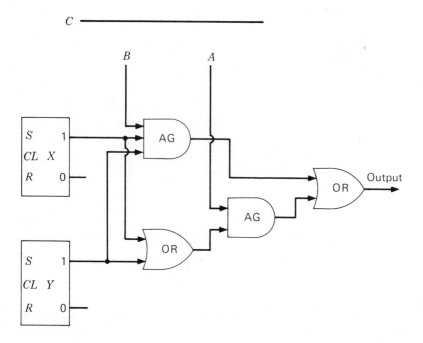

36. In what case will subtracting a negative number from 0 cause an overflow in the 2s complement system?

37. Design a *parallel multiplier* gate network with two inputs A_0A_1 and $B_0B_1B_2$, where A_0A_1 are two binary digits forming a binary number (with decimal values for 0 to 3) and $B_0B_1B_2$ is a 3-bit binary number (with values 0 to 7). Use only AND gates and OR gates and see that no signal passes through more than four levels of gates. (Assume input complements available.)

38. The following is a partial drawing of a combinational network for parallel multiplication of two 3-bit binary integers. The technique used is called *carry save multiplication* and uses a *carry save* adder technique. The two input numbers are $X_0X_1X_2$ and $Y_0Y_1Y_2$. Each are 3-bit binary positive integers, and the output is to be $P_0P_1P_2P_3P_4P_5$, the product of these two integers. The boxes FA are full adders and the products X_iY_j are each formed with AND gates. Assume that all products X_0Y_0, X_0Y_1, ..., X_1Y_1, ..., X_2Y_0, ..., X_2Y_2 have been formed using AND gates and are available. Fill out the diagram with full adders showing the interconnections.

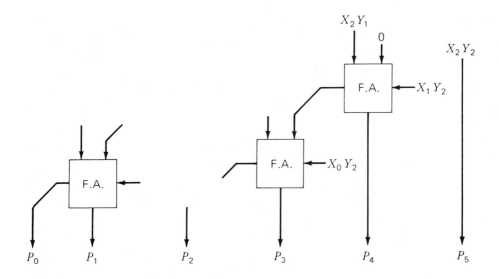

39. Design a gating network for a module in an ALU that will add two 2-bit binary inputs A_i, A_{i+1} and B_i, B_{i+1} and an input carry-in C_i. The network is to generate the two sum digits and a carry-out C_{i+2}. Use only AND or OR gates and inverters, but assume that both complemented and uncomplemented inputs are available. The output carry C_{i+2} should have a delay of no more than three gate delays (that is, a change in an input must pass through no more than three gates in any path to an output).

40. *(a)* In the IBM System 360/370 a 32-bit floating-point word is structured as follows:

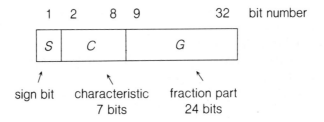

In this word the sign bit and fraction part use a signal-magnitude representation. The value of the characteristic C is simply the binary integer value. The value of the number represented is then $16^{C-64} \times F$. The binary representation for F is normalized in that the four most significant digits always contain a 1 (except for the representation of 0). Give the IBM-360 floating-point representation for decimal 26.25 and −26.25.

(b) The UNIVAC 1108 represents single-precision floating-point numbers in this format:

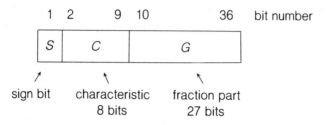

For positive numbers, the characteristic C is treated as a binary integer, the sign bit is a 0, and the fraction part is a binary fraction with value 0.5 $\leqslant F < 1$. The value of the number represented is $2^{128-C} \times F$. The representation for a negative number can be derived by forming the representation for the positive number with the same magnitude and then forming the 1s complement of this representation (considering all 36 bits as a single binary number). Form the UNIVAC 1108 single-precision floating-point representation for $+12$ and -12.

41. (a) Give the IBM 360/370 floating-point representation for $+52.5$ and -52.5.

   (b) Give the UNIVAC 1108 floating-point representation for $+24.0$ and -24.0.

   (c) Compare the ranges, accuracy, and other system design considerations for the above two computer floating-point number systems.

42. If numbers are represented in a 2s complement, 6-bit magnitude plus 1 sign-bit integer system, and we ignore overflow (that is, any result will be stored, even if it requires more magnitude bits), then the largest positive integer which can result from the addition of two numbers is _____, and the largest positive integer which can result from the subtraction of one number from another is _____. The least negative numbers which can result from an addition and subtraction are _____ and _____. As a result, any sum or difference can be stored in _____ bits.

43. Write down all 4-bit 2s complement numbers (that is, sign-plus 3-bit numbers) and their decimal values. Show that there is one more negative number than positive numbers. Consider 0 to be neither negative nor positive.

44. When addition is performed in a binary machine using the 2s complement number system to represent negative numbers, an overflow may occur in a register only when two positive or two negative numbers are added. Show that the addition of a positive number and a negative number cannot result in an overflow condition.

45. Show that there are as many negative as positive numbers in a 1s complement system.

46. The Boolean algebra expressions on the output lines from the gates in Fig. 6·8 are not filled in. Develop the Boolean algebra expressions for the $S1$, $S2$, and $C2$ outputs from the network.

47. Which of the following number systems has two 0s:

(a) Sign-plus magnitude   (b) 1s complement   (c) 2s complement

48. When the 2s complement number system is used and addition is performed, let us designate the carry-out of the full adder connected into the full adder for the sign digits as C_1 (refer to Fig. 6·6). The rule for overflow is that two numbers cause an overflow when they are added if both numbers are positive and C_1 equals a 1, or if both numbers are negative and C_1 does not equal a 1. Therefore, by examining the sign digits of the two numbers being added and the carry-out of the full adder which adds the two most significant digits of the magnitude of the numbers being added, we can form a logic network the output of which will be a 1 when an overflow condition arises and 0 if the addition is legitimate. Let X_0 store the sign digit of the addend, let Y_0 store the sign digit of the augend, and let C_1 again be the carry-out of the full adders connected to the X_1 and Y_1 flip-flops as in Fig. 6·6. Show that the logic equation for an overflow condition is $X_0 Y_0 \overline{C_1} + \overline{X_0}\ \overline{Y_0} C_1$ = overflow.

49. Modify Fig. 6·16 so that the complement of X_{m+1} can be shifted into X_m, that is, so that SHIFT LEFT causes $\overline{X}_{m+1}$ to go into X_m.

50. Show that when we add 7 to 9 in the BCD system using the series-parallel BCD adder in Fig. 6·10, the answer will be correct. Do this by tracing the outputs of the circuit, filling in the binary value for each X and Y shown in the figure, and also by showing the values of Z_8, Z_4, Z_2, and Z_1.

51. Show how the BCD adder in Fig. 6·11 adds $+6$ to $+5$ by calculating each output from the gates and then the final outputs.

52. Check how the gates in Fig. 6·12 form a 9s complement by trying 5 and 3 in BCD at the inputs.

53. Explain the operation of Fig. 6·15 by explaining how 234 can be added or subtracted to or from 523 in this configuration.

54. What is the function of the D flip-flop in Fig. 6·15?

55. Explain how to load the input values on W, X, Y, and Z into the flip-flops in Fig. 6·17.

56. Explain how to cause the flip-flops in Fig. 6·17 to shift right three times. Suppose we (1) make the *reset* input a 0, then a 1, (2) hold J and K at 1 and shift at 1, and then (3) apply three clock pulses to the CLOCK line. Draw the output waveforms for A, B, C, and D for this sequence of inputs.

57. What is the result if we multiply 0.1101 times 0.0011 in our generalized machine in Fig. 6·18? Give the values in each X and B flip-flop.

58. What is the binary number that represents -3 in the 2s complement fractional number system if we represent the number using a sign digit plus four magnitude digits?

59. Using the 8,4,2,1 BCD system with a single digit for the sign digit, write the following numbers using a sign-plus-magnitude number system.

(a) $+0014$ (b) $+0291$

(c) -2346 (d) -0364

60. Using the 8,4,2,1 BCD system, write in binary form the following decimal numbers. Use a single digit for the sign digit, and express the numbers as magnitude plus sign.

(a) $+0043$ (b) -0222 (c) $+1234$ (d) -1297

61. Using the 8,4,2,1 code as in Question 59, give the same numbers but use 9s complement for the negative numbers.

62. Express each of the numbers in Question 60 using the 9s complement and the 8,4,2,1 BCD system. For example, $-1024 = 1.1000\ 1001\ 0111\ 0101$.

63. Write the binary forms of the numbers in Question 60 using 8,4,2,1 but use 10s complements for negative numbers.

64. Write the decimal numbers in Question 60 using the 10s complement number system and again the 8,4,2,1 BCD system to represent these numbers. For example, $-1420 = 1.1000\ 0101\ 1000\ 0000$.

65. If we add two 20-digit binary numbers using the full adders shown in Fig. 6·8, and if 3 ns are required for a signal to pass through a gate, what is the maximum time it will require a CARRY signal to propagate from the lowest order bits to the highest order bits, assuming a full adder which is parallel as in Fig. 6·6? The carry circuit in Fig. 6·8 could be replaced by a "carry bridge" with the expression $C2 = C0 \cdot A1 \cdot A2 + C0 \cdot A1 \cdot B2 + C0 \cdot B1 \cdot A2 + C0 \cdot B1 \cdot B2 + A1 \cdot B1 \cdot A2 + A1 \cdot B1 \cdot B2 + A2 \cdot B2$. Show how this would work and how a carry bridge for 3 bits might work.

66. Explain how you would add gates and inputs to Fig. 6·17 so that the flip-flop register could be shifted left as well as right.

67. If we multiply 6×11 in the registers in Fig. 6·18, show the placement of binary digits at the start and end of the multiplication.

68. Show how 7×9 and 5×5 would be multiplied in the registers in Fig. 6·18.

69. Draw a flowchart (as in Fig. 6·19) for the binary multiplication procedure described.

70. If we divide 23 by 6 in the registers in Fig. 6·18, show the beginning positioning of the numbers (in binary) and the result at the end. (Show where the quotient and the remainder are placed.)

71. Show how to divide 14 by 4 using the registers in Fig. 6·18 and showing how the quotient and the remainder are placed after the division.

72. Go through the division of 14 by 3 using the technique shown in the text.

73. Using the algorithm shown in Fig. 6·19, show how to divide 11 by 4.

74. Show how to represent $+6$ in the 12-bit floating-point word in Fig. 6·22.

75. Show how to represent -14 in the 12-bit floating-point word in Fig. 6·22.

76. *(a)* Give the IBM 360/370 floating-point representation for 57.5 and 54.5.
   (b) Give the Univac 1108 floating-point representation for $+25.0$ and -25.0.
   (c) Compare the ranges, accuracy, and other system design considerations for the above two computer floating-point number systems.

77. Show two decimal numbers which when converted into the IBM 360/370 floating-point number system will have .00110 in bits 9, 10, 11, and 12.

78. Can you give any reasons that might be behind the decision of the systems architects at IBM to use hexadecimal as the base for the 360/370 series floating-point number system instead of conventional base 2? That is, in system 360/370 a floating-point full word of 32 bits has as characteristic a 7-bit integer with value C and as fraction a binary signed-magnitude fraction 25-bit number with value F. The value of the number represented is then $(16^{C-64})F$. Why 16^{C-64} rather than 2^{C-64}? Give system design considerations.

79. Give the value of a positive nonzero *integer* less than 16^{62} which cannot be represented in the IBM 360/370 floating-point number system (using a single 32-bit word). Do not be afraid to use an expression such as $2^{16} + 3$ for your answer, but do give the reason you think your answer is correct.

80. A binary computer with a basic 16-bit code uses an integer 2s complement number system. The arithmetic element contains an accumulator and MQ register, each containing 16 flip-flops (or bits). When a multiply is performed, the 16-bit word taken from the memory is multiplied times the 16-bit word in the accumulator, and the product is stored in the combined ACC-MQ with the least significant bit in the rightmost bit of the MQ. The sign bit of the MQ is set the same as the sign of the ACC and is not used to store a magnitude bit. In what bit of the ACC does the most significant bit of a product appear for numbers of maximum magnitude?

81. For the 74S181 chip in Fig. 6·21, write the Boolean algebra expression for $\overline{F}_0$ in terms of A_0, B_0, and C_n if M, S_3, S_1, S_0 are 1s and S_2 is a 0.

82. For the 74S181 chip in Fig. 6·21, how would you set M and S_0, S_1, S_2, and S_3 to subtract B from A?

83. For the 74S181 chip in Fig. 6·21, if we set $M = 1$, S_3, S_1, $S_0 = 1$, and $S_2 = 0$, the chip will add A to B. Write the Boolean algebra expression for F_1 in terms of the A, B, C_{n+4} inputs.

84. How would you set the M, S_0, S_1, S_2, S_3 inputs to the 74S181 chip in Fig. 6·21 to form the AND of A and B?

85. How would you set the M, S_0, S_1, S_2, S_3 inputs to perform an OR of the A and B inputs for the chip in Fig. 6·21?

86. Explain how the carry output C_n is formed for the chip in Fig. 6·21.

87. In the chapter the statement was made that the maximum delay through the 74S181 chip in Fig. 6·21 is 11 ns. This means, for instance, that if all the inputs are held in the same state except for $\overline{A}_0$, then from the time $\overline{A}_0$ is changed, the maximum time for C_{n+4} to change will be 11 ns. Find the maximum number of gates through which this delay must propagate and then determine typical single-gate delays.

88. The inputs to the 74S181 chip in Fig. 6·21 are each complemented, as are the outputs. Suppose we connect the A and B inputs to the uncomplemented outputs of the A and B flip-flops, also changing the diagram by removing the bars over the A and B inputs and the F outputs. Now if M is a 1, the functions yielded by each S_0, S_1, S_2, and S_3 state (input combination) will be different from those shown in Fig. 6·21. For instance, M, S_3, S_2, $S_1 = 1$ and $S_0 = 0$ will cause the circuit to form $A + B$. Give three more different output functions and their S_0, S_1, S_2, and S_3 values.

89. Repeat the setup with Question 88 and give three more functions.

90. The following is the block diagram for a 74S182 chip in the TTL series. This works with four 74S181 chips as shown in Fig. 6·21. The $\overline{G}_0$, $\overline{P}_0$, $\overline{C}_1$, $\overline{P}_1$, . . . inputs here are connected to the $\overline{G}$ and $\overline{P}$ outputs for the four 74S181 chips to be used. The 74S182 chip forms a carry-look-ahead generator for all four chips, forming high-speed carries for inputs to these chips. A complete 16-bit addition can then be performed in 22 ns. Explain how this works.

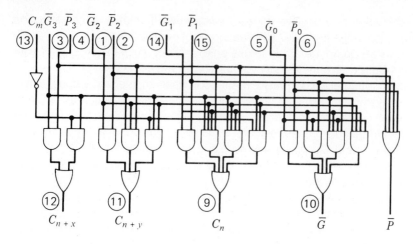

91. For the carry generator in Question 90 and four 74S181 chips as in Fig. 6·21, find the longest carry propagation path and determine how many gates are in it.

92. The following is a block diagram for a 74S283 chip which is a 4-bit full adder with fast carry. This chip can add two 4-bit binary numbers with a maximum

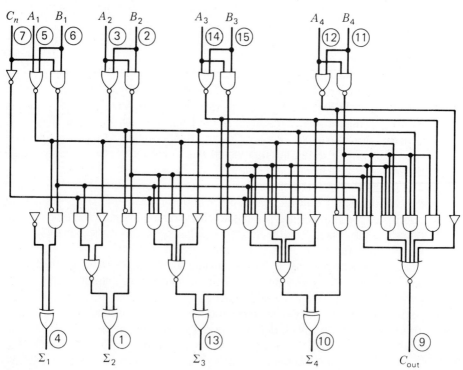

V_{CC} = Pin 16
GND = Pin 8
◯ = Pin numbers

carry time of 8 ns. (from C_{out} back through any path). Find the number of gates in this maximum carry delay path.

93. For the 4-bit full adder above it takes longer to form sum outputs S than the carry output (12 ns maximum for sums). How many gate delays are there in the delay path for the S_4 output?

94. Derive the Boolean algebra expression for the S_1 output in the 4-bit full adder above.

95. Derive the carry output expression (for C_{out}) for the 4-bit full adder above.

96. Why is the delay for C_{out} shorter than are the delays for S_0, S_1, S_2, and S_3 in the 4-bit full adder? When using several chips to make a 16-bit adder, does this make sense? Why?

97. Explain how you would connect the C_{in} and C_{out} inputs and outputs to the 4-bit full adder above if four such chips were used to form a 16-bit adder.

7
THE
MEMORY
ELEMENT

The memory of a computer is not actually concentrated in one place; storage devices are scattered throughout the machine. For instance, the *operation registers* are flip-flop registers which are used in the arithmetic and control units of the computer and arithmetic operations including additions, multiplications, shifts, etc., are all performed in these registers of the machine. The actual processing of information is performed in and at the direction of these registers.

Looking outward, the next category of storage device which is encountered is called the *high-speed memory, inner memory,* or *main memory.* This section of the computer's memory consists of a set of storage registers, each of which is identified with an address that enables the control unit either to write into or read from a particular register.

It is desirable that the operating speed of this section of the computer's memory be as fast as possible, for most of the transfers of data to and from the information processing section of the machine will be via the main memory. For this reason, storage devices with very fast access times are generally chosen for the main memory; unfortunately the presently available devices which are fast enough to perform this function satisfactorily do not possess the storage capacity that is sometimes required. As a result, additional memory, which is called the *auxiliary memory* or *secondary memory,* is added to most computers. This section of the computer's memory is characterized by low cost per digit stored, but it generally has an operating speed far slower than that of either the operation registers or the main memory. This section of the memory is sometimes designated the *backup store,* for its function is to handle quantities of data in excess of those that may be stored in the inner memory.

The final and outermost storage devices are those that are used to introduce information into the computer from the "outside world" and to store results from the computer to the computer user. The storage media in this case generally consist of such input media as punched cards or perforated paper tape, and the outputs from the machine generally consist of printed characters. Again, the cost per bit is low, but the operating speeds of the tape and card readers, printers, etc., are liable to be on the order of 1000 times slower than the speeds of the operation registers. These devices will be described in Chap. 8 under input-output devices. This chapter will be limited to the *internal storage* of the machine, which is defined as those storage devices that form an integral part of the machine and are directly controlled by the machine.

Each of the divisions of memory has certain characteristics. For instance, the premium on speed is very high for the operation registers. These registers must generally perform operations at several times the speed of the main memory. The main memory also requires high operating speeds, but because it is desirable to store larger quantities of data (perhaps 10^4 to 10^9 bits) in this section of the memory, a compromise between cost and speed must generally be made. The same sort of compromise must often be made in the case of the auxiliary memory. In a large machine the auxiliary memory may have to store from 10^8 to 10^{12} binary digits, and in these instances it might prove too expensive to use devices such as those used in the main memory.

An important point to notice when considering operating speed is that, before a word can be read, it is necessary to locate it. The time required to locate and read a word from memory is called the *access time.* The procedures for locating information may be divided into two classes, random access and sequential access. A *random-access* storage device is one in which any location in the device may be selected at random, access to the information stored is direct, and approximately equal access time is required for each location. A flip-flop register is an example of a random-access storage device, as are the IC and magnetic core memories, which will be described. A *sequential-access* device is one in which the arrival at the location desired may be preceded by sequencing through other locations, so that access time varies according to location.† For instance, if we try to read a word stored on a reel of magnetic tape and the piece of tape on which the word is stored is near the center of the reel, it will be necessary to sequence through all the intervening tape before the word can be read.

Another way to subdivide storage devices is according to whether they are static or dynamic storage devices. A *static* storage device is one in which the information does not change position; flip-flop registers, magnetic core registers, and even punched cards or tape are examples of static storage devices. *Dynamic* storage devices, on the other hand, are devices in which the information stored is continually changing position. Circulating registers utilizing charge coupled device (CCD) delay lines are examples of dynamic storage devices.

---

†Sequential-access devices are further separated into *direct-access storage devices* (DASD) and *serial-access devices*. Direct-access storage devices have addresses, but the access time to reach the data at a given address may vary. For instance, the time to locate data on a movable head disk (to be explained) depends on the head position and disk position when the address is given. Serial-access devices are truly serial in their access properties; magnetic tape is the classic example.

This chapter will concentrate on the four most frequently used devices for storing digital information in the internal memory sections of computers. These are (1) IC memories, which are high speed and of moderate cost; (2) magnetic core memories, which are random-access devices used principally in the inner memory because of their high operating speeds and moderate cost per bit; (3) magnetic drum and disk memories, which are direct-access storage devices generally used for auxiliary storage; and (4) magnetic tape memories, which are used exclusively as an auxiliary, or backup, storage but which are capable of storing large quantities of information at low cost. Following the sections on drum, disk, and magnetic tape devices, the techniques used to record digital information on a magnetic surface will be described.

7 • 1 RANDOM-ACCESS MEMORIES

The main memory of a computer is organized in a way which is particularly desirable. Figure 7·1 shows that a high-speed main memory in a computer is organized into words of fixed lengths. As the figure indicates, a given memory is divided into N words, where N generally is some power of 2, and each word is assigned an *address* or *location* in the memory. Each word has the same number of bits, called the *word length,* and if we read, for instance, the word at location 72, we shall receive a word from the memory with this word length.

The addresses or address numbers in the memory run consecutively, starting with the address 0 and running up the largest address. Thus at address 0 we find a word, at address 1 a second word, at address 2 a third word, and so on up to the final word at the largest address.

Generally, the computer can read a word from or write a word into each location in the memory. For a memory with an 8-bit word, if we write the word 01001011

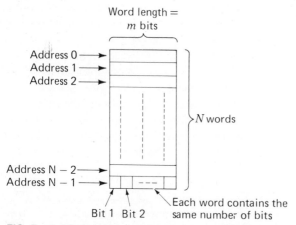

FIG. 7 • 1 Words in high-speed memory.

into memory address 17 and later read from this same address, we shall read the word 01001011. If we again read from this address at a later time (and have not written another word in), the word 01001011 will again be read. This means the memory is *nondestructive read* in that reading does not destroy or change a stored word.

It is important to understand the difference between the *contents* of a memory address and the address itself. A memory is like a large cabinet containing as many drawers as there are addresses in memory. In each drawer is a word, and the address of each word is written on the outside of the drawer. If we write or store a word at address 17, it is like placing the word in the drawer labeled 17. Later, reading from address 17 is like looking in that drawer to see its contents. We do not remove the word at an address when we read, but change the contents at an address only when we store or write a new word.

From an exterior viewpoint, a high-speed main memory looks very much like a "black box" with a number of locations or addresses into which data can be stored or from which data can be read. Each address or location contains a fixed number of binary bits, the number being called the *word length* for the memory. A memory with 4096 locations, each with a different address, and with each location storing 16 bits, is called a *4096-word 16-bit memory,* or, in the vernacular of the computer trade, a *4K 16-bit memory.* (Since memories generally come with a number of words equal to 2^n for some *n*, if a memory has $2^{14} = 16,384$ words, computer literature and jargon would refer to it as a 16K memory, because it is always understood that the full 2^n words actually occur in the memory. Thus, 2^{15}-word 16-bit memory is called a 32K 16-bit memory.)

Memories can be read from (that is, data can be taken out) or written into (that is, data can be entered into the memory). Memories which can be both read from and written into are called *read-write memories.* Some memories have programs or data permanently stored and are called *read-only memories.*

A block diagram of a read-write memory is shown in Fig. 7·2. The computer places the address of the location into which the data are to be read into the *memory address register.* This register consists of *n* binary devices (generally flip-flops), where 2^n is the number of words that can be stored in the memory. The data to be written into the memory are placed in the *memory buffer register,* which has as many binary storage devices as there are bits in each memory word. The memory is told to write by means of a 1 signal on the WRITE line. The memory will then store the contents of the memory buffer register in the location specified by the memory address register.

Words are read by placing the address of the location to be read from into the memory address register. A 1 signal is then placed on the READ line, and the contents of that location are placed by the memory in the memory buffer register.

As can be seen, the computer communicates with the memory by means of the memory address register, the memory buffer register, and the READ and WRITE inputs. Memories are generally packaged in separate modules or packages. It is possible to buy a memory module of a specified size from a number of different manufacturers, and, for instance, an 8K 16-bit memory module can be purchased

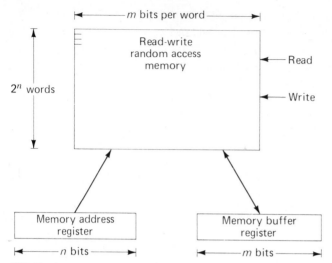

FIG. 7 • 2 Read-write random-access memory.

on a circuit board ready for use. Similarly, if a computer is purchased with a certain amount of main memory, more memory can generally later be added by purchasing additional modules and "plugging them in."

If it is possible to read from or write into any location "at once," that is, if there is no more delay in reaching one location as opposed to another location, the memory is called a *random-access memory* (RAM). Computers almost invariably use random-access read-write memories for their high-speed main memory and then use backup or slower speed memories to hold auxiliary data.

7 • 2 LINEAR-SELECT MEMORY ORGANIZATION

The most used random-access memories are IC memories and magnetic core memories. Both are organized in a similar manner, as will be shown.

In order to present the basic principles, an idealized IC memory will be shown, followed by details of several actual commercial memories.

In any memory there must be a basic memory cell. Figure $7 \cdot 3$ shows a basic memory cell consisting of an *RS* flip-flop with associated control circuitry. In order to use this cell in a memory, however, a technique for selecting those cells addressed by the memory address register must be used, as must a method to control whether the selected cells are written into or read from.

Figure $7 \cdot 4$ shows the basic memory organization for a *linear-select* IC memory. This is a four-address memory with 3 bits per word. The memory address register (MAR) selects the memory cells (flip-flops) to be read from or written into through a *decoder* which selects three flip-flops for each address that can be in the memory address register.

Figure $7 \cdot 5(a)$ shows the decoder in expanded form. It has an input from each

STATIC

this

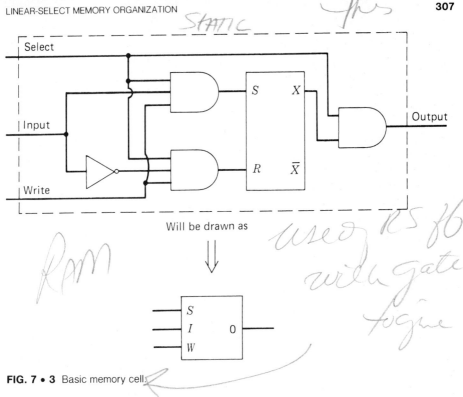

Will be drawn as

used RS f6
with gate
logic

Ram

FIG. 7 • 3 Basic memory cell

flip-flop (bit) to be decoded. If there are two input bits as in Fig. $7 \cdot 5(a)$, then there will be four output lines, one for each state (value) the input register can take. For instance, if the MAR contains 0 in both flip-flops, then the upper line of the decoder will be a 1 and the remaining three lines a 0. Similarly, if both memory cells contain a 1, the lowest output line will be a 1 and the remaining three lines a 0. Similar reasoning will show that there will be a single output line with a 1 output for each possible input state, and the remaining lines will always be a 0.

Figure $7 \cdot 5(b)$ shows a decoder for three inputs. The decoder has eight output lines. In general, for n input bits a decoder will have 2^n output lines.

The decoder in Fig. $7 \cdot 5(b)$ operates in the same manner as that in Fig. $7 \cdot 5(a)$. For each input state the decoder will select a particular output line, placing a 1 on the selected line and a 0 on the remaining lines.

Returning to Fig. $7 \cdot 4$, we now see that corresponding to each value that can be placed in the MAR, a particular output line from the decoder will be selected and carry a 1 value. The remaining output lines from the decoder will contain 0s, not selecting the AND gates at the inputs and outputs of the flip-flops for these rows. (Refer also to Fig. $7 \cdot 3$.)

The memory in Fig. $7 \cdot 4$ is organized as follows: There are four words, and each row of three memory cells comprises a word. At any given time the MAR selects a word in memory. If the READ line is a 1, the contents of the three cells in the selected word are read out on the O_1, O_2, and O_3 lines. If the WRITE line is a 1, the values on I_1, I_2, and I_3 will be read into the memory.

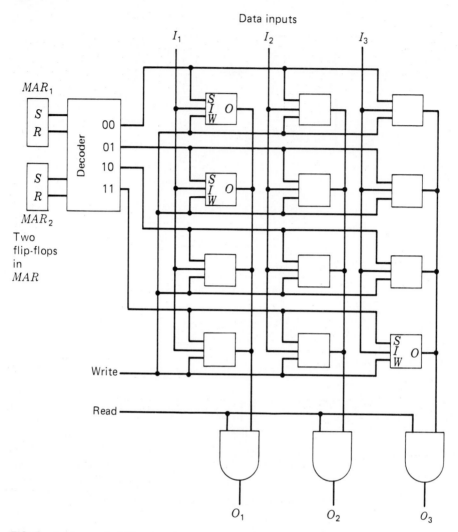

FIG. 7 • 4 Linear-select IC memory.

The AND gates connected to the OUT lines on the memory cells in Fig. 7·3 must have the property that when a number of AND gate output lines are connected together, the output goes to the highest level. (If any OUT is a 1, the line goes to 1, otherwise it is a 0.) This is called a *wired OR*. In Fig. 7·4 all four memory cells in the first column are wire-ORed together, so if any output line is a 1, the entire line will be a 1. (Memory cells in IC memories are constructed in this manner.)

Now if the READ line is a 1 in Fig. 7·4, the output values for the flip-flops in the selected row will all be gated onto the output line for each bit in the memory.

For example, if the second row in the memory contains 110 in the three memory cells, and if the MAR contains 01, then the second output line from the decoder

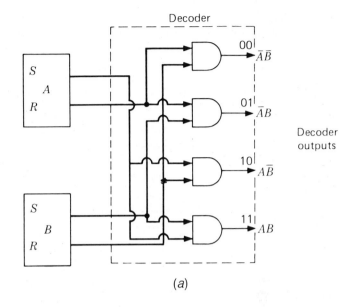

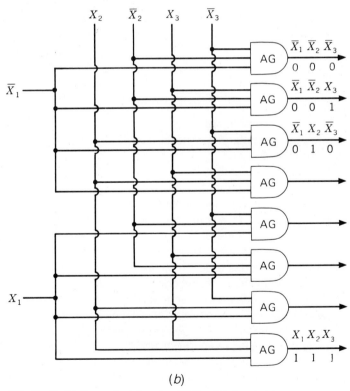

FIG. 7 • 5 (*a*) Four-output decoder. (*b*) Parallel decoder.

(marked 01) will be a 1, and the input gates and output gates to these three memory cells will be selected. If the READ line is a 1, then the outputs from the three memory cells in the second row will be 110 to the AND gates at the bottom of the figure, which will transmit the value 110 as an output from the memory.

If the WRITE line is a 1 and the MAR again contains 01, the second row of flip-flops will have selected inputs. The input values on I_1, I_2, and I_3 will then be read into the flip-flops in the second row.

As may be seen, this is a complete memory, fully capable of reading and writing. The memory will store data for an indefinite period and will operate as fast as the gates and flip-flops will permit. There is only one problem with the memory — its complexity. The basic memory cell (the flip-flop with its associated circuitry) is complicated, and for large memories the decoder will be large in size.

In order to further explore memory organization, we will first examine decoder construction in more detail, the selection schemes that are commonly used, and finally some examples of IC memories now in production.

7 • 3 DECODERS

An important part of the system which selects the cells to be read from and written into is the decoder. This particular circuit is called a *many-to-one decoder,* a *decoder matrix,* or simply a *decoder,* and has the characteristic that for each of the possible 2^n binary input numbers which can be taken by the n input cells, the matrix will have a unique one of its 2^n output lines selected.

Figure 7·5(b) shows a decoder which is completely parallel in construction and designed to decode three flip-flops. There are then $2^3 = 8$ output lines, and for each of the eight states which the three inputs (flip-flops) may take, a unique output line will be selected. This type of decoder is often constructed using diodes (or transistors) in the AND gates. The rule is: the number of diodes (or transistors) used in each AND gate is equal to the number of inputs to each AND gate.† For Fig. 7·5(b) this is equal to the number of input lines (flip-flops which are being decoded). Further, the number of AND gates is equal to the number of output lines, which is equal to 2^n (n is the number of input flip-flops being decoded). The total number of diodes is therefore equal to $n \times 2^n$, and for the binary decoding matrix in Fig. 7·5(b) 24 diodes are required to construct the network. As may be seen, the number of diodes required increases sharply with the number of inputs to the network. For instance, to decode an eight-flip-flop register, we would require 8 $\times 2^8 = 2048$ diodes if the decoder were constructed in this manner.

As a result there are several other types of structures which are often used in building decoder networks. One such structure, called a *tree-type* decoding network, is shown in Fig. 7·6. This tree network decodes four flip-flops and therefore has $2^4 = 16$ output lines, a unique one of which is selected for each state of the flip-flops. An examination will show that 56 diodes are required to build this partic-

---

†The rule for transistors is the same: the number of transistors required equals the number of inputs.

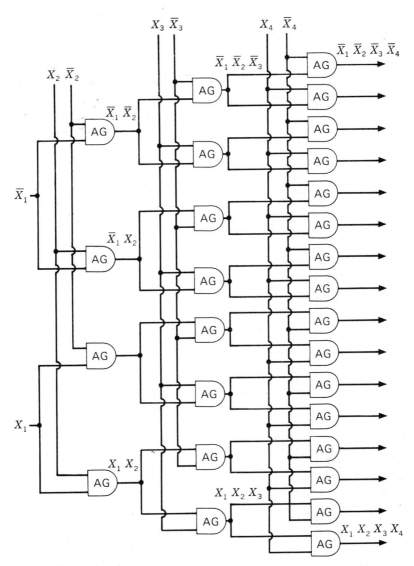

FIG. 7 • 6 Tree decoder.

ular network, while $2^4 \times 4 = 64$ diodes would be required to build the parallel decoder type shown in Fig. 7·5.

Still another type of decoder network is shown in Fig. 7·7. It is called a *balanced multiplicative decoder network*. Notice that this network requires only 48 diodes. It can be shown that the type of decoder network illustrated in Fig. 7·7 requires the minimum number of diodes for a complete decoder network. The difference in the number of diodes, or decoding elements, to construct a network such as shown in Fig. 7·7, compared with those in Figs. 7·5 and 7·6, becomes more significant as the number of flip-flops to be decoded increases. The network shown in Fig.

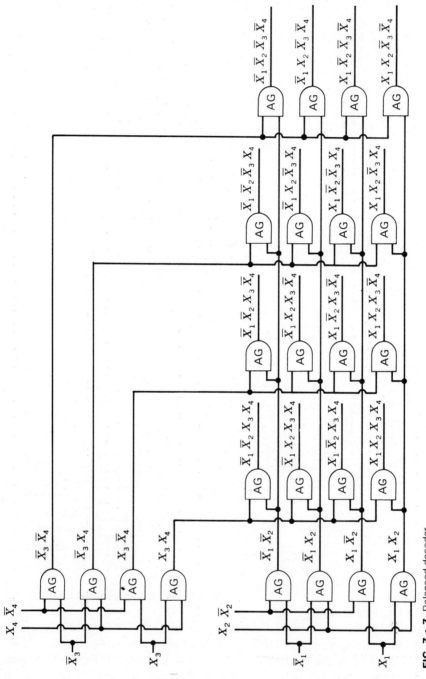

FIG. 7 • 7 Balanced decoder.

$7 \cdot 5$, however, has the advantage of being the fastest and most regular in construction of the three types of networks.

Having studied the three types of decoding matrices which are now used in digital machines, we will henceforth simply draw the decoder networks as a box with n inputs and 2^n outputs, with the understanding that one of the three types of circuits shown in Figs. $7 \cdot 5$–$7 \cdot 7$ will be used in the box. Often only the uncomplemented inputs are connected to decoders, and inverters are included in the decoder package. Then a three-input (or three-flip-flop) decoder will have only three input lines and eight outputs.

7 • 4 DIMENSIONS OF MEMORY ACCESS

The memory organization in Fig. $7 \cdot 4$ has a basic linear-select (one-dimensional) selection system. This is the simplest organization. However, the decoder in the selection system becomes quite large as the memory size increases.

As an example we assume a parallel decoder as shown in Fig. $7 \cdot 5b$. These are widely used in IC packages because of their speed and regular (symmetric) construction.

Consider now a decoder for a 4096-word memory, a common size for an IC package. There will be 12 inputs per AND gate, and 4096 AND gates are required. If a diode (or transistor) is required at each AND gate's input, then $12 \times 4096 = 49,152$ diodes (or transistors) will be required. This large number of components is the primary objection to this memory organization.

Let us now consider a *two-dimensional selection system*. First we will need to add another SELECT input to our basic memory cell. This is shown in Fig. $7 \cdot 8$. Now both the SELECT 1 and the SELECT 2 must be 1s for a flip-flop to be selected.

Figure $7 \cdot 9$ shows a two-dimensional memory selection system using this cell. Two decoders are required for this memory, which has 16 words of only 1 bit per word (for clarity of explanation). The MAR has 4 bits and thus 16 states. Two of the MAR inputs go to one decoder and two to the other.

To illustrate the memory's operation, if the MAR contains 0111, then the value 01 goes to the left decoder and 11 goes to the upper decoder. This will select the second row (line) from the left decoder and the rightmost column from the top decoder. The result is that only the cell (flip-flop) at this intersection of the second row and the rightmost column will have both its SELECT lines (and as a result its AND gates) enabled. As a result, only this particular single cell will be selected, and only this flip-flop can be read from or written into.

As another example, if the MAR contains 1001, the line for the third row of the left decoder will be a 1 as will be the second column line. The memory cell at the intersection of this row and column will be enabled, but no other cell will be enabled. If the READ line is a 1, the enabled cell will be read from; if the WRITE line is a 1, the enabled cell will be written into.

Now let us examine the number of components used. If a 16-word 1-bit memory was designed using the linear-select or one-dimensional system, then a decoder with 16×4 inputs and therefore 64 diodes (or transistors) would be required.

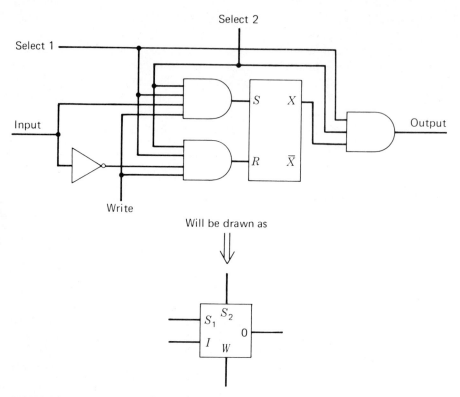

FIG. 7 • 8 Two-dimensional memory cell.

For the two-dimensional system two 2-input 4-output decoders are required, each requiring 8 diodes (transistors); so 16 diodes are required for both decoders.

For a 4096-word 1-bit-per-word memory the numbers are more striking. A 4096-word linear-select (one-dimensional) memory requires a 12-bit MAR. This decoder therefore requires $4096 \times 12 = 49,152$ diodes or transistors. The two-dimensional selection system would have two decoders, each with six inputs. Thus each would require $2^6 \times 6 = 384$ diodes or transistors, that is, a total of 768 diodes or transistors for the decoders. This is a remarkable saving, and extends to even larger memories.

In order to make a memory with more bits per word, we simply make a memory like that shown in Fig. 7·9 for each bit in the word (except that only one MAR and the original two decoders are required).

The above memory employs a classic two-dimensional selection system. This is the organization used in most core memories and in some IC memories. Figure 7·10 shows an IC memory with 256 bits on a single chip. As can be seen, this is a two-dimensional select memory.†

---

†The 256-bit RAM plane in Fig. 7·10 refers to a 16 × 16 two-dimensional array of memory cells. It is common practice to call such an array a *plane*.

MAR_1 MAR_2 MAR_3 MAR_4

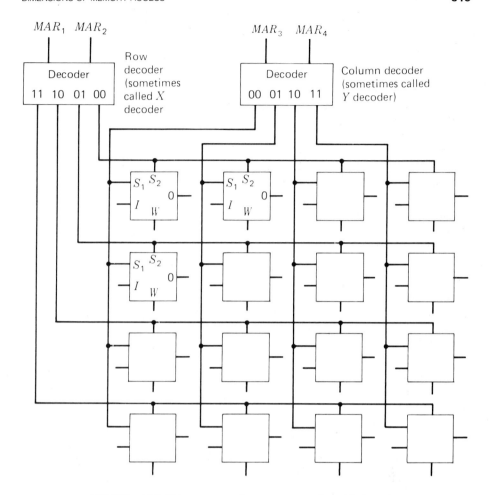

WRITE— (All W inputs on cells are connected to this input)

INPUT— (All I inputs on cells are connected to this input line)

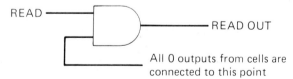

FIG. 7 • 9 Two-dimensional IC memory organization.

In a two-dimensional memory, however, simplification in decoder complexity is paid for with cell complexity. In some cases this extra cell complexity is inexpensive, but it is often a problem, and so a variation of this scheme is used.

A variation on the basic two-dimensional selection system is illustrated in Fig. 7·11. This memory uses two decoders, as in the previous scheme; however, the memory cells are basic memory cells, as shown in Fig. 7·3.

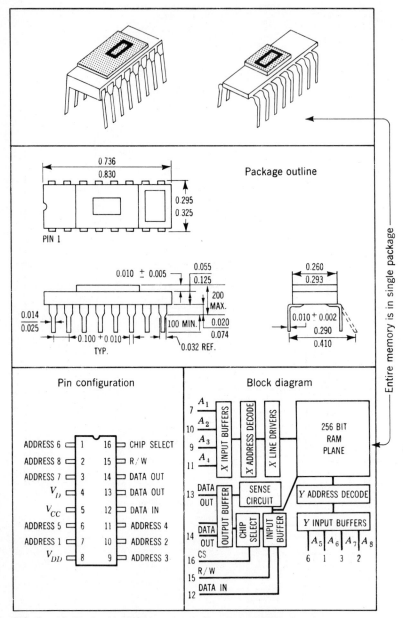

FIG. 7 • 10 Single-chip 256-bit memory. (Courtesy of INTEL Corp.)

The selection scheme uses gating on the READ and WRITE inputs to achieve the desired two-dimensionality.

Let us consider a WRITE operation. First assume that the MAR contains 0010. This will cause the 00 output from the upper decoder to be a 1, selecting the top row of memory cells. In the lower decoder the 10 output will become a 1, and this is gated with an AND gate near the bottom of the diagram, turning the *W* inputs on

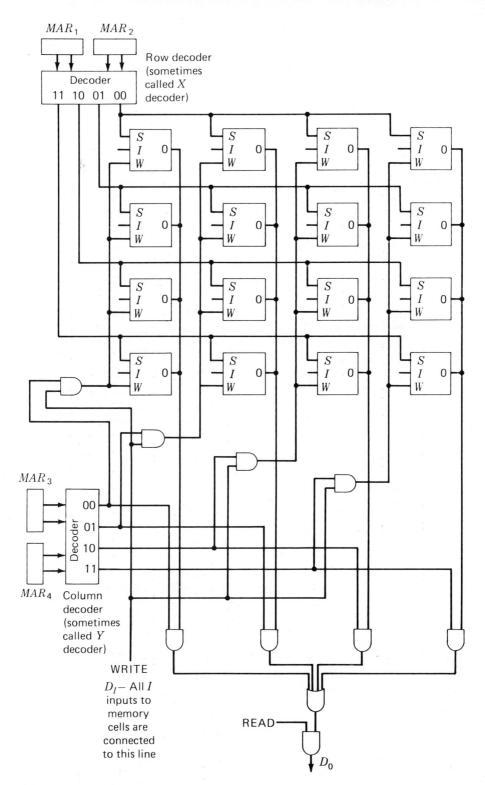

FIG. 7 • 11 IC memory chip layout.

in the third column. As a result, for the memory cell in the top row and third column the S input and the W input will be a 1. For no other memory cell will both S and W be a 1, and so no other memory cell will have its RS flip-flop set to the input value. (Notice that all I inputs on the memory cells are connected to the input value D_i.)

Consideration of other values for the MAR will indicate that for each value a unique memory cell will be selected for the write operation. Therefore for each MAR state only one memory cell will be written into.

The read operation is similar. If the MAR contains 0111, then the upper decoder's 01 line will be a 1, turning the S inputs on in the second row of memory cells. As a result only these four cells in the entire array are capable of writing a 1 on the output lines. (Again, the memory cells are wire-ORed by having their outputs connected together, this time in groups of four.)

The lower decoder will have input 11, and so its lowest output line will carry a 1. This 1 turns on the rightmost AND gate in the lowest row, which enables the output from the rightmost column of memory cells. Only the second cell down has its output enabled, however, and so the output from the rightmost AND gate will have as output the value in the cell. This value then goes through the OR gate and the AND gate at the bottom of the diagram, the AND gate having been turned on by the READ signal.

Examination will show that each input value from the MAR will select a unique memory cell to be read from, and that cell will be the same as would have been written into if the operation were a write operation.

This is basically the organization used by most IC memories at this time. The chips contain up to 64K bits. The number of rows versus the number of columns in an array is determined by the designers who decide upon the numbers that will reduce the overall component count.

All the circuits necessary for a memory are placed on the same chip, except for the MAR flip-flops which quite often are not placed on the chip, but the inputs go directly to the decoders. This will be clearer when interfacing with a bus has been discussed.

7 • 5 CONNECTING MEMORY CHIPS TO A COMPUTER BUS

The present trend in computer memory connection is to connect the computer central processing unit (CPU), which does the arithmetic, generates control, etc.,† to the memory by means of a *bus.* The bus is simply a set of wires which are shared by all the memory elements to be used.

Microprocessors and minicomputers almost always use a bus to interface memory, and in this case the memory elements will be IC chips, which are in IC containers just like those described in Chap. 4 and shown in Fig. 7 · 10.

The bus used to connect the memories generally consists of (1) a set of *address*

---

†A CPU includes the arithmetic and control sections of a computer.

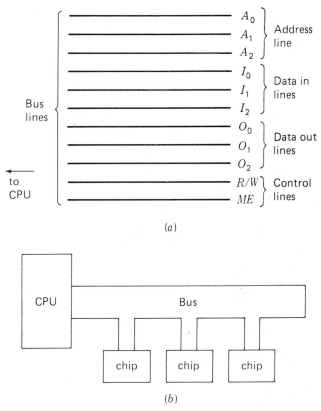

(a)

(b)

FIG. 7 • 12 Bus for computer system. (a) Bus lines. (b) Bus/CPU/memory organization.

lines to give the address of the word in memory to be used (these are effectively an output from a MAR on the microprocessor chip); (2) a set of *data wires* to input data from the memory and output data to the memory; and (3) a set of *control wires* to control the read and write operations.

Figure 7·12 shows a bus for a microcomputer. In order to simplify drawings and clarify explanations, we will use a memory bus with only three address lines, three output data lines, two control signals, and three input data lines. The memory to be used is therefore an 8-word 3-bit-per-word memory.

The two control signals work as follows. When the R/W line is a 1, the memory is to be read from; when the R/W line is a 0, the memory is to be written into.† The MEMORY ENABLE signal ME is a 1 when the memory is either to be read from or to be written into; otherwise it is a 0.

The IC memory package to be used is shown in Fig. 7·13. Each IC package

---

†This is quite similar to the READ and WRITE signals used in prior memory description. An AND gate connected to ME and R/W will generate a READ signal, and an inverted R/W which is ANDed with ME will give a WRITE signal.

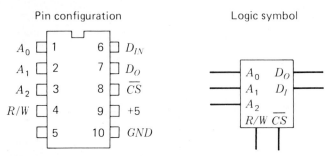

FIG. 7 • 13 IC package and block diagram symbol for RAM chip. (*a*) Pin configuration. (*b*) Logic symbol.

has three address inputs A_0, A_1, and A_2, an R/W input, an output bit D_O, an input bit D_I, and a CHIP SELECT $\overline{CS}$. Each package contains an 8-word 1-bit memory.

The IC memory chip works as follows. The address lines A_0, A_1, and A_2 must be set to the address to be read from or written into (refer to Fig. 7·13). If the operation is a READ, the R/W line is set to a 1, and the $\overline{CS}$ line is brought to 0 (the $\overline{CS}$ line is normally a 1). The data bit may then be read on line D_o. Certain timing constraints must be met, however, and these will be supplied by the IC manufacturer. Figure 7·14 shows several of these. The value T_R is the minimum cycle time a read operation requires. During this period the address lines must be stable. The value T_A is the access time, which is the maximum time from when the address lines are stable until data can be read from the memory. The value T_{CO} is the maximum time from when the $\overline{CS}$ line is made a 0 until data can be read.

The bus timing must accommodate the above times. It is important that the bus not operate too fast for the chip and that the bus wait for at least the time T_A after setting its address lines before reading and wait at least T_{CO} after lowering the $\overline{CS}$ line before reading. Also, the address line must be held stable for at least the period T_R.

For a write operation the address to be written into is set up on the address lines, the R/W line is made a 0, $\overline{CS}$ is brought down, and the data to be read are placed on the D_I line.

The time interval T_W is the minimum time for a WRITE cycle; the time T_H is the time the data to be written into the chip must be held stable. Different types of memories have different timing constraints which the bus must accommodate. We will assume that our bus meets these constraints.†

In order to form an 8-word 3-bit memory from these IC packages (chips), the interconnection scheme in Fig. 7·15 is used. Here the address line to each chip is connected to a corresponding address output on the microcomputer bus. The CHIP ENABLE input of $\overline{CS}$ of each chip is connected to the MEMORY ENABLE output

---

†On the other hand, if a specific microprocessor is used, the memory must be fast enough to accommodate the bus.

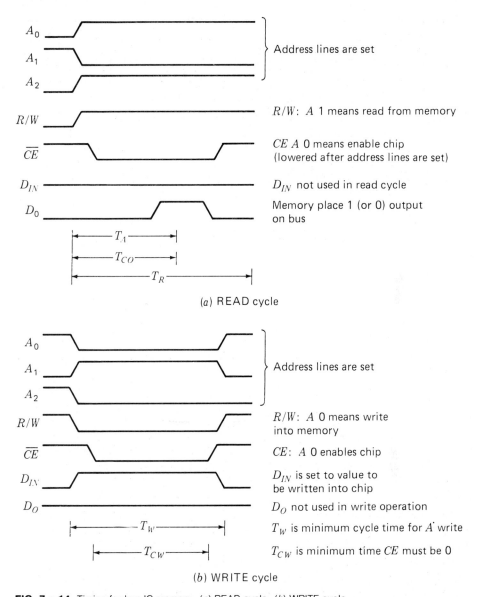

A_0

A_1

A_2

} Address lines are set

R/W R/W: A 1 means read from memory

$\overline{CE}$ CE A 0 means enable chip (lowered after address lines are set)

D_{IN} D_{IN} not used in read cycle

D_0 Memory place 1 (or 0) output on bus

T_A

T_{CO}

T_R

(a) READ cycle

A_0

A_1

A_2

} Address lines are set

R/W R/W: A 0 means write into memory

$\overline{CE}$ CE: A 0 enables chip

D_{IN} D_{IN} is set to value to be written into chip

D_O D_O not used in write operation

T_W T_W is minimum cycle time for $A^{'}$ write

T_{CW} T_{CW} is minimum time CE must be 0

(b) WRITE cycle

FIG. 7 • 14 Timing for bus IC memory. (a) READ cycle. (b) WRITE cycle.

ME from the microprocessor via an inverter, and the R/W bus line is connected to the R/W input on each chip.

If the microprocessor CPU wishes to read from the memory, it simply places the address to be read from on the address lines, puts a 1 on the R/W line, and then raises the ME line. Each chip then reads the selected bit onto its output line, and the CPU can read these values on its I_1, I_2, and I_3 lines. (Notice that a chip's output is a bus input.)

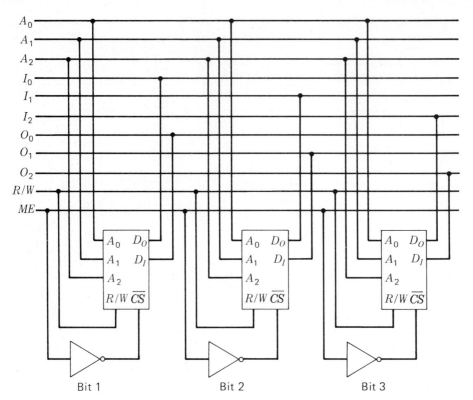

FIG. 7 • 15 Interfacing chips to a bus.

Similarly, to write a word into the memory, the CPU places the address to be written into on the address lines, the bits to be written on the O_1, O_2, O_3 lines, lowers R/W, and then raises ME.

In practice, for microprocessors the memory words now generally contain 8 bits each. (Some new large microprocessors have 16-bit words.) There are generally 16 address lines, and so 2^{16} words can be used in the memory. On the other hand, memory chips tend to have from 8 to 14 (at most) memory address lines. Fortunately there is a simple way to expand memories, and this is shown for our small system in Fig. 7·16.

In this example the chips again have three address lines, but the microprocessor bus has five lines. In order to enable connection, a two-input decoder is connected to the two most significant bits of the address section of the bus, while the three least significant bits are connected to the chip address buses as before.

Now the decoder outputs are each gated with the ME control signal using a NAND gate, so when ME is raised, a single CHIP SELECT line is lowered (the outputs from the NAND gates are normally high). The decoder therefore picks the chip that is enabled, and the address lines on the enabled chip select the memory cell to be written into or read from. The decoding on the chip then selects the particular memory cell to be read from or written into.

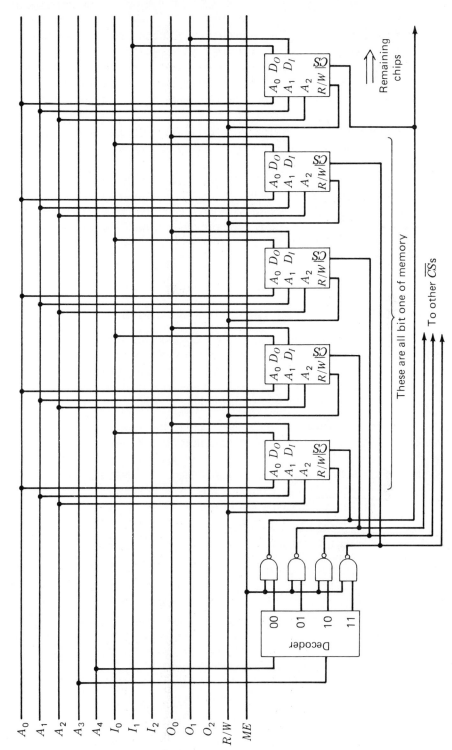

FIG. 7 • 16 Layout for adding memory to bus.

The principle shown in Fig. 7·16 is widely used in computers. Memory chips almost invariably have fewer address inputs than buses, and so this expansion technique is necessary to memory usage. Notice that only 1 bit of the memory word is completely drawn in Fig. 7·16. (One chip from the second bit is also shown.) An entire 32-word 3-bit memory would require 12 chips of the type shown here.

As may be seen, a micro- or minicomputer can be purchased with a minimal memory, and the memory can then be expanded by adding more chips, up to the size that the bus address lines can accommodate.

The remainder of this chapter is structured as follows. The details of some IC memories are presented, followed by the description of core memories. Then disk, drum, and tape memories are covered. Depending on the amount of interest in circuits, the material in the IC memory and core memory sections can be studied. It is, however, possible to skip to the disk, drum, and tape memory sections at this time without loss of continuity.

7 · 6 RANDOM-ACCESS SEMICONDUCTOR MEMORIES

The ability to fabricate large arrays of electronic components using straightforward processing techniques and to make these arrays in small containers at reasonable prices has made semiconductor memories the most popular at this time.

Although there are a number of different schemes and devices available, there are at present six main categories of IC memories.

1. *Bipolar memories*   These are essentially flip-flop memories with the flip-flops fabricated using standard *pn* junction transistors. These memories are fast but tend to be expensive.
2. *Static MOS memories*   These are fabricated using MOS field effect devices to make flip-flop circuits. These memories are lower in speed than the bipolar memories but cost less, consume less power, and have high packing densities.
3. *Dynamic MOS memories*   These are fabricated using MOS devices, but instead of using a flip-flop for the basic memory cell, a charge is deposited on a capacitor (or capacitors) fabricated on the IC chip, and the presence or absence of this charge determines the state of the cell. The MOS devices are used to sense and to deposit the charge on the capacitors used. Since the charge used will slowly dissipate in time, it is necessary to periodically refresh this charge, and the memories are therefore called *dynamic memories.* (MOS or bipolar flip-flop memories are called *static memories.*) These memories tend to be slower than the other types, but they are also less expensive, consume less power, and have a high packing density.
4. *CMOS memories*   CMOS utilizes both *p*- and *n*-channel devices on the same substrate. As a result it involves more complex processing. CMOS has improved speed power output over *n*- and *p*-channel MOS, but is higher in cost.
5. *Silicon on sapphire (SOS) memories*   SOS is similar to CMOS. Devices are

TABLE 7 • 1 SEMICONDUCTOR MEMORY CHARACTERISTICS

CHARACTERISTIC	HIGH SPEED	MOS n-CHANNEL HIGH DENSITY	BIPOLAR
Number of bits per chip	4096	65,536	16,364
Access time, ns	10	100	40
Power dissipation, mW/bit	0.05	0.01	0.1
Average large-quantity cost, cents/bit	0.1	0.05	0.1

formed on an insulating substrate of sapphire. This reduces the device capacitance and improves speed. However, SOS is the highest in cost.

6. *Integrated injection logic (IIL) memories*   The IIL circuits eliminate the load resistors and current sources of TTL circuits. This reduces power consumption over bipolar memories, giving greater packing density than bipolar. As a result, IIL mixes speed of bipolar memories with packing density of MOS. It is medium-cost.

The selection techniques, sensing techniques, and other basic ideas used in core memories also apply to semiconductor memories. Since the storage devices are fabricated on a chip, the sense amplifiers, decoders, etc., can be placed on the same chip, and quite often individual chips contain essentially complete small memories. The following sections cover some of the important features and details of semiconductor memories. Table 7 · 1 lists some key memory characteristics.

7 • 7 BIPOLAR IC MEMORIES*

Bipolar memories are fabricated using high-density versions of the bipolar transistor flip-flop. One problem in increasing the density is isolating individual transistors from one another, but manufacturers have developed processes for reducing the space needed for transistor isolation. An advantage of bipolar devices is the simplicity of the interface circuitry required because of compatibility with bipolar logic. Another is the speed attainable.

Bipolar memories are manufactured using processes similar to those described in Chap. 5, and the primary circuit types include TTL and emitter-coupled logic (ECL).

Figure 7 · 17 shows a basic bipolar memory cell. The circuit consists of two transistors which are cross-coupled to form a conventional flip-flop. Each transistor has two emitters, however, and one of these is used to select the cell in an array. The other emitter is used to sense the state of the flip-flop and to write into the flip-flop.

---

*This section contains some circuit details and can be skipped without loss of continuity. The next two sections can also be skipped over if desired.

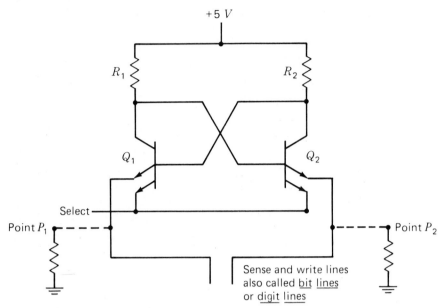

FIG. 7 • 17 Basic bipolar memory cell.

The connections to the top emitters in $Q1$ and $Q2$ form what is called a *digit line*. It is used to both sense the state of the flip-flop and write into it.

The circuit operates as follows. If the SELECT line is low (at about 0 V), the flip-flop will be stable with current from the on transistor being conducted to ground by the emitter connected to the SELECT line. The transmitter will be off. As long as the digit lines are at 0 V or positive, which they normally are, they will not disturb the flip-flop's state.

If the SELECT line is raised positive (to $+5$ V, for instance), the emitters connected to the digit lines now control current flow. Figure $7 \cdot 17$ shows dashed lines to indicate resistors connected to ground from the digit lines.

Now suppose SELECT is high and we wish to read the flip-flop's state. If $Q1$ is on, then current will flow through the left resistor connected to ground. At the same time $Q2$ will be off and so no current will flow through the rightmost resistor. This means that point $P1$ will be positive with regard to $P2$. (The amount that $P1$ will be positive is determined by the value of the resistor in that part of the circuit.)

If $Q2$ is on and $Q1$ is off, current will flow through the rightmost resistor to ground and will not flow through the leftmost resistor, and $P2$ will be positive relative to $P1$.

The above shows that with the SELECT line positive, we can determine the state of the flip-flop by measuring the voltage at $P1$ and $P2$. This is normally done by an amplifier circuit called a *sense amplifier* which measures this difference and outputs a 1 or a 0, depending on whether $P1$ or $P2$ is more positive.

It is also possible to write into the cell using the digit lines. Suppose the SELECT line is high, and if we force $P1$ high with regard to $P2$, then $Q2$ will go on and will force $Q1$ off. Similarly, raising $P2$ with regard to $P1$ will force $Q1$ on and $Q2$ off.

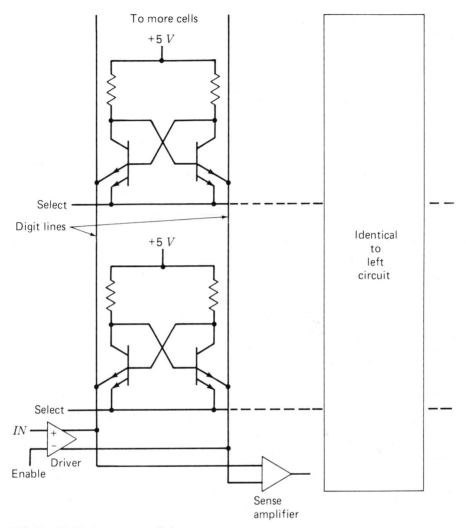

FIG. 7 • 18 Bipolar memory cells in array.

As may now be seen, the same two digit lines can be used to both sense the state of the flip-flop and force a given value into the cell.

Figure 7·18 shows an arrangement with two SELECT lines and two memory cells in order to show how these cells can be combined in memory. As indicated, more cells can be added in either the vertical or the horizontal direction.

Assume that the upper SELECT line is high and the lower SELECT line is low. This selects the upper cell. Now if we wish to read from the memory, the sense amplifier will tell the state of the selected flip-flop because the other cell(s) in that column will have low SELECT lines conducting current to ground for the on transistors, and only the selected cell will have the current flow to ground for its on transistor pass through the sense amplifier. This means that a single cell in each

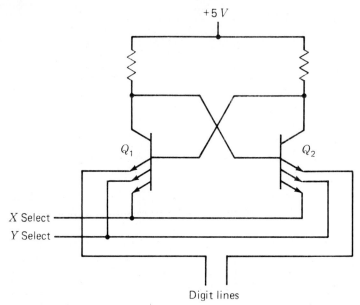

FIG. 7 • 19 Two-dimensional select bipolar cell.

column can be selected and read from by connecting a decoder to the SELECT inputs.

Similarly, we can write a 1 or a 0 into the selected cell in a column using the driver circuit, which will force either one of the digit lines positive with respect to the other.

This memory is organized like that in Fig. 7·11, except that the two digit lines are used to both read from and write into a cell instead of having separate READ and WRITE lines. Also, a sense amplifier is used to read column output values and a column driver (which can be disabled) to write into a cell.

Figure 7·19 shows a bipolar memory cell for a two-dimensional selection system. Both SELECT lines must be high to select the cell. Otherwise the circuit operates like that in Figs. 7·17 and 7·18, using digit lines to both sense the state of the cell and write into a selected cell.

The memory cell in Fig. 7·19 would be used in a memory organized like that in Figs. 7·9 and 7·10.

Table 7·2 lists some characteristics of commercially available bipolar memory chips.

7 • 8 STATIC MOS MEMORIES

It was realized very early in semiconductor memory development that MOS devices offer simplicity of manufacture and economy of layout. (MOS is made with only one diffusion and perhaps two-thirds the number of masks of bipolar devices.)

TABLE 7 • 2 IC BIPOLAR MEMORIES

ORGANIZATION	PART NUMBER	MAXIMUM ACCESS TIME ns	MAXIMUM CURRENT REQUIRED mA
1024 × 4	6250/6251-1	50	175
1024 × 8	6282/6283-2	35	170
	6280/6281-1		
4096 × 1	93L471	45	165
4096 × 1	93F471	30	195

MOS cells take up only one-half to one-fourth the area of bipolar cells, and hence they offer a considerable cost advantage. Figure 7·20 illustrates a MOS flip-flop analogous to the bipolar device of Fig. 7·17.

A cell is selected by simply raising the SELECT line. Q1 and Q3 serve as gates, connecting to the digit lines. Q2 and Q4 form a conventional flip-flop. The state of the storage cell can be read by raising the SELECT line which will turn on either Q1 or Q3, depending on the state of the flip-flop. The write operation is carried out by raising the SELECT line and then setting the desired value in by placing a high and a low voltage on the correct digit lines,† just as in Fig. 7·17.

The predominant type of MOS device in early memories was the *p*-channel enhancement mode (PMOS) unit, where holes are the vehicle of current flow. Although easy to produce, inexpensive, and reliable, PMOS is relatively slow and limited in LSI packing density. *n*-channel devices have now become the most pop-

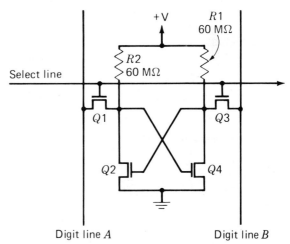

FIG. 7 • 20 MOS static memory cell. (Courtesy of Electronic Memories and Magnetics Corp.)

---

†The resistors *R1* and *R2* are normally realized using MOS transistors.

ular, offering important performance advantages over their *p*-channel counter-parts, such as low operating voltage and higher speed. Because electron mobility is greater than hole mobility, *n*-channel transistors are two to three times faster than *p*-channel transistors, which is equivalent to saying that *n*-channel devices have greater gain than *p*-channel devices of the same size. For equal speeds, *n*-channel units are smaller, permitting greater packing density; and higher substrate doping levels may be employed, increasing density even further. Further, there are many variations in NMOS technology, including VMOS, HMOS, etc.

If we compare bipolar and MOS technologies, bipolar offers a speed advantage, although, until recently, limitations imposed by the need for isolation between transistors have limited packing density and hence per-chip storage capacity. Bipolar components can provide access times of under 10 ns, in contrast with 300 ns or more for PMOS and 20 ns for NMOS. MOS devices have relatively high internal capacitance and impedance, leading to longer time constants and access times. Our schematic symbols will not show the channel connections on the FETs, as is conventional for memory devices. All devices are NMOS.

The operation of a typical 4096-bit static NMOS memory chip is detailed in Figs. 7·21–7·23. The 4096 bits of memory are organized in an array of 64 rows by 64 columns. The memory bits are accessed by simultaneously decoding the *X* address $A_0 - A_5$ for the rows and the *Y* address $A_6 - A_{11}$ for the columns. (Each col-

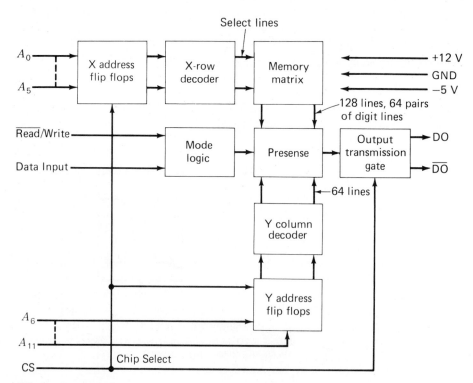

FIG. 7 • 21 Block diagram of MOS static memory. (Courtesy of Electronic Memories and Magnetics Corp.)

Top view

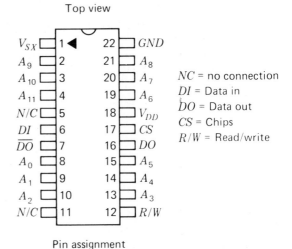

Pin assignment

FIG. 7 • 22 MOS static memory pin assignment.
(Courtesy of Electronic Memories and Magnetics Corp.)

umn contains a *presense amplifier,* the outputs of which are ORed and connected to the output stage.) Each bit or memory cell is a standard flip-flop as shown in Fig. 7·21, consisting of $R1$, $R2$ (which are actually MOS devices), $Q2$, $Q4$, $Q1$, and $Q3$. $Q1$ and $Q3$ are used to connect the cell to the digit lines whenever the X SELECT is high. To read from this cell, the SELECT line is raised; then the cell will pull one of the digit lines low from its normally high state. The sense circuit selected by the Y column decoder will detect the differential voltage on the digit line selected and amplify it. To write into the cell, an X line is selected and forced low by the circuit, and the selected cell assumes the state forced by the selected digit line.

The CHIP SELECT (CS) input controls the operation of the memory.† When CS is low, the input address buffers, decoders, sensing circuits, and output stages are held in the off state, and power is supplied only to the memory elements. When the CS goes high, the memory is enabled. The CS pulse clocks the TTL logic level addresses, READ-WRITE, and DATA input into D flip-flops and enables the output stage. When a cell is read from, one of the two outputs will be a 1 (DO for data originally input as a 1, $\overline{DO}$ for data originally input as a 0).

As shown in Fig. 7·22, this memory chip is packaged in a 22-pin dual in-line package. By assembling a number of these chips, a large, moderately fast memory can be constructed. Memory cycle times for this chip are on the order of 50 ns. Figure 7·23 shows the timing for the memory cycles.

Notice that the basic memory cell in this memory is a device as shown in Fig. 7·3. A two-dimensional selection is obtained by breaking the memory into rows and columns and using many (64) sense amplifiers and INHIBIT, or digit, drivers on

†This is the same as the CHIP ENABLE (CE) line in Figs. 7·13 and 7·16.

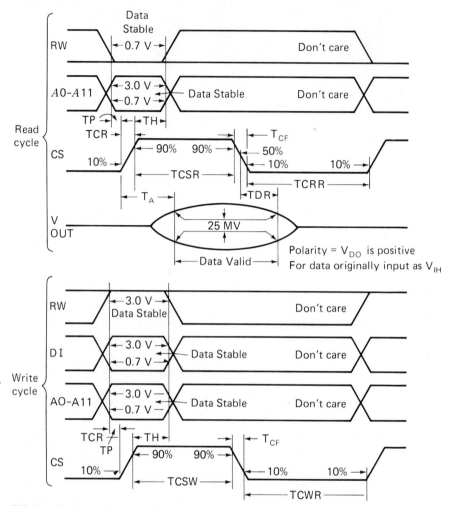

FIG. 7 • 23 Timing diagrams. (Courtesy of Electronic Memories and Magnetics Corp.)

these columns. When a read or write operation is performed, the appropriate digit driver or "presense" amplifier is selected by the *Y* decoder. Thus a row of memory cells is enabled by the ROW SELECT line, but only the cell at the intersection of the enabled row and the selected sense amplifier or digit line driver will be actually used, as was shown in Fig. 7·11. This scheme requires more digit drivers and sense amplifiers, but simplifies construction of the individual flip-flop memory cells. (Two more MOS transistors per cell are required to make a conventional two-dimensional selection as in the bipolar cell previously shown.) In general, two-dimensional selection of semiconductor cells requires more circuitry (generally two transistors per cell) but simplifies the decoders used. A pure one-dimensional (lin-

TABLE 7 • 3 NMOS STATIC MEMORIES

PART NUMBER, MANUFACTURER, ORGANIZATION	POWER DISSIPATION mW	MAXIMUM ACCESS TIME ns	MAXIMUM CYCLE TIME ns	PACKAGE
91L30/AMD (1K × 4)	350	500	840	22-pin
9135/AMD (4K × 1)	675	80	130	18-pin
SEMI 4402 (4K × 1)	500	100	100	22-pin
5256/National (1K × 4)	400	250	400	22-pin
2147H/Intel (4K × 1)	500	45	60	18-pin
TMS4045/TI (1K × 4)	400	150	150	18-pin

ear) selection makes for larger decoders but simpler individual cells. As a result, compromise strategies such as that shown are often used.

The characteristics of several NMOS memories are shown in Table 7·3.

7 • 9 DYNAMIC MEMORIES

MOS cells are generally used as the basis for a dynamic memory system. In a given memory cell, a 1 is written in by placing a charge on a capacitor; not charging or discharging the capacitor stores a 0. Reading then entails sensing the presence or absence of a charge on the capacitor. However, because there is always some leakage of the charge to ground, periodic refreshing is necessary.

Figure 7·24 depicts the simplest and most used type of data storage cell, using a single MOS switching transistor and a storage capacitor (also a MOS device). Although the single-transistor memory cell requires sophisticated sense and write

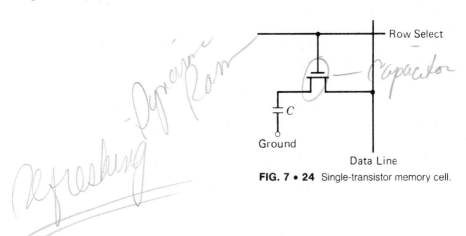

FIG. 7 • 24 Single-transistor memory cell.

circuits, its small size makes it suitable for high-density storage, such as in memories with 64,000 cells per IC chip.

In Fig. 7·24 the ROW SELECT line operates as in other memories: making this line high selects a cell. The DATA line is used to read from the cell. Cells are arranged in a two-dimensional array with sense amplifiers connected to each DATA line and in turn to all the cells in that column. When a row is enabled by the ROW SELECT line, all the transistors in that row conduct (the transistors in other rows are off). These on transistors transfer any charge on the capacitors to the DATA line, destructively reading the data. Each column in the array has its own sense amplifier which detects the charge, amplifying the detected level to a logic 1 (outputting a 0 for no charge). (These sense amplifiers must be carefully designed because the charge is attenuated by the capacitance formed by the entire column's DATA line.)

A cell is written into by forcing the DATA line to a high or low voltage (for 1 or 0) and then raising the ROW SELECT, forcing or not forcing a charge into the capacitor.

Figure 7·25 shows the address timing and pin layout for a 16K-bit dynamic RAM. There are not enough address lines into these chips, and so the addresses are *time multiplexed* (that is, put on in two sections, one right after the other). First the (first half) row address is placed on A_0-A_6 and RAS is lowered, then the column address is placed on A_0-A_6 and $\overline{CAS}$ is lowered. In order to use RAMs of this kind, extra circuitry for multiplexing address lines and to generate the REFRESH signal must be used.† Nevertheless because of the high packing density and low cost, the extra complexity of these specialized circuits is compensated for, and these memories are widely used.

The primary advantages of dynamic MOS memories lie in the simplicity of the individual cells. There is a secondary advantage in the fact that power need not be applied to the cells when they are not being read from or written into. This makes for higher packing densities per chip. The obvious disadvantage lies in the need to refresh these cells every few milliseconds since charge continually leaks from the capacitors (generally less than every 2 ms). External circuitry to control refresh rewrite is generally required, or sometimes the memories may include special circuits to refresh when commanded. As a result, extra refresh memory cycles are required, but these occupy only a small percentage of the overall operating time.‡ Table 7·4 lists some of the characteristics of dynamic memories.

The selection systems and sense and write operations for dynamic memories are similar to those for static memories, except that more complicated timing is required. Dynamic memories are generally slower than static memories but also tend to cost less per bit.

---

†IC manufacturers make special chips for this purpose. For these particular memories refresh is done by extra columns at a line so only all rows must be sequenced through. To refresh a row, the row address is placed on the address lines and the $\overline{RAS}$ is lowered. Each row must be refreshed in each 2-ms period.

‡There are even some interesting internal refresh mechanisms called *charge pumps* which require application of a sine wave on one of the inputs and make refreshing transparent (invisible) to the user. Other refresh strategies rewrite entire rows using a single REFRESH pulse.

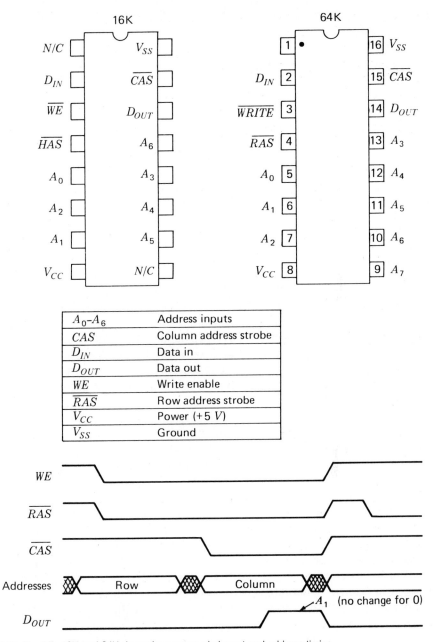

FIG. 7 • 25 16K and 64K dynamic memory pin layout and address timing.

TABLE 7 • 4 SEVERAL COMMERCIALLY AVAILABLE 16K NMOS DYNAMIC MEMORIES

MANUFACTURER	PART NUMBER	ACCESS TIME ns	READ CYCLE TIME ns	WRITE CYCLE TIME ns	OPERATING POWER mW	NUMBER OF PINS	OUTPUTS
Intel	2116	150	375	375	720	16	Latched, 3-state, TTL compatible
TI	TMS4070	150	550	550	550	16	Unlatched, 3-state, TTL compatible
Mostek	MK4116	120	375	375	600	16	Unlatched, 3-state, TTL compatible
Motorola	MCM6616	250	375	375	500	16	Latched, 3-state, TTL compatible

7 • 10 READ-ONLY MEMORIES

A type of storage device called a *read-only memory* (ROM) is widely used. ROMs have the unique characteristic that they can be read from, but not written into. The information stored in these memories is therefore introduced into the memory in some manner such that the information is semipermanent or permanent. Sometimes the information stored in a ROM is placed in the memory at the time of construction, and sometimes devices are used where the information can be changed. In this section we shall study several types of ROMs. These are characteristic of this particular class of memory devices, and most devices are variations on the principles that will be presented.

Basically a ROM is a device with several input and output lines such that for each input value there is a unique output value. Thus a ROM physically realizes a truth table, or table of combinations. A typical (small) one is shown in Table 7·5.

This list of input-output values is actually a list of binary-to-Gray code values. (The Gray code will be discussed in the next chapter.) It is important to see that the list can be looked at in two ways: first as a table for a gating network with four inputs and four outputs, and second as a list of addresses from 0 to 15, as given by the X values, and the contents of each address, as given by the values of Z.

Thus we might construct a gating network as in Fig. 7·26 which would give the correct Z output for each X input. (The boxes with + are mod 2 adders.)

Table 7·5 could also be realized by a 16-word 4-bit-per-word core memory into which we had read 0000 at the address 0; 0001 at the address 1; 0011 in the next address; and so on until 1000 in the last address. If we did not ever thereafter write into this memory, it would be a ROM memory and would serve the same purpose as the gating network in Fig. 7·26.

Figure 7·27(a) shows a scheme for implementing Table 7·5 using a decoder network with four inputs X_1, X_2, X_3, and X_4 and a number of diodes. With a given input combination (or address), a single output line from the decoder will be high. Let us assume that the input value is $X_1 = 0$, $X_2 = 1$, $X_3 = 1$, $X_4 = 1$. This corresponds to 0111 on the decoder output in Fig. 7·27(a). Diodes are connected

TABLE 7 • 5 BINARY-TO-GRAY CODE VALUES

INPUT				OUTPUT			
X_1	X_2	X_3	X_4	Z_1	Z_2	Z_3	Z_4
0	0	0	0	0	0	0	0
0	0	0	1	0	0	0	1
0	0	1	0	0	0	1	1
0	0	1	1	0	0	1	0
0	1	0	0	0	1	1	0
0	1	0	1	0	1	1	1
0	1	1	0	0	1	0	1
0	1	1	1	0	1	0	0
1	0	0	0	1	1	0	0
1	0	0	1	1	1	0	1
1	0	1	0	1	1	1	1
1	0	1	1	1	1	1	0
1	1	0	0	1	0	1	0
1	1	0	1	1	0	1	1
1	1	1	0	1	0	0	1
1	1	1	1	1	0	0	0

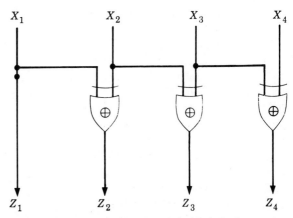

$$X \oplus Y = \overline{X}Y + X\overline{Y}$$

FIG. 7 • 26 Combinational network for binary-to-Gray code.

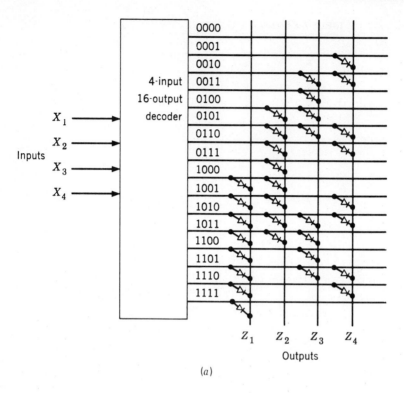

(a)

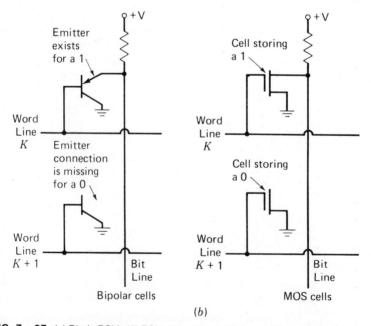

(b)

FIG. 7 • 27 (a) Diode ROM. (b) ROM cells using MOS and bipolar transistors.

at the junction of this line, and the output lines which are 1s, and no diodes are placed where 0s are to appear. Thus for the input 0111 we have a single diode connected to output line Z_2, since the desired output is to be 0100. Similarly, for the input 0110 we connect diodes to Z_2 and Z_4, since the output is to be 0101. The operation of the network is as follows. Only one decoder line output will be high at a time. Current flows from this line to only those output lines to which a diode is connected. Thus for the input 0101, current flows into lines Z_2, Z_3, and Z_4 but not Z_1; so Z_2, Z_3, Z_4 will be 1s and Z_1 a 0.

The entire scheme outlined above realizes the ROM with electronic gates (the diodes form OR gates). By using LSI techniques, arrays of this sort can be inexpensively fabricated in small containers at low prices. 512-word 8-bit memories are of about average size for the LSI ROMs; these memories effectively store 4096 bits in all.

The diodes in Fig. $7 \cdot 27 (a)$ are often transistors, and the manufacturing processes are of various types. Figure $7 \cdot 27 (b)$ shows typical memory cells for semiconductor ROMs using MOS and bipolar transistors. These cells are from a one-dimensional selection system; notice the word-selection lines and the bit line. Both one- and two-dimensional selection is used in ROMs. MOS ROMS generally have 40-ns to 200-ns access times; access times of bipolar memories range from 10 ns to 100 ns.

When a ROM is constructed so that the user can electrically (or using other techniques) write in the contents of the memory, the memory is called a *programmable ROM,* or *PROM.*† Often a scheme is used where a memory chip is delivered with 1s in every position, but 0s can be introduced at given positions by placing an address on the input lines and then raising each output line which is to be a 0 to a specified voltage, thus destroying a connection to the selected cell. (Sometimes the memories contain all 0s, and 1s are written in by the user.) Devices are also manufactured which program PROMs by reading paper tapes, magnetic tapes, punched cards, etc., and placing their contents into the PROM.

Custom ROM manufacturers provide forms whereby a user can fill 1s and 0s on a form that is provided, and the manufacturer will produce a custom-made mask and will then produce LSI chips which will realize the memory contents specified by the user. A single chip may cost more for such a memory, but large production runs generally cost less per chip. These devices come with up to 64R bits per IC package.

Figure $7 \cdot 28$ shows a block diagram of a 64K-bit MOS memory which is organized as a 4096-word 8-bit-per-word memory. The user places the address on the thirteen input lines $A_0 - A_{12}$ and then raises CS_1 and CS_2 ($\overline{CE}$ must be low). This will enable the output, and the desired word will appear on lines $O_0 - O_7$. This is a custom-made memory where the desired memory contents are supplied to the manufacturer by the user on a form. The manufacturer then makes a mask to create the desired bit patterns on an IC chip and manufactures ROMs with this pattern to order. Delay time for the memory is on the order of 75 ns.

---

†These memories are also called *field programmable ROMs.*

PIN CONFIGURATION

Pin	Name		Pin	Name
1	N.C.		28	V_{CC}
2	A_{12}		27	CS_1
3	A_7		26	CS_2
4	A_6		25	A_8
5	A_5		24	A_9
6	A_4		23	A_{11}
7	A_3		22	$\overline{OE}$
8	A_2		21	A_{10}
9	A_1		20	$\overline{CE}$
10	A_0		19	O_7
11	O_0		18	O_6
12	O_1		17	O_5
13	O_2		16	O_4
14	GND		15	O_3

PIN NAMES

$A_0 - A_{12}$	Addresses
$\overline{OE}$	Output enable
$\overline{CE}$	Chip enable
CS	Chip select
$N.C.$	No connection

BLOCK DIAGRAM

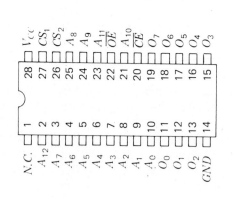

Data outputs $O_0 - O_7$

V_{CC}

GND

CS_1
CS_2
OE
CE

CS, $\overline{OE}$, and $\overline{CE}$ logic

Output buffers

Y Decoder

Y-Gating

X Decoder

65,536-BIT CELL MATRIX

$A_0 - A_{11}$ Address inputs

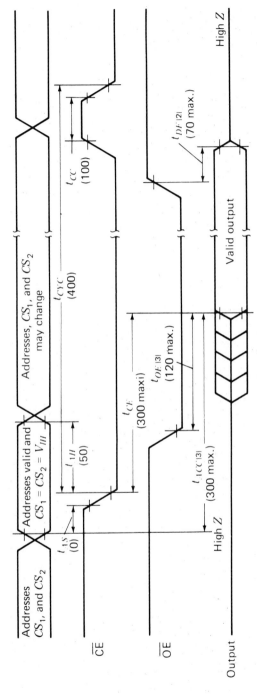

Notes

1. All times shown in parentheses are minimum times and are nonoseconds unless otherwise specified.

2. t_{DF} is specified from $\overline{OE}$ or $\overline{CE}$, whichever occurs first.

3. t_{ACC} may be delayed up to 180 ns after the falling edge of $\overline{CE}$ without impact on t_{ACC}.

FIG. 7 • 28 64K ROM. (Courtesy of INTEL Corp.)

TABLE 7 • 6 ROM CHARACTERISTICS

BIPOLAR ROMS

ORGANIZATION	PART NUMBER†	ACCESS TIME ns	CURRENT REQUIRED mA
512 × 8	6240/6241-1	90	170
1014 × 4	6252/6253-1	60	175
1024 × 8	6282/6283-1	55	170
1024 × 10	6255/6256-1	100	165/175
2048 × 8	6275/6276-1	110	190

MOS EPROMS

MODEL NUMBER	SIZE	ORGANIZATION	MAXIMUM ACCESS TIME (ns)	POWER SUPPLY (V)	MAXIMUM ACTIVE CURRENT (mA)	STANDBY CURRENT (mA)
TI 2716	16K	2048 × 8	450	12, ±5	45	45
Intel 2732	32K	4096 × 8	300	5	40	15
Ti 2532	32K	4096 × 8	450	5	168	10

MOS EAROMS

MODEL NUMBER	SIZE	ACCESS TIME μs
Nitron NC7050	256 × 4	2–5
Nitron NC7051	1024 × 1	2–5
GI ER3402	1024 × 4	0.95
GI ER3800	2048 × 4	2.6

†Courtesy of Monolithic Memories.

When a ROM is manufactured so that the memory's contents can be set as desired by the user and the memory can later have the contents erased and new values written in, the ROM is said to be *erasable and reprogrammable,* and is often called an *EPROM*.

For example, some memory chips are made with a transparent lid. Exposing the chip (through the lid) to ultraviolet light† will erase the pattern on the chip, and a new pattern can be written in electrically. This can be repeated as often as desired.

Table 7·6 shows characteristics of some bipolar ROMs and of several electrically programmable ROMs (EPROMs) which can have their contents erased by exposure to ultraviolet light and can be programmed (written into) by placing designated voltages on inputs. Also shown in Table 7·6 are some characteristics for electrically alterable ROMs (EAROMs) which can have their contents rewritten while in place in a circuit by means of properly applied input voltages.

Several companies make devices for programming PROMs and EPROMs. Some

---

†Standard ultraviolet lamps can be used to erase the memory. About 20- to 30-min exposure is required.

of these devices are operated from a keyboard, some from tape, and some from external inputs such as microprocessors.

When an EPROM or a PROM chip is to be programmed, there is generally a write enable to be raised, which makes output lines able to accept data. Address lines are then set to the location to be written into. Then, for some chips, the output lines to have 1s on them are raised to high voltages (or a sequence of large-amplitude pulses are applied to them) or, for some chips, the normal logic levels are placed on the output lines and a special program input is placed with a sequence of high-voltage (25 V) pulses. In either case each memory location must be written into by setting the address lines and then writing the desired contents into the output lines. Applying an erase (by means of raising the lid to the IC container and applying an ultraviolet light for some specified time) generally erases all the contents of the memory.

7 • 11 MAGNETIC CORE STORAGE

For about 20 years magnetic core memories dominated computer main memory usage. In the past few years, however, IC memories have passed cores in terms of total sales. Total core memory sales increase every year, however, and many existing computers still use them. The invention of the core memory was the technological breakthrough that brought the computer industry to life in the early 1950s.

The basic storage device in a magnetic core memory consists of a small toroidal (ring-shaped) piece of magnetic material, called a *magnetic core.* The magnetic core is generally a solid piece of ferromagnetic ceramic material.

Figure 7·29 illustrates a magnetic core, many times actual size. An input winding (wire) is shown threaded through this core. If current is passed through this winding, magnetic flux will be produced, with a direction dependent on the direction of the current through the winding. The core is ring-shaped and formed of material with high permeability, so that it will present a low-reluctance path for the magnetic flux. Depending on the direction of the current through the input winding, the core will become magnetized in either a clockwise or a counterclockwise direction.†

| Current is applied | Core is magnetized with flux through core in counterclockwise direction | Current is reversed; the core reverses its magnetic state | Current is removed; core remains magnetized with flux in clockwise direction |

FIG. 7 • 29 The magnetic core.

---

†There is a nice rule for determining the direction of the flux around a conductor. Grasp the wire with the right hand with the thumb in the direction of current flow. The fingers then point in the direction of the flux around the conductor. This is called the *right-hand rule.*

The retentivity of the material used in the core is such that when the magnetizing force is removed, the core remains magnetized, retaining a large part of its flux.

The characteristics of a given type of magnetic core are generally studied by means of a graph, with the magnetizing force H produced by the winding current plotted along the abscissa, and the resulting flux density B through the core plotted along the ordinate (Fig. 7·30). If a cyclical current which is alternately positive and negative is applied to the input winding in Fig. 7·29, for each value of the input current there will be a magnetizing force H applied to the core. If the flux density B in the core is then plotted against this magnetizing force, the resulting curve is called a *hysteresis loop.* In Fig. 7·30, the force H applied is sufficient to saturate the core material at both the positive and the negative extremities of the input current. The maximum flux density through the core when the core is saturated with a positive value of H is designated $+B_m$, and the corresponding negative value of H is denoted by $-B_m$.

Notice that for each value of magnetizing force there are two values of flux density. One occurs when the magnetizing force is increasing, and the other when the magnetizing force is decreasing. If the magnetizing force is varied from $-H_m$ to $+H_m$, the flux density will move along the lower part of the curve, and if the magnetizing force is moved from $+H_m$ to $-H_m$, the flux density will move along the upper part of the curve, again following the arrows, to point $-B_m$.

If a current sufficient to cause the core to be saturated is applied at the input winding and then removed, the flux density through the core will revert to either point $+B_r$ or point $-B_r$, depending on the polarity of the current. These two operating points are called the *remanent points,* and when the flux through the core is at either of these points, the core resembles a small permanent magnet. If a core is at the $+B_r$ point of the graph and a current of sufficient amplitude to cause a force of $-H_m$ is applied, the flux produced will be in opposition to the remanent flux in the core $+B_r$, and the flux through the core will be reversed, moving the operating point to $-B_m$. After the current has been removed, the majority of the

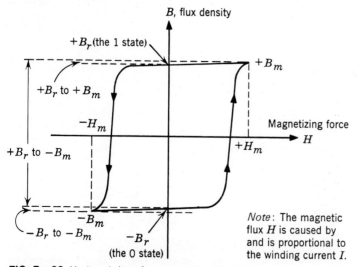

FIG. 7 • 30 Hysteresis loop for a magnetic material.

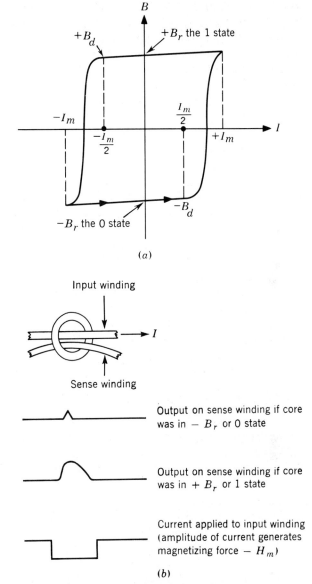

FIG. 7 • 31 (a) Current versus flux density hysteresis loop for a magnetic core. (b) Sense winding.

flux will remain, and the flux density in the core will be at the $-B_r$ point of the curve. The fact that the core can be in either one of two unique states of magnetization makes it possible to consider one state as representing a 0 ($-B_r$ in the figure) and the other state as a 1 ($+B_r$ in the figure).

Another winding, called a *sense winding* [see Fig. 7·31(b)], is used to determine whether a core contains a 0 or a 1. To sense the state of the core, a current sufficient to produce a magnetizing force $-H_m$ is applied to the input winding. If the core was at $+B_r$, the operating point will be moved downward along the arrows in Fig. 7·30 to the $-B_m$ point. If the core was at the $-B_r$ point, the operating point will be moved horizontally to $-B_m$. The amount of change in flux in the core will be quite different for each of these cases. If the core was initially in the 1 state (at point $+B_r$ on the hysteresis curve), the direction of magnetization of the core will be changed, and the flux through the core will change from $+B_r$ to $-B_m$. The magnitude of this change in the magnetization of the core is indicated as $+B_r$ to $-B_m$ on the figure. If, however, the core was originally in the 0 state at $-B_r$ on the curve, the change in magnetization will be small, only from $-B_r$ to $-B_m$, and the magnitude of this change in flux is indicated as $-B_r$ to $-B_m$ on the figure. A change in the flux density through the core will induce a voltage in the sense winding, which is proportional to the rate of change of flux. If the core was originally in the 0 state, the change and rate of change in flux will be small, and therefore the voltage induced in the sense winding will be small. If the core was originally in the 1 state, the amount of change and rate of change in flux will be large, and consequently the voltage induced in the sense winding will be large. A small output from the sense winding will therefore indicate that the core originally contained a 0, and a large output will indicate that the core originally contained a 1.

The difficulty in the use of this technique for sensing the state of a core is that the core is always reset to the 0 state. This readout technique is therefore "destructive" in that the core no longer contains the information that was previously stored in it.

7 • 12 STORAGE OF INFORMATION IN MAGNETIC CORES IN A TWO-DIMENSIONAL ARRAY

The preceding discussion showed how a single bit of information may be stored in and read from a single core. In digital computer systems, however, it is necessary to store many bits of information; some of the larger computers have core memories with over 10 million cores.

Figure 7·31(a) plots the values of flux density for a magnetic core versus current I through the input winding of a core. If the current reaches a value of $+I_m$, which is sufficient to saturate the core, and is then removed, the core will be placed in the $+B_r$, or 1, state. If the operating point on the curve is at $+B_r$ with no input current through the winding, and a negative pulse of current with amplitude $-I_m$ is applied, the core will be switched to the 0 state. The important thing to notice in Fig. 7·31 is that, if the core is in the 1 state and a current of only $-I_m/2$ is applied and then removed, the state of the core will not be changed. Instead, the operating point will move from $+B_r$ to $+B_d$ and, when the current is removed, will move back to approximately $+B_r$. The same principle applies if the core is in the 0 state at point $-B_r$ on the curve. A current of $+I_m$ will switch the core to the 1 state, but a current of $+I_m/2$ will only move the operating point to $-B_d$, and when the current is removed, the core will return to point $-B_r$.

Figure 7·32(a) shows 16 cores arranged in a square array. Each core has two input windings, one from a set of X input lines and one from a set of Y input lines. Assume that all the cores are in the 0 state and a 1 is to be written into core X_2Y_2.

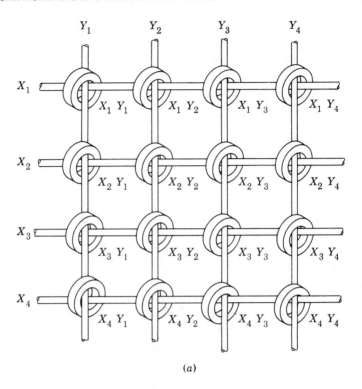

(a)

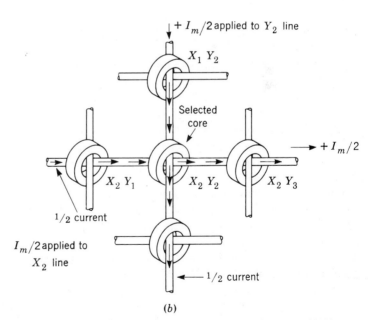

(b)

FIG. 7 • 32 Two-dimensional core plane. (a) Wiring. (b) Selection of $X_2 Y_2$.

If a current with an amplitude of $+I_m$ is applied on the X_2 line, core X_2Y_2 will be switched to the 1 state. However, all the cores connected to the X_2 input line will also be switched to the 1 state. The same holds true if a current of $+I_m$ is applied to input line Y_2, in which case all the cores connected to this Y input line would be switched to the 1 state.

If, however, currents of $+I_m/2$ are applied to both the X_2 line and the Y_2 line at the same time, only core X_2Y_2 will receive a total current of $+I_m$ [Fig. 7·32(b)]. Each of the other cores along the Y_2 input line will receive a current of $+I_m/2$, as will each of the cores along the X_2 input line. Since these cores will have started at point $-B_r$ on the graph and will receive a current of $+I_m/2$, their operating point will be moved as far as $-B_d$ on the curve. However, the operating point will not be moved as far as the steep incline which leads to the $+B_r$ section of the graph. When the current is removed, these cores, with the exception of X_2Y_2, will return to the $-B_r$ point and will be in the 0 state. Therefore only core X_2Y_2 will receive a total current of $+I_m$ and will be switched into the 1 state.

By this technique, any given core can be selected from the array. For instance, core X_1Y_3 can be selected by applying currents of $+I_m/2$ to the X_1 and the Y_3 input lines at the same time. This is known as the coincident-current selection technique. The core which receives a full $+I_m$ current is known as a *fully selected* core, and all the cores which receive a current of $+I_m/2$ are known as *half selected* cores. For instance, if a current of $+I_m/2$ is connected to input lines X_1 and Y_3, core X_1Y_3 will be fully selected, and cores X_1Y_1, X_1Y_2, X_2Y_3, and X_3Y_3 will be half selected.

Notice that regardless of the previous state of each of the cores in the array, a current of $+I_m/2$ applied to one X and one Y input line will result in sufficient current to switch only one core of the array. If cores in the 0 state are half selected, they will remain in the 0 state; and if cores in the 1 state are half selected, they will remain in the 1 state.

The state of any given core can be sensed using the same technique. If currents of $-I_m/2$ are applied to input lines X_2 and Y_2, a full $-I_m$ current will be applied to core X_2Y_2, causing it to change states if it contained a 1 and to remain in the same state if it contained a 0. The fully selected core will be the only core that can change states, and therefore the only core that is capable of causing an appreciable output on a sense winding. A sense winding would be threaded through all the cores; if a certain core is selected, the output at the sense winding will represent the state of that core only.

It may be seen that there are two separate operations involved: first, the writing of information into a core and, second, the reading of information which has been stored in a core. A 0 or a 1 may be written into any core in the array by applying a current of either $-I_m/2$ or $+I_m/2$ to the correct pair of input lines, and the state of any core may be sensed by applying a current of $-I_m/2$ to the correct pair of input lines and sensing the magnitude of the output voltage on the sense winding.

7 · 13 ASSEMBLY OF CORE PLANES INTO A CORE MEMORY

Figure 7·33 illustrates a small *core-memory plane*. Any core in this plane may be selected, and a 0 or a 1 written into the core, or the state of any core may be

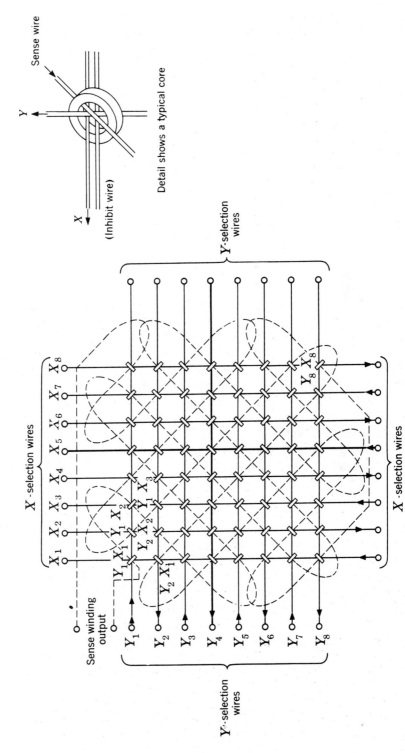

Fig. 7 • 33 Core-memory plane.

sensed by applying the correct currents to one of the X input lines and one of the Y input lines simultaneously. A complete core memory consists of a number of such planes, stacked in a rectangular array. The X windings of each plane are connected in series, so that current applied to the X_1 winding of the first plane must travel through the X_1 winding of the second plane, and so on, until it passes through the X_1 winding for the last plane in the array. If the plane illustrated in Fig. 7·33 were connected in an array, the X_1 winding at the top left of the drawing would be connected to one end of the X_1 winding from the preceding core plane, and the X_1 winding at the bottom left would be connected to the X_1 winding of the following core plane. If 10 core planes of the size shown in Fig. 7·33 were stacked in this manner, a pulse on the X_1 input line would have to travel through 80 cores. The Y windings are connected in the same manner. Each plane has its own sense winding, however, and the sense windings for the planes are not connected together in any way; instead, a *sense amplifier* is connected to the sense-winding output from each plane.

Let us call a $+I_m/2$ current pulse a WRITE 1 pulse, for such a current applied to an X or Y winding tends to write a 1 into the cores along the winding. It may be seen that simultaneously applying a WRITE 1 pulse on a selected Y line and a selected X line will write a 1 into a single core in the same relative position in each of the planes. For instance, if the X_3 and Y_4 input lines are pulsed with a current of $+I_m/2$, the X_3Y_4 core in each plane will receive a $+I_m$ current. If a $-I_m/2$ pulse is then applied to the same X- and Y-selection lines, an output will be sensed on the sense winding† of each plane.

In general there will be as many core planes in the array as bits in the word length of the memory in which the array is used. If the word length is 15 bits, there will be 15 planes in the array; if the word length is 35 bits, 35 planes. There will be a sense winding for each plane, so that the output from each core that is selected will be sensed.

One problem still remains. A WRITE 1 ($+I_m/2$) pulse on a pair of X and Y input lines will write a 1 into the core in the same relative position of each plane, and therefore into every position of the word, and it may be necessary to write 0s into some cores and 1s into others. A fourth winding through each core is therefore added. This winding is called the *inhibit winding,* and it is used to inhibit the writing of a 1 into a given selected core in a plane. A single inhibit winding is threaded through each core in a plane in a direction so that a current of $-I_m/2$ on the winding will oppose the WRITE 1 current. There are therefore as many inhibit windings as core planes. There is also a single driver for each inhibit winding, which can be gated on or off, depending on whether a 1 or a 0 is to be written into the selected core of the plane. The amplitude of the current through the inhibit winding is the same as the $-I_m/2$ current used in the X and Y selection lines. The inhibit winding is threaded through the cores so that the magnetizing force from the current

---

†The sense windings are threaded through the cores diagonal to the other windings to reduce the coupling between drive and sense windings (Fig. 7·33) and to cancel the output signals from half-selected cores caused during a READ pulse.

through the inhibit winding always opposes the magnetizing force of the WRITE 1 currents.

Since the WRITE 1 pulse from the X and Y drivers is of $+I_m/2$ amplitude and the pulse from the INHIBIT driver is of $-I_m/2$ amplitude, if a WRITE 1 pulse is applied from a given pair of X and Y drivers at the same time as an INHIBIT pulse is applied, the total current through the selected core will be $(+I_m/2) + (+I_m/2) + (-I_m/2) = +I_m/2$, which is not sufficient to switch the core to a 1. A 1 or a 0 may therefore be written into the selected core of a given plane by first clearing the cores with a $-I_m/2$ pulse on the correct pair of X and Y SELECT lines, and then turning the inhibit driver on for each plane where a 0 is desired and off for each plane where a 1 is desired, while applying a WRITE 1 pulse to the X and Y SELECT lines.

7 • 14 TIMING SEQUENCE

The same timing sequence is generally used whether the computer is to write information in the core memory or to read information from the core memory. The total time taken by the entire timing sequence is called a *memory cycle,* and is one of the principal speed-determining factors for a core memory. Figure 7·34 shows a complete memory cycle. The operation of writing a word into the memory will be examined first, then the read operation. Assume that there are five core planes in the total array and that each core plane contains 64 cores, as in Fig. 7·33.

1. *Writing into a core memory*   Assume that the binary number 10100 is to be written into core location $X_3 Y_4$ of the memory. Zeros are therefore to be written into the selected cores of planes 2, 4, and 5.

    First the correct drivers are selected. Since core $X_3 Y_4$ in each plane is to be written into, the drivers connected to the X_3 line are enabled, as are the drivers connected to the Y_4 line of the array. When the READ TIME pulses are applied, 0s are written into the $X_3 Y_4$ core in each of the five planes. After 0.4 μs each

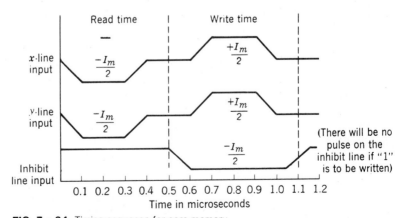

FIG. 7 • 34 Timing sequence for core memory.

of the selected cores will contain a 0. At 0.5 μs after the sequence is initiated, the INHIBIT drivers connected to planes 2, 4, and 5 are turned on; in addition, the write time begins. A 1 will then be written into the selected core in planes 1 and 3, and the subtraction of the inhibit current from the coincident current through the selected cores in planes 2, 4, and 5 will result in the selected cores in these planes remaining in the 0 state. After the sequence of pulses, the selected cores in planes 1 and 3 will contain 1s, the selected cores in planes 2, 4, and 5 will contain 0s, and the computer word 10100 will have been stored in the memory in location $X_3 Y_4$.

2. *Reading from a core memory*   Assume that at a later time the location $X_3 Y_4$, which was written into in the write operation above, is to be read from. The timing sequence illustrated in Fig. 7·34 still applies, although there are several differences in operation. First the read currents are applied to the selected cores (from 0 time to 0.5 μs in Fig. 7·34). If a large signal is received at the sense amplifier connected to a given plane during this period, the selected core in that plane contained a 1; if a small signal is received, the selected core in the plane contained a 0. The sense windings connected to planes 1 and 3 will therefore produce signals indicating 1s, and the sense windings connected to planes 2, 4, and 5 will produce small signals, indicating 0s. The word stored was therefore 10100. This word must now be written back into the memory array. The output of each sense winding is amplified and used to set a storage device to the 0 or 1 state during the read time, and the contents of each of these storage devices are then used to control the INHIBIT drivers during the write time. Only the inhibit drivers connected to planes 2, 4, and 5 will therefore be enabled by signals from the respective storage devices and conduct during the write time, and the selected cores in these planes will remain in the 0 state. After the write time, the selected cores will again contain 10100, just as before the read operation.

7 · 15 DRIVING THE *X*- AND *Y*-SELECTION LINES

Let us examine the sequencing of current through a core memory using a simple idealized model. Flip-flops are generally used as the storage devices for both the memory address register and the memory buffer register. Figure 7·35 illustrates, in block diagram form, the operation of a selection system for a core memory, with each plane the size of the plane illustrated in Fig. 7·33. Since there are eight *X*-selection lines and eight *Y*-selection lines, three flip-flops will be required to select an *X* line and three more to select a *Y* line. There are therefore six flip-flops in the memory address register, so that any one of the 64 (2^6) locations in each plane may be selected. The flip-flops in the register illustrated have been designated X_1, X_2, X_3, and Y_1, Y_2, Y_3 to indicate that the first three are used to select the *X* winding and the second three to select the *Y* winding.

1. *X-selection line drivers*   There are eight *X*-selection line drivers in Fig. 7·35, each of which has two inputs, one from the decoder and one from the READ-

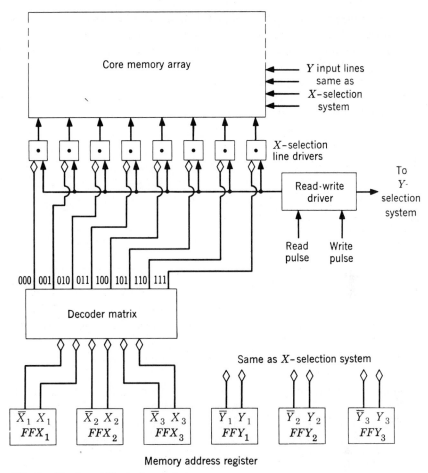

FIG. 7 • 35 *X*- and *Y*-selection system.

WRITE driver. The output currents from the READ-WRITE driver may be either negative or positive; the *X*-selection line drivers are therefore capable of passing current in either direction. The *X*-selection line drivers also function as AND gates, for they will pass current only when the input signal from the decoder matrix represents a 1. Only one of the *X*-selection line drivers will be enabled by the decoder at any given time. For instance, if the *X* flip-flops in the memory address register contain 000, only the leftmost driver in the illustration will be enabled. All the *X*-selection line drivers will receive a READ and then a WRITE current pulse (of opposite polarity) from the READ-WRITE driver. Since only one *X*-selection line driver is enabled by a 1 signal from the decoder, only one of the *X* windings in the array will receive the drive currents. The same holds true for the *Y*-selection line system, which is identical with the *X* system. Since only one *X* line and only one *Y* line are pulsed during each memory cycle, only one core in each plane will receive a full-select READ-WRITE pulse.

2. *READ-WRITE driver*   The READ-WRITE driver receives two clock pulses each memory cycle. The first is the READ pulse, which causes the READ-WRITE driver to deliver a positive HALF-SELECT pulse of current to both the *X*- and *Y*-selection line drivers. The second input pulse to the READ-WRITE driver is the WRITE pulse, which initiates a negative pulse of current to the *X*- and *Y*-selection line drivers. The current supplied by the READ-WRITE drivers is generally on the order of 0.1 to 1 A.

The operation of the memory address register and its associated circuitry causes a single core in each plane of the memory to receive a FULL-READ and then a FULL-WRITE current pulse. The memory address register is generally loaded directly from the instruction which is being interpreted by the machine; that is, the address section of the word is read directly into the memory address register. (This will be described in Chap. 9.)

7 • 16 MEMORY BUFFER REGISTER AND ASSOCIATED CIRCUITRY

The memory buffer register consists of a flip-flop register which contains one flip-flop for each plane in the array. The number of planes in the array, and hence the length of the memory buffer register, is equal to the number of bits in the basic computer word. The arithmetic element and control element of the machine generally communicate directly with the memory buffer, either loading the word to be written in storage into it or reading from it.

Figure 7·36 illustrates two flip-flops of a memory buffer register along with their associated circuitry. Each bit in the memory buffer register has identical circuitry. Two distinct sequences may occur, the first involves the reading of a word from memory and the second the writing of a word into the memory.

1. *Reading from memory*   The location of the word to be read from the memory is first loaded into the memory address register (Fig. 7·35). The memory buffer register is then cleared. During the read time (Fig. 7·34) the selected core in each plane receives a full-current pulse and is set to 0. If the selected core in a given plane contains a 1, a signal is received on the sense winding. This is amplified by the sense amplifier and then used to set a 1 into the memory buffer flip-flop used to control the INHIBIT driver for the core plane. If the selected core in the plane contains a 0, the signal received by the sense amplifier will be small, and no pulse will appear at the output of the sense amplifier, and the flip-flop will remain in the 0 state.

The sense amplifier is "strobed" (Fig. 7·36) with a narrow pulse because, despite the fact that a core containing a 0 will produce a small signal when "sensed," many of the cores in each plane will receive HALF-SELECT pulses, and each will generate a small amount of noise on the sense winding. If this noise is additive, it may approach the level of the signal from a core whose polarity is reversed. It has been found that the noise generated by the half-selected cores dies out shortly after the HALF-SELECT pulses are started. Therefore the sense amplifier is strobed during the latter part of the read time,

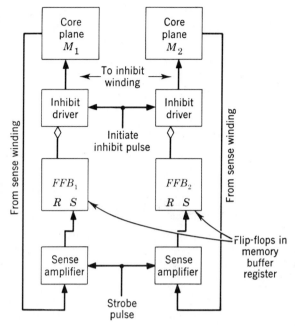

FIG. 7 • 36 Operation of memory buffer register.

when the output from a selected core reversing states is highest in proportion to the noise from half-selected cores. Only the output signal during the strobe pulse is gated into the SET line of the flip-flop.

During write time (Fig. 7·34) each of the selected cores receives a full-select current from the X- and Y-selection system. As a result of the read operation, all these cores have previously been set in the 0 state. However, the memory buffer flip-flops now contain 1s for each plane in which a 1 was stored in the full-selected core. The outputs from these flip-flops are used to enable the INHIBIT drivers for each plane in which a 0 is to remain. All other full-selected cores will be set to the 1 state. The 0 output from each flip-flop is therefore used to enable the INHIBIT driver for the plane associated with the flip-flop. After the write time, the selected core in each plane will be in its original state.

2. *Writing into core memory* The X- and Y-selection system goes through the same timing sequence when a word is to be written into memory as when a word is read from memory. The operation of the memory buffer register differs, however. The word to be written into the selected location is loaded into the memory buffer register, and the address in memory to be written into is loaded into the memory address register. During the read time the sense amplifier is not strobed; so the memory buffer register is not disturbed.

After the read time, all the selected cores will have been set to 0. During the write time, the same cores all receive full-current WRITE pulses from the X- and Y-selection systems. However, the planes in which 0s are to remain have their INHIBIT drivers enabled by the memory buffer flip-flops (Figs. 7·35 and

7·36), and the half-current pulses from these drivers cancel the selection current, leaving the full-selected cores in the 0 state. All other full-selected cores are set to 1.

After the write time, the word in the memory buffer register will have been written into the cores.

7 • 17 CORE-MEMORY ORGANIZATION AND WIRING SCHEMES

The core-memory organization which has been described is the classic *coincident-current four-wire random-access core memory.* Several variations on this basic scheme will be outlined in this section.

First notice that the SENSE-line and the INHIBIT-line windings can be combined into a single winding. The sense amplifier is used only during the read section of the memory timing cycle, while the INHIBIT driver is on only during the write portion of the memory timing cycle. By simply connecting the sense amplifier to the inhibit winding and removing the sense winding, an array with only three wires per core can be formed. To visualize this, picture Fig. 7·33 with the sense winding removed. The sense amplifier is then connected to the inhibit winding, and this winding is called the *digit winding* or *bit winding.* The sense amplifier must, of course, be capable of withstanding the large input from the inhibit driver. A three-wire coincident-current memory of this type is shown in Fig. 7·37, which is a 16-word 4-bit memory.

Aside from simplifying memory construction, reducing the number of windings through the cores has the desirable effect of making it possible to reduce the size of the cores. Smaller cores can be switched faster than larger cores, and the limiting factor on core size is often the number of wires through the cores; so the fastest memories are made with fewer wires. The price that is paid is in additional circuit complexity.

A 16-word 4-bit linear-select memory is shown in Fig. 7·38.

There is another core-memory arrangement called a $2\frac{1}{2}$D memory. One variation of the $2\frac{1}{2}$D memory is used for large inexpensive memories, and another for small fast memories. We shall not study this type of memory in detail except to note that the basic principle consists in making a stack, which is basically a coincident-current selection stack, but where the X windings are continuous from plane to plane. However, each plane has a separate Y winding. During the READ cycle, current is then gated through the selected X winding, which goes through all planes, and also through all Y windings; so each selected Y driver is turned on. During the WRITE cycle only those Y drivers for planes in which a 1 is to be written are turned on, while the X drivers are used in the customary way. CDC has a core memory with 12-mil cores which has a 275-ns memory cycle and a $2\frac{1}{2}$D organization. The organization is basically that illustrated in Fig. 7·11.

The $2\frac{1}{2}$D memory can be three wires with a separate sense winding, or there are some two-wire memories where the output of the selected core is sensed on the Y drive line by a circuit technique. (This is used in a very large IBM memory.) The $2\frac{1}{2}$D memory is a strategy that uses the coincident-current selection technique of

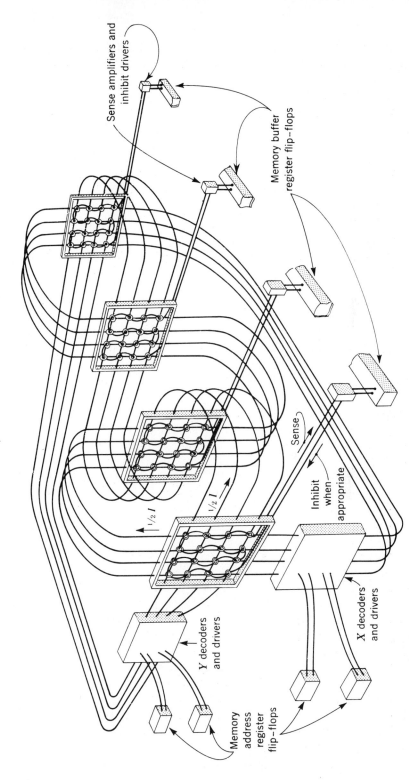

Sense amplifiers and inhibit drivers

Memory buffer register flip–flops

Sense

Inhibit when appropriate

$^{1}/_{2} I$

$^{1}/_{2} I$

Y decoders and drivers

X decoders and drivers

Memory address register flip–flops

FIG. 7 • 37 Three-wire coincident-current memory.

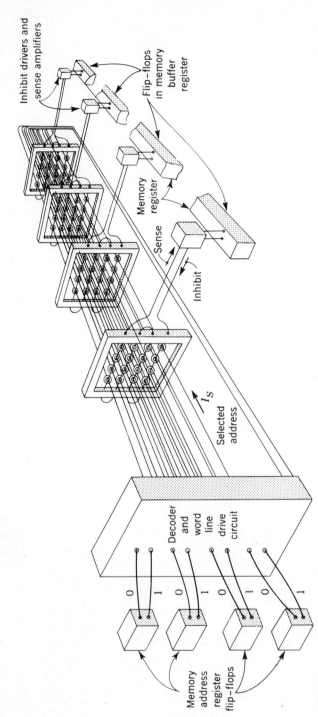

Inhibit drivers and sense amplifiers

Flip-flops in memory buffer register

Memory register

Sense

Inhibit

Memory address register flip-flops

I_S

Selected address

Decoder and word line drive circuit

0
1
0
1
0
1
0
1

FIG. 7 • 38 Linear-select memory.

half currents, but uses a dividend *Y* winding to facilitate writing, using more complicated gating of the *Y* windings rather than inhibit windings.

7 • 18 MAGNETIC DRUM STORAGE

The storage devices which have been described utilize the principle of setting a device that is essentially bistable into one of its two states. Access to the devices was essentially random—once addressed, a core is immediately available and a flip-flop or dynamic cell continuously produces an indication of its state. The limitations on this type of storage are based on the complexity, and therefore the cost and reliability, of storing a large number of bits. While IC memories have been constructed which can store tens of millions of bits, some large machines require the storage of as many as 10^{13} bits. This would require 1 million IC memories. The high speed of IC storage is therefore paid for with the complexity and the cost of the storage.

Magnetic drums were among the first devices to provide a relatively inexpensive means of storing information and have reasonably short access times. A magnetic drum consists basically of a rotating cylinder coated with a thin layer of magnetic material which possesses a hysteresis loop similar to that of the material used in magnetic cores (Fig. 7·30). A number of recording heads [Fig. 7·39(*a*)] are mounted along the surface of the drum. These are used to write and read information from the surface of the drum by magnetizing small areas, or sensing the magnetization of the areas on which information has been recorded. While Fig. 7·39(*a*) shows only a few heads, some magnetic drums have several hundred recording heads scattered about their periphery.

As the drum rotates, a small area continually passes under each of the heads. This area is known as a *track* [Fig. 7·39(*a*)]. Each track is subdivided into cells, each of which can store 1 binary bit.

Generally one of the tracks is used to provide the timing for the drum. A series of timing signals is permanently recorded around this timing track, and each signal defines a *time unit* for the drum system. The timing track is then used to determine the location of each set of storage cells around the tracks. For instance, if the timing track is 60 in. in length and timing pulses are recorded at a density of 100 per inch, there will be 6,000 locations for bits (cells) around each of the tracks. If the drum has 30 tracks plus the timing track, the drum will have the capacity to store a total of 180,000 bits.

Information is written onto the drum by passing current through a winding on the write heads. This current causes flux to be created through the core material of the head. Figure 7·39(*b*) illustrates a head for writing or reading information from a drum. Some drum systems use separate heads for reading and writing, and others use combined read-write heads. The head in Fig. 7·39(*b*) consists of a ring formed of high-permeability material around which wire is wound. When information is to be written on the surface of the drum, pulses of current are driven through the write 0 or write 1 winding. The direction of flux through the head and, in turn,

READ-WRITE heads

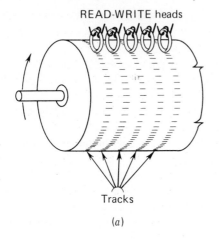

Tracks

(*a*)

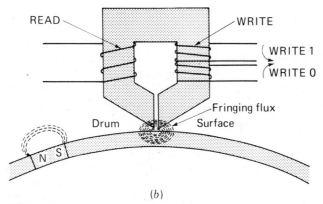

FIG. 7 • 39 Magnetic drum memory. (*a*) Magnetic drum tracks. (*b*) read-write head.

the polarization of the magnetic field recorded on the surface of the drum depend upon whether write 1 or write 0 is on.

The gap in the core presents a relatively high-reluctance path to the flux generated by the current through the coil. Since the magnetic material on the surface of the drum is passing near the gap, most of the flux passes through this material. This causes a small area of the drum surface to be magnetized, and since the material used to coat the surface of the drum has a relatively high retentivity, the magnetic field remains after the area has passed from under the head, or the current through the coil is discontinued. It should be noted that the head does not actually touch the surface of the drum. Instead, to prevent wear, the heads are located very close to the drum surface but not touching it. The drum must therefore be of very constant diameter in order to keep the heads at a constant distance. If the head moves farther from the surface of the drum, the signals recorded will become weaker. In practice the heads are able to move slightly into or away from the surface and are pushed toward the surface by a spring-loading mechanism. A cushion of air between the head and the rotating surface then maintains the required relatively constant distance from the magnetic surface.

The signals recorded on the surface of the drum are read in a similar manner. When the areas which have been magnetized pass under the head, some of the magnetic flux is coupled into the head, and changes in this flux induce signals in the winding. These signals are then amplified and interpreted. A description of the recording techniques used will be found in the final section of this chapter.

The sizes and storage capacities of magnetic drums vary greatly. Small drums with capacities of less than 200,000 bits have been constructed. Drums of this size generally have from 15 to 25 tracks and from 15 to 50 heads. To decrease access time, heads are sometimes located in sets around the periphery of the drum, so that a drum with 15 tracks may have 30 heads divided into two sets of 15 heads, each set located 180° from the other. For very fast access time there may be even more than two sets of heads.†

Much larger drums can store up to 10^9 bits and may have from 500 to 1000 tracks. The larger drums are generally rotated much more slowly than small drums, and speeds vary from 120 rpm up to 75,000 rpm. The access times obviously decrease as the drum speeds increase. However, there is another important factor, the packing density along a track. Most present-day drums have a packing density of from 600 to 2000 bits/in. (By maintaining the heads very close to the drum surface and rotating the drum slowly, packing densities in excess of 1000 bits/in. may be achieved.) One drum system, the IBM 2303, has 800 tracks and 4892 bytes per track (and so about a 3.9 million-byte capacity), and the drum makes a complete rotation in 17.5 ms. Table 7·7 gives some characteristics of present-day drum systems.

TABLE 7 • 7 MAGNETIC DRUM CHARACTERISTICS

CHARACTERISTICS	FH 432 UNIVAC 1108	2301 IBM 360	2303 IBM 360	1964 ICL 1900 SERIES	FASTRAND II UNIVAC 1108
Tracks per drum	144	220	800	512	6,144
Characters per track	12,288	20,483	4,892	4,048	10,752
Characters per unit	1,572,864	4,096,600	3,910,000	2,072,576	132,120,756
Transfer rate, kbits	1,440	1,200	312	100	153
Head arrangement (fixed or movable)	Fixed	Fixed	Fixed	Fixed	Movable
Heads per drum	128	200	800	512	32 × 192 positions
Drum diameter, in.	10.5	10.7		18.5	32.8
Drum speed, rpm	7,100	3,490	3,428	1,500	870
Packing density, bits/in.	627	1,250	1,105	1,000	1,000
Average access time, ms	4.25	8.6	8.75	20.5	93
Approximate cost per 6-bit character stored, cents	8	5	4	3	0.2

†The actual access time can be reduced by clever coding of the computer program. If the computer writes into or reads words near the read or write heads when an instruction is initiated, the access time may be minimized.

7 • 19 PARALLEL AND SERIAL OPERATION OF A MAGNETIC DRUM

It is possible to operate a drum in either a serial or a parallel mode. For parallel operation all the bits of a word may be written simultaneously and read in the same manner. If the basic computer word contains 40 bits, the drum might read from 41 tracks (one for timing) simultaneously, thus reading an entire computer word in 1-bit time. When the drum is read from and written into in parallel, a separate read and write amplifier is required for each track that is used simultaneously, so that to read a 40-bit word in 1-bit time, 40 read amplifiers are required. The correct set of heads is then selected, and the drum system locates the selected set of cells.

Notice that words in a parallel system may be located by means of a timing track. If each track contains 8192 bits, a 13-bit counter may be set to zero at the same position each time the drum revolves, and stepped by one each time a timing pulse appears. In this way location 1096 will be the 1096th slot around the track from the 0 location. If the address of the word to be read is loaded into a register, the signals from the drum can be gated into the computer when the counter agrees with the register's contents. In this way words may be located on the drum.

A magnetic drum may also be operated in a serial mode. In this case only one track will be read from or written into at a given time. Since there are a number of tracks for each drum, the correct track as well as the location of the desired bits around the track must be selected.

Each track is therefore assigned a number. In addition, each track is divided into *sectors,* each sector containing one or more full computer words.

To specify the address of a word on a magnetic drum operated serially, both the track number and the sector number must first be given. If only one word is in a sector, this will suffice; if more than one word is in each sector, this word must be specified also. Consider a drum with 32 tracks plus a timing track and 32 words (sectors) around each track. The address of a word on the drum in a binary machine will consist of 10 bits, 5 bits to specify the track and 5 bits the sector.

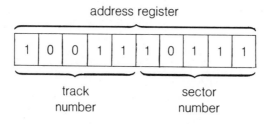

address register

| 1 | 0 | 0 | 1 | 1 | 1 | 0 | 1 | 1 | 1 |

track
number

sector
number

The five flip-flops containing the track number may be connected to a *decoder,* which will then select the correct read-write head.

Several techniques involving the timing tracks may be used to locate the selected sector. One technique involves the use of several timing tracks instead of one. Figure 7·40 shows a technique utilizing three timing tracks. One of the tracks contains a set of signals indicating the location of each bit around the tracks. The second track contains a set of pulses with a pulse at the beginning of each word time. (The word-time signals illustrated are 12 bits apart; so the basic word would

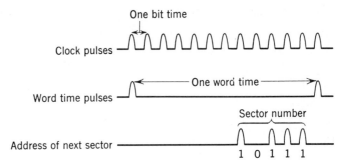

FIG. 7 • 40 Timing signals for a magnetic drum.

be 11 or 12 bits in length.) In addition, the *sector number* of the *next* word around the drum is recorded around a third timing track. The computer reads sector numbers from this track, and when the number read agrees with the sector number in the address, the computer can then read the selected word from the next sector, beginning with the next word-time pulse.

7 • 20 MAGNETIC DISK MEMORIES

Another type of memory, called a *magnetic disk memory,* greatly resembles the magnetic drum memory in operation. The magnetic disk memory provides very large storage capabilities with moderate operating speeds. There are quite a large number of different types of magnetic disk memories now on the market. Although differing in specific details, all of them are based on the same principles of operation.

A magnetic disk memory resembles the coin-operated automatic record player, or "juke box." Rotating disks coated with a magnetic material are stacked with space between each disk (refer to Fig. 7·41). Information is recorded on the surface of the rotating disks by magnetic heads which are positioned against the disks. (Information is recorded in bands rather than on a spiral.) Each band of information around a given disk is called a *track.* On one side of a typical disk there may be from one hundred to several thousand of these data tracks. Bits are recorded along a track at a density of from perhaps 500 to 9000 bits/in. In some systems the outer tracks contain more bits than the inner tracks, because the circumference of an outer track is greater than that of an inner track, but many disks have the same number of bits around each track. The speed at which the disks rotate varies, of course, with the manufacturer, but typical speeds are on the order of 3600 rpm.

Since each disk contains a number of tracks of information and there may be several disks in a given memory, several techniques have evolved for placing the magnetic read-write head in the correct position on a selected track. Since the same head is generally used for reading and for writing, the problem becomes that of placing this head accurately and quickly on the track that has been selected.

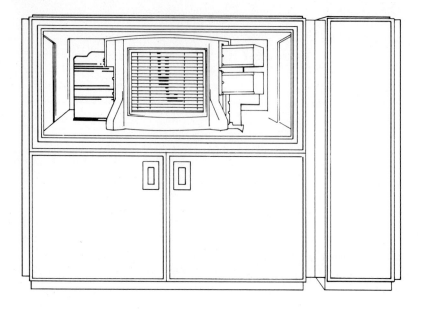

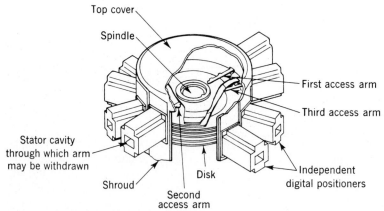

FIG. 7 • 41 Magnetic disk memory system.

There are two basic types of disk head placement systems. The first type of system has its heads fixed in position on each track. These are called *fixed-head systems*. The second kind of system has one or more pairs of read-write heads for each pair of adjacent disk surfaces (because information is generally written on both the top and the bottom of each disk). These read-write heads are mounted on arms which can be moved in and out. These are called *movable-head systems*.†

---

†A few systems have been made with only one pair of read-write heads for the entire memory. In these systems the two recording heads are positioned on an arm which is first moved between the correct pair of disks, and then selects the correct surface of the adjacent surfaces (again because information is written on both the top and the bottom of each disk). The read-write head is finally placed upon the correct selected track of the disk.

The positioning of the heads by means of the mechanical movement of arms is a difficult and tricky business, particularly since the tracks are often recorded less than hundredths of an inch apart on the disk. It should be apparent that disk-file memories with many heads can locate and record or read from a selected track faster than the ones with only a few heads, since the amount of mechanical movement before the track is reached will be less for the multihead system.

The total time it takes to begin reading selected data or to begin writing one selected track in a particular place is called the *access time.*

The time it takes to position a head on the selected track is called the *seek time,* and it is generally somewhere between an average of several milliseconds to fractions of a second. The other delay in locating selected data is the *latency,* or *rotational, delay,* which is the time required for the desired data to reach the magnetic head once the head is positioned. Thus the total access time for a disk is the seek time plus the latency.

For a rotational speed of 2400 rpm, for example, latency is a maximum of 25 ms and averages 12.5 ms. Latency represents a lower limit to access time in systems using fixed heads. As a result, for minimum access time fixed heads are used. Typically heads are arranged in groups of eight or nine, perhaps including a spare, and are carefully aligned in fixed positions with respect to the disk. Although head spacing in each group is typically 8–16/in., track densities of 30–60/in. can be achieved by interlacing groups.

Although they are faster, fixed-head systems provide less storage capacity than moving-head systems having comparable disk recording areas because the moving-head systems have more tracks per inch. Further, the large number of heads required can increase cost for a given capacity.

An important advantage of moving magnetic heads concerns their alignment with very closely spaced data tracks. Although track spacing is limited by "crosstalk" between adjacent tracks and mechanical tolerances, spacing of 10 mils between adjacent tracks is common. Further, track widths of approximately 2.5–5 mils are consistent with head positioning accuracies of 0.5–1.5 mils.

The read-write heads used on magnetic disk memories are almost invariably of the type called *flying heads.* A simplified diagram of a flying head is shown in Fig. 7·42. When a disk rotates at a high speed, a thin but resilient boundary layer of air rotates with the disk. The head is so shaped that it rides on this layer of rotating air, which causes the disk to maintain separation from the head, thus preventing wear on the surface of the disk. In effect, the layer of air rotating with the disk acts like a spring with a stiffness exceeding several thousand pounds per inch, thus forcing the head away from the surface of the disk. To force the head into the correct proximity with the disk, a number of mechanisms have been used. Often compressed air is simply blown into a mechanism which forces the head toward the surface of the disk, using a pistonlike arrangement, as shown in Fig. 7·42.

There are many sizes and speeds for disk memories. Some disks are quite large, running up to 4 ft in diameter. Others are smaller, rotate faster, are changeable, etc. Because of the large market for these memories and the seemingly infinite variety of configurations in which they can be manufactured, the system user is afforded considerable freedom in selection.

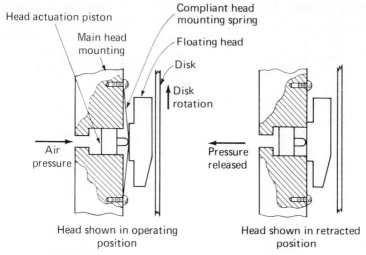

FIG. 7 • 42 Flying head for magnetic drum or magnetic disk memory.

Disk memories which have changeable disk packs (or *modules*†) are very popular. Each disk pack contains a set of disks which rotate together. The IBM 2314 shown in Fig. 7·43(*a*) uses a changeable disk pack, for instance, which contains 20 recording disk surfaces consisting of 10 disks [refer to Fig. 7·43(*b*)]. In this particular configuration the top of the top disk and the bottom of the bottom disk are not used. Eighteen read-write heads are used, two for each surface on which information is recorded. The disks revolve at a speed of 2400 rpm. The heads are mounted in a comblike positioning mechanism as shown. Each disk surface is divided into 200 concentric magnetic tracks per inch, and each track contains about 4400 bits/in.

Figure 7·44 shows characteristics of a lower priced disk system manufactured by Hewlett-Packard.

Table 7·8 lists the characteristics of several of the larger disk pack systems.

In the mid 1970s disk units with changeable packs or modules were the most used devices. At about that time, however, an IBM unit with fixed disks, the 3350,‡ brought in a new disk technology with greater recording density, more tracks per data surface, and faster transfer rate. This disk technology is referred to as *Winchester* technology and features a low head loading force (10 grams versus 300 grams on earlier devices) and a low mass head. Also, since disks are not changeable, alignment and other tracking problems are reduced. Disks are also lubricated so the lightweight heads can "crash" without damage. (They bounce.) The original Winchester disk drives were used for large storage systems; however, the technology was quickly picked up by manufacturers of smaller drives and so Winches-

---

†A *module* is a disk pack which has the read-write heads and positioning arms all packaged together with the disks. These modules are costly, but enable a higher performance system.

‡The 3350 improved an earlier Winchester technology with changeable disk packs (the 3340).

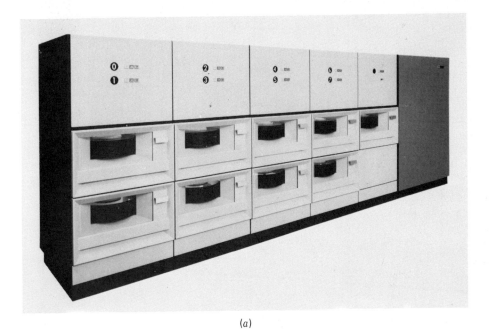

(a)

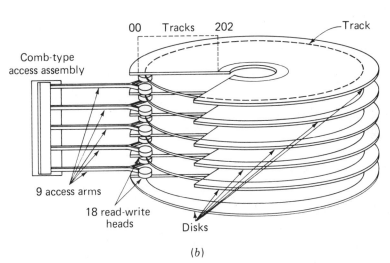

(b)

FIG. 7 • 43 (a) IBM 2314 magnetic disk memory. (b) Disk pack for IBM 2314 (only five disks are shown).

ter drives are now made by many companies, and fixed disk systems are popular with mini- and microcomputer systems as well as with large systems.

Some specifications for a large CDC drive are shown in Table 7·9, while specifications for typical small Winchester drives are shown in Table 7·10.

Because of the relative inexpensiveness per bit of information stored in disk memories and because of the relatively low access times and the high transfer

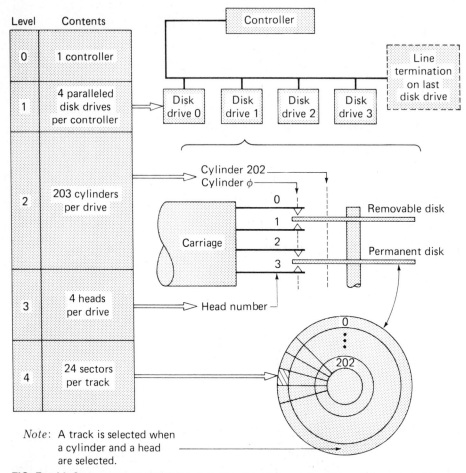

Level	Contents
0	1 controller
1	4 paralleled disk drives per controller
2	203 cylinders per drive
3	4 heads per drive
4	24 sectors per track

Note: A track is selected when a cylinder and a head are selected.

FIG. 7 • 44 Storage system containing up to four disk drives, each with two disks recorded on both sides. (Courtesy Hewlett-Packard Co.)

rates attainable when reading or writing data from or into a disk file, magnetic disk memories have become one of the most important storage devices in modern digital computers.

7 • 21 FLEXIBLE DISK STORAGE SYSTEMS—THE FLOPPY DISK

An innovation in disk storage, originally developed at IBM, uses a flexible, "floppy" disk with a plastic base in place of the more conventional rigid, metal-based disk. This storage medium is approximately the size and shape of a 45-rpm record and can be "plugged in" about as easily as a tape cartridge. Each floppy disk costs only a few dollars.

The floppy disks are changeable, and each disk comes in an envelope as shown in Fig. 7·45. The disks are mounted on the disk drive with the envelope in place,

TABLE 7 • 8 DISK DRIVE/DISK PACK TECHNOLOGY

DISK DRIVE TECHNOLOGY	IBM 2314	CDC 215	UNIVAC 8440	IBM 3330	IBM 3330-11	IBM 3340
Pack design	IBM 2316	IBM 2316	2316†	IBM 3336	IBM 3336-11	IBM 3348
Number of surfaces	20	20	20	19	19	24
Storage capacity, Mbytes	29	54	108	100	200	35 to 70
Tracks per inch	200	200	200	192	384	300
Transitions per inch	4,400	4,400	4,400	4,040	4,040	5,072
Data rate, million bits/s	2.5	2.5	5.0	6.5	6.5	7.1
Average access time, ms	60	30	30	30	30	25
Rpm	2,400	2,400	2,400	3,600	3,600	3,000
Detent	Mechanical‡	Optical	Optical	Servo	Servo	Servo
Actuator	Hydraulic‡	Voice coil	Voice coil	Voice coil	Voice coil	Voice coil
Disk coating, minimum, μin.	90	90	50	50	40	40
Head fly height, minimum, μin.	80	80	70	50	30	30

†Special pack made with 2,316-pack hardware and 3,336 disks.
‡Non-IBM hybrids exist with voice coil and optical mask.

TABLE 7 • 9 LARGE FIXED DISK DRIVE CHARACTERISTICS
FOR CDC 9776†

CHARACTERISTIC	SPECIFICATION
Number of spindles per cabinet	2
Capacity per spindle	400 Mbytes (movable head)
	1.72 Mbytes (fixed head)
Data rate	9.6 MHz
Average access time	25 ms
Rotational speed	3600 rpm
Latency time	8.4 ms

†Courtesy CDC Corp.

TABLE 7 • 10 TYPICAL FIXED DISK
WINCHESTER DRIVE CHARACTERISTICS
(FOR SMALL TO MEDIUM SYSTEMS)

CHARACTERISTIC	SPECIFICATION
Number of disks	1 to 4
Data surfaces	1 to 7
Bit density	6400 bits/in.
Track density	500 tracks/in.
Tracks per surface	690
Surface capacity	7.6 Mbytes
Rotational speed	3600 rpm
4-disk capacity	53.2 Mbytes

and information is written and read through an aperture in the envelope. (Some systems require removing the envelope.) Several manufacturers now provide complete systems for under $500 for use with these disks. Convenience in use and low prices have broadened the use of floppy disk memories in many applications.

On most floppy disk drives the read-write head assembly is in actual physical contact with the recording material. (For increased life, head contact is generally maintained only when reading or writing.) Track life on a diskette is generally on the order of 3 to 5 million contact revolutions. The standard flexible disk is enclosed in an 8-in. square jacket, and the disk has a diameter of 7.88 in. The recording surface is a 100-μin.-thick layer of magnetic oxide on a 0.003-in.-thick polyester substrate. The jacket gives handling protection, and, in addition, it has a special liner that provides a wiping action to remove wear products and other dirt which would be abrasive to the media and head if left on the surface.

In the original IBM version there is a single 0.100-in.-diameter index hole 1.5 in. from the center of the disk to indicate the start of a track. A written track is 0.012-in. wide, and standard track spacing is 48/in. The number of tracks is 77. The capacity of a surface using a standard code and a bit density of 3268 bits/in. on the innermost track is about 400,000 bytes of 8 bits each. Table 7·11 shows some characteristics of this kind of flexible disk system.

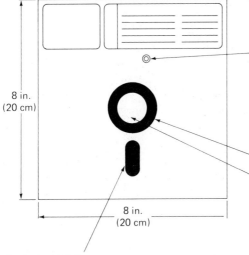

8 in.
(20 cm)

8 in.
(20 cm)

Index hole

The outer circle shows a hole in the jacket;
the inner circle shows the index hole in the
disk. When these two holes are aligned as
the disk revolves during data processing
operations, a beam of light shining on one
side of the diskette is sensed from the other
side and used for timing functions.

Drive access opening in jacket

Drive spindle hole in disk

After the diskette has been placed in the
machine and the disk drive spindle has been
inserted into the drive spindle hole in the
disk, the drive mechanism clamps onto a
portion of the disk exposed by the drive
access opening in the jacket.

Pressure pad slot
(A similar opening on the other side of the
diskette is called the head slot.)

The head slot exposes the recording surface
of the disk as the disk turns in its jacket in
the machine. The data recording and sensing
unit of the disk drive, which is called a *read-
write head* and is similar to the record/play-
back head in a tape recorder, moves to specified positions along the length of the slot.
Moving to a specified position is called
accessing a track. (Data are recorded only
on the side of the diskette that contains the
head slot.)

FIG. 7 • 45 Floppy disk with envelope.

TABLE 7 • 11 CHARACTERISTICS FOR AN IBM COMPATIBLE FLEXIBLE
DISK DRIVE

CHARACTERISTIC	SPECIFICATION
Capacity, bytes†	400,000
Rotational speed, rpm	360
Transfer rate, bits/s	250,000
Track-to-track access time, ms	16–20
Average access time, ms	176
Bit density	
Inner track, bits/in.	3,268
Outer track, bits/in.	1,836
Track density per inch	48
Number of tracks	77

†This is a maximum; using IBM's formatted recording system, only 250,000 bytes
of data are recorded per disk.

TABLE 7 • 12 DISK CHARACTERISTICS

	8-in. DISK DRIVE		5.25 in. DISK DRIVE	
	SINGLE SIDED	DOUBLE SIDED	SINGLE SIDED	DOUBLE SIDED
Capacity (unformatted)				
Single density, kbytes	400	800	110	220
Double density, kbytes	800	1600	220	440
Average access time, ms	225	100	450	300
Transfer rates				
Single density, kbits/s	250	250	125	125
Double density, kbits/s	500	500	250	250
Number of tracks	77	154	35	70
Rotational speed, rpm	360	360	300	300
Track density per inch	48	48	48	48

Disks are also made in $5\frac{1}{4}$-in. and $3\frac{1}{2}$-in. sizes, and these mini disks are becoming increasingly popular. Several companies offer floppy disk systems using adaptations of the flying-head concept. Some floppy disks use an address system (like regular disk) where the disk drive, track, and sector are given. However, other systems write "headers" on each block of recorded data on a track, and the header information is specified for each access.

The "IBM standard" system uses one complete track for formatting information. Sync bits and headers as well as check bits are interlaced with data on the remaining tracks. A complete description of IBM's formatting can be found in *The IBM Diskette for Standard Data Interchange,* IBM Document GA21-9182-01.

In order to increase disk capacity, manufacturers now supply two-sided double-track-density (100 tracks/in.) and double-density (5–6 kbits/in.) drives. Less expensive drives normally have fewer tracks.

Table 7·12 shows some characteristics for small system disks.

7 • 22 MAGNETIC TAPE

At present the most popular medium for storing very large quantities of information is magnetic tape. Although because of its long access time, magnetic tape is not a desirable medium for the main high-speed storage of a computer, modern mass-production techniques have made the cost of tape very low, so that vast quantities of information may be stored inexpensively. Furthermore, since it is possible to erase and rewrite information on tape, the same tape may be used again and again. Another advantage of magnetic tape is that the information stored does not "fade away," and therefore data or programs stored one month may be used again the next.

Another advantage of using magnetic tape for storing large quantities of data derives from the fact that the reels of tape on a tape mechanism may be changed.

In this way the same magnetic tape handling mechanism and its associated circuitry may be used with many different reels of tape, each reel containing different data.

There are four basic parts of a digital magnetic tape system:

1. *Magnetic tape*   This is generally a flexible plastic tape with a thin coating of some ferromagnetic material along the surface.
2. *The tape transport*   This consists of a mechanism designed to move the tape past the recording heads at the command of the computer. Included are the heads themselves and the storage facilities for the tape being used, such as the reels on which the tape is wound.
3. *The reading and writing system*   This part of the system includes the reading and writing amplifiers and the "translators" which convert the signals from the tape to digital signals which may be used in the central computing system.
4. *The switching and buffering equipment*   This section consists of the equipment necessary to select the correct tape mechanism if there are several, to store information from the tape and also information to be read onto the tape (provide buffering), and to provide such facilities as manually directed rewinding of the tape.

The tape transports used in digital systems have two unique characteristics: (1) the ability to start and stop very quickly, and (2) a high tape speed. The ability to start and stop the tape very quickly is important for two reasons. First, since the writing or reading process cannot begin until the tape is moving at a sufficient speed, a delay is introduced until the tape gains speed, slowing down operation. Second, information is generally recorded on magnetic tape in "blocks" or "records." Since the tape may be stopped between blocks of information, the tape which passes under the heads during the stopping and starting processes is wasted. This is called the *interblock* or *interrecord gap.* Fast starting and stopping conserves tape.

Figure 7·46(*a*) shows a typical tape system. To accelerate and decelerate the tape very quickly, an effort is made to isolate the tape reels, which have a high inertia, from the mechanism that moves the tape past the recording heads. Figure 7·46(*b*) shows a high-speed start-stop tape mechanism which uses a set of tension arms around which the tape is laced. The upper and lower tension arms in Fig. 7·46(*b*) are movable, and when the tape is suddenly driven past the heads by the capstan, the mechanism provides a buffering supply of tape. A servomechanism is used to drive the upper and lower reels, maintaining enough tape between the capstan and the tape reels to keep the supply of tape around the tension arms constant. Table 7·13 shows some characteristics of this kind of system.

Another arrangement for isolating the high-inertia tape reels from the basis tape drive is shown in Fig. 7·46(*c*). This system isolates the tape from the capstan drive by means of two columns of tape held in place by a vacuum. A servosystem then maintains the correct length of tape between reel and capstan drive. Both this and the previous systems use continuously rotating capstans to actually drive the tape, and "pressure rolls" to press the tape against the capstan when the transport is

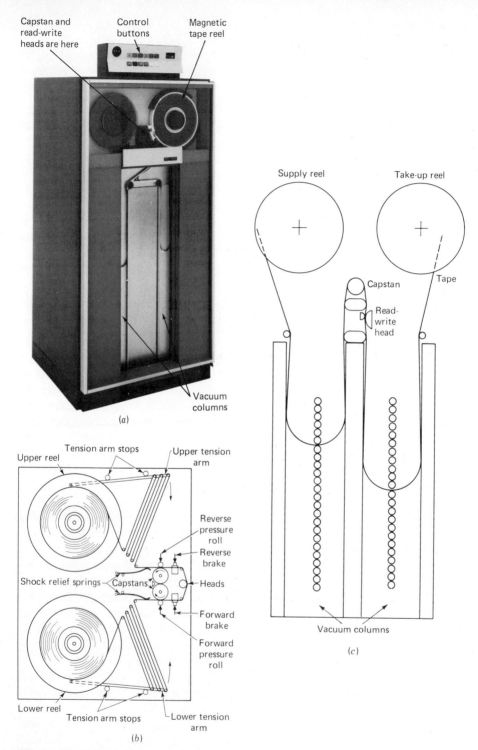

FIG. 7 • 46 (a) IBM 3420 tape system. (b) Magnetic tape mechanism using tension arms. (c) Magnetic tape mechanism using vacuum columns.

TABLE 7 • 13 TYPICAL TENSION ARM TAPE DRIVE CHARACTERISTICS

REEL SIZE in.	bits/in.	DATA RATE kbits	START-STOP TIMES ms	CAPACITY Mbytes	COST OF A TYPICAL REEL OF TAPE $
7	1600	40	15	11.5	7.50
8.5	1600	60	10	23	8.50
10.5	1600	72 kbits/s at 45 in./s; 120 kbits/s at 75 in./s	8.33 (5 ms at 75 in./s)	46	11.00

activated. Brakes are also provided for fast stopping. Table 7·14 shows some typical figures on this kind of system.

Using systems of this sort, the start and stop times can be less than 5 ms. These are the times required to accelerate a tape to a speed suitable for reading or writing and the time required to fully stop a moving tape. The speeds at which the tapes are moved past the heads vary greatly, most tape transports having speeds in the range from 12.5 to 250 in./s. Lincoln Laboratory has constructed a very fast (900 in./s) mechanism in which the tape is driven directly by the reels of the tape transport. A tape system of this sort is designed to transfer only large quantities of data to and from the machine's main fast-access storage in a single operation. The slower tape speeds, combined with fast starting and stopping, are probably more adaptable to systems in which smaller amounts of data must be transferred. Some systems have changeable cartridges with a reel of tape in each cartridge. The manufacturers of these systems feel that this protects the tape and facilitates changing the reels. These will be discussed in a following section.

Most tape systems have two-gap read-write heads. The two gaps (refer to Fig. 7·47) are useful because, during writing, the read gap is positioned after the write gap and is used to check what has been written by reading and comparing.

Tapes vary from $\frac{1}{4}$ to 3 in. in width; however, most tape is $\frac{1}{2}$-in.-wide 1.5-mil-thick Mylar tape. A 10.5-in. reel typically has 2400 or 3600 ft of tape. Generally about nine channels or tracks are used for $\frac{1}{2}$ in. of width. The surface of the tape is usually in contact with the read-write head. Output signals from the read heads are gen-

TABLE 7 • 14 TYPICAL VACUUM COLUMN TAPE DRIVE CHARACTERISTICS FOR 10.5-IN. TAPE REEL SYSTEMS

SPEED in./s	bits/in.	MAXIMUM DATA RATE kbytes/s	START-STOP TIMES ms	CAPACITY Mbytes
50	1600	80	7.5	46
75	1600	120	5	46
200	1600	320	3	62
200	6250	1250	1.2	350

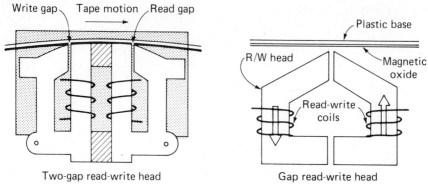

Write gap   Tape motion   Read gap

Plastic base

R/W head

Magnetic oxide

Read-write coils

Two-gap read-write head   Gap read-write head

FIG. 7 • 47 One- and two-gap tape heads.

erally in the 0.1- to 0.5-V range. The recording density varies; however, 200, 556, 800, 1600, 6250, and even 12,500 bits/in. per channel are fairly standard.

Data are recorded on magnetic tape using some coding system. Generally one character is stored per row (refer to Fig. 7·48) along the tape. The tape in Fig. 7·48 has seven tracks, or channels, one of which is a parity bit, which is added to make the number of 1s in every row odd (this will be studied in the next chapter, as will the codes used for magnetic tape). Data are recorded on magnetic tape in blocks, with gaps between the blocks and usually with unique start and stop characters to signal the beginning and the end of a block.

A small piece of metallic reflective material is fastened to the tape at the beginning and end of the reel, and photoelectric cells are used to sense these markers and prevent overrunning of the tape [refer to Fig. 7·49(a)].

The codes used to record on tape vary, but two commonly used IBM codes are shown in Fig. 7·49(b) and (c). IBM standard tape is $\frac{1}{2}$ in. wide and 1.5 milliinch thick, with either seven or nine tracks. The seven-track code is shown in Fig.

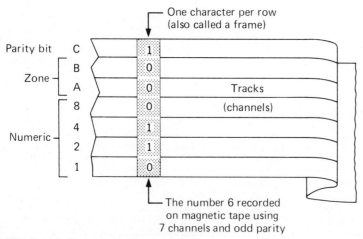

One character per row (also called a frame)

Parity bit   C

Zone — B, A

Tracks (channels)

8

Numeric — 4, 2

1

The number 6 recorded on magnetic tape using 7 channels and odd parity

FIG. 7 • 48 Basic layout of magnetic tape.

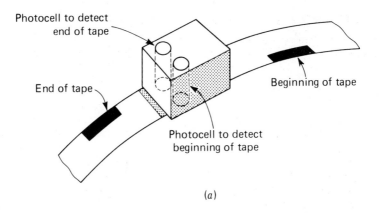

(a)

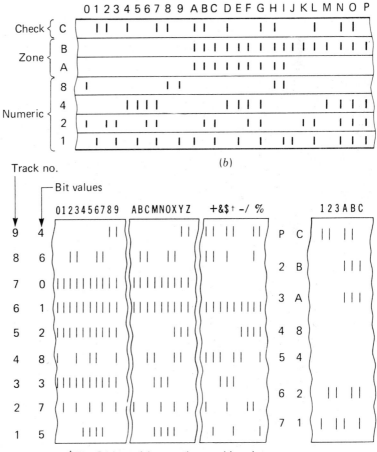

(b)

† The P bit position produces odd parity.

(c)

FIG. 7 • 49 Magnetic tape coding. (a) Beginning and end of tape marking. (b) Magnetic recording of seven-track BCD code on tape. (c) Nine-track (EBCDIC) and seven-track tape data format comparison.

TABLE 7 • 15 VACUUM COLUMN DIGITAL TAPE TRANSPORT CHARACTERISTICS

KENNEDY MODEL 9300†	
CHARACTERISTIC	SPECIFICATION
Data density	9 tracks, 800 characters/in., 1600 characters/in.
Tape velocity	125 in./s
Start-stop time	3 ms at 125 in./s
Start-stop displacement	0.6825 in.
Reel size diameter	10.5 in.
Tape	
Length	2,400 ft
Width	0.5 in.
Thickness	1.5 mil
Rewind speed	300 in./s nominal

†(Courtesy Kennedy Co.)

7·49(*b*), where the 0s are simply blank and 1s are indicated by a vertical line. Figure 7·49(*c*) shows the nine-track code. Recording densities are 200, 556, 800, 1600, or 6250 bits (or rows) per inch [which means 200, 556, 800, 1600, or 6250 characters (or bytes) per inch, since a character is recorded in each row].

Some characteristics of a medium-priced vacuum column tape system are shown in Table 7·15, and Table 7·16 gives the characteristics for an inexpensive tension arm Hewlett-Packard system.

TABLE 7 • 16 HEWLETT-PACKARD 7090E TAPE SYSTEMS

CHARACTERISTIC	SPECIFICATION
Number of tracks	9
Read-write speed	
2100-based systems	25, 37.5, 45 in./s
3000 system	45 in./s
Density	1600 characters/in. (8 bits/character)
Data transfer rate	72,000 characters/s max
Reel diameter	10.5 in. maximum
Tape (computer grade)	
Width	0.5 in.
Thickness	1.5 mils
Rewind speed	160 in./s
Start-stop times	8.33 ms (read-after-write) at 45 in./s
End of tape and beginning of tape reflective strip detection	IBM compatible

tape cassette.

FIG. 7 • 50 Magnetic tape cassette.

7 • 23 TAPE CASSETTES AND CARTRIDGES

The changeable tape cassette used in the familiar home recorder is an attractive means for recording digital data. The cassettes are small, changeable, and inexpensive; they are frequently used in small and "home" computers. The tape moving mechanism in the conventional home tape cassette often used for small systems is not of sufficient quality for larger business and scientific computer usage. However, a number of high-quality digital cassettes with prices in the dollar region ($2 to $15 in general) have been developed. These are of small size — on the order of the familiar cassette — and have a similar appearance.

There are also larger *tape cartridges* which contain long strips of magnetic tape and which resemble large cassettes. These cartridges provide a more convenient way to package tape, and greatly simplify the mounting of tape reels (which can be a problem with conventional reels of tape where the tape must be manually positioned on the mechanism). The tape cartridges also provide protection against dirt and contamination, since the tape is sealed in the cartridge.

Figure 7·50 shows a typical cassette. A number of different digital cassettes and cassette drives are now in production, and each has different characteristics.† As an example, Data General Corporation offers a cassette drive with an average tape speed of 31 in./s, a 282-ft. 0.15-in. magnetic tape per cassette, storage per tape of 800,000 bits, and transfer (reading) rate of 12,800 bits/s. The cassette can rewind in 85 s. A 22-in. reflective leader and trailer are used to mark the beginning and the end of the tape (a photodiode senses this strip).

Cartridges are a high-performance magnetic tape storage medium. There are several cartridge designs available. These vary not only in performance capabilities, but also in the division of hardware between cartridge and transport.‡ The 3M cartridge and drive shown in Fig. 7·51 is representative. The cartridge contains

---

†Standards organizations have attempted to develop standards for cassettes. The Phillips cassette is such a standard.

‡For instance, the heads may or may not be included in each cartridge.

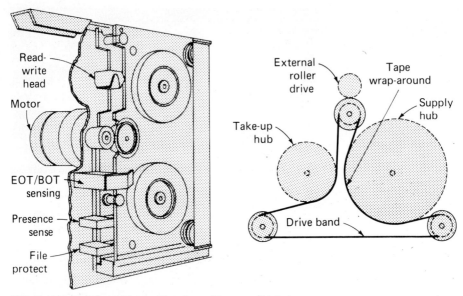

FIG. 7 • 51 Digital cartridge and interface. (Courtesy 3M Co.)

300 ft of $\frac{1}{4}$-in. tape capable of recording up to four tracks at 1600 bits/in. for a maximum storage capacity of more than 2×10^7 bits. The 3M transport operates at 30 in./s when reading or writing, and at 90 in./s in search mode. A novel elastic band drive moves the tape and also supplies tape tension. Tape drive, hub, and guide components are referenced to the base of the cartridge and require no external guidance. There are several new cartridge systems designed to ''back up'' Winchester disk drives.

TABLE 7 • 17 SPECIFICATIONS OF 3M CARTRIDGE AND DCD-3 CARTRIDGE DRIVE

CHARACTERISTIC	SPECIFICATION
Operating speed	
Read-write	30 in./s forward and reverse
Fast forward, rewind, gap search	90 in./s forward and reverse
Packing density	1600 bits/in.
Transfer rate	48 kbits/s maximum
Interrecord gap	1.33 in. typical; 1.2 in. minimum per proposed ANSI standard
Maximum recommended start-stop rate	Three operations per second without forced air cooling
Total speed variation	$\pm 4\%$ max
Tape head	1-, 2-, 4-channel read-while-write heads available
Interface logic	TTL compatible
Power	5 V dc $\pm$ 5%, $\pm$ 18 V dc $\pm$ 5%

†For instance, the heads may or may not be included in each cartridge.

TABLE 7 • 18 STORAGE MEDIA COMPARISONS

	5-in. REEL	PHILLIPS CASSETTE	3M-TYPE CARTRIDGE	FLOPPY DISK	LARGE HARD DISK FIXED MEDIA
Capacity, kbytes	18,500	550	2500	250	571,000
Transfer rate, kbits/s	180	9.6	48	250	14,000
Number of tracks	9	2	4	77	600
Density, bits/in.	880	880	1600	3200	1600
Interrecord gap, in.	0.6	0.8	1.3	Not applicable	Not applicable
Mechanism cost	2000	400	500	400	30,000
Media cost, cents/byte	0.06×10^{-3}	1.2×10^{-3}	0.6×10^{-3}	2.6×10^{-3}	0.185×10^{-3}

(handwritten annotations: $\times 8\,bute = 0.48 \times 10^{-3}$ bit; 9.6×10^{-3}; 4.8×10^{-3}; 20.8×10^{-3}; 1.58×10^{-3})

TABLE 7 • 19 LOW-COST STORAGE SYSTEM CHARACTERISTICS

CHARACTERISTIC	CAPACITY	COST cents/byte	
Floppy disk	2.4 Mbits	2.6×10^{-3}	20.8×10^{-3}
High-performance cassette	1 Mbytes	5×10^{-4}	4×10^{-3}
Phillips cassette	1.44 Mbytes	1.2×10^{-3}	9.6×10^{-3}
Low-performance cassette	200 kbits	20×10^{-4}	1.6×10^{-3}
3M cartridge	11.5 Mbytes	0.6×10^{-3}	4.8×10^{-3}
7-in. tape reels	40 Mbits	0.5×10^{-4}	0.4×10^{-3}

Table 7·17 gives some specifications of the 3M cartridge and the 3M cartridge drive. Table 7·18 compares some of the standard memory devices which have been described. Notice that these are standard systems, and some newer devices exceed these characteristics. Table 7·19 gives some data on the newer low-cost devices suitable for minicomputers and microcomputers as opposed to more expensive devices. These are again representative figures for the latest systems.

7 • 24 MAGNETIC BUBBLE AND CCD MEMORIES

The secondary or backup memory devices that have so far been really successful have all been electromechanical devices (drums, disks, tape, etc.) which store bits as magnetic fields on a surface and rely on mechanical motion to locate the data. However, two devices for secondary storage having no moving parts are now being developed and have started to appear in some commercial applications. These are magnetic bubble and CCD memories.

Magnetic bubble memories are primarily competing with floppy disks, small disks, cartridges, and small tape devices. Bubble memories are more reliable (having no moving parts), consume less power, are smaller, and cost less per unit. However, disks have higher transfer rates, and the cost per bit is lower except for very small systems.

Bubble memories trace their history to research at the Bell Laboratories, which showed that bits can be stored as "bubbles" in a thin magnetic film formed on a crystalline substrate. A bubble device operates as a set of shift registers. The storage mechanism consists of cylindrically shaped magnetic domains, called *bubbles.* These bubbles are formed in a thin film layer of single-crystal synthetic ferrite (or garnet) when a magnetic field is applied perpendicular to the film's surface. A separate rotating field moves the bubbles through the film in shift-register fashion. The presence of a bubble is a 1, no bubble is a 0. The bubbles move along a path determined by patterns of soft magnetic material deposited on the magnetic expitaxial film.

To the user, the physics of the bubble memory's operation are less important than its operating characteristics. The memories appear as long shift registers which can be shifted under external control. Storage is permanent since if shifting is stopped, the bits in the memory will remain indefinitely.

To utilize the shift register characteristics better and reduce access time, the shift registers are generally made of only modest lengths of perhaps 50–100 kbits. A memory package is liable to contain from a few hundred kilobits to several megabits.

The shift rate is relatively slow, perhaps 200 kHz, so access times are on the order of a few milliseconds. (Reading and writing are only performed at the ends of the shift register.)

Bubble memories require relatively complex interface circuitry, but IC manufacturers have produced reasonable IC packages for this purpose.

Charged coupled devices (CCDs) are constructed using IC technology. The bits are stored on capacitors as charges similar to the dynamic IC memories, except that the storage is arranged in a shift register configuration with the charge "packets" being shifted from cell to cell under clock control.

Since the storage mechanism is a charge on a capacitor, if shifting stops for very long (a few milliseconds), the charges will leak from the capacitors and the memory's contents will be lost.

CCD memories generally have from 500 kbits to several megabits of storage. The shift registers are read from and written into from the ends, so access time is dependent on shift-register lengths. The shift rate is generally 200–500 kHz, and so for reasonable-length shift registers access times are in the milliseconds.

Since CCD memories use IC technology, they require less interface circuitry than bubble memories. The strategy involved in determining how long the shift registers should be for both bubbles and CCDs is based on a cost/performance analysis. A greater number of shorter loops results in faster access times, but more interface circuits and more complicated system usage strategies. Long loops give economy but long access times.

Both bubble and CCD technologies are in the early stages, but they are already considered competitive with the smaller more conventional disk memories.

˙7 • 25 DIGITAL RECORDING TECHNIQUES

Although the characteristics and construction of such storage devices as magnetic drums, tape recorders, and magnetic disk storage devices may vary greatly, the fundamental storage process in each consists of storing a binary 0 or 1 on a small area of magnetic material. Storage in each case is dynamic, for the medium on which the information is recorded is moved past the reading or writing device.

Although the process of recording a 0 or a 1 on a surface may appear straightforward, considerable research has gone into both the development of the recorded patterns used to represent 0s and 1s and the means for determining the value recorded. There are two necessities here: (1) the packing density should be made as great as is possible, that is, each cell or bit should occupy as little space as possible, thus economizing, for instance, on the amount of tape used to store a given amount of information; and (2) the reading and writing procedure should be made as reliable as is possible. These two interests are conflicting because, when the recorded bits are packed more and more closely together, the distortion of the playback signal is greatly increased.

In writing information on a magnetic surface, the digital information is supplied to the recording circuitry, which then codes this information into a pattern which is recorded by the write head. The techniques used to write information on a magnetic medium can be divided into several categories, the *return-to-zero* (RZ) technique, the *return-to-bias* (RB) technique, and the *non-return-to-zero* (NRZ) technique. The methods for reading information written using these techniques also vary. The basic techniques will be described below, along with the recorded waveshapes and the waveshapes later read by the read heads and translated by the reading system.

˙7 • 26 RETURN-TO-ZERO AND RETURN-TO-BIAS RECORDING TECHNIQUES

Figure 7·52 illustrates the return-to-zero recording technique. In Fig. 7·52(a) no current goes through the winding of the write head, except when a 1 or a 0 is to be recorded. If a 1 is to be recorded, a pulse of positive polarity is applied to the winding on the write head, and if a 0 is to be written, a negative pulse is applied to the winding. In either case the current through the write-head winding is returned to zero after the pulse, and remains there until the next bit is recorded. The second set of waveforms on this drawing illustrates the remanent flux pattern on the magnetic surface after the write head has passed. There is some distortion in this pattern due to the fringing of flux around the head.

---

*The sections on recording techniques can be omitted without loss of continuity.

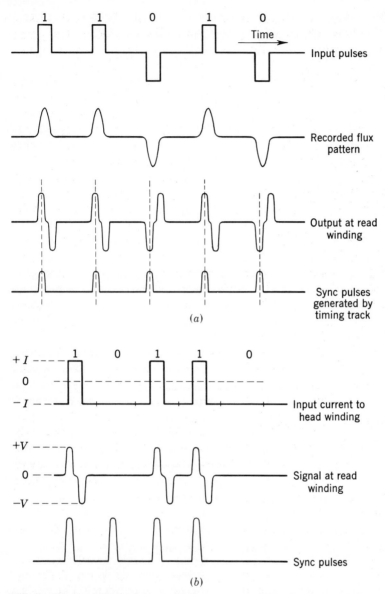

FIG. 7 • 52 Recording techniques. (*a*) Return-to-zero (RZ) recording. (*b*) Return-to-bias (RB) technique.

If this pattern of magnetization is passed under a read head, some of the magnetic flux will be coupled into the core of the head. The flux takes the lower reluctance path through the core material of the head instead of bridging the gap in the head (Fig. 7·39), and when the amount of flux through the core material changes, a voltage will be induced in the coil wound around the core. Thus a change in the amplitude of the recorded magnetic field will result in a voltage being induced in the coil on the read head. The waveforms in Fig. 7·52(a) and (b) illustrate typical output signals on the read-head windings for each of the techniques. Notice that the waveform at the read head is not a reproduction of the input current during the write process, nor of the pattern actually magnetized on the magnetic material.

The problem is, therefore, to distinguish a 1 or a 0 output at the sense winding. Several techniques have been used for this. One consists in first amplifying the output waveform from the output waveform from the read winding in a linear amplifier. The output of this amplifier is then strobed in the same manner that the output from the sense winding of a core plane is strobed. For drum systems the correct timing for the strobe, which must be very accurate, may be determined by the timing signals recorded on the timing track. If the output from the read amplifier is connected to an AND gate, and the strobe pulse is also connected as an input to the same AND gate, the output will be a positive pulse when the recorded signal represents a 1.

It is important that the timing pulse be very sharp and occur at the right time relative to the reading and writing of the bits.

A fundamental characteristic of return-to-zero recording [(Fig. 7·52(a)] is that, for a 1, the output signal during the first half of each bit time will be positive with regard to the second half; and that for a 0, the first half of the output signal during each bit time will be negative in regard to the second half of the signal. This is sometimes exploited in translating the signal read back.

In the return-to-zero system in Fig. 7·52(a) the magnetic field returns to zero flux when a 1 or a 0 pulse is not present. This makes it impossible to write over information which has previously been written, unless the position of each cell is very accurately located. If a 0 pulse is written directly over a previously recorded 1, the flux generated will reverse the polarity of the recorded field only if the write head is in exactly the right position when the 0 is recorded. The timing of the writing of information is therefore very critical for this system, and it is rarely used except with magnetic drums, where the timing may be accurately established by timing tracks. An alternative technique involves erasing all flux before writing new information, but this involves an additional erase head and is seldom used.

The second method for recording information is the return-to-bias system, illustrated in Fig. 7·52(b). In this case the current through the winding maintains the head saturated in the negative direction unless a 1 is to be written. When a 1 is written, a pulse of current in the opposite direction is applied to the winding at the center of the bit time. The outputs at the sense winding are also illustrated in the figure. In this case there will be an output at the sense winding only when a 1 is written. This output may be amplified and strobed just as in the previous case. The timing here is not so critical when information is being ''written over,'' because the negative flux from the head will magnetize the surface in the correct direction, regardless of what was previously recorded. The current through the winding in this case, and in all those which follow, is assumed to be sufficient to saturate the material on which the signals are being recorded. A primary problem here concerns sequences of 0s. For magnetic tape, either a clock track must be used or the code used must be such that at least one 1 occurs in each line of the tape. Notice that this is because only 1s generate magnetic flux changes, and therefore output signals at the read head.

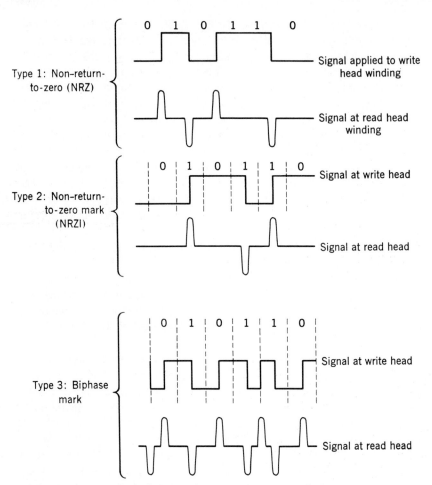

FIG. 7 • 53 Three types of non-return-to-zero recording.

'7 • 27 NON-RETURN-TO-ZERO RECORDING TECHNIQUES

Figure 7·53 illustrates three recording techniques, each of which is classified as a non-return-to-zero system. In the first, the current through the winding is negative through the entire bit time when a 0 is recorded, and is positive through the entire bit time when a 1 is recorded. The current through the winding will therefore remain constant when a sequence of 0s or 1s is being written, and will change only when a 0 is followed by a 1 or when a 1 followed by a 0 is written. In this case a signal will be induced in the sense winding only when the information recorded changes from a 1 to a 0, or vice versa.

The second technique illustrated is sometimes referred to as a *modified non-return-to-zero,* or *non-return-to-zero mark* (NRZI), technique. In this system the

---

* This section can be omitted on a first reading without loss of continuity.

polarity of the current through the write winding is reversed each time a 1 is recorded and remains constant when a 0 is recorded. If a series of 1s is recorded, the polarity of the recorded flux will therefore change for each 1. If a series of 0s is recorded, no changes will occur. Notice that the polarity has no meaning in this system; only changes in polarity. Therefore a signal will be read back only when a 1 has been recorded. This system is often used for tape recording when, in order to generate a clock or strobe, a 1 must be recorded somewhere in each cell along the tape width. That is, if 10 tracks are recorded along the tape, one of these must be a timing track which records a sequence of 1s, each of which defines a different set of cells to be read, or the information must be coded so that a 1 occurs in each set of 10 cells which are read. Alphanumeric coded information† is often recorded on tape, and the code may be arranged so that a 1 occurs in each code group.

The third non-return-to-zero technique in Fig. 7·53 is sometimes called a *phase-encoded, biphase-mark, Harvard, Manchester,* or *split-frequency* system. In this case a 0 is recorded as a $\frac{1}{2}$-bit-time negative pulse followed by a $\frac{1}{2}$-bit-time positive

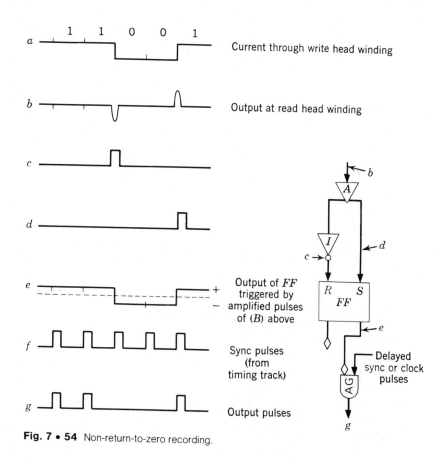

Fig. 7 • 54 Non-return-to-zero recording.

---

pulse, and a 1 is recorded as a $\frac{1}{2}$-bit-time positive pulse followed by a $\frac{1}{2}$-bit-time negative pulse. This technique is often used in high-speed systems.

The reading of information which has been recorded consists of two steps. First the output from the read head is amplified, and then the amplified signals are translated by logic circuitry. Figure 7·54 shows a translation technique for the first non-return-to-zero system illustrated in Fig. 7·53. The output signals may be either from the output flip-flop or from serial pulses. The sync pulses occur each time a cell passes under the read heads in the system.

The flip-flop (Fig. 7·54) responds to positive pulses only. Positive-pulse signals at the recording head will therefore "set" the flip-flop to 1. The inverter at the C input will cause negative pulses to be made positive. These positive pulses then will clear the flip-flop. The output of the flip-flop may be used directly by the computer, or pulse outputs can be generated by connecting an AND gate to the 1 output, delaying the sync pulses, and connecting them to the AND gate. Also, a serial representation of the number stored along the surface may be formed.

QUESTIONS

1. Determine the number of AND gates and OR gates used in a two-dimensional and a one-dimensional IC memory using the techniques in Figs. 7·4 and 7·9. The memory is to have 1 bit per word and 16 words. (Show how you got your numbers.)

2. Determine the complete OR gate and AND gate decoder count for an IC memory with 4096 words of 1 bit each using the selection schemes in Figs. 7·4 and 7·9. (Show how your numbers are derived.)

3. The interface circuitry for dynamic memories is more complicated than for static memories. However, the cost per bit of the actual memory is less for dynamic memories. As a result, for small memories static devices are less expensive and for larger memories dynamic devices are less expensive. If the interface for a static memory costs $1.00 and for a dynamic memory $10.00, and static memory bits cost $0.005 per bit while the dynamic memory bits cost $0.002 per bit, determine how many bits must be in a memory before the dynamic memory is less expensive.

4. Consider decoder matrices which are rectangular, but not square. For instance, to encode a 256-bit memory, we might use a "square" 16 × 16 matrix in two-dimensional form or an 8 × 32 two-dimensional rectangular array. Show that keeping the array "as square as possible" will reduce the number of AND gates in the decoders.

5. Count the number of sense amplifiers for the static memory in Fig. 7·21. What are the sizes of the decoders?

6. As the size of the memory goes up, the advantage of using a two-dimensional selection scheme increases with regard to the number of AND gates used for the decoders. The two-dimensional memory, however, requires more complicated memory cells. For a 4096-bit memory with a single output bit, compare the number of AND gates in the decoder for linear and for two-dimensional memories and also the number of gates in the linear memory cells

versus the two-dimensional memory cells. Try and reach some conclusion regarding which is more economical.

7. Does the two-dimensional selection system in any way slow down operation compared to the linear selection scheme?

8. A 64K word memory is to be assembled with chips having 4096 bits each, using the chip in Figs. 7·21 and 7·22. Explain how a memory bus can be connected so that the full 64K word memory can be implemented (showing only 1 bit in the memory word).

9. The core memory has the advantage over IC memories that if the power goes off, the contents of the core memory remain the same until the power is restored. On the other hand, IC memories, both static and dynamic, lose their contents if the power is removed from the chips. Battery backup power is sometimes used for IC memories. Explain the advantages and disadvantages of this.

10. There is a scheme whereby as the power declines, the contents of the memory are read into a secondary (disk or tape) memory. When the power is returned, the data are reentered into the IC memory. It is important that the power not decline too much before the transfer of information can be made. As a result it is generally necessary to have some sort of backup power to carry the memory through until the contents of the IC memory can be read out. Calculate how long this would take for a 64K memory with a cycle time of 500 ns.

11. Question 10 concerned dumping an IC memory on a disk in case of power failure. It is also necessary to find a spare area on the disk and to transfer the contents of the core memory into the disk. For one of the disk memories described in the chapter discuss this problem for the preceding 64K 500-ns IC memory.

12. Several microcomputers come with a basic 4096-word 8-bit memory. How many flip-flops are in:
(a) The memory address register?
(b) The memory buffer register?

13. How many magnetic cores are required in a core-memory array for a computer with a word length of 35 binary bits and 4096 different addresses in the core memory? How many storage devices (flip-flops) will be required for the memory address register?

14. A 4096-word 12-bit core memory is to be operated in linear-select mode. How many word lines are required? If the memory was coincident-current, how many drive lines are there in the X axis and how many in the Y axis?

15. If we construct a 4096-word 36-bit-per-word coincident-current magnetic-core memory, how many cores will be in the memory? How many sense amplifiers will be required? How many INHIBIT-line drivers? How many word-line drivers? How many X-selection drivers and how many Y-selection drivers? How many planes in the core memory and how many cores per plane?

16. For a two-dimensional IC memory the advantage in gate count decreases over the one-dimensional system as the number of bits in a word increases. Why?

17. The INHIBIT drivers are not used when a word is read from a core memory using a coincident-current selection system. True or false? Why?

18. In a linear-select memory the drivers can be set to "overdrive" cores by applying more current than is necessary to saturate the core. This will make it necessary also to increase the amount of inhibit current that is applied. Why?

19. If we use the coincident-current memory system described, and if the current driver which drives the $-I_m/2$ current through the selection line X_2 in Fig. 7·32 is broken so that no current is ever driven through this line, we will never be able to read from or write satisfactorily into three cores, one of which is core X_2Y_1. What are the designations of the other two cores into which we will never be able to read or write correctly?

20. Draw the input signal, recorded flux pattern, and output at the read head for return-to-zero and for return-to-bias recording if the bits 1001 are recorded.

21. If the INHIBIT driver which is connected to the core plane storing the first binary digit of each computer word fails, what will be the value of the binary digit written into the selected core in this plane during each memory cycle?

22. Draw the waveforms for recording the binary sequence 101, showing the signal applied to the write-head winding and the signal at the read-head winding for the type 1, type 2, and type 3 non-return-to-zero recording techniques.

23. A block diagram of an INTEL MOS LSI memory chip is shown in Fig. 7·10. The A_1 through A_8 lines are for the 256 addresses. R/W tells whether to read or to write (a 0 on this line is READ, a 1 is WRITE). The CHIP SELECT disables the memory for a 1 input and enables the memory with a 0 output. Discuss the construction of a 256-word 8-bit memory using these packages. How many packages are required? Each flip-flop in the address register (external) would have its 1 output connected to how many chips?

24. Draw the schematic for a many-to-one decoder matrix with inputs from four flip-flops and 16 output lines. Use the same basic configuration as is illustrated in Fig. 7·5(a).

25. The INTEL package in Question 23 is representative of several IC manufacturers' products. Show how the CHIP SELECT can be used to add words to a memory.

26. How is it possible to combine the SENSE and INHIBIT lines in a core memory to form a single digit or bit line? Why is this desirable?

27. Answer the following questions on the expansion of a coincident-current magnetic core memory.

   (a) Increasing the number of bits per word in a 4096-word 18-bit memory from 16 to 24 bits increases the number of core planes from _____ to _____.

   (b) Increasing the number of words in a 4096-word 24-bit memory from 4096 to 8192 increases the number of X and Y drive windings from _____ to _____.

   (c) Increasing the number of words in a 4096-word 18-bit memory to 8192 and the number of bits to 24 increases the number of inhibit windings from _____ to _____.

28. *(a)* Explain why the slower, less expensive core memories tend to use a coincident-current selection and the faster, more expensive core memories use linear selection.

(b) How does the number of dimensions in a core memory's selection scheme affect the minimal size of the cores which can be used?

(c) Do IC memories tend to be destructive or nondestructive read memories? Why?

29. (a) Discuss the effects on memory cycle time of destructive versus nondestructive read devices.

(b) Why do the sense amplifiers have to be protected against the inhibit drive current in a three-wire coincident-current core memory but not in a four-wire coincident-current core memory?

30. Discuss the concept of dimensionality in memory-selection techniques and its effects on memory speed, cost, and complexity. (As examples, you might contrast two-dimensional and three-dimensional selection schemes in IC memories or compare linear-select and coincident-current selection in core memories.)

31. What is the purpose of the INHIBIT line in a core memory?

32. Give an advantage of core memory over semiconductor memory.

33. What are the primary advantages of bipolar memory over MOS memory?

34. Explain the operation of the digit line in a linear-select core memory.

35. Explain the difference between a dynamic and a static MOS memory.

36. Contrast the parallel tree and balanced decoder networks for a 32-output decoder. Figure the number of diodes used for each and the delay incurred because of the number of gates a signal must pass through for each, assuming diode AND gates are used.

37. If there is a power failure, most core memories have cutoff circuits so that the computer is stopped after writing its registers into core memory, and the core memory is then stopped before the power drops so low that errors occur. The contents of the core memory are then not lost, and the machine can be restarted. Is this possible with IC memories?

38. Given eight 8-bit registers $A, B, C, \ldots, H$, show how a transfer circuit can be made using multiplexers so that the contents of any register can be selected by a 3-bit register S and transferred into an 8-bit register X.

39. In larger machines, when the ac power drops below a certain level, the contents of the control unit and arithmetic-logic unit are dumped on tape or disks so that the computer can be restarted with no loss of data. If IC memories are used, their contents must also be dumped. Explain why.

40. Explain the operation of the memory cell in Fig. 7·3.

41. Explain the operation of the memory cell in Fig. 7·8.

42. When linear selection is used for IC memories, individual cells tend to be simpler than for two-dimensional cell select systems, but the decoders tend to be more complicated. Explain why.

43. Explain why NMOS is better than PMOS for IC memory use.

44. The memory in Fig. 7·22 uses the organization in Fig. 7·11 and has linear-select memory cells. This simplifies individual memory cell complexity while increasing sense and write circuitry. Explain why this is cost effective for a memory of this type.

45. Dynamic memories that require external refreshing introduce extra complexity into computer operation. Can you give reasons why?

46. Explain the advantages and disadvantages of dynamic IC memories.

47. A magnetic drum has a circumference of 50 in. and a packing density of 1000 bits/in. If the drum has 40 tracks, how many bits can be stored on the surface of the drum?

48. In designing a 256-word 8-bit memory, pin 1 is connected to pin 1 for each container of the chip shown in Fig. 7·10. This applies to all A inputs and to chip select bits and to R/W, but not to data out or data in. Why?

49. A magnetic drum has 256 tracks (exclusive of timing tracks) and 1800 cells or binary bits recorded around each track. If the drum is used in a serial computer with a word length of 32 binary bits, and 1 "spacer bit" is left between words when recording, how many bits will be required to address a word on the drum? How many binary bits will be required to address a track? How many binary bits will be required to address a sector?

50. Show how to expand the 256-word 1-bit memory in Fig. 7·10 to a 2048-word 1-bit memory using the CHIP SELECT and a 3-input, 8-output decoder.

51. For the IBM 3330 disk memory described, how many binary digits can be recorded on one surface of a given disk?

52. Which of the IBM tape units described will transfer data fastest, and how fast can characters and bits be read or written?

53. If a magnetic drum rotates at 18,000 rpm, what is the maximum access time required to read a word in a parallel system, assuming that there is no delay in decoding the address? What is the average random-access time?

54. Make up a formula to calculate how many bits a second can be read for a disk memory that revolves at a rate of r revolutions per second and has b bits per track. What will the average latency time be?

55. Assuming that a disk in the IBM 2314 system rotates at a speed of 2400 rpm as stated and that we read from eight tracks simultaneously, how many bits per second can be read from one of these disks?

56. Explain seek time and latency for disk memories.

57. A magnetic tape system has 7 tracks for each $\frac{1}{2}$-in. width of tape. The packing density per track is 250 bits/in., and the tape is moved at a speed of 75 in./s. If the tape width is 1 in., how many bits may be read per second?

58. Fixed-head disk memories reduce total access time by avoiding either seek time or latency. Which is avoided and why?

59. What is the danger to disk packs when flying heads are used?

60. Contrast three of the disk packs described in Table 7·8, giving your ideas on their desirability. Do you think price might be an important factor in evaluating these systems?

61. Explain the figures given for access times in the HP 2888A disk systems described in Table 7·8.

62. Contrast the floppy disk figures for the 5-in. and the 8-in. systems.

63. Is price a factor in evaluating the systems in Question 62?

64. Compare the Hewlett-Packard 7090E tape system with one of the IBM tape systems.

65. Tape cassettes and tape cartridges have advantages and disadvantages compared to conventional tape systems. Can you give several of each?

66. The table comparing storage media brings out some of the contrasts in price and performance for memory systems. Tell what devices you would choose for the following kinds of computers and why.

(a) Microcomputers

(b) Minicomputers

(c) Large computer systems

67. Draw a diode ROM, as in Fig. 7·27, but which converts from 2, 4, 2, 1 code to the 8, 4, 2, 1 BCD code.

68. If we read or write from a Winchester disk drive as in Table 7·10 using the figures in the table, how many bits per second can we transfer in that system?

69. Draw a diode ROM as in Fig. 7·27 which translates from excess 3 code to BCD.

70. An IC memory could be made three-dimensional by breaking the MAR into three pieces and having three decoders. The memory cell would be more complex, however. Design a 4096-word memory of this type, comparing it with the two-dimensional memory.

71. Design four locations in a diode ROM by adding diodes to the following diagram. The signal C_1 is to be a 1 in locations 01111 and 11110 and is a 0 otherwise; the signal C_2 is to be a 1 in locations 01111 and 10000 and is a 0 otherwise; the signal C_3 is to be a 1 in 01101, 11110, and 01111 and is a 0 otherwise. A given decoder output line is high when selected.

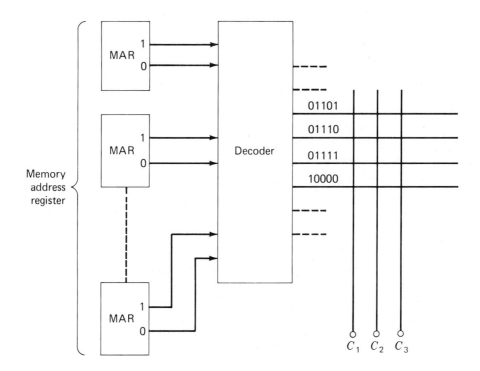

72. Here are some data on a PDP-11 disk pack:

> Number of cylinders, 203
> Tracks per cylinder, 2
> Bytes per track, 6144
> Disk rotation time, 40 ms
> Seek time S to move N cylinders
> > For $N = 0$ to 8, $S = 6 + 2N$
> > For $N = 9$ to 24, $S = 16 + 3N/4$
> > For $N > 24$, $S = 26 + N/3$

Discuss the total search time for finding a specific piece of data, considering the heads to be positioned in the center cylinder when the search order is given. A cylinder is the set of all tracks which can be read from or written on for a given position of the head-positioning mechanism.

73. Design four locations in a diode read-only memory by adding diodes to the diagram of Question 71. The signal C_1 is to be a 1 in locations 01101 and 01111 and is a 0 otherwise; the signal C_2 is to be a 1 in locations 01110 and 01111 and is a 0 otherwise; the signal C_3 is to be a 1 in 01101, 01110, and 10000 and is a 0 otherwise. A given decoder output line is high when selected.

74. Compare a conventional disk memory with the floppy disk memory with regard to operating characteristics and costs.

75. A three-dimensional (coincident-current four-wire random-access) core memory has 4096 words of 16 bits each. The cost of the access circuitry is given by the formula $P = C_1 D_I + C_1 D_{XY} + C_2 D_A$, where D_I is the number of INHIBIT line drivers, D_{XY} is the number of X and Y line drivers, and D_A is the number of sense amplifiers. If $C_1 = \$0.0005$ and $C_2 = \$0.0006$, what is the value of P, the total cost? Explain your answer.

76. If you combine the INHIBIT and SENSE lines in a core memory into a single digit or bit line how does this affect the core wiring?

77. From the figures given, can you estimate how many hours a floppy disk can be reliably operated with the head loaded (that is, reading or writing).

78. The hierarchy of memory systems, disk packs, tape drivers, cassettes, and floppies all have different characteristics. However, in general it can be said that the units with lower entry prices (that is, lower unit prices) have higher bit prices. Can you explain this and give examples using figures in the text?

79. *Hard sectoring* refers to a disk system where sectors are determined by some mechanical technique. For instance, sectors on some floppy disks are determined by punching 32 holes around the disk, and a sector begins when a hole occurs in the disk. *Soft sectoring* refers to a technique where headers are written at the beginning of sectors, and so the reading circuitry locates sectors and information without the use of mechanical devices. Can you give the advantages and disadvantages of these systems?

80. The very high-speed high-bit-packing-density tape drives use an encoding technique where bits are encoded in groups. For instance, in one commonly used technique 4 input bits are encoded into 5 bits. Since the 16 possible combinations of the 4 bits which can occur in the data are mapped into only 16 of the 32 possible combinations of 5 bits, these 16 5-bit patterns can be carefully selected so that the recording characteristics are optimal. When the 5 bits are read back, they are changed back into the original input data. This plus the use of powerful error-correcting codes allow a packing density of 6250 bits/in. (and sometimes more). Give some advantages and disadvantages of a complicated encoding and decoding scheme such as this one with regard to tape drive mechanisms and user characteristics.

81. Formulate a memory system for a microprocessor which has 16K of PROM, 32K of RAM, and an initial backup memory of 0.5 Mbyte with a possibility of expanding to 5 Mbytes. Choose the memory devices you think would be reasonable and justify your choice economically and from a performance viewpoint.

82. Bubble and CCD memories are generally considered to be competitive with floppy disk and small disk packs and are useful in replacing these devices because they require mechanical motion for reading and writing and are thus less reliable than straight integrated circuitry or nonmoving media. Can you give applications where bubble or CCD memories might be particularly useful?

8
INPUT-OUTPUT DEVICES AND INTERFACING

The input-output devices provide the means of communication between the computer and the outer world. To solve problems or process data, the data and instructions must be inserted into the machine, and the machine must deliver the results of its calculations. It has been difficult to produce input and output devices that can keep up with the computer speeds, and there is a constant demand for faster and faster printers, card readers, etc.

In its simplest form, the sequence of events in the processing of information is as follows: First a program is written, describing the sequence of calculations that the computer is to perform. Simultaneously the data are collected and readied for insertion into the machine. Then after the computer has read the program plus the data and stored this information, it is started at the first instruction in the program. After the series of calculations which the computer must perform is completed, the results are printed. The program contains orders that direct the computer to print the final results for the user. (Partial results are sometimes also printed, often for purposes of program checking.)

It is first necessary to insert the program and the data via the input devices. The input devices to an ordinary calculator consist of keys. Numerical data are introduced via these push buttons. When an operation button is pushed, the machine performs the necessary operations.

An input medium proposed by Babbage and still used today is the punched card. A rectangular card is perforated by a number of holes, and the position of each hole determines its meaning. The programs and data are punched into cards. The cards are then placed in a card reader connected to the machine, and the command to read is given. The card reader senses the holes in the cards and transmits this information to the computer, which then stores it. In this manner, either program or data can be read into the machine.

There is now more and more emphasis on online real-time systems. In these systems data, or programs, are inserted directly into the computer, generally by means of a keyboard. (In some systems, particularly real-time control systems, data are introduced using A-to-D converters.) The computer must read these data in "real time" and must not wait too long, or important data (a keystroke, for example) may be missed. The servicing of keyboards is facilitated by techniques where the computer is "interrupted" by the input device; this is discussed in this chapter and in Chap. 10.

When the program has been read and the necessary operations completed, it is necessary for the computer to print out the data so that they may be used. A great variety of output devices are now available. Business applications generally require that the results be printed in tabular form, or perhaps on a series of checks, as in a payroll accounting operation. Scientific results are more likely to consist of numerical data which must be clearly printed with little chance of error (such accuracy is also of prime importance in computers used to calculate payroll checks) or graphs showing the results of the calculations. For any of these applications one type of output device may be more desirable than another. However, the great majority of applications require that the outputs from the machine be printed on a piece of paper. The principal output devices are therefore printers, ranging from electromechanical typewriters, which print one letter or digit at a time, to high-speed printers capable of printing a hundred or more characters at a time. Several of these, as well as several other output devices, such as oscilloscopes, will be described.

In every computer system there is always the problem of connecting the input-output devices to the calculating sections and memory. Many arrangements have been used for this, and some of the newer ideas are discussed in the sections on computer organization. Buses are often used for interfacing, and some material on buses in general as well as on two specific buses is presented. Also specific interfaces for a keyboard and printer are described.

This chapter is organized as follows. First, input devices are discussed, followed by output devices. Then A-to-D converters are described. Keyboard input devices and terminals are covered next. Also a design for an interface between a keyboard and a microprocessor is presented, followed by a microprocessor-to-printer interface. Finally, computer organization, interrupt systems, and then buses are discussed, in that order.

8 • 1 PERFORATED TAPE

Perforated (punched) tape was one of the first popular mediums for storing the programs and data to be read into a digital machine. When the first large computers were designed, telegraph systems had been using perforated paper tapes for some time, and as a result, devices for punching and reading paper tapes had already been fairly well developed. The tape used is of many types and sizes. A medium-thickness paper tape has been used a great deal, and oiled tapes and plastic tapes are also used. The widths of the tapes used have varied from $\frac{1}{2}$ to 3

Channels

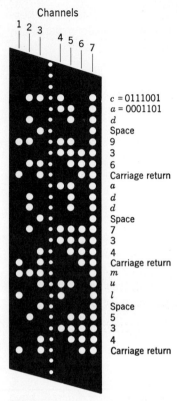

$c = 0111001$
$a = 0001101$
d
Space
9
3
6
Carriage return
a
d
d
Space
7
3
4
Carriage return
m
u
l
Space
5
3
4
Carriage return

FIG. 8 • 1 Punched paper tape.

in. Information is punched into the tape a line at a time. Figure 8·1 illustrates a section of a perforated tape. Multiple channels are used (just as on magnetic tape, a channel runs lengthwise along the tape), and a single character or code is punched as a pattern of bits in each lateral line.

The preparation of these paper input tapes is sometimes referred to as *keyboarding,* and a typical paper-tape-punching machine is shown in Fig. 1·7. In this step the operator of a tape-punching machine is presented with a copy of a program or input data. The operator then punches, by means of the tape-punching machine (tape punch), a number of holes into the tape. The holes represent, in coded form, the input information to the machine. The tape-punching device used may be one of a number of types. The more popular devices resemble a typewriter, and the keyboards of these tape punches contain conventional symbols, similar to those on an ordinary typewriter. The keyboards of many tape-punch machines are identical with the keyboards of manual typewriters used in businesses, and sometimes electric typewriters are converted to tape-punching machines by attaching a punching device which is actuated by the typewriter mechanism.

When a key on the tape-punch keyboard is depressed, the binary-coded symbol for the character selected is punched into the tape, and the tape then advances to

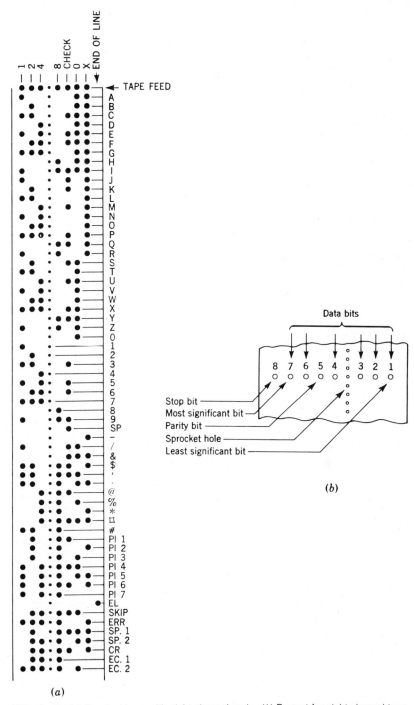

FIG. 8 • 2 (*a*) Punched tape with eight-channel code. (*b*) Format for eight-channel tape.

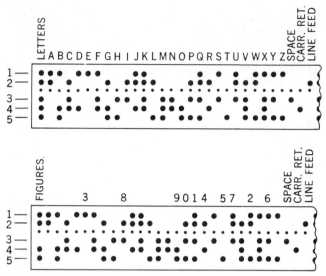

FIG. 8 • 3 Paper tape with five-channel code.

the next line. In most cases, the tape-punch device also prints on a separate piece of paper, in the same manner as a typewriter, the character that was punched, as well as printing the characters along the rows of the tape. There is then a type-written copy of the program, which may be checked for errors in addition to the paper tape punched with the coded symbols. This printed copy of the program is referred to as the *hard copy*. Many of the tape-punch machines are able to read a perforated tape and to type printed copy from this tape. A punched section of tape may be placed in the tape reader attached to the tape-punch machine, and a typed copy of the information which was punched in the tape may be made.

Figures 8·2 and 8·3 show two codes which have been frequently used for paper tape systems. In the eight-channel code shown in Fig. 8·2 eight channels run lengthwise along the tape. A hole in a given one of these channels represents a 1, and the absence of a hole a 0. The 1, 2, 4, and 8 channels are used to represent the digits for 0 to 9. Thus 0s or no holes in positions EL, X, and 0 indicate that the encoded character is a digit with the value given by the sum of the positions 8, 4, 2, 1, in which there are holes. The check position is used for an *odd-parity check*. Its value is determined so that the number of 1s or holes in each character is odd. The 0 and X positions are used in conjunction with the 8, 4, 2, 1 positions to encode alphabetic and special characters.

The code has two special features. A punch in the end-of-line position indicates the end of a record on the tape. When there are punches in all seven of the positions, this indicates a blank character called *tape feed*, and the tape reader skips over such positions. This is useful for correcting mistakes in keyboarding or in editing tapes, because an erroneous character can be eliminated by simply punching in the nonpunched positions.

The five-channel code shown in Fig. 8·3, called the *Baudot* code, was very popular in communications systems. Since five positions are insufficient to encode the requisite number of characters, a special trick is used utilizing two special characters to change the meaning of those characters which follow. Thus a *letters* character followed by a line with a punch in the 1 position indicates an E, while a *figures* character followed by a punch in the 1 position indicates a 3. Whenever a letters character occurs, all following characters are in the letters code until a figures character occurs, and similarly, a figures character means that all following characters are in that mode until a letters character occurs.

8 • 2 TAPE READERS

The function of the paper tape reader is to sense the coded information punched in the tape and deliver this information to the computer. Most of the tape readers used in teletype and office equipment are electromechanical devices. In many of these devices mechanical "sensing pins" are used to determine the symbol punched into each line of the tape. In a system of this type there will be a sensing pin for each information channel, plus a means of moving the tape and positioning it for reading. The tape is not moved continuously, but only a single line at a time, stopped while the coding is sensed, and then moved to the next line. The motion of the sensing pins operates a switch, the contacts of which are opened or closed, depending on whether or not there is a hole in the tape. Another type of reader uses a "star wheel" to sense the absence or presence of holes in the tape, as shown in Fig. 8·4. A complete reader mechanism is shown in Fig. 8·5, indicating the relative complexity of these devices.

When the input is to a digital machine, the motion of the tape through the reader will generally be controlled by the computer. Each time the tape is to be advanced

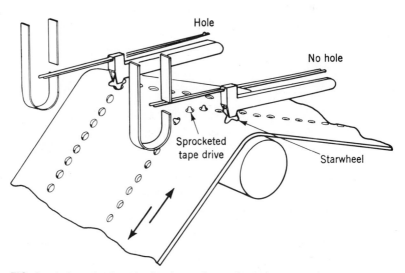

FIG. 8 • 4 Star-wheel mechanism for reading perforated tape.

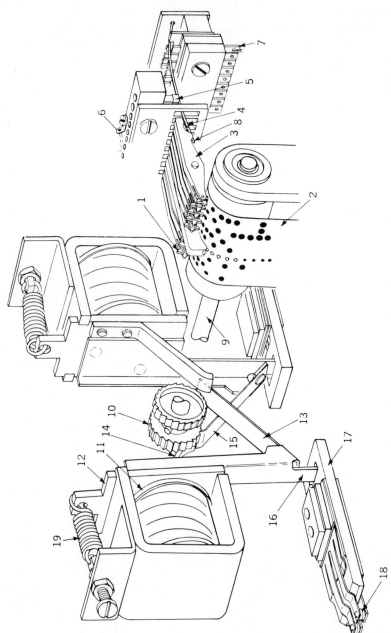

FIG. 8 • 5 Mechanism of electromechanical tape reader. Tape reading and stepping mechanization of Ohr-Tronics-Model 119 tape reader. When star wheel (1) senses hole in paper tape (2), arm (3) is rocked counterclockwise under the urging of contact wires (4) which limit on lower surface of contact screw (5). Electrical circuit is thus completed from common lug (6) to lug (7). Longer wire (8) urges arm (3) against mechanical limit (not shown) to reduce bounce. Drive shaft (9) extends to rear through panel (not shown) and carries bidirectional ratchet (10). Energization of coil (11) attracts armature (12) and engages pawl blade (13) under next tooth. Pawl depressor (14) disengages opposing pawl blade (15). Tip (16) of armature moves card (17) to open interrupter switch contacts (18). Upon deenergization of coil (11), pawl blade (13) steps shaft (9) under urging of spring (19). Interrupter switch recloses near end of armature return. Pulsing of other coil (20) steps tape in reverse direction.

and a new character read, the computer will supply the reader with a pulse which will cause it to advance the tape to the next character. To read characters as fast as possible, a line will generally be read at the same time as the advancing pulse is transmitted. Since there will be a delay due to inertia before the tape is actually moved, the reading of the state of the sensing relays will occur during this delay period. In this case, when a stop character is sensed, the reader will proceed to the next character before actually stopping.

To speed up the reading process, high-speed tape readers use photoelectric cells or photodiodes to read the characters punched into the tape. In this case, a light-sensitive cell is placed under each channel of the tape, including the tape feed hole, or sprocket channel. A light source is placed above the tape, so that the light-sensitive element beneath the hole in the tape will be energized and will produce a signal indicating the presence of the hole. The signals from the light-sensitive elements are then amplified and supplied to the computer as input information.

The tape feed hole will be used in this case to determine when the outputs of the light-sensitive elements are to be sensed. The tape in a reader of this type is generally friction-driven and moved continuously until a stop character is sensed. Extremely fast starting and braking of the tape are very desirable features, and most readers are capable of stopping the tape on any given character.

The operation speeds attainable with various tape readers are generally expressed as the number of characters per second which can be read. Mechanical sensing readers have been designed to operate at speeds as high as 250 characters per second, although speeds of from 10 to 60 characters per second are more common. Present-day photoelectric readers operate at speeds of up to 1000 characters per second.

8 • 3 PUNCHED CARDS

A very widely used input medium is the punched card. While there are a number of sizes of punched cards, the most frequently used card at present is a 12-row 80-column card $3\frac{1}{4}$ in. wide and $7\frac{3}{4}$ in. long (see Fig. 8·6). The thickness of the cards used varies, although at one time most of the cards were 0.0067 in. thick. There is now a tendency to make the card somewhat thinner.

Just as with tape, there are numerous ways in which punched cards may be coded. The most frequently used code is the Hollerith code, an alphanumeric code in which a single character is punched in each column of the card. The basic code is illustrated in Fig. 8·6. As an example, the symbol A is coded by means of a punch in the top row and in the 1 row of the card, and the symbol 8 by a punch in the 8 row of the card. There are other types of cards with different hole positions, just as there are many ways of preparing the cards to be read into the computer. The most common technique is very similar to that for preparing punched tape, in that a card-punch machine with a keyboard like that of a typewriter is used, as was shown in Fig. 1·8. The card punch usually also makes a hard copy of the program as it is punched into the cards. Generally, the card punch also prints the

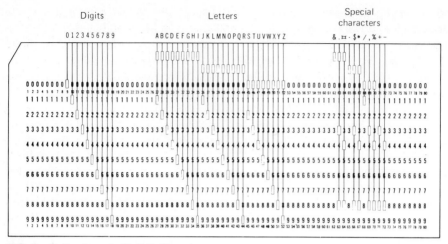

FIG. 8 • 6 Punch card with Hollerith code.

characters punched into a card on the face of the card itself. In this way, a card may be identified without examining the punches. Each character is usually printed at the top of the card directly above the column in which the character is punched.

The card punch machine contains a hopper in which the blank cards are stacked. The operator of the card punch then causes a card to enter the punching area, and the program's list of instructions or the data to be processed are then punched into the card. The card punch punches the card laterally, a column at a time, starting at the left. If a key of the card punch is depressed, the code for the character is punched into a column of the card, and the card is then moved so that the next column on the right is under the punch.

Generally, when a program is punched into cards, only one instruction and its associated address or addresses are punched into each card. Then if an error is made in programming, the erroneous instruction may be changed by throwing the incorrect card away and replacing it with a correct card.

Figure 8·7 shows an IBM/029 card punch, a widely-used device. The IBM 129, a more expensive card punch, has a small memory capable of holding all the data that can be punched into two 80-column records and six program cards. The key-punch operator keyboards the data into the small memory and can backspace and change characters until the data keyboarded are correct. After all the data are in the small memory, an *enter data* key is depressed, and the card is then punched from the characters in the memory. Facilities for controlling the format of the card are included by means of IC logic.

The preparation of cards containing data for business systems is a highly developed area. Large businesses such as insurance companies, credit agencies, and banks must gather and process almost incredible amounts of data. Most of this data processing is now done by electronic computers, but even prior to the advent of the digital computer, punched cards were extensively used, and a considerable technology for handling punched cards was developed.

In any case, the data—information, checking account, income tax rates, or whatever—must first be entered into a punched card by a keypunch operator. To give some idea of the magnitude of this operation, there are over 500,000 keypunching consoles (as shown in Figs. 1·8 and 8·7) in operation at this time.

The preparation of punched cards and some of the operations which can be performed on cards are facilitated by several special devices, as shown in Fig. 8·8. For example, a *verifier* is used to check the keypunching of cards. After a card has been punched, since the alphanumeric characters are printed above the keypunches, some checking can be done by comparing the cards with the input data. A common procedure, however, is to place the deck of cards punched by an operator in the hopper of a verifier and to have a second operator keyboard the same data. The verifier does not punch new cards, but compares what the second operator punches with the deck prepared by the first operator, and if a discrepancy occurs, it notifies the second operator so that the card can be compared against the data.

Other machines shown in Fig. 8·8 are the *sorter,* which is used to sort cards into different sequences according to certain keys in the data, and the *collator* which compares or merges several decks into a single deck according to some instructions wired into the machine.

There are several other card processing machines, such as *summary punches,* which combine data from a number of cards into a few cards, and *reproducers,*

FIG. 8 • 7 IBM 029 card punch.

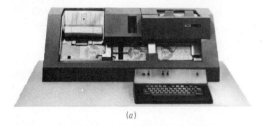

(a)

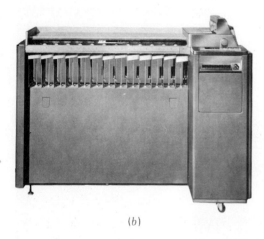

(b)

(c)

FIG. 8 • 8 Punched-card-processing machines.
(a) Verifier. (b) Sorter. (c) Collator.

which duplicate decks. The operations performed by these machines, however, can be performed by electronic machines which, in most cases, cost less to operate and perform the necessary operations faster and more efficiently.

The card punch remains the most frequently used device for entering data into a computer, and the relatively inexpensive card ($\frac{1}{10}$ cent per card, perhaps) is still in widespread use.

8 • 4 CARD READERS

Most card readers are electromechanical devices which read the information punched into a card, converting the presence or absence of a hole into an electric signal representing a binary 0 or 1. The punched cards are placed into a hopper, and when the command to read is given, a lever pushes a card from the bottom of the stack. Generally, the card is then moved lengthwise over a row of 80 *read brushes.* These brushes read the information punched along the bottom row of the card. If a hole is punched in a particular row, a brush makes electrical contact through the hole in the card, providing a signal which may be used by the computer. The next row up is then read, and this process continues until all rows have been read, after which the next card is moved into position on the brushes.

Faster card readers are constructed using photoelectric cells under the 12 punch positions along a column and an illuminating source above the card. As each column on the card is passed over the 12 photoelectric cells, whether or not a given position is punched is determined by the presence or absence of light on the corresponding cell. Card readers operate at speeds of from 12 to 1000 cards per minute.

Notice that when cards are read a row at a time, programs must "decipher" the characters punched in the card. Often "binary" decks are used, particularly for programs, where the computer words are distributed along rows rather than in columns and data may be loaded directly as the rows are read.

8 • 5 ALPHANUMERIC CODES

Data and programs are almost invariably entered in alphanumeric form, and the internal operation of computers, particularly those which involve business records, makes extensive use of alphanumeric codes. Because of the diversity of applications and the many viewpoints on codes and code construction, many different alphanumeric codes have been suggested and used. Computers such as IBM's 1401, 1410, and others, as well as Honeywell's 200 series, have (basically) 6-bit characters with corresponding codes. We have already examined several codes for magnetic tape and 5- and 8-bit codes for paper tape, as well as the 12-bit Hollerith code. Each of these has been widely used. The 6-bit, so-called *BCD code,* used in the IBM 1401, 1410, 7010, 7040, and 7044 and the Honeywell 200 series, as well as many other machines, is shown in Fig. 8·9. This code uses the conventional 8, 4, 2, 1 positions for decimal digits, except that 0 is represented by

CHARACTER Report	Program	C	B	A	8	4	2	1
b		C						
.			B	A	8		2	1
□	)	C	B	A	8	4		
[			B	A	8	4		1
<			B	A	8	4	2	
‡		C	B	A	8	4	2	1
&	+	C	B	A				
$		C	B		8		2	1
*			B		8	4		
]		C	B		8	4		1
;		C	B		8	4	2	
Δ			B		8	4	2	1
−			B					
/		C		A				1
'		C		A	8		2	1
%	(			A	8	4		
m		C		A	8	4		1
\		C		A	8	4	2	
⧺				A	8	4	2	1
b				A				
#	=				8		2	1
@		C			8	4		
:					8	4		1
>					8	4	2	
√		C			8	4	2	1
?		C	B	A	8		2	
A			B	A				1
B			B	A			2	
C		C	B	A			2	1
D			B	A		4		
E		C	B	A		4		1
F		C	B	A		4	2	
G			B	A		4	2	1
H			B	A	8			
I		C	B	A	8			1
!			B		8		2	
J		C	B					1
K		C	B				2	
L			B				2	1
M		C	B			4		
N			B			4		1
O			B			4	2	
P		C	B			4	2	1
Q		C	B		8			
R			B		8			1
‡				A	8		2	
S		C		A			2	
T				A			2	1
U		C		A		4		
V				A		4		1
W				A		4	2	
X		C		A		4	2	1
Y		C		A	8			
Z				A	8			1
Ø		C			8		2	
1								1
2							2	
3		C					2	1
4						4		
5		C				4		1
6		C				4	2	
7						4	2	1
8					8			
9		C			8			1

Low→ ... High→ (COLLATING SEQUENCE)

FIG. 8 • 9 BCD code.

Symbol	Name
‡	Group Mark
‡	Record Mark
⧺	Segment Mark
m	Word Separator
@	At Sign
#	Number Sign
&	Ampersand
+	Plus
*	Asterisk
%	Percent
/	Slash
\	Backslash
□	Lozenge
b	Blank
ƀ	Substitute Blank
(	Left Parenthesis
)	Right Parenthesis
[	Left Bracket
]	Right Bracket
√	Tape Mark
<	Less than
>	Greater than
=	Equal to
;	Semicolon
:	Colon
.	Period or Point
'	Prime or Apostrophe
−	Minus or Hyphen (Dash)
Δ	Delta

a 1 in the 8 and 2 positions. The "report" and "program" are for two different types of systems. Thus for some systems, a 1 in the 8, 2, 1 position yields a # and in other systems a =.

There has been an attempt to standardize on an alphanumeric code which will be agreeable to both manufacturers and users, and the American National Standards Institute has published an American Standard Code for Information Interchange (ASCII code). This code is now widely used in the newer machines, and a number of the major manufacturers are using the code in order that their equipment may be compatible with that of other manufacturers. This code is shown in Fig. 8·10. Notice that the decimal digits are represented by the normal 8, 4, 2, 1 code preceded by the three binary digits 011, so that decimal 1 becomes 0110001, decimal 2 is 0110010, decimal 7 is 0110111, etc. To expand on the code, the letter A is 1000001, B is 1000010, etc. There are various codes such as "end of message," "who are you," "skip," "carriage return," etc., which are very useful in communications systems and in editing data processes in computers. As a result, this is probably the most frequently used code for intercomputer communications systems.

Finally, many IBM computers, and a number of other computer systems, use the extended BCD interchange code (EBCDIC) shown in Fig. 8·11.

8 • 6 DATA PREPARATION

One form of buffering consists in first recording the program to be read in on magnetic tape and then reading from the tape into the machine. A number of devices are available which will read punched tape or cards and transfer the information punched into them onto magnetic tape. This process takes place outside the central computer. Since the magnetic tape may be read much faster than punched cards or paper tape, the time required to read in information will be reduced.

The process of converting from punched cards to magnetic tape has been bypassed by a number of input devices. Several companies now offer a line of keyboard-to-magnetic-tape devices. Figure 8·12 shows a console of this type. In its simplest form, when the operator depresses a key, the character selected appears on a display and is also entered on the tape. When the magnetic tape has been filled or all records have been transcribed, the tape can be read by the computer to be used.

More advanced systems permit the keyboard operator to type a number of characters; these characters are displayed on a console where they may be read and checked and also are stored in a small memory. The characters can be edited (changed), and when the operator is satisfied that the data are correct, a record button is depressed, the data are entered on magnetic tape, and new data may be keyboarded.

Even more complex systems use a number of keyboards, all connected to a small memory and processor equipped with a magnetic tape recorder. This permits extensive editing; checking by the small processor-computer comparing inputs; error detection, particularly format checking of many types; and many sort-

	000	001	010	011	100	101	110	111
0000	$NULL$	DC_0 ①	♭	0	@	P		
0001	SOM	DC_1	!	1	A	Q		
0010	EOA	DC_2	''	2	B	R		
0011	EOM	DC_3	#	3	C	S		
0100	EOT	DC_4 (Stop)	$	4	D	T		
0101	WRU	ERR	%	5	E	U		
0110	RU	$SYNC$	&	6	F	V		
0111	$BELL$	LEM	'	7	G	W	Unassigned	
1000	FE_0	S_0	(	8	H	X		
1001	HT/SK	S_1	)	9	I	Y		
1010	LF	S_2	✳	:	J	Z		
1011	V_{TAB}	S_3	+	;	K	[		
1100	FF	S_4	(Comma) ,	<	L	\		ACK
1101	CR	S_5	−	=	M	]		②
1110	SO	S_6	★	>	N	↑		ESC
1111	SI	S_7	/	?	O	←		DEL

Example: | 100 | 0001 | = A

b_7 --------------- b_1

The abbreviations used in the figure mean:

$NULL$	Null Idle	CR	Carrige return
SOM	Start of message	SO	Shift out
EOA	End of address	SI	Shift in
EOM	End of message	DC_0	Device control ① Reserved for data Link escape
EOT	End of transmission	DC_1-DC_3	Device control
WRU	"Who are you ?"	ERR	Error
RU	"Are you . . . ?"	$SYNC$	Synchronous idle
$BELL$	Audible signal	LEM	Logical end of media
FE	Format effector	S_0-S_7	Separator (information)
HT	Horizontal tabulation		Word separator (blank, normally non-printing)
SK	Skip (punched card)	ACK	Acknowledge
LF	Line feed	②	Unassigned control
V/TAB	Vertical tabulation	ESC	Escape
FF	Form feed	DEL	Delete Idle

FIG. 8 • 10 American Standard Code for Information Interchange.

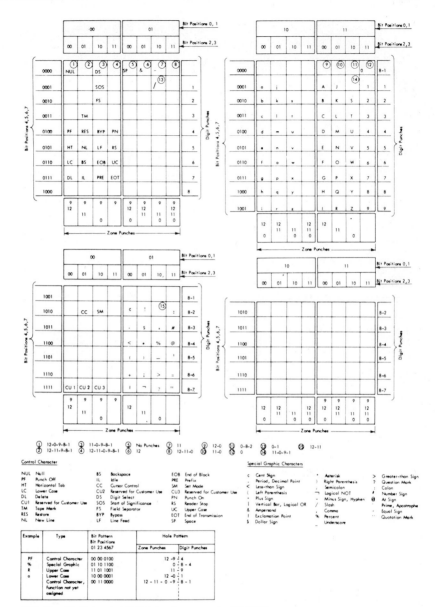

FIG. 8 • 11 Extended BCD interchange code (EBCDIC).

ing and collating operations. The magnetic tape prepared by a system of this sort has had many preprocessing operations already performed, and the data have been subjected to considerable checking and preprocessing. For companies with extensive data processing requirements, such systems are very popular.

Some idea of the importance of input-data preparation can be seen from the fact that 30 to 50 percent of installation cost is often for data preparation. This is

FIG. 8 • 12 Keyboard-to-magnetic-tape console. (Courtesy Honeywell Corp.)

especially true, of course, for the larger business systems, but even strictly scientific installations of modest size find that as much as 20 percent of their system cost can go into preparation of data for computer input.

Numerous special devices and media are used to reduce the cost to business for data entry. For example, agencies such as American Express use a combination of punched cards with printed characters for their billing. The customer returns the card with his or her check, and the card is then directly given to the computer.

Some companies use identification cards with special coding for their employees. In these systems, the employees insert their cards in a special reader which reads the identification and also enters the time from a clock. These data are recorded on tape or a disk, and later the computer reads all the check in and check out data recorded during the day. Still other systems use a time clock to simply punch check in and check out time in a card which has the employee's identification already punched into it. These cards are then collected at the end of each week. Each of these schemes reduces the expense of operators punching the data. Gas pumps which read customers' credit cards and record the amounts of sales, cash registers which carry sales data to a central tape file in a large department store, and many similar techniques are all being used to alleviate the problems and expense of preparing data for computer entry.

8 • 7 CHARACTER RECOGNITION

Techniques for data entry extend in many directions. The reading of handwritten or typewritten characters from conventional paper appears to offer an ideal input system for many applications. The systems currently in use are primarily as follows.

1. *Magnetic ink character reading (MICR)* The recording of characters using an ink with special magnetic properties and with characters having special forms was originally used in quantity by banks. The American Banking Association settled on a type font, and several of their characters are shown in Fig. 8·13. A *magnetic character reader* "reads" these characters by examining their shapes using a 7 × 10 matrix and determines, from the response of the segments of the matrix to the magnetic ink, which of the characters has passed under the reader's head. This information is thus transmitted to the system. The determination of the character which is read is greatly facilitated by the careful design of the characters and the use of the magnetic ink.

2. *Optical character reading (OCR)* This area takes one of two forms. In the first, a special type font (or fonts) is used to print on conventional paper using conventional ink. The printed characters are examined by passing them under a strong light and a lens system which differentiates light (no ink) from inked areas and a logical system which attempts to determine which of the possible characters in the system is being examined. The systems in actual use depend heavily on the fact that only a limited number of characters in a particular font are used, but such systems are still quite useful. The standard type font agreed on by the ANSI optical character committee is shown in Fig. 8·14.

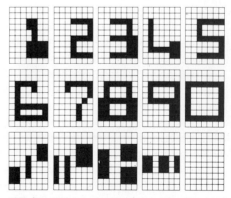

FIG. 8 • 13 A magnetic reader character set.

FIG. 8 • 14 Type font for optical character recognition.

The ideal system would, of course, be able to adapt to many different type fonts. Some systems, particularly one developed by the Post Office, even read handwritten characters. The limited success of these systems is due to the many shapes that a given character can have. Consider the ways you can write an *a* and the similarity between a handwritten *a* and an *o* or a *b* and an *f*. These problems are increased by the optical reader's difficulty with the porosity of paper, ink smearing at the edges of lines, etc. Much work continues in this area, and much more is needed, but the advantages of such systems continue to cause this work to be sponsored and performed.

8 • 8 OUTPUT EQUIPMENT

Although many types of output equipment are now in use in the computer industry, the most popular form of output from a computer is undoubtedly the printed word on paper. Other types of display devices in common use include lights and oscilloscopes, and some computers are even equipped with loudspeakers. (Programs that will play music through the loudspeakers are common, and attempts are often made to compose music using a computer.)

Lights are generally used to indicate the states of the storage devices of the principal registers of the machine (the accumulator, selected in-out registers, etc.). These lights are sometimes used as output devices for simple programs where the answers may then be read visually. However, such lights are generally used as troubleshooting aids, often to troubleshoot the operation of the machine. Figure 8·15 shows the lights on the console of an IBM 370. Each light is connected to a flip-flop output (via a light driver). The outputs of most of the important flip-flops are monitored using the lights. Various sets of flip-flops can be selected using the rotary switches at the bottom of panel, and the toggle switches and push buttons can be used to enter data into flip-flop registers and to sequence operations of the computer (as well as to start and stop the computer). The lights are some-

FIG. 8 • 15 Console of a large computer system. (Courtesy of IBM Corp.)

times used to troubleshoot programs for small machines. If, for instance, a program works itself into an endless loop, the machine can be stopped and the location† of the faulty instruction sequence in the program can be read from the lights on the console of the machine.

8 • 9 PRINTERS

Generally, the most convenient and useful method by which the computer can deliver information is by means of printed characters. For the sake of convenience, the printer should have the ability to print alphabetical characters, decimal digits, and also common punctuation marks.

---

†The program counter contains the address of the instruction being performed. Details of this section of the control element will be presented in the next chapter.

The process in printing is the inverse of the encoding procedure in which a key corresponding to an alphanumeric character is depressed, causing a coded binary character to be punched into a tape or card. In this case, coded groups of binary bits are delivered to the printer, which decodes them and then prints the correct characters. The basic binary-code groups may contain 5 through 9 bits, depending on the coding for alphanumeric characters that the printer provides.

The information delivered to a printer operated online will be in the form of electronic signals directly from the computer. If the printer is operated offline, the reading and decoding of data stored on punched tape, punched cards, or magnetic tape may be a part of the printing operation. Since the electronic circuitry of a computer is able to operate at speeds much higher than those of mechanical printing devices, it is desirable that a printer operated online be capable of printing at a very high speed. Even if the printer is operated offline, speed is highly desirable, since the volume of material to be printed may be quite large.

Most of the original printers were converted electric typewriters, and this type of printer is still popular. If the code used contains 8 bits per character and the printer is operated online, the computer will deliver 8 bits to the printer, which will decode them and energize a solenoid which will actuate the correct key of the typewriter. The codes used generally include coded characters such as those discussed earlier, including codes for spacing between words, carriage return, and other operations necessary to typing. The speed of such typewriter type printers is relatively low, perhaps from 10 to 50 characters per second.

Faster printers are constructed in which the raised characters are distributed around a ''print wheel'' which revolves constantly (see Fig. 8·16). In this case the

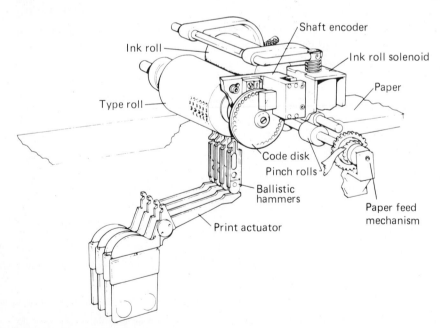

FIG. 8 • 16 Line-at-a-time drum printer.

print wheel does not contain moving parts, but consists of a motor-driven drum with a number of bands equal to the number of characters printed per line. A set of all the characters which are used is distributed around each band. The print wheel is revolved continuously. When the selected character is in position, the print hammer strikes the ribbon against the paper, and thus against the raised character on the print wheel located behind the paper. A printer of this type requires a decoder and a memory for each character position along the line, and also a character-timing encoder for each position, which determines when the selected character is in position. Printers of this type can print up to 1250 lines per minute with 160 characters per line.

Figure 8·16 shows the major mechanical components of the Dian series N printer, which has a type roll or wheel with 17 circular tracks of printed characters and is therefore a 17-character-per-line printer. This type roll is continually revolving, and when a selected character passes by the position it is to be printed in, the print actuator pushes the chosen ballistic hammer against the paper, forcing the paper against the selected character on the type roll. The type roll is continually inked by an ink roll, and no ribbon is used. In this system a code disk and shaft encoder are used to tell which character is currently in a position to be printed. Shaft encoders will be discussed in a later section. Figure 8·16 shows that the paper is moved horizontally after each line is printed.

Figure 8·17 shows the IBM 1403 printer, in which the paper is moved vertically in front of a chain of raised characters of type. This chain is continually moving in the horizontal direction so that each of the 48 different characters continually passes by each of the 100 printer's positions in each line. (Other numbers of characters per line are available.) When a character to be printed passes the position where it is to be printed, the armature hammer magnet is energized, striking a hammer and forcing the paper against the type at that position. An inked ribbon is placed between paper and type so that the character is impressed on the paper in ink.

Figure 1·12 shows a printer for the ledger cards used in accounting systems. This printer is typical of those used in many business-oriented systems. The ledger cards are dropped in the feed slot in the center just above the keyboard. The printer is often used in conjunction with a disk file, automatically posting data from the files in the ledger cards.

In order to provide inexpensive printers for mini- and microcomputers, lower speed "character-at-a-time" printers are often used. Consider the type roll or drum type printer shown in Fig. 8·16. The drum can be reduced to a small cylinder with only one set of characters. This single rotating cylinder can be moved across the paper along with a single hammer, making an inexpensive character-at-a-time printer [see Fig. 8·18(c)]. Sometimes the characters are distributed around a "daisy wheel," as shown in Fig. 8·18(b). A hammer then drives the selected character against the paper when it is in position.

The use of pins which are driven against the paper to print characters also provides low-cost printing. Sometimes the pins are arranged in a complete dot matrix, but sometimes only a single column of seven pins is provided, and this is moved across the paper requiring five positions per character [see Fig. 8·18(a)]. Char-

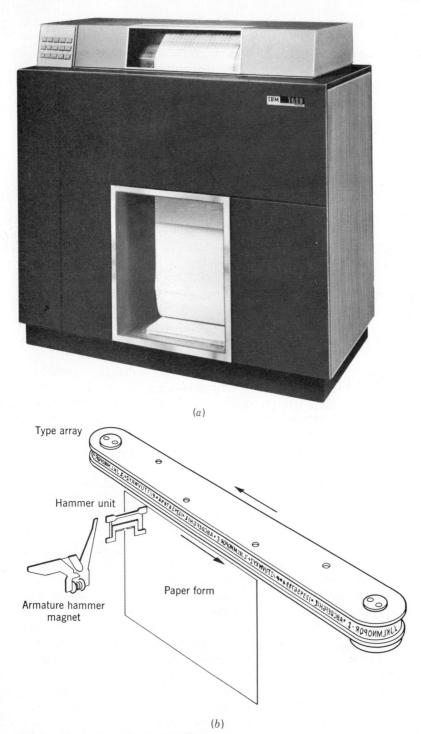

(a)

(b)

FIG. 8 • 17   (a) High-speed line printer. (b) Type chain for the printer.

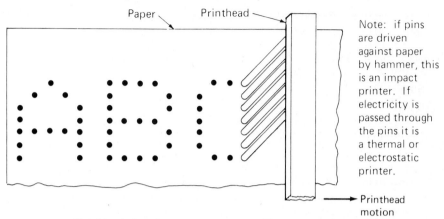

Note: if pins are driven against paper by hammer, this is an impact printer. If electricity is passed through the pins it is a thermal or electrostatic printer.

Matrix printhead moves across page. The correct pins are forced against the paper in the proper sequence to form characters as shown. A 5 × 7 matrix is illustrated here; 7 × 9 is also used.

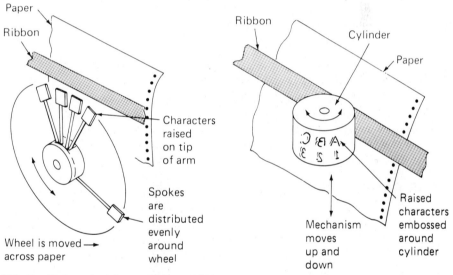

FIG. 8 • 18 Impact printer mechanisms. (*a*) Matrix printhead. (*b*) Daisy wheel printer. (*c*) Cylinder printer.

acter generator logic must sequence the striking of the pins as the print head is moved across the paper.

Microprocessors are often used to control the timing and other functions required in printers. Character buffering can also be provided by microprocessors.

Many inexpensive printers use thermal or electrostatic papers (see below). The printers are inexpensive, but since the paper is not "ordinary" paper its costs are generally greater than for regular paper. However, because of the volume of production, the special papers required are quite reasonable in price.

The natural limitations of speed in electromechanical devices and cost considerations have led to the development of printers called *nonimpact printers.* These printers are primarily in the following categories.

1. *Electromagnetic* Using magnetic recording techniques, a magnetic image of what is to be printed can be written on a drum surface. This surface is then passed through magnetic powder which adheres to the charged areas. The powder is then pressed onto the paper. Speeds of up to 250 characters per second are obtained in such systems.

2. *Electrostatic* For electrostatic printers the paper is coated with a nonconducting dielectric material which holds charges when voltages are applied using writing "nibs" (heads). These heads write dots on the paper as it passes, as shown in Fig. 8·18(*a*). Then the paper passes through a toner which contains material with colored particles carrying an opposite charge to that written by the nibs, and, as a result, particles adhere to the magnetized areas, forming printed characters.

3. *Thermal printers* An electric pulse can be converted to heat on selected sections of a printing head or on wires or nibs. When this heat is applied to heat-sensitive paper, a character is printed, as shown in Fig. 8·18(*a*).

4. *Ink jets* Some printers direct a high-velocity stream of ink toward the paper. This stream is deflected, generally by passing the stream through an electrostatic field such as that used to deflect beams in oscilloscopes. In some systems the ink stream is broken into droplets by an ultrasonic transducer.

The wide variety of printers available and the continuing development of new ideas make the printer field a fascinating area. The cost-performance trade-offs often make selection of a satisfactory printer difficult.

8 • 10 CATHODE-RAY-TUBE OUTPUT DEVICES

Cathode-ray tubes are often used as output devices.The cathode-ray tube is a very fast output device, but does not deliver permanent copy. Therefore such tubes are sometimes used in conjunction with a camera, so that the display on the tube face can be photographed and thereby recorded permanently.

The cathode-ray tubes used in computer displays are the same type as those used in oscilloscopes and television sets, and entire television sets are sometimes used. For these display systems, the displayed points are made by positioning and turning on an electron beam in the tube, just as in television sets or oscilloscopes. The displays are sometimes called *CRT, oscilloscope,* or *scope*, displays. Figure 8·19 shows a cathode-ray-tube display with a keyboard.

Several systems have been used to encode data for transmission to oscilloscope displays. The simplest system consists in simply sending, in binary, the *x, y* coordinates of each point to be displayed. The scope electronics then, using D-to-A converters, convert the binary numbers to voltages, which are used to position the beam.

The above system is simple, but inefficient, in that many points must be transmitted, which takes considerable computer time. Also, if the console or display is

FIG. 8 • 19 Cathode-ray-tube display. (Courtesy of Computek, Inc.)

at a remote location and telephone lines are used, as is often the case, the transmission of the points can be expensive. (In most of these oscilloscope displays the points must be illuminated at least 30, and generally more, times each second. There are, however, *storage scopes,* which hold displayed points and do not require "refreshing." These must be erased, however, before rewriting, and are relatively expensive at present.)

Because of the problem of repeatedly sending data points to the display device, generally the display-device electronics include a small memory which stores the data from the computer and then generates the display from the last data transmitted, changing or updating the display only when the computer so directs.

More complicated but also more efficient techniques for data transmission to oscilloscope displays are generally used in inexpensive displays. If only alphanumeric data are to be displayed, the ASCII code is mostly used for the transmission of each character to be displayed. The display electronics then converts from each 8-bit coded ASCII character to the sequence of points (or lines) required to display the character.† A small memory capable of storing the alphanumeric characters for the entire oscilloscope face is then included in the display, so that the computer must only send characters once, and the scope electronics refreshes the oscilloscope from the memory. Lines for graphic displays such as that shown in Fig. 8·19 are often drawn using a technique by which the computer sends the difference in coordinates between the electronic beam's present location and line segment to be drawn.

8 • 11 OTHER OUTPUT DEVICES

Two other output devices are high-speed card- or tape-punching machines. The information from the computer is punched into either paper cards or tapes, so that the output medium resembles the input medium. If the output is to be used, the punched cards or tapes must then be interpreted and printed; the perforated tapes and cards may therefore be thought of as an intermediate step.

Magnetic tape is also used as an intermediate storage medium for offline output equipment operation. Since magnetic tape may be recorded much faster than either cards or tape may be punched, the computer's output operation is speeded up. In this case, a magnetic tape reader and translator is required to sense and interpret the binary-coded information recorded, and finally a printer is needed to print the information.

One advantage of these devices lies in the speed-to-cost ratio attainable. A high-speed magnetic tape recorder will be much faster than a high-speed printer, and the final printing may then take place on a slower printer, which interprets the recorded tape and prints the final result. This is another case of offline operation, in which the final operation is performed at the speed of a faster output device, and the computer is therefore not slowed down as much as it would be if a low-speed printer were used. Even the magnetic tape recorder devices, however, are inherently much slower than the computer's internal circuitry.

8 • 12 ERROR-DETECTING AND ERROR-CORRECTING CODES

The process of transferring information into the machine and from the machine is especially liable to error. Although card and tape readers are constructed with the

---

†Oscilloscopes are quite often scanned a line at a time, as in television sets, and so some conversion electronics is required. IC packages to generate characters for CRT displays are made by several companies.

highest possible regard for correct operation, and the occurrence of errors is relatively infrequent, errors still do occur, and it is desirable to detect them whenever possible. To facilitate the detection or correction of errors, two classes of codes have been invented, (1) error-detecting codes and (2) error-correcting codes. The first type of code enables the equipment to detect the errors which occur in the coded groups of bits, and the second type of code corrects the errors automatically.

Both error-detecting and error-correcting codes require that redundant information be sent along with the actual information being processed. The most commonly used type of error-detecting code is undoubtedly the parity-check code. Parity-check codes are commonly used for card and tape readers and for the storage of information on magnetic tape.

Parity checking

The parity check is based on the use of an additional bit, known as a *parity bit,* or *parity-check bit,* in each code group. The parity bit associated with each code group in an *even-parity-bit* checking system has such a value that the total number of 1s in each code group plus the parity bit is always even. (An *odd-parity-bit* checking code has a parity bit such that the sum of the 1s in the code group plus the parity bit is always an odd number.) The example shown in Table 8·1, which uses an 8, 4, 2, 1 code, has an even parity bit which makes the sum of the 1s in each code group an even number.

If a single error occurs in transmitting a code group—for instance, if 0010, 1 is erroneously changed to 0011, 1—the fact that there is an odd number of 1s in the code group plus the parity bit will indicate that an error has occurred. If the values of the parity bits had been selected so that the total sum of the 1s in each code group plus the parity bit were odd instead of even, each parity bit would be the complement of the parity bit shown above, and the code would be an odd-parity-bit checking code.

The technique of parity checking is doubtless the most popular method of

TABLE 8 • 1

DECIMAL	BCD	EVEN PARITY BIT
0	0000	0
1	0001	1
2	0010	1
3	0011	0
4	0100	1
5	0101	0
6	0110	0
7	0111	1
8	1000	1
9	1001	0

detecting errors in stored code groups, especially for storage devices such as magnetic tape, paper tape, and even for core-and-drum systems.

If the parity-bit system is used, an additional bit must be sent with each code group. As another example, if the 7-bit ASCII code is used, each line of a punched tape will have an additional hole position which will contain a 1 or a 0. When the tape is read by the tape reader, each code group will be examined, together with the parity bit, and in an odd-parity-bit system, an alarm will be generated if the number of 1s in a group is even.

This type of checking will detect all odd numbers of errors. Suppose that an even-parity check is used as in Table 8·1 and the code group to be sent is 0010; the parity bit in this case will be a 1. If the code group is erroneously read as 0110, the number of 1s in the code group plus the parity bit will be odd, and the error will be detected. If, however, a double error is made and 0010 is changed to 0111, the error will not be detected since the number of 1s will again be even. A parity-bit check will only detect odd numbers of errors. (The above rule will also apply when the parity bit is in error. For instance, consider an even-parity-bit checking system where 0010 is to be sent and the parity bit is 1. If the parity bit is changed to 0, the number of 1s in the code group plus the parity bit will be odd, and the error will be detected.)

There are many types of error-correcting codes, and some very clever and sophisticated coding schemes are used in both communications and computer systems. For instance, magnetic tape is a memory device that is especially prone to errors. Most of these errors are due to either imperfections in the tape or foreign matter which gets between reading heads and the tape, causing the tape to be physically pushed away from the reading head and the recorded signal to be incorrectly interpreted. Such errors are said to be caused by "dropout." These errors tend to lie in a single track, and there are several clever codes which have been used to detect and correct such errors.†

8 · 13 KEYBOARDS

An important data entry device is the keyboard. In some cases keyboards are used to enter data into punched cards or punched tape, for example, and in other cases keyboards enter data directly into a computer. The most familiar keyboards are probably those on teletype consoles (see Fig. 1·7) or on other terminals which include either a printer or an oscilloscope (CRT) display. Sometimes small keyboards with only a few keys (similar to touch-tone telephone dialing keyboards) are used in industrial applications. These small assemblies of keys are generally called *keypads*.

When an operator depresses a key, electrical signals must be generated which will enable the computer (or other device) to determine which key was depressed.

---

†A study of error-correcting and error-detecting codes in some depth may be found in W. W. Peterson, *Error Correcting Codes*, and in G. Birkhoff and T. C. Bartee, *Modern Applied Algebra*.

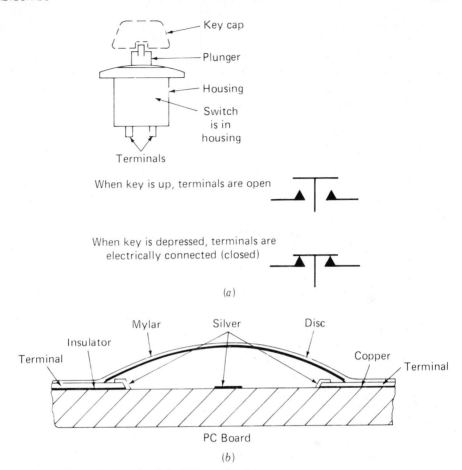

FIG. 8 • 20 (a) Keyboard switch. (b) Keypad switch.

This is called *encoding*. The encoding process is dependent on the mechanism used to make the individual keys in the keyboard.

The most direct method for encoding is based on the use of keyboard switches, which contain a switch similar to the push-button switch used in many electrical devices. Figure 8·20 shows such a switch. When the plunger is depressed, the contacts of the switch in the housing are closed, and the two terminals at the output are effectively connected together. When the plunger is up (key not depressed), the switch in the housing is open, and the terminals are not electrically connected.

In order to encode a keyboard by means of electromechanical switches, diodes (or transistors) can be used. Figure 8·21 shows the layout for encoding three keys into the ASCII code illustrated in Fig. 8·10. An odd-parity-check bit has been added at the right end to make an 8-bit character. Each of the vertical wires on the drawing is normally held at 0 V by the resistor connected to ground. This means that these wires are normally at a 0 logic level. When a key is depressed, however, the switch in its housing is closed, and this connects the wire to +5 V, a logic level of

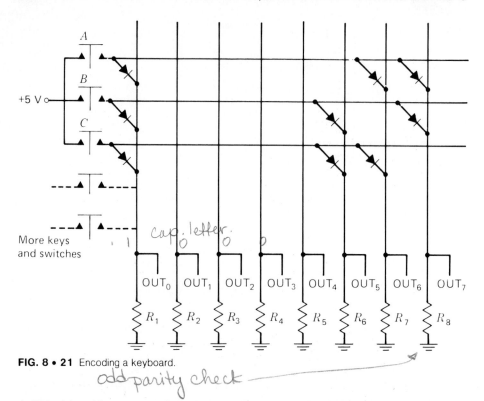

FIG. 8 • 21 Encoding a keyboard.

odd parity check

1. This 1 level is connected to an output line only when a diode exists at the junction of the horizontal and vertical wires in the encoding matrix. Thus if the A key is depressed, the value 10000011 will appear on the output lines, for example, because a diode connects the horizontal wire to the A switch to the leftmost and two rightmost vertical wires. This is the ASCII code for A with a parity bit on the right end.

It is a good idea to load the values on the output lines into a flip-flop register before the computer reads the outputs. This has the advantage of storing the values until the computer can read them, particularly if the keyboard operator raises the key before the computer can respond. Figure 8·22 shows a scheme where a flip-flop is used on each output, and a strobe is generated to load the flip-flops, using a delayed inverted pulse signal generated whenever any one of the output lines from the encoder goes high. The delay is inserted to compensate for signal "skewing" where signals arrive at the output lines at different times because of differing delays through the diodes or through the wires in the system. The delay must be adequate to accommodate the largest delays that may occur. Also, the length of the strobe pulse should be short compared to the least time a key might be depressed. (A delay of 1 ms and a pulse of 1 ms would be reasonable.)

We are here assuming that the switch contacts do not bounce, as is the case with some switches. If the contacts do bounce, the output signals must be "smoothed," and there are various circuits available. When reed relays are used

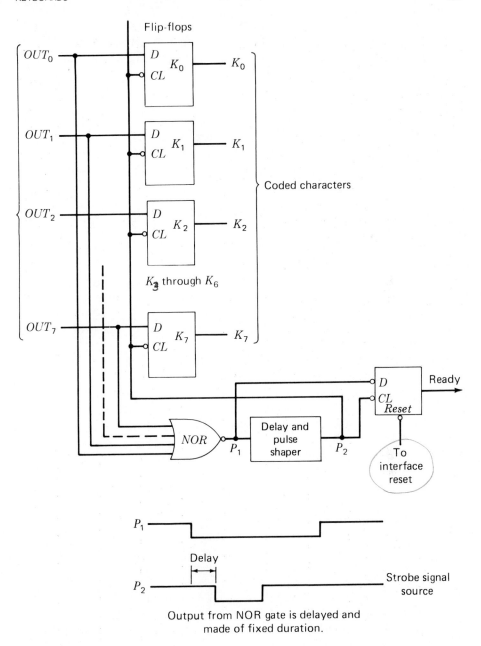

FIG. 8 • 22 Keyboard buffer for interface.

(and these are quite popular), there is little need for this. (The switches are often momentary contact switches which generate a closure of relatively fixed duration.)

In Fig. 8·22 the strobe signal is also used to load a flip-flop, called *ready,* which will be used in an interface design in following sections. Notice that the encoding scheme shown here requires that there be a 1 in the code for each character (so that the strobe pulse will be generated).

The keyboard market is very large, and as a result many kinds of keyboards are now made as manufacturers compete to see who can produce a lower cost, more reliable, more durable keyboard. The basic division of keyboards is (1) the electromechanical keyboard, which includes the switch type just explained and the teletypewriter keyboard (which will be discussed in a later section), and (2) the solid-state keyboard.

There are several basic mechanisms for solid-state keyboards. Capacitor types are low-cost keys, often used in keypads and other cost-conscious keyboards. Hall-effect keyboards are more expensive, but have long life and good key feel, as do the ferrite-core and photooptic keyboards. Each of the basic mechanisms has different problems with regard to encoding the keyprinters' output into a coded form usable by a computer. (The references include discussions of the encoding techniques.)

The encoding technique is often based on a two-dimensional array of keys and wires instead of the "linear" array shown in Fig. 8·21 for reasons of economy. (This is discussed in the Questions.) IC packages for encoding are made by several manufacturers and can include "smoothing" or "debouncing" for contacts and sometimes "key rollover" protection, which protects against two keys being depressed at the same time. (This can happen when an adjacent key is inadvertently depressed or when the next character is struck before a key is released.)

Section 8·21 and the following sections discuss interfacing keyboards and printers in some detail. The overall physical setup for interfacing a mini- or microcomputer will be discussed here.

Figure 8·23 shows the general layout for a typical minicomputer. Printed-circuit boards contain the logic for the CPU, which consists of the arithmetic-logic unit (ALU), the control section, and the high-speed (IC) memory. The high-speed memory is connected to the bus, and the control section controls the high-speed memory using signals it places on the bus. (The bus in Fig. 8·23 consists of a set of wires running under the printed-circuit boards. Printed-circuit-board connectors are mounted to these wires, and the printed-circuit boards are plugged into these connectors, thus making connection to the logic on the boards.)

In order to interface input-output devices with the CPU section boards, *interface boards* are connected to the bus. The boards contain the logic gates and flip-flops to read from and write onto the bus and to control and interface the input-output devices.

In a typical system, in order to interface a keyboard, a keyboard interface board is connected to the bus, using a connector, and a cable then runs from this board to the keyboard. Similar boards are used to interface a tape unit, a disk drive, etc.

Notice that communication between input-output devices and the CPU utilizes the interface boards and the bus. In microprocessors single chips are sometimes

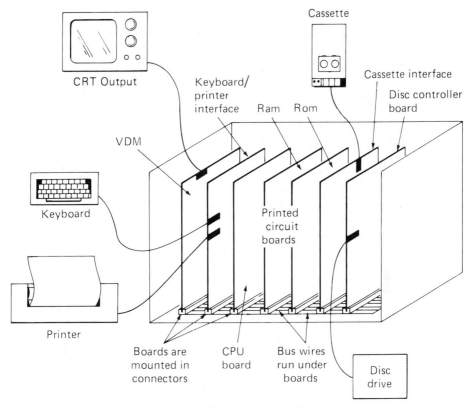

FIG. 8 • 23 Minicomputer interface layout for input-output devices.

used to replace entire boards. (Large-scale integration sometimes makes this possible.) In this case the bus may be on a board in the form of printed-circuit-board wires. In very small systems the CPU and one, two, or more interface chips may be placed on a single board, with the bus on the same board. Cables then connect from this board to the input-output devices.

8 • 14 TERMINALS

When a keyboard is combined with an oscilloscope display or a printing mechanism and suitable electronics is provided so that characters struck on the keyboard can be entered into a computer and the computer can also have the ability to print on the oscilloscope or printing mechanism, the keyboard printer or keyboard oscilloscope is called a *terminal.*

Terminals are widely used to input programs and data to computers. The teletype console shown in Fig. 1·7 was an early terminal which continues to be widely used as a computer terminal. Teletypewriters provide a means for entering alphanumeric characters into a computer. They enable the computer to print responses to a user, and a tape punch and tape reader are generally included so that programs or data can be permanently recorded on paper tape, and so that such programs or data can be read into the computer when desired.

Figure 8·19 shows a terminal consisting of an oscilloscope and a keyboard. Characters struck on the keyboard will appear on the oscilloscope face, and output signals are also provided which are suitable for computer usage. A computer can also print on the oscilloscope, providing for two-way communications. The primary disadvantage is that no "hard copy" or record of what is typed by the terminal operator or printed by the computer remains when the terminal is turned off. Some means of recording selected data are now being introduced in the more expensive systems; these include cameras to photograph the scope face, small printers, and tape cassettes to record data.

Terminals range from minimal systems containing almost no memory to "smart" terminals where a small microcomputer or minicomputer is included. Smart terminals provide many facilities for the user, sometimes including text editing, input formatting, and checking for typing errors made by operators.

Oscilloscope-keyboard combinations almost always contain a small memory in which the present contents of the screen are stored so that the screen can be refreshed by the terminal electronics instead of requiring the computer to continually rewrite data on the screen. In this case, a small memory and some electronics are required, and microprocessors are often used to control the terminal's operation. By enlarging the memory capabilities and program in the microprocessor, a smart terminal can be formed without too much additional cost.

Terminals generally generate output data in serial form and accept input data in serial form. The formats, coding, and electrical properties of the signals generated vary from terminal to terminal, but there are now strong movements to standardize the interface designs.

Teletypewriters and most of the terminals in present-day use generate an 11-bit output in serial form whenever a key on the keyboard is depressed. This same stream is generally used to activate the printer mechanism. However, on teletypewriters and many other devices it is possible to disengage the keyboard from the printing mechanism. In this case, when a key is struck, the code for the character is read by the computer, which must then write this character back into the terminal's printer. This is called *echoing* the character.

Figure 8·24 shows how the present standard character transmission operates. The output line from the keyboard is normally in the high† state, but when a key is depressed, a *start bit* at a low level is generated. This start bit is followed by the proper 8-bit ASCII-coded character, and then two *stop bits* at the high level are inserted before another character can be started (that is, before another start bit can be generated). The start bit, each stop bit, and the bits in the ASCII-coded character are each of the same time duration. For most current systems this is $\frac{1}{110}$ s for each, and since 11 such time periods or *bit times* are required, a single character requires $\frac{11}{110}$ or $\frac{1}{10}$ s.

---

†Communications people call this a *mark* value and the other level a *space*.

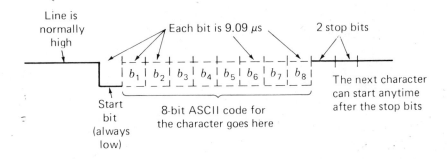

Line is normally high

Each bit is 9.09 μs

2 stop bits

b_1 b_2 b_3 b_4 b_5 b_6 b_7 b_8

The next character can start anytime after the stop bits

Start bit (always low)

8-bit ASCII code for the character goes here

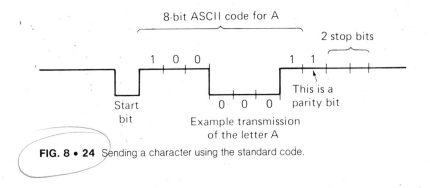

8-bit ASCII code for A

2 stop bits

1 0 0

1 1

Start bit

0 0 0

This is a parity bit

Example transmission of the letter A

FIG. 8 • 24 Sending a character using the standard code.

There are several other speeds which are currently used, including 300, 600, and 1200 bits/s. In each case, the same character construction with start and stop bits is used, and so character rates of $\frac{11}{300}$, $\frac{11}{600}$, and $\frac{11}{1200}$ s are attainable.

The character transmission system described here is called *asynchronous transmission,* for the character and start bits can occur at any time. *Synchronous transmission* systems have the bits clocked into fixed time periods, and characters are also placed in fixed positions in the bit stream. These systems require both bit timing and character timing to be established between the transmitting device and receiver and are therefore more complicated. Character transmission can be at higher rates, however. (Since start and stop bits are not required, the character beginnings and ends are established by the system.) As a result, high-speed data communication is generally in synchronous form.

The output levels and interface requirements for the coded characters are examined in the Questions and several standards are noted.

When terminals are operated at some distance from a computer, the telephone system is often used to provide the necessary communications link. If a terminal is to be operated into the telephone system, special devices are needed to translate the logic levels produced by the terminal into signals acceptable for telephone-line transmission.

Figure 8·25 shows a terminal with an *acoustic coupler.* The handset from the telephone is placed in this acoustic coupler. When a key is depressed, the bits comprising the character are converted into audio tones using a small loudspeaker

Telephone
receiver

When telephone receiver is placed in
acoustic coupler, terminal can
communicate (both ways) with a computer

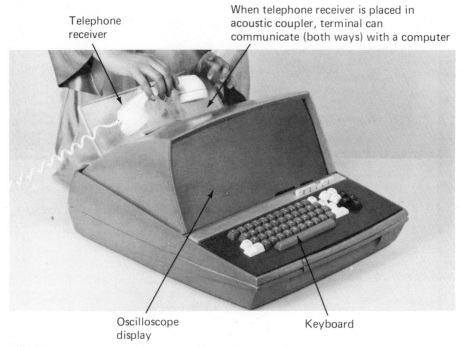

Oscilloscope
display

Keyboard

FIG. 8 • 25 Oscilloscope display and terminal with acoustic coupler.

in the coupler. Generally one frequency is used for a 0 and another for a 1. These
signals enter the transmitter part of the handset and are transmitted into the telephone line. At the computer end these frequencies are received by a microphone
connected to a handset and then converted back to 1s and 0s in electrical form,
so that the electrical logic levels output at the receiver are replicas of the signals
originally generated at the terminal.

The computer "talks" back to the terminal using an acoustic coupler at its end
of the telephone line, and the acoustic coupler at the terminal converts the computer's signals back to logic levels which are used to drive the display.

When output signals in logic-level form are converted directly into electrical signals suitable for telephone transmission using electronic circuitry (instead of
acoustic coupling), the converting device is called a *modem*. A modem can generally convert logic levels into electrical signals for the telephone system and can
convert received signals from the telephone line back into logic levels. This means,
of course, that the connections to the telephone line are made electrically and
directly into the telephone line, and a headset is not used. It also means that the
electrical signals must comply with telephone system regulations. The design of
modems which will (1) send bits through telephone lines at high speeds, (2) make
few errors in transmission, and (3) comply with telephone company regulations is
a highly developed and interesting scientific area.

Like acoustic couplers, modems generally use a (different) frequency for a 1
and a 0. As an example, the Bell 103 modem sends data through telephone lines

at either 110 or 300 bits/s. The modem at one end of a telephone line uses 1070 Hz (for 1s) and 1270 Hz (for 0s) to send, while the modem at the other end uses 2025 Hz (for 1s) and 2225 Hz (for 0s). The reason for the two sets of frequencies is that transmission can be in either direction, and while one modem is transmitting a character, the other will still be sending its high (mark) frequency. (A single telephone line handles communications in both directions. Both ends can "talk" at the same time. You can, for instance, interrupt someone who is talking.)

8 • 15 INPUT-OUTPUT DEVICES FOR SYSTEMS WITH ANALOG COMPONENTS

Not all the inputs to digital machines consist of alphanumeric data which may be directly punched into cards or tape. Computers used in data-reduction systems or in real-time control systems often have inputs which are expressed as the physical position of some device, or as electric signals which are analog in nature. An example of a physical position which might be used as an input to a digital computer is a real-time control system in which a computer is used automatically to point a telescope. If, by some system of gears, the position of the telescope along an axis is related to the position of a shaft, the position of this shaft must be read into the computer. This will involve the translation of the shaft position into a binary-coded number which may be read by the machine.

Changing a physical displacement or an analog electrical signal to a digital representation is called *analog-to-digital* (A-to-D) *conversion*. Two major types of A-to-D converters are: (1) those that convert mechanical displacements into a digital representation and (2) those that convert an electric analog signal into digital-coded signals.

Suppose that an analog device has as its output a voltage which is to be used by a digital machine. Let us assume that the voltage varies within the limits of 0 to 63 V dc. We can then represent the voltage values with a set of 6-bit numbers ranging from 000000 to 111111, and for each value the input voltage may assume, assign a corresponding value of the 6-bit number. If the input voltage is 20 V, the corresponding digital value will be 010100. If, however, the input signal is at 20.249 V dc, the 6-bit binary number will not completely describe the input voltage, but will only approximate the input value. The process of approximating the input value is called *quantizing*. The number of bits in the binary number which represents the analog signal is the *precision* of the coder, and the amount of error which exists between the digital output values and the input analog values is a measure of the *accuracy* of the coder.

Not only are the inputs to the computer sometimes in analog form, but it is often desirable for the outputs of the computer to be expressed in analog form. An example of this lies in the use of a cathode-ray tube as an output device. If the output from the computer is to be displayed as a position on an oscilloscope tube, then the binary-coded output signals from the computer must be converted to voltages or currents, which may be used to position the electron beam, and which are proportional to the magnitude of the output binary number represented by the computer's output signals. This involves D-to-A conversion, and a device that performs this conversion is called a *D-to-A converter.* When digital computers are used in control systems, it is generally necessary to convert the digital outputs from the machine to analog-type signals, which are then used to control the physical system.

8 • 16 ANALOG-TO-DIGITAL CONVERTERS—SHAFT ENCODERS

The first type of coder which will be briefly described below converts a shaft position to a binary-coded digital number. A number of different types of devices will perform this conversion. The type described is representative of the devices now in use, and it should be realized that more complicated coders may yield additional accuracy. Also, it is generally possible to convert a physical position into an electric analog-type signal and then convert this signal to a digital system. For instance, a shaft may be mechanically coupled to a potentiometer with a dc voltage across the ends of the resistance. If the output signal is then taken from the potentiometer tap, the dc output signal will be related to the shaft position. In general, though, more direct and accurate coders can be constructed by eliminating the intermediate step of converting a physical position to an analog electric signal.

Figure $8 \cdot 26(a)$ illustrates a coded-segment disk which is coupled to the shaft. A set of brushes is then attached so that a single brush is positioned in the center of each concentric band of the disk. Each band is constructed of several segments made of either conducting material (the darkened areas) or some insulating material (the unshaded areas). A signal is connected to the conductor, and if a given brush makes contact with a segment of conducting material, a 1 signal will result, but if the brush is over the insulating material, the output from the brush will be a

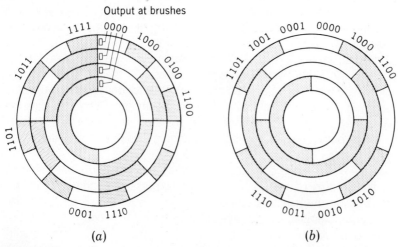

Output at brushes

(a)   (b)

FIG. 8 • 26 Shaft-position encoder disks. (*a*) Binary-coded disks. (*b*) Unit distance code disk.

0. The four output lines of the coder shown will represent a 4-bit binary number. There are 16 distinct intervals around the coder disk, each corresponding to a different shaft-position interval, and each causing the coder to have a different binary number output.

A photoelectric coder may be constructed using a coder disk with bands divided into transparent segments (the shaded areas) and opaque segments (the unshaded areas). A light source is put on one side of the disk, and a set of four photoelectric cells on the other side, arranged so that one cell is behind each band of the coder disk. If a transparent segment is between the light source and a light-sensitive cell, a 1 output will result; and if an opaque area is in front of the photo-toelectric cell, there will be a 0 output. By increasing the number of bands around the disk, more precision may be added to the coder. The photoelectric type of coder has greater resolution than the brush type, and even greater resolution may be obtained by using gears and several disks. The state of the art is about 18 bits or 2^{18} positions per shaft revolution, but most commercial coders have 14 bits or fewer.

There is one basic difficulty with the coder illustrated: if the disk is in a position where the output number is changing from 011 to 100, or in any position where several bits are changing value, the output signal may become ambiguous. Since the brushes are of finite width, they will overlap the change in segments; and no matter how carefully it is made, the coder will have erroneous outputs in several positions. If this occurs when 011 is changing to 100, several errors are possible; the value may be read as 111 or 000, either of which is a value with considerable errors. To circumvent this difficulty, a number of schemes have been used, generally involving two sets of brushes, with one set displaced slightly from the other.

TABLE 8 • 2

DECIMAL	GRAY CODE $a_3 a_2 a_1 a_0$
0	0000
1	0001
2	0011
3	0010
4	0110
5	0111
6	0101
7	0100
8	1100
9	1101
10	1111
11	1110
12	1010
13	1011
14	1001
15	1000

By logically choosing from the outputs available, the "ambiguity" may be eliminated at a slight cost in accuracy.

Another scheme for avoiding ambiguity involves the use of a *Gray,* or *unit-distance,* code to form the coder disk [Fig. 8·26(b)]. In this code, 2 bits never change value in successive coded binary numbers. Using a Gray-coded disk, a 6 may be read for a 7 or a 4 for a 5, but larger errors will not be made. Table 8·2 shows a listing of a 4-bit Gray code.

If the inputs to the machine are from a coder using a Gray code, the code groups must be converted to conventional binary or BCD before use. This conversion may be simply performed, either sequentially or combinationally. The Questions treat the Gray code and conversion in more detail.

8 • 17 DIGITAL-TO-ANALOG CONVERTERS

The problem of converting a digital output to an analog voltage can be resolved by several techniques, the most straightforward of which involves the use of a resistor network. A basic type of resistor-network D-to-A converter is illustrated in Fig. 8·27 which shows a resistor net with four inputs. Each input is converted to a switch which connects a resistor to either 0 V or V_+ When a switch is in the position connecting to V_+, the binary bit represents a 1, and when the switch connects to 0 V, the input bit is a binary 0. The output at E_0 will then be a dc potential in the range of 0 to V_+ and will be proportional to the value of the binary number represented by the inputs.

For instance, if the input number is 0111, the output voltage at E_0 will be $\frac{7}{15}V_+$; if the input is 1111, the output E_0 will be V_+; and if the input is 0001, the output E_0 will be at $\frac{1}{15}V_+$ V dc. To achieve accuracy, the resistors should all be of the precision type. Also, the input voltages representing the binary values must be accurately established, and since the load on the inputs will vary with the value of the input numbers, the input should be capable of delivering the necessary current without a shift in the voltage level. More precision can be added by increasing the number of inputs and adding a resistor for each input.

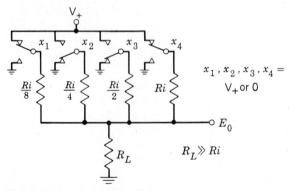

Fig. 8 • 27 D-to-A resistor network.

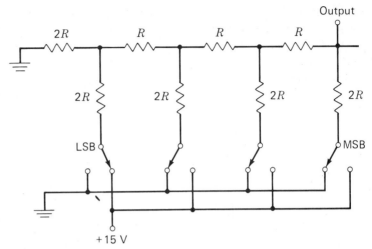

Fig. 8 • 28 $R/2R$ resistor D-to-A converter.

Fig. 8·28 shows another type of resistor network which can be used for D-to-A conversion. The advantage of this network is that only two different values of resistors are used. The inputs are shown as switches, but semiconductor switches or *level-setting amplifiers* are often used. The disadvantage of this converter is that two resistors are required per input.

There are many other types of D-to-A converters, and the design and construction of these devices represent a growing area in the computing field. Many decoders are very specialized, especially those used in control systems. For instance, automatic milling machines are often controlled by a digital computer which must have its digital outputs converted into the mechanical motion of the milling machinery. The use of digital computers in large industries, such as the petroleum industry, paper manufacturing, and camera manufacturing, also involves the utilization of many different types of A-to-D and D-to-A converters.

8 • 18 ELECTRONIC HIGH-SPEED ANALOG-TO-DIGITAL CONVERTERS

There are several techniques used for converting an electric analog signal to digital form. What is basically needed is a device that converts a dc signal to a binary number proportional to the dc level of the signal. Suppose that we have a dc voltage with an amplitude which is in the interval of 0 to $+15$ V. If we wish to convert this to a 4-digit binary number, we will want the number 0000 for 0 to 0.5 V, 0001 for 0.5 to 1.5 V, 0010 for 1.5 to 2.5 V, 1111 for 14.5 V or greater, etc. (Notice that the binary number corresponds to the center of the interval.)

A simple A-to-D converter can be made using a resistor network such as that shown in Fig. 8·27, a START-STOP flip-flop, a 4-flip-flop binary counter, four level converters, and a high-gain dc amplifier.

The basic configuration is shown in Fig. 8·29. The flip-flops X_1, X_2, X_3, and X_4

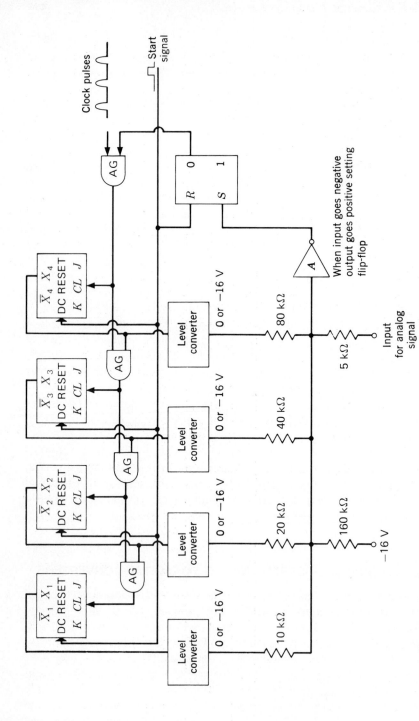

Fig. 8 • 29 A-to-D converter.

are arranged in a binary counter which counts 0000, 0001, 0010, . . . , 1111. Each flip-flop drives a level converter such that, when the flip-flop's output is a 1, the output of the level converter is − 16 V dc; and when the flip-flop's output is a 0, the level-converter output is 0 V dc.

The high-gain dc amplifier is designed so that when the input to the amplifier is positive, the output of the amplifier represents a 0; but when the input is negative, the output goes to a 1, thus setting the START-STOP flip-flop (and stopping the counter).

Now let us assume that a START signal is given, clearing the flip-flop counter to 0000. All the outputs from the level converters will be at 0 V (unless the input analog signal is more than +0.5 V dc, the 160-kΩ resistor to − 16 V will cause the input to the amplifier to be negative†), the amplifier's output will be a 0, and the clock pulse will pass the first AND gate.

If the input signal is 0 to 0.5 V, the amplifier will have a level output of a 1 and will set the START-STOP flip-flop to a 1 so that no clock pulses will pass.

If the input signal is greater than +0.5 V, the counter will count, thereby causing the negative current into the junction of the 10-, 20-, 40-, and 80-kΩ resistors to increase until the input to the amplifier goes negative, thus stopping the counter.

If, for instance, the analog signal input is at +9 V dc, the input to the amplifier will be positive until the counter goes from 1000 to 1001; and when the counter is a 1001, the clock pulses will be stopped, giving the right value for the signal.

There are several other techniques which are used for A-to-D conversion. The most used is the *successive approximation method* because of its combination of high resolution and high speed. The successive approximation converter operates with a fixed conversion time per bit, independent of the value of the analog input. The method can be explained using Fig. 8·28, since it is a variation on this technique.

Consider that we have control of the individual flip-flops in Fig. 8·29 instead of their being in a counter. At the start of the conversion, the D-to-A converter's most significant bit is set to the 1 state, and the converter's output, which is now one-half the full-scale analog input range, is compared with the input. If it is smaller than the input, the most significant bit is left on and the next bit is tried. If the most significant bit output from the level converter to the most significant bit is larger than the input, the most significant bit is turned off when the next least significant bit is turned on.

This process of comparison is continued on each bit in turn down to and including the least significant bit, after which the output register contains the complete output digital number.

Speeds as high as 100 ns/bit can be achieved by this method. Successive approximation converters can also be quite accurate, but the accuracy depends on the stability of the reference voltage, the level converters, the D-to-A resistor network, and the comparator.

---

†The 160-kΩ and − 16-V combination contributes as much current to the junction of resistors at the amplifiers' input as a +0.5-V signal at the input for the analog signal.

The fastest converters are parallel-type converters. These converters can be made to have rates of up to 25 million conversions per second for 4 bits. Sometimes these converters are called *simultaneous* or *flash converters*.

The parallel method of making an *n*-bit converter employs an input quantizer comprised of $2^n - 1$ comparators biased 1 least significant bit apart by resistors connected to a reference voltage; refer to Fig. 8·30, which shows a 2-bit A-to-D converter that therefore has $2^2 - 1$, or 3, comparators. Each comparator looks at the signal input and compares it with its particular reference voltage. If the signal input is less, the comparator turns on; if the signal input is greater, the comparator turns off. As a result, for a given signal input voltage to the comparators, all comparators with inputs from the resistor network which are below the signal input level turn on, while all comparators above it are off. Therefore the quantization process is accomplished in the switching time of a single comparator. The comparator outputs, however, are not in binary code and must, therefore, go through a logic network to be converted to binary, as shown in the figure.

The parallel method has the advantage of the fastest speed but is limited to a relatively few bits, usually 4, due to the large number of comparators required. In order to convert a large number of bits it is necessary to employ a mixed strategy whereby a parallel conversion stage is followed by a fast D-to-A converter, the output of which is subtracted from the input voltage. The difference is then amplified and converted, using another parallel stage. This results in a speed compromise but higher resolution.

A-to-D converters are commonly made to give either 7 to 20 binary digits or 3 to 7 decimal digits for outputs. The fastest converter now on the market makes

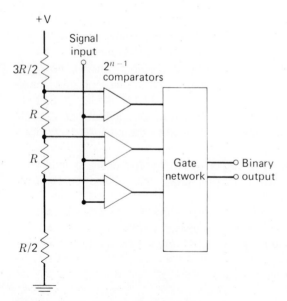

Fig. 8 • 30 Parallel-type A-to-D converter.

TABLE 8 • 3 A-TO-D AND D-TO-A CONVERSION TERMINOLOGY

Resolution   The smallest analog change that can be distinguished by an A-to-D converter or produced by a D-to-A converter. Resolution is the analog voltage value of the least significant bit, which is *full-scale voltage* $\div 2^n$ for an *n*-bit binary converter. Resolution is often specified in percentage of full scale.

Linearity   The maximum deviation from a straight line drawn between the minimum and maximum input levels of the converter. Linearity may be expressed as a percentage of full scale or as a fraction of the least significant bit's voltage size. (The linearity of a good converter is $\pm\frac{1}{2}$ least significant bit.)

Quantizing error   The basic uncertainty associated with digitizing an analog signal, due to the finite resolution of an A-to-D converter. An ideal converter has a maximum quantizing error of $\pm\frac{1}{2}$ least significant bit.

250 million conversions per second; more modestly priced converters operate at much lower frequencies. Slow A-to-D converters primarily intended for manual use or slow-speed recording are called *digital voltmeters*. These almost invariably operate using BCD. Display devices then convert the BCD to a decimal number which is displayed and can be read by an operator or printed.

Table 8·3 lists some of the terms which are used in describing A-to-D and D-to-A converters.

8 • 19 INTERCONNECTING SYSTEM COMPONENTS

The components of a computer system, that is, the memories, input-output devices, etc., must be interconnected to form a computer system. The way these components are put together and how they communicate with each other profoundly affects the system's performance characteristics.

The arithmetic-logic unit and control unit are generally placed physically together and called the central processing unit (CPU). The CPU is then "in charge" of the system's operation, directing the operation of the other parts of the system.

In the earlier computers and in a few present-day smaller computers the CPU is connected directly to each input-output device and memory unit using a separate cable for each connection. This is shown in Fig. 8·31. Then, if a card is to be read from a card reader, the CPU must accept the information, and if it is to be stored in memory, the CPU must store it. The CPU is therefore central and involved directly in each transaction.

The above system has the disadvantage of many different cables (or buses) and considerable interface logic (at each end of each cable).

In order to make interconnection of the system components less expensive and to standardize the interface logic used, a very popular technique involves interconnecting all components using a single *bus*. This bus consists of a number of wires or connections, and in the bus are provisions for addressing the components and transferring data from or to each component.

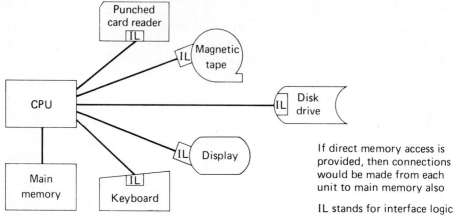

FIG. 8 • 31 Individual connections between computer system units.

Figure 8·32 shows the organization for the DEC PDP-11 bus, which DEC calls a *unibus.* Notice that the same wires are used to transfer data from the CPU to the high-speed main memory as from the CPU to a tape punch or other input-output device.

In the simplest systems, the CPU is the director of all traffic on the bus, and if a transfer of data must be made from, for instance, a disk pack to the core memory, the CPU, under program control, will read each piece of data into its CPU general registers and then store each piece of data in the core memory.

There is a problem here in the computer's ability to know when a *peripheral device*† has performed a given operation. Suppose we wish to find some data on a magnetic tape and are unwilling to wait for the tape to be searched, desiring to perform other calculations while waiting. If the computer must continually look to see if the tape drive now has the right data, time is lost and programming complexity increased. In order to alleviate this, the computer bus is generally provided with control lines which are called *interrupt lines,* and a peripheral device can raise one of these lines‡ when it has completed an action and is ready for attention.

The computer must then be provided with some kind of interrupt facility so that it can "service" the interrupt without losing its place in the program being executed. This problem becomes serious in systems where a number of input-output devices (such as A-to-D converters) must be serviced frequently, and computers are designed to service these interrupts as efficiently as possible.

Even with a good interrupt facility, the computer is still involved in every data transfer, and this can be very time-consuming. It is possible to add a *direct memory access* (DMA) feature to most systems where a disk pack or tape reader transfers data directly into high-speed main memory without passing the data through the

---

†*Peripheral devices* are the input-output devices, disk packs, tape drives, and other devices not including the main (core or IC) memory.

‡The lines are normally 0; to raise a line means to place a 1 on it.

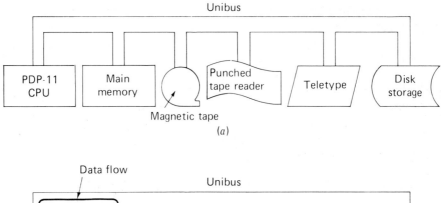

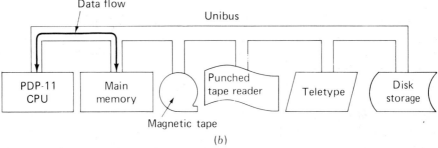

FIG. 8 • 32 Bus for DEC PDP-11. (*a*) CPU, memory, and other devices are connected by a single bus. (*b*) CPU controls transfers of data in normal use. (Courtesy of Digital Equipment Corp.)

CPU (see Fig. 8·33). This is done by "stealing" memory cycles, called *cycle stealing.* The CPU is simply held in its present state for a memory cycle while data are transferred from the disk pack directly into the core memory. The CPU does not "see" each transfer when it occurs, but simply continues executing its program, which is slowed down a little because of the cycle stealing, but not nearly so much as if the CPU had to make each transfer itself. The CPU must, of course, originate these DMA transfers by telling where in the disk pack the data are to be read from and into which locations in the main memory the data are to be read. (Transfers can generally be made in either direction when the DMA feature is added to a system, that is, for example, tape to main memory or main memory to tape.)

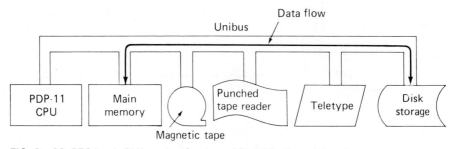

FIG. 8 • 33 DEC bus in DMA mode. (Courtesy of Digital Equipment Corp.)

Because of the economy of operation, a single bus is now the most used way to interconnect components of a microcomputer or minicomputer system.

Large systems have quite different problems from very small systems, and so different interconnection configurations are used. Since large systems contain many components, they are quite expensive, and it is important to utilize the CPU and other components to the maximum. Thus the cost of more expensive interconnection configurations is warranted.

As a result, in order to keep large processor configurations such as that shown in Fig. 8·34 working at their maximum speeds, the systems are operated in a so-called *multiprogramming mode*. This means that several programs are kept in memory at the same time. A given program is then executed until it demands an input-output device or perhaps a disk drive. Since these devices are slow compared to the CPU, the device is started in its function, but the CPU then begins executing another different program until this program asks for input-output. When this happens, the CPU begins executing a third program, and this process continues.

When a program completes execution, another program is read in. As can be seen, the CPU must keep track of where it is in each program and must control all the data transfers between system components but would be hopelessly held up if it had to participate in each transfer.

One way to configure a large system of this sort is shown in Fig. 8·35, which illustrates the IBM 370 configuration. It shows a single 370 CPU and two input-output processors, one of which IBM calls a *multiplexer channel* and the other a

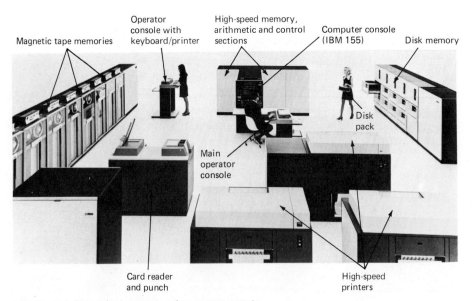

FIG. 8 • 34 Parts of a large general-purpose computer.

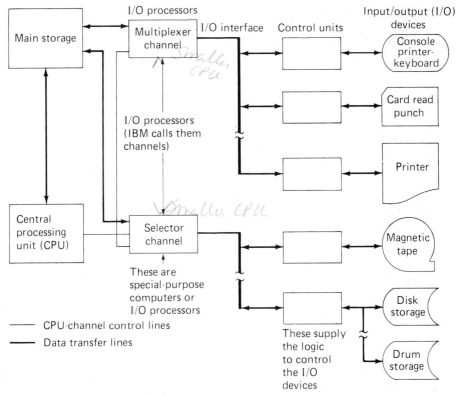

FIG. 8 • 35 Organization of IBM 370 computer series.

selector channel.† Some systems have more input-output processors, and some even have more than one CPU, in which case the system is called a *multiprocessor.*

The system operates as follows: All transfers to and from peripheral devices, such as card readers, printers, tape drives, etc., are initiated by the CPU telling an input-output processor what is to be done. The actual transfers are then made by the special-purpose processors, which work independently of the CPU. To initiate a data transfer, the CPU tells the input-output processor where in memory to put (or find) the data, which input-output device to use, and (if necessary) where in that device the data are located. The actual transferring of data is guided by a *channel program* executed by the input-output processor which has been written in advance, and the CPU also sees that the correct channel program is used.

Once an input-output data transfer has been initiated by the CPU, the CPU can go about executing other programs, and when the input-output processor com-

---

†A multiplexer channel has logic particularly suited to relatively slow devices with random characteristics. Selector channels are for fast bursts of data generated by disk packs and tape drives, for instance.

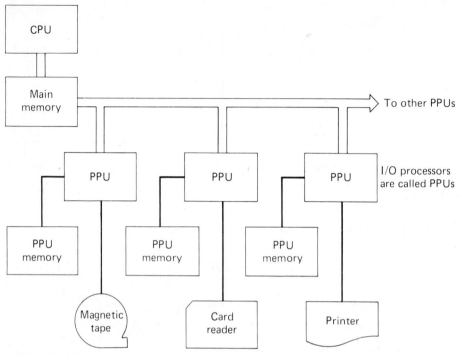

FIG. 8 • 36 Cyber 70 computer organization.

pletes its work, the CPU is notified so it can return and continue where it was in the program which called for the input-output transfer.

Another large computer configuration is that in Fig. 8·36, which shows the organization of the CDC Cyber 70 computer. In this case the input-output operations are all handled by small "computers" called *peripheral processing units* (PPUs). The PPUs have their own memories and programs and work independently of the Cyber 70 CPU. The way the Cyber 70 commands input-output operations is to "plant" messages in a specified area in its memory, telling what it would like. The PPUs then search this memory looking for orders, and when they find one, they execute the necessary operations and plant a message telling the CPU that its orders have been fulfilled and the necessary operations performed.

The reason that complex structures such as the IBM 370 and Cyber 70 make good sense is that a number of peripheral or input-output devices can be operating simultaneously at the relatively low speeds they can maintain, while the CPU races from job to job. In this way the overall throughput for the computer system can be increased because of the parallel operation of all parts of the system.

The idea of providing several CPUs which execute programs in parallel is an attractive one for large systems. As was just mentioned, such systems are called *multiprocessor systems,* and they again have high throughput and make good usage of both large memories and the many input-output devices often found in very large systems. Fig. 8·37 shows such a system.

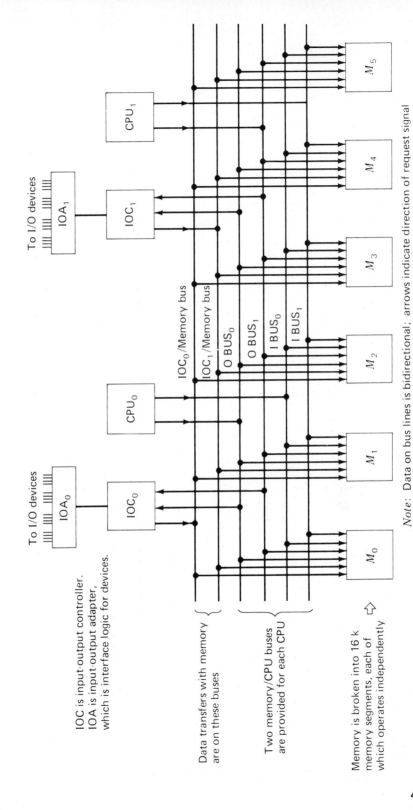

To I/O devices

To I/O devices

IOC is input-output controller.
IOA is input-output adapter,
which is interface logic for devices.

Data transfers with memory
are on these buses

Two memory/CPU buses
are provided for each CPU

Memory is broken into 16 k
memory segments, each of
which operates independently

IOC_0/Memory bus
IOC_1/Memory bus
O BUS_0
O BUS_1
I BUS_0
I BUS_1

Note: Data on bus lines is bidirectional.; arrows indicate direction of request signal

FIG. 8 • 37 Univac AN/UYK-7 multiprocessor.

447

8 · 20 INTERFACING—BUSES

When input-output devices, memory devices, and the arithmetic-logic unit and control unit are all combined to form a computer system, all of these must be connected together. When one device or unit is connected to another, an interface is required which includes the necessary logic.

The primary disadvantages of using a large number of individual cables to interconnect parts of a system are cost and complexity. The necessary interface logic must be repeated for each connection along with cable-driving circuits and receiving circuits.

As has been stated, a widely used technique to interface modules efficiently and with small cost uses a single bus to interconnect all the units. This is shown in Fig. 8·38, where the several lines or conductors which form the bus pass through and connect to a number of units or modules. In general, each module can read from the bus or write into the bus. The bus interface is usually standardized since the same bus connects all units. Since each unit connects only once to the bus, the amount of interface circuitry and logic required tends to be lower than for separate connections between units. As a result, buses are widely used in microcomputers and minicomputers and even in large computer systems for modules where the data flow is not excessive.

Often the modules which are bused together must share the same data lines. It is then necessary that each module be able to both write onto and read from a given wire. There are three general techniques for doing this as shown in Fig. 8·39. (Some of the electrical considerations are treated in the Questions.)

In Fig. 8·39(a) the wire connection to be shared is normally in the high state. A given module can write on this wire by forcing the wire to the 0 or ground level. A typical writing circuit or driver is shown in the inset of the figure. Each module also has a receiver, which is a simple inverter. (Often the high state on the bus wire is made a logical 0 and the low state a 1.)

In Fig. 8·39(b) the bus connection is normally at ground level. The module's writing circuit or driver writes high levels (for logic 1s) on this line, leaving the line low when 0s are to be written. The receiver can consist of either a noninverting amplifier or two inverters in series. In effect, this system wire-ORs the outputs from drivers.

A *most important* type of bus line driver is called a *three-state line driver*. Three-state drivers have a *disable* input as well as a logic level input, as shown in Fig. 8·39(c). When the disable input is low (a 0), the circuit drives the bus wire to the level at the logic input. Thus if the disable input is a 0 and the logic input a 0, the bus wire will be driven to a 0. If the disable input is a 0 and the logic input a 1, the bus wire will be driven high. If the disable input is a 1, however, the circuit presents a very high impedance to the bus wire, which permits another three-state line driver to drive the bus line to whatever level is selected. Receivers are again conventional logic circuits, generally inverters. Manufacturers of TTL, ECL, CMOS, and other circuit lines generally include three-state line drivers in their IC package lines.

Since several units are sharing the same bus lines, the interface procedures for

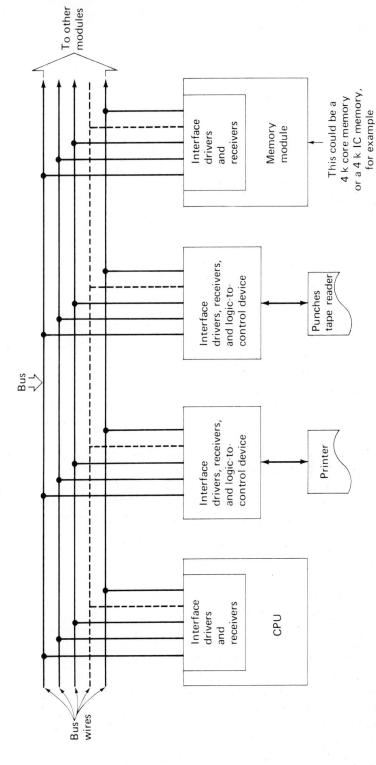

FIG. 8 • 38 Computer organization of single-bus system.

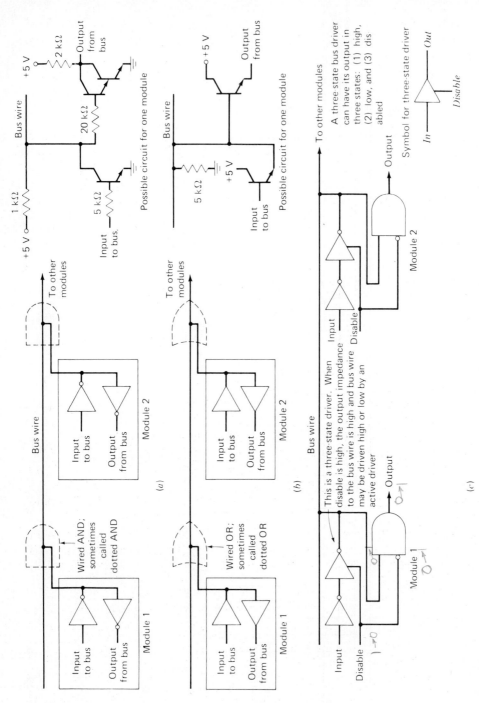

FIG. 8 · 39 Sharing a bus wire. (*a*) Bus connections using wired AND. (*b*) Bus connections using wired OR. (*c*) Three-state bus driver.

bused modules must be carefully worked out so that, for instance, two modules do not attempt to write data on the bus at the same time and that the module for which the data are intended knows it is the selected module, etc.

8 • 21 INTERFACING A KEYBOARD

Section 8·13 described keyboards. In this section we will describe the interfacing of a keyboard with a bus. The bus to be used is that for the 8080 microprocessor. The interface developed will be a straightforward typical design.

Figure 8·40 shows the basic bus for an 8080 microprocessor. The 8080 CPU chip requires a separate chip to generate the clock and several other timing signals. It will not affect the interface design, but for completeness we show a chip developed for this purpose, the 8224 clock generator driver.

An 8228 bidirectional bus driver chip will also be used in this design.† The 8080 output lines have limited drive capabilities, and the 8228 bus driver has TTL levels and drive capabilities which are useful for interfacing. Also, and more importantly, the 8080 bus uses its data lines D_0–D_r for transmitting some control signals (status bits) during an early section of each cycle. These status bits are considered a part of the bus for the 8080. The 8228 driver strobes these values into flip-flops and then outputs them as $\overline{INTA}$, $\overline{MEMR}$, $\overline{I/O\ R}$, $\overline{I/O\ W}$, etc., which are then considered to be a part of the 8080 system bus.

Notice that the 8080 bus has four basic classes of input-output lines: (1) clock-associated lines, (2) address lines A_0–A_{15}, (3) data lines D_0–D_7, and (4) control lines such as $\overline{WR}$, DBIN, and $\overline{I/O\ R}$.

The address signals are used both to address the IC memory and to select which input device is to be written into or read from. The data lines are bidirectional, that is, data are written into the 8080 CPU chip using D_0–D_7, and these same lines are also used to output data to memories, input-output devices, etc. Bidirectional lines are widely used in buses for computers, the main advantage being fewer connections to and from chips and fewer pins on chips. If the data wires D_0–D_7 were not bidirectional, a set of both eight input wires and eight output wires would be required instead of the eight bidirectional wires.‡

Using bidirectional data lines means that the various system components such as memories and keyboards must be carefully controlled and timed in their operations so that only one device writes on a wire at a time and so that system components know exactly when to examine wires with signals on them for their use.

Each input and output device which interfaces an 8080 system is given a unique *device number*. The numbers given devices can have up to 8 bits. Thus 256 different devices can be directly handled.

---

†This is a chip developed by INTEL to facilitate interfacing with input-output devices. Often microprocessor chips have limited power output lines and require extra chips for interfacing.

‡The three-state drivers shown in Fig. 8·39(*c*) are normally used to drive these lines.

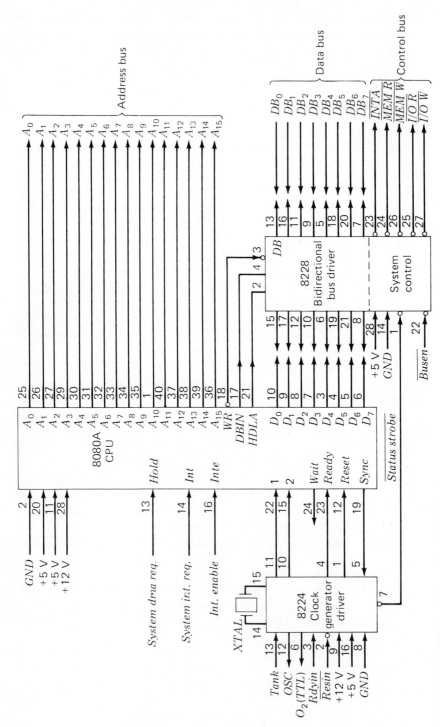

FIG. 8 • 40 8080 bus. (Courtesy of INTEL Corp.)

The 8080 system selects an input-output device as follows:

1. The device number of the selected device is placed on address lines A_0–A_7.
2. (a) If the device is to be read from by the 8080 bus, $\overline{I/O\,R}$ which is normally 1, is made a 0. While $\overline{I/O\,R}$ is a 0, the selected device to be read from places its data on D_0–D_7. When $\overline{I/O\,R}$ goes back to its normal 1 state, the selected device removes the data from the D_0–D_7 lines.

   (b) If the 8080† wishes to output data to a device, it places the device's number on A_0–A_7. Then it places the data to be output on D_0–D_7 and makes $\overline{I/O\,W}$, which is normally 1, a 0. The selected device then reads these data from the bus.

The reading and writing operations for the 8080 are under program control. An OUT instruction executed by the 8080 causes the outputting of data to a device. Executing an IN instruction causes a device to be read from. The accumulator register in the 8080 system receives data during an IN instruction and sends data during an OUT instruction. If an IN instruction is executed, the data from the selected device are read onto D_0–D_7 and from there into the accumulator. If an OUT instruction is executed, the data are read from the 8080 system's accumulator onto D_0–D_7, and the selected device then accepts the data on D_0–D_7. (This accumulator is the same accumulator used for arithmetic operations such as those described in Chap. 6. The internal operation of the 8080 microprocessor is covered in Chap. 10. Section 10·11 covers program operation.)

An interface design for the keyboard of Fig. 8·21 is shown in Fig. 8·41. The keyboard is given the device number 1 or binary 00000001. Therefore the A_0–A_6 lines are 0s and A_7 is a 1 when the keyboard is selected. The NAND gate in Fig. 8·41 shows inputs $\overline{A_0}$–$\overline{A_7}$ to be NANDed along with I/O R. Now, when I/O R is a 1 ($\overline{I/O\,R}$ a 0), the 8080 bus is saying "place the selected device's data on D_0–D_7." In this design, if A_0–A_7 contain 00000001 and $\overline{I/O\,R}$ is a 0, the output of the NAND gate becomes a 0. This enables the 3-state drivers connected to K_0–K_7, the keyboard output from the flip-flops in Fig. 8·21. As a result, the values of K_0–K_7 are placed on the bus lines D_0–D_7 where the 8080 bus can read them (into its accumulator).

Notice that the output of the NAND gate is normally a 1, which disables the 3-state drivers so that they have high impedance and write nothing on the bus lines D_0–D_7.

A major question now arises: At any given time the operator of the keyboard may or may not have depressed a key so that the keyboard may or may not have new information for the 8080. If the keyboard is simply read, the 8080 cannot tell if the character supplied is new or old. (The same key could be pressed twice in succession.) To compensate for this, a system is used where a *keyboard status word* can be read by the 8080 bus which will tell whether or not a new character is ready to be read from the keyboard. The scheme used here is the one most used for this kind of interface.

---

†We will refer to the 8080 microprocessor chips as simply the 8080, as is common practice.

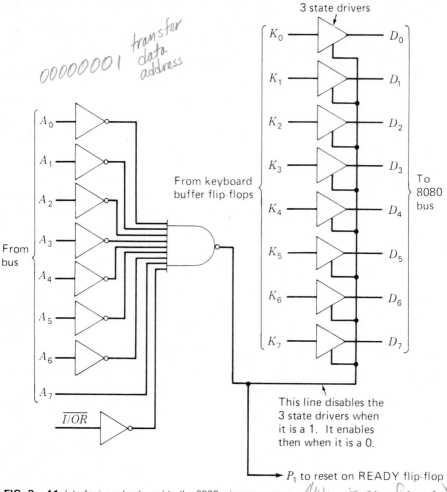

FIG. 8 • 41 Interfacing a keyboard to the 8080 microprocessor. *(like is on figure 8.22, p.427)*

Figure 8·42 shows the status word generator interface for the keyboard. We have given this keyboard status word generator the device number 2. The keyboard status word is used as follows. If a new character is available from the keyboard, the keyboard status word will have a 1 in the D_0 position. If there is no new keyboard character, a 0 will be in the D_0 position. The remaining D_1–D_7 of the keyboard status word will always be 0s.

The interface operates as follows. The program in the 8080 system reads the status word (an IN instruction is executed). The accumulator now contains the status word, and the program sees if it has a 1, in which case the keyboard should be read. If the status word is all 0s, the program goes on to other programs or devices or, if it has nothing else to do, it simply continues to read the status word until a 1 is found.

The operation of the keyboard status word interface is shown in Fig. 8·42. When a key is depressed, the READY flip-flop is set to a 1, as shown in Fig. 8·21. Therefore when the $\overline{I/O\,R}$ is made a 0, indicating a device read, and the device number on A_0-A_7 is 00000010, the NAND gate output in Fig. 8·42 goes to a 0, enabling the 3-state devices so that a 10000000 is placed on D_0-D_7, indicating that the keyboard is ready to be read.

When the keyboard is read, the READY flip-flop is cleared (reset) by the signal generated in Fig. 8·41. Therefore if keyboard status words are read in the interval between when the keyboard has been read and when a key is depressed, the output to the D_0-D_7 lines will be all 0s.

The described use of a status register in the interface circuitry to give the status of an input-output device to the CPU is most widely used technique for interfacing of this sort. In more complicated input-output devices, such as disk memories, there are more status bits in the status word which have a meaning, and these bits are set and reset by the processor and disk controller as operations are sequenced.

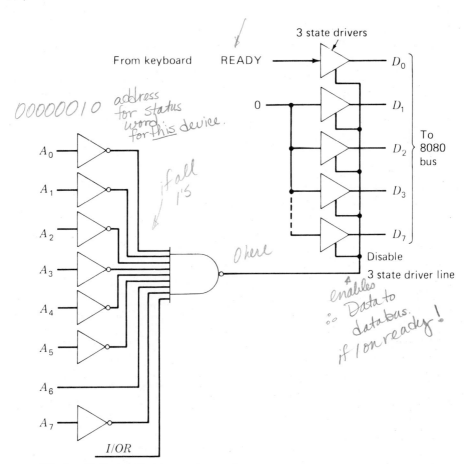

FIG. 8 • 42 Keyboard status word generator.

8 • 22 PROGRAM CONTROL OF KEYBOARD INTERFACE

The interface design for the keyboard is intended to be under program control. This means that a section of the program in the microprocessor will examine the keyboard status register to see if the keyboard has data, and if it does, it will read from the keyboard.

Table 8·4 shows a section of program for the 8080 microprocessor which will read from a keyboard. The 8080 system has an 8-bit *byte* at each address in memory. Each OP (operation) code, which tells what the instruction is to do, is a single byte in memory. There is an IN instruction with OP code 11011011 (binary), which tells the microprocessor to read from an input-output device. The number of the device (device code) immediately follows the IN instruction's OP code in the next byte.

In Table 8·4 the presentation of the program listing is arranged as follows. The program in assembly language is to the right. The program as actually stored is in the two left columns which list addresses in memory followed by the contents of each address in hexadecimal. The *label* column lists names for locations in the memory, enabling programs to use names in memory instead of actual numerical addresses.

For example, this program starts at location 030 in memory. At this location is the value DB, the OP code for the IN instruction. The comments (to the right) are always preceded by a slash; the assembler ignores these comments.

The location 030 in memory is given the name *keystat* in the label column.

In location 031 there is the device number 2; therefore the microprocessor will read location 030, find the IN instruction OP code, and then read location 031, finding in it the device number 2. The microprocesser will then place the value 2 on the address lines and issue an input-output device read sequence on the bus.

This will result in our status register interface placing 00000000 on the data lines if there is no character to be read from the keyboard and 10000000 if there is a character. This value will be read by the microprocessor into its accumulator, completing the instruction.

TABLE 8 • 4

LOCATION IN MEMORY	CONTENTS	ASSEMBLY LANGUAGE			
		LABEL	OP CODE	OPERAND	COMMENTS
030	DB	KEYSTAT	IN	2	/ READ STATUS WORD
031	02				/ INTO ACCUMULATOR
032	E6		ANI	80H	/ AND ACCUMULATOR BITS
033	80				
034	CA		JZ	KEYSTAT	/ JUMP BACK IF ZERO
035	30				
036	00				
037	DB		IN	1	/ READ KEYBOARD
038	01				

The next instruction is an ANI instruction with OP code E6. The ANI instruction performs a bit-by-bit AND of the byte following the instruction, in this case 10000000 (binary), with the accumulator. If the keyboard is ready to be read, this will result in a 1 in the leftmost position; if not, a 0.

The ANI instruction also sets a flip-flop called Z (for zero) in the 8080 to a 1 if the results of the AND contain a 1, and a 0 if not. Therefore if a character is ready to be read, Z will contain a 1; if not, it will contain a 0.

The JZ is the OP code for a "jump-on-zero" instruction in the 8080. If the Z flip-flop is a 0, the microprocessor will take its next instruction word from the address given in the two bytes† following the JZ; if Z is a 1, the instruction following these two bytes will be executed. As a result, if a character is ready to be read, the microprocessor will read the IN instruction 037 next; if no character is ready, the microprocessor will jump back to location 030. Notice that the programmer has used the label *keystat* instead of giving the numerical value in the address part of the instruction, but the actual address appears in the contents column. (The assembler determined the location.) Also, note that a complete address in the 8080 requires 2 bytes. (2^{16} words can be used in memory.) The lower order (least significant) bits come first in an instruction word, followed by the higher order bits.

When the keyboard is to be read, the instruction word beginning at location 037 will be executed. This is an IN instruction, but the device number is 1, so the keyboard itself will be read from.

When this instruction is executed, the 8080 will place the device number 1 on its address lines and then generate a device read sequence of control signals, with the result that the keyboard interface will place the character in the keyboard buffer register on the data lines, and this character will be read into the 8080 accumulator, ending the read process.

8 • 23 INTERFACING A PRINTER

The preceding sections have detailed the reading of data from a keyboard into a microprocessor (CPU). We now examine outputting characters from a microprocessor into a printer.

We assume that the printer uses an ASCII-coded character in 8-bit parallel form to cause the printing of a single character. In 8080 interfacing the printer is first selected. To do this, since different output devices may be connected to the microprocessor, the printer is given a unique device number, and we will assume that the number is 3 (decimal). When the printer is selected, this number will appear on the microprocessor address lines A_0–A_7 in binary.

Figure 8·43 shows an interface design. A NAND gate and six inverters are connected so that the NAND gate will only have a 0 output when the number 3 appears on A_0–A_7 and $\overline{I/O\ W}$ is a 0. This NAND gate's output is used as a GO signal which ultimately causes the printer to print the character on the data lines D_0–D_7. The

---

†The 8080 system address has 2^{16} words of memory; thus two bytes are required for a complete address.

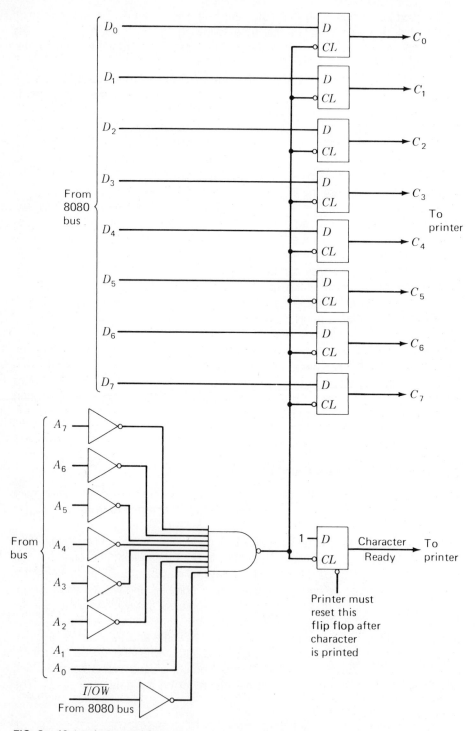

FIG. 8 • 43 Interfacing a printer.

$\overline{\text{I/O W}}$ signal is pulled negative (to a 0) when the character to be printed is available on $D_0 - D_7$ and the device address (3 in this case) is on the $A_0 - A_7$ lines.

A flip-flop called *character ready* is used to signal the printer that a character is ready to be printed. The printer must read this flip-flop and then print the character.

The program instruction which causes this character transfer in the 8080 is called an OUT instruction. The OUT instruction occupies two 8-bit bytes in memory, the second byte containing the device number. When the OUT instruction is executed, the contents of the accumulator are placed on $D_0 - D_7$. Execution of the OUT instruction causes the printer to print a character corresponding to whatever code was stored in the accumulator.

The above implies that the computer program in the 8080 memory has previously stored the ASCII character code for the character to be printed in the accumulator. (A load accumulator instruction to be described in Chap. 10 will effect this. For now we restrict our discussion to the interface strategy.)

There is a basic problem with the above scheme. A printer is a very slow electromechanical device, and the microprocessor, because of its high speed, is capable of flooding the printer with characters which it cannot possibly print. An attempt to print only after a pause between each character will be difficult to implement because the printer may require different time intervals to respond to different characters.

There are two basic solutions to this problem. One is to have the microprocessor examine the printer at regular intervals to see when a new character can be printed. If the printer can print, it "raises a flag" (turns on a flip-flop) which the microcomputer reads. If the flag is a 1, the microcomputer outputs a character to be printed; if the flag is a 0, the microcomputer goes back to what it was doing and then examines the printer again at a later time. (The computer may simply continue to examine the flag until it goes on.)

The other solution to the problem is to have the printer signal the computer with an INTERRUPT line whenever it is able to print. The computer then services this interrupt by feeding the printer a character.

We will use the first technique in our example and explain interrupts in the following section.

All that is required to respond to a query from the 8080 microprocessor is shown in Fig. 8·44. When the printer is clear and able to handle a character, it sets the flag flip-flop on. The flag is then made a bit in a status register of 8 bits.

The program step to read the flag involves transferring an entire 8-bit character placed on the data lines from the status registers into the accumulator. The status register is given device number 4. When an IN instruction with device number 4 is executed by the microprocessor, the number 4 comes up on $A_0 - A_7$, and finally the $\overline{\text{I/O R}}$ line is brought low. This causes the transfer of the flag and its associated 0s into the microprocessor accumulator. Another instruction must then examine the accumulator to see if it is all 0s or contains a 1. If the accumulator sign bit is a 1, the printer is ready for a character; if not, the computer must wait.

The above interfacing technique is widely used because of its simplicity of implementation. Using a flag (or several flags) to determine an output device's sta-

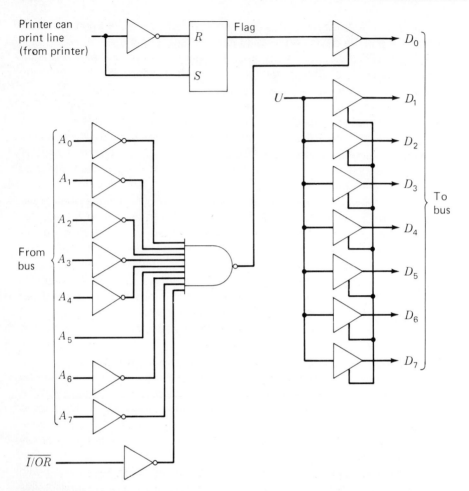

FIG. 8 • 44 Printer status generator.

tus and placing the flag(s) in a status register and then reading the status register using a program is a standard computer interface technique.

8 • 24 INTERRUPTS IN INPUT-OUTPUT SYSTEMS

The preceding examples showing how to interface a keyboard and a printer demonstrated a technique where the program was used to examine flags in status registers to see whether or not an input-output device either had information or could accept information. This technique is widely used, particularly in microcomputer and minicomputer systems where not too many external devices are to be interfaced and where there is sufficient time available so that the program can continually test the devices to see whether they are ready.

In many cases, however, there will be too many devices for this scheme to be successful, or there will be a great amount of computation to be performed, so that continually taking time out to examine the status of input-output devices cannot be tolerated.

In order to deal with this problem, computers have *interrupt systems* for input-output devices, where a given device can cause the program operation to be interrupted long enough for the input-output device to be serviced.

The operation of such a system can best be shown by an example. Suppose that we have a computer system with a keyboard, a printer, and an input from an A-to-D converter measuring temperature in a physics experiment. A great deal of computation is required to process the temperature reading from the A-to-D converter. The operator of the keyboard examines the results of the computation, which are printed on the printer, and occasionally the operator comments using the keyboard. These comments are to be printed by the printer along with the temperature and the results of the calculation.

In this case the keyboard inputs are made infrequently, the printer is kept quite busy, and we will assume that the A-to-D inputs are made at fairly frequent intervals.

The interrupt system works as follows. The computer normally is processing the inputs from the A-to-D converter. Each time a key on the keyboard is depressed, however, an interrupt signal is generated by the keyboard, the program in operation is interrupted, the keyboard is serviced, and the program which was interrupted is then returned to. Similarly, a short list of characters to be printed may be stored in the computer, and the program adds to this list as it gathers results. Whenever the printer can print, it generates an interrupt, current program operation is interrupted long enough to service the printer by giving it another character to print, and the original program operation then continues at the point at which it had been interrupted.

The A-to-D converter will also generate interrupts which must be serviced by reading the output, and the readings would be processed as soon as the time was available.

In order to effect the above, there are some features an interrupt system should have. For instance, it may be necessary to be able to turn off the interrupt feature of the printer, since when there is nothing to print, the printer would simply generate many time-consuming interrupts. (It can always print when there is nothing to print.) It might be necessary to turn the entire interrupt system off for a short period of time, since when servicing the keyboard, an interrupt from the printer might cause an interrupt of an interrupt.

In order to examine the interrupt feature more closely, we note that the following things must be done each time an interrupt is generated:

1. The state of the program in operation when the interrupt is executed must be saved. Then the program can be reentered when the interrupt servicing program is finished.
2. The device that generated the interrupts must be identified.
3. The CPU must jump to a section of the program that will service the interrupt.

4. When the interrupt has been serviced, the state of the program which was interrupted must be restored.

5. The original program's operation must be reinitiated at the point at which it was interrupted.

Discussion of how the program which is interrupted is handled and how returns are made to this program will be deferred to Chap. 10 since more information is required on program execution. The mechanism for interrupt generation and identifying the device that wishes to be serviced can be dealt with here, however.

The interrupts are initiated by a device placing a 1 on an interrupt wire in the bus. This notifies the CPU that a device wishes to be serviced.

The CPU then completes the instruction it is executing and transfers control to a section of program designed to service the interrupt.

In the 6800 microprocessor and in the PDP 8 minicomputer, for example, the various devices are polled by examining the status registers each in turn until the interrupting device is located. This device is then serviced.

In the 8080 microcomputer and in the PDP-11 minicomputer, for example, the location in memory where the service program is located for the particular device that generated the interrupt is read into the CPU by the interrupting device. This is called a *vectored interrupt*. In effect, the device tells the CPU "who did it" and does not wait to be asked.

There can be a problem when several devices generate a 1 signal on the interrupt wire at the same time. If the devices are polled, the polling order determines who gets serviced first, and a device not serviced will continue to interrupt until serviced. For the vectored interrupt, however, if two devices attempted to write their identifier into the CPU at the same time, they might overwrite each other, so a scheme must be devised where only one device tells the CPU whom to service. This is accomplished by chips† external to the CPU, which set a priority on the devices that can interrupt and handle only the highest priority device with its interrupt on.

More details on interrupts are given in the sections on particular computers in Chap. 10.

8 • 25 A STANDARD BUS INTERFACE

Various standards organizations have undertaken to develop interfaces, buses, and interface procedures or, as they are frequently called, *protocols* for digital systems. A widely used bus and its protocol, which has been developed for interfacing instruments and microcomputers, will be briefly outlined as they are representative of the interfaces worked out for buses. This bus, often called the *general-purpose interface bus,* is described in IEEE Std. 488-1978, which is a microcomputer bus standard.

---

†The IC packages used range from gate arrays which examine and allocate priority to programmable interface controllers which contain ROMs with programs for the specific interfaces to be implemented.

Figure 8·45 shows the basic interface and bus lines which can be used to interconnect a number of modules. Each bus line performs at least one interface function, depending on the interface capabilities.

At a given time any particular module connected to the bus may be idle, monitoring the activity on the bus, or functioning as (1) a talker, (2) a listener, or (3) a controller. As a talker, a module sends data over the bus to a listener (or listeners). As a listener, a module receives such data. As a controller, it directs the flow of data on the bus, mainly by designating which modules are to send data and which are to receive data.

Notice that the bus consists of 16 signal lines, grouped functionally into three component buses. The *data bus* (eight lines) is used to transfer data in parallel from talkers to listeners; it also transfers certain commands from the controller to subordinate modules. The *transfer bus* (three lines) is used for the handshaking process by which a talker or controller can synchronize its readiness to receive data. The *general interface management bus* (five lines), as its name suggests, is principally used by the controller.

Each system must have one module to designate listeners and talkers, and this module is called a *controller*. The controller uses a group of commands, referred to as *interface messages,* to direct the other modules on the bus in carrying out their functions of talking and listening.

Normally the controller would be the CPU of a computer, and this unit would generate the command signals on the bus to the other modules which would then respond. Because this interface is designed to handle a large number of different types of modules, the specification is reasonably complicated and general. The basic procedure for generating a transfer of data on this bus is as follows. First, the controller designates a listener by placing the listener's address (each listener is given a 5-bit address) on the data bus and raising the appropriate control lines. A talker is then designated by placing the talker's address on the data lines and raising the appropriate control lines. Finally, the talker and listener are told to proceed, and the talker places data, 8 bits at a time, in parallel on the data lines.

In the transfer of data from talker to listener, certain basic problems arise in the operation of every bus.† These problems are solved by means of a handshaking procedure whereby talker and listener interact using the control lines. It is convenient to describe this procedure using a flowchart, as shown in Fig. 8·46. This diagram shows that three control lines, called DAV, NRFD, and NDAC (defined in Fig. 8·45), are used to control each data byte transfer. The talkers and receivers each raise and lower the control signals, as shown by the flowchart, and the talker places data on the data bus at the appropriate time.

---

†These problems concern: (1) How does the listener know when data are on the bus? (2) How does the talker know when the listener has received the data? The bus described here is an *asynchronous bus*. Microprocessors and minicomputers often use synchronous buses where one wire in the bus contains a clock and the clock signal is used to time data transfers. In these systems, the talker must place the data on the data wires, and the listener must be ready to receive data when the clock edge arrives. A synchronous system is faster and simpler but less flexible.

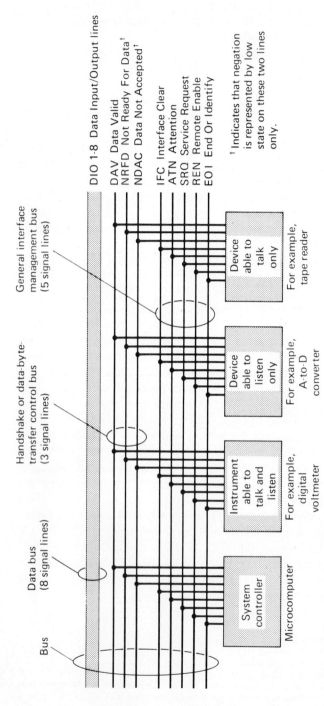

Bus

Data bus
(8 signal lines)

Handshake or data-byte-
transfer control bus
(3 signal lines)

General interface
management bus
(5 signal lines)

DIO 1-8 Data Input/Output lines

DAV Data Valid
NRFD Not Ready For Data[†]
NDAC Data Not Accepted[†]

IFC Interface Clear
ATN Attention
SRQ Service Request
REN Remote Enable
EOI End Or Identify

[†] Indicates that negation
is represented by low
state on these two lines
only.

System
controller

Microcomputer

Instrument
able to
talk and
listen

For example,
digital
voltmeter

Device
able to
listen
only

For example,
A-to-D
converter

Device
able to
talk
only

For example,
tape reader

FIG. 8 • 45 International standard bus.

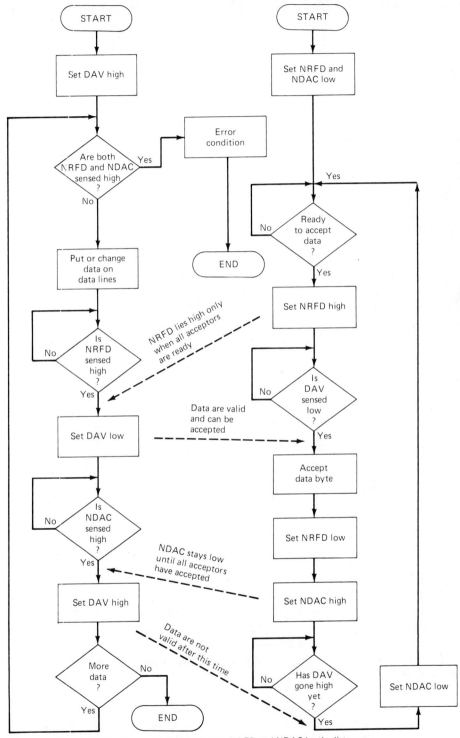

The DAV line is controlled by the talker, NRFD and NDAC by the listeners.

FIG. 8 • 46 Flowchart for handshaking on a bus. (Courtesy of Hewlett-Packard Corp.)

The necessary control circuitry to implement this handshaking and the other required functions must be provided by each module's interface circuitry. It is possible to design a line of input-output equipment including instruments, tape punches, etc., and to interface each of these to the same bus using the interface specification. IC manufacturers often furnish single chips made to provide the necessary logic for an interface.

Even connector types and electrical loading and driving rules are called out so that circuit designers can proceed with the necessary details. Minicomputer and microcomputer manufacturers also provide bus specifications for the buses they use so that peripheral manufacturers can comply with their interface specifications, and so that purchasers of these computers can design their own equipment when necessary. Large computer manufacturers provide similar specifications for their buses and other interfaces.

The bus shown is adequate for most instrument computer purposes. A higher speed bus could be designed by adding more control lines and address lines in parallel with the data lines; many computers have buses with 50 or more lines.

QUESTIONS

1. Using the code in Fig. 8·2, an operator keyboards the following:

    ADD 641
    CAD 932
    SUB 841

How many lines will be punched in the paper tape? How many holes will be punched in the tape?

2. The code in Fig. 8·2 is a parity-checking code. Is the parity check odd or even?

3. Write out in binary form the first line of the program in Question 1, using the code in Fig. 8·3.

4. The code in Fig. 8·2(a) has at least one punch or hole for each character. This makes it possible for the reader to detect when to read. Explain the tape feed character.

5. If the short program in Question 1 is punched into cards according to the code in Fig. 8·6 using normal procedures, how many holes will be punched into the cards used? If a mistake is made during keyboarding, will it be easier to correct if cards or tape are used? Explain why.

6. In EBCDIC, when the first four bits are 1s, the remaining four bits represent a digit. Is the code for these bits BCD or straight binary? Give a reason for your answer.

7. Generally, programs are punched into cards with an instruction word per card. The first line of the program in Question 1 would go on one card. How many holes will be punched in the first card for the code in Fig. 8·6?

8. The tape feed character can be used to take out any character in the code in Fig. 8·2 except one. Which character and why? *Hint:* Remember the parity checks.

9. List the binary-code groups for each decimal digit in the excess 3 BCD code in Chap. 3, and assign a parity bit for an even-parity-bit checking system to each code group. List the values of the parity bits for the same excess 3 code for an odd-parity-bit checking system.

10. Discuss any problems you can foresee in attempting to read characters optically which would not occur for magnetic characters. Do these reasons somewhat explain why banks adopted magnetic readers before optical readers?

11. Each of the following rows of digits consists of a code group in the ASCII code. A single parity check has been added as the rightmost bit in each row, and a single row of parity checks has been added at the end, as explained in Question 15. In addition, errors have been added so that the data are not correct at present. Correct these groups of data, and then convert each 7-digit character to the alphanumeric character it represents. The parity checks are odd-parity checks.

(a)   10101000
        10010001
        10000011
        10101000
        01001111
        10100111
        01100000
        10000100
        10110010
        10001111
        10010001
        10101000
        11000101   parity-check row

(b)   10001001
        10011110
        10011101
        01001111
        10101000
        01001000
        10100111
        10101000
        10011110
        10100001
        01011011
        10111001   parity-check row

12. Using the error-detecting and error-correcting scheme in Question 11, a message has been sent. It arrives as below. Determine if errors have occurred, and correct any you find in the following message:

                10100100
                10000010
                10001101
                10010001
                10101000
                01111111

13. How many bands must a coder disk similar to that shown in Fig. 8·26 have for an A-to-D converter that has a precision of 10 binary digits? List the successive code groups for a 5-bit unit-distance code which counts from 0 to 31_{10}.

14. A 3, 3, 2, 1 code for encoding the 10 decimal digits into 4 binary digits can be made so that no more than two positions change each time a single digit is increased by 1. Write this code down.

15. More powerful parity-check systems can be formed by adding columns with the number of 1s in each column written at the end as a binary number. For instance, if we wish to encode

$$1011$$
$$1101$$
$$1100$$
$$1110$$

we add

$$
\left.\begin{array}{l}0\\0\\1\\0\end{array}\right\} \text{parity checks}
$$

$$
\left.\begin{array}{l}01001\\01110\\10000\end{array}\right\} \text{number of 1s in each column}
$$

┌────indicates two 1s

└indicates four 1s

Adding this to the data forms this encoded block of data:

$$
\begin{array}{l}10110\\11010\\11001\\11100\end{array}
$$

$$
\left.\begin{array}{l}01001\\01110\\10000\end{array}\right\} \text{check digits}
$$

Now if one or more errors occur in the same column, they can be corrected by simply noting that the column does not agree with the number of 1s recorded at the end, and that there are parity checks in the rows of the block of data containing errors. By simply changing these errors, we will convert the message back to its original form. Here are two other blocks of data which include errors. Correct the errors in these blocks of data and write the alphanumeric code for each set of seven digits in a row to the right of the rows. The code is that of Fig. 8·10; so the parity checks are as indicated in the figure, and not in the rightmost column.

(a) 00100011
01101010
01100011
00100001
00110010
00010000
01110110
01111001
01000101
01110101
00010100 ⎫
01001101 ⎬ check digits
01010011 ⎪
00100000 ⎭

(b) 01100010
01000001
01000100
00010000
00100011
01100001
01010111
01110101
00110010
00010000
00110101 ⎫
01100100 ⎬ check digits
01110011 ⎪
00000000 ⎭

16. Explain why the Gray code cannot be used if we are to use a D-to-A resistor network as shown in Fig. 8·27. Explain why the 2, 4, 2, 1 code in Question 14 could be used.

17. If the signals of each of the four inputs to the D-to-A converter resistor network shown in Fig. 8·27 are from the 1 outputs of flip-flops which have +8- and 0-V logic levels (+8 V represents a 1), what will be the potential at E_0 if the flip-flops represent the binary numbers 0101? 1010? 1111?

18. If the ASCII code in Fig. 8·10 is transmitted serially in binary, draw the waveform for the character 6, assuming a 1 is +4 V and a 0 is −4 V.

19. Show an error pattern that the code in Question 15 will not correct but will detect, and one that it will neither correct nor detect.

20. Put errors into the message in Question 12 which the coding will neither correct nor detect.

21. Characters are generally read from punched paper tape a line at a time. When the code in Fig. 8·2(a) is used, the computer will be supplied with information bits each time a line is read. If the computer used is a serial computer, the bits will arrive in parallel and must be changed to serial form. By loading a 7-place shift register in parallel and then shifting the register at the machine's pulse-repetition frequency, the bits representing the character can be converted to serial form. Draw a block diagram of a 7-flip-flop shift register, along with the input lines necessary to load the register. (Assume that there are seven input lines—one to each flip-flop—from the tape reader and that a given input line will contain a pulse if a hole is in the respective position of the tape.)

22. Explain why, in large computer systems, output data to be printed are almost always recorded on magnetic tape for offline printing and not printed at once.

23. Which of the sets or errors in Question 11 would have been detected if the error-catching system in Question 15 had been used? Which of these sets of errors in Question 15 could have been corrected by the error-detecting and error-correcting scheme in Question 11, and which would only have been detected?

24. Design a 6-bit A-to-D converter using the same scheme as shown in Fig. 8·29.

25. For the A-to-D converter in Fig. 8·29, if the 40-kΩ resistor were made 50 kΩ by error, which of the following voltages would be incorrectly converted:

(a) +12 V   (b) +4 V

(c) +2 V   (d) +17 V

(e) +7 V   (f) +15 V

26. Is it possible to invent a 7-binary-bit code which includes an odd-parity-check bit and which contains 70 characters? Give a reason for your answer.

27. The code in Question 15 is not generally able to correct double errors in a row or errors in the checking numbers at the end, but will almost always detect each of these. Explain this statement.

28. Discuss the relationships between accuracy, precision, and speed in an A-to-D converter.

29. Show how a teletypewriter would read out the character *B* when this key was depressed. Draw the output waveform.

30. What is the ASCII code for "line feed," which is also LF in Fig. 8·10?

31. What is the EBCDIC code for *E* in Fig. 8·11?

32. Notice that the characters in the magnetic reader character set in Fig. 8·13 are "blocked," not curved. Why might this be a good idea?

33. Notice the difference in a 0, a Q, and an O in Fig. 8·14. Find other letters that have similar printed shapes and have been altered to make them more machine-readable.

34. What is the difference between an acoustic coupler and a modem?

35. Can you think of any reasons why it might be a good idea for a computer to echo a character struck on a keyboard it is to read from instead of having the character printed immediately?

36. Why are start bits and at least one stop bit necessary for the teletypewriter code transmission explained for terminals?

37. Explain the difference between synchronous and asynchronous transmission of digital data.

38. Explain how the Bell 103 modem described would send the ASCII character *G* on a line in a chosen direction. How would it send in the other direction? Use the teletypewriter scheme to encode using start and stop bits.

39. Use 1- and 2-kΩ resistors and draw the schematic diagram for a D-to-A converter as shown in Fig. 8·28.

40. For the schematic you drew in the preceding question, use +7 and 0 V as the two levels and figure the output for two nonzero digital input values.

41. Repeat the preceding question, but use 5- and 10-kΩ resistors.

42. Design a D-to-A converter that converts using the successive approximation technique. Use a modified version of Fig. 8·29.

43. Show how long it would take a D-to-A converter using the successive approximation technique to convert 7 bits. Assume that it takes 10 ms for the D-to-A converter-resistor network to stabilize its output. Explain by showing how conversions are made for three specific input voltages.

44. Again assuming that it takes 10 ms for the D-to-A converter network to stabilize, show how a 6-bit converter uses the successive approximation technique for three voltages $+9$, $+1$, and $+7$ V, assuming a 0- to 10-V range for inputs (0 and $+10$ V as voltage levels for the level converter outputs).

45. Show how the converter in Fig. $8 \cdot 29$ converts the three voltages in the preceding question and compare the conversion times.

46. Using the information in the preceding three questions, can you compare the average time for conversion for an A-to-D converter as shown in Fig. $8 \cdot 29$ with a successive approximation converter? Assume 6 bits.

47. Show how a flash converter works for a 3-bit system using 10-kΩ resistors. Assume voltages in an interval from 0 to 6 V, so $000_2 = 0$ V, $001_2 = 1$ V, $100_2 = 4$ V, $110_2 = 6$ V, etc. Draw the gates from the comparator outputs to the binary numbers.

48. Explain how the converter in the preceding question converts $+0.5$, $+3.2$, and $+5.4$ V.

49. Discuss resolution, linearity, and quantizing error. Can the quantizing error be less than resolution? Why or why not?

50. Discuss A-to-D converters, bringing out the important characteristics which must be considered in choosing a converter. What is the primary advantage of a "flash" A-to-D converter, and what is its primary disadvantage? Can a flash converter convert an analog input directly into digital form using a Gray code instead of binary? Justify your answer.

51. Explain how computer circuits (gates) both read from and write onto the same wires in a bus.

52. Design a gating network that converts a 3-bit Gray code into a 3-bit conventional binary number. Use only NOR gates in your design.

53. A straightforward technique for encoding a keyboard is shown in this chapter. There are several other methods which are sometimes used, and these are primarily intended to either reduce the number of semiconductors in the decoder mechanism or simplify the wiring.

One technique involves a two-dimensional array similar to the selection systems used in memories. The following figure shows a two-dimensional array. The horizontal wires are connected to the vertical wires by switches which are activated by keys on the keyboard. Thus depressing a key closes a switch which connects a single X wire to a single Y wire. Each key which is depressed produces a unique X wire, or Y wire combination. Determining which key has been closed, however, is nontrivial. A common technique is to raise one of the X or horizontal wires and then scan (i.e., sample) each of the Y wires. If one of the wires is high and the other wires are low, then the particular intersection of the X and Y wires which are connected can be determined. Sometimes a microprocessor is programmed to generate the X wire sequence and sample the Y wires, but special *keyboard encoding chips* are also made for this process. In each case the X wires are normally low except that, one at a time, the microprocessor, or scanner, raises a single X wire and then examines each of the Y wires to see if one is high. If it is, a key has been depressed, and since the microprocessor is aware of which X wire has been raised and also which Y wire was raised, it can determine the unique key that has been depressed. By encoding the X wires with a unique 3-bit code on each wire and the Y wires with a unique 2-bit code, a unique pair of 5-bit combinations can be arranged. For larger keyboards the ASCII code can be used by proper choice of the X and Y values. Draw a simple 8-character encoder which encodes only 8 of the ASCII characters shown in Fig. 8·10, assigning values to the X and Y access wires.

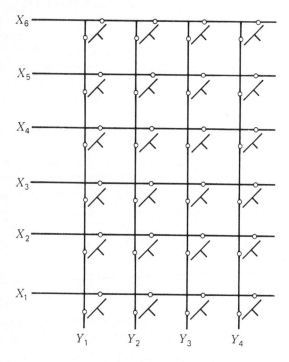

54. Show in flowchart form the procedure for testing and finding which switch is closed, if any, for the encoding scheme described in Question 53.

55. How many steps would it take to scan an entire keyboard for the ASCII code given in Fig. 8·10, using the two-dimensional keyboard scheme?

56. When the encoding scheme in the preceding questions is used, if the switches bounce, that is, if a closure of the switch is not constant but goes on and off when a key is depressed, this complicates the encoding. Explain some of the problems that might arise from contact bounce if the above technique is used.

57. How would you suggest smoothing the bounce from the contacts for the encoding scheme from Question 56.

58. Draw the diode encoder matrix for three ASCII characters not shown in Fig. 8·21.

59. The signal that strobes the values into the flip-flops which read from the encoder of Fig. 8·21 must be slightly delayed. Explain why.

60. In the status register scheme used to interface a microprocessor to a keyboard, only 1 bit is used to determine the status of the keyboard. A status register could have several status bits, however, each with a different mean-

ing. Discuss the use of the AND instruction to test various bits in conjunction with the JUMP instruction for the 8080.

61. The single status bit used in the printer interface status register is set on by the printer and turned off by the interface circuit. It could be controlled completely by the printer. Explain how the interface would work in this case.

62. In an interface such as a printer there is a question as to how the interface should notify the printer when the character to be printed is on the signal wires, and how long the signal should be held there. There are two approaches:

    a. The printer must read the information within a stipulated period of time. In this case signals with data are placed on the interface wires (the interface device address having already been placed there) and are always held for some fixed period of time which is acceptable to all the interface circuitry used.

    b. The device being read into notifies the interface when it has received the characters. In this case another interface wire is used, and a signal is placed on this wire by the device being read into when it has accepted the input data. This is a handshake procedure where the interface device address is placed on the wires, data are then placed on the wires, and a wire to the device is raised which says "the data are on the lines." The interface device then raises another wire, saying "the data have been accepted."

IBM uses technique (a) in its 370 interfaces, whereas the IEEE (and several other standards organizations and computer manufacturers) use the hand-shaking technique. Discuss the advantages and disadvantages of each of these techniques.

63. With the IEEE 488 interface it is possible to read into several devices at the same time. In this case the system controller places the data on the wires and then raises the wire, showing that the data are there. In responding, the devices accepting data use the *open collector* circuit shown in Fig. 8·39(a) so that if any single device has not yet accepted the data the wire will be set to high. Show why for the open collector circuit in Fig. 8·39(a), which ANDs outputs, the devices can only indicate acceptance of data by moving the line to 1 and not to 0.

64. Show how the circuitry in Fig. 8·41 can be modified to interface a keyboard with address 6 (device number 6).

65. Show how the program in Table 8·4 would be modified to service a keyboard with device number 8 and status register number 7.

66. Write a sequence of instructions which will read a keyboard and then print the characters read on a printer. Give the keyboard device number 5 and the printer device number 7. Number the status registers as you please.

67. Design an interface that will accept serial bit strings using the ASCII code and the teletypewriter serial format shown in Fig. 8·24. The interface should buffer this bit string of characters into the 8080 microprocessor.

68. Design an interface that will take a parallel data byte from an 8080 microprocessor bus and convert it to serial for a teletypewriter.

69. If a 10K resistor connected to +5 V is connected to each horizontal wire in the encoding matrix of Question 53 and a 200-Ω resistor to the base of a transistor inverter at each vertical wire, an encoding scheme can be made using a few gates. Show how to do this for a 4 $\times$ 4 matrix.

70. Explain "handshaking" on a bus when data are transferred from a sender to a receiver. How can this be used to prevent errors due to signal skew caused by signals on different wires arriving at different times (skewed) because of the differences in line length and characteristics and differences in delays through IC line drivers, etc.?

71. For the standard instrument interface draw the signals DAV, NRFD, and NDAC for a data transfer from a talker to a listener. Assume that there are no problems in transferring data, and indicate who is raising and lowering each signal.

72. For the standard instrument interface indicate how the controller selects a "talker" and a "listener."

73. How is "signal skew" handled on the standard instrument interface?

74. Explain how peripheral devices interrupt a computer with a single bus organization.

75. Explain the meaning of *direct memory access* (DMA) and why it is desirable in some cases.

76. Can you think of any problems that might arise in multiprocessor systems?

77. If devices and status registers are numbered 1, 2, 4, 8, . . . , and only a few are used (less than or equal to the number of address wires), the gate to determine which device is selected in an interface can be simplified (or omitted). Show why.

THE
CONTROL
UNIT

This chapter describes the control section of digital computers. Preceding chapters illustrated techniques whereby arithmetic and logical operations may be performed and information read into and from various memory devices. To utilize the speeds and information handling capabilities of these techniques and devices, it is necessary to sequence automatically the various operations which occur at speeds compatible with those of the rest of the machine. The control element must therefore be constructed of high-speed circuitry. The basic elements used in the control element of a digital computer are those described in Chaps. 4, 5, and 7, and most of the concepts underlying the functioning of the control element are those presented in Chaps. 3 through 6.

The *control unit* may be defined as "the parts that effect the retrieval of instructions in proper sequence, the interpretation of each instruction, and the application of the proper signals to the arithmetic unit and other parts in accordance with this interpretation."†

The function of the control circuitry in a general-purpose computer is therefore to interpret the instruction words and then sequence the necessary signals to those sections of the computer that will cause it to perform the instruction. Previous chapters have shown how the application of the correct sequence of control signals to the logical circuitry in the arithmetic element enables the computer to perform arithmetic operations, and how binary words may be stored and later read from several types of memory devices. For the computer to function, the operation of its sections must be directed, and the control circuitry performs that function.

---

†From *IEEE Standard Dictionary of Electrical and Electronics Terms,* IEEE Std. 100-1977, Institute of Electrical and Electronics Engineers, Inc.

This chapter first presents some introductory material concerning computer instruction-word execution. Two general-purpose computers are used as examples. Then a small general-purpose computer's control circuitry is described. The basic ideas in the design of control circuitry are presented in these sections. Register transfer concepts are emphasized. The final sections describe microprogrammed computer control concepts, giving the basic ideas used in this class of computers.

9 • 1 CONSTRUCTION OF INSTRUCTION WORD

We have defined a computer word as an ordered set of characters handled as a group. Also, the computer word is considered to be a basic unit of information in a machine.† Basically all words consist of a set of binary digits, and the meaning of the digits depends upon several different factors. For instance, the bits 01000100 could represent the decimal number 68 in a pure binary computer, and the decimal number 44 in a BCD computer which uses an 8, 4, 2, 1 code. Thus the meaning of a set of digits is sometimes determined by its usage. In addition, other interpretations are possible, for instruction words are stored just as are data words, and the digits could represent an instruction to the computer. Since memory locations can store either instruction words or data words, the programmers and system operators must see that the instruction words are used to determine the sequence of operations which the computer performs, and that reasonable meanings are assigned to the data words.

If we assume that each memory location can contain a single instruction word, a computer will start with the word stored in some specified address, interpret the contents of this location as an instruction, and then continue taking instruction words from the memory locations in order, unless a HALT or BRANCH instruction is encountered. The data to be used in the calculations will be stored in another part of the memory. Since the computer can store either instructions or data in the same storage registers, considerable flexibility of operation results. For instance, if the computer memory element can store only 8000 words, one program might contain 5000 instructions, leaving 3000 locations for the storage of data, while another program might use only 1000 instruction words, leaving 7000 locations for data. The computer user is therefore free to allocate the memory as necessary, and problems with many instructions and few numbers, or with many data and few instructions, can be handled by the same computer.

It should be noted that computers which have both a high-speed inner memory and a lower speed auxiliary memory will use the high-speed inner memory for the instruction words and for intermediate results, and the lower speed storage devices for any data that cannot be accommodated in the high-speed memory. For

---

†Some of the new computers will handle words of different lengths, in which case the "basic word" is generally considered to be the word normally handled as a unit. Some computers have completely variable word lengths.

instance, if a computer has a high-speed IC memory plus a number of magnetic tape devices, the program instructions may be stored in the IC memory and the data to be used in the tape storage. Then as portions of the data are read into the IC memory and calculations are performed, more data are read from tape to IC memory, and more calculations are performed until all the data have been processed. The machine takes its instruction words only from the "inner" IC memory; if instructions are stored on tape, they must be transferred into the inner memory before they are performed by the computer.

An instruction word in a digital machine generally consists of several sections. The number of divisions in the word depends on the type of computer. Because of its wide usage and simplicity, we will describe what are called *single-address instruction words* in this and the following sections, leaving more complicated formats to later sections. The single-address instruction word is widely used in microcomputers and minicomputers, as well as in many of the larger computers; it serves as a good basis for introducing control unit operations. Basically each single-address instruction word contains two sections; the *operation code* (OP code), which defines the instruction to be performed, such as addition, subtraction, etc.; and the *address part,* which contains the location of the number to be added or subtracted or otherwise used (the operand).

If 5 binary digits of the word are used to specify which instruction is to be performed, there must be some coding system to indicate each of the various instructions. Since 5 bits have been allocated to designate which instruction is to be performed, 2^5, or 32, different instructions could be used, and a different binary number would be associated with each. Each type of instruction will then have a specific OP code consisting of the set of binary digits that the computer is to interpret.

As an example computer we will now examine a classic single-address computer, the PDP-8. This was the first "big winner" in the minicomputer area, and for some years the PDP-8 outsold all other minicomputers. Even today it remains a substantial computer in DEC's line and is used in many of their products. Further, "micro" versions of the PDP-8 are available, and thus it has the distinction of being available in both minicomputer and microcomputer form.

The PDP-8 has a basic memory word and instruction word of 12 bits. The instruction word is comprised of two sections, an OP code part and an address part, as shown in Fig. 9·1(*a*). There are only 3 bits in the OP code part, and so only eight basic instruction types are possible. In this section we will describe only three of these, leaving the remainder for Chapter 10. The instructions we will study are the TAD (2s complement add), the DCA (deposit and clear), and the JMP (jump) instructions.

The TAD instruction [Fig. 9·1(*b*)] has an OP code of 001 (in binary). It tells the computer to add the number located in memory at the address given in the address part of the instruction to the number currently in the accumulator and to place the sum in the accumulator.

Thus if the address part of the instruction was 000100110, this would reference the number at address 38 (decimal) in memory. The computer instruction word that

1 2 3   4   5   6   7   8   9 10 11 12

OP code	Address part

(a)

001	Address part

OP code for
TAD instruction
is 001

001000000111   Example: This instruction
word tells computer to
add word at location 7
in memory into
the accumulator

(b)

011	Address part

OP code for DCA
instruction is 011

011000001101   Example: This instruction
word tells computer to
deposit the contents of
the accumulator at
the address in memory
given in the address
section which is 13_{10}

(c)

FIG. 9 • 1 PDP-8 instruction words. (a) Instruction-word format.
(b) TAD instruction format. (c) DCA instruction format.

will cause the 12-bit number at address 38 (decimal) memory to be added to the number in the accumulator will be 001000100110. Words are generally written in octal in the PDP-8, and this word would be 1046 in octal.

The DCA instruction has OP code 011 in binary. This instruction tells the CPU to deposit or store the present contents of the accumulator at the address given by the address part of the instruction. Thus the instruction word 011000001101 tells the CPU to store the current contents of the accumulator at location 13 in the memory. The DCA instruction also clears the accumulator to all 0s.

Let us now examine two program steps, a DCA followed by a TAD. Let these two instruction words be at memory locations 41 and 42 (octal). Let the DCA refer to location 50 (octal) and the TAD to location 51. The arrangement is therefore as follows:

LOCATION IN MEMORY (OCTAL)	MEMORY CONTENTS (OCTAL)	MEMORY CONTENTS (BINARY)
41	3050	011000101000
42	1051	001000101001
50	0222	000010010010
51	0243	000010100011

We now analyze the action of the computer as it executes these two instructions. Suppose that the accumulator contains 0102 (octal) when the instruction at 41 is executed. The value 0102 will then be deposited (stored) at location 50, overwriting or destroying the value 0222 which was in location 50. The accumulator will then be cleared to all 0s.

Next, the instruction at location 42 in memory will be executed. This instruction will add the value at location 51, which is 0243 (octal), to the current value in the accumulator.

Therefore, when execution is begun on the instruction word at location 43 (not shown), the accumulator will contain 0243, and the contents of memory location 50 will be 0102.

Another instruction in the PDP-8's repertoire is the JMP instruction with OP code 101. This instruction causes a jump in memory to the address (location) given in the address part of the instruction word.

For example, suppose the content at location 71 (octal) in memory is 101001000011 (binary) or 5103 (octal). When the CPU reads this as the instruction word JMP 0103, it will cause the next instruction to be taken from location 103 in memory and not from location 72.

Table 9·1 shows the three instructions so far introduced, combined into a 5-instruction-word section of program. Assembly language and octal values are both shown in this table.

TABLE 9 • 1 SECTION OF PDP-8 PROGRAM

ADDRESS IN MEMORY (OCTAL)	CONTENTS (OCTAL)	LABEL	OP CODE	ADDRESS	COMMENTS
0041	3051		DCA	LOC1	/CLEARS ACC
0042	1052		TAD	LOC2	/LOADS 0200
0043	1053		TAD	LOC3	/ADDS 212
0044	3054		DCA	LOC4	/STORES AT 54
0045	5071		JMP	71	/GO TO 71
. . .	. . .		. . .		
0051	0600	LOC1	0600		
0052	0200	LOC2	0200		
0053	0212	LOC3	0212		
0054	0310	LOC4	0310		

The operation of these instructions by a CPU would be as follows. When location 41 is read, the DCA instruction stores the current contents of the accumulator, which is then cleared to 0s. The next instruction word is TAD LOC2,† which causes the number 0200 at location 52 to be added to the accumulator, giving 0200 in the accumulator. Notice that 0200 is in the OP code column but is actually an octal number.

When the TAD LOC3 instruction is read, it causes the number 0212 at location 53 in memory to be added to the number 0200 in the accumulator, giving 0412 in the accumulator. The CPU then executes the instruction DCA LOC4, causing the value in the accumulator, which is 0412, to be stored at address 54 in the memory. The CPU then reads the JMP 71 instruction, causing it to fetch the next instruction word from location 71 in the memory (and not from location 46).

After this section of the code has been executed, the sum of the numbers at locations 52 and 53 will be stored in location 54, and the CPU will have jumped to location 71 in memory.

The PDP-8 has several addressing features which will be discussed in the next chapter. Also, because of the short OP code (3 bits), several of the other instructions are very clever (and somewhat tricky). More details of this will also be given in Chap. 10.

We will now describe, for reference and study purposes, a small single-address computer, the DDP-24, which is manufactured by Minneapolis-Honeywell. Details of the addressing modes and other features will be given in Chap. 10. However, a study of this instruction repertoire will indicate the number and variety of instructions available in computers of this type.

The complete set of instructions for the DDP-24 is shown in Table 9·2. In this table, A refers to the accumulator, B to the register used to store the least significant digits of products, etc., and EA is the address portion of a computer instruction word. Octal OP codes, as well as the mnemonic codes, are given. To explain a typical instruction, the addition instruction has an octal OP code of 10; the binary code is 001000. The mnemonic code is ADD, and the notation $(A) + (EA) \rightarrow (A)$ says that the sum of the accumulator plus the word in memory at the address given by EA (which is the location given by the address part of the instruction word) is placed in the accumulator.‡

As a further example, JMP with a binary OP code of 111100 causes the machine to take the next instruction word from the address given by the address portion of the JMP instruction word. Notice that the multiplication instruction multiplies a word in memory by the B register, not the accumulator, which was a characteristic of many earlier IBM computers.

Subscripts such as in $(A)_{2-24}$ are very useful notational devices. They indicate the bits of the register involved, so that, for instance, STD in Table 9·2 causes

---

†LOC2 is a label or symbolic address, giving a memory. Refer to Chap. 1 for details.

‡The parentheses are used to indicate "the contents of." Therefore the notation (A) means "the contents of the accumulator" and the notation (A) → (B) means "the contents of register A are transferred into register B." [This is often written (A) → B, but Honeywell uses (A) → (B).]

TABLE 9 • 2 OPERATION CODES FOR DDP-24 COMPUTER

| | OP CODE | | | | |
	MNEMONIC	OCTAL	FUNCTION	X	I	O'F
LOAD AND STORE	CRA	60	$O \rightarrow (A)$			
	IAB	57	$(A)\ (B)$			
	LDA	24	$(EA) \rightarrow (A)$	X	X	
	LDB	23	$(EA) \rightarrow (B)$	X	X	
	STA	05	$(A) \rightarrow (EA)$	X	X	
	STB	03	$(B) \rightarrow (EA)$	X	X	
	STC	04	$(A)_{1-9} \rightarrow (EA)_{1-9}$	X	X	
	STD	06	$(A)_{10-24} \rightarrow (EA)_{10-24}$	X	X	
	TAB	55	$(A) \rightarrow (B)$			
ARITHMETIC	ADD	10	$(A) + (EA) \rightarrow (A)$	X	X	X
	ADM	20	$(A) + |(EA)| \rightarrow (A)$	X	X	X
	BCD*	36	(EA) BCD $\rightarrow (A)$ binary	X	X	
	BIN*	37	(EA) binary $\rightarrow (A)$ BCD	X	X	(X)
	DIV	35	$(A, B)/(EA) \rightarrow$ (quotient to B, remainder to A)	X	X	(X)
	MPY	34	$(B) \times (EA) \rightarrow (A, B)$			X
	RND	62	$(A) + 1 \rightarrow (A)$, if $(B)_2 = 1$			
	SBM	21	$(A) - |(EA)| \rightarrow (A)$	X	X	X
	SUB	11	$(A) - (EA) \rightarrow (A)$	X	X	X
LOGICAL	ANA	15	$(A) \cap (EA) \rightarrow (A)$	X	X	
	ERA	17	$(A) \oplus (EA) \rightarrow (A)$	X	X	
	ORA	16	$(A) \cup (EA) \rightarrow (A)$	X	X	
SHIFT	ALS**	41	Shift $(A)_{2-24}$ left, positions specified by $(EA)_{19-24}$	X	X	
	ARS**	40	Shift $(A)_{2-24}$ right, positions specified by $(EA)_{19-24}$	X	X	
	LGL**	47	Shift $(A)_{1-24}$ left, positions specified by $(EA)_{19-24}$	X	X	
	LLR**	43	Rotate $(A, B)_{1-24}$ left, positions specified by $(EA)_{19-24}$	X	X	
	LLS**	45	Shift $(A, B)_{2-24}$ left, positions specified by $(EA)_{19-24}$	X	X	
	LRR**	42	Rotate $(A, B)_{1-24}$ right, positions specified by $(EA)_{19-24}$	X	X	
	LRS**	44	Shift $(A, B)_{2-24}$ right, positions specified by $(EA)_{19-24}$	X	X	
	NRM	46	Shift $(A, B)_{2-24}$ left until $(A)_2 = 1$			
	SCL**	65	Shift $(A, B)_{2-24}$ left and decrement index register, positions specified by $(EA)_{19-24}$	X	X	
	SCR**	64	Shift $(A, B)_{2-24}$ right and increment index register, positions specified by $(EA)_{19-24}$	X	X	

X—indexable; I—indirectly addressable; O'F—overflow possible; (X)—improper divide possible; $\cap$—symbol for AND; $\cup$—symbol for OR.

*Optional.

**If indirect address not specified (I = O), address portion of instruction is effective operand.

TABLE 9 • 2 (CONTINUED)

	OP CODE		FUNCTION	X	I	O'F
	MNEMONIC	OCTAL				
JUMP	JMP	74	Jump to EA	X	X	
	JOF	73	Jump to EA, if overflow indicator set	X	X	
	JPL	70	Jump to EA, if sign (A) = 0	X	X	
	JRT	25	Jump to location specified by $(EA)_{11-24}$, restore interrupt	X	X	
	JST	27	Jump to EA + 1 and store location in (EA)	X	X	
	JZE	71	Jump to EA, if (A) = 0	X	X	
	SKG	12	Skip next instruction, if (A) > (EA)	X	X	
	SKQ	13	Skip next instruction, if (A) ≥ (EA)	X	X	
INDEX	ADX**	54	$(X) + (EA)_{11-24} \rightarrow (X)$	X	X	
	IRX	67	$(EA)_{11-24} + 1 \rightarrow (EA)_{11-24}$ and (X)	X	X	
	JIX	72	Jump to EA, if (X) ≠ 0	X	X	
	JXI	75	$(X) + 1 \rightarrow (X)$, jump to EA, if resultant (X) = 0	X	X	
	LDX**	56	$(EA)_{11-24} \rightarrow (X)$	X	X	
	STX	66	$(X) \rightarrow (EA)_{11-24}$	X	X	
	TAX	63	$(A)_{11-24} \rightarrow (X)_{11-24}$			
INPUT-OUTPUT	DMB	32	Dump memory starting at EA	X	X	
	FMB	31	Load memory starting at EA	X	X	
	INA**	52	Input → (A), according to mask in (EA)	X	X	
	INM	07	Input → (EA)	X	X	
	ITC**	51	Inhibit or enable interrupt, according to mask in (EA)	X	X	
	OCP**	53	Select I/O, according to mask in (EA)	X	X	
	OTA**	50	(A) → output, according to mask in (EA)	X	X	
	OTM	22	(EA) → output	X	X	
	SKS**	61	Skip next instruction, if sense line not set sense line specified by $(EA)_{11-24}$	X	X	
CONTROL	HLT	00	Stop computer operation until start button pressed			
	NOP	77	Perform no operation			
	XEC	02	Execute instruction at EA	X	X	

Word formats

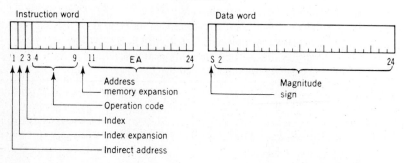

482

only the bits in the tenth to the twenty-fourth positions in the accumulator to be stored at the location given by the address (EA) in the instruction word, and these go into the tenth through the twenty-fourth positions in that word of the memory.

9 • 2 INSTRUCTION-CYCLE AND EXECUTION-CYCLE ORGANIZATION OF CONTROL REGISTERS

A digital computer proceeds through the execution of a program with a basic rhythm or pattern in its sequence of operation which is produced by the necessity of drawing both instructions and operands from the same memory. Let us examine the single-address-type computer, bearing in mind that the two-address, as well as three- and four-address machines, operate in essentially the same manner and require essentially the same control registers, although the pattern of the execution of an instruction differs according to the number of operands in the particular machine and the format of the instruction word.

The basic pattern or sequence of operations for most instructions in a digital computer of the single-address type consists of an alternation of a time period called the *instruction cycle,* followed by a period of time called the *execution cycle.* During the instruction cycle, an instruction word is obtained from the memory and interpreted, and the memory is given the address of the operand to be used. During the execution cycle, the memory obtains the operand to be used (for instance, the multiplier if the instruction is a multiplication, or the augend if the instruction is an addition), and the operation called out by the instruction word is then performed upon this operand.

Almost all computers now being made use either an IC or a core memory for the storing of both instruction words and operands or data. In both cases the cycle time for the memory is fixed, and once we tell the memory that we wish to read from it or write into it, a certain period of time will elapse before we can instruct the memory that we are again ready to read or write. If we are reading from the memory, the selected word will be delivered a short time after the memory has been given the address of the word to be read and instructed to read.

If the memory is to be written into, the word to be written as well as the address at which we wish to write it must be given to the memory. A WRITE signal must also be given, telling it to write this word at the location or address which we have given. As discussed in Chap. 7, the address at which we write into or read from in the memory is given by means of a *memory address register,* and the word to be written into the memory is delivered to a register called the *memory buffer register.* When we read from the memory, the word is also delivered to a memory buffer register.

During the instruction cycle, the instruction word is transferred by the memory into the memory buffer register. To obtain this word, we must tell the memory to read and give the memory the address to read from. During the instruction cycle the instruction word which was read into the memory buffer register is interpreted, and the address of the operand to be used is delivered to the memory address register. For many instructions this will be the address part of the instruction word which was read from the memory during the instruction cycle. During the execution time or execution cycle, an operand is obtained from the memory or written into the memory, depending upon the instruction word which was interpreted during the previous instruction time period.

If the instruction being interpreted is an ADD instruction, the location of the augend is given in the address part of the instruction word, and this address must be given the memory address register. The memory then obtains the desired word from the memory and puts it into the memory buffer register. The computer must add this word to the word already in the accumulator. Afterward the computer must give the memory the address of the next instruction word to be used and command the memory to read this word.

Notice that the machine alternates between instruction cycles and execution cycles. Also notice that during an execution cycle we must store somewhere in our control circuitry the OP code of the instruction word which was read from the memory, the address of the operand to be used (which was a part of the instruction word read from the memory), and also the address of the next instruction word to be read from the memory and used.

As a result there are several registers which are basic to almost every digital computer. These are shown in Fig. 9·2 and are described as follows:

1. *The instruction counter*†   This is a counter of the same length as the address section of the instruction word. The counter can be either reset or incremented. A typical logic diagram for the instruction counter could consist of the counter shown in Fig. 4·10(*a*), having a RESET line and an INCREMENT or ENABLE line. This counter keeps track of the instructions to be used in the program, so that normally, during each instruction time, the counter will be incremented by 1, which will give the location of the next instruction word to be used in the program. If, however, the instruction is a BRANCH or JUMP instruction, we may wish to place part of the *B* register's contents into this counter, and the MB INTO IC line does this. The counter can be reset to 0 when a program is started.‡

   It must also be possible to transfer the contents of this counter into the memory address register, which is used to locate a word in memory. Normally the instruction counter will be increased by 1 during the performance of each instruction, and the contents of the counter will be transferred into the memory address register at the beginning of each instruction time.

2. *The OP-code register*   When an instruction word is read from the memory, the OP-code section of this word must be stored in order to determine what instruction is to be performed. If the computer has an OP code with a length of 5 binary digits, the operation register will be 5 binary digits in length and will contain the OP-code part of the instruction word which is read from the memory. We must therefore be able to transfer a section of the memory buffer register into the OP-code register during the instruction time period.

---

†In some computers the instruction counter is called the *program counter.*

‡Most computers make it possible to load a selected address into the operation counter and thereby start the machine at that selected address.

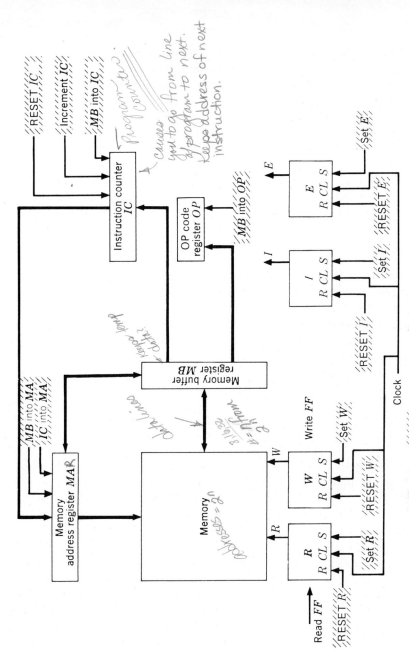

Note: Control signals are shaded thus ///Set *E*///

FIG. 9 • 2 Control registers.

3. *The memory address register* This register contains the location of the word in memory to be read or the location to be written into.

4. *R flip-flop* When this flip-flop is turned on, it tells the memory to read a word. (The flip-flop can be turned off shortly thereafter, for it need not be on during the entire memory cycle.)

5. *W flip-flop* Turning this flip-flop on tells the memory to write the word located in the memory buffer register at the location given by the memory address register.

6. *I flip-flop* When this flip-flop is on, the computer is in an instruction cycle.

7. *E flip-flop* When this flip-flop is on, the machine is in an execution cycle.

9 • 3 SEQUENCE OF OPERATION OF CONTROL REGISTERS

Let us further consider the construction of the control circuitry of a digital computer, again using the block diagram of the control registers, memory, memory address register, and memory buffer register shown in Fig. 9·2.

The control signals necessary to the operation of this small single-address computer are also shown on the diagram and are as follows. There is a RESET IC line which will clear the instruction counter to 0. (This is often connected to a push button which clears the counter when the program is to be started.) There is an MB INTO IC control signal which causes the contents of the memory buffer register to be transferred into the instruction counter, and there is an INCREMENT IC control signal which causes the instruction counter to be incremented by 1. Another control signal is the MB INTO OP, which transfers the first five digits of the memory buffer register that contains the OP code of an instruction word into the five flip-flops in the operation register. The memory address register has two control signals. The IC INTO MA control signal causes the contents of the instruction counter to be transferred into the memory address register, and the MB INTO MA control signal causes the last 16 digits of the memory buffer register (which constitute the address part of an instruction word) to be transferred into the memory address register.

During each instruction cycle of the computer, we must first turn the READ flip-flop on, and at the same time (or earlier) transfer the contents of the instruction counter into the memory address register. The memory will now read an instruction word into the memory buffer register, after which time we can enable the MB INTO OP line, transferring the OP-code section of the instruction word into the OP-code register. The next actions that the computer will take will now be dependent upon the contents of the OP-code register.

9 • 4 CONTROLLING ARITHMETIC OPERATIONS

Consider the problem of directing the arithmetic element as it performs an instruction word. Let us add an accumulator and a *B* register to the registers shown in Fig. 9·2, thus forming the block diagram shown in Fig. 9·3. Five more control

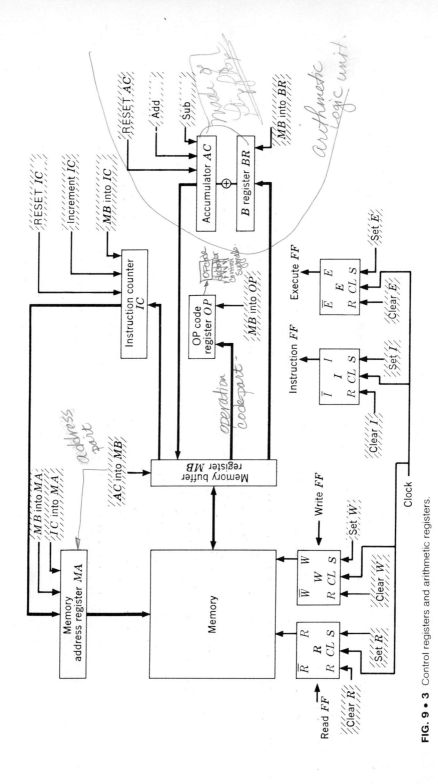

FIG. 9 • 3 Control registers and arithmetic registers.

487

signals are required to perform such instructions as ADD, SUBTRACT, CLEAR AND ADD, and STORE:

1. *RESET ACC*   This signal sets all the flip-flops in the accumulator to 0.
2. *ADD*   This signal causes the *B* register to be added to the accumulator and the sum transferred into the accumulator.
3. *SUBTRACT*   This signal causes the *B* register to be subtracted from the accumulator and the difference placed in the accumulator.
4. *MB INTO BR*   This signal transfers the memory buffer register into the *B* register.
5. *AC INTO MB*   This causes the contents of the accumulator to be transferred into the memory buffer register.

Figure 9·4 shows a single accumulator flip-flop and a single *B*-register flip-flop, along with the control signals and gates required for these operations. The accumulator and *B* register are basically composed of as many of these blocks as there are bits in the basic computer word. (The carry into the least significant bit is connected to the SUBTRACT signal when 2s complement addition is used, or to the carry-out of the sign digit when the 1s complement system is used.)

One further thing is needed. We must distribute our control signals in an orderly manner. Some sort of a time base, which will indicate where we are in the sequence of operations to be performed, is required. To do this, each memory cycle is broken into four equal time periods, the first of which we call T_0, the second T_1, the third T_2, and the fourth T_3. If we are in the first of these time periods, we need a signal which will tell us that it is now time T_0; then during the second period, we need a signal which will tell us that it is time T_1, etc.

Figure 9·5 shows a way of generating such timing signals. There is a clock signal input, and the clock is assumed to be running so that during a memory cycle we obtain four clock pulses. If it requires 1 μs to read into or write from the memory, a clock pulse should be generated every $\frac{1}{4}$ μs. Therefore the clock will run at a rate of 4 MHz.

The circuit has four output lines designated T_0, T_1, T_2, and T_3. When the computer is in time period T_0, the output line T_0 will carry a 1 signal, and T_1, T_2, and T_3 will be 0s; at time T_1 only, line T_1 will have a 1 signal on it, etc.

Let us now write, in a short table, the sequence of operations which must occur during each of the ADD, SUBTRACT, CLEAR AND ADD, and STORE instructions. Notice that when the instruction-cycle flip-flop *I* is on, the operations during times T_0 and T_1 are always the same. In Table 9·3 the control signal to be turned on or made a 1 is listed to the left, and what the signal does is listed to the right.

From this table of operations it is possible to design the control section of this small computer. The inputs are the OP code stored in the OP-code register, the timing-signal distributor, and the *I* and *E* flip-flops.

Notice, for instance, that when it is time T_0 and we are in an instruction cycle, we always turn the READ flip-flop on, telling the memory to read the instruction word located at the address in the memory address register. Then we assume that the memory places this word in the memory buffer register before time T_1, so at time T_1 we transfer the OP-code part of the instruction word into the OP-code

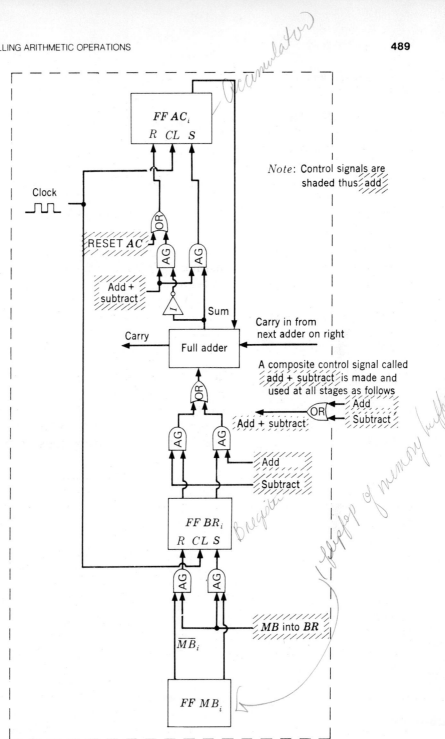

FIG. 9 • 4 Accumulator flip-flop and *B*-register flip-flop with control signals.

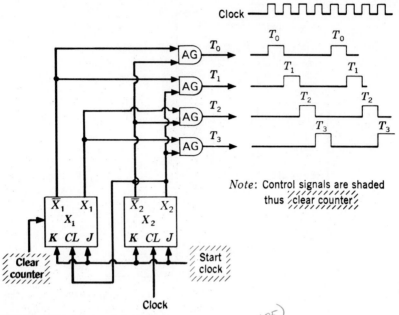

FIG. 9 • 5 Timing signal distributor.

(goes with p. 485)
p. 487

(address of instruction in memory is initially address register)

TABLE 9 • 3 SEQUENCING OF CONTROL SIGNALS

INSTRUCTION	LIST OF CONTROL SIGNALS TO BE TURNED ON	COMMENTS
~~ADD~~		
I and T_0	SET R	Tells memory to read instruction word.
I and T_1	MB INTO OP, RESET R	Transfers OP-code part of instruction word into OP-code register; turns READ flip-flop off.
I and T_2	INCREMENT IC	Adds 1 to the instruction counter, preparing for the next instruction.
I and T_3	MB INTO MA, RESET I, SET E *(address for data)*	Transfers the address part of the instruction word (which is in the memory buffer register) into the memory address register. Puts the computer in the execution cycle.
E and T_0	SET R	Turns the READ flip-flop on, telling the memory to read a word.
E and T_1	MB INTO BR, RESET R	Transfers the contents of the memory buffer register into the B register. Since the memory buffer register now contains what was read from the memory, the addend is transferred into the B register; also turns READ flip-flop off.

TABLE 9 • 3 (CONTINUED)

INSTRUCTION	LIST OF CONTROL SIGNALS TO BE TURNED ON	COMMENTS
E and T_2	ADD	The contents of the B register are added to the accumulator and the sum is placed in the accumulator.
E and T_3	IC INTO MA, SET I, RESET E	The contents of the instruction counter are transferred into the memory address register giving the location of the next instruction word to the memory. The instruction-cycle flip-flop is turned on and the execution-cycle flip-flop turned off.
CLEAR AND ADD		
I and T_0	SET R	Tells memory to read instruction word.
I and T_1	MB INTO OP, RESET R	Transfers OP-code part of instruction word into OP-code register; turns READ flip-flop off.
I and T_2	INCREMENT IC	Adds 1 to the instruction counter, preparing for the next instruction.
I and T_3	MB INTO MA, RESET I, SET E	Transfers the address part of the instruction word (which is in the memory buffer register) into the memory address register.
E and T_0	SET R	Turns the READ flip-flop on, telling the memory to read a word.
E and T_1	MB INTO BR, RESET AC, RESET R	Transfers the memory buffer register into the B register and also clears the accumulator, so if the B register is now added to the accumulator, the accumulator will contain the word read from memory.
E and T_2	ADD	The contents of the accumulator are added to the B register and the sum placed in the accumulator.
E and T_3	IC INTO MA, SET I, RESET E	The contents of the instruction counter are transferred into the memory address register, giving the location of the next instruction word to the memory. The instruction-cycle flip-flop is turned on and the execution-cycle flip-flop turned off.
SUBTRACT		
I and T_0	SET R	Tells memory to read instruction word.
I and T_1	MB INTO OP, RESET R	Transfers OP-code part of instruction word into OP-code register; turns READ flip-flop off.
I and T_2	INCREMENT IC	Adds 1 to the instruction counter, preparing for the next instruction.

TABLE 9 • 3 (CONTINUED)

INSTRUCTION	LIST OF CONTROL SIGNALS TO BE TURNED ON	COMMENTS
I and T_3	MB INTO MA, RESET I, SET E	Transfers the address part of the instruction word (which is in the memory buffer register) into the memory address register. Puts the computer in the execution cycle.
E and T_0	SET R	Turns the READ flip-flop on, telling the memory to read a word.
E and T_1	MB INTO BR, RESET R	Transfers the contents of the memory buffer register into the B register. Since the memory buffer register now contains what was read from the memory, the subtrahend is transferred into the B register; also turns READ flip-flop off.
E and T_2	SUB	The contents of the B register are subtracted from the accumulator, and the difference is placed in the accumulator.
E and T_3	IC INTO MA, SET I, RESET E	The contents of the instruction counter are transferred into the memory address register, giving the location of the next instruction word to the memory. The instruction-cycle flip-flop is turned on and the execution-cycle flip-flop turned off.
STORE		
I and T_0	SET R	Tells memory to read instruction word.
I and T_1	MB INTO OP, RESET R	Transfers OP-code part of instruction word into OP-code register; turns READ flip-flop off.
I and T_2	INCREMENT IC	Adds 1 to the instruction counter, preparing for the next instruction.
I and T_3	MB INTO MA, RESET I, SET E	Transfers the address part of the instruction word (which is in the memory buffer register) into the memory address register.
E and T_0	SET W, AC INTO MB	Transfers word to be read into memory from accumulator into the memory buffer register.
E and T_1	RESET W	Turns WRITE flip-flop off.
E and T_2		Contents of memory buffer register written into memory.
E and T_3	IC INTO MA, SET I, RESET E	The contents of the instruction counter are transferred into the memory address register, giving the location of the next instruction word to the memory. The instruction-cycle flip-flop is turned on and the execution-cycle flip-flop turned off.

register. These two facts tell us that we should logically AND the output line T_0 from the timing-signal distributor with the 1 output of the I flip-flop, and connect the $T_0 \cdot I$ signal to the set input of the READ flip-flop. Then we should connect a $T_1 \cdot I$ signal to the control line that transfers the first 5 bits of the memory buffer register into the OP register. This is shown in Fig. 9·6.

What happens next is always dependent on the OP-code register. We now connect a decoder with $2^5 = 32$ outputs to that register (assuming that we will use all the combinations by adding more instructions). We then have a set of signal lines, so that line 00000 = ADD will carry a 1 signal when we are adding (since the operation code for ADD is 00000); 00001 = SUB will carry a 1 if and only if we are subtracting, since the OP code for subtract is 00001; 00010 = CLA will be a 1 only when we clear and add, etc. We combine these lines and the timing-signal distributor lines and the I and E flip-flop lines to give us all the control signals needed to run the computer. Figure 9·6 shows the complete control circuitry required. A comparison of this figure with the timing and control-signal chart in Table 9·3 will show how the control circuitry works and signals are manufactured when they are needed.

More instructions can be added by adding to the timing and control-signal chart and also by adding the required gates to the control circuitry. Analyzing the computer in this way, we can readily see how the control circuitry directs the operations performed in the machine, alternating the acquiring of instructions from the memory and the performance of the instructions.

9 • 5 TYPICAL SEQUENCE OF OPERATIONS

It will be instructive to analyze the control circuitry in Fig. 9·6 during both an ADD instruction and a STORE instruction. Each instruction will be started with the I (instruction-cycle) flip-flop on, and with the timing-signal distributor having an output on line T_0 so that the AND gate at the upper right of the figure will be turned on by I and T_0, thus setting the READ flip-flop to the 1 state and initiating a READ from the memory. At this time, the memory address register is assumed to have the address of the instruction that will be read into the memory buffer register.

By time T_1 the word read from the memory will have been read into the memory buffer register, so that when we have the control state I and T_1, the contents of the memory buffer register which constitute the OP-code section of the instruction will be transferred into the OP-code register, and the computer will be in a position to decode the OP code and determine what instruction is to be performed.

At time I and T_2 the instruction counter is incremented by 1, so that the instruction counter now contains the address of the next instruction to be read from the memory. The AND gate connected to the I and T_2 input signals is used in turn on the INCREMENT IC control signal, and its output is designated by the name of the control signal.

Similarly, at time I and T_3 the memory buffer register is transferred into the memory address register by the MB INTO MA signal, thus transferring the address part of the instruction word into the memory address register. The next word read from

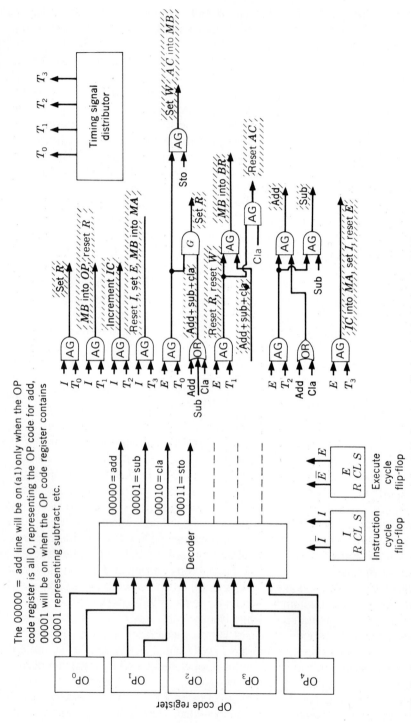

FIG. 9 • 6 Control circuitry for four-instruction computer.

the memory or written into the memory will then be at the address designated by the address part of the instruction word which was just read from the memory.

At the same time the instruction-cycle flip-flop is cleared by the RESET I signal, and the execution flip-flop is set on by the SET E signal, thus changing the state of the computer from an instruction cycle to an execution cycle.

At time E and T_0, then, during an ADD instruction, we set the R flip-flop on, thus telling the memory to read the word at the address currently in the memory address register. In this case this address will be the address part of the instruction word that is being executed. Then at time E and T_1 we transfer the contents of the memory buffer register into the B register. The memory buffer register at that time contains the word which has been read from the memory, so that we now have the word which has been addressed by the instruction word in the B register for the addition. At the same time we reset the READ flip-flop.

Notice that the RESET R and RESET W lines are used to reset both the READ and the WRITE flip-flops simultaneously. There is no harm in resetting both flip-flops, since only one will be on at any given time.

If the instruction is an ADD instruction at time E and T_2, we shall add the contents of the B register to the contents of the accumulator. The B register contains the word which has been read from the memory and the accumulator has not been changed, so their sum will be transferred into the accumulator. Thus the sum of the word read from the memory and the previous contents of the accumulator will be placed in the accumulator. Then, at time E and T_3, we transfer the instruction counter into the memory address register (thus giving the address of the next instruction to be performed to the memory), at the same time clearing the EXECUTE flip-flop, setting the instruction-cycle flip-flop on, and changing the computer from an execution cycle to an instruction cycle.

Since the I flip-flop is on and it is time T_0, the SET R control line will now go high, thus telling the memory to read a word. The next instruction word will be read from the memory and can then be interpreted.

Let us also examine the operation of the STORE instruction which was just described. When the instruction flip-flop is on and we are in an instruction cycle, when time T_0 arrives, the R flip-flop will be set on, telling the memory to read just as for an addition, subtraction, or clear and add; the same thing will happen during time I and T_1. Since the memory-buffer-register flip-flops now contain the OP code of the instruction at time I and T_1, it will be transferred into the OP-code register.

At time I and T_2 we will increment the instruction counter so that the address of the next instruction in memory now lies in the instruction counter; and at time I and T_3 we will reset the instruction flip-flop and turn on the execution-cycle flip-flop, thus putting the computer in an execution cycle.

At time E and T_1, however, if the instruction is a STORE instruction, we will set the WRITE flip-flop on instead of the READ flip-flop, thus initiating a WRITE into the memory. We will also transfer the contents of the accumulator into the memory buffer register, so that the word written into the memory will be the current contents of the accumulator register, and so that after the WRITE cycle has been terminated, the accumulator will have been written into the memory at the address that was given by the instruction word.

At time E and T_1 we reset the WRITE flip-flop, since we have already told the memory to write; nothing need be done at E and T_2, for we are now writing the word into the memory. At time E and T_3 the instruction counter is transferred into the memory address register by the IC INTO MA control signal, thus giving the address of the next instruction to the memory. The instruction-cycle flip-flop is turned on and the execution-cycle flip-flop turned off, thus turning the computer to the instruction-cycle state. The machine will now execute an instruction cycle by reading the next instruction word from the memory, interpreting it, and continuing onward in the program.

The preceding example demonstrates how it is possible to design a computer that will execute a given sequence of operations and thereby cause it to perform each instruction word that is read from the memory. Although only four instructions were demonstrated in this particular example, more instructions can be added in exactly the same manner by simply writing down what must be done when an instruction word is read from the memory, listing the operations that must be performed, and providing gates which will generate the control signals necessary to the performance of each instruction. Subsequent sections will discuss shifting instructions, branching instructions, floating-point instructions, and indexing instructions. All these may be incorporated into the computer shown by simply adding gates to the control circuitry and providing for the additional gates necessary for the transfers and operations between its registers.

The general form of the control-signal generating scheme is shown in Fig. 9·7. It shows a timing-pulse distributor with eight different time divisions, in which case each time period would be one-eighth of the memory-cycle time.

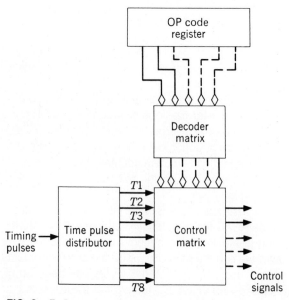

FIG. 9 • 7 General configuration of control circuitry.

9 • 6 BRANCH, SKIP, OR JUMP INSTRUCTIONS

The BRANCH, SKIP, or JUMP instruction varies from the normal instruction in several ways.† For single-address machines only one word, the instruction word, must be located in memory. Also, the contents of the instruction counter may be modified instead of being simply increased by 1. There are two types of BRANCH instructions, conditional and unconditional. For the unconditional BRANCH instruction the contents of the address portion of the memory buffer register are always transferred into the instruction counter. The next instruction performed will then be the instruction at the location indicated by the address section of the instruction word. In most single-address computers, however, the conditional BRANCH instruction will cause the machine to branch only if the number stored in the accumulator register of the arithmetic element is negative. If the number in the accumulator is positive, the contents of the instruction counter will simply be increased by 1, and the next instruction will be taken in the normal order.

During a conditional BRANCH instruction, the sign bit of the accumulator of the arithmetic element must be examined by control circuitry. If the sign bit is a 1, the number stored is negative, and so the number in the address part of the instruction word is transferred into the instruction counter. If the sign bit is a 0, a 1 is added to the instruction counter, and the computer proceeds.‡

To demonstrate how a typical BRANCH-ON-MINUS instruction (BRM) operates in a single-address computer, we will modify the control circuitry shown in Fig. 9·6 so that the small machine will also include a BRM instruction. Let us give the OP code 00100 to BRM, so that the line beneath the 00011 = STO line will be high from the decoder attached to the OP-code register in Fig. 9·6 when a BRM instruction is in the register.

The first two time periods of the instruction cycle are the same for all instructions. First the memory is told to read, and then the instruction word is read from memory into the memory buffer register. The OP-code part is then transferred into the OP-code register, so that, after time T_1 and the beginning of time T_2, the line 00100 = BRM will be high and all the other output lines from the decoder will be low. Now let us make a small table for a BRM instruction, showing what must be done in order to carry out this instruction. Table 9·4 shows the steps that must be taken.

If at time T_2 during the instruction cycle a BRM instruction OP code is in the OP-code register, one of two things must happen. Either we wish to increment the instruction counter and give this number as the address of the next instruction to be taken from the memory, or we wish to transfer the contents of the address portion of the instruction word into the instruction counter. Which of the two choices we take depends upon the sign bit of the accumulator, called AC_0. If the

---

†A survey indicates that some manufacturers call these instructions BRANCH instructions, others call them TRANSFER instructions, while still others call them SKIP or JUMP instructions. All are the same thing.

‡Many computers have a set of *status bits* (flip-flops) which are set and reset depending on the results of operations performed. Jumps or transfers are then taken based on these flip-flops. The Questions and Chap. 10 cover this in detail.

TABLE 9 • 4

BRANCH ON MINUS	LIST OF CONTROL SIGNALS TO BE TURNED ON	COMMENTS
I and T_0	SET R	Tells memory to read instruction word.
I and T_1	MB INTO OP, RESET R	Transfers OP-code part of instruction word into OP-code register; turns READ flip-flop off.
I and T_2 and $\overline{AC_0}$	INCREMENT IC	If the sign digit of the accumulator AC_0 is a 0, we want to increment the instruction counter and use its contents as the address of the next instruction.
I and T_2 and AC_0	MB INTO IC	If the sign digit of the accumulator is a 1, the accumulator is negative, and we want to use the address in the instruction word as the address of the next instruction word.
I and T_3	IC INTO MA	This transfers the instruction counter into the memory address register. Notice that the E flip-flop is not turned on as we are ready to read another instruction word; an EXECUTE cycle is not needed.

accumulator contains a negative number, it will have a 1 in AC_0, and if it contains a positive number, it will have a 0 in flip-flop AC_0. Therefore if I AND T_2 AND $\overline{AC_0}$, we want to increment the instruction counter. If I AND T_2 AND AC_0 happens to be the case, we wish to transfer the memory buffer register into the instruction counter. This is shown in the table. During time T_3 of this instruction cycle we want to transfer the instruction counter into the memory address register. We do not need to put the machine in an execution cycle, but can simply continue on to another instruction cycle, taking the word at the address which has been transferred into the memory address register as the next instruction. Therefore we do not clear the instruction-cycle flip-flop or put a 1 in the execution-cycle flip-flop, but simply transfer the instruction counter into the memory address register.

The control circuitry which will implement these operations is shown in Fig. 9·8. This means that the two particular AND gates in Fig. 9·6, which are connected to the I, T_2 and I, T_3 inputs, will be replaced with the two circuits shown in Fig. 9·8. Notice that this logical circuitry, plus the circuitry in Fig. 9·6, is all that is needed to generate the control signals required for the BRM instruction.

Notice also that a $\overline{BRM}$ signal (the complement of BRM) is used rather than ORing together the instructions which are not BRM instructions. This saves control circuitry in that $\overline{BRM}$ can be made as shown in the figure by simply connecting the BRM signal to an inverter and designating this as $\overline{BRM}$.

Notice that the BRM instruction requires only one access to memory, and therefore only one instruction cycle for its execution.

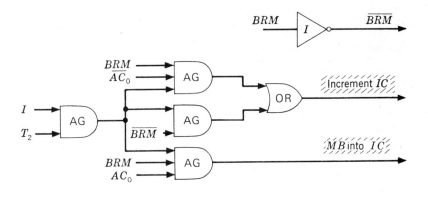

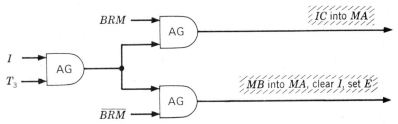

FIG. 9 • 8 Modification of control circuitry for BRANCH instruction.

9 • 7 SHIFT INSTRUCTIONS

The instructions we have examined to date have been instructions that were always performed within a basic fixed number of memory cycles; that is, the ADD, SUBTRACT, CLEAR AND ADD, and STORE instructions were performed within exactly two memory cycles and the TRANSFER and BRANCH instructions required only one memory cycle. There are several classes or types of instructions that may require several memory cycles, because the instruction cannot be performed within, say, two memory cycles. Typical of these instructions are multiplication and division, which generally require more time than the two memory cycles. Similarly, an instruction such as SHIFT RIGHT or SHIFT LEFT could conceivably be performed in a single memory cycle, since the operand is in the accumulator when the instruction word is obtained. However, if the instruction calls for a large number of shifts, more than a memory cycle may be needed to complete the number of operations required. In this case we could not initiate another memory cycle until we had finished shifting the requisite number of times. Similarly, for multiplication and division we could not initiate another memory cycle until we had finished our multiplication and division process.

To implement these types of instructions, we will therefore turn over our control of the computer to a simple control element which is dominated by a counter. This counter will sequence and count the number of steps that must be performed until the instruction has been completed, and it will then put the computer in an instruction cycle and tell the memory to read the next instruction word.

The SHIFT-RIGHT instruction consists of two parts, an OP code and an address part. The OP code of 00101 tells the machine to shift the word in the accumulator right the number of times given in the address part, so that if we write 00101 for the OP code in an instruction word and then write 8 in binary form in the address part, the computer has been instructed to shift the binary number in the accumulator right 8 binary digits.

Assuming that we have an accumulator with gates so that we can shift the accumulator digits right, as was explained in Chap. 6, all we need is to apply eight consecutive SHIFT-RIGHT control signals to the accumulator and we will have shifted the number right 8 places. Since there are only four pulses per memory cycle, we will not want to use the memory until we have completed our shifting. If, for instance, the instruction said SHIFT RIGHT 1, we could finish in one pulse time and start the next instruction cycle immediately after; but if the instruction word said SHIFT RIGHT 4, 5, or 15 or more times, we would have to wait until we had completed shifting before we could initiate another instruction cycle and fetch the next instruction word from the memory.

To do this, we first prepare the computer for the shifting operation by incrementing the instruction counter so that the next word obtained from the instruction counter will contain the address of the next instruction word; and in order to count the number of shifts that we perform, we add another register, called *step-counter register,* which is a counter that counts downward from a given number to 0. We then transfer the memory-buffer-register address part into the step counter, so that the step counter contains the number of shifts to be performed. Then each time we shift, we decrement the counter by 1, so that when the counter reaches 0, we will have performed the requisite number of shifts.

Figure 9·9 shows two stages of a decrementing counter and also the gates necessary to transfer the memory-buffer-register contents into the step counter, designated *SC*. The two rightmost, or least significant, digits of the counter are shown (SC_{n-1} and SC_n), as are also the two rightmost digits of the memory buffer register (MB_{n-1} and MB_n).

The actual number of stages in the step counter will be determined by the maximum number of shifts which the machine must ever make, and since we will also use the same counter for multiplication and division, by the maximum number of steps that will ever be required to multiply or divide. For a computer containing 21 binary digits in the basic computer word, the counter might well contain 5 flip-flops. For a computer with a basic computer word of perhaps 35 or 36 binary digits, the step counter might well contain 6 or even 7 flip-flops.

Consider a sequence of operations for a SHIFT instruction. Times I AND T_0 and I AND T_1 are as usual. At I AND T_2 we increment the instruction counter and transfer count to the step counter. At I AND T_3, we set a flip-flop called *SR* (shift right) on, which tells the computer to start shifting. At the same time we clear the I flip-flop, so that the machine is in neither an instruction nor an execution cycle, although it

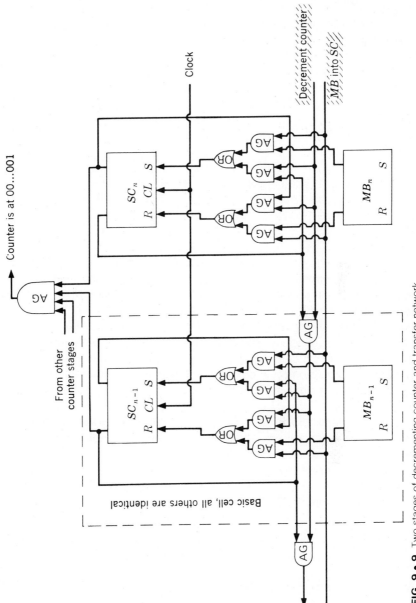

FIG. 9 • 9 Two stages of decrementing counter and transfer network.

TABLE 9 • 5

SHIFT RIGHT	CONTROL SIGNAL TURNED ON	COMMENTS
I and T_0	SET R	Tells memory to read.
I and T_1	MB INTO OP, RESET R	OP code of instruction word is transferred into OP-code register. READ flip-flop is turned off.
I and T_2	INCREMENT IC, MB INTO SC	The instruction counter is prepared to obtain the next instruction word. The address part of the instruction word is transferred into the step counter.
I and T_3	RESET I, SET SR	The instruction-cycle flip-flop is turned off. The SHIFT-RIGHT flip-flop is turned on.

is actually executing an instruction. Thus we do not initiate subsequent memory cycles, and the machine effectively freezes in the shifting state until the step counter has counted to 0, indicating that the requisite number of shifts has been performed. (Actually notice that the step counter counts only to binary 1 rather than to 0 before the order to stop counting is given, for counting when the counter is at 0 would introduce an extra shift.) If we turn the counter SR flip-flop off when the output of the counter is at the 00 . . . 001 signal, and if we at the same time turn the I or instruction cycle on, the computer will proceed to the next instruction cycle, fetching the next instruction word from the memory and performing it. Table 9·5 shows this.

When the SR flip-flop is on, it will be necessary to stop the timing-signal distributor. Thus we arrange to disable this circuit, using the SR flip-flop's output for this purpose.

Implementation of the above procedure is straightforward. A three-input AND gate with inputs I, T_3, and 00101 = SHR (the output from the decoder in Fig. 9·6) can be used to turn an SR flip-flop on and the STOP output from the step counter to turn it off, also turning I on. The input to the clock can be turned off when SR is on.

˙9 • 8 MICROPROGRAMMING

In the preceding sections the control signals which sequence the operations that are performed to execute computer instructions were generated using gates. There is another method, called *microprogramming,* which is also used to generate the control signals in an orderly fashion. This method generally involves use of a ROM to effectively store the control signals in a manner that will be described.

When a computer is microprogrammed, the individual operations between and

---

˙This section can be omitted in a first reading.

on registers are called *microoperations*. For instance, transferring the program counter's contents into the memory address register is a microoperation. Similarly, incrementing the program counter is a microoperation, as is transferring the accumulator's contents into the memory buffer register. In each of these cases a microoperation is initiated by raising a single control signal. Thus sequencing microoperations involves sequencing the appropriate control signals.

Figuring out a sequence of microoperations to do something is called *microprogramming*. The microprogrammer generally writes the list of operations or *microprogram*, using a special language, and quite often a computer program is used to translate this microprogram into a listing describing the appropriate contents for a ROM which will be used to store the microprogram. The statements that the microprogrammer writes are therefore in a microprogramming language. This language can be very primitive or it can be very complex. (Variations of the PL/1 compiler language are used in some systems.) Also, ROM manufacturers often provide a service where a punched paper tape with the desired contents of the ROM punched into it can be automatically placed in the ROM.

In order to explain microprogramming, we will use the computer layout and instructions given in the previous sections and redo the design using a ROM to store the control signals. Therefore the registers and control signals in Fig. 9·3 will be used in the design. First we note that the basic list of microoperations needed is shown in Table 9·6. Each microoperation is described using a symbolic notation (in effect, a microprogramming language), and the corresponding control signal which will cause this operation to occur is also shown.

TABLE 9 • 6 MICROOPERATIONS

MICROOPERATION	CONTROL-SIGNAL NAME	BIT IN READ-ONLY CONTROL MEMORY
$0 \rightarrow IC$	RESET IC	C_7
$IC + 1 \rightarrow IC$	INCREMENT IC	C_8
$MB \rightarrow IC$	MB INTO IC	C_9
$0 \rightarrow AC$	RESET AC	C_{10}
$AC + BR \rightarrow AC$	ADD	C_{11}
$AC - BR \rightarrow AC$	SUBTRACT	C_{12}
$1 \rightarrow W$	SET W	C_{13}
$0 \rightarrow W$	RESET W	C_{14}
$1 \rightarrow R$	SET R	C_{15}
$0 \rightarrow R$	RESET R	C_{16}
$0 \rightarrow AC$	CLEAR AC	C_{17}
$MB_{5-21} \rightarrow MA$	MB INTO MA	C_{18}
$IC \rightarrow MA$	IC INTO MA	C_{19}
$AC \rightarrow MB$	AC INTO MB	C_{20}
$MB_{0-4} \rightarrow OP$	MB INTO OP	C_{21}
$MB \rightarrow BR$	MB INTO BR	C_{22}
$IAR + 1 \rightarrow IAR$	INCREMENT IAR	C_{23}
$C_{0-6} \rightarrow IAR$	C INTO IAR	C_{24}
$OP + IAR + 1 \rightarrow IAR$	ADD OP TO IAR	C_{25}
$0 \rightarrow IAR$	RESET IAR	C_{26}

For instance, the microoperation MB → BR, which means "transfer the contents of the memory buffer register (MB) into the *B* register (BR)," is made to occur by raising the control signal MB INTO BR. Notice the considerable similarity between the description in the microprogramming language and the control signal's name. This is a convenient practice although the control signals could be named X_1, A_1, or anything desired, of course.

Figure 9·10 shows a block diagram for the control system as it will be implemented. There is a ROM with 64 locations and 30 bits per address and an address register for this memory called *IAR* (microinstruction address register). Each output bit from the ROM is a control signal which will generate a microoperation, and these control signals are named C_0–C_{26}. Seven of these outputs are special as they are *next addresses* which can be loaded into the IAR and which will be used to sequence the IAR in several cases. (This ROM is often called a *control memory*.)

The following operations can be performed on this control unit. A 1 can be added to the IAR (in microprogramming language IAR + 1 → IAR, the control signal is called INCREMENT IAR), and the output bits from the control memory labeled C_0–C_6 can be transferred into the IAR. It is also possible to add the value in OP (see Fig. 9·3) plus 1 to the current contents of the IAR.

Now the basic scheme is this: The control signals to generate a given computer instruction, say ADD, are stored in a section of the control memory. The IAR sequences through this section, and at each location the outputs from the control memory will comprise the control signals. These ROM outputs then replace the control signals generated by the gates in Fig. 9·6.

The first problem is that the IAR must be set to the correct address at the beginning of that section in control memory which contains the bits storing the control signals for the instruction to be executed. To do this, we must examine the OP-code register's contents after we have read the instruction word from memory and

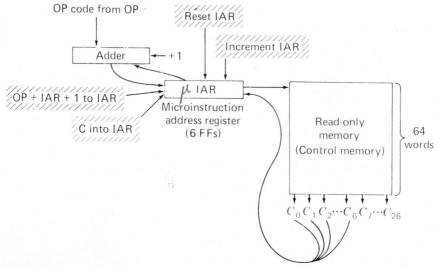

FIG. 9 • 10 Block diagram for control system.

then moved the OP-code section from the memory buffer register into the OP-code register. The complete microprogram for the control memory is shown in Table 9·7. Notice that the first microoperations performed are as follows:

LOCATION IN CONTROL MEMORY	MICROPROGRAM	
0	$1 \rightarrow R$	$IAR + 1 \rightarrow IAR$
1	$MB_{0-4} \rightarrow OP$	$IAR + 1 \rightarrow IAR$
2	$OP + IAR + 1 \rightarrow IAR$	
3	$C_{0-6} \rightarrow IAR$	
4	$C_{0-6} \rightarrow IAR$	
5	$C_{0-6} \rightarrow IAR$	
6	$C_{0-6} \rightarrow IAR$	

The operation here is as follows. First the memory is told to read. (The prior instruction has loaded the memory address register with the location of the instruction word.) The instruction word is then in the memory buffer register when the next microoperation is performed. This microinstruction loads the OP-code register with the first 5 bits in the memory buffer register. Next this value is added to the IAR register plus 1. Now if the instruction is an ADD instruction with OP code 00000, then 1 will be added to the current IAR's contents (which will give 3 in decimal). Thus the next word in the control memory to be accessed would be at location 3, and in location 3 the value for C in the first 7 bits is 20. When C is loaded into the IAR, the next microinstruction word addressed will be that at address 20 in the ROM, which contains the first microinstruction in the ADD section. If the instruction in OP was a SUBTRACT, the OP code will be 00001, and so the next word in the control memory to be used will be at location 4 decimal, which will cause a transfer to location 25, which in turn contains the microinstructions for the SUBTRACT instruction.

Therefore an ADD instruction will cause a jump to location 20 (decimal) in the control memory, and a SUBTRACT will cause a branch to location 25. In each case these locations begin the section of memory containing the microinstructions which will cause the instruction to be executed.

At the end of each microprogram section which causes an instruction to be executed, the IAR is set to 0, which is the starting point for the operations that lead to reading in the next instruction and branching to the correct section in the control memory to cause the instruction to be executed.

9 • 9 VARIATIONS IN MICROPROGRAMMING CONFIGURATIONS

Figure 9·11 shows the microprogram of Table 9·7 stored in a memory. The implementation here has the control memory in Fig. 9·10 with its contents as shown in Fig. 9·11. This basic configuration is used in most modern microprogrammed computers. There are many variations on this idea, however, and there are many microprogramming languages. The references contain further descriptions and information in this area.

TABLE 9 • 7 MICROPROGRAM FOR FOUR-INSTRUCTION COMPUTER

LOCATION IN CONTROL MEMORY	MICROPROGRAM	COMMENTS
0	$1 \rightarrow R$, IAR $+ 1 \rightarrow$ IAR	Tell memory to read, increment IAR.
1	$MB_{0-4} \rightarrow OP$, IAR $+ 1 \rightarrow$ IAR	Place OP code in instruction in OP.
2	OP $+$ IAR $+ 1 \rightarrow$ IAR	Add OP code to 3, this gives next address in IAR to be used.
3	$C_{0-6} \rightarrow$ IAR, C_{0-6} has value 20 decimal	Instruction was ADD go to location 20 in ROM.
4	$C_{0-6} \rightarrow$ IAR, C_{0-6} has value 25 decimal	Instruction was SUBTRACT go to location 25 in ROM.
5	$C_{0-6} \rightarrow$ IAR, C_{0-6} has value 30 decimal	Instruction was CLA go to location 30 in ROM.
6	$C_{0-6} \rightarrow$ IAR, C_{0-6} has value 35 decimal	Instruction was STO go to location 35 in ROM.
7		
8		
9		
10	Left blank to add more instructions	
11		
12		
13		
14		
15		
16		
17		
18		
19		
20	$0 \rightarrow I$, $1 \rightarrow E$, $MB_{5-21} \rightarrow MA$	Begin ADD instruction microoperations; place address of augend in memory address register.

No.	Microoperation	Comment
21	$1 \rightarrow R$, $IC + 1 \rightarrow IC$	Read augend from memory, increment instruction counter.
22	$MB \rightarrow BR$, $0 \rightarrow R$	Place augend in B register.
23	$AC + BR \rightarrow AC$	Add and place sum in accumulator.
24	$IC \rightarrow MA$, $1 \rightarrow I$, $0 \rightarrow E$, $0 \rightarrow IAR$	Set up for next instruction by placing instruction counter in memory address register and going to location 0 in control memory.
25	$MB_{5-21} \rightarrow MA$, $0 \rightarrow I$, $1 \rightarrow E$	Begin SUBTRACT instruction microoperations.
26	$1 \rightarrow R$, $IC + 1 \rightarrow IC$	
27	$MB \rightarrow BR$, $0 \rightarrow R$	Place subtrahend in B register.
28	$AC - BR \rightarrow AC$	Subtract and place difference in accumulator.
29	$IC \rightarrow MA$, $1 \rightarrow I$, $0 \rightarrow E$, $0 \rightarrow IAR$	Place address of next instruction word in memory address register and go to 0 in control memory.
30	$MB_{5-21} \rightarrow MA$, $0 \rightarrow I$, $1 \rightarrow E$	Begin CLA instruction operations.
31	$1 \rightarrow R$	
32	$MB \rightarrow BR$, $0 \rightarrow AC$, $0 \rightarrow R$	Reset accumulator.
33	$AC + BR \rightarrow AC$	Add B register to accumulator.
34	$IC \rightarrow MA$, $1 \rightarrow I$, $0 \rightarrow E$, $0 \rightarrow IAR$	End CLA instruction; place address of next instruction in memory address register and go to 0 in control memory.
35	$0 \rightarrow I$, $1 \rightarrow E$, $MB_{5-21} \rightarrow MA$	Begin STO instruction.
36	$1 \rightarrow W$, $AC \rightarrow MB$	Place accumulator's contents in memory buffer register so that it can be stored; tell memory to write.
37	$0 \rightarrow W$	
38	$IC + 1 \rightarrow IC$	Set up for next instruction.
39	$IC \rightarrow MA$, $1 \rightarrow I$, $0 \rightarrow E$, $0 \rightarrow IAR$	End of instruction, place address of next instruction in memory address register and go to 0 in control memory.

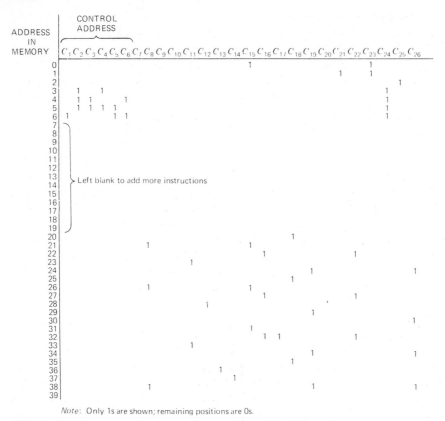

Note: Only 1s are shown; remaining positions are 0s.

FIG. 9 • 11 Microprogram in memory. Control address C_0 has 0s in all positions.

The microprogramming configuration shown in Fig. 9·11 has an output bit from the memory for each control signal. This is called *horizontal microprogramming*. For larger computers there may be many control signals, and thus there would be many bits in the control memory. (In general, the number of control signals varies from about 60 for small computers to about 3000 for the largest machines.) Since this would involve too large a control memory, the control signals are examined, and an attempt is made to reduce the number of outputs from the memory. After this is done, the resulting configuration is said to use *vertical microprogramming*.

As an example of how the number of outputs might be reduced, consider that in some cases when one control signal is raised, another is always raised, and so these two signals could be combined into a single signal.

In some cases different control signals are never turned on at the same time. If N such signals can be found, then only M control lines, where $2^M > N$, will be required, and a decoder can be used to provide the necessary control signals. For instance, the ADD, SUB, RESET AC, and MB INTO BR signals are never turned on at the same time. Thus two control output lines with a four-output decoder could be used to generate these signals.

When vertical microprogramming is used, the system becomes less flexible, since if a microprogram is to be changed or enlarged, fewer options in control signal generation will be available. As a result most commercial computers are arranged so they are somewhere between horizontal and vertical in their construction. (Many schemes have been used, and several are described in the Questions.)

Microprogramming is widely used in the new computer lines. Since the instruction repertoire for the computer is effectively stored in the ROM, the instructions provided can be changed or added to by changing or adding to the ROM.

Further, microprogramming is useful in simulating one computer on another. This means that we have a computer which has a basic set of registers and operations between registers, and we have the ability to microprogram this computer. Further, we have a second computer with a certain set of instructions and a set of programs written to run on this second computer. We now wish to make the first computer run these programs and deliver the same results as the second computer would have delivered. This is called *simulation,* and the first computer is said to *simulate* the second computer. To do this, we microprogram the simulator computer so that a given instruction has the same effect as the same instruction in the second machine.†

As can be seen, a computer which is microprogrammed can be made to simulate another computer. Clearly some computers have architectures which are much better suited for simulation than others. A computer that is very well adapted for simulation is, for instance, the Burroughs 1700, which has great flexibility in its operations between registers and a considerable set of microoperations available.

The microprograms provided by a manufacturer (or anyone else) to be used on its microprogrammed computer are generally called *firmware.* The instructions that a microprogrammed computer provides can be very complex and can be carefully designed to satisfy the programmer's needs. The primary objections to microprogramming are: (1) speed, because the logic gates used in a "conventional" computer will be faster than the ROM in most cases, and so the conventional machine may run faster; and (2) the gates can be minimized in number since the instructions are to be fixed, and thus the total amount of equipment can often be made smaller. (This is not always the case; however, ROMs are quite compact and inexpensive so that the advantage of gates decreases as time passes.) As a result, most large, fast "super" computers tend to use logic gates for control, while the medium and smaller computers now tend to be microprogrammed.

QUESTIONS

1. A single-address, one-instruction-per-word computer has a word length of 22 binary digits. The computer can perform 32 different instructions, and it has three index registers. The inner memory is a 16,000-word magnetic core

---

†This is often called *emulation* when microprogramming is used. It is necessary to rename registers and arrange for other changes to really effect this, but the principle is essentially given here.

memory. Draw a diagram of the computer word, allocating space for each part of the basic instruction word (OP-code part, address part, index-register part). Do not use the sign digit (leftmost digit) of the word.

2. The octal code 15 (for ANA) causes the contents of the accumulator to be ANDed, with the contents (word) at the address given in the instruction word in the DDP-24 in Table 9·2. Make bits 1 through 3 each a 0, and also make bit 4 a 0. Then write, in binary, the instruction word that will AND the accumulator with the contents of address 12 in the memory.

3. If the basic computer word in a machine has 24 binary digits and we have 55 different instructions, make up an instruction-word format for a single-address machine. How many different memory locations can be directly addressed by the address portion of this computer instruction word? Make up the computer instruction word for a double-address computer with 24 binary digits in the computer word and 55 instructions. How many different locations can now be addressed directly by a single instruction word?

4. If the accumulator of the DDP-24 computer contains all 1s (has a 1 in each bit) and address 30 in the memory contains all 0s, an STC 30_{10} instruction, in which 30 refers to (decimal) location 30, will result in what in location 30 in the memory?

5. Write a simple program, using the operation codes for the DDP-24, which will evaluate $a + b + c$, given that a, b, and c are in memory addresses 23, 24, and 26, respectively. Store the result in 30.

6. Would you expect the instruction counter of a single-address computer to have as many bits as the address portion of the computer word? Why?

7. The instruction code for the DDP-24 is listed in Table 9·2, along with a diagram of the basic instruction word. Write in binary form the instruction word that will cause the contents of the B register to be multiplied by the word stored at location 24 of the computer's inner memory.

8. Design a single stage of an accumulator and B register which will add and shift left in one operation (step) or will simply shift left in one step. Use SHIFT LEFT and ADD AND SHIFT LEFT as control signals, a full adder, AND and OR gates, and RS flip-flops.

9. Make out a timing table and modify the control circuitry in Fig. 9·6, including the modification in Fig. 9·8, so that the machine has an unconditional BRANCH instruction BRA, as well as a conditional BRANCH instruction BRM, generating the necessary control signals.

10. Explain the RND instruction in Table 9·2.

11. Write a program for the DDP-24, using the OP codes in Table 9·2, which will evaluate the expression $(x + y^2)/z$, assuming that x, y, and z are at addresses 301, 302, and 303 in the memory. Assume that no scaling is necessary and store the result at address 304 in the memory.

12. Explain the STD instruction in Table 9·2. This is called an *address-modifying* instruction. Why?

13. Explain the SBM instruction in Table 9·2.

14. The microprogramming language outlined in this chapter is generally called a *register-transfer language*. Discuss how you would expand or perhaps improve this language. Do you think that microprogramming in a higher level language, such as PL/1 or one of its variations, would yield an efficient microprogram in the control memory? Discuss this.

15. Show how to modify Fig. 9·8 so that the BRM instruction becomes a BRP instruction, meaning that the computer jumps or branches when the ACC is positive instead of negative.

16. Show how to generate timing signals (such as T_0, T_1, T_2, and T_3 in Fig. 9·5) using a shift register with the rightmost stages' outputs connected to the leftmost stages' inputs. This is called a *ring counter*. In what states would you set the flip-flops to start?

17. Why is the instruction counter always placed in the memory address register at time T_3 during the execution part of an instruction in Table 9·3?

18. Explain why some instructions require both execution and instruction cycles and some require only instruction cycles. Give examples of both kinds of instruction.

19. Why can the SET W and AC INTO MB control signals be combined in Fig. 9·6?

20. Why can the IC INTO MA, SET I, and CLEAR E control signals be combined in Fig. 9·6?

21. Show how to add a push button connected to a reset and start wire which will (using DC SETs and DC RESETs on the flip-flops) cause the computer in Fig. 9·6 to start executing a program beginning at location 0 in the memory when depressed.

22. Add a BRANCH ON ZERO instruction similar to that in Table 9·4 and Fig. 9·8, except that the computer branches when the accumulator value is all 0s.

23. Add a SHIFT-LEFT instruction to the example computer control using a technique as shown in Table 9·5 and Figs. 9·8 and 9·9.

24. When microprogramming is used to generate control signals and a ROM is used, how can the instruction repertoire of the computer be changed?

25. In Fig. 9·10 the control signals could be loaded into D flip-flops and the flip-flops' outputs used as the actual control signals. Give advantages and disadvantages of this.

26. Explain the difference between a microoperation and the control signal which implements it.

27. In order to implement BRANCH or JUMP ON ACCUMULATOR NEGATIVE instructions, another control signal C_{30} can be added which, when it is a 1, causes a test of the sign bit of the accumulator and a jump in the control memory to a section of microoperations which cause the desired change in the computer sequence of operations. Design this instruction.

28. In writing microprograms it is convenient to have an IF microoperation. For instance, to write a microprogram to implement a branch instruction, we might like an IF($AC_0 = 1$) THEN $C_{0-6} \rightarrow$ IAR ELSE IAR $+$ 1 $\rightarrow$ IAR microoperation. This says if AC_0 is a 1, then place the current value of $C_0 - C_6$ in IAR, which means that the next microinstruction will be from the address given in $C_0 - C_6$. If AC_0 is a 0, the next microinstruction will be from the next location in the control store. Write a microprogram for the branch-register-memory instruction using this microoperation.

29. Write a microprogram for a BRP (branch or positive) instruction using the information in the preceding question.

30. Show how to implement the instruction in the preceding question.

31. Write a microprogram for a SHIFT-RIGHT instruction using the IF type of statement just described. (You will also need a counter.)

32. Show how to implement the microprogram in the preceding question.

33. Write a microprogram to implement a multiplication instruction.

34. Show how to implement the multiplication instruction in the preceding question.

35. Write a microprogram to implement a DIVIDE instruction.

36. Show how to implement your DIVIDE instruction from the preceding question.

37. Reduce the number of control signals used in Fig. 9·11.

38. Explain what features you might like in a computer which is to be microprogrammed to simulate several other computers.

39. Discuss some of the advantages and disadvantages of microprogramming as you see them.

40. Some computers now use a branch or jump scheme where status bits are continually being set during arithmetic and logical operations. For instance, status bits Z and N are commonly used to indicate if the result of an operation is "all zero" or "negative." Show how to add such status bits to the arithmetic section of the computer shown in Fig. 9·6.

41. When status bits are used, jump instructions are of the form "jump on zero," meaning jump if the Z flip-flop is a 1, or "jump negative," meaning jump if the N flip-flop is a 1. Design these two instructions using the Z and N circuitry from the preceding question.

42. Discuss the advantages and disadvantages of *random logic* (gate-generated logic) versus microprogramming for a computer control section. Assume that the computer is a minicomputer.

43. Compare the microprogramming and conventional random logic techniques for generating the control signals in a general-purpose digital computer. Assume that the computer is to be sold in a large market where both business and scientific programs are to be run. Give the advantages and disadvantages of both techniques for implementing control logic.

44. The control of a single-address small computer normally passes through two major phases or cycles in executing an instruction which fetches a single operand from memory (an ADD or SUBTRACT instruction, for example). We call these the *instruction cycle* and the *execution cycle*. In order for control to know which phase or cycle it is in, a conventional random logic control unit uses an E flip-flop and an I flip-flop.

   (a) Why are two flip-flops used instead of one?

   (b) Why does a microprogrammed version of the same computer not require an E and an I flip-flop?

19
COMPUTER
ORGANIZATION

Computers are now available in a wide range of sizes and capabilities. The smallest computers are called microcomputers, the next largest are minicomputers, followed by small, medium-sized, and finally the large, super, or "maxi" computers. The prices range from a few dollars (for a chip set for a microcomputer) to several million dollars. Speeds are from tens of microseconds per instruction (or operation) to tens of instructions per microsecond.

The microcomputer is the newest addition in the computer hierarchy, and a given microcomputer generally consists of several integrated-circuit (IC) chips, including a central processing unit (CPU) chip (or chips), called a *microprocessor chip* (or chips), several memory chips, and one or more input-output interface chips. These sets of chips can be quite inexpensive (a few dollars in large quantities) or fairly expensive (several hundred dollars for high-speed chip sets). The familiar hand calculators are often assembled from IC chips including one of the lower priced microprocessor chips. Fully assembled microcomputers can cost as little as several hundred dollars.

Microprocessor chips are widely used in so-called original equipment manufacturer (OEM) devices or systems. Traffic lights, printers, communications controllers, automatically controlled instrument complexes, cash registers, and automatic checkout facilities in grocery and department stores, for example, all make wide use of microprocessors.

Similarly, minicomputers, which generally have prices from one thousand to tens of thousands of dollars (including memory and input-output devices), are widely used in control systems and OEM systems as well as in scientific applications and business data processing for small businesses, schools, laboratories, etc. The minicomputer preceded the microcomputer in time, and it continues to be widely used since computers in this price range provide many users with enough additional capabilities to warrant the extra cost.

The small- and medium-scale computer market finds applications in businesses and laboratories of all kinds as well as in hospitals, warehouses, small banks, etc. The largest computers are to be found in large corporations such as insurance companies, large banks, large scientific laboratories, and large universities. These "super" computers range from scientific-application-oriented "number crunchers" to large complexes of input-output devices and memories used in businesses where emphasis is on maintaining large files of data, producing management reports, billing, automatic ordering, inventory control, etc.

The characteristics of these different kinds of computers differ considerably from category to category and also from design to design. Computers for business data processing have different systems features than those for scientific work. There is also considerable variation in opinion as to how computers for the same application area should be configured, which leads to differing computer designs.

The subject of *computer architecture* ranges through almost every aspect of computer organization. Included are the lengths of the instruction words, whether the length is variable or there are several different lengths, and how many addresses in memory are referenced by an instruction word. Other architectural considerations concern the number of bits in each memory word, whether instructions and data words are of the same size as the memory words, whether numbers are handled in 1s or 2s complement form or in BCD or some combination of these. What are the instructions provided, how are the memories organized, and how are input-output devices interfaced? As can be seen, computer architecture is a large and rich subject which deals with most aspects of computer design and organization and interacts with every aspect of the computer.

This chapter will first describe some of the instruction-word formats now in use. Then some typical computer architectures will be covered. Actual details of real computers will be used to illustrate the principles covered. Enough information is given so that the architecture and operation of most computers can be readily understood. Examples of program sections are also included to illustrate the principles covered and to introduce machine language and assembly language concepts. The intent is therefore to concentrate on the principles involved, using actual computers to illustrate these principles.

10 • 1 INSTRUCTION WORD FORMATS—NUMBER OF ADDRESSES

A given computer has one or more basic formats for its instruction words. We have emphasized the single-address instruction word, which is very popular for microcomputers. There are also several other formats in use, however.

Two-address instructions

The number of divisions in the basic computer instruction word is determined primarily by the number of addresses which are referred to. The single-address

Single address instruction

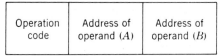

Two address instruction

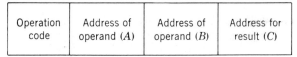

Three address instruction

Operation code	Address of operand (A)	Address of operand (B)	Address for result (C)	Address of next instruction (D)

Four address instruction

FIG. 10 • 1 Formats for instructions.

instruction has been covered. Many computers, however, have two-address instruction words with three sections (Fig. 10·1), the first consisting of the OP code and the second and third sections each containing the address of a location in the memory.

Different computers use these addresses differently. Generally, both addresses in a two-address machine specify operands, and the result is stored at the first of the addresses.* The Minneapolis-Honeywell 200 and the IBM 1400 and 360/370 series have two-address instructions which provide examples in which each address refers to an operand in the memory.

In many computers, instead of a single accumulator, there are two or more registers which are called either *multiple accumulators* or *general-purpose registers*. An instruction word will then have the first address section (the "address of operand *A*" section in Fig. 10·1) tell which general register contains one of the operands. The second address section of the instruction word will then give the address in memory of the second operand. If only two accumulators or general registers are provided, only 1 bit is needed for the first address section; if 16 general registers are used, then 4 bits will be needed for the first address. Results are generally stored in the general register (accumulator) specified by the first address.

---

*In several computers the result of the calculation is stored at the second of the two addresses.

In some computers instruction words are provided in which each of the two addresses refers to general registers. Thus, for instance, in a computer with 16 general registers an instruction word would consist of the OP code plus two 4-bit address sections.

Two-address instruction words in which one or both addresses refer to general registers are shorter than two-address instruction words where both addresses refer to the memory, and this format is popular in microcomputers and mincomputers.

Zero-address instructions—stacks

There is a type of instruction word that does not specify any location in memory for an operand, but which relies on what is called a *stack* to provide operands.

Basically a stack is a set of consecutive locations in a memory into which operands (data items) can be placed. The name *stack* is derived from the fact that the memory is organized like a stack of plates in a cafeteria. (Each operand can be thought of as a plate.) The first operand placed on the stack is said to be at the bottom of the stack. Placing an operand on the stack is called *pushing,* and removing an operand is called *popping* the operand. The operand most recently placed on the stack is said to be on the *top* of the stack. Only this top operand is immediately available.

If we push operands *A, B,* and *C* onto an empty stack and then pop an operand, *C* will be removed. If we push *A, B,* and *C* in order and then pop three operands, first *C* will be popped, then *B,* and finally *A.* (This last-in first-out principle leads to stacks sometimes being called *LIFO lists.*)

Figure 10·2 shows the operation of a stack. Stacks are generally maintained as a set of words in a memory. Each word therefore has a fixed length (number

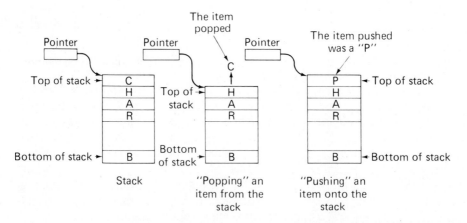

Note: In this case each item in the stack is a single character. The stack items could be numbers, words, records, etc. The pointer contains the address of the "top of the stack."

FIG. 10 • 2 Stack operations.

of bits) and an address. The *stack pointer* is a register that contains the address of the top operand in the stack. The stack pointer is incremented or decremented when an operand is pushed or popped.

If an ADD instruction is given a computer using a stack architecture, the top two operands in the stack will be removed and added and the sum then placed on the top of the stack. Similarly, a MULTIPLY instruction would cause the top two operands to be multiplied together and the product placed on the stack.

Since only the OP-code section of an arithmetic instruction need be given to specify an arithmetic operation, these instruction words can be very short. It will still be necessary, however, to move operands from memory onto the stack and from the stack back into the memory, and the instruction words for this will be longer since memory addresses must be specified. (These instruction words will be like single-address instruction words, except that the operands are moved to and from the stack instead of to and from the accumulator.)

The advocates of stacked computer architecture have some convincing arguments, but problems do exist. Stacked computers include the Burroughs 5500 and 1700 and the Hewlett-Packard 3000. Stacks are widely used in other sections of computers, as will be shown.

10 • 2 REPRESENTATION OF INSTRUCTIONS AND DATA

Important features of a computer's architecture concern the number of bits in instruction words, the size of memory words, and the way data are represented in the computer. In most early computers and in some present-day computers the high-speed memory contains the same number of bits at each address (in each location) as the instruction words. Similarly, numbers are represented again using the same number of bits. This makes for straightforward implementation. An example of a computer with this structure can be found in the PDP-8, which has a 12-bit-per-word memory, and 12-bit instruction words with a 3-bit OP code, and numbers are represented using a 12-bit signed 2s complement number system. Many large computers were and are made with this structure; the IBM 700, 704, 709, 7094, and the Honeywell 6000 and 60 series of computers all have 36-bit memory words and 36-bit instruction words, and binary numbers are represented using 2s complement signed 36-bit numbers (floating-point numbers are basically 36 bits, also). Most of the large scientific number-crunching machines also use this structure, and CDC produces a number of 64-bit-per-word large computers with this basic structure as well as some smaller 24-bit-per-word computers.

There is a desire to be efficient with the length of instruction words. Also, business data processing involves much manipulation using character strings (names, addresses, text, etc.). The desire to create computer architectures that conserve on instruction word length and also permit storing of strings of characters of arbitrary length efficiently has led to a number of computer architectures with (1) only 8 bits at each address in memory, so a single alphanumeric character can be stored at each address, and (2) instruction words with variable lengths (each word length is generally some multiple of 8 bits).

The IBM 1400 and 1600 series of computers, as well as the Honeywell 200 series, all have 8 (or 9) bits per word in the high-speed memory, and instruction-word OP codes are one alphanumeric character (8 bits) plus whatever bits are needed to provide the two memory addresses required for each instruction. This kind of computer is described in Sec. 10·14.

The IBM 360/370 series has 8 bits per word in the memory and a number of different instruction word lengths ranging from 16 to 48 bits.

In many of the newer computers, numbers can be represented in BCD as well as in binary and floating point, and calculations can be performed in each of these number representation systems.

Microcomputers tend to have data words and memory words of 4, 8, or 16 bits. Instruction words are generally variable in length, but the lengths are almost always multiples of the number of bits in the memory.

10 • 3 ADDRESSING TECHNIQUES

When an address in memory is given in an instruction word, the most obvious technique is simply to give the address in memory in binary form. This is called *direct addressing,* and the instruction words in the examples in Chap. 9 all use direct addressing.

While direct addressing provides the most straightforward (and fastest) way to give a memory address, several other techniques are also used. These techniques are generally motivated by one of the following considerations:

1. *Desire to shorten address section*   For instance, if we have a minicomputer with 16-bit words and a 32K memory, 15 bits will be required for each direct address and addressing techniques are used to reduce this number.
2. *Programmer convenience*   There are several addressing techniques (such as index registers, which will be described) which provide a convenience to the programmer in writing programs.
3. *System operation facilities*   In most large computer systems the computer will have several different programs in its memory at a given time and will alternate the running of these programs. In order to efficiently load and remove these programs from memory in differing locations, addressing techniques are provided which make the programs *relocatable,* meaning that the same program can be run in many different sections of memory.

The following sections describe the basic addressing techniques now in use. Included are (1) direct addressing, (2) immediate addressing, (3) paging, (4) relative addressing, (5) indirect addressing, and (6) indexed addressing.

10 • 4 DIRECT ADDRESSING

Simply giving the complete binary address in memory is the most direct way to locate an operand or to give an address to jump to. As a result, most computers have some form of *direct addressing*. The following examples are for computers that will also be used in the sections on more complex addressing strategies.

Example

The 8080 micropressor has a single 8-bit accumulator. The 8080's memory is organized into words of 8 bits per word which are called *bytes*. An OP code for this microprocessor occupies 8 bits or 1 byte, an entire memory location. The address bits are then located in the following memory locations, and since 2^{16} words can be used in a memory, 2 bytes are required for a direct address. As a result, a direct-address instruction requires 3 bytes in memory—one for the OP code and two for the direct address.

In executing an instruction, the 8080 CPU† always obtains the OP code from memory first, and this tells how many bytes are required for the address. The 8080 CPU then reads the necessary bytes from memory and assembles a complete instruction word in its registers, which it then proceeds to execute.

A typical direct-access instruction in the 8080 is the LDA (load accumulator) instruction with OP code 00111010 (3A hexadecimal). This OP code is followed by 2 bytes giving the address in memory of the 8-bit word to be loaded into the accumulator. The low-order (least significant) bits of the address are given in the first byte of the address and the high order bits in the second byte.

Assume that the memory contains these values:

ADDRESS (HEXADECIMAL)	CONTENTS (HEXADECIMAL)
0245	3A
0246	49
0247	03
. . .	. . .
0349	23

The 3 bytes in locations 245, 246, and 247 contain a single LDA instruction which when executed will cause the value 23_{16} to be transferred into the accumulator of the 8080 microprocessor.

Example

The 6800 microprocessor has two 8-bit accumulators which are referred to as accumulator *A* and accumulator *B*. The microprocessor has 8 bits per memory word. The OP code of an instruction occupies 8 bits and therefore a complete memory word. The address bits for an instruction word are in the memory location(s) following the OP code. The memory can be up to 2^{16} locations in size. As an example of direct addressing, the OP code for ADDA, which causes the con-

---

†The 8080 CPU is constructed on a single chip. This chip, which is sometimes called the *8080 microprocessor chip*, interprets and executes instructions. Memory is on separate chips, as are input-output interface circuits.

ADDA OP code is *BB* for direct addressing

ADDB OP code is *FB* for direct addressing

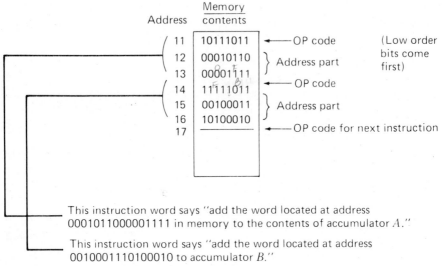

FIG. 10 • 3 6800 microprocessor instruction execution.

tents of the address referenced to be added to and then stored in accumulator *A*, is BB (hexadecimal) or 10111011 (binary). If the microprocessor reads this OP code, it knows that the address is given in the following 16 bits. As a result, if the 6800 CPU reads an OP code of BB, it then reads the next 2 bytes in memory to obtain the address. The microprocessor then reads from this address and performs the required addition. The next OP code is then read from the memory location following the two locations that contained the address.†

The OP code for an ADDB instruction, which causes the number stored in the memory location referenced by the next 16 bits to be added to accumulator *B*, is FB (hexadecimal). Now examine Fig. 10·3. If the microprocessor reads the two instruction words shown, it will cause addition into first accumulator *A*, then accumulator *B*, and will take the next instruction word from location 17 in the memory.

In the 6800 microprocessor, instruction words can have addresses with 1 byte or 2 bytes, as will be seen. [Some instructions have only "implied addresses" (no address bits); HALT is such an instruction.] The microprocessor must therefore read the OP code before it can determine how many more locations from the mem-'ory need to be read to form the instruction word.

One note is necessary here. The 6800 microprocessor has instructions with only 8-bit addresses. In this case an address has only 8 bits, and thus only the first 256 bytes in the memory can be referenced. As an example, an instruction to add the number at the location given in the following 8 bits to accumulator *A* has OP code 9B. An instruction to add to accumulator *B* the number at the location given in the

---

†Notice that the 6800 places the most significant bits in the address in the second byte and the least significant bits in the third byte. (The 8080 does the reverse.)

following byte has OP code DB. The OP code tells whether a complete 16-bit or an 8-bit address is to be read from the memory. (In its manuals Motorola calls the 8-bit address instruction words *direct-addressing instructions* and the 16-bit address instruction words *extended direct-addressing instructions*.) The 16-bit addresses have been used to illustrate the direct-addressing technique because they are more natural and all of the memory can be reached.

Example

The PDP-11 is a DEC minicomputer series with sizes ranging from small to large. A particular size is designated by the model number, so that a PDP-11/05 is a small computer, the PDP-11/45 is a medium-sized machine, and the PDP-11/70 is a fairly large system. This series of minicomputers is typical of what is offered by DEC and other manufacturers.

The PDP-11 has eight 16-bit general registers (accumulators). It is common practice to name these general registers $R0$–$R7$, and we will follow this practice.

The PDP-11 memory is organized into 8-bit words, so 1 byte is in each memory location. The PDP-11 has a number of addressing modes and, as a result, a fairly complex instruction-word format.

A typical direct-address instruction in the PDP-11 involves adding the numbers in two general registers together and storing the sum in one of the registers. The instruction word to do this has three sections: (1) the OP code, (2) the source address, and (3) the destination address. (In an ADD, the number in the source register is added to that in the destination register, and the sum is placed in the destination register.) Since the source and destination are each general registers and there are 8 general registers, 3 bits are required to give each address. However, since the PDP-11 has a number of addressing modes, three extra bits are included in each of the source and destination addresses to tell which addressing mode is to be used. The instruction-word format is therefore as follows:

OP code	Source address	Destination address
15 12	11 6 5	0

The first (leftmost) 3 bits in the source and destination addresses give the mode, and for direct addressing these will be all 0s. The next 3 bits give the register number. The OP code for ADD in the PDP-11 is 0110, and so the instruction word which will add register 3 to register 5 and store the sum in register 5 is

0110	000011	000101

Another example of direct addressing is the increment instruction which simply adds 1 to a selected general register. The instruction word to accomplish this has two sections: an OP code and an address section. The address section has 3 bits to tell the mode and 3 bits to designate the register. The OP code for an INC (increment) instruction is 0000101010. Thus an instruction that will increment general register 5 is

0000101010	000101

OP code   Address part

Notice that this OP code is larger than the ADD OP code. This is because only one operand is required here. (The first 4 bits are not duplicated in any of these larger OP codes; they tell the class of operation.)

10 • 5 IMMEDIATE ADDRESSING

A straightforward way to obtain an operand is simply to have it follow the instruction word in memory. Suppose that we want to add the number 7 to the accumulator in a single accumulator computer, and suppose that the memory is organized in 8-bit bytes. A direct way to cause this addition would be to have an 8-bit OP code which says to ADD and that the augend follows "immediately" in memory (the next byte). The computer would then read the OP code, get the byte to be added from memory (which would contain 7), add it into the accumulator, and then take the next instruction word's OP code from the byte following the byte containing the augend. This is essentially how the 8080 (and 6800) computers operate.

In general, immediate addressing simply means that an operand immediately follows the instruction word in memory.

Example

For the 8080 microprocessor the instruction ADI (add immediate) has OP code 11000110 and tells the CPU to take the byte following this OP code and add it into the accumulator. Consider:

ADDRESS	CONTENTS
16_{16}	11000110
17_{16}	00001100
. . .	. . .

When the computer reaches address 16_{16} in memory, it reads the OP code, sees that this instruction is an ADI instruction, takes the next byte from the memory which is 00001100, adds this into the accumulator, and then takes the next OP code from location 18_{16} in memory.

Example

The 6800 microcomputer has two accumulators, and so the OP code must tell which accumulator is to be used. The instruction ANDA with OP code 84_{16} will cause the byte following the OP code to be ANDed bit by bit with accumulator A, while the instruction ANDB with OP code $C4_{16}$ will cause the byte following the OP code to be ANDed bit by bit with accumulator B.

Suppose that accumulator A contains 01100111 and accumulator B 10011101. Then consider this in memory:

ADDRESS	CONTENTS
10_{16}	10000100
11_{16}	11010101
12_{16}	11000100
13_{16}	10100101
14_{16}	. . .

The 6800 will read the ANDA at location 10_{16}, AND the next byte with accumulator A giving 0100101, which will be placed in accumulator A. It will then read the ANDB in location 12_{16}, AND the next byte with B, giving 10000101, place this in accumulator B, and then read the next OP code for an instruction from location 14_{16}.

Example

The PDP-11 has 8 accumulators and so must tell which accumulator to use when an addition instruction uses immediate addressing. The OP code for ADD is 0110, and an instruction word for an immediate add looks like this:

0110	010111	000011
OP code	Source	Destination

The source bits say that the add is an immediate add and that the augend is in the 2 bytes (since the accumulators have 16 bits) following this word. The destination section here refers to general register 3, so the next 16 bits will be added into general register 3. (Placing 101 in the rightmost bits instead of 011 will cause an addition into general register 5, etc.)

Now if general register 4 contains 000061_8, the memory is as follows (all these numbers are in octal, which is DEC's practice):

ADDRESS	CONTENTS
1020–1021	062704
1022–1023	000012
. . .	. . .

Execution of these by the CPU will result in 12_8 being added into general register 4, giving 73_8 in that register.

Notice in the PDP-11 that the ADD instruction OP code is the same for immediate and for direct addressing. It is the first 3 bits in the source and destination address sections that tell the addressing mode, not the OP code.

10 • 6 PAGING

Microcomputers and minicomputers sometimes alleviate the problem of addressing a large memory with a short word by using a technique that actually arose in a large computer called Atlas. This technique is called *paging*. When paging is used, the memory is divided into pages, each of a fixed length. An instruction word then designates a page and a location on that page.

Example

For the PDP-8 mentioned in Chap. 9 the basic memory of 4096 words of 12 bits each is divided into 32 *pages* of 128 words each. Thus page 0 contains the memory locations from 0 to 127 (decimal), page 1 refers to the memory locations from 128 to 255,. . ., and, finally, page 31 refers to the locations from 3968 to 4095, as shown in Fig. 10·4. Then 5 bits are required to reference a page, and 7 bits to reference a location within a page.

The addressing of data in a computer with paging varies from computer to computer. Generally the address given in the instruction word can refer either to the page in which the instruction word lies or possibly to some other particular page previously specified.

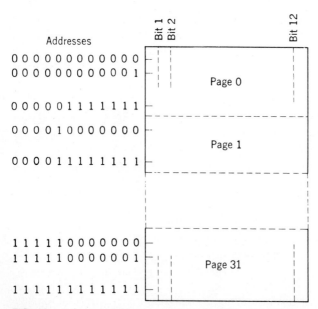

FIG. 10 • 4 Layout of 31-page memory with 4096 words of 12 bits.

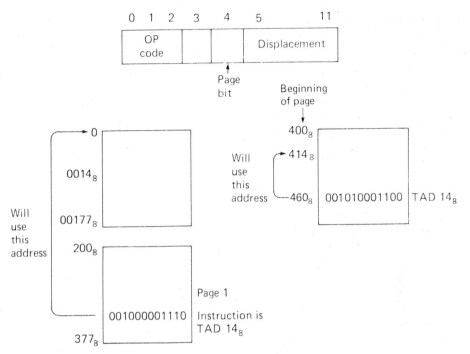

FIG. 10 • 5 Paging examples.

Example

For the PDP-8 the fourth bit in a 12-bit instruction word is called the *page bit.* This bit tells whether the 7-bit address in the instruction word refers to the page in which the instruction lies, in which case the bit is a 1, or to the first page in the memory, in which case the bit is a 0.

Fig. 10·5 shows the page bit in the instruction word for the PDP-8. If this bit is a 0 in a TAD (or other) instruction, the address given by bits 5–11 refers to an address on page 0 (see Fig. 10·4). Therefore the instruction word 001000001110 refers to location 14_8 in memory, regardless of where in memory the instruction is placed. (The first 3 bits are 001, the OP code for TAD.)

If the instruction word has a 1 in the page bit position, and if the final bits give the number 14_8, the address to be used is the 14_8th address on the page in which the instruction lies. This is shown in Fig. 10·5 where the instruction word 001010001100, when located at address 000100110000 in memory, points to location 000100001100 in memory, and the augend for the TAD would be fetched from that address.

Paging shortens the length of the address part. For the PDP-8 a 4096-word memory, which would require 12 address bits if a direct address were used, is addressed using a page bit and 8 more bits. Some addresses are not reachable from a given instruction word, however. To reach addresses not on page 0 or the page containing the instruction word, a technique called indirect addressing is used, as will be shown.

10 • 7 RELATIVE ADDRESSING

Relative addressing is quite similar to paging, except that the address referred to is relative to the instruction word. In general, when relative addressing is used, the address part of the instruction word gives a number to be added to the address following the instruction word. Thus in relative addressing, the address section contains a displacement from the instruction word's location in the memory. Giving only a displacement reduces the number of address bits but makes only a part of the memory available. For instance, if the instruction word uses relative addressing and the address part contains 8 bits, then only 256 memory locations are available to a given instruction.

Relative addressing is best explained by using examples.

Example

The 6800 microprocessor can have up to 2^{16} memory words. Therefore 16 bits are required to address the entire memory in a direct mode. When relative addressing is used, this address is reduced to an 8-bit displacement, shortening the instruction word when relative addressing is used.

In the 6800 a relative-address instruction word contains only the OP code and an 8-bit address, so only two locations in memory (bytes) are required. (The OP code tells what kind of addressing is to be used.) When the addressing is relative, the address in the second byte of the instruction is added to the address at which the OP code lies, plus 2. The address in the second byte is considered as a signed 2s complement number, however, so the address referenced can be at a higher or lower address in memory than the instruction word. In fact, the address can be from -125 to $+129$ memory words from the address of the OP code.

Figure 10·6 shows this. The OP code for a BRA (branch) instruction using relative addressing is 20 (hexadecimal). The microprocessor would read the OP

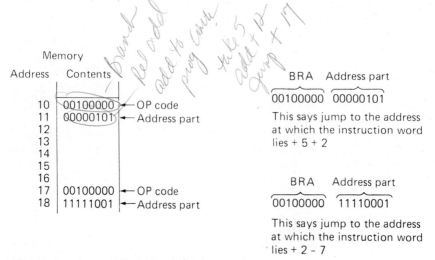

FIG. 10 • 6 Relative addressing in 6800 microprocessor.

code at location 10, see that it is a BRA instruction, get the bits 00000101 from the next memory location, add this 5 (decimal) to 2 plus 10 (where the OP code lies), giving 17. The next OP code would then come from location 17. In Fig. 10·6 this OP code is again a BRA, and location 18 contains 11111001, which is −7 decimal, and since $17 + 2 - 7 = 12$, the next OP code would come from location 12.

Example

In the PDP-11 a relative addressing mode can be used for the INC (increment) instruction. The OP code for an INC in the PDP-11 is 0052_8, and 27_8 in the address part indicates a relative addressing mode.

Assume that we have the following situation in memory:

ADDRESS (OCTAL)	CONTENTS (OCTAL)
1020	005627
1022	000012
1024	. . .

The relative addressing feature operates as follows. The displacement, 12_8 in the example, is added to the address following the instruction word, in this case 1024. This gives 1036, and so the number at location 1036 in memory would be incremented.

10 • 8 INDIRECT ADDRESSING

Another widely used variation in addressing is called *indirect addressing*. When used, indirect addressing causes the instruction word to give the address, not of the operand to be used, but of the address of the operand. As an example, if we write ADD 302 and the instruction is a conventional direct-addressing addition instruction, the number at location 302 will be added to the word currently in the accumulator.

If the addition instruction is indirectly addressed and we write IAD 302 (indirect add), then the number stored at address 302 will give the *address* of the operand to be used. As an example, when the instruction word at address 5 in the memory in the following program is performed, it will cause the number 164 to be added to the current contents of the accumulator.

MEMORY ADDRESS	CONTENTS
5	IAD 302
. . .	
302	495
. . .	. . .
495	164

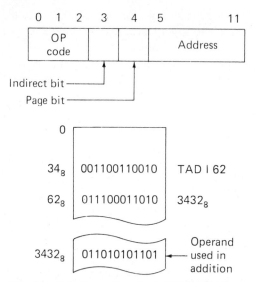

FIG. 10 • 7 Indirect addressing in PDP-8 minicomputer.

Example

The PDP-8 has a 12-bit instruction word as shown in Fig. 10·7. The instruction word contains a 3-bit OP code, a page bit, an indirect bit, and a 7-bit unsigned binary number. The page bit has been explained. There is also an indirect bit. A 0 in the indirect bit says, "This is not an indirect address." However, a 1 in the indirect bit indicates the address referenced is indirect.

As an example refer again to Fig. 10·7. The TAD instruction with OP code 001 is again used. The figure shows a case where the instruction word is a TAD with the page bit a 0, so the address is on page 0 in the memory, and the indirect bit is a 1. Since the 7 address bits point to location 62_8, that location contains the address of the operand. Again, referring to the figure, at location 62_8 we find a 3432_8, and it is this location, at which the operand 0213_8 is located, that is added to the accumulator.

Notice that the entire 4096_{10} word memory is accessible to an instruction word through the use of indirect addressing because each memory word contains 12 bits. Placing an address on page 0 where it can be reached from anywhere in the memory makes that address always available in programming.

There is one variation on the indirect-addressing scheme used by Varian, Data General, and several others. If the memory address referenced contains a 0 in the sign bit, the remaining bits contain the address of the number to be added to the present value of the accumulator. If, however, the sign bit at the memory address referenced is a 1, this says, "Use the remaining bits as the address of the next place to look for an address." The contents of this memory location are treated similarly. If the sign bit is a 0, the remaining bits give the address of the operand to be added to the accumulator; if the sign bit is a 1, the address formed from the remaining bits gives the address of the next place to look for the operand's address.

This indirect-addressing scheme permits indefinite chaining of indirect addresses and is useful in some programs.

Notice that when indirect addressing is used, an entire word can be used as an address. This is very useful in a paged computer since the entire word will be larger than the address part of an instruction word, and most if not all of the memory will be addressable. For the PDP-8 this is particularly advantageous.

Example

In the 8080 microprocessor there are several registers in the CPU in addition to the accumulator. These are called *scratchpad registers* and may be used in several types of instructions. The scratchpad registers are named *B, C, D, E, H,* and *L.* The registers are each 8 bits in length. Sometimes they can be handled in pairs with a resultant length of 16 bits, thus forming a complete address. Then an indirect-address mode can be used where the number in the register pair points to the address where the operand lies.

For example, in the 8080 there is a MOV (move) instruction which moves an 8-bit word from the memory into a designated register. The format for this instruction word is as follows:

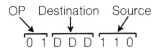

The DDD section here is 3 bits,* which simply call out the register into which the 8-bit word from memory is to be moved. The accumulator has number 111, register *B* has number 000, scratchpad register *C* has number 001, etc. The location in the memory from which the word to be moved is taken is always given by the register pair *H, L.* Thus if register pair *H, L* contains $45A2_{16}$ (*H* contains 45, *L* contains A2), then the address in memory used will be $45A2_{16}$.

If the instruction word is 01111110 and register pair *H, L* contains 3742_{16}, then the word at location 3742_{16} will be moved into the accumulator. If the instruction word is 01001110 and the *H, L* pair contains 2379_{16}, then the word at location 2379_{16} in memory will be moved into scratchpad register *C.*

Moving an address into the *H, L* registers in the CPU makes the word at that address available to an instruction word through the use of indirect addressing. Complete details and how to load the *H, L* pair are given in the Sec. 10·11 on 8080 microprocessors.

---

*Each D stands for a single destination bit that can be either a 0 or a 1.

10 · 9 INDEXED ADDRESSING

There is a variation on conventional direct memory addressing which facilitates programming, particularly the programming of sequences of instructions that are to be repeated many times on sets of data distributed throughout the machine. This technique is called *indexing*.

Indexing was first used in a computer developed at the University of Manchester. A register named the *B-box* was added to the control section. The contents of the B-box could be added to the contents of the memory address register when desired. When the B-box was used, the address of the operand located in memory would be at the address written by the programmer plus the contents of the B-box. The American term for B-box is *index register,* and this term will be used. Index registers are so useful that computers sometimes provide several of them.

Use of index registers eases writing programs that process data in tables, such as those described in Chap. 1, greatly reducing the number of instructions required in an iterative program. The index registers permit the automatic modification of the addresses referred to without altering the instructions stored in memory.

When index registers are included in a computer, a section of the instruction word tells the computer if an index register is to be used, and if so, which index register to use. The basic instruction word is therefore broken, for a single-address computer, into three parts instead of two. A typical division is shown in Fig. 10·8.

Generally two additional instructions are also added. One is used to load the index register, and the other modifies the number stored in the specified index register or causes the computer to branch.

If an index register is not to be used, the programmer places 0s in the index-register-designation section of the word. If there are three index registers, there will be two binary digits in the index-register section of the word, and the index register desired can be selected by placing the correct digits in the index-register-designation section.

To describe the operation of the index registers, two new instructions will be introduced. We will designate one of these by the mnemonic code SIR (set index registers), and this instruction will cause the address section of the instruction word to be transferred into the index register designated by the index-register-designation bits in the word. For instance, 01 SIR 300 will load the number 300 into index register 01. Since the address section normally contains the address section of the computer word, all that is required is that the contents of the address register be transferred into the index register designated.

We will designate the second instruction with the mnemonic code BRI (branch

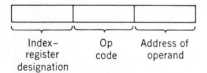

| Index–
register
designation | Op
code | Address of
operand |

FIG. 10 · 8 Index-register instruction word.

on index). This instruction will cause the contents of the index register designated to be decreased by 1 if the number stored in the index register is positive. At the same time, the computer will branch to the address in the address section of the instruction word, taking its next instruction from that address. If the index register designated contains a 0, the computer will not branch but instead will perform the next instruction in normal order.

The index registers may be used during any normal instruction by simply placing the digits indicating the index register to be used in the index-register-designation section of the computer word. For instance, if index register 01 contains 300, and we write a CAD (clear and add) instruction as follows:

01 CAD 200

the computer will add the contents of index register 01 to the contents of the address section, and the address used will be the total of these two. Since index register 01 contains 300 and the address section contains 200, the address from which the operand will be taken will be address 500 in memory.

An example of the use of an index register may be found in the short program shown in Table 10·1, which will add together all the numbers stored in memory addresses 201 to 300 and store the sum in address 301.

The program repeats the instructions at addresses 1–4 until index register 01 is finally at 0. Then the computer does not branch and is halted by the next instruction.

TABLE 10 • 1

ADDRESS IN MEMORY	INSTRUCTION WORD			COMMENTS
	INDEX-REGISTER DESIGNATION	OP CODE	ADDRESS SECTION	
0	01	SIR	99	The number 99 is placed in index register 01.
1	01	CAD	201	Picks up number to be added.
2	00	ADD	301	Adds to total thus far.
3	00	STO	301	Stores the current sum.
4	01	BRI	1	Subtracts 1 from index register 01 and then branches to first instruction until index register 01 contains 0, then proceeds to next instruction.
5	00	HLT	0	
201 to 300	Contain numbers to be added.			
301	Location at which sum is stored.			

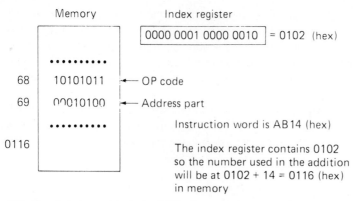

FIG. 10 • 9 Index register in the 6800 microprocessor.

Example

The 6800 microprocessor mentioned before has a single 16-bit index register. For the ADDA instruction, when indexing is used, the OP code is AB (hexadecimal). This instruction has only one 8-bit address part, so an entire instruction word requires only 16 bits (two memory locations).

Figure 10·9 shows an example for the 6800 microprocessor. The instruction word is at locations 68 and 69 in memory and is an indexed ADDA instruction. The 8-bit address part contains 14 (hexadecimal), and the index register in the CPU contains 0102. This results in the number at location 116 in memory being added into accumulator *A*.

The 6800 has instructions to load, increment, or decrement the index register, and these are covered in Sec. 10·12.

10 • 10 SINGLE-ADDRESS COMPUTER ORGANIZATION

A straightforward example of a single-address computer is the DEC PDP-8 minicomputer. It continues to be an important computer (in terms of sales) for DEC. This computer will be used to point out some basic principles in computer architecture.

The basic organization of the PDP-8 is shown in Fig. 10·10. It has a 12-bit instruction word as shown in Fig. 10·11. The memory is also organized in 12-bit words, and a basic memory block consists of $2^{12} = 4096$ words. Since the instruction word is very short, the designers have allowed only 3 bits for the OP-code part, and thus, as shown in Fig. 10·11, there are only 8 basic classes of instruction words.

Several of the basic instructions are very straightforward. For instance, the TAD instruction (for 2s complement ADD) simply performs a 2s complement addition of the operand addressed in memory to the operand currently in the 12-bit single accumulator and places the sum in this accumulator. There is an extra flip-flop

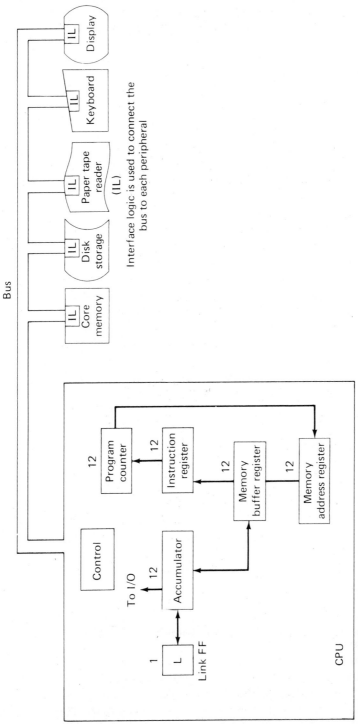

FIG. 10 • 10 Organization of PDP-8 minicomputers.

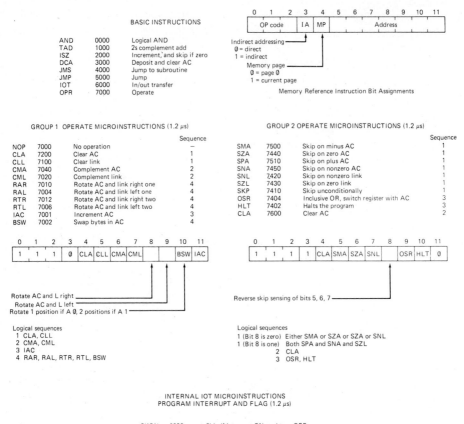

BASIC INSTRUCTIONS

AND	0000	Logical AND
TAD	1000	2s complement add
ISZ	2000	Increment, and skip if zero
DCA	3000	Deposit and clear AC
JMS	4000	Jump to subroutine
JMP	5000	Jump
IOT	6000	In/out transfer
OPR	7000	Operate

0	1	2	3	4	5	6	7	8	9	10	11
OP code			IA	MP			Address				

Indirect addressing
0 = direct
1 = indirect
Memory page
0 = page 0
1 = current page

Memory Reference Instruction Bit Assignments

GROUP 1 OPERATE MICROINSTRUCTIONS (1.2 μs)

			Sequence
NOP	7000	No operation	—
CLA	7200	Clear AC	1
CLL	7100	Clear link	1
CMA	7040	Complement AC	2
CML	7020	Complement link	2
RAR	7010	Rotate AC and link right one	4
RAL	7004	Rotate AC and link left one	4
RTR	7012	Rotate AC and link right two	4
RTL	7006	Rotate AC and link left two	4
IAC	7001	Increment AC	3
BSW	7002	Swap bytes in AC	4

0	1	2	3	4	5	6	7	8	9	10	11
1	1	1	0	CLA	CLL	CMA	CML			BSW	IAC

Rotate AC and L right
Rotate AC and L left
Rotate 1 position if A 0, 2 positions if A 1

Logical sequences
1 CLA, CLL
2 CMA, CML
3 IAC
4 RAR, RAL, RTR, RTL, BSW

GROUP 2 OPERATE MICROINSTRUCTIONS (1.2 μs)

			Sequence
SMA	7500	Skip on minus AC	1
SZA	7440	Skip on zero AC	1
SPA	7510	Skip on plus AC	1
SNA	7450	Skip on nonzero AC	1
SNL	7420	Skip on nonzero link	1
SZL	7430	Skip on zero link	1
SKP	7410	Skip unconditionally	1
OSR	7404	Inclusive OR, switch register with AC	3
HLT	7402	Halts the program	3
CLA	7600	Clear AC	2

0	1	2	3	4	5	6	7	8	9	10	11
1	1	1	1	CLA	SMA	SZA	SNL		OSR	HLT	0

Reverse skip sensing of bits 5, 6, 7

Logical sequences
1 (Bit 8 is zero) Either SMA or SZA or SZA or SNL
1 (Bit 8 is one) Both SPA and SNA and SZL
2 CLA
3 OSR, HLT

INTERNAL IOT MICROINSTRUCTIONS
PROGRAM INTERRUPT AND FLAG (1.2 μs)

SKON	6000	Skip if interrupt ON, and turn OFF
ION	6001	Turn interrupt ON
IOF	6002	Turn interrupt OFF
SRQ	6003	Skip on interrupt request
GTF	6004	Get interrupt flags
RTF	6005	Restore interrupt flags
SGT	6006	Skip on Greater Than flag
CAF	6007	Clear all flags

0	1	2	3	4	5	6	7	8	9	10	11
1	1	0		Device selection						IOT	

External device
Generates an IOP4 pulse if A 1
Generates an IOP2 pulse if A 1
Generates an IOP1 pulse if A 1

IOT Instruction Bit Assignments

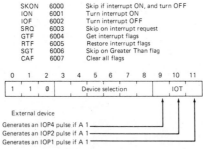

FIG. 10 • 11 Instruction repertoire for PDP-8. (Courtesy of Digital Equipment Corp.)

called the *link* or *L bit* which receives any overflow from this addition. The OP code for TAD is 001_2 or 1_8.

Similarly, the AND instruction simply performs a bit-by-bit AND on the operand addressed in memory and the contents of the accumulator, placing the result in the accumulator. The OP code for AND is 000_2 or 0_8.

The addressing techniques used in the 9 bits to form addresses have been described. The 3 bit in an instruction word is a 0 if the address is direct and a 1 if indirect (the address of the address). The 4 bit is a 0 if the remaining 7 bits (bits 5 to 11) give the actual address on page 0 of the memory and a 1 if the address is on the same page as the instruction word.

There is an ISZ (increment and skip if zero) instruction which simply increments the word addressed and returns it to memory. However, if this word becomes a 0, the next instruction following the ISZ instruction is not executed. Instead, the computer next executes the word in memory following this word. This particular instruction is very useful in indexing through tables when using indirect addressing and is provided as a substitute for index registers.

The DCA (deposit and clear accumulator) instruction stores the accumulator in the memory at the address specified and also clears the accumulator to all 0s. The OP code for DCA is 011 or 3_8.

The JMS (jump to subroutine) brings up an important feature in instruction repertoires for computers. It is good form in writing a computer program to break the program into as many subprograms (separable pieces of the program) as possible. These subprograms or subroutines† are then jumped to whenever the function they perform is required [refer to Fig. 10·12(a)].

The problem confronting the computer designer is that a given subprogram can be jumped to from several different locations in the program. This is shown in Fig. 10·12(b). For instance, in minicomputers and microcomputers no square root instruction is provided. If many square roots are called for in a program, the programmer writes a single square root subprogram (or subroutine), and whenever the program must find a square root, a jump is made to this subprogram. After the square root has been formed, the subprogram then causes a jump back to the instruction following the JMS subprogram instruction in the original program section. The subprogram is then said to be *called,* and it exits by returning to the *calling program.*

The problem is to arrange for a smooth jump to the called subprogram and to make it easy for the subprogram to return or jump back to the original program. To implement this it is necessary to "plant" the address of the instruction to be returned to when the subprogram is finished in some convenient place for the subprogram. Since the program counter (instruction counter) contains this address when the jump is made, most computers provide a JMS instruction that will store the program counter before the jump is made.

The JMS instruction in the PDP-8 operates as follows. The program counter is stored at the address given in the address portion of the JMS instruction. The computer then jumps to the next address in memory, that is, if we write JMS 50_8 (where 50_8 is the 50th location in memory) and if our instruction word is at 201_8 in the memory, when the JMS 50_8 instruction is executed, the value 202_8 will be stored at location 50_8 in the memory, and the computer will actually jump to or execute the word at location 51_8 next.‡

---

†We will use the words subroutine and subprogram to mean the same thing. Different manufacturers use different words.

‡DEC uses octal numbers almost exclusively in PDP-8 programming.

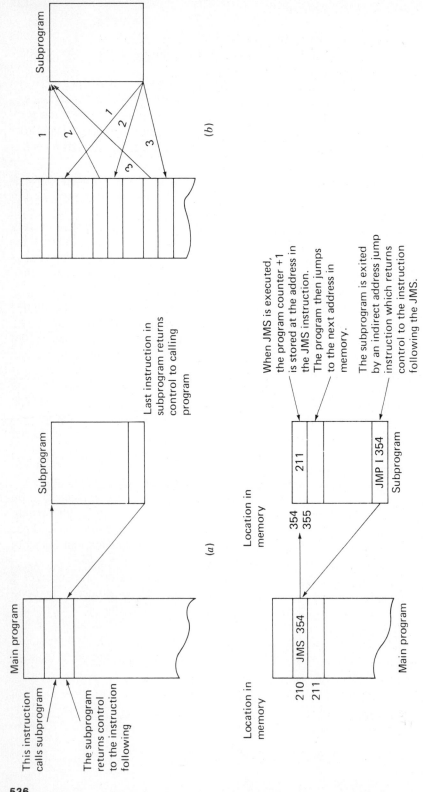

This instruction calls subprogram

The subprogram returns control to the instruction following

Main program

Subprogram

Last instruction in subprogram returns control to calling program

(a)

(b)

Location in memory

210 | JMS 354
211 |

Main program

When JMS is executed, the program counter +1 is stored at the address in the JMS instruction.

The program then jumps to the next address in memory.

The subprogram is exited by an indirect address jump instruction which returns control to the instruction following the JMS.

Location in memory

354 | 211
355 |

JMP I 354

Subprogram

(c)

FIG. 10 • 12 (a) Calling a subprogram. (b) The same subprogram may be called several times. (c) How the PDP-8 handles subprogram calls and returns.

Planting the program counter's contents at location 50_8 in the above example enables the writer of the subroutine to exit from the subprogram by placing a JMP (jump) instruction at the end of the subprogram using address 50_8 in the address section, but making the address an indirect address. Therefore the computer will actually jump to the address stored at location 50_8, which will be 202_8, and the next instruction executed will be that at location 202_8.

Notice that a subprogram set up in this way can be jumped to by a JMS and exited using a JMP indirectly from any place in memory, and the return will always be correct.

The above scheme is a good one and has been used (with variations) in several computers, but it has the problem that if a subprogram calls another subprogram, which then calls the first subprogram, the return address for the original return will be wiped out. While this may seem unlikely, programs can become very complicated, and this must be guarded against.

If a subprogram can call itself or can call another program which then calls it without damage, then the subprogram is said to be *recursive*.

A scheme whereby jumps to subprograms can be made so that a subprogram can call itself will be given in a later section.

The PDP-8 is a bused computer, and input-output devices are connected to this bus. Input-output in the PDP-8 is provided by the IOT (input-output transfer) instruction. The input-output devices are each assigned a number from 0 to $2^6 - 1$, and when an IOT instruction is given, the number in bits 3 to 8 of the IOT is placed on six wires in the bus which each input-output device inputs to see if it is being addressed. The remaining 3 bits are also transmitted on the bus and tell the input-output device what it is to do (read, write, rewind, etc.). The selected input-output device responds to the bus signals generated by the IOT instruction using logic circuits in its interface to interpret the instruction and to place data on the data section of the bus, read from it, etc.

The input-output devices are allowed to interrupt the processor and demand service during program operation, using the computer's interrupt facility. There is an instruction, the ION (interrupt on) instruction, which raises a bus wire called ION to the input-output devices telling them it is their right to raise the INTERRUPT line on the bus and demand service.

If an input-output device raises its INTERRUPT line while the computer is operating a program, the address of the next instruction word which would normally be executed is placed in location 0 in the memory, and the next instruction executed is at location 1 in the memory. (This is generally a jump to the subprogram which services input-output devices.)

Since the address of the next instruction word in the program which was interrupted is in location 0, the interrupt service program† can exit using that address to return to the original program. This is shown in Fig. 10·13.

Again, an interrupt of an interrupt will cause the original return address (at 0 in the memory) to be destroyed. The programmer must see that this does not occur,

---

†The program (or subprogram) which handles the peripheral that generates the interrupt is called an *interrupt service program*.

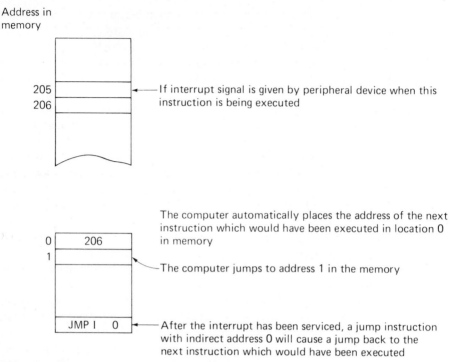

Address in
memory

205 — If interrupt signal is given by peripheral device when this
206   instruction is being executed

The computer automatically places the address of the next
instruction which would have been executed in location 0
0   206   in memory
1
       — The computer jumps to address 1 in the memory

JMP I   0 — After the interrupt has been serviced, a jump instruction
       with indirect address 0 will cause a jump back to the
       next instruction which would have been executed

FIG. 10 • 13 Interrupts in the PDP-8 minicomputer.

and the right of devices to interrupt is revoked as soon as an interrupt occurs. (The bus line for ION is lowered.) The program must issue another ION in order to restore the interrupt privilege to input-output devices.

The PDP-8 has a number of features which have helped to make it attractive, but which are outside the context of this description. For instance, since there is only a single arithmetic instruction, the TAD, it is necessary to complement an operand and then add in order to subtract. To perform this complement and also to provide ROTATE or SHIFT instructions, some SKIP instructions, and some other logical operations, the OP code 111 is a "no address" instruction class where the remaining 9 bits tell which of a number of different possible operations can be made to occur. (Details can be found in the manufacturers' manuals listed in the Bibliography.)

Table 10·2 shows a section of an assembler listing for a PDP-8. The leftmost two columns (or digits) list the addresses in memory and their contents. The columns to the right of these were written by the programmer. The programmer fed the assembler language statements to the assembler program, which then generated the complete listing shown here. All material to the right of the slashes are comments and are ignored by the assembler program.

The purpose of this subroutine, or subprogram, is to read from a keyboard into the PDP-8's accumulator. Another program enters this subprogram with a JMS statement, which deposits the address of the next instruction to be operated when the subroutine is completed in the first address of the subprogram. Thus the

TABLE 10 • 2 PDP-8 SUBPROGRAM

ADDRESS	CONTENTS	LABEL	OP CODE		COMMENTS
Ø251	ØØØØ	LISN,	Ø		/INPUT SUB
Ø252	6Ø31		KSF		
Ø253	5252		JMP	#252	
Ø254	6Ø36		KRB		
Ø255	5651		JMP	I LISN	

address to be returned will be stored at location 251 in the memory when the sub-routine is entered, and the first statement executed will be the statement at location 252 in the memory.

The statement at 252 in the memory is a KSF statement, which is a special input statement which reads from the keyboard's status register (see Chap. 8 for details). If the status bit is a 1 in this register, the program skips over the next instruction. As a result, when the KSF statement is executed, if there is a character to be read from the keyboard, the next statement read will be the one at location 254. If the status word is all 0, then the statement executed after the KSF will be the JMP instruction at 253 in the memory.

The JMP instruction causes the computer to jump to location 252 in the memory. Notice that the OP code for JMP is 5, and the instruction has assembled into a word as follows:

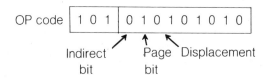

This instruction word says, "jump to the word at location 52 on the same page as the instruction lies." The first address on this page is 200 (octal), so the final address for the jump is 252 (octal).

When a character is to be read, the KRB instruction selects the keyboard, using the bus, the keyboard places its character on the data wires in the bus, and the character is read by the PDP-8 into its accumulator. After this instruction is read, the accumulator contains the character from the keyboard. (The status bit in the status word is also turned off.)

The JMP I LISN instruction causes a jump to the address given at the location LISN. This will return control to the location in the memory after the JMS which called this subroutine.

The JMP I LISN instruction word is as follows:

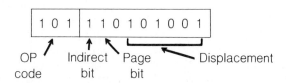

This instruction word says "since the page bit is a 1, use the location on the same page, which is the 51st location on that page." Since the beginning of the page is location 200, the address generated is 251. Now the indirect bit is a 1, so the number at location 251 is the actual address to be used for the jump, as desired.

Another short segment of a PDP-8 program is shown in Table 10·3. This first calls the subroutine just described using a JMS LISN instruction. Therefore when the DCA STORE instruction is executed, the accumulator contains the character from the keyboard. The purpose of this section of program is to see if the character read is a period.

First, the DCA STORE deposits the character at an address with label (name) STORE. In another section of the program, STORE has been located at 264 in the memory, so the DCA STORE instruction is to store the accumulator at 264. The assembled instruction looks like this:

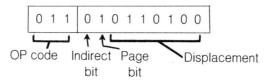

The indirect bit is a 0, the page bit is a 1, so the address is on the same page as the instruction word. This page begins with location 200 so the actual address will be 200 plus the displacement, which is 64, and thus the address used will be 264.

The next instruction, the TAD PD, loads the accumulator with the negative (2s complement) of the keyboard code for a period. This has already been loaded by the program at location 265, so the function of the IAD PD is to read from location 265. As an examination of the assembled value 1265 will indicate, the page bit is a 1, and 65 is therefore added to 200, the first address of the page on which the instruction lies, giving 265.

The value in STORE, which is that of the character read, is now added to the negative of the character code for a period, and if the resulting value in the accumulator is a 0, the character just read is a period. The SZA instruction is a special PDP-8 instruction which tests the accumulator for "all zero" and skips the next

TABLE 10 • 3 SECTION OF PDP-8 PROGRAM

ADDRESS IN MEMORY	CONTENTS	LABEL	OP CODE	ADDRESS	COMMENTS
0200	6032	START,	KCC		/CLEAR KB
0201	4251		JMS	LISN	/ENTER SUB
0202	3264		DCA	STORE	/
0203	1265		TAD	PD	/GET NEG PD
0204	1264		TAD	STORE	/ADD INPUT
0205	7440		SZA		/SKIP IF EQ
0206	5213		JMP	A	/

instruction if it is 0, but does not skip otherwise. (The PDP-8 uses skip instructions instead of conditional jump instructions with addresses.) As a result, if the character is a period, the instruction at location 207 will be executed next. If not, control will jump to location A because the JMP A will be executed.

This section of the program shows some of the good and bad features of the PDP-8. Since there is no subtract instruction, a 2s complement of the period character value had to be formed and added. Since there is no conditional jump instruction, a skip and then a jump instruction were required. On the other hand, the code is very compact and reasonably clear.

10 • 11 A SINGLE-ADDRESS MICROPROCESSOR

The INTEL 8080 is an example of a microprocessor chip series. A basic 40-pin IC chip is used to package the 8080 CPU. Other chips available include RAMs, ROMs, interface chips, etc. The chips are interconnected using a bus which contains 8 data lines, 16 address lines, and 6 control lines. This microprocessor has been so successful that various "upward compatible" microprocessors have grown out of it, including the 8085 and the Z-80. Even the 16-bit 8000 uses much of its design.

The 8080 CPU is basically a single-accumulator organization, but a number of other scratchpad registers are provided, as illustrated in Fig. 10·14(a). The instruction-word formats are shown in Fig. 10·14(b), and a functional block diagram of the 8080 is shown in Fig. 10·15.

The INTEL 8080 has a good set of addressing modes (see Table 10·4). At the beginning of each instruction cycle, the 8-bit OP code is read by the 8080 CPU, and this determines how many more fetches from memory the CPU must make to execute the instruction. Some instructions require only the 8-bit OP code, while some require 8-bit and some 16-bit addresses or operands, and so the CPU must make the necessary accesses to perform the instruction.

Since 8 bits are used for the OP code, a large instruction repertoire has been provided. A short list of the instructions used in examples is presented in Tables 10·5 and 10·6. Table 10·7 shows the complete instruction set.

The 8080 has conditional JUMP instructions which jump or do not jump, depending on the values in the so-called *condition flags*. These consist of 5 flip-flops (see Table 10·8) which are set to the 0 or 1 state by the results of arithmetic instructions. For instance, if an addition is performed and the result is 0, then the Z flag will be set to 1 and the S, P, and C flags to 0 (provided no carry was generated). A conditional JUMP instruction which tests the Z flag for a 1 state would then cause a jump, whereas a conditional JUMP instruction which tests the S, P, or C flags would not cause a jump. (Refer to the BRANCH instructions in Table 10·6.)

In programming the 8080 considerable use is made of the scratchpad registers B, C, D, E, H, and L as well as accumulator A. In some instructions the scratchpad registers are used in pairs. For instance, the INR M instruction, a 1-byte instruction, uses the two 8-bit registers H and L to form a 16-bit address. The 8-bit number in the memory at this address is then incremented by the instruction. The Z, S, P, and AC flags are all set and reset by the instruction, so a 0 result at that location will set the Z flag, a negative result would set the S flag, etc.

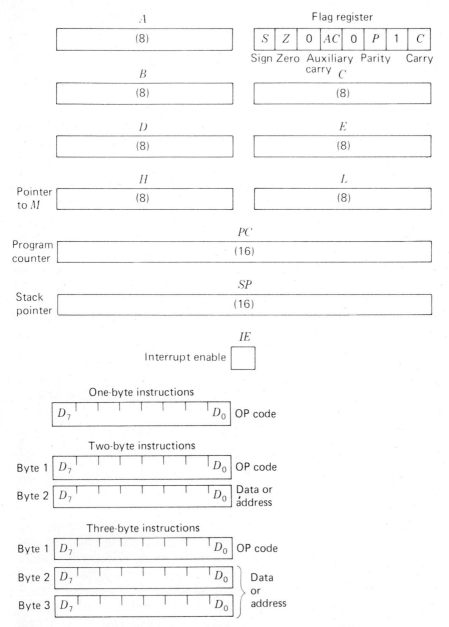

FIG. 10 • 14 (*a*) 8080 CPU registers. (*b*) Instruction-word formats for 8080 CPU.

Parentheses are used to indicate "the contents of" in Tables 10·5 and 10·6. For example, the notation (H) $\longleftrightarrow$ (D) used in the XCHG instruction means, "the contents of register H and register D are exchanged." Similarly, ((H)(L)) $\leftarrow$ (byte 2) in the description of the MVI instruction means, "the contents of byte 2 of the instruction word are transferred into the location in memory whose address is

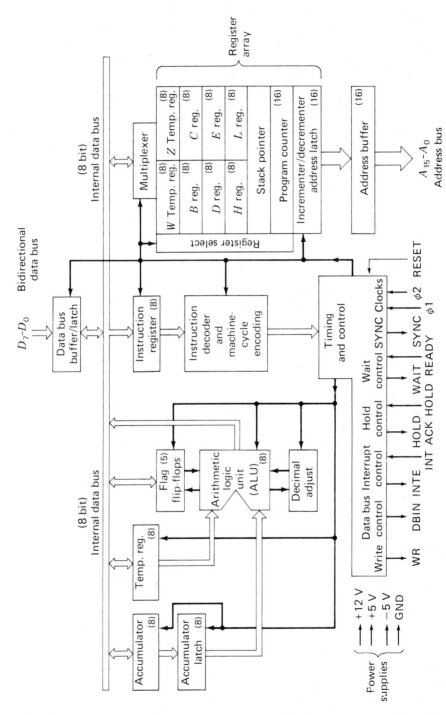

FIG. 10 • 15 8080 CPU functional block diagram. (Courtesy of INTEL Corp.)

TABLE 10 • 4 ADDRESSING MODES FOR THE 8080 CPU

When multibyte numeric data are used, the data, like instructions, are stored in successive memory locations, with the least significant byte first, followed by increasingly significant bytes. The 8080 has four different modes for addressing data stored in memory or in registers:

1. *Direct* Bytes 2 and 3 of the instruction contain the exact memory address of the data item (the low-order bits of the address are in byte 2, the high-order bits in byte 3).

2. *Register* The instruction specifies the register or register pair in which the data are located.

3. *Register indirect* The instruction specifies a register pair that contains the memory address where the data are located (high-order bits of the address are in the first register of the pair, low-order bits in the second).

4. *Immediate* The instruction contains the data. This is either an 8-bit quantity or a 16-bit quantity (least significant byte first, most significant byte second).

Unless directed by an INTERRUPT or a BRANCH instruction, the execution of instructions proceeds through consecutively increasing memory locations. A BRANCH instruction can specify the address of the next instruction to be executed in one of two ways:

1. *Direct* The BRANCH instruction contains the address of the next instruction to be executed. (Except for the RST instruction, byte 2 contains the low-order address and byte 3 the high-order address.)

2. *Register indirect* The BRANCH instruction indicates a register pair that contains the address of the next instruction to be executed (high-order bits of the address are in the first register of the pair, low-order bits in the second).

formed by writing the contents of register H to the left of the contents of register L." This notation is widely used and worth examining in some detail.

Table 10·9 shows an 8080 program in assembly language and also a listing of the hexadecimal values for memory location and contents as generated by the assembler. The programmer wrote the columns: label, OP code, operand, and comments. The assembler generated the two leftmost columns.

The purpose of the program is to find the largest of two 8-bit numbers in locations 50 and 51 in the memory and to store this number at location 52.

The first instruction LXI H, 50H loads the number 50_{16} into registers H and L. When the 8080 assembler is used, writing an H to the right of a number means the number is hexadecimal. Therefore 50H means 01010000_2 or 50_{16} to the assembler. This LXI therefore loads 00000000 into register H and 01010000 into register L. (Notice that the least significant byte is first in the memory in an instruction word in the 8080.)

The MOV A, M instruction† moves the byte in the memory pointed to by the address in registers H and L into accumulator A. Since H and L point to location 50, the byte at that location will be moved into the accumulator.

The INX H instruction adds 1 to the register pair H, L, giving 51 in H and L.

---

†M is used in assembler language to indicate the byte in the memory pointed to by the H, L pair of registers. These must have been properly set before such an instruction is used.

TABLE 10 • 5 NOTATION FOR 8080 CPU INSTRUCTION REPERTOIRE LISTING IN TABLE 10·6

SYMBOL	MEANING
Accumulator	Register A
Addr	16-bit address quantity
Data	8-bit data quantity
Data 16	16-bit data quantity
Byte 2	Second byte of the instruction
Byte 3	Third byte of the instruction
Port	8-bit address of an input-output device
r, r1, r2	One of the registers A, B, C, D, E, H, L
DDD, SSS	Bit pattern designating one of the registers A, B, C, D, E, H, L (DDD = destination, SSS = source):

DDD or SSS	Register name
111	A
000	B
001	C
010	D
011	E
100	H
101	L

rh	First (high-order) register of a designated register pair
rl	Second (low-order) register of a designated register pair
rp	One of the register pairs:
	B represents the B, C pair with B as the high-order register and C as the low-order register
	D represents the D, E pair with D as the high-order register and E as the low-order register
	H represents the H, L pair with H as the high-order register and L as the low-order register
	SP represents the 16-bit stack pointer register
RP	Bit pattern designating one of the register pairs B, D, H, SP:

RP	Register pair
00	B, C
01	D, E
10	H, L
11	SP

PC	16-bit program counter register (PCH and PCL are used to refer to the high-order and low-order 8 bits, respectively)
SP	Stack pointer
r_m	Bit m of register r (bits are numbered 7 through 0 from left to right)
Z, S, P, CY, AC	Condition flags: zero, sign, parity, carry, and auxiliary carry, respectively
( )	Contents of memory location or registers enclosed in the parentheses
←	"Is transferred to"
∧	Logical AND
$\veebar$	Exclusive OR
∨	Inclusive OR
+	Addition
−	2s complement subtraction
*	Multiplication
⟷	"Is exchanged with"
−	1s complement [e.g., $(\overline{A})$]
n	Restart numbers 0–7
NNN	Binary representation 000–111 for restart numbers 0–7, respectively

TABLE 10 • 6 INSTRUCTION REPERTOIRE FOR 8080 CPU

MOV r1, r2 (move register)

(r1) ← (r2)

Content of register r2 is moved to register r1.

0	1	D	D	D	S	S	S

Addressing: register   Flags: none

MOV r, M (move from memory)

(r) ← ((H)(L))

Content of memory location, whose address is in registers H and L, is moved to register r.

0	1	D	D	D	1	1	0

Addressing: register indirect   Flags: none

MOV M, r (move to memory)

((H)(L)) ← (r)

Content of register r is moved to memory location whose address is in registers H and L.

0	1	1	1	0	S	S	S

Addressing: register indirect   Flags: none

ADD r (add register)

(A) ← (A) + (r)

Content of register r is added to content of accumulator. Result is placed in accumulator.

1	0	0	0	0	S	S	S

Addressing: register   Flags: Z, S, P, CY, AC

ADD M (add memory)

(A) ← (A) + ((H)(L))

Content of the memory location, whose address is contained in registers H and L, is added to content of accumulator. Result is placed in accumulator.

1	1	0	0	0	1	1	0

Addressing: register indirect   Flags: Z, S, P, CY, AC

ADI data (add immediate)

(A) ← (A) + (byte 2)

Content of second byte of instruction is added to content of accumulator. Result is placed in accumulator.

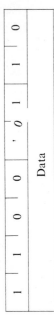

1	1	0	0	0	1	1	0
Data							

Addressing: immediate   Flags: Z, S, P, CX, AC

INR M (increment memory)

$((H)(L)) \leftarrow ((H)(L)) + 1$

Content of the memory location, whose address is contained in registers H and L is incremented by 1. *Note:* All condition flags except CY are affected.

0	0	1	1	0	1	0	0

Addressing: register indirect   Flags: Z, S, P, AC

LDA addr (load accumulator direct)

$(A) \leftarrow ((byte\ 3)\ (byte\ 2))$

Content of memory location, whose address is specified in byte 2 and byte 3 of instruction, is moved to register A.

0	0	1	1	1	0	1	0
Low-order addr							
High-order addr							

Addressing: direct   Flags: none

STA addr (store accumulator direct)

$((byte\ 3)\ (byte\ 2)) \leftarrow (A)$

Content of accumulator is moved to memory location whose address is specified in byte 2 and 3 of instruction.

0	0	1	1	0	0	1	0
Low-order							
High-order addr							

Addressing: direct   Flags: none

SUB M (subtract memory)

$(A) \leftarrow (A) - ((H)(L))$

Content of memory location, whose address is contained in registers H and L, is subtracted from content of accumulator. Result is placed in accumulator.

1	0	0	1	0	1	1	0

Addressing: register indirect   Flags: Z, S, P, CY, AC

SUI data (subtract immediate)

$(A) \leftarrow (A) - (byte\ 2)$

Content of second byte of instruction is subtracted from content of accumulator. Result is placed in accumulator.

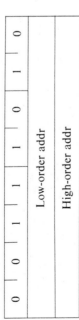

Addressing: immediate   Flags: Z, S, P, CY, AC

SBB r (subtract register with borrow)

$(A) \leftarrow (A) - (r) - (CY)$

Content of register r and content of CY flag are both subtracted from accumulator. Result is placed in accumulator.

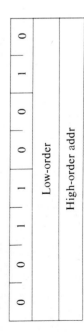

Addressing: register   Flags: Z, S, P, CY, AC

TABLE 10·6 • (CONTINUED)

CMP M (compare memory)

(A) − ((H) (L))

Content of memory location, whose address is contained in registers H and L, is subtracted from accumulator. Accumulator remains unchanged. Condition flags are set as a result of subtraction. Z flag is set to 1 if (A) = ((H) (L)). CY flag is set to 1 if (A) < ((H) (L)).

1	0	1	1	1	1	1	0

Cycles: 2   States: 7
Addressing: register indirect   Flags: Z, S, P, CY, AC

INX rp (increment register pair)

(rh) (rl) ← (rh) (rl) + 1

Content of register pair rp is incremented by 1. *Note:* No condition flags are affected.

0	0	R	P	0	0	1	1

Cycles: 1   States: 5
Addressing: register   Flags: none

DCX rp (decrement register pair)

(rh) (rl) ← (rh) (rl) − 1

Content of register pair rp is decremented by 1. *Note:* No condition flags are affected.

0	0	R	P	1	0	1	1

Cycles: 1   States: 5
Addressing: register   Flags: none

RST n (restart)

((SP) − 1) ← (PCH)   ((SP) − 2) ← (PCL)

(SP) ← (SP) − 2   (PC) ← 8* (NNN)

The high-order 8 bits of next instruction address are moved to memory location whose address is 1 less than content of register SP. The low-order 8 bits of next instruction address are moved to memory location whose address is 2 less than content of register SP. Content of register SP is decremented by 2. Control is transferred to instruction whose address is eight times the content of NNN.

1	1	N	N	N	1	1	1

Cycles: 3   States: 11
Addressing: register indirect   Flags: none

15	14	13	12	11	10	9	8	7	6	5	4	3	2	1	0
0	0	0	0	0	0	0	0	0	N	N	N	0	0	0	0

Program counter after restart

LXI rp, data 16   (load register pair immediate)

(rh) ← (byte 3)   (rl) ← (byte 2)

Byte 3 of instruction is moved into high-order register rh of register pair rp. Byte 2 of instruction is moved into low-order register rl of the register pair rp.

0	0	R	P	0	0	0	1
Low-order data							
High-order data							

Addressing: immediate   Flags: none

This group of instructions alters normal sequential program flow. *Condition flags are not affected by any instruction in this group.*

The two types of branch instructions are unconditional and conditional. Unconditional transfers simply perform the specified operation on register PC (the program counter). Conditional transfers examine the status of one of the four processor flags to determine if the specified branch is to be executed. The conditions that may be specified are as follows:

CCC		Condition
000	NZ	Not zero ($Z = 0$)
001	Z	Zero ($Z = 1$)
010	NC	No carry ($CY = 0$)
011	C	Carry ($CY = 1$)
100	PO	Parity odd ($P = 0$)
101	PE	Parity even ($P = 1$)
110	P	Plus ($S = 0$)
111	M	Minus ($S = 1$)

JMP addr (jump)
$(PC) \leftarrow$ (byte 3) (byte 2)
Control is transferred to instruction whose address is specified in byte 3 and byte 2 of current instruction.

1	1	0	0	0	0	1	1
Low-order addr							
High-order addr							

Addressing: immediate   Flags: none

Jcondition addr   (conditional jump)
If (CCC), $(PC) \leftarrow$ (byte 3) (byte 2)
If specified condition is true, control is transferred to instruction whose address is specified in byte 3 and byte 2 of current instruction; otherwise control continues sequentially.

1	1	C	C	C	0	1	0
Low-order addr							
High-order addr							

Addressing: immediate   Flags: none

DCR r   (decrement register)
$(r) \leftarrow (r) - 1$
Content of register r is decremented by 1. *Note:* All condition flags except CY are affected.

0	0	D	D	D	1	0	1

Addressing: register   Flags: Z, S, P, AC

LDAX rp (load accumulator indirect)
$(A) \leftarrow ((rp))$
Content of memory location, whose address is in register pair rp, is moved to register A. *Note:* Only register pairs rp = *B* (registers *B* and C) or rp = *D* (registers *D* and *E*) may be specified.

0	0	R	P	1	0	1	0

Addressing: register indirect   Flags: none

TABLE 10·6 • (CONTINUED)

STAX rp (store accumulator indirect)
((rp)) ← (A)
Content of register A is moved to memory location whose address is in register pair rp. *Note:* Only register pairs rp = B (registers B and C) or rp = D (registers D and E) may be specified.

0	0	R	P	0	0	1	0

Addressing: register indirect   Flags: none

XCHG (exchange H and L with D and E)
(H)   (D)
(L)   (E)
Contents of registers H and L are exchanged with contents of registers D and E.

1	1	1	0	1	0	1	1

Addressing: register   Flags: none

INR r (increment register)
(r) ← (r) + 1
Content of register r is incremented by 1. *Note:* All condition flags except CY are affected.

0	0	D	D	D	1	0	0

Addressing: register   Flags: Z, S, P, AC

MVI M, data (move to memory immediate)
((H) (L)) ← (byte 2)
Content of byte 2 of instruction is moved to memory location whose address is in registers H and L.

0	0	1	1	0	1	1	0
Data							

Addressing: immediate register indirect   Flags: none

CALL addr (call)
((SP) − 1) ← (PCH)   (SP) ← (SP) − 2
((SP) − 2) ← (PCL)   (PC) ← (byte 3) (byte 2)
The high-order 8 bits of next instruction address are moved to memory location whose address is 1 less than content of register SP. The low-order 8 bits of next instruction address are moved to memory location whose address is 2 less than content of register SP. Content of register SP is decremented by 2. Control is transferred to instruction whose address is specified in byte 3 and byte 2 of current instruction.

1	1	0	0	1	1	0	1
Low-order addr							
High-order addr							

Addressing: immediate/register indirect   Flags: none

RET (return)
(PCL) ← ((SP))   (PCH) ← ((SP) + 1)
(SP) ← (SP) + 2
Content of memory location, whose address is specified in register SP, is moved to low-order 8 bits of register PC. Content of memory location, whose address is 1 more than content of register SP, is moved to high-order 8 bits of register PC. Content of register SP is incremented by 2.

| 1 | 1 | 0 | 0 | 1 | 0 | 0 | 1 |

Addressing: register indirect   Flags: none

STACK, INPUT-OUTPUT, AND MACHINE CONTROL GROUP

This group of instructions performs input-output, manipulates the stack, and alters internal control flags.

Unless otherwise specified, *condition flags are not affected by any instruction in this group.*

PUSH rp (push)

$((SP) - 1) \leftarrow (rh)$ $((SP) - 2) \leftarrow (rl)$ $(SP) \leftarrow (SP) - 2$

Content of high-order register of register pair rp is moved to memory location whose address is 1 less than content of register SP. Content of low-order register of register pair rp is moved to memory location whose address is 2 less than content of register SP. Content of register SP is decremented by 2. *Note:* Register pair rp = SP may not be specified.

| 1 | 1 | R | P | 0 | 1 | 0 | 1 |

Addressing: register indirect   Flags: none

PUSH PSW (push processor status word)

$((SP) - 1) \leftarrow (A)$
$((SP) - 2)_0 \leftarrow (CY)$, $((SP) - 2)_1 \leftarrow 1$
$((SP) - 2)_2 \leftarrow (P)$, $((SP) - 2)_3 \leftarrow 0$
$((SP) - 2)_4 \leftarrow (AC)$, $((SP) - 2)_5 \leftarrow 0$
$((SP) - 2)_6 \leftarrow (Z)$, $((SP) - 2)_7 \leftarrow (S)$
$(SP) \leftarrow (SP) - 2$

Content of register *A* is moved to memory location whose address is 1 less than register SP. Contents of condition flags are assembled into a processor status word, and word is moved to memory location whose address is 2 less than content of register SP. Content of register SP is decremented by 2.

| 1 | 1 | 1 | 1 | 0 | 1 | 0 | 1 |

Addressing: register indirect   Flags: none

POP rp (pop)

$(rl) \leftarrow ((SP))$ $(rh) \leftarrow ((SP) + 1)$ $(SP) \leftarrow (SP) + 2$

Content of memory location, whose address is specified by content of register SP, is moved to low-order register of register pair rp. Content of memory location, whose address is 1 more than content of register SP, is moved to high-order register of register pair rp. Content of register SP is incremented by 2. *Note:* Register pair rp = SP may not be specified.

| 1 | 1 | R | P | 0 | 0 | 0 | 1 |

Addressing: register indirect   Flags: none

POP PSW (pop processor status word)

$(CY) \leftarrow ((SP))_0$ $(P) \leftarrow ((SP))_2$ $(AC) \leftarrow ((SP))_4$
$(Z) \leftarrow ((SP))_6$ $(S) \leftarrow ((SP))_7$
$(SP) \leftarrow (SP) + 2$

Content of memory location, whose address is specified by content of register SP, is used to restore condition flags. Content of memory location, whose address is 1 more than content of register SP, is moved to register *A*. Content of register SP is incremented by 2.

| 1 | 1 | 1 | 1 | 0 | 0 | 0 | 1 |

Addressing: register indirect   Flags: Z, S, P, CY, AC

TABLE 10 • 7 8080 INSTRUCTION REPERTOIRE

MNEMONIC	DESCRIPTION	INSTRUCTION CODE*							
		D_7	D_6	D_5	D_4	D_3	D_2	D_1	D_0
MOV r1, r2	Move register to register	0	1	D	D	D	S	S	S
MOV M, r	Move register to memory	0	1	1	1	0	S	S	S
MOV r, M	Move memory to register	0	1	D	D	D	1	1	0
HLT	Halt	0	1	1	1	0	1	1	0
MVI r	Move immediate register	0	0	D	D	D	1	1	0
MVI M	Move immediate memory	0	0	1	1	0	1	1	0
INR r	Increment register	0	0	D	D	D	1	0	0
DCR r	Decrement register	0	0	D	D	D	1	0	1
INR M	Increment memory	0	0	1	1	0	1	0	0
DCR M	Decrement memory	0	0	1	1	0	1	0	1
ADD r	Add register to A	1	0	0	0	0	S	S	S
ADC r	Add register to A with carry	1	0	0	0	1	S	S	S
SUB r	Subtract register from A	1	0	0	1	0	S	S	S
SBB r	Subtract register from A with borrow	1	0	0	1	1	S	S	S
ANA r	AND register with A	1	0	1	0	0	S	S	S
XRA r	Exclusive OR register with A	1	0	1	0	1	S	S	S
ORA r	OR register with A	1	0	1	1	0	S	S	S
CMP r	Compare register with A	1	0	1	1	1	S	S	S
ADD M	Add memory to A	1	0	0	0	0	1	1	0
ADC M	Add memory to A with carry	1	0	0	0	1	1	1	0
SUB M	Subtract memory from A	1	0	0	1	0	1	1	0
SBB M	Subtract memory from A with borrow	1	0	0	1	1	1	1	0
ANA M	AND memory with A	1	0	1	0	0	1	1	0
XRA M	Exclusive OR memory with A	1	0	1	0	1	1	1	0
ORA M	OR memory with A	1	0	1	1	0	1	1	0
CMP M	Compare memory with A	1	0	1	1	1	1	1	0
ADI	Add immediate to A	1	1	0	0	0	1	1	0
ACI	Add immediate to A with carry	1	1	0	0	1	1	1	0
SUI	Subtract immediate from A	1	1	0	1	0	1	1	0
SBI	Subtract immediate from A with borrow	1	1	0	1	1	1	1	0
ANI	AND immediate with A	1	1	1	0	0	1	1	0
XRI	Exclusive OR immediate with A	1	1	1	0	1	1	1	0
ORI	OR immediate with A	1	1	1	1	0	1	1	0
CPI	Compare immediate with A	1	1	1	1	1	1	1	0
RLC	Rotate A left	0	0	0	0	0	1	1	1
RRC	Rotate A right	0	0	0	0	1	1	1	1
RAL	Rotate A left through carry	0	0	0	1	0	1	1	1
RAR	Rotate A right through carry	0	0	0	1	1	1	1	1
JMP	Jump unconditional	1	1	0	0	0	0	1	1
JC	Jump on carry	1	1	0	1	1	0	1	0
JNC	Jump on no carry	1	1	0	1	0	0	1	0
JZ	Jump on zero	1	1	0	0	1	0	1	0
JNZ	Jump on no zero	1	1	0	0	0	0	1	0

TABLE 10 • 7 (CONTINUED)

MNEMONIC	DESCRIPTION	D_7	D_6	D_5	D_4	D_3	D_2	D_1	D_0
JP	Jump on positive	1	1	1	1	0	0	1	0
JM	Jump on minus	1	1	1	1	1	0	1	0
JPE	Jump on parity even	1	1	1	0	1	0	1	0
JPO	Jump on parity odd	1	1	1	0	0	0	1	0
CALL	Call unconditional	1	1	0	0	1	1	0	1
CC	Call on carry	1	1	0	1	1	1	0	0
CNC	Call on no carry	1	1	0	1	0	1	0	0
CZ	Call on zero	1	1	0	0	1	1	0	0
CNZ	Call on no zero	1	1	0	0	0	1	0	0
CP	Call on positive	1	1	1	1	0	1	0	0
CM	Call on minus	1	1	1	1	1	1	0	0
CPE	Call on parity even	1	1	1	0	1	1	0	0
CPO	Call on parity odd	1	1	1	0	0	1	0	0
RET	Return	1	1	0	0	1	0	0	1
RC	Return on carry	1	1	0	1	1	0	0	0
RNC	Return on no carry	1	1	0	1	0	0	0	0
RZ	Return on zero	1	1	0	0	1	0	0	0
RNZ	Return on no zero	1	1	0	0	0	0	0	0
RP	Return on positive	1	1	1	1	0	0	0	0
RM	Return on minus	1	1	1	1	1	0	0	0
RPE	Return on parity even	1	1	1	0	1	0	0	0
RPO	Return on parity odd	1	1	1	0	0	0	0	0
RST	Restart	1	1	A	A	A	1	1	1
IN	Input	1	1	0	1	1	0	1	1
OUT	Output	1	1	0	1	0	0	1	1
LXI B	Load immediate register pair *B*, *C*	0	0	0	0	0	0	0	1
LXI D	Load immediate register pair *D*, *E*	0	0	0	1	0	0	0	1
LXI H	Load immediate register pair *H*, *L*	0	0	1	0	0	0	0	1
LXI SP	Load immediate stack pointer	0	0	1	1	0	0	0	1
PUSH B	Push register pair *B*, *C* on stack	1	1	0	0	0	1	0	1
PUSH D	Push register pair *D*, *E* on stack	1	1	0	1	0	1	0	1
PUSH H	Push register pair *H*, *L* on stack	1	1	1	0	0	1	0	1
PUSH PSW	Push *A* and flags on stack	1	1	1	1	0	1	0	1
POP B	Pop register pair *B*, *C* off stack	1	1	0	0	0	0	0	1
POP D	Pop register pair *D*, *E* off stack	1	1	0	1	0	0	0	1
POP H	Pop register pair *H*, *L* off stack	1	1	1	0	0	0	0	1
POP PSW	Pop *A* and flags off stack	1	1	1	1	0	0	0	1
STA	Store *A* direct	0	0	1	1	0	0	1	0
LDA	Load *A* direct	0	0	1	1	1	0	1	0
XCHG	Exchange *D*, *E* and *H*, *L* registers	1	1	1	0	1	0	1	1
XTHL	Exchange top of stack, *H*, *L*	1	1	1	0	0	0	1	1
SPHL	*H*, *L* to stack pointer	1	1	1	1	1	0	0	1

TABLE 10 • 7 (CONTINUED)

MNEMONIC	DESCRIPTION	D_7	D_6	D_5	D_4	D_3	D_2	D_1	D_0
				INSTRUCTION CODE*					
PCHL	H, L to program counter	1	1	1	0	1	0	0	1
DAD B	Add B, C to H, L	0	0	0	0	1	0	0	1
DAD D	Add D, E to H, L	0	0	0	1	1	0	0	1
DAD H	Add H, L to H, L	0	0	1	0	1	0	0	1
DAD SP	Add stack pointer to H, L	0	0	1	1	1	0	0	1
STAX B	Store A indirect	0	0	0	0	0	0	1	0
STAX D	Store A indirect	0	0	0	1	0	0	1	0
LDAX B	Load A indirect	0	0	0	0	1	0	1	0
LDAX D	Load A indirect	0	0	0	1	1	0	1	0
INX B	Increment B, C registers	0	0	0	0	0	0	1	1
INX D	Increment D, E registers	0	0	0	1	0	0	1	1
INX H	Increment H, L registers	0	0	1	0	0	0	1	1
INX SP	Increment stack pointer	0	0	1	1	0	0	1	1
DCX B	Decrement B, C	0	0	0	0	1	0	1	1
DCX D	Decrement D, E	0	0	0	1	1	0	1	1
DCX H	Decrement H, L	0	0	1	0	1	0	1	1
DCX SP	Decrement stack pointer	0	0	1	1	1	0	1	1
CMA	Complement A	0	0	1	0	1	1	1	1
STC	Set carry	0	0	1	1	0	1	1	1
CMC	Complement carry	0	0	1	1	1	1	1	1
DAA	Decimal adjust A	0	0	1	0	0	1	1	1
SHLD	Store H, L direct	0	0	1	0	0	0	1	0
LHLD	Load H, L direct	0	0	1	0	1	0	1	0
EI	Enable interrupts	1	1	1	1	1	0	1	1
DI	Disable interrupt	1	1	1	1	0	0	1	1
NOP	No-operation	0	0	0	0	0	0	0	0

Note: DDD or SSS are numbered as follows: 000-B; 001-C; 010-D; 011-E; 100-H; 101-L; 110-memory; 111-A. For example, 01010001 instructs the computer to move the contents of register C into register D.

The CMP M instruction compares the byte in the memory pointed to by the H, L pair with the contents of accumulator A and sets the status flags accordingly. In effect, the flags are set as if the byte in memory had been subtracted from accumulator A. However, neither memory nor accumulator are changed. As a result, if the byte in the memory equals that in A, the Z bit will be set to 1; if A is less than the byte in the memory, the C flag will be set to 1.

The JNC FINIS instruction causes a jump to FINIS if the C flag is a 0. (In this case the content of A is larger than or equal to that in location 51 in the memory.)

If no jump is taken, the MOV A, M instruction moves the byte at location 51 (now pointed to by H, L) into the accumulator.

The INX H instruction adds 1 to the H, L register pair, giving 52, and the MOV M, A instruction moves the contents of the accumulator into location 52 in the memory.

This computer employs what is now becoming the most used technique for subroutine calls and for servicing interrupts.

For a subroutine jump a CALL instruction is used. The address of the subroutine is in the 16 bits (2 memory addresses) following the CALL OP code. This instruction first increments the program counter to the address of the next instruction in sequence and then places (pushes) the contents of the program counter on a stack in the memory. The stack pointer (see Fig. 10·16) is adjusted to point to this address on the stack. The jump to the subroutine is then made.

At the end of the subroutine a RETURN instruction is used. This instruction specifies no address but simply causes a return to the address currently on top of the stack and then pops this address.

An investigation of this scheme will show that if a subroutine calls another subroutine which calls another subroutine which then calls the first subroutine, the successive addresses needed are stacked one on the other, and the subprograms will finally work their way back to the original calling program without loss of any of the necessary address links.

After a discussion of interrupts we will return to subroutine calls. First it should be pointed out that in preparing subroutines, some method must be agreed on for "passing parameters" into the subroutine. For example, if the subroutine's function is to find the square root of a number, the original number must be passed to the subroutine, and the square root calculated by the subroutine must be passed back to the calling program. In this case the accumulator is a logical place to use for passing the number involved. Thus more than likely each time the subroutine is to

TABLE 10 • 8 FLAGS USED IN 8080 CPU

Flag word							
D_7	D_6	D_5	D_4	D_3	D_2	D_1	D_0
S	Z	O	AC	O	P	1	CY

There are five condition flags associated with the execution of instructions on the 8080. They are zero, sign, parity, carry, and auxiliary carry. Each is represented by a 1-bit register in the CPU. A flag is "set" by forcing the bit to 1 and "reset" by forcing the bit to 0.

Unless indicated otherwise, when an instruction affects a flag, it affects it in the following manner:

1. *Zero* If the result of an instruction has the value 0, this flag is set; otherwise it is reset.
2. *Sign* If the most significant bit of the result of the operation has the value 1, this flag is set; otherwise it is reset.
3. *Parity* If the modulo 2 sum of the bits of the result of the operation is 0 (i.e., if the result has even parity), this flag is set; otherwise it is reset (i.e., if the result has odd parity).
4. *Carry* If the instruction resulted in a carry (from addition) or a borrow (from subtraction or a comparison) out of the high-order bit, this flag is set; otherwise it is reset.
5. *Auxiliary carry* If the instruction caused a carry out of bit 3 and into bit 4 of the resulting value, the auxiliary carry is set; otherwise it is reset. This flag is affected by single precision additions, subtractions, increments, decrements, comparisons, and logical operations.

TABLE 10 • 9 8080 PROGRAM TO FIND LARGEST NUMBER

MEMORY ADDRESS	CONTENTS	LABEL	OP CODE	OPERAND	COMMENTS
00	21		LXI	H, 50H	LOAD *H* AND *L*
01	50				
02	00				
03	7E		MOV	A, M	GET 1ST OPERAND
04	23		INX	H	
05	BE		CMP	M	IS 2ND OPERAND LARGER?
06	D2		JNC	FINIS	
07	0A				
08	00				
09	7E		MOV	A, M	2ND OPERAND IS LARGER
0A	23	FINIS	INX	H	
0B	77		MOV	M, A	

be used, the number whose square root is to be formed will be placed in the accumulator, the subroutine will be called, and at the end of the subroutine the square root will be in the accumulator.

In this computer interrupts are handled in a way similar to subroutine calls. The program being executed is interrupted, and the address of the next instruction which was to be executed is placed on top of the stack maintained by the stack pointer. The interrupting device places an RST instruction on the data lines of the bus, and the 8080 next performs this instruction. The address section (NNN in Table 10·6) of this instruction contains the address in memory where the subroutine to service the interrupt is located. Returns from the interrupt servicing subroutine can then use the RETURN instruction to return to the original program. This is shown in Fig. 10·16.

When this kind of stacking of subprogram and interrupt addresses is used, it is possible to have subroutines interrupted, interrupts interrupted, and so on, and still return to each strip of instructions correctly as long as the stack does not overflow the area in memory allocated for it.

It is also necessary to save the registers in the CPU when interrupts occur if they are changed by the interrupt servicing subroutine. (The same applies for subroutine calls.) The interrupt program must take care of this saving and restoring of registers. Some idea of how this is done using a stack can be gathered by examining the PUSH and POP instructions, and the Questions treat this in more detail.

We now examine a program using a subroutine call. The subroutine is to search a table for a specific character. If the character is found, the position of the character in the table is to be passed back to the calling routine.

Examination of the problem indicates that the following information must be passed to the subroutine: (1) the location of the table in the memory, (2) the length of the table (number of characters in the table), and (3) the character to be searched for. To pass these three parameters, we choose registers *H* and *L* to point to the ending location of the table, put the number of characters into register

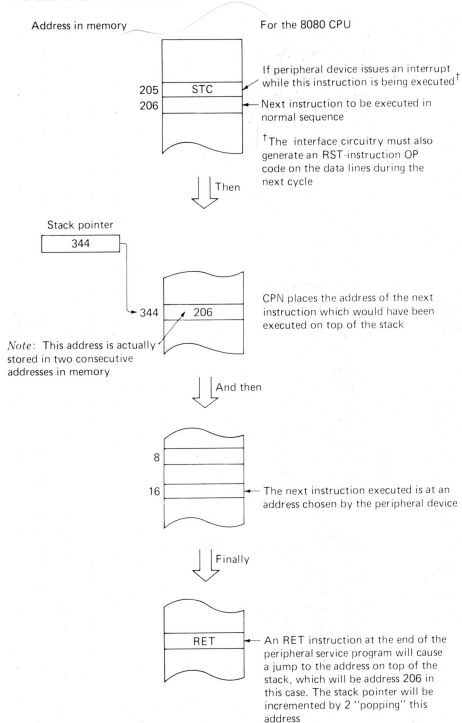

Address in memory

For the 8080 CPU

205   STC   If peripheral device issues an interrupt while this instruction is being executed[†]

206   Next instruction to be executed in normal sequence

[†]The interface circuitry must also generate an RST-instruction OP code on the data lines during the next cycle

Then

Stack pointer

344

344   206   CPN places the address of the next instruction which would have been executed on top of the stack

Note: This address is actually stored in two consecutive addresses in memory

And then

8

16   The next instruction executed is at an address chosen by the peripheral device

Finally

RET   An RET instruction at the end of the peripheral service program will cause a jump to the address on top of the stack, which will be address 206 in this case. The stack pointer will be incremented by 2 "popping" this address

FIG. 10 • 16 Interrupt servicing using a stack.

TABLE 10 • 10 A SEARCH SUBROUTINE

LABEL	OP CODE	OPERAND	COMMENTS
	ORG	30H	
SRCH	CMP	M	;IS CHAR = TABLE ENTRY?
	JZ	FINIS	;YES
	DCX	H	;GO TO NEXT ENTRY
	DCR	B	;DECREMENT B
	JNZ	SRCH	;IS SEARCH OVER?
FINIS	RET		;RETURN

B, and place the character to be searched for in the accumulator. The subroutine is then entered, and its job is to find the character, place its position in the table in register *B,* and then return to the calling program. If the character is not in the table, *B* is made a 0.

A subroutine to perform this function is shown in Table 10·10. When the subroutine is entered, the register pair *H, L* points to the table's last location in memory, *B* gives the number of characters, and *A* contains the character to be located.

The name of the subroutine is SRCH. The ORG 30H statement, which occurs first, is an *assembler directive* which tells the assembler to "locate this subroutine beginning at location 30_{16} in memory."

The label SRCH identifies the subroutine. The CMP M instruction compares the last entry in the table (which is pointed to by the *H, L* pair) with the accumulator. If they are equal, the *Z* status flag will be set, and the JZ instruction will cause a jump to FINIS. If they are not equal, the DCX H instruction subtracts 1 from the *H, L* pair, and then the DCR B subtracts 1 from *B*. When the DCR B instruction is executed, if *B* becomes 0, the *Z* flag will be set. The JNZ instruction tests this, and if another location is to be checked, it jumps back to SRCH; otherwise the subroutine ends.

A possible calling sequence is shown in Table 10·11. The location of the end of the table is at TBEND in the memory, and the number of items is 20_{16}. These are loaded into the *H, L* pair and *B,* and the character to be searched for, here called CHAR, is loaded into the accumulator. Finally the subroutine is entered, using a CALL SRCH instruction.

TABLE 10 • 11 CALLING PROGRAM FOR SEARCH SUBROUTINE

LABEL	OP CODE	OPERAND	COMMENTS
	LXI	H, TBEND	;LOAD TABLE END ADDRESS
	MVI	B, 20H	;LOAD NO OF CHARS
	LDA	CHAR	;LOAD CHARACTER
	CALL	SRCH	;CALL SUBROUTINE
	LDR	40H	;RETURN IS TO HERE
	. . .	. . .	

When the RET instruction in the subroutine is executed, the return will be to the LDR 40H instruction, which would be executed next. (This statement is placed in the program only for completeness and does not affect any operation discussed.)

10 • 12 THE 6800 MICROPROCESSOR

Another widely used example of a microcomputer is the 6800 microprocessor-microcomputer system first developed by Motorola. (Chips for this system are also available from a number of other manufacturers.) The basic CPU is on a single 40-pin IC chip, as shown in Fig. 10 · 17. The 6800 has an 8-bit data bus and a 16-bit address bus (see Fig. 10 · 17). From a programming viewpoint, the CPU chip contains 6 basic registers which are shown in Fig. 10 · 18.

1. *Accumulator A*   This is an 8-bit accumulator.
2. *Accumulator B*   This is an 8-bit accumulator.
3. *Index register*   This is a single 16-bit index register.
4. *Stack pointer*   This is a 16-bit register which points to a stack in memory.
5. *Program counter*   This is the instruction counter or program counter and contains 16 bits.
6. *Status register*   This is a 6-bit register containing 6 flip-flops *H, I, N, Z, V,* and *C.* The results of arithmetic and other operations are stored in these bits, as will be described.

The instruction repertoire for this CPU chip includes over 100 different instructions. The operation code is 8 bits, the size of a word in memory. There are seven different addressing modes, which are described in Table 10 · 12. A list of the instructions for this microprocessor chip is shown in Tables 10 · 13– 10 · 15.

The way that conditional branch instructions operate deserves mention. When an arithmetic or Boolean operation is performed, the status bits are set according to the result of this operation. Tables 10 · 16 and 10 · 17 show the status bits and detail their function. The branch instructions use the values of these bits to determine whether or not a branch is to be made.

For instance, if an arithmetic addition is performed, let us say accumulator *A* is added to accumulator *B,* then if the sum is negative, the *N* bit will be set to a 1. We also assume no overflow, so *V* will be set to a 0. Now if a BLT (branch if LT 0) instruction follows, the computer will branch to the address given in the address part of the instruction. If the result of the addition had been 0 or positive, no branch would have occurred, and the next instruction in sequence would be taken.

The *interrupt mask bit (I)* in the status register is set on when external input-output devices are allowed to interrupt the computer. When an interrupt occurs, the computer jumps to an interrupt servicing routine (program) which is stored in the memory. To simplify and shorten the interrupt servicing program, this microprocessor automatically transfers the values in all the CPU registers into a stack in the memory and places the address of these stored register contents in the stack pointer. The interrupt servicing program can then simply service the printer, reader,

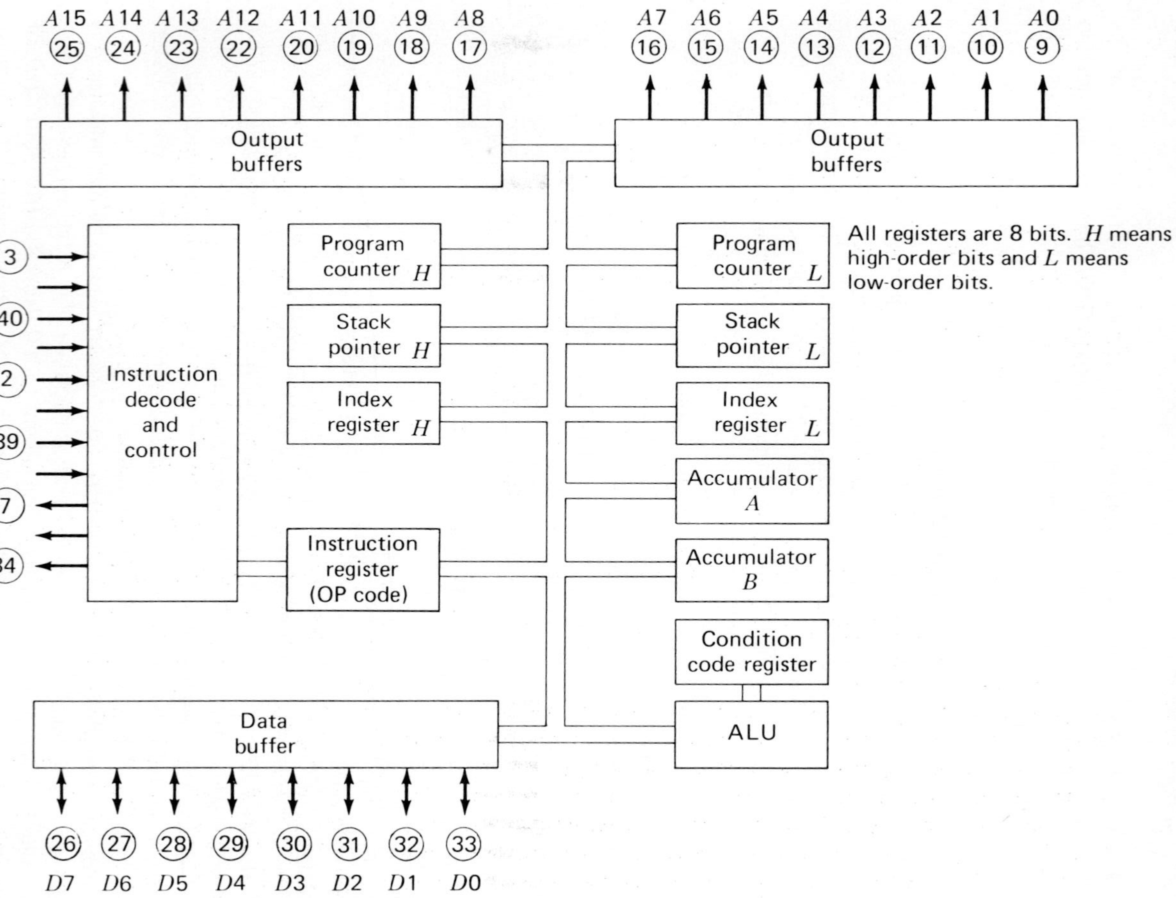
A15 A14 A13 A12 A11 A10 A9 A8
25 24 23 22 20 19 18 17
A7 A6 A5 A4 A3 A2 A1 A0
16 15 14 13 12 11 10 9
Output buffers
Output buffers
All registers are 8 bits. H means high-order bits and L means low-order bits.
Clock ϕ1 3
Clock ϕ2 37
$\overline{\text{Reset}}$ 40
$\overline{\text{Nonmaskable Interrupt}}$ 6
$\overline{\text{Halt}}$ 2
$\overline{\text{Interrupt Request}}$ 4
Three-state Control 39
Data Bus Enable 36
Bus Available 7
Valid Memory Address 5
Read/Write 34
Instruction decode and control
Program counter H
Stack pointer H
Index register H
Instruction register (OP code)
Program counter L
Stack pointer L
Index register L
Accumulator A
Accumulator B
Condition code register
ALU
Data buffer
26 27 28 29 30 31 32 33
D7 D6 D5 D4 D3 D2 D1 D0

Note: Circled numbers are pin numbers on IC container.

FIG. 10 • 17 Block diagram of CPU chip for 6800 microprocessor. (Courtesy of Motorola Corp.)

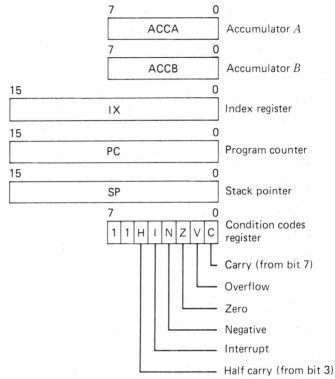

FIG. 10 • 18 Basic registers used in programming the 6800 microprocessor.

or whatever generated the interrupt and can later return the contents of the CPU registers to their status when interrupted and restart the program where it was interrupted.

Maintaining these stored registers in a stack also enables the interrupt servicing program to be interrupted, since the contents of the registers are again placed in the stack. In this way several interrupts can follow one another, and the program can still service each interrupt in turn and then return to the original program, which was operating when the first interrupt occurred.

Details of the operating features of this CPU can be found in the manufacturers' manuals listed in the Bibliography.

Table 10·18 shows a short program for the 6800 microprocessor. Its purpose is to add a table of 8-bit bytes located in the memory starting at address 51_{16}. The number of bytes in the table is in location 50_{16}. The sum of the numbers is to be stored at location 0F in the memory. Carries from the addition are ignored.

The programmer wrote the columns from label to the right. The assembler generated the leftmost two columns.

The first instruction CLRA simply clears accumulator A. The LDAB instruction gets the number of bytes in the table from location 50_{16} in the memory and stores that number in register B. Notice that in 6800 assembly language a hexadecimal number is designated by placing a $ in front of the number. Also notice that the 50

TABLE 10 • 12 ADDRESSING MODES FOR MICROPROCESSOR

MODE	OPERATION
Accumulator (ACCX) addressing	In accumulator-only addressing either accumulator A or accumulator B is specified. These are 1-byte instructions.
Immediate addressing	In immediate addressing the operand is contained in second byte of instruction, except LDS and LDX, which have operand in second and third bytes of instruction. The 6800 addresses this location when it fetches the immediate instruction for execution. These are 2- or 3-byte instructions.
Direct addressing	In direct addressing the address of the operand is contained in second byte of instruction. Direct addressing allows user to directly address lowest 256 bytes in machine, i.e., locations 0 through 255. Enhanced execution times are achieved by storing data in these locations. In most configurations it would be a random-access memory. These are 2-byte instructions.
Extended addressing	In extended addressing the address contained in second byte of instruction is used as higher 8 bits of address of the operand. Third byte of instruction is used as lower 8 bits of address for the operand. This is an absolute address in memory. These are 3-byte instructions.
Indexed addressing	In indexed addressing the address contained in second byte of instruction is added to index register's lowest 8 bits. Any carry generated is then added to higher order 8 bits of index register. This result is then used to address memory. The modified address is held in a temporary address register so there is no change to index register. These are 2-byte instructions.
Implied addressing	In the implied addressing mode the OP code gives the address (i.e., stack pointer, index register, etc.). These are 1-byte instructions.
Relative addressing	In relative addressing the address contained in second byte of instruction is added to program counter's lowest 8 bits plus 2. The carry or borrow is then added to high 8 bits. This allows user to address data within a range of -125 to $+129$ bytes of present instruction. These are 2-byte instructions.

occurs in the second memory address of the instruction word, and the addressing mode is immediate.

The LDX#$01 loads the value 1 in the index register. The symbol # tells the assembler to use this as an actual number, not as an address. The resulting immediate address operand requires 2 bytes since the index register contains 16 bits. Also note that the least significant byte is the last byte in the 3-byte instruction word.

The ADDA $50, X is an *indexed*-addressing-mode addition instruction. In the 6800 the indexed mode is indicated by the X in the statement. The $50 (for hexadecimal 50) gives the offset. The actual address used is formed by adding the offset to the contents of the index register. In this case, the first time through the loop, the address will be the offset 50_{16} plus 1, and therefore 51_{16}. Notice that the offset is loaded in the memory following the OP code and is a single byte. (A check of the OP codes will indicate that AB is the OP code for an indexed-mode addition). After this instruction is executed, accumulator A will contain the number at location 51.

The INX adds 1 to the index register, which will now contain 2. The DECB decrements register B and also sets the status bits. In particular, if B becomes 0, the Z status bit will be set to a 1, and this will indicate that the entire table has been processed.

The BNE LOOP instruction tests the Z bit and branches if Z is *not* a 1. When Z becomes 1, the program control "falls through" the BNE to the STAA instruction.

When the program control loops back the first time, the index register plus the offset now equal 52, so the number at that address will be added into accumulator A by the ADDA $50, X instruction. This process continues with numbers at successive locations being added into A until the table end is reached. Then the STAA $0F instruction stores the sum at location F in the memory.

Subroutine calls for the 6800 are made by a JSR (jump subroutine) instruction which pushes the program counter's contents (2 bytes)† on top of the stack (also adjusting the stack pointer). When an RTS (return from subroutine) instruction is given, the address (2 bytes) on top of the stack is placed in the program counter, causing return to the instruction after the initial JSR.

An example of a subroutine is shown in Table 10·19. The ORG $30 is an *assembler directive* which tells the assembler to place the subroutine starting at location 30_{16} in the memory.

The purpose of this subroutine is to find where in a table in the memory a character lies. The parameters are passed‡ as follows: (1) the address of the end of the table must be in the index register before the subroutine is entered, (2) the number of entries in the table is placed in accumulator B, (3) the character to be searched for must be in accumulator A.

The subroutine is entered at SRCH where the CMPA 0, X instruction causes the byte at the memory address given by the index register (notice that the offset is 0) to be compared with accumulator A. If they are equal, the Z status bit will be set to 1, and the BEQ FINIS instruction will test this instruction and branch to FINIS. Otherwise the index register will be decremented so that it points to the next lowest entry in the table. Accumulator B will then be decremented by the DECB, and if this sets the Z flag to 1, indicating a 0 in B, the search will be ended. Otherwise the return to SRCH will cause the next entry in the table to be compared with the character in accumulator A. This will be repeated until all table entries have been examined.

---

†After the program counter has already been updated to point to the next instruction.
‡See description of the 8080 for a discussion of parameter passing.

TABLE 10 • 13 ACCUMULATOR AND MEMORY INSTRUCTIONS (COURTESY OF MOTOROLA CORP.)

OPERATIONS	MNEMONIC	IMMED OP	DIRECT OP	INDEX OP	EXTND OP	IMPLIED OP	BOOLEAN ARITHMETIC OPERATION* (ALL REGISTER LABELS REFER TO CONTENTS)
Add	ADDA	8B	9B	AB	BB		$A + M \rightarrow A$
	ADDB	CB	DB	EB	FB		$B + M \rightarrow B$
Add accumulators	ABA					1B	$A + B \rightarrow A$
Add with carry	ADCA	89	99	A9	B9		$A + M + C \rightarrow A$
	ADCB	C9	D9	E9	F9		$B + M + C \rightarrow B$
And	ANDA	84	94	A4	B4		$A \cdot M \rightarrow A$
	ANDB	C4	D4	E4	F4		$B \cdot M \rightarrow B$
Bit test	BITA	85	95	A5	B5		$A \cdot M$
	BITB	C5	D5	E5	F5		$B \cdot M$
Clear	CLR			6F	7F		$00 \rightarrow M$
	CLRA					4F	$00 \rightarrow A$
	CLRB					5F	$00 \rightarrow B$
Compare	CMPA	81	91	A1	B1		$A - M$
	CMPB	C1	D1	E1	F1		$B - M$
Compare accumulators	CBA					11	$A - B$
Complement 1s	COM			63	73		$\overline{M} \rightarrow M$
	COMA					43	$\overline{A} \rightarrow A$
	COMB					53	$\overline{B} \rightarrow B$
Complement 2s (negate)	NEG			60	70		$00 - M \rightarrow M$
	NEGA					40	$00 - A \rightarrow A$
	NEGB					50	$00 - B \rightarrow B$
Decimal adjust, A	DAA					19	Converts binary addition of BCD characters into BCD format
Decrement	DEC			6A	7A		$M - 1 \rightarrow M$
	DECA					4A	$A - 1 \rightarrow A$
	DECB					5A	$B - 1 \rightarrow B$

Operation	Mnemonic	IMMED	DIRECT	INDEX	EXTND	IMPLIED	Boolean/Arithmetic Operation
Exclusive OR	EORA	88	98	A8	B8		$A \oplus M \rightarrow A$
	EORB	C8	D8	E8	F8		$B \oplus M \rightarrow B$
Increment	INC			6C	7C		$M + 1 \rightarrow M$
	INCA					4C	$A + 1 \rightarrow A$
	INCB					5C	$B + 1 \rightarrow B$
Load accumulator	LDAA	86	96	A6	B6		$M \rightarrow A$
	LDAB	C6	D6	E6	F6		$M \rightarrow B$
Inclusive OR	ORAA	8A	9A	AA	BA		$A + M \rightarrow A$
	ORAB	CA	DA	EA	FA		$B + M \rightarrow B$
Push data	PSHA					36	$A \rightarrow M_{SP}, \ SP - 1 \rightarrow SP$
	PSHB					37	$B \rightarrow M_{SP}, \ SP - 1 \rightarrow SP$
Pull data	PULA					32	$SP + 1 \rightarrow SP, \ M_{SP} \rightarrow A$
	PULB					33	$SP + 1 \rightarrow SP, \ M_{SP} \rightarrow B$
Rotate left	ROL			69	79		M $\quad \leftarrow \fbox{$\fbox{}\fbox{}\fbox{}\fbox{}\fbox{}\fbox{}\fbox{}\fbox{}$} \leftarrow$
	ROLA					49	A $\quad C \quad b_7 \qquad\qquad b_0$
	ROLB					59	B
Rotate right	ROR			66	76		M $\quad \rightarrow \fbox{$\fbox{}\fbox{}\fbox{}\fbox{}\fbox{}\fbox{}\fbox{}\fbox{}$} \rightarrow$
	RORA					46	A $\quad C \quad b_7 \qquad\qquad b_0$
	RORB					56	B
Shift left, arithmetic	ASL			68	78		M $\quad \leftarrow \fbox{$\fbox{}\fbox{}\fbox{}\fbox{}\fbox{}\fbox{}\fbox{}\fbox{}$} \leftarrow 0$
	ASLA					48	A $\quad C \quad b_7 \qquad\qquad b_0$
	ASLB					58	B
Shift right, arithmetic	ASR			67	77		M $\quad \fbox{$\fbox{}\fbox{}\fbox{}\fbox{}\fbox{}\fbox{}\fbox{}\fbox{}$} \rightarrow \fbox{}$
	ASRA					47	A $\quad b_7 \qquad\qquad b_0 \quad C$
	ASRB					57	B
Shift right, logic	LSR			64	74		M $\quad 0 \rightarrow \fbox{$\fbox{}\fbox{}\fbox{}\fbox{}\fbox{}\fbox{}\fbox{}\fbox{}$} \rightarrow \fbox{}$
	LSRA					44	A $\qquad\quad b_7 \qquad\qquad b_0 \quad C$
	LSRB					54	B
Store accumulator	STAA		97	A7	B7		$A \rightarrow M$
	STAB		D7	E7	F7		$B \rightarrow M$
Subtract	SUBA	80	90	A0	B0		$A - M \rightarrow A$
	SUBB	C0	D0	E0	F0		$B - M \rightarrow B$

TABLE 10 • 13 (CONTINUED)

| OPERATIONS | MNEMONIC | ADDRESSING MODES | | | | | BOOLEAN ARITHMETIC OPERATION* |
| | | IMMED | DIRECT | INDEX | EXTND | IMPLIED | (ALL REGISTER LABELS REFER TO CONTENTS) |
		OP	OP	OP	OP	OP	
Subtract accumulator	SBA					10	A − B → A
Subtract with carry	SBCA	82	92	A2	B2		A − M − C → A
	SBCB	C2	D2	E2	F2		B − M − C → B
Transfer accumulators	TAB					16	A → B
	TBA					17	B → A
Test, zero or minus	TST			6D	7D		M − 00
	TSTA					4D	A − 00
	TSTB					5D	B − 00

*OP Operation code (hexadecimal)
+ Arithmetic plus
− Arithmetic minus
· Boolean AND
M_{SP} Contents of memory location pointed to by stack pointer
+ Boolean inclusive OR

⊕ Boolean exclusive OR
$\overline{M}$ Complement of M
→ Transfer into
0 Bit = zero
00 Byte = zero

Note: Accumulator addressing mode instructions are included in the column for implied addressing.

TABLE 10 · 14 INDEX REGISTER AND STACK MANIPULATION INSTRUCTIONS

| POINTER OPERATIONS | MNEMONIC | ADDRESSING MODES | | | | | BOOLEAN ARITHMETIC OPERATION* |
		IMMED OP	DIRECT OP	INDEX OP	EXTND OP	IMPLIED OP	
Compare index register	CPX	8C	9C	AC	BC		$X_H - M, X_L - (M + 1)$
Decrement index register	DEX					09	$X - 1 \rightarrow X$
Decrement stack pointer	DES					34	$SP - 1 \rightarrow SP$
Increment index register	INX					08	$X + 1 \rightarrow X$
Increment stack pointer	INS					31	$SP + 1 \rightarrow SP$
Load index register	LDX	CE	DE	EE	FE		$M \rightarrow X_H, (M + 1) \rightarrow X_L$
Load stack pointer	LDS	8E	9E	AE	BE		$M \rightarrow SP_H, (M + 1) \rightarrow SP_L$
Store index register	STX		DF	EF	FF		$X_H \rightarrow M, X_L \rightarrow (M + 1)$
Store stack pointer	STS		9F	AF	BF		$SP_H \rightarrow M, SP_L \rightarrow (M + 1)$
Index register → stack pointer	TXS					35	$X - 1 \rightarrow SP$
Stack pointer → index register	TSX					30	$SP + 1 \rightarrow X$

*See footnotes to Table 10·13.

TABLE 10 • 15 JUMP AND BRANCH INSTRUCTIONS

OPERATIONS	MNEMONIC	RELATIVE OP	ADDRESSING MODES INDEX OP	EXTND OP	IMPLIED OP	BRANCH TEST*
Branch always	BRA	20				None
Branch if carry clear	BCC	24				$C = 0$
Branch if carry set	BCS	25				$C = 1$
Branch if $= 0$	BEQ	27				$Z = 1$
Branch if ≥ 0	BGE	2C				$N \oplus V = 0$
Branch if > 0	BGT	2E				$Z + (N \oplus V) = 0$
Branch if higher	BHI	22				$C + Z = 0$
Branch if ≤ 0	BLE	2F				$Z + (N \oplus V) = 1$
Branch if lower or same	BLS	23				$C + Z = 1$
Branch if < 0	BLT	2D				$N \oplus V = 1$
Branch if minus	BMI	2B				$N = 1$
Branch if not equal 0	BNE	26				$Z = 0$
Branch if overflow clear	BVC	28				$V = 0$
Branch if overflow set	BVS	29				$V = 1$
Branch if plus	BPL	2A				$N = 0$
Branch to subroutine	BSR	8D				
Jump	JMP		6E	7E		
Jump to subroutine	JSR		AD	BD		
No operation	NOP				02	Advances program counter only
Return from interrupt	RTI				3B	
Return from subroutine	RTS				39	
Software interrupt	SWI				3F	
Wait for interrupt	WAI				3E	

*See footnotes to Table 10·13.

TABLE 10 • 16 CONDITION CODE REGISTER BITS

Condition code register   The condition code register indicates the results of an arithmetic-logic-unit operation: negative (N), zero (Z), overflow (V), carry from bit 7 (C), and half carry from bit 3 (H). These bits of the condition code register are used as testable conditions for the conditional branch instructions. Bit 4 is the interrupt mask bit (I). The unused bits of the condition code register (b_6 and b_7) are 1s.

TABLE 10 • 17 CONDITION CODE REGISTER MANIPULATION INSTRUCTIONS

OPERATIONS	MNEMONIC	OP CODE	BOOLEAN ARITHMETIC OPERATION
Clear carry	CLC	0C	$0 \to C$
Clear interrupt mask	CLI	0E	$0 \to 1$
Clear overflow	CLV	0A	$0 \to V$
Set carry	SEC	0D	$1 \to C$
Set interrupt mask	SEI	0F	$1 \to I$
Set overflow	SEV	0B	$1 \to V$
Accumulator $A \to$ CCR	TAP	06	$A \to$ CCR
CCR $\to$ accumulator A	TPA	07	CCR $\to A$

TABLE 10 • 18 A 6800 PROGRAM

MEMORY ADDRESS	CONTENTS	LABEL	OP CODE	OPERAND	COMMENTS
0000	4F		CLRA		CLEAR A
0001	D6		LDAB	$50	GET NO OF ENTRIES
0002	50				
0003	CE		LDX	#$01	LOAD INDEX REGISTER
0004	00				
0005	01				
0006	AB	LOOP	ADDA	$50, X	
0007	50				
0008	08		INX		INCREMENT IR
0009	5A		DECB		DECREMENT B
000A	26		BNE	LOOP	
000B	FA				
000C	97		STAA	$0F	
000D	0F				

TABLE 10 • 19 6800 SUBROUTINE FOR TABLE LOOKUP

LABEL	OP CODE	OPERAND	COMMENTS
	ORG	$30	SET ORIGIN
SRCH	CMPA	X	CHAR = TABLE ENTRY?
	BEQ	FINIS	YES QUIT
	DEX		INCREMENT IR
	DECB		DECREMENT B
	BNE	SRCH	TEST FOR END
	RTS		RETURN TO CALLER

TABLE 10 • 20 CALLING 6800 SUBROUTINE

LABEL	OP CODE	OPERAND	COMMENTS
	LDX	#ENDTA	LOAD IR WITH TABLE END
	LDAB	#20	LOAD B WITH NO OF ENTRIES
	LDAA	CHAR	LOAD A WITH CHAR
	JSR	SRCH	
	STAA	MABEL	

The RTS will cause a return to the calling program with accumulator *B* containing the number in the table at which the matched character lies.

A possible calling program segment is shown in Table 10·20. The LDX loads the index register with the address of the end of the table, which is assumed to be at ENDTA. The number of table entries is assumed to be 20_{10}, and the LDAB loads *B* with that value. (No $ symbol means decimal.) The HSR causes a jump to the subroutine, and the jump back from the subroutine using the RTS will cause the STAA instruction to be executed next.

When a set of chips for a microprocessor of this kind is used with a fixed program, such as in an industrial controller, the program is generally developed using system software which is provided by the chips' manufacturer and software vendors and placed in a ROM memory. A ROM memory can be addressed and used just like a RAM memory when connected to a microprocessor CPU (except, of course, that one cannot write into a ROM). It is common practice to write the program for the microprocessor and assemble this program using another computer. The program is sometimes tested using this larger computer, which runs it on a simulator. The larger computer then produces a punched tape which is used to set up the ROM in which the program will be stored.

Considerable effort is made by the manufacturers of the microprocessor chips to facilitate programming the microprocessor and to facilitate preparing the ROMs and loading the RAMs, when required. Sometimes higher level languages are provided, enabling programs to be written in Fortran, PL/M, or other compiler languages, which are then translated into the program for the microcomputer.

10 • 13 THE PDP-11

The PDP-11 is a minicomputer series. These computers have 16-bit words, each containing two 8-bit bytes (see Fig. 10·19). Notice, however, that each address in memory contains 1 byte. The eight general registers are 16 bits each, and a computer word normally has 16 bits.

The PDP-11 reads from and writes into external input-output devices in the same manner that it reads from and writes into high-speed (IC or core) memory. Each input-output device is simply given an address in memory, and to read from an address, and in turn an input-output device, the computer uses not a special input-output instruction, but a MOVE instruction, an ADD instruction, or whatever is

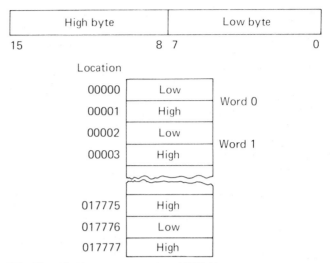

FIG. 10 • 19 Memory organization of PDP-11.

desired. This means that status registers must be used by the CPU (as in Chap. 8) to determine if a device can be written into, has something to read, etc.

There is a complex interrupt structure in the PDP-11 where the CPU continually puts a status number on 3 wires of its bus. Each external device has a status number, and if that status number is greater than the CPU status number, it has the right to interrupt. Setting a CPU's status number to its maximum stops all interrupts. The CPU's status number is set under program control and therefore can be changed as the program operates.

Interrupts are "vectored" (see Chap. 8 and the description of the 8080, Sec. 10·11) in that an interrupting device places data (an interrupt vector) on the bus lines which enable the CPU to transfer control directly to a service program for the interrupting device.

The general registers of the PDP-11 are shown in Fig. 10·20(a). Notice that register R6 is a stack pointer and R7 is the program counter. These can be used and addressed just like the other general-purpose registers, making for interesting instruction variations.

The CPU in the PDP-11 includes a status register as shown in Fig. 10·20(b). This status register contains the priority number just discussed, which is placed on the bus in bits 5–7. Bits 11–15 in Fig. 10·20(b) are used by the operating system to control program operations in the 11/45, one of the larger PDP-11 models, and will not be discussed here. (Details are given in the manuals listed in the Bibliography.)

The N, Z, V, C bits in the status word are set and reset as instructions are operated. For example, the N bit indicates when a result is negative. If an ADD instruction is performed and the result is negative, the N bit will be set to a 1; otherwise it will be a 0. Similarly, the Z bit indicates a zero result and will be set on if an instruction's result is zero. (V is for overflow and C is for carry.)

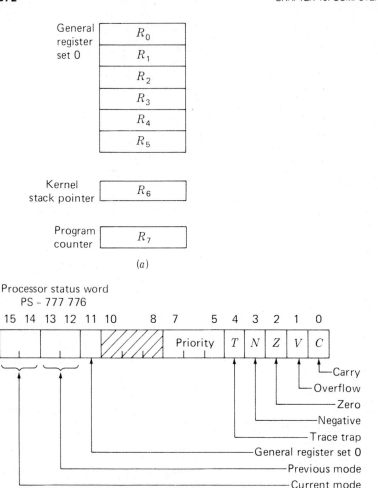

FIG. 10 • 20 PDP-11 organization. (*a*) General registers. (*b*) Processor status word.

The conditional jump or branch instructions in the PDP-11 use these bits to determine if a jump is to be taken. For instance, a BNE (branch or negative) instruction will cause a branch only if the N bit is a 1. As another example, the BEQ (branch or equal) instruction causes a branch only if the Z bit is a 1.

Table 10·21 lists the addressing modes for the PDP-11. The addressing mode number is placed before the register number in an instruction word and indicates how the designated register is to be used. Table 10·22 gives the instructions for the computer.

Table 10·23 shows a sample section of a program for a PDP-11. This is a subroutine, or subprogram, which reads from a teletypewriter keyboard. There is a status byte (interface register) at address 177030 in the memory which tells when

TABLE 10 · 21 ADDRESSING MODES FOR PDP-11 MINICOMPUTER

ADDRESS	MODE	NAME	SYMBOLIC	DESCRIPTION
General register	0	Register	R	(R) is operand [e.g., R2 = %2]
Mode *R*	1	Register deferred	(R)	(R) is address
	2	Auto increment	(R)+	(R) is address; (R) + (1 or 2)
	3	Auto increment deferred	@(R)+	(R) is address of address; (R) + 2
	4	Auto decrement	−(R)	(R) − (1 or 2); (R) is address
	5	Auto decrement deferred	@−(R)	(R) − 2; (R) is address of address
	6	Index	X(R)	(R) + X is address
	7	Index deferred	@X(R)	(R) + X is address of address
Program counter, Reg = 7	2	Immediate	#n	Operand *n* follows instruction
Mode 7	3	Absolute	@#A	Address *A* follows instruction
	6	Relative	A	Instruction address + 4 + X is address
	7	Relative deferred	@A	Instruction address + 4 + X is address of address

TABLE 10 · 22 PDP-11 INSTRUCTION REPERTOIRE

LEGEND

OP CODES		OPERATIONS		BOOLEAN		CONDITION CODES	
■	0 for word/1 for byte	( )	Contents of	$\wedge$ = AND		*	Conditionally set/cleared
SS	Source field (6 bits)	s	Contents of source	$\vee$ = Inclusive OR		−	Not affected
DD	Destination field (6 bits)	d	Contents of destination	$\not\vee$ = Exclusive OR		0	Cleared
R	General register (3 bits) 0 to 7	r	Contents of register	$\sim$ = Not		1	Set
XXX	Offset (3 bits) +127 to −128	←	Becomes				
N	Number (3 bits)	X	Relative address				
NN	Number (6 bits)	%	Register definition				

SINGLE OPERAND: OPR dst

15	OP CODE	6 5	DD	0

MNEMONIC	OP CODE	INSTRUCTION	dst RESULT	N	Z	V	C
General							
CLR(B)	■ 050DD	Clear	0	0	1	0	0
COM(B)	■ 051DD	Complement (1s)	~d	*	*	0	1
INC(B)	■ 052DD	Increment	d + 1	*	*	*	−
DEC(B)	■ 053DD	Decrement	d − 1	*	*	*	−
NEG(B)	■ 054DD	Negate (2s complement)	−d	*	*	*	*
TST(B)	■ 057DD	Test	d	*	*	0	0
Rotate and Shift							
ROR(B)	■ 060DD	Rotate right	→ C, d	*	*	*	*
ROL(B)	■ 061DD	Rotate left	C, d ←	*	*	*	*
ASR(B)	■ 062DD	Arithmetic shift right	d/2	*	*	*	*
ASL(B)	■ 063DD	Arithmetic shift left	2d	*	*	*	*
SWAB	0003DD	Swap bytes		*	*	0	0

Multiple Precision

MNEMONIC	OP CODE	INSTRUCTION	OPERATION	N	Z	V	C
ADC(B)	■055DD	Add carry	d + C	*	*	*	*
SBC(B)	■056DD	Subtract carry	d − C	*	*	*	*
▲SXT*	0067DD	Sign extend	0 or −1	—	*	—	—

DOUBLE OPERAND: OPR src, dst   OPR src, R or OPR R, dst

```
 15      12 11        6 5        0
┌─────────┬──────────┬──────────┐
│ OP CODE │    SS    │    DD    │
└─────────┴──────────┴──────────┘

 15        9 8      6 5          0
┌───────────┬───────┬────────────┐
│  OP CODE  │   R   │  SS OR DD  │
└───────────┴───────┴────────────┘
```

MNEMONIC	OP CODE	INSTRUCTION	OPERATION	N	Z	V	C
General							
MOV(B)	■1SSDD	Move	d ← s	*	*	0	—
CMP(B)	■2SSDD	Compare	s − d	*	*	*	*
ADD	06SSDD	Add	d ← s + d	*	*	*	*
SUB	16SSDD	Subtract	d ← d − s	*	*	*	*
Logical							
BIT(B)	■3SSDD	Bit test (AND)	s ∧ d	*	*	0	—
BIC(B)	■4SSDD	Bit clear	d ← (∼s) ∧ d	*	*	0	—
BIS(B)	■5SSDD	Bit set (OR)	d ← s ∨ d	*	*	0	—
▲*Register*							
MUL	070RSS	Multiply	r ← r×s	*	*	0	*
DIV	071RSS	Divide	r ← r/s	*	*	*	*
ASH	072RSS	Shift arithmetically		*	*	*	*
ASHC	073RSS	Arithmetic shift combined		*	*	*	*
XOR	074RDD	Exclusive OR	d ← r ∨ d	*	*	0	—

TABLE 10 · 22 (CONTINUED)

BRANCH: B—location

If condition is satisfied:
Branch to location,
New PC ← updated PC + (2 × offset)

$\underbrace{\qquad}$ address of branch instruction + 2

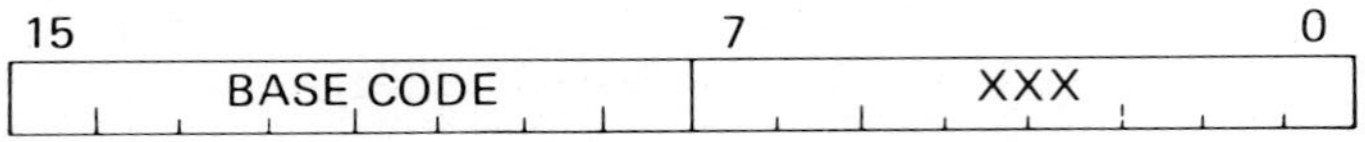

| 15 | BASE CODE | 7 | XXX | 0 |

OP code = base code + XXX

MNEMONIC	BASE CODE	INSTRUCTION	BRANCH CONDITION	
Branches				
BR	000400	Branch (unconditional)	(always)	
BNE	001000	Branch if not equal (to 0)	$\neq 0$	$Z = 0$
BEQ	001400	Branch if equal (to 0)	$= 0$	$Z = 1$
BPL	100000	Branch if plus	$+$	$N = 0$
BMI	100400	Branch if minus	$-$	$N = 1$
BVC	102000	Branch if overflow is clear		$V = 0$
BVS	102400	Branch if overflow is set		$V = 1$
BCC	103000	Branch if carry is clear		$C = 0$
BCS	103400	Branch if carry is set		$C = 1$
Signed Conditional Branches				
BGE	002000	Branch if greater or equal (to 0)	≥ 0	$N \veebar V = 0$
BLT	002400	Branch if less than (0)	< 0	$N \veebar V = 1$
BGT	003000	Branch if greater than (0)	> 0	$N \vee (N \veebar V) = 0$
BLE	003400	Branch if less or equal (to 0)	≤ 0	$Z \vee (N \veebar V) = 1$
Unsigned Conditional Branches				
BHI	101000	Branch if higher	$>$	$C \vee Z = 0$
BLOS	101400	Branch if lower or same	$\leqslant$	$C \vee Z = 1$

MNEMONIC	OP CODE	INSTRUCTION	NOTES		
BHIS	103000	Branch if higher or same	$\geqslant$		C = 0
BLO	103400	Branch if lower	$<$		C = 1

JUMP AND SUBROUTINE

MNEMONIC	OP CODE	INSTRUCTION	NOTES
JMP	0001DD	Jump	PC ← dst
JSR	004RDD	Jump to subroutine	Use same R
RTS	00020R	Return from subroutine	
▲MARK	0064NN	Mark	Aid in subroutine return
▲SOB	077RNN	Subtract 1 and branch (if ≠ 0)	(R) − 1, then if (R) ≠ 0:
			PC ← updated PC − (2 × NN)

TRAP AND INTERRUPT

MNEMONIC	OP CODE	INSTRUCTION	NOTES
EMT	104000 to 104377	Emulator trap (not for general use)	PC at 30, PS at 32
TRAP	104400 to 104777	Trap	PC at 34, PS at 36
BPT	000003	Breakpoint trap	PC at 14, PS at 16
IOT	000004	Input-output trap	PC at 20, PS at 22
RTI	000002	Return from Interrupt	
▲RTT	000006	Return from Interrupt	Inhibit T bit trap

CONDITION CODE OPERATORS

15				5	4	3	2	1	0
OP CODE BASE = 000240						H	Z	V	C

0 = CLEAR SELECTED CONDITION CODE BITS
1 = SET SELECTED CONDITION CODE BITS

MNEMONIC	OP CODE	INSTRUCTION	N	Z	V	C
CLC	000241	Clear C	–	–	–	0
CLV	000242	Clear V	–	–	0	–

TABLE 10 • 22 (CONTINUED)

MNEMONIC	OP CODE	INSTRUCTION	N	Z	V	C
CLZ	000244	Clear Z	–	0	–	–
CLN	000250	Clear N	0	–	–	–
CCC	000257	Clear all condition code bits	0	0	0	0
SEC	000261	Set C	–	–	–	1
SEV	000262	Set V	–	–	1	–
SEZ	000264	Set Z	–	1	–	–
SEN	000270	Set N	1	–	–	–
SCC	000277	Set all condition code bits	1	1	1	1

MISCELLANEOUS

MNEMONIC	OP CODE	INSTRUCTION
HALT	000000	Halt
WAIT	000001	Wait for interrupt
RESET	000005	Reset external bus
NOP	000240	(No operation)
●SPL	00023N	Set priority level (to N)
▲MFPI	0065SS	Move from previous instruction space
▲MTPI	0066DD	Move to previous instruction space
●MFPD	1065SS	Move from previous data space
●MTPD	1066DD	Move to previous data space

NOTE: ▲ Applies to 11/35, 11/40, and 11/45 computers. ● Applies to 11/45 computer.

TABLE 10 • 23 A PDP-11 PROGRAM SEGMENT

MEMORY ADDRESS	CONTENTS	LABEL	OP CODE	ADDRESS PART	COMMENTS
000524	105767 177030	READ:	TSTB	KSR	;READY
000530	100375		BPL	READ	;NO
000532	116710 177024		MOVB	KSB, @R0	;MOVE IT INTO THE TABLE
000536	005267 000200		INC	COUNT	;INCREASE COUNT
000542	122027 000256		CMPB	(R0)+, #256	;IS IT A PERIOD
000546	001366		BNE	READ	;NO

the keyboard has a new character. The subprogram places characters in a table until a period is typed, at which time control is transferred to another subprogram.

The section shown in Table 10·23 is from an actual assembler listing for a PDP-11, and all numbers are in octal. The programmer writes all text from the label column to the right. Semicolons indicate comments, and everything to the right of a semicolon is a comment and is ignored by the assembler.

The listing was prepared by the programmer who wrote the assembly language program and then fed it into the assembler program which generated this listing.

The leftmost column lists locations in the memory and the next column the contents of these locations. For instance, a TSTB (test byte) instruction has OP code 105767, and the assembler has read the programmer's TSTB instruction and converted it into octal value.

The statement TSTB tests the byte at the address given, and if the value there is negative, places a 1 in the N bit; if it is zero, a 1 is placed in the Z bit. KSR designates the address in memory, 177030, where the status byte for the keyboard is located. The programmer has (in an earlier section of the program) told the assembler the value of KSR. If the keyboard has a character ready, the sign bit of the KSR byte will be a 1, causing the N bit to go on.

The next instruction, BPL READ, says branch to READ if $N = 0$. This means that if no character is available, the program goes back to READ and looks again. This continues until a character is ready and $N = 1$.

The BPL has an OP code of 100. The next byte contains the displacement or offset for the branch in 2s complement form. The address for the branch is equal to two times the offset byte's value (375) added to the address of the next instruction. In this case the offset value is negative, and a branch would go back to location 524.

When $N = 1$, the instruction word at location 532 will be executed. This is a MOVB (move byte) instruction which causes a byte to be moved from KSB, which is 177024 (the address of the keyboard's buffer, the value of which the program has already given to the assembler), to the value pointed to by R0. This is an example of indirect addressing, where R0 is used to point to the actual address.

Prior to this section of the program the programmer has loaded R0 with the starting location of the table in the memory where the input characters are to be stored.

The program now checks to see if the input character is a period, which has octal code 256, by comparing it with the character just loaded in the memory. Notice that indirect addressing is again used. The + sign causes the value in R0 to be incremented. Only if the character pointed to is equal to 256 will the Z bit be set to 1.

The BNE (branch on not equal) instruction checks this, and if the character is a period, it transfers control to another program; otherwise control is transferred back to the READ, where another character is then read from the keyboard.

The variety and complexities of the PDP-11's instruction repertoire can only be appreciated through a study of the manuals for this computer. The preceding example should point out the kind of efficient programs which can be written for this computer.

10 • 14 IBM 370 COMPUTER SERIES

We will now consider the IBM 370 series of computers. This line ranges from small to very large computers. The designs are arranged so that the computers are *upward compatible*. This means that a program written for a small computer will run on any computer in the 370 series that is larger. (The general way in determining "larger" is that the 40 is larger than the 30, the 50 is larger than the 40, etc., the 370/158 is larger than any of these, and, in general, a larger model number means a larger computer.) To keep the computers upward compatible, the instruction repertoire of a small computer is made a subset of the instruction repertoire of a larger computer.

The various models are designed in different IBM labs and use differing circuit lines and memory technologies, and some are microprogrammed and some are not. Nevertheless, keeping the architectures consistent and standardizing the instruction repertoires enable this upward compatibility to work. Other manufacturers do the same thing, and, for example, DEC's PDP-11 series and Honeywell's 60 series are all lines of computers where the instruction repertoires and general capabilities of the larger computers are expanded versions of the instruction repertoires and capabilities of the small ones.

The IBM 370 series is also designed so that it can compete effectively in both the scientific computing market and the business-data-processing computer market. The scientific-application area calls for an instruction repertoire including numeric instructions which operate (add, subtract, multiply, etc.) on both integer representation and floating-point numbers. These calculations must be performed on operands that are relatively long (in this case long is 32 and 64 bits per operand). The business applications, on the other hand, demand instructions that operate on character strings (as in the 1400 series) which consist of 8-bit alphanumeric characters and are of arbitrary length, as might be found in names, addresses, inventory descriptions, etc. It is also a good idea for business-data-processing computers to be able to calculate using BCD (since this reduces conversion time), and such numbers are also liable to be of different lengths and are generally stored in strings.

IBM's answer to these demands is to have a very large instruction repertoire which includes the necessary instructions to satisfy both application areas. Then Fortran compilers—which generally handle the numerical-type problem—generate the word-oriented binary arithmetic instructions, while Cobol compilers generate character-string handling instructions.

Another important consideration in large systems is the use of a programmed *operating system* to control the operation of the computer. An operating system consists of a set of programs which are used to control the running of the *user,* or *applications, programs.* To use the system, the operating system programs are first read in, and then these programs start and "operate" other programs by reading them into the memory, starting them, stopping programs which run too long or use too much memory, etc. These programs effectively aid the manual operators of the system to achieve maximum system throughput. The operating system sometimes types commands to operators on systems printers, telling them to mount tapes or disk packs, to add paper to printers, etc.

In order for large systems to be employed to their utmost potentiality, they are generally used in the *multiprogramming* mode where the operating system reads in one program, and if it calls for some slow operation (an input-output operation, for instance), the operating system then reads in and starts another program. This continues, and programs are restarted where they were last interrupted by the operating system when input-output is available or when other programs end.

In order to aid the writer of the operating system and to make computer operation more efficient, many computers now have architectures that permit the following:

1. A given program is *relocatable*. This means that a program can be placed in different locations in the memory at different times, and it will still run. This permits the operating system to locate several different programs in different parts of the memory and to operate first on one and then others, as convenient.

2. There must be some way for the operating system to set upper and lower bounds on the memory used by a given program. By allocating a specific area in the memory to a program and not permitting the program to use other locations in the memory, the program can be prevented from damaging the operating of other programs which are in the memory at the same time. This also aids in what is called *security,* which refers to preventing programs from deliberately reading other programs or otherwise interfering with them. For instance, one user might try and read another user's files, steal that user's programs, send himself a check, etc.

In order to help achieve the above goals, the IBM 370 series (and most manufacturers' larger computers) have two classes of instructions: *supervisory mode instructions* and *user mode instructions*. The operating system programs use the *supervisory mode instructions,* and when they are being executed, a flip-flop is on in the CPU so that the computer knows it is in this mode. When user or application mode programs are being executed, certain privileged instructions are not available to the program. Included in supervisory mode instructions but not in application mode instructions are those that set the upper and lower bounds in the memory where a program can operate and control input-output—in particular the reading of files—and a number of special instructions to handle emergencies, signal operators, etc.

Because of its size and complexity, we will only examine some of the more important aspects of the IBM 370 computer series. The manufacturer's manuals carry complete details.

In the 370 series, instruction words come in various sizes and lengths, and Fig. 10·21 shows three different types of instruction words and their lengths. Notice that the computer is basically a two-address machine. The computer has 16 accumulators, which are called *general registers,* and these are shown in Fig. 10·22. Each of these general registers consists of 32 bits, and each is addressable. There are also four *floating-point registers,* each consisting of 64 bits, and these are given the addresses 0, 2, 4, and 6, respectively. There are instructions so that one can load any of the general registers from the memory or one can transfer the contents of any general register into the memory, and the same may be said for each of the floating-point registers.

The memory is organized with 8 bits at each address. Thus the memory is said to be *character,* or *byte, addressable.* The basic computer word consists of 32 bits, and so four consecutive memory locations are required to form a single word. There are also *halfwords* and *doublewords,* as shown in Fig. 10·23. There are instructions that operate on words, instructions that use halfwords, instructions that use doublewords, and instructions that operate on character strings.

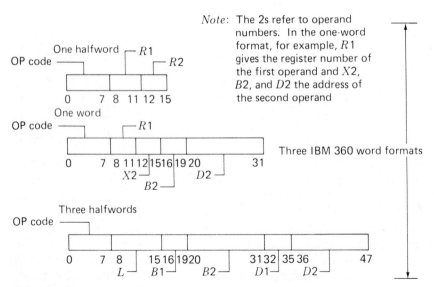

Note: The 2s refer to operand numbers. In the one-word format, for example, $R1$ gives the register number of the first operand and $X2$, $B2$, and $D2$ the address of the second operand

Three IBM 360 word formats

FIG. 10 • 21 Typical three IBM 360 instruction-word formats.

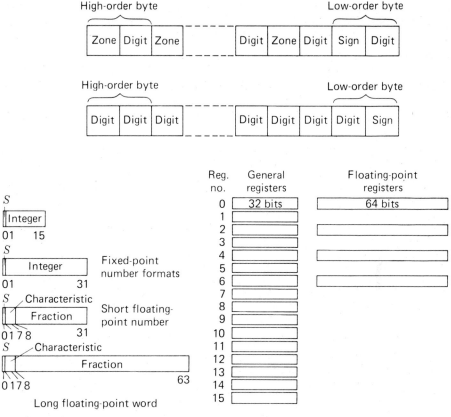

FIG. 10 • 22 General registers.

In general, when we add one 32-bit word to another word, we can (1) add one of the general registers to another general register and store the sum in one of the general registers, or (2) add one of the general registers to a word located in the memory and store the sum in the general register.

Further, there are floating-point and fixed-point instructions, so that a floating-point word located in the memory can be multiplied by the contents of one of the floating-point registers and the product stored in one of the floating-point registers. As noted in Chap. 6, for floating-point words the word addressed in memory will consist of either 32 or 64 digits. These consist of a sign digit plus a 7-digit characteristic and a 24-digit fraction if a short floating-point instruction is used, or of a sign digit plus a 7-digit characteristic and a 56-digit floating-point fraction or mantissa if a long floating-point word is used.

The general registers not only contain operands, but they are also used to store addresses, so that many instructions form an address by adding a number in a general register to another number to form the number of the location to be used in an operand.

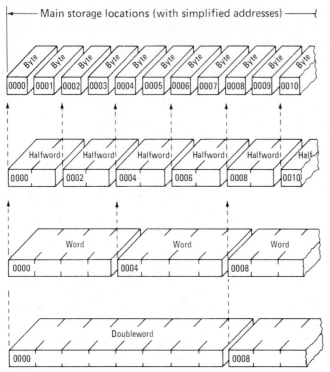

FIG. 10 • 23 Organization of memory—halfwords, words, doublewords, and bytes.

Let us examine several typical words in this system to see how various instructions operate. The first instruction shown in Fig. 10·24 is an ADD instruction, the OP code for which is 1A (base 16) lying in bits 0 through 7. Two operands are then designated. These operands are located in general register 7 and general register 9, so that the number in general register 7 will be added to the number in general register 9 and the sum stored in general register 7. Notice that the two addresses given in this particular type of instruction actually indicate directly the locations of the two words to be added.

The second instruction shown, which is a STORE instruction, is more complicated. The OP code for store in this system is 50. This OP code is followed in the instruction word by four numbers in the system. The first number, which lies in bits 8 through 11, gives the number of one general register to be used; the contents of this register are to be stored in the memory. The second set of three numbers occupies bits 12 through 31 in the instruction word and gives the address in memory where this number is to be stored. However, this address is not given directly. It is instead formed by adding the number in general register 10 to the number in general register 14, taking the 24 least significant digits of this number, and adding these to the number stored in bits 20 through 31 in the instruction word, which in this case is 310. For instance, if general register 10 contains the number 400 and if general register 14 contains the number 200, we add these two numbers, giving 600, and add that to 310, giving the number 910, so that the word in general register 3 is stored in location 910 in the memory.

SUBTRACT instructions operate somewhat similarly. The SUBTRACT instruction is indicated by the OP code 5B, and the particular type of instruction shown in Fig. 10·24 subtracts the number stored at an address which is determined by adding the number stored in general register 9 to the number stored in general register 8, and adding to this the number lying in bits 20 to 31 of the SUBTRACT instruction. When these three numbers are combined to form an address in the memory, the word located at that address is then subtracted from the word located in general register 4, and the difference is stored in general register 4.

For instance, if general register 4 contains 300, general register 9 contains 100, general register 8 contains 200, and in the memory the location 800 contains the word 1000, we will form the address number 800 by adding the number 200 lying in general register 8 to the number 100 lying in general register 9, and then adding this to the 500 given in bits 20 through 31 in the instruction word, giving the number 800. We then look in the memory at location 800 and find the word 1000. If this number is subtracted from 300, which lies in general register 4, the difference, 700, will be stored in general register 4 when the instruction is completed.

As one last example of the instruction code for this computer, let us examine a SHIFT RIGHT instruction, the OP code for which is 88. In this case the general register indicated by bits 8 through 11 in the instruction word is to be shifted right. The number of times the word is to be shifted is calculated by adding the number

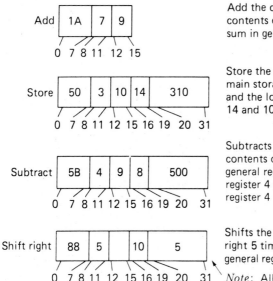

Add the contents of general register 7 to the contents of general register 9 and store the sum in general register 7

Store the contents of general register 3 at the main storage address given by the sum of 310 and the low-order 24 bits of general registers 14 and 10

Subtracts the word located at 500 plus the contents of the 24 least significant digits of general registers 8 and 9 from the word in register 4 and stores the difference in general register 4

Shifts the word in general register 5 to the right 5 times plus the number located in general register 10

Note: All characters are hexadecimal, for example, 1A is 0001 1010

FIG. 10 • 24 Typical instruction words.

in bits 20 through 31 of the instruction word to the number in the register designated by bits 16 through 19 of the instruction word.

In the example shown, general register 10 is called out by bits 16 through 19;
so the number stored in general register 10 will be added to the 5 stored in bits 20
through 31, and general register 5 will be shifted right this many times. If, for
instance, general register 10 contains the number 7, then we would add 7 to 5,
saying that the word in general register 5 should be shifted right a total of 12 times.

There are several reasons for the complicated addressing technique used here.
The use of two general-purpose registers to form each address is (1) to permit the
operating system programs to relocate user programs in memory, and (2) to permit
the programmer to use one of the registers as an index register. Common practice
in the 370 series is for the second register in each address (the one specified in
bits 12 to 15) to be used only by the operating system. This register is then called
the *base register,* and if the base register is the same, say register 5, in each
instruction word in a program, then the number in this register will be added to
each address generated. By placing an appropriate number in this register, the
operating system can cause a given program to be loaded at locations in memory
of its choice, and the program will operate there because each instruction word
and data word address will be appropriately located. This then leaves the remaining register, that specified by bits 11 to 13, to be used by the programmer as an
index register.

This series is typical of the computers used in large systems in that it has a rich
instruction repertoire and many features which the designers feel are useful to the
computer's user. Some computer lines are much more scientific-application oriented and some are almost exclusively business oriented. A good blend is maintained by several computer firms, however.

QUESTIONS

1. Discuss the advantages and disadvantages of the following addressing strategies in a microcomputer: *(a)* Paging. *(b)* Indirect addressing. *(c)* Index
   registers.
2. Describe some advantages and disadvantages of multiple-accumulator (general-purpose registers) versus single-accumulator computer architecture.
   Include effects on instruction word length, convenience in programming, etc.
3. *(a)* The PDP-8 series uses the original paging scheme for addressing. The
       PDP-11 and other computers use a relative address or sliding page. Dis-
       cuss the advantages and disadvantages of these two techniques.
   (b) What is the obvious problem in indirect addressing of 8K or larger mem-
       ories which arises in the PDP-8 but does not occur for 16-bit-word com-
       puters such as the NOVA, PDP-11, or Varian?
4. Discuss the desirability of the following computer architectural features for a
   microcomputer to be used as a traffic light controller: *(a)* Paging of memory.
   (b) Floating-point arithmetic. *(c)* Indirect addressing.

5. The following is a short program in assembly language for the PDP-8:

```
*700
        CLA  CLL   /CLEARS AC AND LINK
        TAD  DAT1
GO,     ISZ  DAT2
        JMP  GO
        RAL           /RIGHT SHIFT AC AND LINK
        JMP  GO
DAT1,   0077
DAT2,   0
$
```

After this program has been assembled and loaded, it appears as follows in memory (all digits are octal), except that the contents of two addresses in memory need to be filled in:

ADDRESS NUMBER	
0700	
0701	CONTENTS
0702	2307
0703	5302
0704	7004
0705	5302
0706	0077
0707	0000

Supply the contents of (octal) locations 700 and 701 in memory.

6. The program in Question 5 rotates a sequence of 0s and 1s through the accumulator link.

(a) How many 0s and how many 1s? In what order?

(b) How many instructions must be executed for a complete cycle of a given 0 and 1 pattern?

7. A microcomputer has a bus with a single INTERRUPT line which an external device is to raise when it wishes to be serviced. The bus is controlled by the microcomputer's CPU chip. Explain the CPU's problem in determining which input-output device(s) generated an interrupt, and discuss two possible solutions.

8. The following is a short program for the 6800 which was written to compute $Y = 32(9 - 7)$ and store it. The programmer then converted the program into hexadecimal and is now prepared to enter it into the computer. There are several mistakes in the program. Find as many as possible and explain each.

#	ADDRESS	OP	OPER	LABEL	MNEMONICS	OPERAND	COMMENTS
01	0200	4F		START	CLRA		;CLEAR REGISTER A
02	0201	86	OE		LDA	X	;LOAD X INTO REGISTER A
03	0203	43			COMA		;COMPLEMENT X
04	0204	8B	09		ADDA(IM)	#09	;ADD 9
05	0206	CE	05		LDX(IM)	#05	;LOAD INDEX REGISTER WITH 5
06	0208	49		LOOP	ROLA		;ROTATE LEFT 1 BIT (MULTIPLY BY 2)
07	0209	09			DEX		;DECREMENT INDEX REGISTER
08	020A	26	FD		BNE	LOOP	;ROTATE AGAIN IF INDEX REGISTER $\neq$ 0
09	020C	97	0F		STAA	Y	;AFTER MULTIPLYING BY $2^5 = 32$, STORE THE RESULT IN Y
10	020E	07		X	DATA	1 BYTE	
11	020F	00		Y	DATA	1 BYTE	;DATA IN THIS LOCATION WILL BE REPLACED BY VALUE OF Y

9. A short program has been written for the 6800 to determine the number of bytes in a table which have 1s in their sign bits. The number of elements in the table is stored at location 50, and the table begins in location 60. The number of bytes with 1 in the sign bit is to be stored in location 51. Modify this program so that the number of nonzero bytes with a 0 in the sign bit is stored in location 55.

```
        LDX     #$50     /LOAD I REGISTER
        CLRB
LOOKN   LDAA    X        /CHECK FOR NEGATIVES
        BPL     HOUS
HOUS    INCB
        INX
        DEC     $60
        BNE     LOOKN    /DONE?
        STAB    $51
```

10. A two-address computer has a large IC memory with a 0.5-μs memory cycle time and a small high-speed memory with a 0.25-μs memory cycle time. An addition instruction word looks like this:

ADD	1st address	2d address

The first address refers to the small high-speed memory and the second address to the large memory. The sum is placed in the high-speed memory at the first address. How long will it take to perform an addition instruction? Why?

11. Using the index instructions given in Sec. 10·9, write a program that adds 40 numbers located in the memory, starting at address 200 and storing the sum in register 300.

12. If we use 3 binary digits in the instruction word to indicate which index register is used, or if one is to be used, how many index registers can be used in the machine?

13. Modify the program in Sec. 10·9 so that the numbers located at memory addresses 353 through 546 are added together and stored at address 600.

14. Modify the program in Sec. 10·9 so that the numbers located at addresses 300 through 305 are multiplied together and the product is stored at address 310.

15. The use of paging enables the relocation or moving around of programs in the memory without extensive modification of the addresses in the program. Explain why.

16. Explain how paging and indirect addressing can be useful in relocating sub-programs when a program is rewritten. What are some disadvantages of paging and indirect addressing?

17. Discuss the architecture of the 6800 versus the 8080 microprocessors.

18. Compare the PDP-11 addressing to the 8080 addressing modes.

19. Evaluate the use of multiple general registers and an IBM 370 format in addressing versus the use of index registers in the DDP-24 (described in Chap. 9) for adding together numbers arranged in three tables.

20. Explain how paging as an addressing technique can be useful in relocating programs, and then explain how small pages can sometimes force programmers to "think in segments." Are the above characteristics desirable or undesirable?

21. Explain the addressing of pages in the PDP-8 series and the displacement-plus-instruction-location addressing technique used by the PDP-11. Give reasons why you think systems architects have elected to use these systems.

22. The following is a section of program and memory contents from an assembly listing for a PDP-8. The programmer who wrote this contends that after the instruction at location 255_8 is executed, the location 256_8 in memory will contain the difference $A - B$ of the numbers A and B at locations 260_8 and 2053_8. Is the programmer correct? Give the reason for your answer, explaining the program operation.

*250

0250	7300	CLA	CLL	
0251	1657	TAD	I	F
0252	7040	CMA		
0253	1260	TAD	A	
0254	3256	DCA	C	

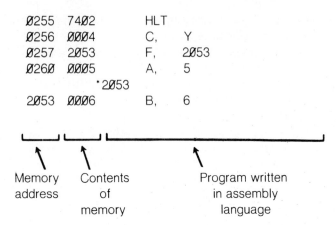

23. Sketch, describe, and discuss the merits of one of the machine architectures that have been presented, or of any other machine with which you are familiar (or with which you would like to be familiar—including any of your own "ideal" designs, if you have any such notions).

24. A real-time system for manufacturing control is to be constructed using a computer. The system is to perform two functions:
    (a) The computer has to automatically test cameras as they are manufactured. This involves, among other things, reading 1000 values each second from several A-to-D converters and checking to see if the values are within prescribed limits.
    (b) The computer has to service four terminals which run inquiries against the data base maintained on the cameras, and it also has to run some Fortran and Cobol programs.

25. Show how a recursive subroutine call can erase the return location planted at the beginning of a subroutine when the PDP-8 JMS instruction is used.

26. Show how the 6800 microprocessor subroutine call will not destroy the return address in a recursive subroutine call because of the use of the use of the stack.

27. Show how the 8080 jump to a subroutine will not destroy the return location in a recursive subroutine call because of the stack.

28. Write a program in assembly language for the 6800 microprocessor which will multiply Y by 16 and then subtract 15 from the result. (Ignore overflows.)

29. Write a program in assembly language for the 8080 microprocessor which will multiply a number X by 32 and then subtract 14 from the result. (Ignore overflows.)

30. Write a subroutine for the 8080 microprocessor which will double the number in the accumulator and then subtract 5. (Ignore overflows.)

31. Write a subroutine for the 6800 which will add accumulator A to accumulator B, store the result in accumulator A, and then subtract 12 from this result, storing that in accumulator B. (Ignore overflows.)

32. Write a subroutine call for the 6800 which will utilize the subroutine written in Question 31. Before this subroutine call, place 13 in accumulator A and 23 in accumulator B.

33. Discuss PDP-11 addressing [where the addressing mode (or modes) is carried in the address section] versus placing that information in the OP code.

34. Show the mode information in the two 3-bit fields in a PDP-11 instruction word which uses both source and destination registers in a direct addressing mode.

35. Write a program for the PDP-11 which will add the number in R_1 to the number in R_3 and then store this number at location 63_8 in the memory.

36. Why is it not a good idea to store data at location 0 in the PDP-8 memory?

37. Explain why placing often used data in the first 256 words of the memory in a 6800 will shorten some instruction words.

38. Explain the following sentence: The 6800 has one index register, the PDP-1 can use any general register as an index register, and the 8080 has no index register.

39. Explain how the auto-increment and auto-decrement instruction modes in the PDP-11 can be useful in processing tables.

40. In the 8080 an interrupt is serviced as follows. The device which is being serviced places on the data lines of the 8080 bus an instruction word which is a special instruction, called RST. Three bits of this instruction give the address of the next instruction to be executed. The interrupting device places the correct 3 bits in the section of the RST instruction on the bus, and the 8080 then takes the next instruction from that location. (See OP-code description of RST.) In that location is a jump to the subroutine which actually services the device generating the interrupt. Discuss the advantages and disadvantages of this procedure.

41. The IBM series of computers uses a priority delegation scheme where interrupt devices are interconnected as shown below. When an interrupt service is issued by the 360, the leftmost point of the "daisy-chain" wire is raised. If a device wishes to be serviced, it does not forward this 1 to the device on the right. If it does not wish to be serviced, it forwards this 1 to the device on the right. Each device in turn makes this decision, either passing the 1 to the right or passing a 0. (A 0 on the left is always passed right.) Design a logic circuit to effect this. Use an interrupt flip-flop which is turned on by the device utilizing the interface and which has a 1 output if the device wishes service and a 0 if not.

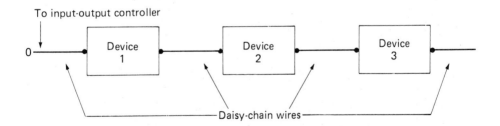

42. The daisy-chain interrupt scheme in Question 41 assigns interrupt priorities according to the position in the daisy chain. Explain this statement.

43. The passing of a 1 or a 0 along the daisy chain by each device must be carefully controlled with regard to time. Strict standards are given as to how long maximum delays can be for each device. Explain the advantages and disadvantages of the daisy-chain scheme in assigning priorities and determining which device has generated an interrupt.

44. Notice that when the daisy-chain scheme explained in Question 41 is used, a device can then place its identity or interrupt vector on the bus without the danger of other devices placing their vectors on at the same time and over-writing at the same time. In some microcomputers combinational logic is used to determine which device is to be serviced first. Explain how this might be done, assuming that each device uses an interrupt flip-flop as in Question 41.

45. Compare the disadvantages and advantages of using combinational logic versus the daisy-chain technique for interrupt servicing.

46. When DMA (direct memory access) is used on a bus, a line to the CPU on the bus is raised by the device wishing to read into memory using the bus. The CPU then stops, executing instructions at the first possibility, and raises another line on the bus, indicating that it has stopped execution of instructions. The device wishing access to the bus then uses the bus, and when done it lowers the wire that was used to stop the CPU. The CPU then continues to execute instructions. Explain the danger of having several devices able to generate interrupts of this kind at the same time.

47. The PDP-8 uses an input-output instruction to test and see if a device has data ready or can accept data. Incorporated in this instruction is a jump if the device is not ready. In the 6800 and 8080 computers it is necessary to check a status bit and then use a conventional jump on condition instruction to see whether or not a device can be serviced. Discuss the advantages and disadvantages of these approaches to seeing whether the device is ready.

48. Show how indirect addressing can be used in the PDP-8 to access a word located at address 4322_8 in the memory when an instruction word is on page 1 of the memory.

49. Translate the following program into hexadecimal for the 6800:

```
           ORG    $50
           LDX    #$79
           LDAA   #$20
    BLKC   INX
           CMPA   X
           BEQ    BLKC
           STX    $55
```

50. The program in Question 49 stores the address of the first nonspace character in a string at location 55 in the memory. Analyze the program operation instruction by instruction.

51. Translate the following program into hexadecimal for the 8080 showing the contents of each memory location:

```
ORG   50H
LXI   H, 50H
MOV   A, M
INX   H
ADD   M
INX   H
MOV   M, A
```

52. Analyze the operation of the section of program given in Question 51 instruction by instruction, explaining what it does.

53. Translate the following PDP-11 program into octal. What does this short section of program do?

```
READ    TSTB    KSR          ; READY
        BPL     READ         ; NO
        INC     R5           ; INC BUFFER PTR
        MOVB    KSB;@R5      ; STORE INPUT
        MOV     @R5; R4      ; STORE LASCHR IN RY.
        JSR     PC, PRINT    ; PRINT INPUT
        BR      READ         ; READ NEXT CHAR
PRINT   CMPB    R4, #212
```

Place the read statement at location 500_8. KSB is at location 177562_8.

54. In the IBM 370, how many binary digits are required to store the following decimal numbers in BCD and in binary? (In BCD, sign requires 4 bits, and BCD numbers are always organized into bytes.)

(a) 20   (b) 10,241   (c) 984   (d) 6

55. Describe the calculation of an effective address for the IBM 370, and outline logical hardware which will implement this calculation (control signals, data paths, registers, etc.).

56. Suppose that we push A, B, D, and F on a stack, pop the stack twice, and then push M and then N onto the stack. If we then pop letters from the stack three times, what letters and in what order will be popped?

57. Explain extended addressing, implied addressing, and relative addressing in the 6800 microprocessor.

58. Explain how the "branch if zero" instruction works on the 6800 microprocessor.

59. Explain the difference in an ADD accumulator (ABA) and an ADD (ADDA or ADDB) instruction for the 6800 microprocessor.

60. Explain a ROTATE RIGHT instruction on the 6800 microprocessor.

61. What are the differences between ROTATE and SHIFT instructions on the 6800 microprocessor? Why are both useful?

62. Explain the "branch to subroutine" and the "return from subroutine" instructions for the 6800 microprocessor, and explain how they would be used to enter and then exit from a subroutine.

63. Contrast the JMS instruction in the PDP-8 with the JSR instruction in the 6800.

64. Explain the register indirect and immediate addressing modes for the 8080 microprocessor.

65. Explain how two of the arithmetic-type instructions for the 8080 microprocessor affect the setting of the condition flags.

66. Explain how conditional JUMP instructions work in the 8080 microprocessor.

67. Explain the PUSH and POP instructions in the 8080 microprocessor.

68. Explain the CALL and RET instructions for the 8080 microprocessor and compare these with the JSR and RTS instructions for the 6800 microprocessor.

69. Explain the STA and LDA instructions for the 8080 microprocessor.

70. Explain the ADI instruction for the 8080 microprocessor and contrast it to the ADM instruction.

71. Compare the ADM instruction for the 8080 microprocessor with the ADDA and ADDB instructions for the 6800 microprocessor.

72. Contrast the PUSH and POP instructions for the 8080 microprocessor with the DES and INS instructions for the 6800 microprocessor.

73. Compare the BRANCH instructions for the 6800 microprocessor with those for the 8080 microprocessor.

74. Write a program to service the printer interface in Chap. 8 for the 8080 microprocessor.

75. Show how the BPL instruction in Table 10·23 operates by calculating the value of the offset for the branch, adding it to the program counter to see if the branch goes to the right place.

76. The plus before the indirect address in Table 10·23 for the MOVB instruction indexes through the table where index characters are to be stored. Explain how this is accomplished using Table 10·14 as background information.

77. Explain how the assembler calculated the value for the TSTB instruction in Table 10·23.

78. Explain how the assembler calculated the binary translation of the BNE LOOP instruction in Table 10·18.

79. Modify Tables 10·19 and 10·20 so that the parameter being passed from calling program to subroutine is a pointer to the beginning of the table to be searched instead of the end of the table.

80. Explain how the BNE LOOP instruction operates in Table 10·18, calculating the value of the jump in the computer word and seeing whether it points to the right location in the memory.

81. Modify the program in Table 10·10 so that the number of characters in the table are passed using register *D* instead of register *B*.

82. Modify the programs so that Table 10·11 passes the lowest table address in memory instead of the end of the table. This will require modification to both Tables 10·10 and 10·11.

83. Explain how the JZ instruction operates in Table 10·10.

84. Convert the program in Table 10·10 into binary as an assembler would.

85. For the 8080 or 6800 microprocessor, explain how you would pass parameters if two tables should both be searched for an input character and the start or end points of each table must be given the subroutine as well as the character to be searched for and the number of characters in each table.

86. Explain how the bracket notation is used for the LDA instruction in the instruction repertoire table for the 8080 (Table 10·7).

87. Write a program like that in Table 10·9 with the aim to find the smallest number instead of the largest.

88. Modify the program in Table 10·2 so that it checks for all 1s in the character transferred as well as for periods, jumping to the same section of program if all 1s are found.

89. What is the character code for a period in the PDP-8?

90. Change the JMP I LISN instruction in Table 10·2 so that it causes a jump to location 254 in the memory and not to 252. Change memory contents also.

91. Explain how the index instruction in the 6800 microprocessor can be used to sequence through two tables, each of which is located at a different position in the memory, but has the same number of elements.

92. The MOVE M instruction in the 8080 microprocessor uses register pair *H, L* as a pointer to the memory. Explain how register pair *H, L* can be loaded.

93. Find two examples of relative addressing in the sample programs given for the computers in this chapter.

94. Compare paging to relative addressing as an address strategy.

BIBLIOGRAPHY

CHAPTER 1

American National Standards Committee, X3/TR-1-77: *American National Dictionary for Information Processing,* Computer and Business Equipment Manufacturers Assoc., Washington, D.C., 1977.

Bartee, T. C.: *Introduction to Computer Science,* McGraw-Hill Book Company, New York, 1975.

Bass, C.: Microsystems: PLZ—A Family of System Programming Micro-Processors, *Computer,* March 1978.

Bennett, W. R.: *Scientific and Engineering Problem Solving with the Computer,* Prentice-Hall, Englewood Cliffs, N.J., 1976.

Bibbero, R. S.: *Microprocessors in Instruments and Control,* John Wiley and Sons, New York, 1977.

Brown, W.: Microsystems: Modular Programming in PL/M, *Computer,* March 1977.

Conway, R., and D. Gries: *Primer in Structural Programming in PL/1,* Winthrop Publ., Cambridge, Mass., 1977.

Eikhouse, R. H., and L. R. Morris: *Minicomputer Systems,* Prentice-Hall, Englewood Cliffs, N.J., 1979.

Hennefeld, J.: *Using Basic,* Prindle, Weber and Schmidt, Boston, Mass., 1978.

Klingman, E. E.: *Microcomputer Systems Design,* Prentice-Hall, Englewood Cliffs, N.J., 1977.

Leventhal, L. A.: *Introduction to Microprocessors: Software, Hardware, Programming,* Prentice-Hall, Englewood Cliffs, N.J., 1979.

McCracken, D. D.: *A Guide to PL/M Programming for Microcomputer Applications,* Addison-Wesley, Reading, Mass., 1979.

Pollack, S. V., and T. D. Sterling: *A Guide to PL/1,* Holt, Rinehart and Winston, New York, 1979.

Powers, V. M., and J. H. Hernandez: Microprogram Assembler for Bit-Slice Micro-
    processors, *IEEE Transactions on Computers,* July 1978.

CHAPTER 2

Bell, C. G., J. C. Mudge, and J. E. McNamara: *Computer Engineering,* Digital
    Equipment Corp., Maynard, Mass., 1978.
Booth, T. L., and Y. T. Chien: *Computing,* Hamilton, Santa Barbara, Calif., 1974.
Gschwind, H. W., and E. J. McCluskey: *Design of Digital Computers,* Springer-Ver-
    lag, New York, 1975.
Hill, F. J., and G. R. Peterson: *Digital System Hardware Organization and Design,*
    John Wiley and Sons, New York, 1978.
Hwang, K., *Computer Arithmetic,* John Wiley and Sons, New York, 1979.
Sippl, G. S.: *Microcomputer Handbook,* Van Nostrand, New York, 1977.

CHAPTER 3

Bell, C. G., J. C. Mudge, and J. E. McNamara: *Computer Engineering,* Digital
    Equipment Corp., Maynard, Mass., 1978.
Birkhoof, G., and T. C. Bartee: *Modern Applied Algebra,* McGraw-Hill Book Com-
    pany, New York, 1970.
Boole, G.: *An Investigation of the Laws of Thought,* Dover Publications, New York,
    1966. (First published 1854.)
Culliney, J. N., et al.: Results of the Synthesis of Optimal Networks of AND and OR
    Gates for Four-Variable Switching Functions, *IEEE Transactions on Computers,*
    January 1979.
Kline, R. M.: *Digital Computer Design,* Prentice-Hall, Englewood Cliffs, N.J., 1979.
McCluskey, E. J., Jr.: *Introduction to the Theory of Switching Circuits,* McGraw-Hill
    Book Company, New York, 1975.
Muroga, S., and H. C. Lai: Minimization of Logic Functions under a Generalized
    Cost Function, *IEEE Transactions on Computers,* September 1976.
Prother, R. E., and H. T. Casstevens: Realization of Boolean Expressions by
    Atomic Digraphs, *IEEE Transactions on Computers,* August 1978.
Thayse, A.: Meet and Joint Derivatives and Their Use in Switching Theory, *IEEE
    Transactions on Computers,* August 1978.

CHAPTER 4

Brzozowski, J. A., and M. Yoeli: *Digital Networks,* Prentice-Hall, Englewood Cliffs,
    N.J., 1975.
Current, K. W., and D. A. Mow: Implementing Parallel Counter with Four-Valued
    Threshold Logic, *IEEE Transactions on Computers,* March 1979.
Fairchild Semiconductor: *TTL Data Book,* Mountain View, Calif., 1979.
Gaitanis, N., and C. Halatsis: A New Double-Rank Realization of Sequential
    Machines, *IEEE Transactions on Computers,* December 1978.

Halatsis, C., et al.: Polylinear Decomposition of Synchronous Sequential Machines, *IEEE Transactions on Computers,* December 1978.

Hemmati, F., and D. S. Costello: An Algebraic Construction for q-ary Shift Register Sequences, *IEEE Transactions on Computers,* December 1978.

Intel Corporation: *Intel 8080 Microcomputer System User's Manual,* Santa Clara, Calif., 1979.

Kartashev, S. P., and S. I. Kartashev: On Modular Networks Satisfying the Shift-Register Rule, *IEEE Transactions on Computers,* December 1978.

Kline, R. M.: *Digital Computer Design,* Prentice-Hall, Englewood Cliffs, N.J., 1979.

Motorola Corporation: *M6800 Microprocessor Applications Manual,* Phoenix, Ariz., 1979.

Texas Instruments, Inc.: *The TTL Data Book,* Dallas, Tex., 1979.

CHAPTER 5

American Microsystems, Inc.: *Guide to Standard MOS Products,* Santa Clara, Calif., 1979.

Barnes, D.: CMOS Performance, Cost Make Digital Just Part of Its Story, *Electronic Design,* November 1978.

Bingham, D.: CMOS: Higher Speeds, More Drive and Analog Capability Expand Its Horizons, *Electronic Design,* November 1978.

Cuswell, H. L., et al.: Basic Technology, *Computer,* September 1978.

Fairchild Semiconductor: *TTL Data Book,* Mountain View, Calif., 1979.

Hodges, D. A.: Trends in Computer Hardware Technology, *Computer Design,* February 1976.

Intel Corporation: *Intel 8080 Microcomputer System User's Manual,* Santa Clara, Calif., 1979.

Motorola Corporation: *M6800 Microprocessor Applications Manual,* Phoenix, Ariz., 1979.

Motorola Semiconductor Products, Inc.: Semiconductor Data Library, Phoenix, Ariz., 1979.

Texas Instruments, Inc.: *The TTL Data Book,* Dallas, Tex., 1979.

CHAPTER 6

Agrawal, D. P.: High Speed Arithmetic Arrays, *IEEE Transactions on Computers,* March 1979.

Flores, I.: *The Logic of Computer Arithmetic,* Prentice-Hall, Englewood Cliffs, N.J., 1963.

Freiman, C. V.: Statistical Analysis of Certain Binary Division Algorithms, *Proceedings of the IRE,* January 1961.

Garner, H. L.: Theory of Computer Additions and Overflows, *IEEE Transactions on Computers,* April 1978.

Hwang, K.: *Computer Arithmetic,* John Wiley and Sons, New York, 1979.

Jullien, G. A.: Residue Number Scaling and Other Operations Using ROM Arrays, *IEEE Transactions on Computers,* April 1978.

MacSorley, O. L.: High Speed Arithmetic in Binary Computers, *Proceedings of the IRE,* January 1961.

Sippl, G. S.: *Microcomputer Handbook,* Van Nostrand, Princeton, N.J., 1977.

Smith, L.: Adapting Control and Arithmetic Subroutines to Single-Chip Microsystems, *Computer Design,* August 1979.

Waser, S.: State of the Art in High-Speed Arithmetic Integrated Circuits, *Computer Design,* July 1978.

CHAPTER 7

American Microsystems, Inc.: *Guide to Standard MOS Products,* Santa Clara, Calif., 1979.

Barnes, D.: ROMs and PROMs Are Moving to Greater Densities, Compatibility, *Electronic Design,* July 1978.

Bhandarkar, D. P., J. B. Barton, and A. F. Tasch: Charge-Coupled Device Memories: A Perspective, *Computer,* January 1979.

Bursky, D.: New 64K RAM Jumps Ahead With On-Chip Refresh Control, *Electronic Design,* February 1979.

Carothers, J. D.: A New High Density Recording System: The IBM 1311 Disc Storage Drive with Interchangeable Disc Packs, *Proceedings of the 1963 Fall Joint Computer Conference,* American Federation of Information Processing Societies.

Chandra, A. K., and C. K. Wong: The Movement and Permutations of Columns in Magnetic Bubble Lattice Files, *IEEE Transactions on Computers,* January 1979.

Cupice, R. P.: The Race Heats Up in Fast Static RAMs, *Electronics,* April 1979.

Deem, W., K. Muchow, and A. Zeppa: *Digital Computers, Circuits and Concepts,* Reston Publishing Company, Reston, Va., 1979.

Fird, D. C., D. Brunner, and J. Moench: 64K Dynamic RAM has Pin that Refreshes, *Electronics,* February 1979.

George, P.: As Bubble Density Approaches 1 Mbit, Material Design, Packaging Problems Mount, *Electronic Design,* May 1979.

Intel Corporation: *Intel 8080 Microcomputer System User's Manual,* Santa Clara, Calif., 1979.

Koung, S.: Memories Have Hit a Density Ceiling But New Processes Will Push Through, *Electronic Design,* October 1978.

MacKenzie, K. F.: Get Top Memory System Performance with MOS RAMs, *Electronic Design,* March 1979.

McCormick, B.: Take the Dynamics Out of Dynamic RAM with an IC Controller Handling Refresh, *Electronic Design,* December 1978.

Metzger, J.: Earoms, *Electronics Products,* September 1977.

Motorola Corporation: *M6800 Microprocessor Applications Manual,* Phoenix, Ariz., 1979.

Postoriza, J.: Tradeoffs among Binary Codes in Magnetic Tape Cassettes, *Computer Design,* no. 1, 1976.

Young, D. C.: Guidelines for Designing Battery Backup Circuits, *Computer Design,* August 1979.

CHAPTER 8

Bell, C. G., J. C. Mudge, and J. E. McNamara: *Computer Engineering,* Digital Equipment Corp., Maynard, Mass., 1978.

Burton, D. P., and A. L. Dexter: Handle Microcomputer I/O Efficiently, *Electronic Design,* June 1978.

Burton, D. P., and A. L. Dexter: Know Microcomputer Bus Structures, *Electronic Design,* June 1978.

Eiifinger, R. J.: Integrating Peripherals into Processor Systems, *Computer Design,* December 1978.

Elinoff, G.: Inexpensive Printers: Hard-Copy Link Between Man and Microcomputer, *Electronics Products,* August 1978.

Gryston, B. K.: A Software Approach to Priority Interrupts, *Computer Design,* August 1979.

Institute of Electrical and Electronics Engineers: *IEEE Standard 488-1978, Digital Interface for Programmable Instrumentation,* New York, 1978.

Larsen, D. G., and P. R. Rony: Interfacing Fundamentals: The 8085 Processor, *Computer Design,* July 1978.

Larsen, D. G., and P. R. Rony: Interfacing Fundamentals: Assembly Language or Basic, Which Way to Go, *Computer Design,* November 1978.

Leseen, A., and Z. Rodney: *Microprocessor Interfacing Techniques,* Sybex, Inc., Berkeley, Calif., 1977.

Nissian, J.: DMA Controller Capitalizes on Clock Cycles to Bypass CPU, *Computer Design,* January 1978.

Peatman, J. B.: *Microcomputer Basic Design,* McGraw-Hill Book Company, New York, 1977.

Postoriza, J.: Tradeoffs Among Binary Codes in Magnetic Tape Cassettes, *Computer Design,* no. 1, 1976.

Rony, P. R., D. G. Larsen, and J. A. Titus: *The 8080A Bugbook,* Howard W. Sams, Indianapolis, Ind., 1977.

Talambrias, P. P.: Digital-to-Analog Converters: Some Problems in Producing High-Fidelity Systems, *Computer Design,* January 1975.

Titus, C., and J. A. Titus: Interfacing Fundamentals: The 8080 Family of Memory Devices, *Computer Design,* August 1978.

CHAPTER 9

Bartee, T. C.: *Introduction to Computer Science,* McGraw-Hill Book Company, New York, 1975.

Boulage, G., and J. Mermet (Eds.): *Microprogramming,* Hermann & Cie, Paris, 1972.

Logan, J. D., and P. S. Kreager: Using a Microprocessor, *Computer Design,* September 1975.

Marchin, P.: Multi-Level Nesting of Subroutines in a One-Level Microprocessor, *Computer Design,* September 1975.

Waldecker, D. E.: Comparison of a Microprogrammed and a Non-Microprogrammed Computer, *Computer Design,* June 1970.

CHAPTER 10

Bishop, R.: *Basic Microprocessors and the 6800,* Hayden Book Company, Rochelle Park, N.J., 1979.

Bowra, J. W., and H. C. Torng: The Modeling and Design of Multiple Function Unit Processors, *IEEE Transactions on Computers,* March 1976.

Cowry, F. F.: Advanced Architecture and Applications of Microcomputers, *Computer,* January 1976.

Digital Equipment Corporation: *Introduction to Programming,* Maynard, Mass., 1972.

Digital Equipment Corporation: *PDP-11 Processor Handbook,* Maynard, Mass., 1977.

Durham, S. J.: Fast LSI Arbiters Supervise Priorities for Bus-Access in Multiprocesses Systems, *Electronic Design,* May 1979.

Durnick, A.: VLSI Shakes the Foundations of Computer Architecture, *Electronics,* May 1979.

Fleisher, H., and L. I. Maissel: An Introduction to Array Logic, *IBM Journal of Research and Development,* March 1975.

Hertz, W.: Indexed Addressing for Microcomputers, *Computer Design,* January 1979.

Intel Corporation: *Intel 8080 Microcomputer System User's Manual,* Santa Clara, Calif., 1979.

Leseen, A., and Z. Rodney: *Microprocessor Interfacing Techniques,* Sybex, Inc., Berkeley, Calif., 1977.

Leventhal, L. R.: *6800 Assembly Language Programming,* Adam Osborne and Assoc., Berkeley, Calif., 1978.

Leventhal, L. A.: *8080A/8085 Assembly Language Programming,* Adam Osborne and Assoc., Berkeley, Calif., 1978.

Metzger, J.: Peripheral ICs for Microprocessors, *Electronics Products,* March 1979.

Motorola Corporation: *M6800 Microprocessor Applications Manual,* Phoenix, Ariz., 1979.

Rony, P. R., D. G. Larsen, and J. A. Titus: *The 8080A Bugbook,* Howard W. Sams, Indianapolis, Ind., 1977.

Salisbury, A. B., *Microprogrammable Computer Architecture,* Macdonald American Elsevier, New York, 1976.

Vilteran, J. F.: Handling Multilevel Subroutines and Interrupts in Microcomputers, *Computer Design,* January 1978.

ANSWERS TO SELECTED ODD-NUMBERED QUESTIONS

CHAPTER 1

7.

ADDRESS	OP CODE	ADDRESS PART
1	CLA	40
2	ADD	41
3	ADD	42
4	STO	43
5	HLT	000
40	contains	X
41	contains	Y
42	contains	Z
43	contains	0

9.

ADDRESS	OPERATION	OPERAND
1	CLA	20
2	MUL	20
3	STO	40
4	CLA	21
5	MUL	21
6	ADD	40
7	STO	40
8	CLA	22
9	MUL	22
10	ADD	40
11	STO	40
12	HLT	
20	contains	X
21	contains	Y
22	contains	Z
40	contains	0

13.

ADDRESS	OPERATION	OPERAND
1	CLA	20
2	STO	21
3	CLA	21
4	MUL	20
5	STO	21
6	CLA	50
7	ADD	51
8	STO	50
9	BRM	3
10	CLA	21
11	ADD	20
12	STO	21
13	HLT	
20	contains	X
21	contains	0
50	contains	-5
51	contains	1

We will store our sum $X^5 + X$ in the address assigned by the assembler to the variable D.

ADDRESS	OPERATION	OPERAND
A	DEC	0
B	DEC	-5
C	DEC	1
D	DEC	0
	CLA	X
	STO	D
E	CLA	D
	MUL	X
	STO	D
	CLA	B
	ADD	C
	STO	B
	BRM	E
	CLA	D
	ADD	X
	STO	D
	HLT	

19.

If we assume that the integers are in ascending or descending order only,

ADDRESS	OPERATION	OPERAND
1	CLA	30
2	SUB	31
3	BRM	5
4	HLT	
5	HLT	

The computer stops at address 4 if the numbers are in ascending order and at 5 if the numbers are in descending order.

We must check to see whether the numbers are in ascending or descending order.

ADDRESS	OPERATION	OPERAND
1	CLA	30
2	SUB	31
3	BRM	10
4	CLA	31
5	SUB	32
6	BRM	13
7	HLT	
10	CLA	31
11	SUB	32
12	BRM	15
13	HLT	
15	HLT	

This program stops at address 13 if the numbers are in neither ascending nor descending order, at address 7 if the numbers are ascending, and at address 15 if the numbers are descending.

23.

ADDRESS	OPERATION	OPERAND
1	CLA	26
2	SUB	25
3	BRM	300
4	BRA	400

25.

ADDRESS	OPERATION	OPERAND
P	CLA	A
	SUB	B
	BRM	M
	CLA	A
	SUB	C
	BRM	M
	CLA	A
	STO	X
	HLT	
M	CLA	B
	SUB	C
	BRM	N
	CLA	B
	STO	X
	HLT	
N	CLA	C
	STO	X
	HLT	

27. A = 10;
      B = 20;
      C = 5;
      D = (A * B) ** C;
      END;

29. 72

31. Z = 0
      A = 0
      LOOP. DO WHILE Z LE A
      X = −X
      Y = −Y
      Z = X − Y
      END LOOP
      PRINT (Z)
      END

33.

ADDRESS	OPERATION	OPERAND	ADDRESS	OPERATION	OPERAND
1	CLA	300	13	CLA	6
2	BRM	5	14	ADD	400
3	STO	300	15	STO	6
4	BRA	7	16	CLA	401
5	SUB	300	17	ADD	400
6	SUB	300	18	STO	401
7	CLA	3	19	BRM	1
8	ADD	400	20	HLT	
9	STO	3	300 ⎫	contains numbers	
10	CLA	5	329 ⎭		
11	ADD	400	400	contains 1	
12	STO	5	401	contains − 30	

35. *(a)* 45   *(b)* 2000   *(c)* 55   *(d)* 70

37. *(a)* A ** C / B ** D   *(b)* A ** 2 + B ** 2 + C * D
      (c) A/B + (C/D) ** E   *(d)* (A * B) ** C + (B * D)/E

CHAPTER 2

1. (a) 101011   (b) 1000000   (c) 100000000000   (d) 0.011
   (e) 0.11011   (f) 0.0111   (g) 1000000000.1   (h) 10000011.1001
   (i) 10000000000.0001

3. (a) 13   (b) 27   (c) 23   (d) 0.6875   (e) 0.203125   (f) 0.212890625
   (g) 59.6875   (h) 91.203125   (i) 22.3408203125

5. (a) 11   (b) 36   (c) 19   (d) 0.8125   (e) 0.5625   (f) 0.3125
   (g) 11.1875   (h) 9.5625   (i) 5.375

7. (a) 10100.11 = 20.75   (b) 1001010 = 74   (c) 1.1 = 1.5
   (d) 10101 = 21

9. (a)   1101.1   13.5   (b)   101101   45
         1011.1   11.5   110110   109
         11001.0   25   1100011   154

   (c) 0.0011   0.1875   (d)   1100.011   12.375
        0.1110   0.875   1011.011   11.375
        1.0001   1.0625   10111.110   23.750

11. (a)   1000000   (b)   1111111
           − 100000   − 111111
            100000   1000000

   (c)   1011101.1   (d)   1010100.01001
         − 101010.11   − 110000.01010
          110010.11   100011.11111

13. (a)   100101   (b) 10000000
           − 100011   01000000
            000010   1000000

   (c) 1011110.1   (d) 11111111
        101011.11   1111111
        110010.11   10000000

15. (a) 100100000   (b) 11111100   (c) 100   (d) 1.1   (e) 10100000001.101
   (f) 10.1

17. (a)   1111   (b)   1111
                  1101   1010
                  1111   11110
                 11110   11110
                 1111   10010110
               11000011

   (c)   100   (d)   11.1
        1011) 101100   1100) 101010.0
              1011   1100
               000   10010
                                         1100
                                         1100
                                         1100
                                            0

(e)   111.11   (f)   10110.1
          10.1   100.11
          11111   101101
         111110   101101
       10011.011   10110100
                                  1101010.111

19.   **9s COMPLEMENT**   **10s COMPLEMENT**
(a)   4563   4564
(b)   8067   8068
(c)   54.84   54.85
(d)   81.706   81.707

21.   **9s COMPLEMENT**   **10s COMPLEMENT**
(a)   6345 *4563*   6346 *4564*
(b)   7877   7878
(c)   45.80   45.81
(d)   62.736   62.737

23.   **1s COMPLEMENT**   **2s COMPLEMENT**
(a)   0100   0101   *?*
(b)   00100   00101
(c)   0100.10   0100.11
(d)   00100.10   00100.11

25.   **1s COMPLEMENT**   **2s COMPLEMENT**
(a)   010000   010001
(b)   011011   011100
(c)   01000.01   01000.10
(d)   01100.00

27.   **9s COMPLEMENT**   **10s COMPLEMENT**
(a)   948   948
        765   766
      1 713   714
       └──→1
        714

(b)   347   347
        736   737
      1 083   084
       └──→1
        084

(c)   349.5   349.5
        754.6   754.7
      1 104.1   104.2
       └──→1
        104.2

(d)   412.7   412.7
        590.7   590.8
      1 003.4   3.5
       └──→1
        3.5

29.   **9s COMPLEMENTS**   **10s COMPLEMENTS**

(a)   1024   1024
     9086   9087
     0110   0111
       → 1
     111

(b)   249   249
     862   863
     111   112
       → 1
     112

(c)   24.1   24.1
     86.5   86.6
     10.6   10.7
       → 1
     10.7

(d)   239.3   239.3
     880.5   880.6
     119.8   119.9
       → 1
     119.9

31.   **1s COMPLEMENT**   **2s COMPLEMENT**

(a)   1011   1011
     1010   1011
   1 0101   0110
       → 1
     0110

(b)   11011   11011
     00110   00111
   1 00001   00010
       → 1
     10

(c)   10111.1   10111.1
     01100.0   01100.1
   1 00011.1   100.0
       → 1
     100.0

(d)   11011.00   11011.00
     01100.00   01100.01
   1 00111.00   111.01
       → 1
     111.01

33. $2^6 = 64$

35. 1000 different numbers in each case (from 0–999, for instance)

37. 0, 1, 2, 3, 10, 11, 12, 13, 20, 21

39. 0, 1, 2, 3, 4, 5, 6, 7, 8, 9, A, 10, 11, 12, 13, 14, 15, 16, 17, 18, 19, 1A, 20, 21, 22

41. (a)   .1001   (b)   .1110   (c)   01111

          .1001   .1001   10110

          0010   0111   00101

              →1   →1   →1

          .0011   .1000   .00110

    (d)   11011   (e)   1110101

          00110   0101101

          00001   1 0100010

              →1   →1

          00010   0100011

45. (a) 45056   (b) 24576

        1536   1024

         192   160

           7   12

      46791   25772

    (c) 40960   (d) 851968

        1024   8192

         144   1792

           2   96

      42130   3

                   862051

49. (a) 55 (b) 556 (c) 267 (d) 66.3 (e) 3.554

53. (a) 1644. (b) 514 (c) 1041.3 (d) 1170.76051. (e) 10515.5

57. (a) B7 (b) 9C (c) 5F (d) 0.7E (e) B7A

61. (a) 15_8 (b) 24_8 (c) 126_8

       $+14_8$ $+36_8$ $347_8.$

        31_8 62_8 475_8

    (d) 67_8 (e) 136_8

        45_8 636_8

     134_8 774_8

CHAPTER 3

1. (a)

X	Y	Z	XYZ	$X\bar{Y}\bar{Z}$	$XYZ + X\bar{Y}\bar{Z}$
0	0	0	0	0	0
0	0	1	0	0	0
0	1	0	0	0	0
0	1	1	0	0	0
1	0	0	0	1	1
1	0	1	0	0	0
1	1	0	0	0	0
1	1	1	1	0	1

(b)

A	B	C	ABC	ABC̄	ĀBC̄	ABC + ABC̄ + ĀBC̄
0	0	0	0	0	1	1
0	0	1	0	0	0	0
0	1	0	0	0	0	0
0	1	1	0	0	0	0
1	0	0	0	1	0	1
1	0	1	0	0	0	0
1	1	0	0	0	0	0
1	1	1	1	0	0	1

(c)

A	B	C	BC̄	B̄C	BC̄ + B̄C	A(BC̄ + B̄C)
0	0	0	0	0	0	0
0	0	1	0	1	1	0
0	1	0	1	0	1	0
0	1	1	0	0	0	0
1	0	0	0	0	0	0
1	0	1	0	1	1	1
1	1	0	1	0	1	1
1	1	1	0	0	0	0

(d)

A	B	C	A + B	A + C	Ā + B̄	(A + B)(A + C)(Ā + B̄)
0	0	0	0	0	1	0
0	0	1	0	1	1	0
0	1	0	1	0	1	0
0	1	1	1	1	1	1
1	0	0	1	1	1	1
1	0	1	1	1	1	1
1	1	0	1	1	0	0
1	1	1	1	1	0	0

3. Only the values of the expressions are listed:

(a)

A	B	AB̄ + ĀB
0	0	0
0	1	1
1	0	1
1	1	0

(b)

A	B	C	AB̄ + BC̄
0	0	0	0
0	0	1	0
0	1	0	1
0	1	1	0
1	0	0	1
1	0	1	1
1	1	0	1
1	1	1	0

(c)

A	C	$A\bar{C} + AC$
0	0	0
0	1	0
1	0	1
1	1	1

(d)

A	B	C	$A\bar{B}C + AB\bar{C} + \bar{A}BC$
0	0	0	0
0	0	1	0
0	1	0	0
0	1	1	1
1	0	0	0
1	0	1	1
1	1	0	1
1	1	1	0

(e)

A	B	C	$A(\bar{A}\bar{B}C + A\bar{B}\bar{C} + AB\bar{C})$
0	0	0	0
0	0	1	0
0	1	0	0
0	1	1	0
1	0	0	1
1	0	1	1
1	1	0	1
1	1	1	0

7. (a) $\overline{BC} + \overline{AC} + \overline{AB}$ (b) $\overline{C} + \overline{B} + \overline{A}$

    (c) $A(B + C)$ (d) A is a minimal expression

9. (a) $ABC(AB\overline{C} + A\overline{B}C + \overline{A}BC) = 0$, for no assignment of binary values will make this expression take the value 0

    (b) $AB + A\overline{B} + \overline{A}C + \overline{A}\,\overline{C} = 1$, for every assignment of values will give this expression the value 1

    (c) $XY + XYZ + XY\overline{Z} + \overline{X}YZ = XY + YZ$

    (d) $XY(\overline{X}YZ + X\overline{Y}Z + \overline{X}\,\overline{Y}\overline{Z}) = 0$

11. (a) $\overline{A}(\overline{B} + \overline{C})(\overline{A} + B) = \overline{A}B + \overline{A}\,\overline{C}$ or $\overline{A}(\overline{B} + \overline{C})$

     (b) $\overline{A}B + \overline{B}\overline{C} + \overline{A}C$

     (c) $(\overline{A} + \overline{B})(B + \overline{C})(\overline{C} + D) = \overline{A}B\overline{C} + \overline{A}\,\overline{C} + \overline{A}BD + \overline{A}\overline{C}D$
       $= \overline{A}\,\overline{C} + \overline{B}\,\overline{C} + \overline{A}BD$

     (d) $(\overline{A} + \overline{B}) + (C + \overline{D})(B + \overline{C}) = \overline{A} + \overline{B} + BC + B\overline{D} + \overline{C}\overline{D}$
       $= \overline{A}\,\overline{B} + C + \overline{D}$

     (e) $\overline{A} + \overline{B}\overline{C} + CD$

13. The important columns in these tables are as follows:

X	Y	Z	$(\overline{X + Y + Z})$	$\overline{X}\,\overline{Y}\,\overline{Z}$
0	0	0	1	1
0	0	1	0	0
0	1	0	0	0
0	1	1	0	0
1	0	0	0	0
1	0	1	0	0
1	1	0	0	0
1	1	1	0	0

X	Y	Z	$(\overline{XYZ})$	$\overline{X} + \overline{Y} + \overline{Z}$
0	0	0	1	1
0	0	1	1	1
0	1	0	1	1
0	1	1	1	1
1	0	0	1	1
1	0	1	1	1
1	1	0	1	1
1	1	1	0	0

15. (a) $\overline{A}BC + A\overline{B}C + AC + BC = AC + BC$

(b) $A\overline{B} + A\overline{C} + ABC + AB\overline{C} + \overline{A}BC + \overline{B}C$ (This can be simplified to $\overline{B}C$)

(c) $A\overline{B} + A\overline{B}C = A\overline{B}$

17. Rule 13

19. (a) $AB + AD + BC + CD$

(b) $AB + AD + AC + BC + CD + C + BD + D + DC = C + D + AB$

(c) $ABC + ABD + AC + BC + DC + ADC + BDC + DC$
     $= AC + BC + DC + ABD$

(d) $A\overline{B} + A\overline{C}$

21. $\overline{X}\overline{Y}Z + XY\overline{Z}$

23. $(X + Y)(X + Z) = X + XZ + YZ$
                        $= X + Z + YZ$
                        $= X + Z$

25. $XY + X\overline{Z}$

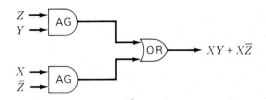

27.

X	Y	X + X̄Y	X + Y
0	0	0	0
0	1	1	1
1	0	1	1
1	1	1	1

29. $Y\overline{Z} + \overline{Y}Z$ is the sum-of-products expression and $(Y + Z)\,(\overline{Y} + \overline{Z})$ is the product-of-sums expression

35. *(a)*

	$\overline{X}$	X
$\overline{Y}$	1	
Y	1	

$\overline{X}\,\overline{Y} + \overline{X}\,Y$

(b)

	$\overline{X}\,\overline{Y}$	$\overline{X}\,Y$	XY	$X\overline{Y}$
$\overline{Z}$	1		1	
Z				

$\overline{X}\,\overline{Y}\,\overline{Z} + XY\overline{Z}$

(c)

	$\overline{X}\,\overline{Y}$	$\overline{X}\,Y$	XY	$X\overline{Y}$
$\overline{Z}$	1	1		
Z	1			

$\overline{X}\,Y\overline{Z} + \overline{X}\,\overline{Y}$

(d)

	$\overline{X}\,\overline{Y}$	$\overline{X}\,Y$	XY	$X\overline{Y}$
$\overline{Z}$	1	1		1
Z				

$\overline{X}\,\overline{Y}\,\overline{Z} + \overline{X}\,Y\overline{Z} + X\overline{Y}\,\overline{Z}$

(e)

	$\overline{X}\,\overline{Y}$	XY	XY	$X\overline{Y}$
$\overline{Z}$	1	1		1
Z				

$X\overline{Z} + \overline{Y}Z$

(f)

	$\overline{A}\,\overline{B}$	$\overline{A}B$	AB	$A\overline{B}$
C				
C				

$AB(\overline{A}\,\overline{B}\,\overline{C} + \overline{B}C)$

39. *(a)* 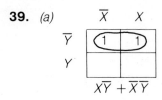   *(b)*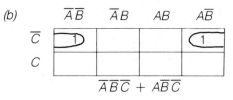

(c)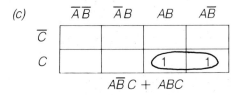

(d)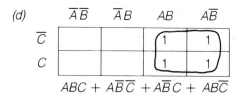

(e)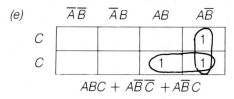

(f)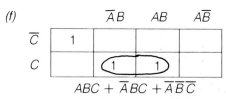

41. *(a)*   *(b)*

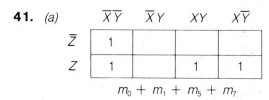

45. *(b)*

	$\overline{W}\,\overline{X}$	$\overline{W}X$	WX	$W\overline{X}$
$\overline{Y}\,\overline{Z}$	1	1	1	1
$\overline{Y}Z$			1	1
YZ				1
$Y\overline{Z}$	1			1

$m_0 = \overline{W}\,\overline{X}\,\overline{Y}\,\overline{Z}$ $m_{10} = W\overline{X}\,Y\overline{Z}$

$m_2 = \overline{W}\,\overline{X}\,Y\overline{Z}$ $m_{11} = W\overline{X}\,YZ$

$m_4 = \overline{W}X\overline{Y}\,\overline{Z}$ $m_{12} = WX\overline{Y}\,\overline{Z}$

$m_8 = W\overline{X}\,\overline{Y}\,\overline{Z}$ $m_{13} = WX\overline{Y}Z$

$m_9 = W\overline{X}\,\overline{Y}Z$

$m_0 + m_2 + m_4 + m_8 + m_9 + m_{10} + m_{11} + m_{12} + m_{13}$

$\overline{X}\,\overline{Z} + \overline{Y}\,\overline{Z} + W\overline{X} + W\overline{Y}$

$\overline{Z}(\overline{X} + \overline{Y}) + W(\overline{X} + \overline{Y})$

$(\overline{Z} + W)\,(\overline{X} + \overline{Y})$

47. *(a)* $m_1 + m_3 + m_5 + m_7 + m_{12} + m_{13} + m_8 + m_9$

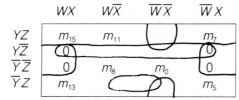

	WX	$W\overline{X}$	$\overline{W}\,\overline{X}$	$\overline{W}X$
YZ	0	0	m_3	m_7
$Y\overline{Z}$	0	0	0	0
$\overline{Y}\,\overline{Z}$	m_{12}	m_8	0	0
$\overline{Y}Z$	m_{13}	m_0	m_1	m_5

product-of-sums:

$\overline{(WY + W\overline{Z})} = (\overline{W} + \overline{Y})\;(W + Z)$

sum-of-products:

$W\overline{Y} + \overline{W}Z$

(b) $m_0 + m_5 + m_7 + m_8 + m_{11} + m_{13} + m_{15}$

	WX	$W\overline{X}$	$\overline{W}\,\overline{X}$	$\overline{W}X$
YZ	m_{15}	m_{11}		m_7
$Y\overline{Z}$	0			0
$\overline{Y}\,\overline{Z}$	0	m_8	m_0	0
$\overline{Y}Z$	m_{13}			m_5

product-of-sums:

$(X\overline{Z} + Y\overline{Z} + \overline{W}\,\overline{X}Z + \overline{X}\,\overline{Y}Z)$

$= (\overline{X} + Z)\,(\overline{Y} + Z)\,(W + X + \overline{Z})$

$(X + Y + \overline{Z})$

don't-cares

49. *(a)* $\overline{A}\,\overline{B}\,\overline{C} + A\overline{B}\,\overline{C} + \overbrace{ABC + \overline{A}B\overline{C} + \overline{A}BC}^{} = \overline{B}\,\overline{C}$

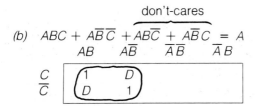

	AB	$A\overline{B}$	$\overline{A}\,\overline{B}$	$\overline{A}B$
C	D		D	
$\overline{C}$		1	1	D

don't-cares

(b) $ABC + A\overline{B}\,\overline{C} + \overbrace{A\overline{B}\,\overline{C} + \overline{A}\,\overline{B}C}^{} = A$

	AB	$A\overline{B}$	$\overline{A}\,\overline{B}$	$\overline{A}B$
C	1	D		
$\overline{C}$	D	1		

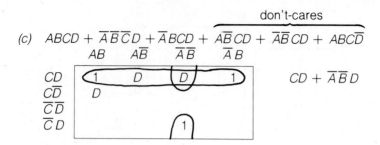

(c) $ABCD + \overline{A}\,\overline{B}\,\overline{C}D + \overline{A}BCD + \overline{A}\,\overline{B}\,CD + \overline{A}\,\overline{B}\,CD + ABC\overline{D}$

$$CD + \overline{A}\,\overline{B}\,D$$

CHAPTER 4

1.

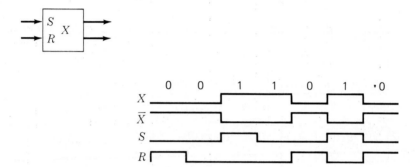

5.

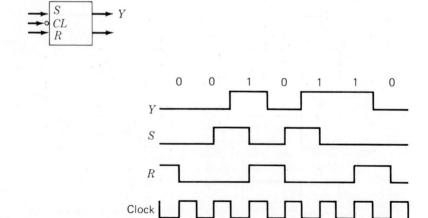

9.

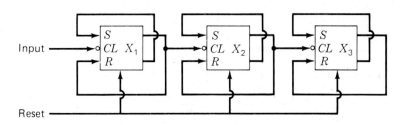

13.

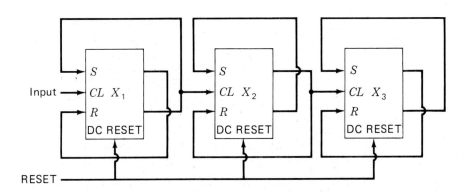

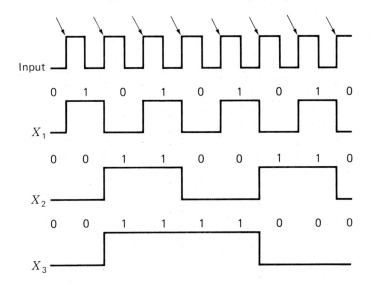

15.

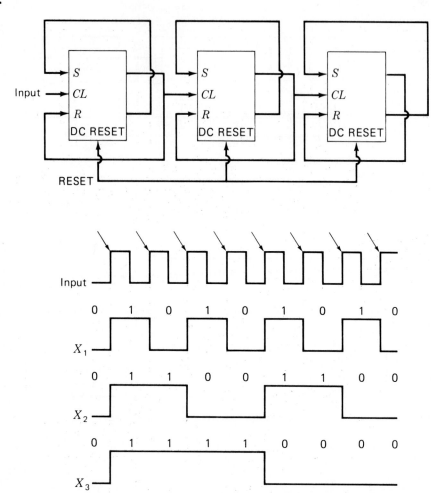

17.

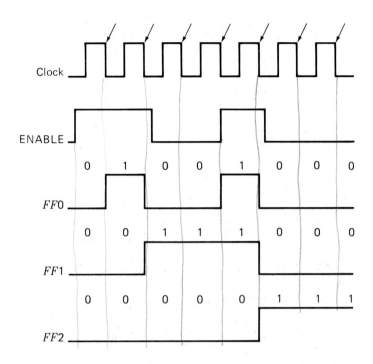

CHAPTER 5

9.

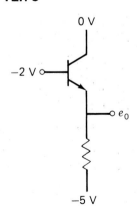

(a) $e_0 = -2.75$ V

(b) Yes; the emitter-base junction is forward biased (*npn* base more positive than emitter)

13.

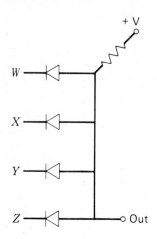

15. +0.1 V
25. T3 and T5
31. 8.333 mA maximum
41. $\overline{X}$ will be a 1 when X is a 0 and a 0 when X is a 1
47. Both will be 0s (at about ground)

49.

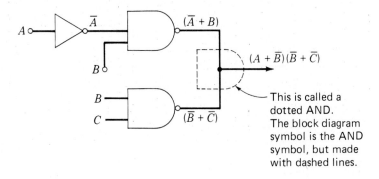

51.

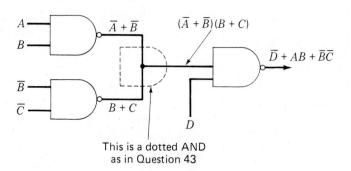

55. 200 μA

CHAPTER 6

1.

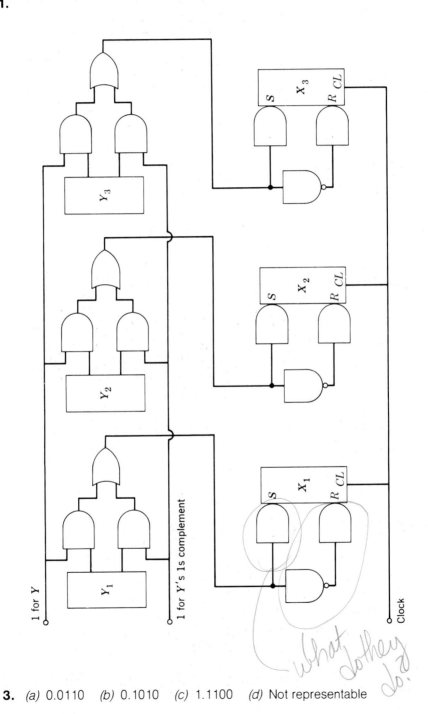

3. *(a)* 0.0110   *(b)* 0.1010   *(c)* 1.1100   *(d)* Not representable

5. -4 would be stored 1.0100 in the magnitude system, 1.1011 in the 1s complement system, and 1.1100 in the 2s complement system

7. $S = 1$ and $C = 1$

9. -12 in 1s complement; -13 in 2s complement

11. The sum will overflow the register and cause an incorrect addition. Most machines sense for this and turn on an "addition overflow" or indicate the overflow in some manner.

15.

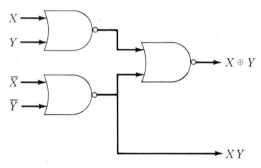

29. Logical addition, 0.111011
Logical multiplication, 0.100010
Exclusive OR, 0.011001

31. The logical MULTIPLY will clear those digits of X where 0s occur in Y, and the logical ADD will add 1s into the places in X where 1s occur in Y

48.

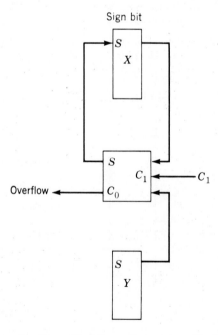

Overflow $= (A > \emptyset) \cdot (B > \emptyset) \cdot (C_1 = 1) + (A < \emptyset) \cdot (B < 0) \cdot (C_1 = \emptyset)$
Overflow $= \overline{X}\overline{Y}C_1 + XYC_1$

50. The general scheme is:

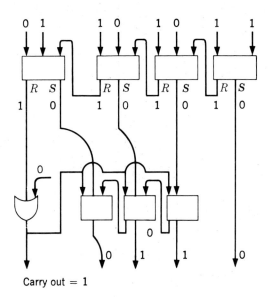

Carry out = 1

CHAPTER 7

13. 143,360 cores, 12 flip-flops for address register, 35 flip-flops for memory buffer register
15. 147,456 cores, 36 sense amplifiers, 36 inhibit drivers, 64 X drivers, 64 Y drivers, 36 planes, and 4096 cores per plane
17. False, because all the selected cores are set to the 0 state and 1s must be rewritten
19. $X_2 Y_2$, $X_2 Y_3$
21. 1
22.

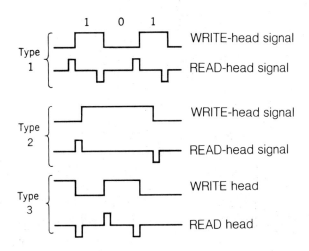

53. 40 μs, 20 μs
55. 3,600,000 bits/s
57. 262,500 bits/s

CHAPTER 8

3. 01100001
01100100
01100100
00010000
00010110
00000100
00000001
10000000   Carriage return is perhaps optional
5. 27 holes in three cards. Easier to correct if cards are used, for erroneous cards may simply be replaced.
7. Nine holes

9.

DECIMAL	EXCESS 3 CODE	EVEN-PARITY CHECK	ODD-PARITY CHECK
0	0011	0	1
1	0100	1	0
2	0101	0	1
3	0110	0	1
4	0111	1	0
5	1000	1	0
6	1001	0	1
7	1010	0	1
8	1011	1	0
9	1100	0	1

11. (a) The errors are in the seventh, eighth, and ninth rows; the sixth digit in each row is in error, and the message is "that's right"
(b) The error is the fourth digit in the sixth row, and the message is "don't stop"
13. 10—One such code can be formed by adding a leading 0 to each of the 4-binary-digit Gray code groups listed in Chap. 8 and then adding another 16 rows with the 4 rightmost binary digits the same as those in Chap. 8 but with their order reversed and with a leading 1 added to each of these code rows.
15. (a) Errors are in the second, third, and fourth rows, the seventh digit in. The message is "that's fine."
(b) Errors are in the second and third rows, the third digit in, and the message is "bad tapes." Notice that we corrected a double error in a column.

17. 0101 gives $+2\frac{2}{3}$ V
       1010 gives $+5\frac{1}{3}$ V
       1111 gives $+$ 8 V

19. The code will detect but not correct errors occurring in two different columns. It will not detect or correct four errors occurring in two rows and two columns, that is, two errors in each of two rows with errors in the same two columns in each row. There are many other patterns of these types, and analysis of these codes is very subtle.

27. Double errors in a row lead to detection via the check digits. Since there are essentially no checks on the check digits, errors in these result in data loss.

CHAPTER 9

1.

S	OP code	Index register	Address
1	5	2	14
digit	digits	digits	digits

3. Single address

OP code	Address	
1	6 7	24

2^{18} different addresses

Double address

OP code	Address A	Address B	
1	6 7	15 16	24

2^9 different addresses

7. Sign

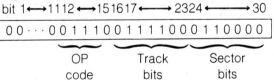

bit 1⟷1112⟷1516 17⟷2324⟷30

00··· 0 0 1 1 1 0 0 1 1 1 1 0 0 0 1 1 0 0 0 0

| OP | Track | Sector |
| code | bits | bits |

11.

CRA	302
MPX	302
ADD	301
DIV	303
STA	304

13. The SBM instruction subtracts the magnitude of the number stored in the location given by the address part of the instruction word from the number in the accumulator and places this difference value in the accumulator. The instruction is indexable and indirectly addressable and can result in an overflow.

15. Change each AC_0 to $\overline{AC}_0$, each $\overline{AC}_0$ to AC_0, and BRM to BRP.

CHAPTER 10

11.

ADDRESS	INDEX REGISTER	OP CODE	ADDRESS PART
0	01	SIR	39
1	01	CAD	200
2	00	ADD	300
3	00	STO	300
4	01	BRI	1
5	00	HLT	0
Location of data	200		
	239		
	300	contains 0 when program is started	

INDEX